HISTORICAL DICTIONARY OF POLAND, 1945–1996

HISTORICAL DICTIONARY OF POLAND, 1945–1996

Piotr Wróbel

With editing by
Anna Wróbel

Greenwood Press
Westport, Connecticut

Library of Congress Cataloging-in-Publication Data

Wróbel, Piotr.
  Historical dictionary of Poland : 1945–1996 / [by] Piotr Wróbel ;
with editing by Anna Wróbel.
    p.   cm.
  Includes bibliographical references and index.
  ISBN 0–313–29772–X (alk. paper)
    1. Poland—History—1945– —Dictionaries.   I. Wróbel, Anna.
II. Title.
  DK4433.W76   1998
  943.805—dc21   97–40855

British Library Cataloguing in Publication Data is available.

Library of Congress Catalog Card Number: 97–40855
ISBN: 0–313–29772–X

First published in 1998

Greenwood Press, 88 Post Road West, Westport, CT 06881
An imprint of Greenwood Publishing Group, Inc.

Printed in the United States of America

The paper used in this book complies with the
Permanent Paper Standard issued by the National
Information Standards Organization (Z39.48–1984).

10 9 8 7 6 5 4 3 2 1

CONTENTS

PREFACE

Poland is the eighth largest nation of Europe and the largest one in East-Central Europe—located between the former Soviet Union and the German-speaking countries. After the fall of communism the importance of Poland has grown rapidly. Poland has the potential to become a political and economic "bridge" between the East and the West. Located in the heart of Europe, Poland is crucial to European security and stabilization. The last millennium of European history has proven clearly that without peace in Central Europe, in the region of Poland, there can be no peace on the entire European continent. Thus, it is important to have at least a basic knowledge of the Polish contemporary and historical situation. Yet the list of reference books on the recent history of Poland is very short. The *Historical Dictionary of Poland, 1945–1996* constitutes an attempt to fill this lacuna and is a sequel to the *Historical Dictionary of Poland, 966–1945*, published by Greenwood Press in 1996. It is helpful to use both dictionaries together because some movements or individuals active after 1945 but more important in the pre-1945 period have their entries in the first volume, whereas others have entries in both volumes. Both volumes address an English audience rather than a Polish one. An asterisk (*) indicates that an individual name, event, or term appears as an entry in this book. Every entry has a short bibliography of English-language works. If there are no important books on a given topic in English, bibliographies contain Polish-language references. The contemporary history of Poland is very controversial. Even single words are controversial. The words "communism" and "communist," for example, might be contested as inadequate, but the terms "socialism," "real socialism," or "totalitarianism" are not perfect either. My intention has been to make this dictionary as objective and impartial as possible. The readers will judge whether this goal has been achieved.

_____ NOTES ON THE POLISH ALPHABET

The Polish alphabet consists of thirty-two letters: a, ą, b, c, ć, d, e, ę, f, g, h, i, j, k, l, ł, m, n, ń, o, ó, p, r, s, ś, t, u, w, y, z, ź, ż. **The entries of this dictionary are arranged in the sequence of the Polish alphabet**. Accordingly, letters with diacritical markings (for example Łódź) follow the ordinary English alphabet letters.

The Polish letters are pronounced in the following way: ą and ę are nasals and correspond, respectively, to the French *on* (= ą) and *ain* (= ę). The nearest English equivalents are the vowel sounds in "don't" and "sand," without the *n* that follows being heard separately.

a is pronounced like *a* in art

c like *ts* in its

e like *ai* in air

g like *g* in good

h and *ch* like *h* in hard

i like *ee* in been

j like *y* in you

l like *l* in battle

n like *ng* in singing

ó and *u* like *u* in full

w like *v* in never

y like *i* in fin, tin, but guttural

rz and *ż* like *zh* in Brezhnev

cz like *tsch* or *ch* in chalk

sz like *sh* in shop

ć, ń, ś and *ź* like soft *c, n, s*, and *z* followed by *y*

Because of variations in the spelling of Polish names and terms, consultation of the index for helpful cross-references is advised.

TIMETABLE

1944–1948: COMMUNIST SEIZURE OF POWER*

January 1, 1945   Provisional Government of the Republic of Poland* is established.

June 28, 1945   Provisional Government of National Unity (TRJN)* is formed.

June 30, 1946   Referendum.*

January 19, 1947   First postwar parliamentary elections.*

December 15–21, 1948   Unification Congress* of the Polish United Workers' Party (PZPR).* Beginning of the collectivization* program is announced.

1949–1956: STALINIST PERIOD*

January 1949   Comecon* is founded.

November 1949   K. Rokossowski* becomes the Minister of National Defense and Marshall of Poland. W. Gomułka* is ejected from the Party leadership.

July 22, 1952   Stalinist Constitution* is accepted by the Sejm.*

September 26, 1953   Primate* S. Wyszyński* is arrested.

May 14, 1955   Warsaw Treaty* is signed.

1956: "POLISH OCTOBER" OF 1956*

February 14–25, 1956   Twentieth Congress of the Communist Party of the Soviet Union.

June 28, 1956   Poznań* uprising.

October 21, 1956   W. Gomułka* is appointed First Secretary of the Polish United Workers' Party (PZPR).*

1956–1970: GOMUŁKA* PERIOD

March 14, 1964   "Letter of 34"* protesting against the cultural policies of the government.

May–June 1966   Millennium celebrations.*

March 1968   March events:* students' riots and anti-Semitic campaign.

December 1970   December events:* workers' riots in Gdańsk* and Gdynia.*

1970–1980: GIEREK* PERIOD

May 1975   Administration* reform is implemented.

February 1976   1952 Constitution* is amended.

June 1976   June events:* workers' riots in Radom,* Ursus,* and elsewhere.

September 1976   Workers' Defense Committee (KOR)* is established.

October 16, 1978   Cardinal Karol Wojtyła is elected as Pope John Paul II.*

June 2–10, 1979   First Papal visit* to Poland.

1980–1981: SOLIDARITY* PERIOD

August 16, 1980   Inter-Factory Strike Committee (MKS)* is organized in Gdańsk* (Lenin) Shipyard with L. Wałęsa* as its chairman.

August 31, 1980   Gdańsk Agreement* is signed.

December 1980   Soviet military maneuvers around Poland.

October 1981   Gen. W. Jaruzelski* replaces S. Kania* as Party First Secretary.

December 12–13, 1981   Martial Law* is implemented.

1982–1989: JARUZELSKI* PERIOD

July 22, 1983   Martial Law* officially ends.

October 19, 1984   Fr. J. Popiełuszko* murdered by secret police.

August 1988   Wave of strikes; the authorities and the opposition begin to talk.

February 6–April 5, 1989   Round Table Negotiations.*

1989 AND AFTER: RE-DEMOCRATIZATION

June 1989   Solidarity* wins the first postwar partially free parliamentary elections.*

August 24, 1989   First postwar, noncommunist government, of T. Mazowiecki,* is formed.

November–December 1990   L. Wałęsa* wins the presidential elections.*

October 27, 1991   Parliamentary elections; 29 parties enter the Sejm.*

September 19, 1993   Victory of the left in the parliamentary elections.*

November 1995   A. Kwaśniewski* defeats L. Wałęsa* in the presidential elections.*

MAPS

Poland and its neighbors before World War II.

Source: Stephen Borsody, *The New Central Europe*. New York: Columbia University Press, 1993, p. 89.

Poland and its neighbors after World War II.

Source: Stephen Borsody, *The New Central Europe*. New York: Columbia University Press, 1993, p. 197.

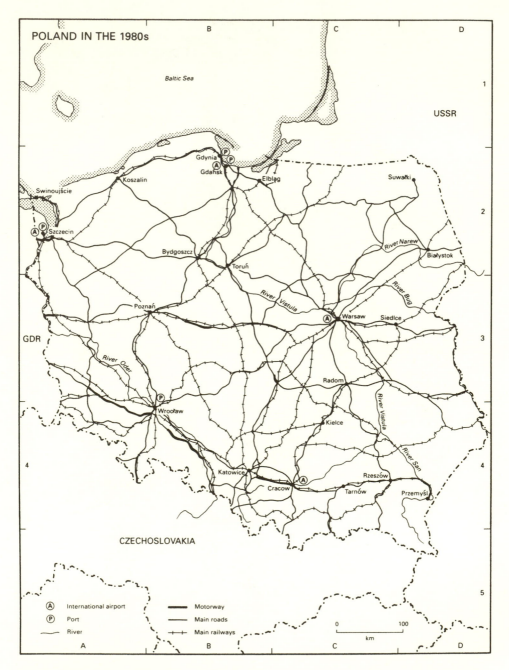

POLAND IN THE 1980s

Baltic Sea

USSR

Gdynia
Gdańsk
Elbląg
Suwałki
Koszalin
Świnoujście
Szczecin
Bydgoszcz
Toruń
River Narew
Białystok
Poznań
River Vistula
Warsaw
Siedlce
River Bug
GDR
River Oder
Radom
River Vistula
Wrocław
Kielce
Katowice
Cracow
Rzeszów
River San
Tarnów
Przemyśl

CZECHOSLOVAKIA

Ⓐ   International airport
Ⓟ   Port
　 River

▬▬ Motorway
── Main roads
+-+ Main railways

0   100
km

Source: Richard and Ben Crampton, *Atlas of Eastern Europe in the Twentieth Century*. London: Routledge, 1996, p. 206.

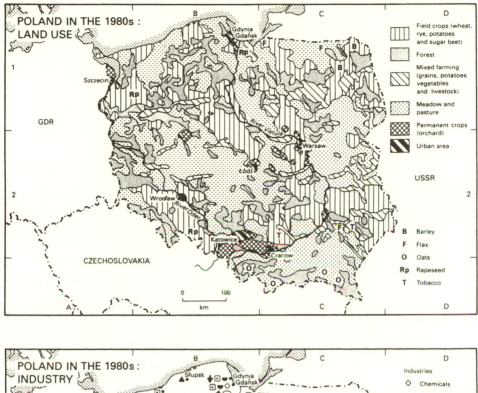

POLAND IN THE 1980s :
LAND USE

Field crops (wheat,
rye, potatoes
and sugar beet)

Forest

Mixed farming
(grains, potatoes
vegetables
and livestock)

Meadow and
pasture

Permanent crops
(orchard)

Urban area

B   Barley
F   Flax
O   Oats
Rp Rapeseed
T   Tobacco

GDR
USSR
CZECHOSLOVAKIA

0   100
km

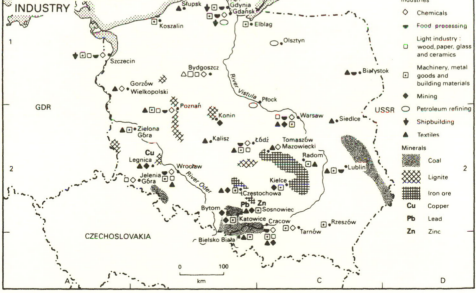

POLAND IN THE 1980s :
INDUSTRY

Industries

◇   Chemicals
◆   Food processing
Light industry :
□   wood, paper, glass
and ceramics
Machinery, metal
▣   goods and
building materials
◆   Mining
○   Petroleum refining
▼   Shipbuilding
▲   Textiles

Minerals

Coal
Lignite
Iron ore
Cu Copper
Pb Lead
Zn Zinc

GDR
USSR
CZECHOSLOVAKIA

0   100
km

Source: Richard and Ben Crampton, *Atlas of Eastern Europe in the Twentieth Century*. London: Routledge,
1996, p. 208.

xix

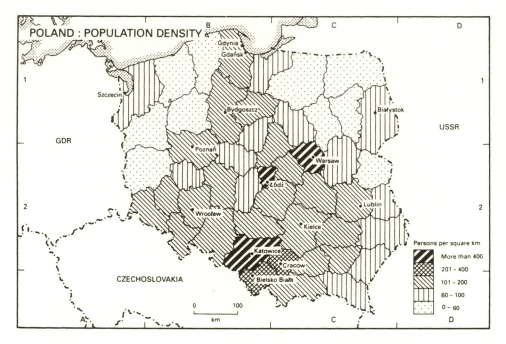

POLAND : POPULATION DENSITY

Gdynia
Gdańsk
Szczecin
Bydgoszcz
Białystok
GDR
USSR
Poznań
Warsaw
Łódź
Wrocław
Lublin
Kielce
Persons per square km
Katowice
Cracow
More than 400
CZECHOSLOVAKIA
Bielsko Biała
201 – 400
101 – 200
0   100
60 – 100
km
0 – 60

Source: Richard and Ben Crampton, *Atlas of Eastern Europe in the Twentieth Century*. London: Routledge, 1996, p. 207.

ABAKANOWICZ, MAGDALENA (1930–), painter, sculptor, and professor at the Academy of Fine Arts in Warsaw.* She won international acclaim and numerous awards for her three-dimensional compositions and created her own unique weaving techniques. *Who's Who in the Socialist Countries of Europe*, ed. by J. Stroynowski, vol. 1 (Munich, 1989), 1.

ABORTION, serious moral and social issue that has divided Polish public opinion. In 1956 a flexible legislation, which relaxed restrictions on abortion, was passed in Poland. Abortions became very numerous, and the 1956 law was strongly criticized by its opponents. In January 1993 the Sejm* approved access to abortion, but only for medical and criminal reasons. The new law did not ban the procedure completely, as the Roman Catholic Church* in Poland had urged. Nonetheless, the strict abortion law was strongly criticized by liberal segments of public opinion, including several women's organizations. In January 1997 a relaxed abortion law was introduced again. However, numerous state hospitals continue to refuse to perform abortion, though the procedure is allowed by law. D. Ost, *Solidarity and the Politics of Anti-Politics* (Philadelphia, 1990), 159, 214; *Sytuacja kobiet w Polsce*, ed. by Polish Committee of Non-Governmental Organizations, Beijing 1995 (Warsaw, 1995).

ABRAMOW-NEWERLY, JAROSŁAW (1933–), playwright, writer, satirist, and son of I. Newerly.* One of the founders of the Students' Satirical Theater (STS),* he wrote numerous satirical pieces, short plays, and comedies, all of which enjoyed considerable success. He also authored historical and contemporary novels, worked for TV,* and composed songs. *Who's Who in the Socialist Countries of Europe*, ed. by J. Stroynowski, vol. 1 (Munich, 1989), 2; *Dictionary of Polish Literature*, ed. by E. J. Czerwinski (Westport, Conn., 1994), 1–2.

ACTION WISŁA (VISTULA), large operation of the Polish People's Army*
and civilian authorities who in spring and summer 1947 deported about 140,000
Ukrainians* and Lemkos* from their homeland in southeastern Poland to northwestern territories newly acquired from the Germans.* From 1945 the Ukrainian
Insurgent Army (UPA)* concentrated its operations on both sides of the new
Polish-Soviet border and clashed with the Polish communist-controlled armed
forces. Supported by the local Ukrainian and Lemko population, the UPA continued its fighting during 1946. In May 1947 the Polish Vice Minister of Defense, Gen. K. Świerczewski,* was killed in a skirmish, apparently an ambush
organized by the UPA. The Polish authorities answered with mass deportation
of the local non-Polish population, arguing that the transfer of the Ukrainian
population was the only way to stop popular support for the UPA and to terminate its activities. Almost all Ukrainian and Lemko nationals were forcibly
transferred to the depopulated "Recovered Territories."* The operation was
brutally executed. Deportees were allowed to take with them only limited farming equipment and private property. They were dispersed in small groups
throughout northern and western Poland to facilitate their assimilation. P. R.
Magocsi, *A History of Ukraine* (Toronto, 1996), 648; E. Misiło, *Akcja Wisła* (Warsaw,
1993); E. Pasternak, *The Outline of History of the Kholm and Podlachia Lands* (Toronto,
1968); A. B. Szczęśniak and W. Z. Szota, *Droga do nikąd: Działalność Organizacji
Ukraińskich Nacjonalistów i jej likwidacja w Polsce* (Warsaw, 1973); *Litopys UPA*, vols.
17, 22, 23 (Toronto, 1988–92); B. Huk (ed.), *Zakierzonia. Wspomnienia żołnierzy
Ukraińskiej Powstańczej Armii*, vol. 1 (Warsaw, 1994); A. Chojnowska, "Operacja
Wisła," *Zeszyty Historyczne*, no. 102 (Paris, 1992).

ADMINISTRATION, institutions and activities involved in the implementation
of policies laid out by the Sejm* and, before 1989, the Party. The Council of
Ministers (Rada Ministrów) constitutes the chief organ of administration, has
been appointed by, and is responsible to, the Sejm, and consists of a Premier,*
several Deputy Premiers, and ministers chairing individual ministries or similar
central offices. The government controls two networks of administration: economic and territorial; before 1989 both were supervised by the third network
created by the Party. Territorially, Poland is divided into 49 provinces (województwo), including three self-governing cities. Each province consists of numerous communes (gmina). Altogether, there are 2,468 of them. Before the
administrative reform of 1973–75,* 17 provinces (initially 14) were divided into
counties (powiat*). The population of every administrative district elected its
National Council (Rada Narodowa), which included, or was supervised by, a
governmental official. In 1983 the administration employed 135,500 persons,
including 43,400 in the central administration (16,200 in ministries and similar
offices) and 92,000 in provincial administration. J. Kapliński, "The Communist
Party and the Control of Local Administration," *Poland since 1956*, ed. by T. N. Cieplak
(New York, 1972), 230–239.

ADMINISTRATIVE REFORM OF 1973–75, reorganization of the territorial administration, which had been implemented by the Central Committee* of the Polish United Workers' Party (PZPR)* in 1973–75, was approved by the Sejm* on May 28, 1975, and became effective on June 1, 1975. The first introductory stage of the reform started in 1973, when over 4,300 rural communes (gromada) were merged into some 2,350 larger consolidated rural communes (gmina). During the last stage of the reform, the existing government structure consisting of the three tiers of commune (gmina), county or district (powiat), and province or voivodship (województwo) was replaced by a two-tiered structure: provinces and rural communes or towns; 314 districts and 17 voivodships (plus five large cities with provincial status) were replaced by 46 new voivodships and three autonomous cities, namely, Warsaw,* Łódź,* and Cracow.* Under the new system each province consists of about 50 rural communes and towns. According to First Secretary E. Gierek's* announcement, the reform was implemented to simplify the administrative system, to improve local self-government, and to increase the participation of the local population. Yet most observers saw the reform not as "the basis of socialist democracy" but as a strengthening of centralism, responsible for "the reduction in the distance between the centers of control at national level and the base units [of administration]." Instead of dealing with powerful first secretaries of large provinces, the central authorities faced much weaker first secretaries of new, small voivodships. Supporters of Party factions unfriendly toward Gierek, such as M. Moczar's* sympathizers, were purged, and obedient officials were promoted. After the reform, chief editors of provincial newspapers were directly appointed by the Central Committee's press section and no longer by the voivodships' secretaries. The reform involved relocation of some 120,000 civil servants, was the cause of significant trouble, and contributed considerably to the growing political crisis in Poland. *Keesing's Contemporary Archives*, July 21–27, 1975, p. 27235; M. K. Dziewanowski, *Poland in the Twentieth Century* (New York, 1977), 225–227; *The History of Poland since 1863*, ed. by R. F. Leslie (Cambridge, 1980), 423–425.

AGRICULTURAL FOUNDATION OF THE EPISCOPATE (Fundacja Rolnicza Episkopatu or Kościelna Fundacja Rolnicza), institution organized on the initiative of Solidarity.* The Roman Catholic Church* in Poland helped to negotiate this "little Marshall Plan" with the Germans and the European Union, but eventually the initiative burned out without delivering the expected results. J. Karpiński, *Polska, Komunizm, Opozycja* (London, 1985), 58–59; L. Wałęsa, *Droga nadziei* (Cracow, 1989), 260–261.

AGRICULTURE. Polish agriculture was unique in the Soviet bloc. The communist authorities did not manage to collectivize farming in Poland. Traditional agriculture proved to be more efficient than communist forms of farming, and the peasants managed to defend themselves against collectivization.* Yet the state's attempt to implement collectivization while the peasants fought to preserve their old way of farming had a negative long-term effect. The Polish countryside did not undergo modernization until the 1980s, when it entered the period of democratization and integration with Western Europe in poor condition.

Interwar Poland was a predominantly agricultural state. The peasantry constituted a considerable social power and had a developed political agenda. During World War II the economic status of the peasants improved, although the Polish countryside was seriously damaged by military activities. Immediately after the Germans were ejected from the regions of Lublin,* Białystok,* and Rzeszów,* the Polish Committee of National Liberation (PKWN), installed there as a provisional government by the Soviets, had to secure foodstuffs for the Red and Polish People's Armies* and for the town population. To do so the PKWN issued a decree concerning obligatory deliveries and, on September 6, 1944, a decree on land reform.* After the liberation of territories west of the Vistula River,* land reform was extended to those regions. Yet the parceling proceeded slowly; in central and eastern Poland the hunger for land could not be satisfied: Land was distributed in small plots, new farms could not become independent ones, and many peasants did not consider the reform a legitimate operation. Large landowners disappeared as a social group, and their estates ceased to produce foodstuffs for the market. In former German territories land reserves exceeded requirements, and a network of state farms, later called PGRs,* was established. In general, however, Polish agriculture was dominated by peasant farms. The state assisted with the reconstruction of the agricultural sector, and Poland received important aid from the United Nations Relief and Rehabilitation Administration (UNRRA). Land reform did not solve all the problems of Polish agriculture, however, and in 1949 its total production reached 91% of the 1934–38 value. The government maintained obligatory quota deliveries until summer 1946, when they were abolished just prior to the referendum.* Economic results of the reform were nil: There was no real improvement in agrarian structure, rural overpopulation decreased only slightly, and the well-being of peasants hardly improved. Yet the communists considered the land reform and the postwar "agrarian revolution" one of their greatest achievements.

In the second half of 1948, the government changed its agricultural policy, based its new policy on the Soviet patterns of the 1930s, and started collectivization. Polish agriculture had developed between 1945 and 1947 in spite of all obstacles and had fulfilled the Three-Year Plan (1947–49); there were no economic reasons for announcing collectivization. Yet the ideologically driven authorities expected collectivization to raise production and thus enable the workforce to migrate to industry. There was no well-prepared plan for collectivization. In addition, between 1951 and 1953 total investment in farming diminished by about 24%, building materials supplied to farming dropped by almost 75%, and tractor and fertilizer supplies did not meet demand. As a consequence, gross agricultural product fell and obligatory deliveries were reintroduced. In 1952 they accounted for over 90% of grain sold by farmers. Police, administrative, and economic pressure forced individual farmers to join collectivized farms. The law was frequently violated. In September 1956 the number of cooperatives reached 10,510 and covered an area of 1,963,000 hectares, whereas individual farmers owned 15,630,000 hectares. Peasants answered the governmental policy with passive resistance; some farms collapsed, and masses of the countryside population left for the towns. In 1954 the authorities began to change agricultural policy. They slowed down collectivization and invested more in agriculture. In 1956 the Party leadership accepted that forced collectivization of agriculture was a complete failure.

The "Polish October" of 1956,* as this period was known, was followed by an immediate dissolution of most cooperatives. By the end of 1957, only 1,700 survived, and from then about 200 cooperatives disappeared every year. In 1965 the collective farms cultivated only 1% of agricultural land and produced about 1% of total output. The separate Ministry of State Farms was abolished in December 1956, when the PGR network was decentralized and put under the supervision of the Ministry of Agriculture. The authorities had never abandoned their ideological goal of communist transformation of agriculture, but facing foodstuff shortages, they decided to save private farming and to elaborate a system by which it could be controlled. Peasants still had to make obligatory deliveries; they had to purchase minimum amounts of fertilizers. Meanwhile, government investments in agriculture grew. The authorities were entitled to take over land from decaying farms, to protect arable land, and to restrict its takeover for non-agricultural purposes. The farmers were to be stimulated by administrative measures and penalties. A system of supply contracts was developed. All these measures brought diminishing results, however. The increase of agricultural product was lower than the economic plans and resolutions of the Party congresses expected. Animal husbandry grew very slowly and required a growing amount of feed to be imported from the West. The smallness of most farms made mechanization impracticable, and farms continued to be worked with horses. Agriculture suffered from increasing workforce shortages. The "socialized" sector of agriculture and state farms needed growing subsidies. Working conditions in the countryside were much worse than in non-agricultural jobs. As a result, younger generations were leaving for the cities and farming was dominated by older people.

The Gierek* period brought positive changes to agriculture. In 1972 obligatory deliveries and administrative means of stimulating agricultural production were repealed, tax reductions were introduced, and farmers were included in free medical care and old-age benefit systems like employees from other branches of the national economy. Purchasing prices were rising, and some specialization in farming appeared. Yet many Party and state leaders remained distrustful of individual farming, and the governmental agricultural policy lacked consistency. Poland switched from its original role of foodstuffs exporter, in 1949, to that of importer and remained in that position until the fall of communism. From 1946 to 1988, the countryside population declined from 68% to 38.8% of all Polish citizens. In 1989 about 4,068,000 people were employed in private sector agriculture compared to 745,000 in the state sector.

After 1989 Polish agriculture faced another series of challenges: the removal of subsidies and price controls, the decrease in purchasing power of incomes, and a rise in costs of credits, farming equipment, fertilizers, and other inputs. Farm incomes dropped by one-half in the early 1990s; so the peasants became frustrated, organized frequent protests, and demanded state intervention. This dissatisfaction accounted for the spectacular victory of the Polish Peasant Party (PSL)* in the elections of 1993.* There are some grounds for optimism over the future of Polish agriculture, although the 1990s constitute a period of its transformation. Z. Landau and J. Tomaszewski, *The Polish Economy in the Twentieth Century* (London, 1985), 187–321; A. Korbonski, *Politics of Socialist Agriculture in Poland, 1945–1960* (New York, 1965); A. Korbonski, "Peasant Agriculture in Socialist Poland since 1956: An Alternative to Collectivization," *Soviet and East European Agriculture*, ed. by J. F. Karcz (Berkeley, Calif., 1967), 411–435; *Eastern Europe and Commonwealth of Independent States, 1994* (London, 1994), 476; J. Wilkin, "Private Agriculture and Socialism: The Polish Experience," *Poland: The Economy in the 1980s*, ed. by R. A. Clarke (London, 1989), 61–71; M. Nadolski, *Komuniści wobec chłopów w Polsce 1941–1956* (Warsaw, 1993).

AJDUKIEWICZ, KAZIMIERZ (1890–1963), logician and semanticist, chief contributor to the Warsaw School of Philosophy and Logic. J. Wolenski, *Logic and Philosophy in the Lvov-Warsaw School* (Dordrecht, 1989).

AK. See **Home Army.**

AKTYW (active [segment of the Party]), members of the Party or of any affiliated organization who, according to the beliefs of the Party leadership, are easy to mobilize and to use in an action. *Aktyw* was supposed to support Party propaganda and was used as fighting squads. In 1968 *aktyw* participated in "anti-Zionist" demonstrations and beat students. J. Karpiński, *Polska, Komunizm, Opozycja* (London, 1985), 10.

ALBRECHT, JERZY (1914–   ), communist official. A member of the communist youth movement in interwar Poland, he joined the Polish Workers' Party (PPR)* in 1942 and became its secretary of the Warsaw* district. Arrested by the Germans in 1942, he returned to his post in 1945. At the same time, he became a member of the PPR Central Committee* and remained until 1968. During 1948–50 he chaired its propaganda department; during 1950–56 he presided over the Warsaw City Council; in 1955–57 he was a member of the State Council (Rada Państwa)* and in 1957–60 became its Deputy President. From 1945 to 1969, he was a member of the Sejm,* from 1960 to 1968, serving as Minister of Finance. One of the main PPR reformers of the "Polish October" of 1956,* he signed the "Letter of 14," criticizing the Gierek* regime. T. Mołdawa, *Ludzie Władzy 1944–1991. Władze państwowe i polityczne Polski według stanu na dzień 28 II 1991* (Warsaw, 1991), 329–330; Z. Błażyński, *Mówi Józef Światło. Za kulisami bezpieki i partii* (London, 1985), 137–139.

ALCOHOLISM, one of the most threatening plagues of Polish society. Alcoholism would increase every time Poland underwent a period of oppression or crisis and was especially acute under communism. By the end of the 1970s, a statistical Pole drank about six liters of 100% spirit per year. In 1980–81 this amount diminished, but it later increased. However, statistical data are not exact because a large segment of Polish society used to bypass the state monopoly and distill liquor in secret. J. Karpiński, *Polska, Komunizm, Opozycja* (London, 1985), 11.

ALL-POLAND ALLIANCE OF TRADE UNIONS (Ogólnopolskie Porozumienie Związków Zawodowych [OPZZ]), federation of trade unions organized by the Jaruzelski* regime in 1985. After Martial Law* legislation of October 1982 banned all trade unions, the regime created new unions to oppose and replace Solidarity.* Led by A. Miodowicz,* a member of the communist Politburo,* they never reached the strength of either the pre-1980 communist trade unions or Solidarity. The OPZZ formally registered on April 12, 1985, and received funds taken from suspended Solidarity. The Alliance, which emphasized the autonomy of member unions, reached nearly 7 million members (63% of the Polish workforce) by the mid-1980s. It criticized some governmental policy, managing to win price reductions in March 1987 and a wage increase for state employees in February 1988. Yet the Alliance did not support the strikes of 1988. After 1989 the OPZZ became an important sector of the post-communist left. It joined the Democratic Left Alliance (SLD)* and created its own political arm—the Movement of the Working People (RLP)—but the OPZZ's membership dropped to 4.5 million (40.5% of the workforce) by July 1991. In 1990 Miodowicz was succeeded by E. Spychalska.* G. Sanford and A. Gozdecka-Sanford, *Historical Dictionary of Poland* (Metuchen, N.J., 1994), 25; J. Campbell (ed.), *European Labor Unions* (Westport, Conn., 1992), 351.

ALSTER, ANTONI (1904–   ), activist of the interwar Communist Party of Poland (KPP), member of the Central Committee* of the Polish United Workers' Party (PZPR)* between 1948 and 1964, member of the Security Committee during 1955–56, Deputy Minister of Internal Affairs from 1956 to 1961. Z. Błażyński, *Mówi Józef Światło. Za kulisami bezpieki i partii* (London, 1985), 289.

AMBROZIAK, JACEK W. (1941–   ), lawyer and judge in a Warsaw* district court during 1965–79. Later he served as an adviser to the Polish Episcopate* and to Solidarity.* A participant of the Round Table Negotiations,* he served as an Undersecretary of State in Premier T. Mazowiecki's* government in Au-

gust and September 1989 and as a minister-director of the Mazowiecki cabinet
from September 1989 to December 1990. *Kto jest kim w polityce polskiej*, ed. by
R. Ignasiak (Warsaw, 1993), 10; T. Mołdawa, *Ludzie Władzy 1944–1991. Władze państwowe i polityczne Polski według stanu na dzień 28 II 1991* (Warsaw, 1991), 330.

AMERICAN-POLISH UNION (Unia Amerykańsko-Polska), small, loose political organization founded in October 1989, aimed at the establishment of close
American-Polish relations. *Partie Polityczne w Polsce*, ed. by A. Gargas and M. Wojciechowski (Gdańsk, 1991), 160–161.

AMNESTY, an act of oblivion granted by government usually for political
crimes. The first amnesties in communist Poland were granted August 2, 1945,
and February 22, 1947. They were combined with a call for Poles to leave the
anti-communist underground and to disclose themselves. After each amnesty
about 40,000 persons returned to legal life. The next amnesties were granted in
1952, 1956, 1969, 1974, 1977, 1981, 1983, and 1984. J. Karpiński, *Polska, Komunizm, Opozycja* (London, 1985), 12.

ANARCHIST FEDERATION (Federacja Anarchistyczna), small anarchist
group that left the organization of Polish anarchists, the Anarchist International
(Miedzynarodówka Anarchistyczna), in 1989. The Federation supports peaceful
methods of fighting for the anarchist system. *Partie Polityczne w Polsce*, ed. by A.
Gargas and M. Wojciechowski (Gdańsk, 1991), 21.

ANDERS, WŁADYSŁAW (1892–1970), general from 1934 and leader of
post–World War II Polish emigration to England. Originally an officer in the
Russian Army, he joined the Polish units in Russia in 1917, distinguished himself in the Polish-Soviet War of 1919–21, opposed the 1926 Piłsudski coup
d'état, and served on various positions in the interwar Polish Army.* In 1939
he participated in the defense of Poland and was imprisoned by the Soviets.
Liberated in 1941, he commanded the Polish Forces in the USSR, moved with
them to the Middle East, and during 1943–45 commanded the Second Polish
Army Corps in Africa and Italy. Between February 26 and the end of May 1945,
he served as the acting commander-in-chief and the general inspector of Polish
forces in the West. He ordered the organization of the clandestine Delegation
of the Armed Forces in the Country* and saved the Świętokrzyska Brigade from
being given away to the NKVD. On October 31, 1946, he left Italy for England
and became general inspector of the Polish Corps of Training and Distribution
(Polski Korpus Przysposobienia i Rozmieszczenia). That same year he was
stripped of his Polish citizenship by the communist-controlled Provisional Government of National Unity.* He tried to save structures of the Polish forces in
the West as long as possible, supported the anti-communist movement in Poland
from England, and became an important leader of the Polish community in exile
after World War II and a member of the Council of Three (Rada Trzech)* from

1954. On June 16, 1947, Gen. T. Bór-Komorowski* turned over to Anders the
honorary position of commander-in-chief of the Polish Army. Anders is buried
at the Polish Military Cemetery at Monte Cassino. J. Lerski, *Historical Dictionary
of Poland, 966–1945*, with special editing and emendations by P. Wróbel and R. J. Kozicki (Westport, Conn., 1996), 12; *Słownik Historii Polski, 1939–1948*, ed. by A.
Chwalba and T. Gąsowski (Cracow, 1994), 21–27; W. Hładkiewicz, *Przywódcy "Polskiego" Londynu, 1945–1972* (Zielona Góra, 1993), 10–13.

ANDRZEJEWSKI, JERZY (1909–83), writer and journalist. He made his de-
but in the late 1930s when he wrote for the rightist papers *ABC* and *Prosto z
Mostu* ("Straight from the Shoulder") and became a member of the Polish
Writers Union in 1936. During the war Andrzejewski participated in the anti-
German resistance and wrote several works, among which was *Wielki Tydzień*
("Holy Week"), a novel about the 1943 uprising in the Warsaw* Ghetto. In
1947 he published his best-known work, *Popiół i Diament* ("Ash and Dia-
mond"), filmed by A. Wajda* after 1956. In 1949 Andrzejewski joined the
Polish United Workers' Party (PZPR)* and propagated Socialist Realism.* He
served as a member of the Sejm* during 1952–56 and then, bitterly disillusioned
with communism, participated in the de-Stalinization of Polish culture. Later he
parted with Marxism, left the PZPR, and in 1976 helped found the Workers'
Defense Committee (KOR),* becoming a member of the political opposition.*
C. Miłosz, *The History of Polish Literature* (Berkeley, Calif., 1983), 490–493; M. Kuncewicz, *The Modern Polish Mind* (Boston, 1962); M. H. Bernhard, *The Origins of Democratization in Poland* (New York, 1993); *Dictionary of Polish Literature*, ed. by E. J.
Czerwinski (Westport, Conn., 1994), 2–4.

ANEKS, political quarterly published first in Uppsala and then in London from
1973. It presented translations of well-known foreign scholars and writers, forbidden in Poland, and articles on subjects censored by the communist authorities.
In 1975 a publishing house, *"Aneks,"* appeared. Among other works, it used
to reprint two Polish underground periodicals: *Krytyka** (from 1978) and *Res
Publica** (in 1979–81). J. Karpiński, *Polska, Komunizm, Opozycja* (London, 1985),
13.

ANTCZAK, JERZY (1930–   ), film director, chief producer of the Polish
State TV* Network in 1964–74, and deputy member of the Central Committee*
of the Polish United Workers' Party (PZPR)* between 1971 and 1980. He made
such well-known films as *Hrabina Cosel* ("Countess Cosel") and *Noce i Dnie*
("Nights and Days"). After imposition of Martial Law* in 1981, he did not
return to Poland and lives in New York. *Who's Who in the Socialist Countries of
Europe*, ed. by J. Stroynowski, vol. 1 (Munich, 1989), 23.

ANTHEM. See **National Symbols.**

ANTI-SEMITISM, hostility toward Jews* based on a belief that they constitute a "social parasite," conspire against the rest of the population to exploit it, are racially inferior, are invariably anti-Christian, and are unable to assimilate. Among the factors that contributed to anti-Semitism were economic competition and the teaching of the Christian churches that the Jews killed Jesus Christ. Medieval and early modern Poland was less anti-Semitic than West European countries, and as a result, masses of Jews migrated to Polish lands. In the 17th century relative Polish tolerance began to disappear, and starting in the late 19th century, anti-Semitism in Poland grew rapidly. During World War II most Polish Jews were murdered by the Germans.* After the war Jews were very visible in the communist establishment, and many Poles associated them with the new Soviet-sponsored system and were thus unfriendly toward them. During the civil war of 1945–47, about 1,500 Jews were killed and anti-Semitism reached its apogee in the Kielce pogrom* of 1946. After their escape in the late 1940s and their emigration in the late 1950s, only several thousand Jews remained in Poland, and the Jewish issue disappeared from public attention. Yet numerous communists in Poland put anti-Semitism on their agenda, and led by Minister of the Interior M. Moczar,* they organized the anti-Jewish purge of the late 1960s. During 1980–81, the Solidarity* era, Polish attitudes toward Jews changed in a positive way, although communist propaganda tried to show Solidarity leaders as anti-Polish. After democratization in 1989, anti-Semitism once again became overt. Many people, negatively affected by economic transformation in Poland, blamed their situation on suspected secret activities of Jews, masons, Western bankers, and others. Several politicians continue to use anti-Semitic slogans, especially during parliamentary and presidential elections. Yet none of the parties that base their programs on anti-Semitism managed to receive any parliamentary seats after 1989. During the presidential election of 1990,* a widely circulated rumor held that Premier T. Mazowiecki* had secret Jewish ancestry, and the Star of David appeared on posters advertising Mazowiecki's candidacy. *Antisemitism World Report, 1996* (New York: Institute for Jewish Policy Research and American Jewish Committee, 1996), 189–197; *Facts on File*, Nov. 30, 1990, p. 895.

ANTI-SOCIALIST FORCES OR ELEMENTS, term used in government propaganda, especially in the 1970s and 1980s, to refer to all activities and events not in accordance with communist policies. The Jaruzelski* regime used the term so often and sometimes so paradoxically that members of the democratic opposition* in Poland agreed half-jokingly, half-seriously that, yes, they were anti-socialist elements. Underground and private enterprises produced colorful buttons displaying this term. J. Karpiński, *Polska, Komunizm, Opozycja* (London, 1985), 14.

APARAT (apparatus). State apparatus was understood as the administration, the Army,* and the police (Citizen's Militia [Milicja Obywatelska or MO]*). Party apparatus encompassed all political employees hired by the Party and assigned as leaders of its important units. Usually, these were trusted and experienced older members. J. Karpiński, *Polska, Komunizm, Opozycja* (London, 1985), 15.

APPEAL CONCERNING THE 1975 CONSTITUTION AMENDMENT, public protest against a new version of the Constitution, sponsored by the leadership of the Polish United Workers' Party (PZPR).* By the end of 1975, Party leaders announced they were going to amend the Constitution. Among several proposed changes was an affirmation of the socialist character of the Polish state, a statement on the guiding principles of the Bolshevik revolution, an assertion of the leading role of the PZPR, and a declaration of unshakable fraternal bonds between Poland and the USSR. The proposal provoked public outrage. Fifty-nine intellectuals headed by E. Lipiński* delivered to the Sejm* a petition demanding that the democratic right recognized in the Helsinki Declaration be included in the new Constitution. Several hundred people signed an open letter protesting the changes and supporting the petition. Surprised by the intensity of the protest, the Party leadership moderated the changes. The PZPR was described as "the leading political force of the society in the building of socialism," which did not decree a monopoly of communist power. The proposed "unshakable fraternal bonds" were replaced with strengthening of friendship and cooperation with the USSR. The statements about the Bolshevik revolution and about citizens' rights depending on their fulfillment of civic duties disappeared. The adoption of this "compromise" version was followed by protests of the Episcopate* and intellectuals. The conflict contributed significantly to the demise of the Gierek* regime. *The History of Poland since 1863*, ed. by R. F. Leslie (Cambridge, 1980), 431–432; A. Paczkowski, *Pół wieku dziejów Polski, 1939–1989* (Warsaw, 1995), 429; D. Ost, *Solidarity and the Politics of Anti-Politics* (Philadelphia, 1990).

APPEAL OF THE 34 INTELLECTUALS. See **Letter of 34.**

ARCHITECTURE. Post–World War II Polish architecture was shaped by two phenomena: reconstruction of war damages and communist ideology. During 1945–47, Polish architects concentrated on reconstruction. In Warsaw* 85% of which had been destroyed by the Germans, the Bureau of the Reconstruction of the Capital* was founded. It rebuilt the most important prewar objects and designed several large housing estates. Architectural and urbanistic concepts of this period reflected contemporary tendencies in Western architecture. In 1948 some projects were changed in the middle of the construction process, and the 1949 conference of architects—members of the Polish United Workers' Party (PZPR)*—announced the beginning of "Polish socialist architecture." The Stalinist architecture of 1948–56 followed the rules of Socialist Realism.* Architectural designs were obliged to be "socialist in content, national in form," which meant that heavy classicist compositions were decorated with elements from historical Polish architecture. Between 1952 and 1955 the Palace of Culture and Sciences, a Soviet gift to Poland, was built in Warsaw, as were Constitution Square and the building of the Ministry of Agriculture, all constructed in the same style. Nowa Huta* housing project near Cracow,* and Kościuszko Square in Wrocław* followed this formula. Those architects who rejected "Sociorealism" concentrated on the reconstruction of historical sites. In 1947–53 the Old Town, and in 1954 the New Town, was rebuilt in Warsaw. The historical centers of Gdańsk,* Wrocław, Opole,* and Poznań* were reconstructed in 1949–55, and the charming town of Kazimierz Dolny was rebuilt in 1955. Polish historical preservation and Polish landscape schools were born during these years.

In March 1956 the All-Polish Conference of Architects decided to break with Socialist Realism. What followed were new simple designs and experimental constructions, like "Supersam" in Warsaw. By 1959 Polish architects began to win prestigious prizes in international competitions. They designed spectacular objects abroad, like the Art Museum in Skopje, Yugoslavia, and the University of Dublin in Ireland. Yet the Stalinist period* had a visible negative impact on Polish architecture, which needed years to recover. Often Polish construction enterprises were technologically underdeveloped and thus unable to incorporate bolder designs into their buildings. Frequently, as in the cases of the Hotel Forum (1972–73) and the Intraco building (1973–75) in Warsaw and the Hotel Kasprowy (1974) in Zakopane, Polish buildings were erected by foreign constructors. Then in the 1960s large housing estates were constructed with prefabricated residential blocs. Some of these projects gained international acclaim, but most of them, especially those of the late 1970s, when Poland experienced a long economic crisis, received the dull, stereotypical modernist form. Only a few constructions, such as churches, hotels, and academic buildings, were designed differently. The fall of communism in Poland revolutionized Polish architecture, which reverted to its Western tendencies. B. Knox, *The Architecture of Poland* (London, 1971); B. Lisowska, *Modern Architecture in Poland* (Warsaw, 1968); T. Barucki, *Architektura Polski* (Warsaw, 1985); T. P. Szafer, *Współczesna architektura polska. Contemporary Polish Architecture* (Warsaw, 1988), 5–8.

ARCHIWUM WSCHODNIE. See **Eastern Archives.**

ARCISZEWSKI, TOMASZ (1877–1955), politician and one of the most important leaders of the Polish Socialist Party (PPS).* Minister in the first two governments of interwar Poland during 1918–19, he served as a Sejm* deputy during 1919–34 and 1938–39, and as PPS Chairman during 1931–39. During 1939–44 he was active in the leadership of the clandestine PPS in German-occupied Poland. Then in July 1944 he moved to England; in November 1944, after Mikołajczyk's* return to Poland, he became Premier* of the Polish Government-in-Exile.* On July 5, 1945, the United States and Great Britain withdrew their recognition for this government, but Arciszewski continued to serve as its Premier until 1947. Later, until his death, Arciszewski belonged to the leadership of the PPS in exile, and in 1954–55 he was a member of the Council of Three (Rada Trzech).* *Słownik Historii Polski 1939–1948*, ed. by A. Chwalba and T. Gąsowski (Cracow, 1994), 27–30.

ARENDARSKI, ANDRZEJ J. (1949–   ), Solidarity* activist, member of the Sejm* in 1989–91, and Minister of International Cooperation and the Marine Industry in the Suchocka* government from June 1992 to October 1993. *Kto jest kim w polityce polskiej*, ed. by R. Ignasiak (Warsaw, 1993), 10.

ARKA, underground periodical published in Cracow* from 1983, devoted to literary criticism and contemporary history of Poland. D. Cecuda, *Leksykon opozycji politycznej 1976–1989* (Warsaw, 1989), 145.

ARŁAMÓW, heavily guarded, lonely hunting lodge near the Soviet border in the Przemyśl region. In March 1982 L. Wałęsa* was moved to Arłamów after his arrest on December 13, 1981, and various interrogations in Warsaw.* He was imprisoned and isolated in Arłamów until November 1982, when he was released and returned via Warsaw to Gdańsk.* L. Wałęsa, *A Way of Hope* (New York, 1987), 228–237; M. Craig, *The Crystal Spirit: Lech Wałęsa and His Poland* (London, 1986), 245.

ARMY. By the end of World War II, the Polish armed forces constituted the fourth largest military power in the anti-German coalition (after the Soviet, U.S., and British armies). Yet the Polish forces were divided and controlled by two political adversaries: the Polish Government-in-Exile* and the Soviet-sponsored Provisional Government of the Republic of Poland.* The Polish People's Army (Ludowe Wojsko Polskie [LWP]), created by the merger of the communist guerrilla movement, known as the People's Army (AL), and the Polish Army in the USSR, had about 350,000 soldiers in May 1945. At the same time, the Polish Armed Forces (Polskie Siły Zbrojne [PSZ]) in the West were about 230,000 soldiers strong. The PSZ was dissolved in 1946, and only a small number of its soldiers and officers returned to Poland. Some of them joined the LWP. In 1946 it was demobilized, and during 1947–48 became largely neglected by the communist authorities, concentrated on developing strong internal security forces necessary to fight the anti-communist opposition.* One security unit was the Internal Security Corps (Korpus Bezpieczeństwa Publicznego [KBW])* formed in May 1945. This situation changed after 1948, during the Stalinist period.* Facing escalation of the Cold War,* the USSR began a massive military buildup of its own army and of the armed forces of its satellites. After the conscription of 1949, the Polish People's Army increased to nearly 400,000 soldiers. More modern Soviet equipment replaced World War II armament. The new Polish commander-in-chief and Minister of Defense, Soviet Marshal K. Rokossowski,* replaced thousands of Polish officers with Soviet "advisers," who by 1950 constituted almost 50% of the entire officer corps and roughly 90% of the top positions in the Defense Ministry. The Polish Army was purged: Hundreds of officers were arrested and many were tried. All in all, there were 55 military trials in the early 1950s, and 37 defendants were given death sentences. The Polish Army was reorganized to conform to the Soviet model and was commanded directly from Moscow.

Yet during the "Polish October" of 1956* a portion of the Polish Army did not obey Rokossowski's orders. The Internal Security Corps took up defensive positions around Warsaw* to resist the approaching Soviet units. Several important Polish military commanders, located outside the capital, prepared their units to fight the Soviets. After W. Gomułka's* return to power the "de-Sovietization" and the "re-nationalization" of the Polish Army began. Rokossowski and most Soviet officers returned to the USSR. If they survived, purged "pre-Stalinist" officers regained their posts, and Rokossowski's place was given to Gomułka's assistant and friend, Gen. M. Spychalski,* who served as Minister of Defense until 1968, when he was replaced by Gen. W. Jaruzelski.* Polish national uniforms and songs were reintroduced, and ideological indoctrination and direct Party control over the army were limited. Nonetheless, the Polish People's Army continued to constitute an important segment of the communist military bloc. The 1955 Warsaw Pact strengthened Polish-Soviet military ties. Soviet officers who had previously served in the Polish Army were replaced by a network of Soviet "liaisons missions" who supervised the Polish military. Obsessed with the threat to Poland from West Germany, the Polish leadership claimed that only an alliance with the USSR could guarantee Poland's territorial integrity.

In the 1960s, belief that future war would be nuclear prompted reorientation of operational doctrine from defense to rapid offensive against NATO territory. Poland's 15 divisions had their role in the Soviet offensive scenario against Western Europe. Plans were that the Polish Army would create a separate front, would attack through northern Germany, and would occupy Denmark. At the same time, Polish Army theorists elaborated the "Defense of National Territory" (Obrona Terytorialna Kraju [OTK]) concept. In 1965 a segment of the Polish armed forces was excluded from Warsaw Pact operations, or from the regular forces called the "operational army," and prepared for action on the "internal front"—mostly defense against massive nuclear air attack. The Internal Security Corps was renamed the Internal Defense Forces (Wojska Obrony Wewnętrznej [WOW]), transferred from the jurisdiction of the Interior Ministry to the Defense Ministry, and subordinated to the Inspectorate of the "Defense of National Territory." New impetus was given to civil defense efforts. Also, modernization of the Polish Army started in the 1960s. Many Polish officers complained that the standards of the Warsaw Pact armies lagged behind the Western level of military modernization. This became obvious during the 1967 Arab-Israeli war when Soviet equipment and tactics, used by the Arabs, proved to be ineffective in comparison with Western military products and thought. The 1967 Six-Day War led to a political crisis in Poland, known as the March events of 1968.* Hundreds of officers of Jewish background, among them 14 generals and 200 colonels, were ousted from the Army as early as 1967. In 1968 the Polish Army participated in the communist invasion of Czechoslovakia. Two years later about 61,000 troops were used against the civilian population during the December events of 1970.* All these events and actions discredited the Polish Army in the eyes of the population. As early as the late 1950s, however, officers' schools had had problems with recruitment. The invasion of Czechoslovakia was followed by a dramatic decline in the number of applications to military academies.

In 1971 after rearrangement of the Polish political leadership, the Polish Army was again purged, this time of its commanders' tied to the Gomułka* regime. Jaruzelski, though elected to the Party Central Committee* in 1968 and to the Politburo* in December 1970, remained in his position, extended his influence, and worked toward the recovery of the Army after the events of 1967–70. He desperately tried to diminish the damage done to the Polish Army's morale and image. During the June events of 1976,* the Army stayed in its barracks; yet in 1981 the eroding Polish communist authorities were unable to deal with the next crisis through political means alone. The Party asked the Army for help against Solidarity.* PZPR leaders believed the Army would rebuild "order" and return to the barracks, as it had in 1970. This time, however, Army commanders did not want to play this role; they had their own political ambitions and had lost confidence in the effectiveness of the Party. Only Jaruzelski was able to assume leadership, and only the Army, among all government-controlled organizations, retained its cohesion and discipline and enjoyed the trust of the Polish people. Martial Law* and the military dictatorship of General Jaruzelski constituted a last desperate and unsuccessful attempt to save communism in Poland.

In 1989 the Polish Army, together with Polish society in general, entered a difficult period of transformation. The Army, which continues to suffer from material problems, has been reduced from about 350,000 individuals in the mid-1980s to less than 300,000 in 1995, has become an object of struggle for control among various political forces in Poland, and is looking forward to joining NATO. G. C. Malcher, *Poland's Politicized Army* (New York, 1984); A. R. Johnson, R. W. Dean, and A. Alexiev, *East European Military Establishments: The Warsaw Pact Northern Tier* (New York, 1982); A. A. Michta, *Red Eagle: The Army in Polish Politics, 1944–1988)* (Stanford, Calif., 1990).

ART. Post–World War II Polish art reflected political changes and conflicts in Poland. In the years immediately following the war, the prewar style of patronage and the prewar artistic tendencies prevailed. In 1949, when the communist seizure of power* was completed, state authorities extended their dominance over artistic life. Adopted as an official doctrine, Socialist Realism* was imposed on artists by the Ministry of Culture and Art, which controlled all subsidies and ran the Central Bureau of Artistic Exhibitions, museums, and art schools. Political pressure and intimidation supported this system of art control. As a consequence, Polish artists became isolated and lost contact with artistic changes in the West. Polish sculptors produced massive monumental and portrait works in the academic Soviet style. Yet Polish artists managed to find a narrow margin of freedom, and in the early 1950s the Polish school of poster art was born. By 1955 the Stalinist system of art control began to collapse. The 1955 exhibition in the Arsenal of Warsaw, for example, showed that Polish artists were allowed to deviate from official doctrine; during the next three decades Polish artists broke out of isolation and tried to catch up with contemporary artistic tendencies in the West. W. Hasior* formed his first assemblages in 1957, T. Kantor* arranged his first happening in 1965, and Polish conceptual art was launched in the early 1970s. Sculptors returned to smaller and more individualistic forms, painters first embraced non-representational art and then returned to such realistic idioms as Photorealism and Neo-Expressionism, and architects turned to experimental designs, forbidden before 1956. The real end of administrative control over art came in the late 1980s, when Poland saw the democratization of its political life. The political situation of the early 1990s and the collapse of central state patronage prompted patriotic, religious, and national tendencies in Polish art. *The Dictionary of Art*, ed. by J. Turner, vol. 25 (New York, 1996), 91–143.

ARTISANS' SOLIDARITY (Independent Self-Managing Trade Union of Individual Artisans "Solidarity" [Niezależny Samorządny Związek Zawodowy Indywidualnego Rzemiosła "Solidarność"]), artisans' branch of the Solidarity* movement. Established at congresses in Koszalin on March 13, 1981, and Warsaw* on April 30, 1981, it was officially registered on June 9, 1981. The organization was divided in factions; the artisans' unions of southern Poland refused to recognize the Warsaw congress and arranged their own meeting in Katowice* on September 12–13, 1981. This internal conflict continued until imposition of Martial Law* in December 1981. J. Holzer, *Solidarność, 1980–81. Geneza i historia* (Warsaw, 1983), 91.

AS, bulletin of the Press Agency Solidarity. It published documents of Solidarity* and material from local Solidarity newsletters. J. Karpiński, *Polska, Komunizm, Opozycja* (London, 1985), 22.

ASH, TIMOTHY GARTON (1952–   ), fellow of St. Antony's College, Oxford, and author of several important books on Germany and East-Central Europe. He was with the strikers in the Lenin Shipyard in Gdańsk* and later described his experiences there in *The Polish Revolution*, recounting the birth of Solidarity. 1996 Sanford S. Elberg Lecturer: Timothy Garton Ash, <http://globe trotter.berkeley.edu/Elberg/gartonash.html>

ASSOCIATION OF JOURNALISTS OF THE PEOPLE'S REPUBLIC OF POLAND (Stowarzyszenie Dziennikarzy PRL), organization of journalists established in March 1982 to replace the dissolved Association of Polish Journalists (SDP).* The SDPRL consisted of individuals obedient toward the Jaruzelski* regime. The organization was just a purged version of the former SDP. J. Karpiński, *Polska, Komunizm, Opozycja* (London, 1985), 265.

ASSOCIATION OF POLISH JOURNALISTS (Stowarzyszenie Dziennikarzy Polskich [SDP]), professional organization of Polish journalists established in 1951 after communist authorities disbanded the Journalists' Trade Union. The SDP reached about 8,000 members in 1980, when some of them were active in the democratic opposition and the organization, as a whole, was no longer totally controlled by the authorities. As a consequence, the SDP was suspended after imposition of Martial Law* in December 1981 and officially dissolved on March 20, 1982. J. Karpiński, *Polska, Komunizm, Opozycja* (London, 1985), 264.

ASSOCIATION OF SCIENTIFIC COURSES (Towarzystwo Kursów Naukowych [TKN]), semi-clandestine organization created in January 1978 to support an independent educational movement free from communist domination and indoctrination. The TKN was preceded by the so-called Flying University,* established on the initiative of the Workers' Defense Committee (KOR)* in October 1977. A TKN declaration was signed by 58 persons, including a group of outstanding scientists. Jan Kielanowski* presided over the TKN's Program Council, and A. Celiński* and Wojciech Ostrowski were its secretaries. The TKN organized courses taught first at universities and then in private homes. A. Michnik* oversaw the courses on communist Poland; Tadeusz Kowalik, history of economics; Jerzy Jedlicki, contemporary political ideologies; Tadeusz Burek, literature as a manifestation of social consciousness; and Andrzej Tyszka, tradition and present socialist culture. The organization supported independent research, edited non-censored *Zeszyty Naukowe* (''Scientific Journals''), organized conferences and colloquia, maintained Ph.D. studies, and funded scholars persecuted by communist authorities. Among individuals instrumental in promoting TKN activities were B. Geremek,* W. Kunicki-Goldfinger,* Aldona Jawłowska, Jan Waszkiewicz, A. Drawicz,* J. Woźniakowski,* and Stefan Amsterdamski. The birth of Solidarity in 1980–81 allowed the TKN to work more openly, usually at the universities. J. J. Lipski, *KOR: A History of the Workers' Defense Committee in Poland, 1976–81* (Berkeley, Calif., 1985); D. Cecuda, *Leksykon Opozycji Politycznej 1976–1989* (Warsaw, 1989), 115–117.

ATHEISM, doctrine supported by communist authorities, who interpreted it as militant activity against religions. Initially after World War II, Polish communists tried to hide their anti-religious attitude. Important figures of the communist regime participated in religious ceremonies and emphasized their openness and tolerance. After 1948 the communists, secure and in full control, started an intense atheist propaganda campaign combined with severe anti-Church persecutions. In October 1956 these activities were tempered, but in the early 1960s they again intensified. In 1945 the prewar Polish Association of Free Thought (Polski Związek Myśli Wolnej) had been rebuilt but was discontinued in 1949; it was replaced by the Society of Atheists and Freethinkers (Stowarzyszenie Ateistów i Wolnomyślicieli) and the Society of Secular School (Towarzystwo Szkoły Świeckiej) in 1957. In 1959 both organizations merged into the Society for Propagation of Secular Culture (Towarzystwo Krzewienia Szkoły Świeckiej). It had about 370,000 members by the end of the 1970s and published two periodicals: *Argumenty* ("Arguments") and *Fakty i Myśli* ("Facts and Thoughts"). During the 1980–81 Solidarity* period it lost over one-half its members and later deteriorated further. J. Karpiński, *Polska, Komunizm, Opozycja* (London, 1985), 23.

AUDERSKA, HALINA (1904–   ), writer and political activist, member of the Sejm,* and leader of the Union of Polish Writers.* She made her debut in the 1930s, participated in the anti-German resistance during World War II, and fought in the Warsaw Uprising. After the war she edited several periodicals and wrote novels, plays, and television scenarios based mostly on the contemporary history of Poland. P. Kuncewicz, *Leksykon Polskich Pisarzy Współczesnych*, vol. 1 (Warsaw, 1995), 18–22.

AUTONOMOUS TRADE UNIONS (autonomiczne związki zawodowe), trade unions that belonged neither to Solidarity* nor to state-controlled trade unions in 1980–81. After imposition of Martial Law,* they were suspended and, in October 1983, declared illegal. J. Karpiński, *Polska, Komunizm, Opozycja* (London, 1985), 23.

AXER, ERWIN (1917–   ), theater director and producer, chief of several state theaters after 1945, and professor at the State Higher Theatrical School in Warsaw* between 1949 and 1981. *Who's Who in the Socialist Countries of Europe*, ed. by J. Stroynowski, vol. 1 (Munich, 1989), 35.

BABIUCH, EDWARD (1927–) communist politician, Premier* between February and August 1980, and E. Gierek's* major political assistant. Babiuch joined the Polish Workers' Party (PPR)* in 1948. He worked in the apparatuses of the communist Union of Polish Youth (ZMP)* during 1949–55, of the Central Committee* of the Polish United Workers' Party (PZPR)* in 1955–59, and the PZPR's Warsaw* Provincial Committee during 1959–63. He became a member of the Central Committee of the PZPR in 1964 and of the Politburo* in 1970. Between 1972 and 1976 he was a member of the State Council (Rada Państwa),* and from 1976–80 its Deputy President. Appointed Premier to stop the 1980 crisis, he was politically destroyed during its course: In October 1980 he was ejected from the Central Committee, in July 1981 from the PZPR, and in December 1980 from the Sejm,* where he had served since 1969. In his memoirs Gierek accused Babiuch of conspiring against him. G. Sanford and A. Gozdecka-Sanford, *Historical Dictionary of Poland* (Metuchen, N.J., 1994), 34; T. Mołdawa, *Ludzie Władzy 1944–1991. Władze państwowe i polityczne Polski według stanu na dzień 28 II 1991* (Warsaw, 1991), 330.

BACEWICZ, GRAŻYNA (1909–69), violinist and composer, professor at the Warsaw* Conservatory of Music. *Encyklopedyczny Słownik Sławnych Polaków* (Warsaw, 1996), 9.

BACZKO, BRONISŁAW (1924–), professor of philosophy. Expelled from Warsaw University* after the March events of 1968,* he left Poland and taught at the Universities of Clermond-Ferrand and Geneva. *Nowa Encyklopedia Powszechna PWN*, vol. 1 (Warsaw, 1995).

BADYLARZE ("stalk growers"), half-derogatory nickname for flower and vegetable growers. They farmed close to large Polish cities and prospered supplying them, whereas state-controlled agriculture* was unable to do so adequately. J. Wilkin, "Private Agriculture and Socialism: The Polish Experience," *Poland: The Economy in the 1980s*, ed. by R. A. Clarke (London: 1989), 61–71.

BAFIA, JERZY (1926–91), lawyer, professor at Cracow* (1950–53), Warsaw* (1954–68, 1970–91), and Silesian Universities (1969–70), and important functionary of the communist judicature. In 1950 he joined the Polish United Workers' Party (PZPR)* and started his career in the state judicial apparatus. Initially, he served in a district (powiatowy) and provincial (wojewódzki) courts of justice. In 1953–54 he served on the Supreme Court and during 1972–76 was its First President. Between 1976 and 1981 he was a Minister of Justice. An MP during 1972–80, he served as the President of the Sejm* Legislative Committee. T. Mołdawa, *Ludzie Władzy 1944–1991. Władze państwowe i polityczne Polski według stanu na dzień 28 II 1991* (Warsaw, 1991), 331.

BAGIŃSKI, KAZIMIERZ (1890–1966), one of the 16 leaders of the Polish underground state arrested by the Soviet secret police in 1945. A member of the Polish Socialist Party (PPS)* and the Polish Military Organization (POW) before 1918, he was one of the most important peasant leaders during the interwar period and World War II, when he was a member and then deputy president of the Council of National Unity (Rada Jedności Narodu). Arrested on March 28 and sentenced in Moscow to one year in prison, he returned to Poland and became an important leader of the Polish Peasant Party (PSL).* In 1946 he was rearrested and sentenced to eight years in prison. Released after a year, he left Poland together with St. Mikołajczyk* in October 1947. He died in Phoenix, Arizona. R. F. Staar, *Poland, 1944–1962: The Sovietization of a Captive People* (New Orleans, 1962); *Sprawa 16-tu. Protokoły przesłuchań gen. Leopolda Okulickiego "Niedźwiadka" i współoskarżych*," ed. A. Chmielarz and A. K. Kunert (Warsaw, 1993).

BAIRD, TADEUSZ (1928–81), Polish composer and a co-organizer of the "Warsaw Autumn" music festival. G. Sanford and A. Gozdecka-Sanford, *Historical Dictionary of Poland* (Metuchen, N.J. 1994), 34; *Encyklopedyczny Słownik Sławnych Polaków* (Warsaw, 1996), 11.

BAKA, WŁADYSŁAW (1936–), state official and professor of economics who taught at Warsaw University* from 1959. He joined the Polish United Workers' Party (PZPR)* in 1955 and made a career as a Party economist. During 1973–77 he served as a deputy director of the Economic Division of the Party Central Committee,* deputy director of its Division of Planing and Economic Analyzes between 1977 and 1980, and a deputy director of the Division of Trade and Finances in 1980–81. During 1980–86 he served as a secretary of the Committee for Economic Reform, and during 1981–85 as Minister of Economic Reform. From 1985 to 1988, he was a president of the National Polish

Bank, a position he held again in 1989–1991. In 1988 he became a member of the Party Central Committee, and a year later, its secretary. *Who's Who in the Socialist Countries of Europe*, ed. by J. Stroynowski, vol. 1 (Munich, 1989), 44; A. Kępiński and Z. Kilar, *Kto jest kim w Polsce inaczej* (Warsaw, 1985), 9–26.

BALAZS, ARTUR K. (1952–), politician and agronomist. A leader of Rural Solidarity* and peasant strikes, he was interned in 1981–82. He participated in the Round Table Negotiations,* and from September 1989 to December 1990, he served as a minister for rural social matters in the government of T. Mazowiecki.* In June 1989 Balazs was elected to the Sejm,* where he presided over the Committee of Agriculture and Food Industry. Since 1993 he has been a member of the Senate.* T. Mołdawa, *Ludzie Władzy 1944–1991. Władze państwowe i polityczne Polski według stanu na dzień 28 II 1991* (Warsaw, 1991), 331.

BALCEROWICZ, LESZEK (1947–) professor of economics and author of the "Balcerowicz Plan." During 1970–89 he taught at the Main School of Planning and Statistics in Warsaw* and unsuccessfully promoted a radical marketization reform of Polish industry. During 1972–74 he studied at St. John's University in New York. A member of the Polish United Workers' Party (PZPR)* since 1969, he became an economics consultant for Solidarity* in 1981, worked closely with the Network of Leading Workplaces, "Sieć," established in April 1981, and left the Party that same year. In 1988 he joined the Citizen Committee of Solidarity in Warsaw. On September 12, 1989, he became the Deputy Prime Minister, Finance Minister, and president of the Economic Committee of the Ministers Council in the government of T. Mazowiecki.* Between January 12, 1991, and December 22, 1991, he held the same positions in the cabinet of J. K. Bielecki.*

Balcerowicz created the so-called Balcerowicz Plan, aimed to transform Poland's communist economic system to a free market economy. Its author intended to incorporate Poland quickly into the global economy and supported tight monetary policies. Despite its obvious success, however, the plan was widely criticized for its harsh and rapid implementation. Enthusiasts of the plan argue that it gained the support of Western economic powers and the International Monetary Fund and led to a debt-restructuring advantageous to Poland. Balcerowicz authored some 50 scholarly works, was a candidate for the Nobel Prize in Economics in 1991, and was elected president of the Freedom Union (UW)* in 1995. G. Sanford and A. Gozdecka-Sanford, *Historical Dictionary of Poland* (Metuchen, N.J., 1994), 34–35; T. Mołdawa, *Ludzie Władzy 1944–1991. Władze państwowe i polityczne Polski według stanu na dzień 28 II 1991* (Warsaw, 1991), 157, 160, 331; L. Balcerowicz, *800 dni. Szok kontrolowany* (Warszawa, 1992); *Encyklopedyczny Słownik Sławnych Polaków* (Warsaw, 1996), 12; T. Torańska, *My* (Warsaw, 1994), 5–28.

BANACH, KAZIMIERZ (1904–85), peasant politician who served as a Sejm* deputy between 1945 and 1972, vice-president of the United Peasant Party

(ZSL)* during 1969–71, and member of the State Council (Rada Państwa)* in 1957–71. T. Mołdawa, *Ludzie Władzy 1944–1991. Władze państwowe i polityczne Polski według stanu na dzień 28 II 1991* (Warsaw, 1991), 332.

BANDEROWCY, popular name for members of the Ukrainian Insurgent Army (UPA).* In fact, "banderists" constituted only one faction of the UPA, led by Stepan Bandera. A. B. Szczęśniak and W. Z. Szota, *Droga do nikąd: Działalność Organizacji Ukraińskich Nacjonalistów i jej likwidacja w Polsce* (Warsaw, 1973); *Litopys UPA*, vol. 17, 22, 23 (Toronto, 1988–92); B. Huk (ed.), *Zakierzonia. Wspomnienia żołnierzy Ukraińskiej Powstańczej Armii*, vol. 1 (Warsaw, 1994).

BANKS. See **Finance.**

BAŃCZYK, STANISŁAW (1903–88), teacher and leader of peasant movement. He joined the Polish Peasant Party "Liberation" (PSL "Wyzwolenie"), in 1919 and was a leader of the underground Peasant Party during World War II. In 1944 he co-organized the Peasant Party "People's Will" and, in 1945, became its President. In late 1945 it merged with the Polish Peasant Party (PSL)* and Bańczyk became a deputy president of its Executive Committee. Threatened with an arrest by communists, Bańczyk left Poland in 1948 and was stripped of his Polish citizenship by the government in Warsaw.* In 1966 he became president of the Polish Peasant Party in Exile. T. Mołdawa, *Ludzie Władzy 1944–1991. Władze państwowe i polityczne Polski według stanu na dzień 28 II 1991* (Warsaw, 1991), 332; A. K. Kunert, *Illustrowany przewodnik po Polsce podziemnej, 1939–1945* (Warsaw, 1996), 451.

BAR (adwokatura). In the early 1980s there were about 6,000 attorneys in Poland. To receive a license to practice law, they had to graduate from the law department of a Polish university,* work as an apprentice for a specified period, and be accepted by the Attorneys' Council. In the 1950s and 1960s Polish attorneys were under heavy pressure; their position was very difficult and frequently dangerous. By the 1970s the attorneys' role in political trials was growing. On January 3–4, 1981, the first All-Polish Convention of Attorneys took place. The attorneys demanded real self-government and independence of the Bar. The next convention, held on October 1–3, 1983, repeated these demands, and soon, in 1984, the state authorities and the press began to attack the attorneys for "irresponsibility." J. Karpiński, *Polska, Komunizm, Opozycja* (London, 1985), 8.

BARAŃCZAK, STANISŁAW (1946–   ), poet, dissident, master of translation, scholar, professor and holder of the Chair of Polish Language and Literature at Harvard University, and author of many outstanding works. One of the founders of the Workers' Defense Committee (KOR)* in 1976, he became its representative to Greater Poland (Wielkopolska), and joined the editorial board of the underground *Zapis* ("The Record").* He was not allowed to publish, though, and was forbidden to carry out his duties at the University of Poznań,* where he had worked since his graduation. In August 1980 he left Poland to assume a professorship at Harvard. He has published many volumes of poetry, essays, and translations and remains an outstanding contemporary Polish theoretician of literature. *Who's Who in the Socialist Countries of Europe*, ed. by J. Stroynowski, vol. 1 (Munich, 1989), 57; M. H. Bernhard, *The Origins of Democratization in Poland* (New York, 1993); *Dictionary of Polish Literature*, ed. by E. J. Czerwinski (Westport, Conn., 1994), 10–12.

BARCIKOWSKI, KAZIMIERZ (1927–   ), agronomist, economist, and communist politician. He joined the Polish United Workers' Party (PZPR)* in 1953 and started a successful Party career. He served as a secretary of the Main Board of the communist Union of Polish Youth (ZMP)* in 1956–57, as deputy president and then president of the Union of Peasant Youth (ZMW)* in 1957–65, as a provincial Party secretary in Poznań* during 1968–70, as a member of the Party Central Committee* in 1968–90, its secretary in 1970–74 and 1980–85, Minister of Agriculture in 1974–77, member of the Politburo* in 1980–89, Deputy Premier* between February and October 1980, member of the State Council (Rada Państwa)* in 1980–85 and its Vice-President in 1985–89, and Sejm* deputy in 1965–89. He played an important role during the political crisis of 1980: As Politburo member and Deputy Premier he led the government delegation during negotiations with the Szczecin* strike committee and signed the Szczecin agreement of August 30, 1980. After imposition of Martial Law* on December 13, 1981, Barcikowski became a close assistant of Gen. W. Jaruzelski* and a member of the so-called Directorate, a small, unofficial cabinet. T. Mołdawa, *Ludzie Władzy 1944–1991. Władze państwowe i polityczne Polski według stanu na dzień 28 II 1991* (Warsaw, 1991), 333; N. Ascherson, *The Polish August* (New York, 1981), 151, 155, 170–172, 184, 189, 263, 272; *Who's Who in Poland* (Warsaw, 1982), 26; A. Micewski, *Ludzie i opcje* (Warsaw, 1993), 197–201.

BARDINI, ALEKSANDER (1913–95), actor, theater director, and professor who educated several generations of Polish actors. *Who's Who in Poland* (Warsaw, 1982), 27; *Encyklopedyczny Słownik Sławnych Polaków* (Warsaw, 1996), 16.

BARTELSKI, LESŁAW M. (1920–   ), poet, writer, and literary critic. After basing his first works on his experience during World War II, he immersed himself in Socialist Realism.* In the 1960s and 1970s he wrote about Polish history and culture and, in literary and documentary form, about his life obsession: the Warsaw Uprising. *Who's Who in the Socialist Countries of Europe*, ed. by J. Stroynowski, vol. 1 (Munich, 1989), 65.

BARTOSZCZE, MICHAŁ (1914–   ), farmer and veteran of the Home Army (AK)* and the peasant movement. A co-organizer of Rural Solidarity,* he was beaten by the Citizens' Militia (MO)* at the Provincial People's Council Office in Bydgoszcz* in March 1981, an event that started a political crisis. His son, Piotr, was murdered under unexplained circumstances. *Who's Who in the Socialist Countries of Europe*, ed. by J. Stroynowski, vol. 1 (Munich, 1989), 67.

BARTOSZCZE, ROMAN (1946–), farmer, son of M. Bartoszcze,* and activist of Rural Solidarity* and the Polish Peasant Party (Wilanów Group). In 1989 he was elected to the Sejm.* He became chairman of the reunited Polish Peasant Party (PSL)* and its candidate in the presidential election of 1990.* He received only 7.15% of the vote, was eliminated from the leadership of his party, and organized a new one: Polish "Patrimony" Party (Polska Partia "Ojcowizna"). G. Sanford and A. Gozdecka-Sanford, *Historical Dictionary of Poland* (Metuchen, N.J., 1994), 36–37; *Kto jest kim w polityce polskiej*, ed. by R. Ignasiak (Warsaw, 1993), 17.

BARTOSZEWSKI, WŁADYSŁAW (1922–), writer, historian, politician, Minister of Foreign Affairs in the cabinet of J. Oleksy* from May 1995 to December 22, 1995. After a year in Auschwitz (1940–41), he was active in the anti-German resistance, belonged to the Council for Aid to Jews, "Żegota," fought in the Home Army (AK),* and participated in the Warsaw Uprising. After the war Bartoszewski worked in the state's Committee for the Investigation of German Crimes in Poland and wrote for an opposition newspaper. During 1946–48 and 1949–54 he was imprisoned by the communist authorities. Later he co-edited *Tygodnik Powszechny* ("The Universal Weekly"),* taught at the Catholic University of Lublin (KUL),* presided over the Polish PEN Club in 1972–82, and researched World War II history in Poland and abroad. He also taught at the Universities of Munich, Eichstaett, and Augsburg (1983–90). In 1963 the Holocaust Remembrance Institute of Jerusalem named him Righteous among the Nations of the World, and in 1992 he became an honorary citizen of Israel. Member of Solidarity,* he was interned in 1981. During 1991–95 he served as Polish ambassador to Austria. As Minister of Foreign Affairs, he energetically supported the Polish application for membership in NATO and the European Union. He resigned after the 1995 presidential election* in Poland and the Oleksy spy affair. A prolific writer, Bartoszewski has published a number of books, dealing mostly with the history of Warsaw during the war, the Polish Jews, and the rescue of Jews by Polish gentiles. They include *Warsaw Death Ring, 1939–1944* and *Righteous among Nations: How Poles Helped the Jews*. K. Iranek-Osmecki, *He Who Saves One Life* (New York, 1971), 140, 288; A. Micewski, *Ludzie i opcje* (Warsaw, 1993), 126–129; *Kto jest kim w polityce polskiej*, ed. by R. Ignasiak (Warsaw, 1993), 17–18.

BATOWSKI, HENRYK (1907–), professor of history at the Jagiellonian University* in Cracow,* member of the Polish Academy of Sciences (PAN),* and author of many books and articles on East-Central Europe in the 19th and

20th centuries. *Who's Who in the Socialist Countries of Europe*, ed. by J. Stroynowski, vol. 1 (Munich, 1989), 72.

BAUMAN, ZYGMUNT (1925–), sociologist. Expelled from Warsaw University* in 1968, he emigrated to Israel and England, where he taught at the University of Leeds and became one of the most outstanding sociologists of the 20th century. D. Ost, *Solidarity and the Politics of Anti-Politics* (Philadelphia, 1990).

BĄK, HENRYK (1930–), anti-communist peasant leader and deputy speaker of the Sejm* in 1991. *Kto jest kim w polityce polskiej*, ed. by R. Ignasiak (Warsaw, 1993), 19–20.

BBWR. See **Non-Party Bloc for the Support of Reform.**

BEDNARKIEWICZ, MACIEJ (1940–), lawyer who defended political prisoners before the fall of communism in Poland. During 1989–91 he served as a Sejm* deputy, since 1989 as President of the Main Attorneys' Council (Naczelna Rada Adwokacka), and, since 1991 as a member of the State Tribunal. *Nowa Encyklopedia Powszechna PWN*, vol. 1 (Warsaw, 1995).

BELORUSSIAN DEMOCRATIC UNION (Białoruskie Zjednoczenie Demokratyczne), the largest Belorussian political party in Poland. In February 1989 the first Belorussian Territorial Councils appeared in the Białystok* region. On February 10, 1990, they were officially transformed into this party. Its aims are the introduction of Belorussian as the second official language in the ethnic Belorussian territories of Poland and their faster economic and cultural development. Led by S. Janowicz* and Wiktor Stachwiuk, the party cooperates with the Freedom Union (UW).* *Partie Polityczne w Polsce*, ed. by A. Gargas and M. Wojciechowski (Gdańsk, 1991), 9–10.

BELORUSSIANS, national minority of about 300,000 people living mostly in Białystok* Province (województwo). After World War II about 150,000 Belorussians found themselves within the new borders* of Poland. They survived so many political changes in the 20th century that most Belorussians were indifferent to their state affiliation. They were recognized as full citizens of Poland but did not receive special minority status. The Polish Committee of National Liberation (PKWN) allowed schools with Belorussian language of instruction to be organized. In November 1944, there were 117 such schools on the liberated territories. There were also two Belorussian high schools in Hajnówka and Bielsk Podlaski and one Russian-Belorussian high school in Białystok. Most of these schools were closed between 1945 and 1947. In September 1944 the PKWN and the Soviet authorities signed an agreement for the mutual exchange of Polish and Belorussian populations. Rumors spread that the Belorussians would like to separate their territories from Poland and attach them to the Belorussian Soviet Republic. The Polish-Soviet agreement was to end the "Belorussian problem" in Poland, but repatriation was not popular. Most Belorussians did not want to abandon their possessions, and only 36,388 persons left Poland through the end of 1946. Several thousands moved to Poland's newly acquired Western Territories and large cities in central Poland. In the late 1940s and the 1950s a wave of Belorussians, especially the young, moved from the countryside to local towns, mostly Białystok, Bielsk Podlaski, Hajnówka, and Siemiatycze. Rumors about Belorussian separatism surfaced during every political crisis in Poland.

In 1949 Polish authorities resumed development of Belorussian education. By 1954 there were 66 Belorussian elementary schools and 2 high schools. Those numbers grew, and eventually 90 elementary schools and several high schools taught Belorussian. A nucleus of Belorussian intelligentsia was revived and in 1955–56, during de-Stalinization, it established the Belorussian Social-Cultural Association (Białoruskie Towarzystwo Społeczno-Kulturalne [BTSK]), which became the center of Belorussian activities in Poland. At the same time, the weekly *Niva* ("The Realm") appeared and a chair of Belorussian language and literature was established at Warsaw University.* Since then a Belorussian yearbook has been published, Belorussian programs have been broadcasted on radio, and choirs and amateur theaters have been active in almost every village. In 1967–68, at the height of Belorussian educational development, 12,504 children were learning Belorussian at school. Yet the BTSK and all other Belorussian activities were officially supervised by the Polish Interior Ministry. In the late 1960s Polish authorities began to limit Belorussian activities and cultural life. As a result, Belorussian schools disappeared gradually, and in 1980–91 only 4,068 children were learning Belorussian. In 1972 the largest Belorussian dance ensemble, Lavonicha, was dissolved. In 1973 the Regional Belorussian Ethnographic Museum in Białowieża was closed. In the early 1980s Polish authorities tried to settle Polish peasants from central and southern Poland in eastern parts of the Białystok region. At the same time, however, the 1980 Solidarity* period witnessed a revival of Belorussian cultural and political life. Belorussian student movements appeared in the academic centers of Poland. Martial Law* and the Jaruzelski* regime stopped these changes only partially and temporarily. Belorussian press continued to print underground. New Belorussian organizations were established in 1988 and 1989. J. Zaprudnik, *Belarus: At a Crossroads in History* (Boulder, Colo., 1993), 215–218; E. Mironowicz, *Białorusini w Polsce 1944–49* (Warsaw, 1993); W. Choruży, *Białoruski drugi obieg w Polsce 1981–90* (Białystok, 1994), 7–58; K. Podlaski, *Białorusini, Litwini, Ukraińcy* (London, 1985).

BENDER, RYSZARD J. (1932–   ), professor of history at the Catholic University of Lublin (KUL)* and a Christian-National politician. A leader of several Christian organizations before 1989 and the Chairman of Lublin's* Club of Catholic Intelligentsia,* he represented the *Znak** group in the Sejm* during 1976–80 and 1985–89. In 1989 he participated in the Round Table Negotiations* and in 1990–91 was a member of the Civic Committee (KO).* He became a leader of the Christian-National Union (ZChN),* headed its caucus in the Senate,* where he sat during 1990–93, and was a member of the Radio and TV Council (Krajowa Rada Radiofonii i Telewizji) in 1993–94 (president in 1994). *Who's Who in Poland* (Warsaw, 1982), 38; *Kto jest kim w polityce polskiej*, ed. by R. Ignasiak (Warsaw, 1993), 22; G. Polak, *Kto jest kim w Kościele katolickim?* (Warsaw, 1996), 22.

BENTKOWSKI, ALEKSANDER (1941–   ), lawyer and politician. He joined the United Peasant Party (ZSL)* in 1962 and participated in its reform in 1989. He became a leader of the Polish Peasant Party "Revival" ("Odrodzenie") and, after May 1990, of the reborn Polish Peasant Party (PSL).* He served as a Minister of Justice in the Mazowiecki* government (September 1989–December 1990) and as attorney general (prokurator generalny) in 1990. In 1989 and 1993 he was elected to the Sejm,* where he served as chairman of the PSL caucus and of the Justice Committee. T. Mołdawa, *Ludzie Władzy 1944–1991. Władze państwowe i polityczne Polski według stanu na dzień 28 II 1991* (Warsaw, 1991), 335.

BERLING, ZYGMUNT (1896–1980), general and commander of the first Army of the Polish People's Army.* Veteran of the Piłsudski Legions during World War I, he joined the Polish Army in 1918, supported the 1926 Piłsudski coup d'état, and served in various military positions until his retirement in July 1939. During World War II he cooperated with the NKVD, co-organized and took command of the communist-controlled First Kościuszko Division in 1943 (from March 1944, of the First Polish Army in the USSR). In July 1944 he became a deputy defense minister in the Polish Committee of National Liberation (PKWN). In September 1944 as a commander of the First Polish Army, he tried to help the Warsaw Uprising, was removed from his position, and, in January 1945, was sent to a Military Academy in Moscow. In 1947 he returned to Poland and during 1948–53 commanded the General Staff Academy of the Polish Army in Warsaw.* Later he served as a Deputy Minister of the State Agricultural Enterprises and in several secondary administration positions. *Słownik Historii Polski 1939–1948*, ed. by A. Chwalba and T. Gąsowski (Cracow, 1994), 30–34.

BERMAN, JAKUB (1901–84), lawyer, communist official, and one of the three most important Stalinist officials in Poland. An activist of the Communist Party of Poland (KPP) since 1928, he spent World War II in the Soviet Union, where he was active in the communist-controlled Union of Polish Patriots (ZPP) and the Central Bureau of the Polish Communists in the USSR. In 1944 he returned to Poland with the Red Army,* joined the Polish Workers' Party (PPR),* and became a member of its Central Committee* and Politburo.* After the forced unification of the Polish Socialist Party (PPS)* and the PPR in 1948, he served in the same positions in the Polish United Workers' Party (PZPR).* Until he resigned from the Politburo on May 4, 1956, and was ejected from the Central Committee and the Party on May 18, 1957, Berman occupied several crucial positions in the Polish communist apparatus: deputy director of the Foreign Affairs Department of the Polish Committee of National Liberation (PKWN) in 1944, undersecretary of state in the Ministry of Foreign Affairs in 1945, undersecretary of state in the Presidium of the Ministers' Council in 1945–52, a member of this Presidium in 1950–52, a Sejm* deputy in 1944–56, and Vice Premier from March 18, 1954 to May 4, 1956. Responsible for security in the Politburo, Berman was hated by most Poles. Because of his Jewish family background, many Poles believed that he epitomized the theory of "Judeocommunism" (Żydokomuna). After 1956 Berman left politics and worked in the history department of the Party's publishing house until his retirement in 1969. In 1984, shortly before Berman's death, a journalist, T. Torańska,* interviewed him and a group of leading Polish Stalinists. She published these interviews in a book that is both exceptionally interesting and crucial to an understanding of the Stalinist period.* T. Torańska, *"Them": Stalin's Polish Puppets* (New York, 1987), 201–355; K. Kersten, *The Establishment of Communist Rule in Poland, 1943–48* (Berkeley, Calif., 1991).

BETON (cement), derogatory nickname for hard-line communists, made popular in 1980 and used frequently in the 1980s. The representatives of Beton—such as A. Żabiński* and T. Grabski,* a prosecutor general and his assistants, the military newspaper *Żołnierz Wolności* ("The Soldier of Freedom"),* the journal *Rzeczywistość* ("The Reality"), *Biuletyn Aktualności* ("News Bulletin"), which was published by the Warsaw Party committee, and Katowice's Party Forum—opposed any contacts with Solidarity* and other organizations of the political opposition, and were ready to ask the Soviet Union to intervene in Polish affairs. J. Karpiński, *Polska, Komunizm, Opozycja* (London, 1985), 24.

BEYLIN, KAROLINA (1899–1977), journalist and contributor to the most popular Polish periodicals. M. Dąbrowska, *Dzienniki Powojenne 1945–1965*, vol. 1, ed. by T. Drewnowski (Warsaw, 1996), 167.

BĘBENEK, STANISŁAW (1920–), journalist and editor. A long-time Polish Workers' Party (PPR)* and Polish United Workers' Party (PZPR)* official, he directed several state publishing houses, a theater, and a TV* program. He made his name after 1975 as president and editor-in-chief of the *Czytelnik* ("Reader") Publishing House. *Who's Who in Poland* (Warsaw, 1982), 36.

BIAŁOSZEWSKI, MIRON (1922–83), poet and writer, author of shocking works. His *Pamiętnik z powstania warszawskiego* ("Memoir of the Warsaw Uprising"), cruel and anti-heroic, became a literary sensation. P. Kuncewicz,

Leksykon Polskich Pisarzy Współczesnych, vol. 1 (Warsaw, 1995), 53–56; *Dictionary of Polish Literature*, ed. by E. J. Czerwinski (Westport, Conn., 1994), 20–22.

BIAŁYSTOK, capital city of Białystok Province (województwo) in northeastern Poland. Founded by the Lithuanians* in the Middle Ages, it was incorporated by Russia after the Partitions of Poland. In 1918 it was returned to the Polish state as a large textile industry center. During World War II, the Germans killed half the Białystok population, including about 40,000 Jews.* After the war the city was rebuilt as a center of the textile, food, and metallurgical industries. Warsaw University* has a campus in Białystok. In 1982 the city reached a population of 230,000, including a large group of Belorussians,* who consider the town their main center in Poland. *Encyklopedia Historii Gospodarki Polski*, ed. by A. Mączak, vol. 1 (Warsaw, 1981), 36–37.

BIELECKI, CZESŁAW (Maciej Poleski) (1948–), architect, publisher, prolific publicist, and activist of democratic opposition before 1989. Political prisoner in 1968, 1983, and 1985–86, he wrote for Paris *Kultura,** organized an underground publishing house, the *CDN,** and participated in the *Porozumienie Ponad Podziałami* (Agreement beyond Divisions). *Who's Who in the Socialist Countries of Europe*, ed. by J. Stroynowski, vol. 1 (Munich, 1989), 98.

BIELECKI, JAN KRZYSZTOF (1951–), economist, politician, and Premier* from January 1991 to December 1991. A faculty member of Gdańsk* University in 1973–74 and a professor at a governmental management school during 1975–82, he was active in Solidarity* in 1980–81 and after imposition of Martial Law* was removed from work for political reasons. Later he was active as a private entrepreneur, and in 1988 he co-organized the Liberal-Democratic Congress (KLD)* and became the president of its Political Council. Elected to the Sejm* in June 1989, Bielecki followed T. Mazowiecki* as a Premier. Later he served as a minister in charge of European integration and foreign help to Poland in the government of H. Suchocka.* T. Mołdawa, *Ludzie Władzy 1944–1991. Władze panństwowe i polityczne Polski według stanu na dzień 28 II 1991* (Warsaw, 1991), 337; *Kto jest kim w polityce polskiej*, ed. by R. Ignasiak (Warsaw, 1993), 25–26; T. Torańska, *My* (Warsaw, 1994), 29–88; *Rodem z Solidarości*, ed. by B. Kopka and R. Żelichowski (Warsaw, 1997), 15–31.

BIELIŃSKI, KONRAD (1949–), mathematician, member of the Workers' Defense Committee (KOR)* since October 1977, and Solidarity* activist. He participated in the Lenin Shipyard strike in Gdańsk* in August 1980. An experienced editor of underground periodicals, such as *Krytyka* ("The Critique")* and *Głos* ("The Voice"),* he helped to organize *Tygodnik Solidarność* ("The Solidarity Weekly"),* the main organ of the Solidarity Trade Union, and headed its Commission for Information and Mass Communication, Mazovian Regional Board. After imposition of Martial Law* in 1981, he went underground as a member of the Provisional National Commission of Solidarity. *Who's Who in the Socialist Countries of Europe*, ed. by J. Stroynowski, vol. 1 (Munich, 1989), 98; D. Ost, *Solidarity and the Politics of Anti-Politics* (Philadelphia, 1990); M. H. Bernhard, *The Origins of Democratization in Poland* (New York, 1993).

BIEŃ, ADAM (1899–1998), one of the 16 leaders of the Polish underground state arrested by the NKVD in 1945. A judge of a district court in Warsaw,* he was active in peasant youth organizations during the interwar period, belonged to the leadership of the underground peasant movement during World War II, and served as a deputy delegate of the Polish Government-in-Exile* in Poland (1943) and as a minister of this government (May 1944). Arrested in March 1945, he was sentenced to five years in prison. In 1949 he returned to Poland and settled in his native village. In the late 1980s he participated in the reconstruction of an authentic peasant movement in Poland. R. F. Staar, *Poland, 1944–1962: The Sovietization of a Captive People* (New Orleans, 1962); *Sprawa 16-tu. Protokoły przesłuchań gen. Leopolda Okulickiego "Niedźwiadka" i współoskarżonych,"* ed. A. Chmielarz and A. K. Kunert (Warsaw, 1993); A. K. Kunert, *Ilustrowany przewodnik po Polsce podziemnej, 1939–1945* (Warsaw, 1996), 454.

BIEŃKOWSKI, WŁADYSŁAW (1906–91), philosopher, communist, and dissident. Active in the communist movement during the interwar period, he joined the Polish Workers' Party (PPR)* in 1942, and in December 1943 he co-organized the National Home Council (KRN).* In 1945 he became a member of the Central Committee* of the PPR, served as an undersecretary of state in the Ministry of Education in 1945–46, a director of the Propaganda Department of the Central Committee of the Polish United Workers' Party (PZPR),* and a member of the secretariat of the Central Committee in 1946–48. During 1948–56 he was a director of the National Library, and in 1956–59, Minister of Education. A member of Parliament during 1943–52 and 1957–69, he was removed from politics after a conflict with W. Gomułka* and began to cooperate with the democratic opposition. M. H. Bernhard, *The Origins of Democratization in Poland* (New York, 1993); T. Mołdawa, *Ludzie Władzy 1944–1991. Władze państwowe i polityczne Polski według stanu na dzień 28 II 1991* (Warsaw, 1991), 337.

BIERIEZIN, JACEK (1947–93), rebellious poet, activist of the Workers' Defense Committee (KOR),* and editor of Puls Publishing House.* J. J. Lipski, *KOR: A History of the Workers' Defense Committee in Poland, 1976–81* (Berkeley, Calif., 1990).

BIERUT, BOLESŁAW (1892–1956), the most important official in Poland during the Stalinist period.* Born in a peasant family in the Lublin* region, he joined the Polish Socialist Party–Left (PPS-Lewica) in 1912; after the 1918 unification of the Polish radical left, he continued his activities in the Communist Party of Poland (KPP), serving in several important positions. During 1925–26 and 1928–30 he trained in Moscow, and in 1930–32 he worked as a Comintern emissary in Austria, Czechoslovakia, and Bulgaria, organizing communist cells there. Arrested by the Polish police, he was imprisoned in 1933–38. In 1939 he moved to the USSR. Then in July 1943 he returned to Poland, joined the Polish Workers' Party (PPR),* and became a member of its Central Committee* secretariat. After the creation of the communist-dominated underground National Home Council (KRN)* on December 31, 1943, he became its president; as such, he was designated the head of the Soviet-controlled Polish puppet state in September 1944. On February 21, 1947, the newly elected Sejm* appointed Bierut President* of Poland and later chairman of the State Council (Rada Państwa).* He became First Secretary of the Central Committee of the PPR in September 1948. After the forced unification of the Polish political left in December 1948, Bierut headed the Central Committee and the Politburo* of the Polish United Workers' Party (PZPR).* Starting in 1950, he unofficially directed the Presidium of the Polish government, but on November 20, 1952, he left the presidency and served as Premier* of Poland until March 18, 1954. He died in Moscow on March 12, 1956, immediately after the 20th Congress of the Communist Party of the Soviet Union. Many Poles believe that he was killed by Stalin's successors because he embodied Stalinism in Poland. Dogmatic Stalinist and obedient follower of the directives from Moscow, Bierut was instrumental in the communist seizure of power* in Poland. L. B. Bain, *The Reluctant Satellites* (New York, 1960); *The Cold War, 1945–1991*, vol. 2, "Leaders and Other Important Figures in the Soviet Union, Eastern Europe, China, and the Third World," ed. by B. Frankel (Detroit, 1992), 32–34; K. Kersten, *The Establishment of Communist Rule in Poland, 1943–48* (Berkeley, Calif., 1991); R. Spasowski, *The Liberation of One* (New York, 1986).

"BIM-BOM," satiric student theater opened in November 1954 in Gdańsk* as a part of cultural "thaw"* and de-Stalinization in Poland. Among those collaborating with "Bim-Bom" were such renowned artists as Z. Cybulski,* Bogumił Kobiela, Jacek Federowicz, Wowo Bielicki, and Jerzy Afanasjew. The theater developed its own style of humorous song and gained international fame. *Wkład Polaków do kultury świata*, ed. by M. A. Krąpiec (Lublin, 1976), 726.

BIULETYN INFORMACYJNY (Information Bulletin), underground organ of the Workers' Defense Committee (KOR),* reporting on its activities. Its 41 issues appeared between 1976 and 1980. M. H. Bernhard, *The Origins of Democratization in Poland* (New York, 1993); J. Karpiński, *Polska, Komunizm, Opozycja* (London, 1985), 26.

BLISS LANE, ARTHUR (1894–1956), diplomat and U.S. ambassador to Poland from July 5, 1945, to March 31, 1947. Starting his career in 1916, he served in various diplomatic positions in Rome, London, Paris, Berne, Mexico, Nicaragua, Estonia, Latvia, Lithuania, and Poland (second secretary to the Warsaw* legation, 1919–20). Appointed minister to Yugoslavia in 1937, he was instrumental in evacuating U.S. citizens and the U.S. legation from Belgrade, bombed by the Germans in 1941. Later he represented his country in Costa Rica and Colombia. In September 1944 he was designated ambassador to the Polish Government-in-Exile,* but it had lost U.S. recognition before Lane went to London. Instead, Lane was sent to Warsaw as ambassador to the Provisional Government of National Unity (TRJN)* immediately after it was recognized by Washington. After the faked election of 1947,* Lane resigned his post; in protest against U.S. policy toward Eastern Europe, he retired from diplomatic service. He devoted his life to the fight against communism and wrote several books about Soviet imperialism, including *I Saw Poland Betrayed: An American Ambassador Reports to the American People*, which is an important primary source on postwar Polish history. Lane was also an active member of the National Committee for a Free Europe, the Committee for a United Europe, the American Committee to Investigate the Katyń* Massacre, and the Paderewski Testimonial Fund. *The National Cyclopaedia of American Biography*, vol. 45 (New York, 1962) 146.

BLOC OF DEMOCRATIC PARTIES (BLOK STRONNICTW DEMOK-RATYCZNYCH). See Elections of January 19, 1947.

BLUMSZTAJN, SEWERYN (1946–   ), Solidarity* activist. Harassed and arrested many times by the communist authorities, he was an important member of several organizations of the democratic opposition in Poland, including the Workers' Defense Committee (KOR).* Organizer and head of the Solidarity Press Agency (AS), he established the Coordinating Bureau of Solidarity Abroad in Paris, where he was when Martial Law* was imposed in Poland on December 13, 1981. In 1985 he was forbidden to return to Poland by its communist authorities. *Who's Who in the Socialist Countries of Europe*, ed. by J. Stroynowski, vol. 1 (Munich, 1989), 111; D. Ost, *Solidarity and the Politics of Anti-Politics* (Philadelphia, 1990); M. H. Bernhard, *The Origins of Democratization in Poland* (New York, 1993).

BŁOŃSKI, JAN (1931–   ), writer, professor of Polish literature at the Jagiellonian University,* and member of the Polish PEN Club. He contributed significantly to Polish-Jewish studies and dialogue. His article "The Poor Poles Look at the Ghetto," published in *Tygodnik Powszechny* ("The Universal Weekly")* in January 1987, started a fierce polemic about anti-Semitism* in Poland. *Who's Who in the Socialist Countries of Europe*, ed. by J. Stroynowski, vol. 1 (Munich, 1989), 110; M. C. Steinlauf, *Bondage to the Dead: Poland and the Memory of the Holocaust* (Syracuse, N.Y., 1997), 113–116.

BOBROWSKI, CZESŁAW (1904–96), economist. A graduate of Warsaw University* and the École des Sciences Politiques in Paris, he directed the Department of Economics of the Polish Ministry of Agriculture during 1935–39. A veteran of the September 1939 Campaign and the French campaign of 1940, he was interned in Switzerland but escaped to France and was active in the Resistance. A member of the Chief Council of the Polish Socialist Party (PPS)* in 1946–48, he served as president of the Central Planning Office and deputy chairman of the Economic Committee of the Council of Ministers during 1945–48. He co-authored the postwar Three-Year Plan of Reconstruction. Removed from top state positions during the Stalinist period,* he resumed his position as acting deputy chairman of the governmental Economic Committee in 1957–63. In the 1960s and 1970s he taught at Polish and foreign universities and worked as an expert for the United Nations. In 1981, shortly after imposition of Martial Law,* he accepted Gen. W. Jaruzelski's* invitation to chair the regime's Consultative Economic Council. Although criticized for this act by his opponents, Bobrowski was prized by his supporters for his devotion to the interests of Poland. *Who's Who in Poland* (Warsaw, 1982), 56; W. Wilczyński, "Zawsze dla Polski," *Polityka*, no. 22 (2039), June 1, 1996.

BOCHEŃSKI, ALEKSANDER (1904–   ), writer and journalist. He started publishing in the 1930s in conservative and Catholic periodicals and was associated with the *Bunt Młodych* ("Rebellion of the Young") group. After the war he co-organized the PAX Association,* was its representative in the Sejm* during 1947–52, and contributed to the PAX papers. A prolific writer and publicist, he authored such interesting works as *Dzieje głupoty w Polsce* ("History of Stupidity in Poland") and *Rzecz o psychice narodu polskiego* ("On the Psyche of the Polish Nation"). *Who's Who in the Socialist Countries of Europe*, ed. by J. Stroynowski, vol. 1 (Munich, 1989), 113; M. Dąbrowska, *Dzienniki powojenne 1945–49*, vol. 1, ed. by T. Drewnowski (Warsaw, 1996), 53.

BOCHEŃSKI, JACEK (1926–   ), writer whose works evolved from Socialist Realism* to anti-communism. He joined the Polish Workers' Party (PPR)* in 1947, but in 1966 he left the Polish United Workers' Party (PZPR)* in protest against the ousting of L. Kołakowski* from the Party. In 1976 Bocheński signed an appeal concerning the 1975 Constitution amendment* and the appeal of 13, defending the workers of Ursus* and Radom.* As a consequence, censors blocked all publications by Bocheński, who became editor of the underground *Zapis* ("The Record")* and a lecturer of the Association of Scientific Courses (TKN).* In spring 1997 he was elected president of the Polish PEN Club. *Who's Who in the Socialist Countries of Europe*, ed. by J. Stroynowski, vol. 1 (Munich, 1989), 113.

BOGUTA, GRZEGORZ (1952–   ), dissident and activist of the Workers' Defense Committee (KOR),* instrumental in organizing the independent publishing movement in Poland in the late 1970s. J. J. Lipski, *KOR: A History of the Workers' Defense Committee in Poland, 1976–81* (Berkeley, Calif., 1985); M. H. Bernhard, *The Origins of Democratization in Poland* (New York, 1993).

BONI, MICHAŁ J. (1954–   ), Solidarity* leader and politician. During 1977–90 he taught at Warsaw University.* After imposition of Martial Law,* he became a leader of the underground Solidarity in Warsaw.* A chairman of Solidarity, Mazowsze Region in 1991, he served as Minister of Labor in the government of J. K. Bielecki* in 1991 and Deputy Minister of Labor in the cabinet of H. Suchocka* in 1992–93. During 1991–93 he represented the Liberal Democratic Congress (KLD)* in the Sejm.* Since 1994 he has been a city alderman of Warsaw, and since mid-1995 he has worked in the Institute of Public Affairs (Instytut Spraw Publicznych). *Kto jest kim w polityce polskiej*, ed. by R. Ignasiak (Warsaw, 1993), 33.

BORDERS. After World War II Poland lost large territories to the USSR and gained some former German provinces, called by the Poles the "Recovered Territories"* or "Recovered Lands." As a result, Poland's frontiers were shifted about 200 kilometers to the west. The present borders of Poland are marked by the coast of the Baltic Sea in the north, the Oder-Neisse Line* in the west, the Sudetic Mountains and the Carpathian Mountains to the south, and the Curzon Line in the east. The frontiers of Poland stretch for 3,538 kilometers (2,198 miles). N. Davies, *God's Playground: A History of Poland*, vol. 2 (New York, 1984), 492–535; J. Lerski, *Historical Dictionary of Poland, 966–1945*, with special editing and emendations by P. Wróbel and R. J. Kozicki (Westport, Conn., 1996), 91–92.

BOREJSZA, JERZY (1905–52), journalist, communist official, and brother of J. Różański.* Born Benjamin Goldberg to a Zionist journalist in Warsaw,* Borejsza joined the Communist Party of Poland (KPP) in 1929 and worked for its editorial and propaganda department. In 1939–40 he directed *Ossolineum* Publishing House in Soviet-occupied Lvov. He became an officer in the Red Army* in 1941. In 1944 he served in the Polish People's Army* and, in August, became editor of *Rzeczpospolita* ("The Republic"), the press organ of the Polish Committee of National Liberation (PKWN). In October 1944 Borejsza established *Czytelnik* ("The Reader"), a large publishing house, officially a cooperative. A member of the Polish Workers' Party (PPR)* since 1944, he became a deputy member of its Central Committee* in 1947. Borejsza was an *eminence grise* of the Party, responsible for its cultural policy. Yet in October 1948 he was removed from his post as president of *Czytelnik* and, in 1950, from all the other positions he held. B. Fijałkowska, *Borejsza i Różański. Przyczynek do dziejów stalinizmu w Polsce* (Olsztyn, 1995); *Nowa Encyklopedia Powszechna PWN*, vol. 1 (Warsaw, 1995), 521.

BOROWSKI, MAREK S. (1946–   ), economist and politician. A member of the Polish United Workers' Party (PZPR)* during 1967–68 and 1975–90, he served in the Ministry of Internal Trade as a deputy director during 1982–91 and a deputy minister in the Mazowiecki* government from September 1989 to January 1991. In 1990 he joined the Social-Democracy of the Polish Republic

(SdRP),* becoming one of its leaders. In 1991 he was elected to the Sejm.* In the Pawlak* government, between October 1993 and February 1994, Borowski served as Deputy Premier and Minister of Finance; in the Oleksy* cabinet he served as minister-director of the Council of Ministers' Office (URM). In February 1996 he became Deputy Speaker of the Sejm. *Kto jest kim w polityce polskiej*, ed. by R. Ignasiak (Warsaw, 1993), 34; *Polska on Line* (Internet), "Polish Politicians" <http://www.polityka.pol.pl>

BOROWSKI, TADEUSZ (1922–51), famous and controversial writer who immortalized Auschwitz in two series of stories, *Pożegnanie z Marią* ("Farewell to Maria") and *Kamienny świat* ("World of Stone"). He made his debut in the early 1940s with two volumes of catastrophist poetry. Arrested by the Germans in 1943, he was imprisoned in Auschwitz and Dachau. In his stories he described everyday life in the death camps and explored the depths of human degradation. By the late 1940s he was one of the most radical Stalinist writers in Poland. Caught between remembrances of Auschwitz and the inhuman alienation of the Stalinist system, he committed suicide. *Dictionary of Polish Literature*, ed. by E. J. Czerwinski (Westport, Conn., 1994), 28–31; P. Kuncewicz, *Leksykon Polskich Pisarzy Współczesnych*, vol. 1 (Warsaw, 1995), 84–90.

BORUSEWICZ, BOGDAN (1949–), Solidarity* leader. Imprisoned in 1968 for his participation in the March events,* he was later active in the Workers' Defense Committee (KOR)* and the Social Self-Defense Committee "KOR" (KSS KOR) and edited several underground periodicals. An organizer of independent trade unions in the late 1970s, a leader of the 1980 strikes, and a personal friend of L. Wałęsa,* Borusewicz helped to coordinate the strike in the Lenin Shipyard in Gdańsk* and participated in negotiations with Polish authorities in August 1980. After imposition of Martial Law,* he helped to rebuild Solidarity in the underground but was imprisoned in 1986. In 1989 he was elected to the Sejm,* where he was active in the National Minorities Committee and the Foreign Affairs Committee. *Who's Who in the Socialist Countries of Europe*, ed. by J. Stroynowski, vol. 1 (Munich, 1989), 128; D. Ost, *Solidarity and the Politics of Anti-Politics* (Philadelphia, 1990); M. H. Bernhard, *The Origins of Democratization in Poland* (New York, 1993).

BÓR-KOMOROWSKI, TADEUSZ (1895–1966), general and commander-in-chief of the Home Army (AK)* in 1943–44. After World War II he settled in London, served as the commander-in-chief of the Polish Army in the West from May 1945 to September 1946 and became a leader of the Polish community in England. During 1955–72, he was a member of the Council of Three (Rada Trzech).* J. Lerski, *Historical Dictionary of Poland, 966–1945*, with special editing and emendations by P. Wróbel and R. J. Kozicki (Westport, Conn., 1996), 47; T. Radzik, *Z dziejów społeczności polskiej w Wielkiej Brytanii po drugiej wojnie światowej, 1945–*

1990 (Lublin, 1991); *Warszawa nad Tamizą,* ed. by A. Friszke (Warsaw, 1994); A. K. Kunert, *Ilustrowany przewodnik po Polsce podziemnej, 1939–1945* (Warsaw, 1996), 507.

BRANDSTAETTER, ROMAN (1906–87), playwright, poet, and writer whose works are frequently based on motifs taken from the Bible and history. *Dictionary of Polish Literature,* ed. by E. J. Czerwinski (Westport, Conn., 1994), 34–35; P. Kuncewicz, *Leksykon Polskich Pisarzy Współczesnych,* vol. 1 (Warsaw, 1995), 93–94.

BRANDYS, KAZIMIERZ (1916–), writer who wrote primarily about the Polish intelligentsia and its dilemmas. His first books, such as *Drewniany koń* ("Hobby Horse") and the famous *Miasto niepokonane* ("Invincible City"), a portrait of World War II Warsaw,* were devoted to Polish war experiences. Brandys became one of the leading communist writers and co-edited the Marxist weekly *Kuźnica* ("The Forge") in 1950–52 and *Nowa Kultura* ("The New Culture"). His worldview began to change in the mid-1950s, when he became the pillar of intellectual resistance against communism in Poland. His *Obrona Grenady* ("Defense of Grenada") was one of the first ice-breaking works to come from the period of de-Stalinization. Later his stance evolved from a mild criticism of communism to uncompromising political opposition. In 1966 he returned his Party card as a protest against the ousting of L. Kołakowski* from the Polish United Workers' Party (PZPR).* In the 1970s he signed several letters and appeals protesting the policies of the communist authorities in Poland. As a result, his books were kept from being published. His works, such as *Wariacje pocztowe* ("Postal Variations"), *Niewrzeczywistość* ("Unreality"), and *Miesiące* ("Months"), became obligatory reading for every intellectual in Poland. *Who's Who in the Socialist Countries of Europe,* ed. by J. Stroynowski, vol. 1 (Munich, 1989), 136; *Dictionary of Polish Literature,* ed. by E. J. Czerwinski (Westport, Conn., 1994), 35–36; P. Kuncewicz, *Leksykon Polskich Pisarzy Współczesnych,* vol. 1 (Warsaw, 1995), 94–97.

BRANDYS, MARIAN (1912–), history writer and journalist, brother of K. Brandys,* and husband of H. Mikołajska.* An Army officer and participant in the September Campaign in 1939, he spent the war in a German POW camp. After the war he began his writing career as a newspaper reporter; eventually he became an important and popular Polish author of books and essays on history. He renounced his Party membership in 1966 to protest the expulsion of L. Kołakowski* from the Polish United Workers' Party (PZPR).* In the 1970s he signed most protests against the regime's policies and was constantly harassed by the secret police. His *Nieznany książę Poniatowski* ("The Unknown Prince Poniatowski"), *Kozietulski i inni* ("Kozietulski and Others"), and *Koniec świata szwoleżerów* ("End of the Light Cavalry Era") belong to the classics of Polish historical writing. *Who's Who in the Socialist Countries of Europe,* ed. by J. Stroynowski, vol. 1 (Munich, 1989), 136; *Dictionary of Polish Literature,* ed. by E. J.

Czerwinski (Westport, Conn., 1994), 36–38; P. Kuncewicz, *Leksykon Polskich Pisarzy Współczesnych*, vol. 1 (Warsaw, 1995), 97–99.

BRATKOWSKI, STEFAN (1934–   ), journalist and important member of the democratic opposition* in Poland before 1989. He started his journalistic career in *Po Prostu* ("Plainly Speaking")* and then either contributed to or was on the editorial staff of several leading periodicals. His favorite subject was the modernization of life in Poland, and he headed a weekly supplement to *Życie Warszawy* ("Warsaw Life"),* entitled *Życie i Nowoczesność* ("Life and Modernity"). In the late 1970s he was a co-organizer and animator of the conversatory Doświadczenie i Przyszłość DiP ("Experience and Future").* In 1980 he was elected president of the Association of Polish Journalists (SDP)* and tried to defend its independence. Expelled from the Polish United Workers' Party (PZPR)* in October 1981, he remained unemployed after the imposition of Martial Law* on December 13, 1981. *Who's Who in the Socialist Countries of Europe*, ed. by J. Stroynowski, vol. 1 (Munich, 1989), 138.

BRATNIAK ("Fraternity"), underground periodical created by young political dissidents from Gdańsk* in October 1977. Later it became the organ of the Young Poland Movement* and gained new contributors from Łódź,* Poznań,* and Warsaw.* Among *Bratniak*'s most important editors were A. Hall,* Marian Piłka, Jacek Bartyzel, and Arkadiusz Rybicki. In 1981 the periodical sold 20,000 copies. The periodical was discontinued after imposition of Martial Law* in December 1981. D. Cecuda, *Leksykon Opozycji Politycznej 1976–1989* (Warsaw, 1989), 151.

BRATNY, ROMAN (1921–   ), nom de guerre of Roman Mularczyk, officer of the Home Army (AK)* and participant of the Warsaw Uprising. He made his debut as a poet during the war but became famous in 1957, when *Kolumbowie rocznik 20* ("The Columbus of 1920") was published. The book was considered a manifesto of the AK veterans and a testimony to their tragic fate. Yet most books by Bratny are consistent with the cultural policy of the communist authorities. *Who's Who in the Socialist Countries of Europe*, ed. by J. Stroynowski, vol. 1 (Munich, 1989), 138; P. Kuncewicz, *Leksykon Polskich Pisarzy Współczesnych*, vol. 1 (Warsaw, 1995), 99–103.

BRAUN, ANDRZEJ (1923–   ), poet, writer, and researcher of Joseph Conrad's heritage. A former Home Army (AK)* soldier, he became one of the main writers of the Stalinist period.* Later he wrote his great novel, *Zdobycie nieba* ("The Conquest of the Sky"), and numerous works on Joseph Conrad and the Asian continent. *Who's Who in the Socialist Countries of Europe*, ed. by J. Stroynowski, vol. 1 (Munich, 1989), 139; P. Kuncewicz, *Leksykon Polskich Pisarzy Współczesnych*, vol. 1 (Warsaw, 1995), 104–105.

BREZA, TADEUSZ (1905–70), writer and diplomat. Most of his novels are devoted to the problems of the Polish intelligentsia.* After several years in Rome as a Polish cultural attaché, he wrote the famous *Spiżowa brama* ("The Bronze Gate") and *Urząd* ("The Office"), describing the bureaucratic structures and policies of the Vatican. *Dictionary of Polish Literature*, ed. by E. J. Czerwinski (Westport, Conn., 1994), 38; P. Kuncewicz, *Leksykon Polskich Pisarzy Współczesnych*, vol. 1 (Warsaw, 1995), 109.

BREZHNEV DOCTRINE, concept developed by L. I. Brezhnev to justify the invasion of Czechoslovakia in 1968. Often called a doctrine of "limited sovereignty" in the West and of "socialist internationalism" in the East, it condoned armed intervention by the USSR and its satellites in the internal affairs of a socialist state that would like to depart from socialism. This idea had always been crucial to Soviet policy vis-à-vis the socialist states, but it was explicitly declared by Brezhnev for the first time in his speech to the Fifth Congress of the Polish United Workers' Party (PZPR)* on November 13, 1968. The Soviet leader explained the Soviet-led East German, Polish, Hungarian, and Bulgarian intervention in Czechoslovakia on August 20–21, 1968: "When a threat arises to the cause of socialism in one country—a threat to the security of the Socialist Commonwealth as a whole—this is no longer a problem for that country's people, but a common problem, the concern of all socialist states." The Soviet government concluded that the changes in Czechoslovakia in 1968, the so-called Prague Spring, constituted a threat to communist control over the country. In spite of Brezhnev's explanation, repeated many times by the official Soviet press, Moscow denied the existence of this doctrine until the late 1980s. In October 1989 Mikhail S. Gorbachev announced that his country had no right to interfere in the affairs of other states. His spokesperson, G. I. Gerasimov, added a joke, saying that the "Brezhnev Doctrine" had been replaced by the "Sinatra Doctrine" ("I Did It My Way"). The Brezhnev Doctrine was an important factor in Polish politics, especially during the Solidarity* period when the Polish communist authorities threatened Poles with Soviet intervention. *The Cold War, 1945–1991*, vol. 3, "Resources: Chronology, History, Concepts, Events, Organizations, Bibliography, Archives," ed. by B. Frankel (Detroit, 1992), 118–121; *Political and Economic Encyclopedia of the Soviet Union and Eastern Europe*, ed. by S. White (London, 1990), 40.

BRONIEWSKI, WŁADYSŁAW (1897–1962), romantic and revolutionary poet, author of great historical, personal, and catastrophic lyrics. He fought in the Piłsudski Legions during World War I and as a Polish Army* officer during the Polish-Soviet War of 1919–21. In the 1920s he began to write revolutionary poems. After the outbreak of World War II, he was arrested by the Soviets in Lvov and sent to a labor camp in northern Russia. "Amnestied" in 1941, he left the USSR with the Polish Army commanded by Gen. W. Anders.* After the war he returned to Poland via Jerusalem and London. He became a celebrated poet, although he never joined the Party. *Dictionary of Polish Literature*, ed. by E. J. Czerwinski (Westport, Conn., 1994), 40–42; P. Kuncewicz, *Leksykon Polskich Pisarzy Współczesnych*, vol. 1 (Warsaw 1995), 112.

BROSZKIEWICZ JERZY (1922–93), writer, playwright, and member of the editorial staff of the weekly *Przegląd Kulturalny* (''The Cultural Review'') and several other important literary journals. Very active in the post-1956 period, he authored several novels about World War II about outstanding individuals from Polish history. *Dictionary of Polish Literature*, ed. by E. J. Czerwinski (Westport, Conn., 1994), 42–43; *Who's Who in the Socialist Countries of Europe*, ed. by J. Stroynowski, vol. 1 (Munich, 1989), 146; P. Kuncewicz, *Agonia i nadzieja. Literatura polska od 1939*, vol. 2 (Warsaw, 1994), 431–433.

BRUS, WŁODZIMIERZ (1921–   ), professor of modern Russian and East European studies in Oxford and an expert on socialist economy. A former director of the Research Bureau of the Polish State Planning Commission, he was vice-chair of the Economic Council until 1963 and professor of political economy at Warsaw University.* Removed from his academic position in 1968, he left Poland in 1972. *Who's Who, 1996* (London, 1996), 262; D. Ost, *Solidarity and the Politics of Anti-Politics* (Philadelphia, 1990).

BRYLL, ERNEST (1935–   ), poet, prose writer, and playwright. He started his writing career as a journalist in *Po Prostu* (''Plainly Speaking'')* in 1955–56. Later he directed several theaters and state film production enterprises. In 1990–91 he was an editor in *Tygodnik Solidarność* (''The Solidarity Weekly''),* and in 1991 he was appointed ambassador to Ireland. *Who's Who in the Socialist Countries of Europe*, ed. by J. Stroynowski, vol. 1 (Munich, 1989), 150; *Dictionary of Polish Literature*, ed. by E. J. Czerwinski (Westport, Conn., 1994), 43–45; *Kto jest kim w polityce polskiej*, ed. by R. Ignasiak (Warsaw, 1993), 37.

BRYSTYGIER, JULIA (1902–80), director of the Ministry of the Public Security Fifth Department responsible for Stalinist policy toward the Roman Catholic Church* in Poland between 1944 and 1956, member of the Polish United Workers' Party's (PZPR)* Central Control Commission during 1948–54, and member of the Committee for Public Security. A dogmatic communist, she aimed at the destruction of the Church using all possible methods. Active in the Communist Party of western Ukraine before 1939, she spent World War II in the communist underground in Lvov and later served on the Executive Committee of the Union of Polish Patriots in the USSR. In September 1956, removed from the communist apparatus, she retired to private life and attempted a writing career. A. Micewski, *Ludzie i opcje* (Warsaw, 1993), 51–54; A. Polonsky and B. Drukier, *The Beginnings of Communist Rule in Poland* (London, 1980).

BRZEZIŃSKI, ZBIGNIEW (1928–   ), scholar and U.S. National Security Adviser to President Jimmy Carter during 1977–81. A graduate of McGill University in Montreal and of Harvard, he was named director of Columbia University's Institute of Communist Affairs in 1961. In his writings he supported a firm policy toward the USSR. He served as a member of the State Department's Policy Planning Staff, as an adviser to Vice-President Hubert H. Humphrey during the Lyndon B. Johnson administration, and in 1973 as the first director of the Trilateral Commission, which aimed at strengthening relations among the United States, Europe, and Japan. During the presidential campaign, Brzeziński became Carter's foreign policy adviser and President-elect Carter appointed him U.S. National Security Adviser. Brzeziński served in this position during 1977–80 and contributed decidedly to the creation of the Carter Doctrine: the guarantee of U.S. assistance to countries facing communist aggression. After 1981 he continued his scholarly activities and published prolifically. *The Cold War, 1945–1991*, vol. 1, "Leaders and Other Important Figures in the United States and Western Europe," ed. by B. Frankel (Detroit, 1992), 65–70.

BUG RIVER, right tributary of the Vistula River.* About 125 miles of the course of the Bug became the frontier between Poland and the USSR. During 1939–41, the river served as a border between Nazi- and Soviet-occupied Poland. In 1920 Lord Curzon made the same part of the Bug a fragment of the famous Curzon Line, an alleged ethnic border between Polish and non-Polish territories. Before 1915 the river was the eastern frontier of the Congress Kingdom of Poland; from 1795 to 1807, it was the frontier between the Austrian- and Russian-partitioned Polish-Lithuanian Commonwealth. *The New Encyclopaedia Britannica*, vol. 2 (Chicago, 1990), 609.

BUGAJ, RYSZARD (1944–   ), leader of Solidarity* and the Union of Labor (UP).* He was expelled from the Union of Socialist Youth (ZMS)* in 1967 and from Warsaw University* in 1968, in both cases for political reasons. Cooperating with the Workers' Defense Committee (KOR)* after 1976, he joined Solidarity in 1980, became a member of the Mazowsze Region leadership, and participated in the First Congress of Solidarity in Gdańsk.* Interned in 1981, he was active in the underground Solidarity after he was released from an internment camp. In 1989 he participated in the Round Table Negotiations* and was elected to the Sejm* in 1989 and 1993. He co-organized and presided over the Labor Solidarity (Solidarność Pracy) and the Union of Labor. D. Ost, *Solidarity and the Politics of Anti-Politics* (Philadelphia, 1990); *Kto jest kim w polityce polskiej*, ed. by R. Ignasiak (Warsaw, 1993), 40.

BUJAK, ZBIGNIEW (1954–   ), former Solidarity* leader and a politician of the Union of Labor (UP).* A worker at the "Ursus"* tractor factory, he organized the 1980 strike there and became one of the most important Solidarity leaders. After imposition of Martial Law,* he became active in the underground;

during 1981–89 he served as chairman of Solidarity, Mazowsze Region. In 1989 he participated in the Round Table Negotiations* and was elected to the Sejm.* Bujak was an organizer of the Citizens' Movement for Democratic Action (ROAD)* and supported T. Mazowiecki* during the presidential elections of 1990.* After Mazowiecki's defeat ROAD was reshaped into the Democratic Union (UD)* and in April 1991 Bujak attempted, unsuccessfully, to establish the leftist Democratic-Social Movement (Ruch Demokratyczno-Społeczny [RD-S]). Eventually, he joined the Union of Labor. D. Ost, *Solidarity and the Politics of Anti-Politics* (Philadelphia, 1990); M. H. Bernhard, *The Origins of Democratization in Poland* (New York, 1993); *Kto jest kim w polityce polskiej*, ed. by R. Ignasiak (Warsaw, 1993), 41; *Rodem z Solidarności*, ed. by B. Kopka and R. Żelichowski (Warsaw, 1997), 33–54.

BUND (General Union of Jewish Workers), the Jewish Socialist party in Poland organized in 1897 as the *Algemeyner Yiddisher Arbeter Bund im Lite, Poyln un Rusland* (General Jewish Workers' Union in Lithuania, Poland, and Russia). After 1917 it was destroyed by the Bolsheviks in Russia and developed into an independent party in Poland. In the 1930s the Bund, fighting for democracy and for cultural-national autonomy for Jews,* became the largest Jewish party in Poland. It was destroyed during World War II. In September 1944 the first Bundist survivors, returning from either the USSR or hidings in Poland, appeared in already liberated Lublin* and began to rebuild their party. By 1947 the Bund reached 1,500 members and was one of eleven Jewish parties in Poland. It was the only Jewish party that clearly opposed Jewish emigration from Poland. In 1948 the Bund was forced to join the Polish United Workers' Party (PZPR).* B. K. Johnpoll, *The Politics of Futility: The General Jewish Workers Bund of Poland, 1917–1943* (Ithaca, N.Y., 1967); *Najnowsze dzieje Żydów w Polsce*, ed. by J. Tomaszewski (Warsaw, 1993), 433–439.

BUREAU FOR THE RECONSTRUCTION OF THE CAPITAL (Biuro Odbudowy Stolicy), governmental institution supervising the reconstruction of Warsaw* after World War II. Established on February 14, 1945, it edited its own periodical and consisted of over 1,500 architects, engineers, urbanists, economists, lawyers, and other professionals. In 1951 it was dissolved and replaced by the Urbanistic Bureau of Warsaw. *Encyklopedia Warszawy*, ed. by B. Petrozolin-Skowrońska (Warsaw, 1994), 70.

BYDGOSZCZ (German Bromberg), capital city of Bydgoszcz Province (województwo) in northern Poland. Established as a Polish border stronghold in the Middle Ages, it was incorporated into Prussia after the Partitions of Poland, returned to the Polish state after 1918, and lost about 50,000 people during World War II. An important transportation junction, it became a center for textile, metallurgical, chemical, electronic, and machine industries. Bydgoszcz has grown steadily since the war, and now the city has two institutions of higher learning and a population that reached 352,000 in 1982.

In 1980–81 Bydgoszcz became an important Solidarity* center. In March 1981, the police brutally assaulted a group of Solidarity activists who had been petitioning the Bydgoszcz City Council on behalf of farmers demanding registration of their own independent union. Solidarity responded to the beatings by scheduling a general strike, called off at the last moment by L. Wałęsa.* D. Ost, *Solidarity and the Politics of Anti-Politics* (Philadelphia, 1990), 125; *Encyklopedia Historii Gospodarczej Polski*, ed. by A. Mączak, vol. 1 (Warsaw, 1981), 80.

C

CATHOLIC CHURCH. See **Roman Catholic Church.**

CATHOLIC UNIVERSITY OF LUBLIN (Katolicki Uniwersytet Lubelski [KUL]), Catholic private university established in Lublin* in 1918. After World War II it was the only university in Poland and all Soviet-bloc states that worked partially outside the control of state authorities. Communist authorities tried to influence the activities of KUL, whose independence varied in various periods. In 1951 the university was forced to close its Department of Law and its Department of Social Sciences. In 1952 KUL had to accept Rev. J. Iwanicki as its rector, and during his tenure seven KUL professors were removed from their positions. After the Stalinist period* ended, KUL became almost completely independent and developed into an important academic center. Among KUL's professors were such outstanding scholars as K. Wojtyła,* S. Świeżawski, M. A. Krąpiec,* and J. Kłoczowski.* *Dictionary of Polish Literature*, ed. by E. J. Czerwinski (Westport, Conn., 1994), 51–53; J. Karpiński, *Polska, Komunizm, Opozycja* (London, 1985), 84.

CAT-MACKIEWICZ, STANISŁAW. See **Mackiewicz, Stanisław.**

CDN, underground publishing house organized in winter 1982 by C. Bielecki.* Its first book, *Solidarity under Martial Law*, soon appeared; by the mid-1980s, CDN had published some 50 titles. The CDN also produced videos and films and edited two journals: *Myśl Niezależna* ("The Independent Thought") and *Obóz* ("The Camp"). The publishing house was represented abroad by London Information Bureau of Solidarity, Puls Publication,* and Paris's *Instytut Literacki,* among others. The CDN published works by such authors as A. and L. Ciołkosz,* J. J. Lipski,* Juliusz Mieroszewski, S. Kisielewski,* Raymond Aron, and Alain Besançon. *Dictionary of Polish Literature*, ed. by E. J. Czerwinski (Westport, Conn., 1994), 95–97; D. Cecuda, *Leksykon Opozycji Politycznej 1976–1989* (Warsaw, 1989), 129; Karpiński, *Polska, Komunizm, Opozycja* (London, 1985), 29.

CEGIELSKI, LONGIN (1920–87), peasant activist and state official. A soldier of the Union of Armed Struggle (ZWZ) and the Peasant Battalions (BCh) during World War II, he joined the Peasant Party (SL)* in 1946 and became one of the most important leaders of the United Peasant Party (ZSL).* In 1968–71 he served as Deputy Minister of Agriculture, and during 1976–80 as Deputy Premier. T. Mołdawa, *Ludzie Władzy 1944–1991. Władze państwowe i polityczne Polski według stanu na dzień 28 II 1991* (Warsaw, 1991), 339.

CELIŃSKI, ANDRZEJ B. (1950–   ), deputy chairman of the Democratic Union (UD)* and its representative in the I and II Senate* after 1989 and 1991. Expelled from Warsaw University* after the March events of 1968,* he was active in the Workers' Defense Committee (KOR)* and co-organized the ''Flying University''* and the Association of the Scientific Courses (TKN).* An important Solidarity* leader and a close assistant of L. Wałęsa,* Celiński was interned in 1981–82. He continued his opposition activities in the 1980s, was on the Civic Committee,* and participated in the Round Table Negotiations* in 1989. After the ''war on the top''* he became a leader of the Democratic Union and, later, of the Freedom Union (UW).* In 1993 he was elected to the Sejm* from the Płock electoral district, where he was involved in ''organic work'' and modernization of the local economy. During 1993–95 he presided over the foundation ''Poland Now'' (Teraz Polska). *Who's Who in the Socialist Countries of Europe*, ed. by J. Stroynowski, vol. 1 (Munich, 1989), 171; *Kto jest kim w polityce polskiej*, ed. by R. Ignasiak (Warsaw, 1993), 50–51; M. H. Bernhard, *The Origins of Democratization in Poland* (New York, 1993).

CENSORSHIP, colloquial name for the Central Office for Control of the Press, Publications, and Public Performances and, simultaneously, popular term for all the state and Party institutions and activities aimed at control of information. Although the 1945 and 1952 Polish Constitutions guaranteed the right to freedom of expression, the communist regime in Poland constructed a large apparatus to keep this freedom within the limits of the ''interests of society.'' The limitations were defined by the Central Committee* of the Polish Workers' Party (PPR)*; after 1948 the Polish United Workers' Party (PZPR)* set the political ''line'' of all publications in Poland. The Central Committee decided on appointment to the Council of Ministers, which in turn nominated members to the institutions that controlled the scope and ''ideological purity'' of all information given to the public. Throughout the communist period these institutions varied in name and duties, but their functions remained constant. The most important institutions were the Central Office for Control of the Press, Publications, and Public Performances (created by a governmental decree on July 5, 1946), the Central Office for Publishers, Printing Industry, and Bookselling (created in

1951), the Polish Press Agency (PAP), the Central Administration of Motion Pictures, the Committee on Broadcasting Affairs, the Ministry of Culture and Art, and the Central Administration of Libraries. The provincial and local offices of each were controlled by provincial and local Party committees. Central institutions were controlled by the appropriate sections of the Central Committee: the Propaganda, Radio, Press, Publications, Culture, and Science Sections.

These state and Party institutions decided on personnel appointments in the Polish press, TV,* radio,* theater, film production enterprises, scientific institutes, and other institutions that created opinions and distributed information. Only loyal and trusted individuals, mostly Party members, were placed in key positions. They were responsible for the so-called internal censorship of articles and books, film and theater scenarios, and television and radio scripts. After this self-censorship, the Central Office for Control of the Press, Publications, and Public Performances read every text before it was printed and distributed in the country. The Central Office received instructions from the Party on what subjects and information to remove from print. First on a long list of forbidden names and topics were remarks critical of the USSR and the Party and the word "censorship" itself. Frequently, outstanding writers or public figures who were not obedient enough were punished by the communist regime in such a way that their works or even their names were removed from print. Also, anti-Russian, anti-communist, and anti-Soviet historical or contemporary writers or public figures were wiped out by censorship. Most Poles had never heard of C. Miłosz,* for example, before he received the Nobel Prize. Every institution engaged in publishing had to obtain a special license from the Central Office for Control of Publications and Public Performances (Głowny Urząd Kontroli Publikacji i Widowisk) or, before 1981, from the Central Office for Control of the Press, Publications, and Public Performances.

In some periods, like in the 1940s, the early 1950s, and after imposition of Martial Law* in 1981, correspondence and phone conversations were also controlled. The most oppressive period started in 1948. Starting in 1954, censorship was progressively curtailed; after July 1956 it vanished almost completely. Then in early 1957 censorship was again tightened, to be slightly moderated only in the early 1970s. By the late 1970s the so-called second circulation appeared: More and more books and periodicals published underground made censorship inefficient. In 1977 a censorship employee, Tomasz Strzyżewski, smuggled 1974–77 censorship documents to Switzerland. They were published abroad and in the underground. During the 1980–81 Solidarity* era, some publications were beyond the reach of the censors. Censorship was an important element of the communist system; a quest for freedom of expression contributed greatly to its fall. C. R. Barnett, *Poland: Its People, Its Society, Its Culture* (New York, 1958), 143–147; J. Karpiński, *Polska, Komunizm, Opozycja* (London, 1985), 31.

CENTER ALLIANCE (Porozumienie Centrum [PC]), center-right political party formed in spring 1990 as a weapon in the "war on the top,"* a political maneuver by L. Wałęsa* that split Solidarity* into several camps. The PC was organized around J. Kaczyński,* editor-in-chief of *Tygodnik Solidarność* ("The Solidarity Weekly"),* and his brother, Lech. The Kaczyński group fought domination of Solidarity by the political left and against a reshaping of the Solidarity movement into a mono-party similar to the Polish United Workers' Party (PZPR).* The Round Table Agreement* had lost its validity because of the disappearance of the PZPR, the group claimed, and new, faster, and more dynamic changes were necessary. The organizers of the Alliance believed that Poland needed political pluralism. The Mazowiecki* government had no valid economic plan, they argued, and the government's economic reform was detrimental to the majority of Poles. These claims were presented on May 12, 1990, as the "Declaration of the Center Alliance," publication considered to mark the beginning of the party. The PC supported Wałęsa's candidacy in the 1990 presidential elections and supplied the presidential chancellery with key officials, such as the Kaczyński brothers, S. Siwek,* Teresa Liszcz, Jacek Maziarski, and Maciej Zalewski. In late 1990 the Alliance proposed to replace Premier T. Mazowiecki with J. Olszewski.* The latter did not want to accept L. Balcerowicz* as Deputy Premier, however, and the project failed. Two Alliance representatives joined the cabinet of J. K. Bielecki.* A conflict between Wałęsa and the Kaczyńskis led to a decline of the PC, which received only 8.7% of the votes in the 1991 parliamentary elections (44 Sejm and 9 Senate seats). In addition, the Alliance leadership opposed the evolution of their party into a Catholic and nationalistic organization. Eventually, the PC became one of numerous secondary splinter parties and failed to win any parliamentary seats in the election of 1993.* G. Sanford and A. Gozdecka-Sanford, *Historical Dictionary of Poland* (Metuchen, N.J., 1994), 46; *Political Handbook of the World, 1995–1996*, ed. by A. S. Banks, A. J. Day, and T. C. Muller (New York, 1996), 764; J. Puchalski, *Polskie polityczne partie, stronnictwa, stowarzyszenia, związki i kluby* (Warsaw, 1991), 110–112; *Polskie partie polityczne*, ed. by K. A. Paszkiewicz (Warsaw, 1996), 173–181.

CENTKIEWICZ, ALINA (1907–93) and **CZESŁAW** (1904–96), popular writers specializing in books about the Arctic region. *Encyklopedyczny Słownik Sławnych Polaków* (Warsaw, 1996), 47.

CENTRAL BUREAU OF PLANNING (Centralny Urząd Planowania [CUP]), institution of the Economic Committee of the Council of Ministers (Komitet Ekonomiczny Rady Ministrów) established in 1945. The CUP prepared economic plans,* coordinated activities of ministries dealing with the economy, and controlled the realization of economic plans. It prepared the Three-Year Plan of Economic Reconstruction, 1947–49, and the first draft of the Six-Year Plan, 1950–55. Among the economists working for the CUP was a group of planners who were close to the Polish Socialist Party (PPS),* including C. Bobrowski,* the president of the Bureau. In 1948, they were sharply criticized and then eliminated by the communists. In 1949 the CUP was dissolved and replaced by the State Commission for Economic Planning. J. Karpiński, *Polska, Komunizm, Opozycja* (London, 1985), 31.

CENTRAL BUREAU OF THE POLISH COMMUNISTS IN THE USSR, secret organization of the most trusted Polish communists living in the Soviet Union during World War II. Established on February 1, 1944 by the Bolshevik Party, it paralleled all other communist-controlled Polish organizations in the Soviet Union and played a special role during the imposition of the Soviet system in Poland in 1944. Among its best-known members were J. Berman,* H. Minc,* A. Zawadzki,* and S. Radkiewicz.* *Słownik Historii Polski 1939–1948*, ed. by A. Chwalba and T. Gąsowski (Cracow, 1994), 112.

CENTRAL COMMITTEE, the highest Party authority between congresses and the most authoritative continuing body in the communist system. Both the Polish Workers' Party (PPR)* and the Polish United Workers' Party (PZPR)* were organized along lines established in the Soviet Communist Party and included a Central Committee. According to the PZPR statute, "The Central Committee represents the Party externally, establishes Party institutions, directs their activities, nominates the editorial boards of Party newspapers, controls Party cadres, disposes of Party property and funds." It also "directs and controls the activities of Party members who occupy leading positions of national importance" and who issue party resolutions and decisions. It was required to hold plenary sessions no less than once every four months, but it did not. Plenary sessions were scheduled irregularly, usually before major events, such as the introduction of an economic plan. The Central Committee's power and authority were limited by its large membership and infrequent meetings, and responsibility for policymaking was delegated to the much smaller secretariat of the Committee and the Politburo.* In 1945 the Central Committee consisted of only 47 members, but over the years it grew to about 200 full and candidate members, most of whom were full-time employees of the Party apparatus. During every political turning point in postwar Poland—in 1956, in 1970, and in 1980–81—the Central Committee usually divided into competing factions, thus changing dramatically. R. F. Staar, *Poland, 1944–1962: The Sovietization of a Captive People* (New Orleans, 1962), 152; B. P. McCrea et al., *The Soviet and East European Political Dictionary* (Oxford, 1984), 91.

CENTRAL COUNCIL OF TRADE UNIONS. See **CRZZ.**

CHAJN, LEON (1910–83), lawyer, journalist, state official, and member of the State Council (Rada Państwa)* from February 1957 to June 1965. He joined the Communist Party of Poland (KPP) in 1932 and spent World War II in the Soviet Union, where he was active in the Union of Polish Patriots (ZPP) and served as a political officer in the communist-controlled First Polish Army.* In 1944, he joined the satellite Democratic Party (SD),* becoming one of its main leaders until 1965. A deputy director of the Justice Department of the Polish Committee of National Liberation (PKWN) and a Deputy Minister of Justice during 1945–49, he occupied several important state positions and represented his party in the Sejm* in 1944–69. The chairman of the Main Directory of the State Archives (NDAP) during 1965–76, he wrote numerous articles and several books on the contemporary history of Poland. R. F. Staar, *Poland, 1944–1962: The Sovietization of a Captive People* (New Orleans, 1962), 236–237; T. Mołdawa, *Ludzie Władzy 1944–1991. Władze państwowe i polityczne Polski według stanu na dzień 28 II 1991* (Warsaw, 1991), 340.

CHAŁASIŃSKI, JÓZEF (1904–79), professor of sociology at the Universities of Łódź* (1945–66) and Warsaw* (1966–74) and a specialist in the sociology of culture and nation. A. Kaleta (ed.), *Józef Chałasiński, sociolog i humanista* (Toruń, 1984).

CHEŁCHOWSKI, HILARY (1908–83), Party and state official, member of the State Council (Rada Państwa)* from April 1955 to February 1957. An activist of the Communist Party of Poland (KPP) since 1932, he joined the Polish Workers' Party (PPR)* in 1942, became a member of its Central Committee* in 1943, commanded a communist guerrilla unit in Poland, and chaired the Lublin,* Radom,* and Kielce* Party districts. After the war he remained a member of the PPR's and then Polish United Workers' Party's (PZPR)* Central Committees. A deputy member of the Politburo* from 1948 to 1956, he served as chairperson of the Central Committee Agricultural Department in 1948–50, Deputy Premier in 1950–52, and minister of the State Agricultural Enterprises (PGR) from 1951 to 1954. His promotion to the State Council was, in fact, a political retirement. T. Mołdawa, *Ludzie Władzy 1944–1991. Władze państwowe i polityczne Polski według stanu na dzień 28 II 1991* (Warsaw, 1991), 340.

CHEŁM, provincial town in the Lublin* region, near the River Bug,* one of the medieval Czerwień castles. One of the first towns on the left bank of the River Bug to be taken by the Red Army* in July 1944, Chełm became the seat of the Polish Committee of National Liberation (PKWN), and it was there the PKWN issued its manifesto on July 22. Soon the PKWN, a communist government-in-waiting, was moved to Lublin. After the war the town was rebuilt and extended. By 1990 its population reached 64,000 inhabitants. G. Sanford and A. Gozdecka-Sanford, *Historical Dictionary of Poland* (Metuchen, N.J., 1994), 47.

CHOJECKI, MIROSŁAW (1949–   ), important member of the democratic opposition in Poland and creator of NOWa* Publishing House. He worked as a scientist in the Institute of Nuclear Research (Instytut Badań Jądrowych) until 1976, when he was fired for his involvement in the Workers' Defense Committee (KOR).* His managerial talents, diligence, and persistence were crucial in creating NOWa. In the late 1970s he became a target for the secret police. Frequently arrested, searched, beaten, and threatened, he persevered as a symbol of resistance for his peers. After imposition of Martial Law* he stayed abroad and continued his activities in Paris, where he established and headed a publishing house and its journal, *Kontakt*. Chojecki returned to Poland after the fall of communism and in 1992 organized the Warsaw New TV. J. J. Lipski, *KOR: A History of the Workers' Defense Committee in Poland, 1976–1981* (Berkeley, Calif., 1985), 56; M. H. Bernhard, *The Origins of Democratization in Poland* (New York, 1993).

CHRISTIAN CIVIC MOVEMENT (Chrześcijański Ruch Obywatelski), small, loose political organization created in September 1990 by Solidarity* activists opposed to its leftist leadership, supported L. Wałęsa* and the idea of a strong presidential system in Poland, opposed the Balcerowicz* Plan, and cooperated with the Catholic Electoral Action (Wyborcza Akcja Katolicka [WAK]). *Partie Polityczne w Polsce*, ed. by A. Gargas and M. Wojciechowski (Gdańsk, 1991), 13–14.

CHRISTIAN-DEMOCRATIC LABOR PARTY (Chrześcijańsko-Demokratyczne Stronnictwo Pracy), political party that considers itself a direct continuation of the Labor Party (SP),* established in 1937, discontinued in Poland after 1946, and active exclusively in exile. In 1989 several SP activists reactivated its leadership; during the May 1990 congress they rebuilt the party. In fall 1990 it split into two organizations when a group of party leaders did not support W. Siła-Nowicki* as a party candidate during the presidential election of 1990* but instead backed L. Wałęsa.* The secessionists organized the Christian-Democratic Party "Union" (Chrześcijańsko-Demokratyczne Stronnictwo "Zjednoczenie").* The Christian-Democratic Labor Party, led by W. Siła-Nowicki and Tadeusz Przeciszewski, has no parliamentary representation. In 1991 the party had about 3,000 members. *Political Handbook of the World: 1995–1996*, ed. by A. S. Banks, A. J. Day, and T. C. Muller (New York, 1996), 764; *Partie Polityczne w Polsce*, ed. by A. Gargas and M. Wojciechowski (Gdańsk, 1991), 15–16; *Polskie partie polityczne*, ed. by K. A. Paszkiewicz (Warsaw, 1996), 22–27.

CHRISTIAN DEMOCRATIC PARTY (Partia Chrześcijańskich Demokratów [PChD]), moderate Catholic party established in December 1990 in Poznań* by former Solidarity* activists. Since February 1994 the PChD, which resembles West European Christian Democratic parties, has been headed by P. Łączkowski,* the former Deputy Premier in the Suchocka* government. *Political Handbook of the World: 1995–1996*, ed. by A. S. Banks, A. J. Day, and T. C. Muller (New York, 1996), 764; *Polskie partie polityczna. Charakterystyki i dokumenty*, ed. by K. A. Paszkiewicz (Wrocław, 1996), 72–80.

CHRISTIAN-DEMOCRATIC PARTY "UNION" (Chrześcijańsko-Demokratyczne Stronnictwo "Zjednoczenie"), small political party that split from the Christian-Democratic Labor Party* on October 24, 1990. With about 1,000 members at large and led by J. Zabłocki* and R. Bender,* the party supported L. Wałęsa* during the presidential election of 1990,* bases its program on national, Catholic, and democratic principles, and has no parliamentary representation. *Partie Polityczne w Polsce*, ed. by A. Gargas and M. Wojciechowski (Gdańsk, 1991), 17–18.

CHRISTIAN LABOR PARTY (Chrześcijańska Partia Pracy), small political party organized on March 31, 1990, in the Warsaw Artisans' House (Dom Rzemiosła) by small-business representatives. The party has no parliamentary representation, and its program is based on the sociopolitical doctrine of the Roman Catholic Church.* *Partie Polityczne w Polsce*, ed. by A. Gargas and M. Wojciechowski (Gdańsk, 1991), 12–13.

CHRISTIAN-NATIONAL UNION (Związek Chrześcijańsko-Narodowy [ZChN]), nationalist, religious conservative party established in September 1989 by W. Chrzanowski,* J. Łopuszański,* S. Niesiołowski,* A. Macierewicz,* and a group of other rightist activists of Solidarity* and about 20 small Christian and nationalist organizations. The party program aims at rebuilding an independent and strong Polish state integrated into a united Europe, understood as a "community of fatherlands." The party wants to base national revival on national and Catholic ethnic values: It stresses family and moral values, supports criminalization of abortion,* and strongly opposes birth control. During the 1991 parliamentary elections the Catholic Electoral Action (WAK),* organized by the ZChN, received 8.73% of all votes, which gave it 49 seats in the Sejm,* 9 in the Senate.* Supported by the ZChN, the Olszewski* government (December 1991–June 1992), collapsed after its Minister of Interior, Macierewicz, announced a list of secret police spies and informers, which included names of numerous pre-1989 opposition leaders. First on the Macierewicz list was L. Wałęsa,* accused earlier by Olszewski's Minister of Defense, J. Parys, of plotting a military coup. The ZChN became especially unpopular among the younger generation, who considered the party the embodiment of obscurantism. G. Sanford and A. Gozdecka-Sanford, *Historical Dictionary of Poland* (Metuchen, N.J., 1994), 48–49; *Political Handbook of the World: 1995–1996*, ed. by A. S. Banks, A. J. Day, and T. C. Muller (New York, 1996), 763; *Partie Polityczne w Polsce*, ed. by A. Gargas and M. Wojciechowski (Gdańsk, 1991), 180–181.

CHRISTIAN PEASANT ALLIANCE (Sojusz Ludowo-Chrześcijański [SLCh]), small party developed from the Polish Peasant Party–Solidarity (PSL-S)* in spring 1992 and representing the most right-wing peasant electorate. It participated in the government of J. Olszewski* but opposed its lustration policy and supported the no-confidence vote against the government. During the elections of September 1993,* the SLCh formed the Fatherland (*Ojczyzna*) coalition with the Christian-National Union (ZChN),* the Conservative Party (PK),* and the Party of Christian Democracy (PChD).* This group did not pass the coalition threshold of 8%, nor did it gain any seats in the Sejm.* B. Szajkowski (ed.), *Political Parties of Eastern Europe, Russia, and the Successor States* (London, 1994), 329.

CHRISTIAN SOCIAL ASSOCIATION (Chrześcijańskie Stowarzyszenie Społeczne [ChSS]), group of Catholic intellectuals and politicians who gathered around J. Frankowski and his weekly *Za i przeciw* ("For and Against") in 1957. The group, partially created by the Party apparatus, wanted to cooperate with the communist authorities in Poland but opposed B. Piasecki* and left his PAX* Association. Frankowski and his supporters hoped they would constitute a third ideological and political power between the Party and the Roman Catholic Church,* but the plan failed and their Association did not play an important role in Polish politics. The ChSS ran a publishing institute, *Novum*, which published *Tygodnik Polski* ("The Polish Weekly") from 1982 and the quarterly *Studia i Dokumenty Ekumeniczne* ("Ecumenical Studies and Documents"). By 1983 the ChSS had grown to about 10,000 members. A. Micewski, *Kościół—Państwo 1945–1989* (Warsaw, 1994), 42–43; J. Karpiński, *Polska, Komunizm, Opozycja* (London, 1985), 33.

CHROSTOWSKI, WALDEMAR (1951–   ), priest, theologian, director of the Institute of Catholic-Judaic Dialogue at the Academy of Catholic Theology in Warsaw,* deputy chairman of the Polish Episcopate* Committee for Dialogue with Judaism, and member of the International Council of the Auschwitz Museum. G. Polak, *Kto jest kim w Kościele katolickim* (Warsaw, 1996), 47.

CHRUŚCIEL, ANTONI (1895–1960), general since September 1944 and commander-in-chief of the Polish forces fighting against the Germans during the 1944 Warsaw Uprising. After the war he was active in the Polish armed forces and its veteran organizations in the West. *Encyklopedyczny Słownik Sławnych Polaków* (Warsaw, 1996), 52.

CHRZANOWSKI, WIESŁAW M. (1923–   ), organizer and president of the Christian-National Union (ZChN)* in 1989, speaker of the Sejm* since October 27, 1991, Minister of Justice in the government of J. K. Bielecki* from January to November 1991, and professor of law at the Catholic University of Lublin (KUL)* since 1982. A member of the underground National Party (Stronnictwo Narodowe)* and later of the Labor Party (Stronnictwo Pracy),* he participated in the anti-German resistance during World War II. As a soldier of the Home Army (AK),* he fought in the Warsaw Uprising. A co-organizer of the Catholic-national movement after the war, he was imprisoned by the communists during 1948–54. Still persecuted by communist authorities after his release, he continued his activities in the Catholic movement. During 1965–81 he served on an informal information committee helping the Primate* of Poland, S. Wyszyński.*

In 1983–84 Chrzanowski served on the Primate's Social Council (Prymasowska Rada Społeczna). A member of Solidarity,* he served as an adviser to its leadership, was instrumental in the gaining of official recognition for this trade union, and joined Solidarity's Civic Committee.* As Minister of Justice, Chrzanowski attempted to criminalize abortion,* following a religious-conservative line; he became unpopular among liberal circles of Polish society, which considered him a religious fundamentalist. His political career was damaged when his ZChN rival and the Olszewski* cabinet Minister of Internal Affairs, A. Macierewicz,* announced that Chrzanowski was a communist secret police informer. *Kto jest kim w polityce polskiej*, ed. by R. Ignasiak (Warsaw, 1993), 49–50; G. Sanford and A. Gozdecka-Sanford, *Historical Dictionary of Poland* (Metuchen, N.J., 1994), 49; *Who's Who in the Socialist Countries of Europe*, ed. by J. Stroynowski, vol. 1 (Munich, 1989), 183; A. Micewski, *Ludzie i opcje* (Warsaw, 1993), 7–13.

CIASTOŃ, WŁADYSŁAW (1929–   ), officer of Counter-Espionage, undersecretary of state in the Ministry of Internal Affairs, and chief of Security Service since 1983. He authorized action against the priest J. Popiełuszko* in 1985. *Who's Who in the Socialist Countries of Europe*, ed. by J. Stroynowski, vol. 1 (Munich, 1989), 185

CIBOROWSKI, ADOLF (1919–87), architect and member of the State Council (Rada Państwa)* during 1985–87. Chairman of the State Committee of Urbanistics and Architecture in 1954–56 and chief architect of Warsaw* during 1964–67, he directed the U.N. reconstruction of Skopje, Yugoslavia, in 1964–67, served as urban-planning adviser to the U.N. Secretariat during 1974–77, and was a member of numerous international organizations of architects and urban planners. In 1981 he joined the Patriotic Movement for National Rebirth (PRON)* and beginning in 1983 chaired its Warsaw Council. *Who's Who in the Socialist Countries of Europe*, ed. by J. Stroynowski, vol. 1 (Munich, 1989), 185.

CIESZYN (German Teschen, Czech Tešin), town on the Olza River divided by the Polish-Czech border. The industrial region of Cieszyn was a bone of contention between Poland and Czechoslovakia. In 1918 the Duchy of Cieszyn of the Habsburg Empire was divided along ethnic lines, which gave the entire town of Cieszyn and a small territory on the left bank of the Olza to Poland. In 1919, when Poland was involved in the war against Bolshevik Russia, the Czechs annexed the left bank Cieszyn. It was taken by the Poles in 1938, during the Nazi-led partition of Czechoslovakia. After World War II the Polish-Czechoslovak dispute resurfaced. In June 1945 Polish troops seized Cieszyn and it seemed likely Poland would receive the entire region in exchange for the Kłodzko (Glatz) region in Silesia.* Polish and Czech foreign ministers were summoned to Moscow, however, where Stalin decided that the pre-1938 border should be preserved: There would be no territorial exchange. The Polish Army returned Cieszyn to the Czechs, and over 100,000 ethnic Poles remained in this region of Czechoslovakia. *The New Encyclopaedia Britannica*, vol. 3 (Chicago, 1990), 318; *The History of Poland since 1863*, ed. by R. F. Leslie (Cambridge, 1980), 285.

CIMOSZEWICZ, WŁODZIMIERZ (1950–), lawyer, politician, Premier* of Poland since January 1996, and key leader of Social-Democracy of the Polish Republic (SdRP).* A member of the Polish United Workers' Party (PZPR)* since 1971, he graduated from the Law Department at Warsaw University* and taught there during 1972–85. In 1980–81 he held a Fulbright Scholarship at Columbia University in New York. Beginning in 1985 he ran a farm. An experienced leader of socialist youth organizations, he was elected to the Sejm* in 1989 as a representative of the PZPR and became the chairman of its Parliamentary Club. A member of several Sejm committees—Foreign Affairs, National Minorities, Constitution, Territorial Self-Government, and the Extraordinary Committee of the Ministry of Internal Affairs—he became popular among his party colleagues, was a candidate in the presidential election of 1990,* and won fourth place after L. Wałęsa,* S. Tymiński,* and T. Mazowiecki,* gaining 9.21% of the vote. He was also elected to the Sejm in 1991 and 1993. Serving as Deputy Premier and Minister of Justice in the Pawlak* government from October 1993 to March 1995, he became a Deputy Speaker in the Sejm. In December 1995, he was appointed chairman of the Constitutional Committee of the National Assembly; in January 1996 he became Premier of Poland. *Kto jest kim w polityce polskiej*, ed. by R. Ignasiak (Warsaw, 1993), 53–54; G. Sanford and A. Gozdecka-Sanford, *Historical Dictionary of Poland* (Metuchen, N.J., 1994), 49–50.

CIOŁKOSZ, ADAM (1901–78) and **LIDIA** (1902–), veterans of wars for independence and restored borders of Poland during 1918–21, activists of the Polish Socialist Party (PPS),* and prolific political writers. In 1940 Adam Ciołkosz became a member of the National Council (Rada Narodowa)—the Polish Parliament-in-Exile in London; during 1947–57 he presided over the PPS in England. Adam and Lidia Ciołkosz edited London's *Robotnik* ("The Worker") and authored numerous important works on the history of socialism. *Encyklopedyczny Słownik Sławnych Polaków* (Warsaw, 1996), 54; W. Hładkiewicz, *Przywódcy "Polskiego" Londynu, 1945–1972* (Zielona Góra, 1993), 16.

CIOSEK, STANISŁAW (1939–), Polish ambassador to Moscow since November 1989, member of the Central Committee* of the Polish United Workers' Party (PZPR)* in 1985–86, and a reform-minded minister in Gen. W. Jaruzelski's* government. In 1960 he began work in the apparatuses of socialist youth organizations and the PZPR. During 1975–80 he served as First Secretary of the provincial Party organization in Jelenia Góra. Minister in charge of cooperation with trade unions during 1980–85, he was also Minister of Labor in 1983–84 and after 1985 also a director of a Central Committee department. In 1980–81 and 1988–89 he negotiated with Solidarity* and mediated both agreements between the independent trade union and the communist Polish authorities. As ambassador to Moscow he established Poland's new relationship with the Kremlin during the particularly dangerous period of the breakup of the Soviet Union. Despite his Party career, he enjoyed L. Wałęsa's* trust. He belongs to a group of officials who both served the old regime and now serve the new democratic authorities in Poland. *Kto jest kim w polityce polskiej*, ed. by R. Ignasiak (Warsaw, 1993), 54–55; G. Sanford and A. Gozdecka-Sanford, *Historical Dictionary of Poland* (Metuchen, N.J., 1994), 50; *Who's Who in the Socialist Countries of Europe*, ed. by J. Stroynowski, vol. 1 (Munich, 1989), 189.

CITIZENS' COMMITTEE OF THE CHAIRMAN OF SOLIDARITY (Komitet Obywatelski przy Przewodniczącym Solidarności [KO]), forum of opposition leaders organized by L. Wałęsa* in December 1988. The KO was instrumental before and during the Round Table Negotiations.* Its regional and local committees contributed greatly to Solidarity's* victory in the elections of June 1989* and helped Premier T. Mazowiecki* to form the non-communist regime. The KO's *spiritus movens* was its secretary, the experienced Solidarity leader H. Wujec.* He was replaced by Z. Najder,* who was appointed by Wałęsa in June 1990. In February 1991 the KO was transformed into the National Citizens' Committee (Krajowy Komitet Obywatelski [KKO]). G. Sanford and A. Gozdecka-Sanford, *Historical Dictionary of Poland* (Metuchen, N.J., 1994), 50.

CITIZENS' MILITIA. See **Militia.**

CITIZENS' MOVEMENT FOR DEMOCRATIC ACTION. See **ROAD.**

CITIZENS' PARLIAMENTARY CLUB (Obywatelski Klub Parlamentarny [OKP]), Solidarity* caucus in the Sejm* and the Senate,* formed after the elections of June 1989.* It consisted of 161 Sejm deputies and 99 senators and was first chaired by B. Geremek.* In November 1990 he was replaced by M. Gil,* who was appointed by L. Wałęsa,* and the OKP soon disintegrated into several Parliamentary Clubs. G. Sanford and A. Gozdecka-Sanford, *Historical Dictionary of Poland* (Metuchen, N.J., 1994), 50; B. Szajkowski (ed.), *Political Parties of Eastern Europe, Russia, and the Successor States* (London, 1994), 314; R. Taras, *Consolidating Democracy in Poland* (Boulder, Colo., 1995), 138–142.

CIVIL LIBERTIES, several privileges and immunities, such as freedom of speech, press, assembly, and worship (conscience), usually enshrined in constitutions of democratic states. Both the 1936 Soviet Constitution and its 1952 Polish copy included these liberties. Yet the day-to-day defense of civil liberties can be secured only through an independent bar and judiciary, which did not exist either in the USSR or in the Polish People's Republic. At the same time, the ideology* of class struggle denied liberties to members of the "reactionary" classes; as a consequence, civil liberties were not observed in communist Poland. R. L. Perry (ed.), *Sources of Our Liberties* (New York, 1952).

CIVIL SOCIETY, term often used in discussions on democratization. Usually civil society is understood as a network of independent professional, cultural, and social associations, political parties, and movements, all of which are able to organize themselves outside the official political sphere. Totalitarian systems have no place for such groups. The communist authorities of Poland almost succeeded in destroying civil society. Reconstruction of civil society in the 1970s and 1980s became crucial to the societal transformation that led to the fall of communism. Civil society contested the communist establishment and state power and made possible the existence of truly representative forms of government. D. Ost, *Solidarity and the Politics of Anti-Politics* (Philadelphia, 1990); M. H. Bernhard, *The Origins of Democratization in Poland: Workers, Intellectuals, and Oppositional Politics, 1976–1980* (New York, 1993); R. Taras, *Consolidating Democracy in Poland* (Boulder, Colo., 1995).

CLUBS OF CATHOLIC INTELLIGENTSIA (KIK), organizations of lay Catholics established in October 1956 as part of the political "thaw"* in Poland. Initially called the All-Polish Club of Progressive Catholic Intelligentsia, they had about 20 local branches. The communist authorities refused to register all of them. In March 1957 a compromise was reached: Five Clubs of Catholic Intelligentsia were legally established, one each in Warsaw,* Cracow,* Poznań,* Toruń,* and Wrocław.* The clubs developed intensive cultural and educational activities and created well-bonded, informal groups of people unfriendly toward communism. In the 1970s the KIK helped to create the anti-communist opposition, and in 1980–81 it enthusiastically supported Solidarity.* Yet the KIK's position was peculiar: Considered nests of reactionary opposition by the communists, they were also mistrusted by the Episcopate* and most priests of the Roman Catholic Church* in Poland as too liberal and "ideologically" suspicious. During the Solidarity period, the number of the clubs grew rapidly, but they were suspended after imposition of Martial Law* in December 1981 and later most of them were dissolved. Since the mid-1980s, however, their number increased again. In 1989 members of 54 Clubs of Catholic Intelligentsia helped to prepare the Round Table Negotiations* and the parliamentary elections. Many KIK activists, such as K. Łubieński,* T. Mazowiecki,* A. Stelmachowski,* J. Turowicz,* and J. Zawieyski,* belonged to the democratic opposition before 1989 and to the political elite of Poland after the fall of communism. In 1991 over 100 KIKs had about 25,000 members. M. H. Bernhard, *The Origins of Democratization in Poland* (New York, 1993); J. Karpiński, *Polska, Komunizm, Opozycja* (London, 1985), 88; *Nowa Encyklopedia Powszechna PWN*, vol. 3 (Warsaw, 1995), 379–380; A. Friszke, *Oaza na Kopernika. Klub Inteligencji Katolickiej, 1956–1989* (Warsaw, 1997).

COALITION FOR THE REPUBLIC (Koalicja dla Republiki [KdR]), coalition established by J. Olszewski's* Movement for the Republic (RdR),* A. Macierewicz's* Polish Action (AP), and K. Morawiecki's* Freedom Party (Partia Wolności), formerly Fighting Solidarity,* in September 1992. During the elections of September 1993* the KdR received only 2.7% of the vote and no parliamentary seats. B. Szajkowski (ed.), *Political Parties of Eastern Europe, Russia, and the Successor States* (London, 1994), 334.

COHN, LUDWIK (1902–81), attorney and defender in many political trials. A veteran of the 1920 Polish-Soviet War, a member of the Polish Socialist Party (PPS),* and an activist of the leftist movement before World War II, he participated in the September Campaign of 1939 and spent the war in a POW camp in Germany. An activist in the Crooked Circle Club,* he was an organizer and leader of the Workers' Defense Committee (KOR).* J. J. Lipski, KOR: *A History of the Workers' Defense Committee in Poland, 1976–1981* (Berkeley, Calif., 1985), 53; R. Stefanowski, *PPS 1892–1992* (Warsaw, 1992); M. H. Bernhard, *The Origins of Democratization in Poland* (New York, 1993).

COLD WAR, major ideological and political conflict between the Soviet bloc and the Western countries, led by the United States. The term was first used in April 1947 by a U.S. presidential adviser, Bernard Baruch, after the announcement of the Truman Doctrine. After several turning points, such as the 1948 communist coup in Czechoslovakia, the Berlin blockade, the establishment of NATO and the Warsaw Treaty Organization,* the 1962 Cuban missile crisis, and the 1968 invasion of Czechoslovakia, the Cold War entered its final phase in the late 1980s. With the fall of communism in East-Central Europe in 1989 and the dissolution of the USSR in 1991, the Cold War came to an end. The conflict had an important impact on the postwar history of Poland; simultaneously, Poland's internal situation significantly affected the course of the Cold War. It started, in part, over the Soviet occupation of Poland in the mid-1940s. The 1980–81 Solidarity* period and the failure of Martial Law* contributed considerably to the fall of communism and the end of the Cold War. *The Cold War, 1945–1991*, vols. 1–3, ed. by B. Frankel (Washington, D.C., 1992).

COLLECTIVIZATION, expropriation of privately owned land by communist state authorities to create large collective farms whose profits are, theoretically, shared by the members of these collective farms. An important part of communist ideology, collectivization was introduced in the USSR in the 1930s. It failed to establish efficient and productive agriculture* and led to hardship and famine. In the late 1940s, it was imposed on East-Central European Soviet satellites. In Poland, collectivization started in the second half of 1948, when its opponent, W. Gomułka,* was purged. Transformation of the Polish economy and society was accelerated by Yugoslavia's defection from the Soviet bloc and by escalation of the Cold War.* In July 1948 the Minister of Trade and Industry,

H. Minc,* gave the signal for collectivization. During a meeting of the Party leadership, he announced: "Within the socioeconomic system of a people's democracy farm cooperatives are the simplest and easiest way within the grasp of a common peasant, to develop a new system of large-scale economy, capable of utilizing all the benefits of modern technology and agricultural knowledge." Initiation of the collectivization program was announced at the First Congress of the Polish United Workers' Party (PZPR)* in December 1948. By the end of 1949, there were 243 cooperatives, composed mostly of farms created during the land reform* and in the "Recovered Territories."* State Centers of Agricultural Machines were established to help the cooperatives.

Favorable tax rates and compulsory deliveries gave farmers an incentive to join collective farms. Already in 1949, peasants felt administrative pressure. Encouraged by the good harvest in 1949, the authorities set very high targets for agriculture in the Six-Year Plan and hoped collectivization would result in more rational utilization of machinery and land and promote modern cultivation methods; large farms would invest more economically, the authorities reasoned, and would use less workers, now needed in industry. Thus, collectivization became important to the communist strategy in Poland. At the same time, state investments in agriculture and supplies of goods required in the countryside were insufficient and even diminishing in 1951–53. Polish peasants, spiritually attached to their land, saw no reason to join the cooperatives. Farming production stagnated, and the food supply to towns was negatively influenced as a result. The so-called planned purchase of grain came in 1950, and obligatory deliveries of grain were reintroduced in 1951. Simultaneously, the development of cooperative farms accelerated. Local administrative organs received centrally designed plans indicating how many collective farms should be created in a specified time. Young Party activists intimidated peasants and tried to persuade them of the superiority of collective farming. Brigades purchasing farm products illegally searched peasant property and sometimes destroyed it. Groundless administrative penalties and unlawful detentions were harassments used by Security and the Citizens' Militia (MO).* Abuses of power became well known and were criticized even in the Party.

Collective farms developed rapidly. In 1950 there were 2,199, but by September 1956 that number grew to 10,510. Cooperatives in some parts of the "Recovered Territories" covered most arable land, whereas in central and southeastern Poland their role was marginal. Altogether, they encompassed 8.6% of Polish land under cultivation. The 1960 target for development of cooperatives was between 25% and 30% of arable land. Yet it soon became obvious that traditional, non-collectivized farming was more efficient than "socialist forms of agriculture." As early as 1954 the Party leadership knew that collectivization was a failure. The alternative was clear: collectivization and hunger or traditional farming and relative abundance of food. When the political "thaw" came, the authorities had to abandon collectivization, and most cooperatives disappeared in late fall and winter 1956–57. R. F. Staar, *Poland, 1944–*

1962: The Sovietization of a Captive People (New Orleans, 1962), 88–93; B. P. McCrea, J. C. Plano, and G. Klein, *The Soviet and East European Dictionary* (Oxford, 1984), 185; Z. Landau and J. Tomaszewski, *The Polish Economy in the Twentieth Century* (London, 1985), 193–231.

COMECON, another name for the Council for Mutual Economic Assistance (Rada Wzajemnej Pomocy Gospodarczej [RWPG]). Established in January 1949 to coordinate the economic activities of communist states and to maintain Soviet hegemony, it included the Soviet Union, Bulgaria, Czechoslovakia, Hungary, Poland, Romania, Albania (from February 1949 until the end of 1961), the German Democratic Republic (from September 1950), Mongolia (from June 1962), Cuba (from 1972), and Vietnam (from 1978). From 1964 Yugoslavia participated in some Comecon activities. In the Stalinist period* Moscow used Comecon to control and exploit the economies of the communist states. In the late 1950s Comecon promoted industrial specialization among its members and developed a semi-barter exchange system. Early in the 1960s the economic plans of Comecon members were coordinated, and in 1963 the International Bank of Economic Cooperation was founded for common investment projects. Some members, especially Romania, opposed "international socialist division of labor" and were afraid it might handicap their industrial development. East Germany and Hungary pressed for greater national specialization, hoping that some branches of their relatively developed industries could dominate communist markets. Poland called for better distribution of investments among members. Because Comecon limited economic exchange with the West, the communist states manufactured outdated products that could not compete on the world market; as a consequence, Comecon countries became exporters of mostly cheap raw materials. After the fall of communism in East-Central Europe in 1989, the economic system created by Comecon collapsed. During Comecon's 45th session on January 9–10, 1990, in Sofia, the representatives of East-Central European countries bitterly criticized Comecon as an economically inefficient "product of political division in Europe" that deprived them of opportunities to promote their industries to the world. On June 28, 1991, at a meeting in Budapest, Comecon was formally dissolved. B. P. McCrea, J. C. Plano, and G. Klein, *The Soviet and East European Dictionary* (Oxford, 1984), 317; *The New Encyclopaedia Britannica*, 15th edition, vol. 8, p. 459; *1991 Britannica Book of the Year*, 169; *1992 Britannica Book of the Year*, 140.

COMINFORM, abbreviation designating the Information Bureau of Communist and Workers' Parties, founded on September 22–27, 1947, in the town of Szklarska Poręba in Silesia. The organizational meeting was attended by representatives of nine communist parties: E. Kardelj and M. Djilas from Yugoslavia; V. Chervenkov and V. Poptomov from Bulgaria; G. Gheorghiu-Dej and A. Pauker from Romania; M. Farkas and J. Revai from Hungary; H. Minc* and W. Gomułka* from Poland; R. Slansky and St. Bastovansky from Czechoslovakia; A. Zhdanov and G. Malenkov from the Soviet Union; J. Duclos and E. Farjon from France; and L. Longo and E. Reale from Italy. Officially, the Cominform was a forum for information exchange; in practice, it was established by Stalin to control East-Central Europe and the world's communist movement. The Cominform filled the vacuum created by the dissolution of the Comintern in May 1943, was an answer to the Truman Doctrine and the Marshall Plan, and constituted a deepening of the Cold War* and a new stage of Soviet domination over East-Central Europe. The Cominform rejected an individual, national approach to communism, criticized Czechoslovak communists for their failure to take power, and condemned the French and Italian communist parties for "permitting" their exclusion from ruling coalitions. The Information Bureau headquarters was in Belgrade; after the Soviet-Yugoslav conflict and Yugoslavia's expulsion from the Cominform in June 1948, it was moved to Bucharest, Romania. The Information Bureau met only five times, and its activities were mostly secret. In April 1956 the Cominform was dissolved by N. S. Khrushchev. H. Minc and enthusiastic hard-core Polish communists sympathized with the establishment and activities of the Cominform. W. Gomułka and his supporters were against it, however. They considered the Cominform part of Stalin's dangerous plan for total centralization and Russification of the world's communist movement. *The Cold War, 1945–1991*, vol. 3, "Resources: Chronology, History, Concepts, Events, Organizations, Bibliography, Archives," ed. by B. Frankel (Detroit, 1992), 131–134; P. Mosely, *The Kremlin and World Politics: Studies in Soviet Policy and Action* (New York, 1960); K. Kersten, *The Establishment of Communist Rule in Poland, 1943–1948* (Berkeley, Calif., 1991).

COMMAND ECONOMY, economic and political system in which the state authorities seek to control all aspects of economic activities; an indispensable element of the communist system. Its model was established by the Stalin regime in the USSR during 1929–53 and copied in the Soviet satellite states after 1945. It relies on tight central control and the mobilization of all resources. Its most important characteristics are state ownership, centrally determined state allocation, mobilization and full utilization of all resources, long-range economic planning, high rates of capital investment, especially in heavy industry, and state enforcement of economic plans. In Poland the central state organs had never managed to control the entire economy. Disintegration of the command economy became one of the most important factors leading to the fall of communism. B. P. McCrea, J. C. Plano, and G. Klein, *The Soviet and East European Dictionary* (Oxford, 1984), 187.

"COMMANDOS." See **"Komandosi."**

COMMUNIST INFORMATION BUREAU. See **Cominform.**

COMMUNIST SEIZURE OF POWER IN POLAND. The Bolsheviks had always planned to introduce communism to Poland because worldwide revolution was fundamental to their ideology. The first attempt to do this came in 1920 when the Red Army* invaded Poland and the Provisional Polish Revolutionary Committee (Tymczasowy Komitet Rewolucyjny Polski [TKRP]), a communist government-in-waiting, was organized in Białystok.* The Red Army's defeat in Poland, the civil war, the international intervention, and an internal crisis in the Soviet Union stopped Bolshevik expansion, but the plan was never abandoned. Communist revolution was also an ultimate goal of the Communist Party of Poland (KPP), organized in 1918 and sponsored by the USSR until 1938. During the Soviet-Nazi cooperation of 1939–41, Stalin made unclear plans concerning Poland, but the catastrophe of 1941 stopped him. During 1941–42 Soviet leaders were too busy to prepare world revolution and foster communism in Poland. Nonetheless, the Soviets managed to organize the Polish Workers' Party (PPR)* in Warsaw on January 5, 1942. The PPR was initially very small, was fought by the Polish underground state, and was isolated from its Soviet sponsors by a several hundred mile wide territory occupied by the Germans.

After the battle of Stalingrad (November 1942–January 1943), which became the turning point of World War II in Europe, Stalin returned to his Polish plans. In April 1943 the USSR discontinued diplomatic relations with the Polish Government-in-Exile,* using as a pretext the controversy following the discovery of Katyń* graves. In 1943 the Union of Polish Patriots (ZPP) and the communist-controlled First Division of the Polish Army* were formed. The Central Bureau of the Polish Communists in the USSR (CBKP)* was established in February 1944. Then on December 31, 1943, the PPR organized the National Home Council (KRN),* a conglomerate of underground political groups active in German-occupied Poland ready to cooperate with the communists. All these organizations helped to create the Polish Committee of National Liberation (PKWN), another communist-controlled government-in-waiting. The KRN and the PKWN decreed and began to introduce land reform* and nationalization* of industry* in Poland. The Home Army (AK)* and the civil sectors of the Polish underground state, directed by the Government-in-Exile, were paralyzed by the terror of the Red Army and the Soviet-sponsored Polish communist institutions. On January 1, 1945, the PKWN was reshaped into the Provisional Government of the Republic of Poland.* Dominated and fully controlled by communists, the Polish government was not recognized by the Western Allies, who were opposed to its establishment. Yet in Yalta* the Allies compromised with the Soviets.

The Provisional Government, supplemented by several non-communist politicians, was reshaped into the Provisional Government of National Unity (TRJN).* The communists and their allies held the most important portfolios, however. The TRJN was obliged to arrange "free and unfettered elections" as soon as possible, to create a parliament, which would then decide the political and economic profile of postwar Poland. Because the communists knew they would lose free and early elections, the 1946 elections were preceded by a June referendum,* during which the communists organized a campaign of terror against the democratic opposition.* In addition, the authorities falsified the referendum results. The PPR and the Soviets considered the referendum a rehearsal before a decisive parliamentary election. Thus the elections of January 1947* were even more oppressive. The opposition managed to gain a small number of parliamentary seats, but its organization and leadership were broken after mass arrests preceding the elections and the referendum. Political pluralism was over. The most important leaders of the Polish Peasant Party (PSL)* either were arrested or left the country. Remnants of their party merged with the Peasant Party (SL)* into the United Peasant Party (ZSL).* The Polish Socialist Party (PPS)* incorporated with the PPR during the so-called Unification Congress of December 1948,* when the Polish United Workers' Party (PZPR)* was established. Smaller parties and almost all independent institutions were de-legalized, and the entire political system was adjusted to precisely resemble the Soviet one. K. Kersten, *The Establishment of Communist Rule in Poland, 1943–1948* (Berkeley, Calif., 1991); J. Coutouvidis and J. Reynolds, *Poland, 1939–1947* (Leicester, 1986); M. K. Dziewanowski, *Poland in the Twentieth Century* (New York, 1977); *The History of Poland since 1863*, ed. by R. F. Leslie (Cambridge, 1980); N. Davies, *God's Playground: A History of Poland*, vol. 2 (New York, 1984).

CONFEDERATION FOR AN INDEPENDENT POLAND (Konfederacja Polski Niepodległej [KPN]), political party organized in 1979 by L. Moczulski* and his followers, who opposed the political line of the Workers' Defense Committee (KOR)* and accused it of leftist and conciliatory policy. In 1989 the KPN opposed the Round Table Negotiations,* claiming they constituted an unnecessary and harmful compromise. The KPN leadership believed the communist system was doomed and would fall within several months. During the hard transitionary period after 1989, the KPN's support grew quickly as a result of rising popular frustration and unemployment. The KPN strongly favored lustration and interventionist economic policy. It advocated slower privatization and a mixed economy of public and private ownership. Although it supported Polish membership in NATO and the European Union,* it also favored an activist Eastern policy. Moczulski claimed his eclectic program was based on the political heritage of J. Piłsudski. Moczulski, who aspired to a special position on the Polish political scene, asked an unrealistically high price for participation in a governmental coalition. As a consequence, the KPN landed mostly outside such coalitions. During the presidential elections of 1990,* Moczulski gained 2.5% of the vote. In the elections of 1991,* the KPN received 7.5% of the vote, which meant 46 seats in the Sejm* and 4 in the Senate.* During the elections of September 1993,* it gained only 5.8% of the vote and 22 parliamentary seats. This failure and Moczulski and his family's autocratic position in the party led to internal conflicts and the 1996 split, which produced two KPNs and marginalized both of them. G. Sanford and A. Gozdecka-Sanford, *Historical Dictionary of Poland* (Metuchen, N.J. 1994), 52; B. Szajkowski (ed.), *Political Parties of Eastern Europe, Russia, and the Successor States* (London, 1994), 330; *Political Handbook of the World: 1995–1996*, ed. by A. S. Banks, A. J. Day, and T. C. Muller (New York, 1996), 763; *Polskie partie polityczne*, ed. by K. A. Paszkiewicz (Warsaw, 1996), 43–54.

CONGRESS OF INTELLECTUALS FOR PEACE (Kongres Intelektualistów w Obronie Pokoju), meeting of about 600 prominent cultural and scientific figures from 45 countries on August 25–28, 1948, in Wrocław.* A permanent liaison committee was formed, and an appeal to people of good will to organize national committees in defense of peace was issued. *Twenty Years of the Polish People's Republic* (Warsaw, 1964), 302; B. Fijałkowska, *Borejsza i Różański. Przyczynek do dziejów stalinizmu w Polsce* (Olsztyn, 1995), 142–145.

CONSERVATIVE COALITION (Koalicja Konserwatywna [KK]), small political party established on February 7, 1994, by K. M. Ujazdowski* and his supporters, who left the Conservative Party (PK)* in January 1994. *Polskie partie polityczne*, ed. by K. A. Paszkiewicz (Warsaw, 1996), 37–42.

CONSERVATIVE PARTY (Partia Konserwatywna [PK]), political party that rose from a right-wing faction of the Democratic Union (UD).* The faction, led by A. Hall,* left the UD in September 1992 to form a Western-style Christian Democracy as opposed to the Christian-National Union (ZChN).* Most members of the PK and its leader, A. Hall, initially belonged to the Forum of Democratic Right established in spring 1990 to support the candidacy of T. Mazowiecki* for President.* In May 1991 the Forum of Democratic Right and the Citizens' Movement for Democratic Action (ROAD)* merged into the UD. Yet Hall and his followers were too conservative for most UD leaders. Hall stressed classic laissez-faire economic policy and Christian values, including strong opposition to abortion* and support for religious education at school. During the elections of 1993,* the PK formed a coalition with the ZChN and the Christian Peasant Alliance (SLCh).* This coalition, called *Ojczyzna* ("The Fatherland") did not manage to cross the 8% electoral threshold and failed to gain seats in the Sejm.* In January 1994 the PK was additionally weakened by a secession of a group of activists, led by K. M. Ujazdowski* and called the Conservative Coalition. The entire PK had about 1,000 members. B. Szajkowski (ed.), *Political Parties of Eastern Europe, Russia, and the Successor States* (London, 1994), 331; *Political Handbook of the World: 1995–1996*, ed. by A. S. Banks, A. J. Day, and T. C. Muller (New York, 1996), 764; *Polskie partie polityczne*, ed. by K. A. Paszkiewicz (Warsaw, 1996), 81–85.

CONSTITUTION CRISIS OF 1975. See **Appeal Concerning the 1975 Constitution Amendment.**

CONSTITUTION OF THE POLISH PEOPLE'S REPUBLIC, constitution accepted by the communist-controlled Sejm* on July 22, 1952. It replaced the 1947 "Little Constitution" and was amended several times. Immediately after World War II Poland operated theoretically on the 1921 Constitution. The approval of a new Constitution was a major goal of the Sejm formed after the elections of January 1947.* On February 19 the newly "elected" Sejm passed a law "On the System and Prerogatives of the Highest Authorities of the Republic of Poland," commonly called the "Little Constitution." This act, which stipulated the prerogatives of the Sejm, the President* who chaired the State Council (Rada Państwa),* and the government, was in force until the full-fledged Constitution was accepted. The "Little Constitution" reflected the political situation in Poland in 1947 and was very flexible; it maintained the appearance of a traditional parliamentary system but at the same time sanctioned a new form of government.

The first steps toward accepting a full Constitution were taken in mid-1951, when the Sejm established a drafting commission, chaired by President B. Bierut.* By the end of 1951, the commission approved the first draft. On January 27, 1952, the draft, revised and polished, was published by all Polish newspapers, which called for nationwide discussion. In July, Bierut announced that 11.0 million persons (out of 25.5 million Polish citizens) participated in this discussion. Yet the final text, accepted on July 22 by a unanimous vote, included only a few very minor changes, compared to the draft. The Constitution was modeled on the 1936 Stalinist Constitution, although Poland—like other Soviet European satellites—was not declared a communist state but a People's Republic, a state form placed, according to Marxism-Leninism, between capitalism and socialism. This state form was based on a rule presented in the Constitution: "from each according to his ability, to each according to his work." The text of the Constitution opened with a preamble that referred neither to God nor Providence, invoked neither national unity nor historical Polish achievements of the Poles. It stated: "The historic victory of the USSR over fascism liberated the Polish land, enabled the Polish working people to assume power, and created the conditions for the national rebirth of Poland within new and just borders." Then the preamble announced: "The alliance of the working class with the working peasants constitutes the basis for the present people's rule in Poland. In this alliance, the directing role belongs to the working class as the leading class of society, basing itself on the revolutionary achievements of the Polish and international workers." The preamble was followed by 10 chapters, including 91 articles. Article I defined Poland as a "people's democratic state" ruled by the working people. Their representatives elected by general, equal, direct, and secret suffrage (Article II) constituted the supreme organ of state authority, the Sejm. The State Council (Rada Państwa) substituted for the Sejm between its sessions. The Constitution defined competencies and structure of the Council of Ministers, local administration, and judicial system and listed the fundamental rights and duties of citizens.

The 1952 Constitution was amended several times. Some changes were less important than others, but Gierek's initiative provoked widespread public protests and an appeal concerning the 1975 Constitution amendment.* The last amendments of 1989 abolished the leading role of the Polish United Workers' Party (PZPR)* and transformed the Polish People's Republic into the Polish Republic. The entire text of the 1952 Constitution proved inadequate given the new political conditions, and a new Constitution was accepted in 1997. G. Sanford and A. Gozdecka-Sanford, *Historical Dictionary of Poland* (Metuchen, N.J., 1994), 53; J. Karpiński, *Poland since 1944: A Portrait of Years* (Boulder, Colo., 1995), 22; R. F. Staar, *Poland, 1944–1962: The Sovietization of a Captive People* (New Orleans, 1962), 27–48; J. Karpiński, *Polska, Komunizm, Opozycja* (London, 1985), 107; K. Kersten, *The Establishment of Communist Rule in Poland, 1943–1948* (Berkeley, Calif., 1991), 351–354.

CONTRACT SEJM. See **Elections of June 4 and 18, 1989.**

COOPERATIVE MOVEMENT (Spółdzielczość). Poland had a rich tradition of cooperative movements well before the imposition of cooperatives by the communist regime. Immediately after World War II numerous successful cooperatives were rebuilt. Yet in the 1950s they were subjected to intense state control, and their cooperative character practically disappeared. Like the large Housing Cooperatives, they became state enterprises. J. Karpiński, *Polska, Komunizm, Opozycja* (London, 1985), 258.

COUNCIL OF THREE (Rada Trzech), political body established in August 1954 in London to lead Polish emigration and Polish institutions in exile. The Council of Three acted as a "collegial President-in-Exile" and consisted of E. Raczyński,* Gen. W. Anders,* and T. Arciszewski*; the latter was replaced after his death in 1955 by Gen. T. Bór-Komorowski.* The Council of Three discontinued its activities in 1972. T. Radzik, *Z dziejów społeczności polskiej w Wielkiej Brytanii po drugiej wojnie światowej, 1945–1990* (Lublin, 1991); *Warszawa nad Tamizą*, ed. by A. Friszke (Warsaw, 1994).

COVENANT FOR POLAND (Przymierze dla Polski [PdP]), "confederation" established by the leaders of five parties from Poland's fragmented right wing on May 12, 1994. The PdP included the Center Alliance (PC),* the Christian-National Union (ZChN),* the Peasant Accord,* the Movement for the Republic (RdR),* and the Conservative Coalition.* In the elections of September 1993,* the PdP polled an aggregate vote of about 15%, but no one party had passed the 5% threshold necessary to win seats. *Keesing's Record of World Events*, May 1944, p. 40016; *Political Handbook of the World: 1995–1996*, ed. by A. S. Banks, A. J. Day, and T. C. Muller (New York, 1996), 763.

CRACOW (Kraków), capital city of Cracow Province (województwo) in southern Poland on the upper Vistula River.* One of the oldest towns of Poland and its capital between the mid-11th and the early 17th centuries, Cracow is the third largest city of the country (with 750,000 inhabitants in 1990) and one of the two most important cultural centers of Poland. Liberated in a surprise Soviet attack on January 17, 1945, Cracow was not destroyed by the Germans during World War II. Site of the most impressive concentration of historical monuments in Poland, Cracow was transformed into an industrial center when the giant steel works of Nowa Huta* were built in the late 1940s. The concentration of the workers there, which made the city more "proletarian," turned into a disadvantage for the communist authorities. Cracow became a center of industrial unrest and dissident activities supported by numerous students and intellectuals. Cracow is the seat of several institutions of higher learning, including the oldest and the most prestigious Polish university, called Jagiellonian University.* *International Dictionary of Historic Places*, ed. by T. Ring, vol. 2 (Chicago, 1995), 389; G. Sanford and A. Gozdecka-Sanford, *Historical Dictionary of Poland* (Metuchen, N.J., 1994), 104.

CRIMINAL CODE (Kodeks Karny), body of written rules defining and classifying criminal activities and their punishment. The 1932 Polish criminal code was in force during 1945–69. The code was amended with some special decrees, their regulations incorporated into the new criminal code passed by the Sejm* in 1969. The new code included a special chapter devoted to "crimes against the basic political and economic interests of the Polish People's Republic" and stipulated that these crimes could be punished with death. In 1982 and 1983 tough regulations were added directed against members of illegal organizations and protesters and demonstrators. J. Karpiński, *Polska, Komunizm, Opozycja* (London, 1985), 90–91.

CROOKED CIRCLE CLUB (Klub Krzywego Koła), the most successful of many young intelligentsia discussion clubs organized in 1955 and 1956 on the initiative of the weekly *Po Prostu* ("Plainly Speaking").* The first meeting of the Crooked Circle Club took place in 1955 in a private apartment in Crooked Circle Street in Warsaw.* Soon the Club changed its character, expanded greatly, and moved its meetings to a public hall in the Warsaw Old City Market, where the Club met every Thursday at 6:00 P.M. until its closing in 1962. Before 1957 the Club flourished and played an important political and intellectual role during the Polish de-Stalinization era. It coordinated the activities of other discussion clubs, established a network of contacts with the workers of Warsaw factories, and helped to organize clubs within the factories. In 1957 the Club participated intensly in the parliamentary electoral campaign. Attended by writers, artists, professors, judges, politicians, and even members of government, the Club initiated discussions on subjects previously forbidden or still banned from print by the censorship.* It encouraged people to speak out sincerely and openly, opposed conformity and opportunism, brought together groups of different worldviews, and broke the Stalinist barrier of fear. In 1957 W. Gomułka* tightened his policies and limited the activities of the discussion clubs. Their members were arrested, fired from work, and threatened by the police. The Crooked Circle Club also went through a crisis, but the energetic activities of its director, J. J. Lipski,* enabled it to survive as the only discussion club in Poland. It was revived in 1958. Several sections—artistic, sociological, architectural, and four others—were organized within the Club, which established independent awards for outstanding creative work. In 1960 P. Jasienica* was awarded for his historical writings and Jan Wolski for his studies on collective labor; in 1961, W. Bartoszewski* for his research on World War II, L. Kołakowski* for his philosophical works, and Henryk Stażewski for his painting. In March 1962 the communist authorities finally liquidated the Club, which had only 292 members but invited to its meeting about 2,000 people representing different fields of endeavor. The Club, which held about 300 meetings during its tenure, was a bulwark of independent thought and a school for many future intellectuals and politicians. W. Jedlicki, ''The Crooked Circle Club,'' *Poland since 1956*, ed. by T. N. Cieplak (New York, 1972), 120–129.

CRZZ (Centralna Rada Związków Zawodowych [Central Council of Trade Unions]), supreme leadership of the official trade unions, sponsored and controlled by the Polish communist authorities. The CRZZ was established in July 1949 as a continuation of the Central Committee of Trade Unions (Komisja Centralna Związków Zawodowych) during the Stalinization of Poland. All legal trade unions had to belong to the CRZZ. Fully controlled by the state, it was a mockery of workers' representation and self-government. It represented Polish trade unions abroad and published several periodicals. Presided over by K. Witaszewski* during 1945–48, E. Ochab* in 1948–49, A. Zawadzki* in 1949–50, K. Witaszewski during 1950–56, I. Loga-Sowiński* during 1956–71, W. Kruczek* during 1971–80, and R. Jankowski in 1980, the CRZZ was dissolved on December 5, 1980, as an outcome of the Solidarity* rebellion. J. Karpiński, *Polska, Komunizm, Opozycja* (London, 1985), 30.

CULTURE. See **Architecture; Art; Censorship; Literature; Music; Socialist Realism.**

CYBIS, JAN (1897–1977), painter and professor at several artistic academies in postwar Poland. *Encyklopedyczny Słownik Sławnych Polaków* (Warsaw, 1996), 54.

CYBULSKI, ZBIGNIEW (1927–67), popular film actor considered by many to be the Polish ''James Dean.'' He died tragically in a railway accident. G. Sanford and A. Gozdecka-Sanford, *Historical Dictionary of Poland* (Metuchen, N.J., 1994), 54; T. Cawkwell and J. Smith, *The World Encyclopedia of Film* (New York, 1972).

CYRANKIEWICZ, JÓZEF (1911–89), socialist politician, Premier* of Poland from February 1947 to November 1952, Deputy Premier from November 1952 to March 1954, Premier again from March 1954 to December 1970, and Chairman of the State Council (Rada Państwa)* from December 1970 to March 1972. A Polish Socialist Party (PPS)* activist since 1931, he was a prisoner at Auschwitz and Mauthausen and a member of camp resistance in 1941–45. After the war he led the PPS branch that supported cooperation and merger with the Polish Workers' Party (PPR)* in 1948. After the unification of the Polish workers' movement, he was a member of the Politburo* of the Polish United Workers' Party (PZPR)* until December 1971. A servilist and opportunist, he survived several political changes in Poland as a top official, serving before the Stalinist period,* throughout the Stalinist period, during de-Stalinization, throughout the entire Gomułka* period, and during the first two years of the Gierek* period. At the same time, he was considered a jovial author of numerous political jokes and a lover of a rich social life. G. Sanford and A. Gozdecka-Sanford, *Historical Dictionary of Poland* (Metuchen, N.J., 1994), 54; T. Mołdawa, *Ludzie Władzy 1944– 1991. Władze państwowe i polityczne Polski według stanu na dzień 28 II 1991* (Warsaw, 1991), 342.

CYWIŃSKA, IZABELLA (1935–   ) theater director and Minister of Culture in the Mazowiecki* cabinet from September 1989 to January 1991. She had directed several theaters in Poland and had won numerous awards for her artistic activities but became a public figure when she was designated a minister and a leader of the Democratic Union (UD).* *Kto jest kim w polityce polskiej*, ed. by R. Ignasiak (Warsaw, 1993), 55.

CYWIŃSKI, BOHDAN (1939–   ), journalist and historian working closely with the Clubs of Catholic Intelligentsia,* the Flying University,* and the *Znak* ("The Sign")* group. He published several important books on the history of Poland and the Roman Catholic Church,* edited *Znak* ("The Sign") monthly during 1973–77, and was an important figure in the democratic opposition in Poland. *Who's Who in the Socialist Countries of Europe*, ed. by J. Stroynowski, vol. 1 (Munich, 1989), 208; P. S. Wandycz, "Historiography of the Countries of Eastern Europe: Poland," *American Historical Review*, Oct. 1992, p. 1022; E. Kridl Valkenier, "The Rise and Decline of Official Marxist Historiography in Poland, 1945–1983," *Slavic Review*, vol. 44, no. 4 (winter 1985), 661–680.

CZAPSKI, JÓZEF (1896–1993), painter, writer, officer of the Polish Army,* co-founder of, and contributor to, the Paris *Kultura*.* A veteran of World War I, he distinguished himself during the 1919–20 Polish-Soviet War, studied at art academies in Warsaw* and Cracow,* and led the Kapist painters group. In 1939 he was taken a POW by the Soviets and spent almost two years in the infamous Starobielsk camp. Released in 1941, he joined the Anders* army, headed its Propaganda and Education Department, and directed the search for lost Polish officers. After the war he wrote about his experiences in the Soviet Union and on the history of art. First he settled in Paris, where he helped to edit *Kultura*, and then he moved to England, where he became one of the most outstanding personalities of the Polonia.* *Dictionary of Polish Literature*, ed. by E. J. Czerwinski (Westport, Conn., 1994), 71–72; *Encyklopedyczny Słownik Sławnych Polaków* (Warsaw, 1996), 57.

CZARNECKI, RYSZARD (1963–   ), leader of the Christian-National Union (ZChN).* A historian by profession, he worked in the underground Solidarity* Archives in the late 1980s and then for *Dziennik Polski* (''Polish Daily'') in London. Since 1990 he has been one of the main leaders of the ZChN and, temporarily, its spokesperson. *Kto jest kim w polityce polskiej*, ed. by R. Ignasiak (Warsaw, 1993), 56.

CZESZKO, BOGDAN (1923–88), writer, member of the communist underground during World War II, editor of several literary journals in postwar Poland, Sejm* deputy, and author of many novels and short stories about the war and about politics. *Encyklopedyczny Słownik Sławnych Polaków* (Warsaw, 1996), 63.

CZĘSTOCHOWA, city of 160,000 people and a provincial capital in south-central Poland, center of textile, chemical, food, and metallurgic industries. Częstochowa is the seat of Jasna Góra (''Shining Mountain'') monastery, which contains the painting ''The Black Madonna,'' the holiest picture of Catholic Poles, who consider St. Mary their queen. Every year Roman Catholic pilgrimages are made to Częstochowa, which has become an unofficial capital of the Roman Catholic Church* in Poland. J. Lerski, *Historical Dictionary of Poland, 966–1945*, with special editing and emendations by P. Wróbel and R. J. Kozicki (Westport, Conn., 1996), 97; *The New Encyclopaedia Britannica*, vol. 3 (Chicago, 1990), 838.

CZUBIŃSKI, ANTONI STEFAN (1928–   ), professor of history at Poznań University,* appointed deputy rector of the Higher School of Social Sciences by the Central Committee* of the Polish United Workers' Party (PZPR)* in 1971–74, and one of those who shaped official historiography in Poland before the fall of communism. *Who's Who in the Socialist Countries of Europe*, ed. by J. Stroynowski, vol. 1 (Munich, 1989), 213.

CZUBIŃSKI, LUCJAN (1930–   ), party official and Polish Army* general since 1970. In the military prosecutor's office since 1950, he became the chief military prosecutor in 1968, the chief state prosecutor in 1972, a director general in the Ministry of Internal Affairs during 1981–83, a deputy minister in the same ministry during 1983–90, and a deputy chairman of the Governmental Committee for Law Enforcement and Social Discipline, where he was especially harsh on the political opposition. *Who's Who in the Socialist Countries of Europe*, ed. by J. Stroynowski, vol. 1 (Munich, 1989), 213; M. H. Bernhard, *The Origins of Democratization in Poland* (New York, 1993).

CZUMA, ANDRZEJ (1938–   ), political dissident, co-organizer and leader of the *Ruch** group, and member of the Movement for the Defense of Human and Civil Rights (ROPCiO),* arrested and imprisoned many times. *Who's Who in the Socialist Countries of Europe*, ed. by J. Stroynowski, vol. 1 (Munich, 1989), 214; M. H. Bernhard, *The Origins of Democratization in Poland* (New York, 1993).

CZYREK, JÓZEF (1928–   ), communist official close to Gen. W. Jaruzelski* and momentarily considered his possible successor. Minister of Foreign Affairs in 1980–82, Czyrek was Secretary of the Central Committee* of the Polish United Workers' Party (PZPR)* during 1980–90, Politburo* member in 1981–89, and deputy president of the Patriotic Movement of National Revival (PRON)* during 1982–89. He was instrumental in organizing the Round Table Negotiations.* In 1989–90 he served as Minister of State in General Jaruzelski's presidential chancellery. G. Sanford and A. Gozdecka-Sanford, *Historical Dictionary of Poland* (Metuchen, N.J., 1994), 57; *Who's Who in the Socialist Countries of Europe*, ed. by J. Stroynowski, vol. 1 (Munich, 1989), 214; A. Kępiński and Z. Kilar, *Kto jest kim w Polsce inaczej* (Warsaw, 1985), 63–80; D. Ost, *Solidarity and the Politics of Anti-Politics* (Philadelphia, 1990).

D

DĄBROWSKA, MARIA (1889–1965), writer. Born into a family of impoverished landowners, she studied in Switzerland and Belgium and made her debut in the early 1920s with books for children and short stories about agricultural laborers and poor peasants. Gradually, her writing became more philosophical and intellectual. Dąbrowska studied Joseph Conrad's works, wrote about the cooperative movement, and in 1932–34 published her major work, *Noce i dnie* (''Nights and Days''). This large four-volume ''family saga'' tells the story of a gentry couple. It shows how Polish society transformed in the late 19th and early 20th centuries. Dąbrowska spent World War II in Warsaw.* After the war she did not support the new authorities but kept silent during the Stalinist period.* She became more visible after the 1956 political changes and published new stories, essays, and theatrical plays. Her works, reprinted in mass editions, became classics of Polish literature, and her *Dzienniki* (''Dairies'') constitutes an interesting primary source on interwar Poland, World War II, and postwar Poland. C. Młosz, *The History of Polish Literature* (Berkeley, Calif., 1983), 420–423; *Dictionary of Polish Literature*, ed. by E. J. Czerwinski (Westport, Conn., 1994), 77–81; T. Drewnowski, *Rzecz russowska. O pisarstwie Marii Dąbrowskiej* (Cracow, 1981).

DĄBROWSKI, BRONISŁAW (1917–   ), Archbishop, secretary of the Polish Episcopate* in 1969–93, and one of the closest collaborators of Primate S. Wyszyński.* Dąbrowski served as a liaison and negotiator between the Roman Catholic Church* and the communist authorities in Poland and, frequently, as a messenger to the West. The important law on the status of the Polish Church, accepted by the Sejm* in May 1989, was an outcome of his persistent activities. He retired in 1993. A. Micewski, *Ludzie i opcje* (Warsaw, 1993), 79–82; G. Polak, *Kto jest kim w Kościele katolickim* (Warsaw, 1996), 58.

DĄBROWSKI, KONSTANTY (1906–75), communist official and member of the State Council (Rada Państwa)* during 1969–72. A leader of the pro-communist faction of the Polish Socialist Party (PPS),* he became a member of the Central Committee* of the Polish United Workers' Party (PZPR)* after the 1948 forced unification of the socialist movement in Poland. He served as a finance minister several times. T. Mołdawa, *Ludzie Władzy 1944–1991. Władze państwowe i polityczne Polski według stanu na dzień 28 II 1991* (Warsaw, 1991), 344.

DAVIES, NORMAN (1939–   ), British historian, professor at the School of Slavonic and East European studies in London during 1985–97, and author of several important works on Polish history, including the magisterial *God's Playground: A History of Poland*. *Nowa Encyklopedia Powszechna PWN*, vol. 2 (Warsaw, 1995).

DĄB-KOCIOŁ, JAN (1898–1976), leader of the Polish Peasant Movement and Minister of Agriculture. During 1944–69 he was a member of the Sejm,* and during 1961–65, of the State Council (Rada Państwa).* T. Mołdawa, *Ludzie Władzy 1944–1991. Władze państwowe i polityczne Polski według stanu na dzień 28 II 1991* (Warsaw, 1991), 343.

DEATH PENALTY. In 1944–46, the communist authorities, installed in Poland by the USSR, decreed that capital punishment could be used against those people who belonged to illegal organizations, resisted land reform,* owned a transmitting radio device, did not inform the authorities about a committed crime, and opposed the government in other ways. Before 1956 several thousand people were systematically sentenced to death and executed as opponents of communism. The "Polish October" of 1956* ended the procedural killing of political prisoners. Yet W. Gomułka* supported capital punishment for heavy economic crimes. In 1965, for example, an official responsible for a "meat swindle" was executed. Although the execution provoked public protests, capital punishment persisted during the Gierek* period. In 1972 Polish courts set a record, passing 33 death sentences. After imposition of Martial Law* on December 13, 1981, the Jaruzelski* regime issued a decree, officially dated December 12, 1981, that extended the list of crimes punishable by death. Several people were sentenced to death in absentia, among them the Polish ambassadors to Japan and the United States, Z. Rurarz* and R. Spasowski,* for defection. In 1988 the authorities announced a moratorium on the application of capital punishment, and since then nobody has been executed, although the Polish courts sentenced 14 people to death during 1989–96. J. Karpiński, *Polska, Komunizm, Opozycja* (London, 1985), 82; P. Pytlakowski, "Pożegnanie z katem," *Polityka*, April 19, 1997, pp. 3–8.

DECEMBER EVENTS OF 1970 (wydarzenia grudniowe), grave political crisis in Poland triggered by the December 13 announcement of major increases in the price of food and fuel. During December 14–18, demonstrations and strikes in Gdańsk,* Gdynia,* and Szczecin* developed into violent riots, accompanied by heavy loss of life. On December 20, First Secretary of the Polish

United Workers' Party (PZPR)* W. Gomułka* resigned and was succeeded by E. Gierek.* On December 23 the Premier,* J. Cyrankiewicz,* was replaced by P. Jaroszewicz,* who formed a new cabinet. Most Gomułka supporters were removed from the Politburo,* which was then formed by Gierek's assistants. The crisis began a new era in the history of communist Poland—the Gierek period.

By the late 1960s the Polish authorities faced serious economic problems. Both industry* and agriculture* were not working well. Manufactured consumer goods and food products had failed to keep up with demand. Two bad harvests in 1969–70 destroyed the balance of international trade, since meat products were among Poland's most profitable exports. This prompted government-planned reforms aimed at partial marketization of the Polish economy. Yet conditions at the start of reforms were poor. Therefore, the Gomułka regime decided to "reshape the structure of production and consumption" to gain money necessary for new investments and to terminate a situation in which retail prices of most food and some industrial goods were lower than the cost of production. On December 13, 1970, the government announced increases in the price of meat (17.6% on average), lard (33.4%), fish (11.7%), flour (16%), milk (8%), cheese (25%), jam (26.8%), hard coal (10%), brown coal (14%), and other foodstuffs and goods. Reductions in prices of consumer goods such as medicines, TV sets, radios, vacuum cleaners, and sewing machines were intended to balance increases in food prices. The latter, which added 20% to the average family's food bill, were introduced just before Christmas and, a significant fact in the case of fuel price increases, in the middle of winter.

On December 14 Gdańsk shipyard workers approached PZPR representatives to ask them to withdraw the increases and to raise their wages. Party officials called the workers "provocateurs." The workers left the meeting and marched to Party headquarters, singing the "Internationale" and the national anthem. A rumor circulated that their delegation was arrested. Fighting broke out, rioting and arson spread throughout the city, and a general strike of shipyard and dockworkers began. On December 15 the riots continued; the PZPR headquarters, the central railway station, and other targets were set on fire. The rioters stormed the prison, looted shops, and fought with police, who fired into the crowds. Some people were killed. Riots continued in Gdańsk and on December 16 spread to Gdynia and Elbląg.* S. Kociołek,* a Deputy Premier and a Politburo member sent to Gdańsk to deal with the situation, asked the workers to return to work and promised them an immediate 20% wage increase. Those who tried to return, however, were shot at by soldiers in Gdynia. Gdańsk and Gdynia were sealed off, and all foreigners and foreign ships were ordered to leave the two ports. Go-slow strikes started in the main industrial centers of Poland. On December 17 the fighting spread to Słupsk and Szczecin, where a general strike was declared. The strike committee took control of the city and formed workers' militias to maintain order. Declaring a state of emergency, the government authorized the police to use weapons. A speech by J. Cyrankiewicz was broadcast in which the Premier stated, "Criminal and anarchist elements on the one hand, and enemies of socialism and Poland on the other, have exploited the situation to loot, burn and destroy" and have tried to "disorganize the life of the country." By December 18 the situation in Gdańsk and Gdynia was slowly returning to normal. Universities all over the country closed for Christmas earlier than usual, and the police moved into the most important large factories on the Baltic coast. Then on December 20 Gomułka, suffering from cardiovascular problems, resigned and was replaced by Gierek. At the same time, four officials closely associated with Gomułka—M. Spychalski,* B. Jaszczuk,* Z. Kliszko,* and R. Strzelecki*—were dropped from the Politburo.* M. Moczar,* P. Jaroszewicz, S. Olszowski,* E. Babiuch,* and J. Szydlak entered the Politburo. H. Jabłoński,* Gen. W. Jaruzelski,* and J. Kępa* were promoted as its alternate members. In a broadcast that evening Gierek claimed the crisis had been caused, among other reasons, by "ill-considered economic ideas"; he promised to improve the lot of the workers. The media, having earlier claimed the riots were provoked by "adventurers and hooligans," changed their attitude completely. Immediately after Gomułka's resignation, they shifted the responsibility to failures of his government and called for a fundamental reshaping of economic and social policy. Finally, on December 21 Gdańsk and Gdynia workers returned to work. In Szczecin, completely sealed off by the military, workers demanded that army and police units be withdrawn first. Once forces withdrew, they resumed work on December 24. Before that, on December 23, the Sejm had accepted Cyrankiewicz's resignation and endorsed Jaroszewicz as the new Premier. Most ex-ministers kept their portfolios. Only Kociołek ceased to be Deputy Premier to assume a new position at the Central Committee* Secretariat. Jaroszewicz added four new ministerial positions, taken by his supporters. Gierek promised the Sejm that price increases would be withdrawn, prices would be frozen for the next two years, families with low incomes would receive special aid, and credits granted to peasantry, pensions, disability allowances, and minimum wages would be increased. Jaroszewicz also stated that his government would work toward full normalization of relations with the Roman Catholic Church.* Similar promises were repeated in New Year messages broadcasted by TV* and radio.* Gierek and Jaroszewicz visited Moscow on January 5, 1971, to talk with L. Brezhnev and A. Kosygin; there followed a common communiqué stating that Polish and Soviet leaders had "complete identity of views" on all discussed problems.

Yet stoppages and strikes resumed in January 1971 in Gdańsk, Szczecin, and Łódź. On January 15 the chairman of the Central Council of Trade Unions, I. Loga-Sowiński,* resigned, followed by Minister of Internal Affairs K. Świtała. In January Gierek received representatives from various social groups; on January 24 he met with striking workers in the Szczecin shipyard. The next day he and Jaroszewicz visited workers at the Gdańsk shipyard. They answered Gierek's question, "Will you help us?" with the legendary "We will." The workers had no political demands, and the intellectuals kept silent, terrorized by the

"March events" of 1968.* The crisis was over. J. Karpiński, *Poland since 1944: A Portrait of Years* (Boulder, Colo., 1995), 159–168; *Keesing's Contemporary Archives*, Jan. 16–23, 1971, pp. 24389–24393; J. L. Curry and L. Fajfer (eds.), *Poland's Permanent Revolution: People vs. Elites, 1956 to the Present* (Washington, D.C., 1996), 55–108; M. K. Dziewanowski, *Poland in the Twentieth Century* (New York, 1977), 206–209; *The History of Poland since 1863*, ed. by R. F. Leslie (Cambridge, 1980), 384–406.

DECEMBER 13, 1981. See **Martial Law.**

DEJMEK, KAZIMIERZ (1924–   ), theater director and Minister of Culture in the governments of W. Pawlak* and J. Oleksy* during 1993–96. In 1968 he staged A. Mickiewicz's drama *Dziady* ("Forefathers' Eve"),* with strong anti-Russian sentiments. The banning of the play provoked student demonstrations and started the "March events" of 1968.* Dejmek's ministerial performance was considered by many to be autocratic and controversial and was sharply criticized. G. Sanford and A. Gozdecka-Sanford, *Historical Dictionary of Poland* (Metuchen, N.J., 1994), 58; W. Filler, *Contemporary Polish Theatre* (Warsaw, 1977).

DELEGACY FOR THE ARMED FORCES IN POLAND (Delegatura Sił Zbrojnych na Kraj), clandestine organization established in Poland on May 7, 1945, by the commander-in-chief of Polish forces in the West. The Delegacy was based on the organizational structure of the Home Army (AK),* dissolved on January 19, 1945. Headed by Col. Jan Rzepecki,* the Delegacy informed the Polish military leadership in London about the situation in Poland and tried to demobilize the AK in a way that would minimize casualties and allow the creation of a smaller and better-hidden clandestine military structure. In August and September 1945 Rzepecki ordered the Delegacy to be replaced by the "Freedom and Independence" (WiN)* organization. The Delegacy failed to control the post-AK underground. Several former AK districts and numerous guerrilla groups declared independence and continued the armed struggle against the Soviets. S. Korboński, *The Polish Underground State: A Guide to the Underground, 1939–1945* (New York, 1978), 226–227; J. Coutouvidis and J. Reynolds, *Poland, 1939–1947* (Leicester, 1986); *Słownik Historii Polski 1939–1948*, ed. by A. Chwalba and T. Gąsowski (Cracow, 1994), 39–41.

DELEGACY OF THE GOVERNMENT OF THE REPUBLIC OF POLAND (Delegatura Rządu na Kraj), clandestine organization established by the Polish Government-in-Exile* to coordinate non-military activities of the Polish underground state in Nazi-occupied Poland during World War II. Anti-German military resistance organized very soon after the fall of Poland. Creation of civil resistance was slower. On February 26, 1940, the Political Coordination Committee (Polityczny Komitet Porozumiewawczy [PKP]) was established by the underground Polish Socialist Party–Freedom, Equality, Independence (Polska

Partia Socjalistyczna–Wolność, Równość, Niepodległość [PPS-WRN]), the Peasant Party (SL),* and the National Party (SN).* The Government-in-Exile wanted to establish better contact with, and control over, the resistance, to separate the civil and military underground leadership, and to establish an office of the Delegate of the Government of the Republic of Poland. Special government emissary Jan Skorobohaty-Jakubowski traveled to Poland from London in May 1940 to organize the Collective Delegacy, consisting of representatives of the clandestine parties and the commander-in-chief of the underground army. After the fall of France in June 1940, the Collective Delegacy lost contact with the Government-in-Exile (which moved from France to London) and was dissolved by it in September 1940. On December 3, 1940, the Government-in-Exile nominated Cyryl Ratajski from the Labor Party (SP)* as its delegate. In summer 1942 Ratajski resigned and was replaced by Jan Piekałkiewicz from the SL. Arrested by the Germans on February 19, 1943, Piekałkiewicz was succeeded by Jan Stanisław Jankowski from the SP. Jankowski served until his arrest by the NKVD on March 27, 1945. Subsequently, the SL's S. Korboński* took the office.

The Delegacy developed and headed a sophisticated underground apparatus. Local delegacies administered the provinces and districts of occupied Poland. Thirteen departments, resembling prewar ministries, were in charge of internal affairs, information and press, education and culture, work and social affairs, industry and trade, agriculture, justice, liquidation of the consequences of the war, finances, and mail and communication. The Delegacy established several specialized organizations, such as the Directorate of Civil Resistance (Kierownictwo Walki Cywilnej). On May 3, 1944, the delegate became the chairman of the Home Cabinet (Krajowa Rada Ministrów). The Polish underground state tried to cooperate with the Red Army* entering Poland in mid-1944. The Soviets, however, did not intend to cooperate. They imprisoned local military commanders and clandestine administrative directors who came out of hiding. On March 27, 1945, the Soviets arrested and sent to Moscow 16 leaders of the Polish underground state. Those leaders not arrested by the Soviets decided to continue their fight for freedom on April 7, 1945. The Delegacy reorganized and adapted to the new conditions. In June 1945 the Provisional Government of National Unity (TRJN),* including S. Mikołajczyk* and several "London Poles," was created. Meanwhile, the Polish underground state disintegrated. On July 1, 1945, the clandestine Council of National Unity (Rada Jedności Narodu [RJN]) issued its manifesto to the Polish nation, the Testament of the Fighting Poland, which announced the end of the Polish underground state. Nonetheless, numerous clandestine organizations and guerrilla units continued their activities during the following several years. S. Korboński, *The Polish Underground State: A Guide to the Underground, 1939–1945* (New York, 1978), 43–54, 223–226; J. Coutouvidis and J. Reynolds, *Poland, 1939–1947* (Leicester, 1986); *Słownik Historii Polski 1939–1948*, ed. by A. Chwalba and T. Gąsowski (Cracow, 1994), 35–39.

DELEGATE FOR THE ARMED FORCES. See **Delegacy for the Armed Forces in Poland.**

DELEGATE OF THE GOVERNMENT OF THE REPUBLIC OF PO-LAND. See **Delegacy of the Government of the Republic of Poland.**

DEMBOWSKI, BRONISŁAW (1927–   ), Bishop of Włocławek, professor of philosophy, and member of the Polish Episcopate* Commission, on which he was responsible for a dialogue with non-believers. He was also involved in the Ecumenical Movement and politics; in 1989 he participated in the Round Table Negotiations.* G. Polak, *Kto jest kim w Kościele katolickim* (Warsaw, 1996), 60.

DEMOCRATIC CENTRALISM, basic organizational principle of communist parties. It was supposed to reconcile democracy with centralism. The democratic element allegedly existed in elections of Party leadership and the predominance of majority over minority. The latter was strictly forbidden from forming inter-Party factions or opposition. According to the rule of centralism, once the elected leading bodies were formed, their decisions were binding to Party members and Party units of a lower level. Democratic centralism was one of the main principles of the program of the Polish United Workers' Party (PZPR).* Cleverly manipulated, it became a tool of despotic Party leadership. M. Waller, *Democratic Centralism: An Historical Commentary* (Manchester, 1981).

DEMOCRATIC LEFT ALLIANCE (Sojusz Lewicy Demokratycznej [SLD]), alliance of leftist political organizations established in July 1991, before the elections of 1991,* as the National Electoral Committee of the Left Alliance (Krajowy Komitet Wyborczy Sojuszu Lewicy Demokratycznej). It gathered 15 trade unions, political parties, and other organizations, including the All-Poland Alliance of Trade Unions (OPZZ)* and the reborn Polish Socialist Party (PPS),* but was dominated by the Social Democracy of the Republic of Poland (SdRP),* a successor party of the Polish United Workers' Party (PZPR),* dissolved in January 1990. The 1991 elections gave the SLD 60 out of 460 seats in the Sejm* and 4 out of 100 seats in the Senate.* On November 4, 1991, the Parliamentary Club of the SLD was formed and A. Kwaśniewski* was elected its chairman. Before the elections of 1993,* a new Coalition Agreement was signed by representatives of 28 leftist parties and organizations. The extended SLD received 20.5% of the vote and this spectacular victory doubled its representation in the Sejm. The SLD formed a coalition with the Polish Peasant Party (PSL),* which received an even larger share of votes, and created a government headed by the PSL leader W. Pawlak.* During the presidential election of 1995,* the leader of the SLD, Kwasniewski, was elected President* of Poland. Polish public opinion generally considers the SLD a "post-communist" incarnation of the PZPR. General information about Poland at <http://bmb.ippt.gov.pl/poland/partone.html>

DEMOCRATIC-NATIONAL PARTY (Stronnictwo Demokratyczno-Narodowe), small party established in Warsaw* in April 1991. It has had no parliamentary representation. *Partie Polityczne w Polsce*, ed. by A. Gargas and M. Wojciechowski (Gdańsk, 1991), 146–147.

DEMOCRATIC PARTY (Stronnictwo Demokratyczne [SD]), liberal democratic party established in 1937 and, after the war, accepted by the communists as an allied and fully controlled organization, representing the intelligentsia,* small traders, and artisans. As such, it received seats in the Sejm* and local councils from the communist authorities. After the 1989 election the SD and the United Peasant Party (ZSL)* unexpectedly reversed their alliances to support Solidarity,* thus making the organization of the Mazowiecki* government possible. Jan Jankowski became Deputy Premier in the Mazowiecki government, two other leaders of the SD served as ministers. However, the SD lost in its competition with numerous newly established parties and practically disintegrated. Membership diminished from 130,000 in 1990 to 60,000 in 1991, and the party had only one minister in the Bielecki* cabinet. During the 1991 parliamentary election it received only one seat in the Sejm. G. Sanford and A. Gozdecka-Sanford, *Historical Dictionary of Poland* (Metuchen, N.J., 1994), 59; *Partie Polityczne w Polsce*, ed. by A. Gargas and M. Wojciechowski (Gdańsk, 1991), 142–145.

DEMOCRATIC-SOCIAL MOVEMENT (Ruch Demokratyczno-Społeczny [RDS]), a group withdrawn from the Democratic Action Civic Movement (ROAD)* by Z. Bujak* in early 1991, after T. Mazowiecki* lost in the presidential 1990 elections.* Later, the RDS merged with Labor Solidarity* into the Union of Labor (UP).* B. Szajkowski (ed.), *Political Parties of Eastern Europe, Russia, and the Successor States* (London, 1994), 340.

DEMOCRATIC UNION (Unia Demokratyczna [UD]), party established immediately after the presidential election of 1990,* on December 2, as a merger of the Electoral Committees of T. Mazowiecki,* the Citizens' Movement for Democratic Action (ROAD),* and the Forum of Democratic Right (FPD).* Registered on December 28, 1990, it was finally shaped during its Unification Congress on May 13–14, 1991. Led by T. Mazowiecki, B. Geremek,* J. Kuroń,* A. Hall,* J. Rokita,* Z. Kuratowska,* and W. Frasyniuk,* it remained the largest Parliamentary club after the Civic Parliamentary Club (OKP)* disintegrated. In the 1991–93 Parliament, which included 49 organizations, the UD was the strongest club with 62 seats in the Sejm and 21 in the Senate.* However, it translated into only 12.31% of the vote in the 1991 election. In addition, the party was visibly divided into social democratic and Christian democratic factions. The UD is close to the *Gazeta Wyborcza* ("The Electoral Gazette")* and was the main force of the coalition supporting the Suchocka* government from July 1992 to October 1993. Enemies of the UD believed that it cooperated with former communists, monopolized Polish mass media, assumed an elitist attitude, and denigrated other parties as representatives of an uneducated crowd. In 1991 the UD had about 15,000 members. G. Sanford and A. Gozdecka-Sanford, *Historical Dictionary of Poland* (Metuchen, N.J., 1994), 59; *Partie Polityczne w Polsce*, ed. by A. Gargas and M. Wojciechowski (Gdańsk, 1991), 164–167.

DIP. See **"Experience and Future."**

DISSIDENTS, term used to identify non-Catholic Christians in Poland during the Reformation and Counter-Reformation. In the late 1960s the Western press began to use this term to describe a small group of people who opposed official communist doctrine in the USSR. In Poland the term was not popular, since in the eyes of most Poles dissidents were communists who constituted a small group with an unusual worldview. J. Karpiński, *Polska, Komunizm, Opozycja* (London, 1985), 46.

DOBRACZYŃSKI, JAN (1910–94), prolific Catholic writer who became a communist state official. He made his debut in the 1930s; during World War II he participated in the anti-German resistance and the Warsaw Uprising. After the war he cooperated with the communist-sponsored Catholic PAX Association* and edited its first organ, *Dziś i Jutro* ("Today and Tomorrow"). During 1953–56 Dobraczyński served as editor-in-chief of *Tygodnik Powszechny* ("The Universal Weekly"),* taken by the communists from its previous owners. During 1952–56 and 1985–89 he served as a Sejm* deputy, and from 1983 to November 1989, as president of the Patriotic Front for National Revival (PRON),* a window-dressing organization created by the Jaruzelski* regime after Martial Law.* *Who's Who in the Socialist Countries of Europe*, ed. by J. Stroynowski, vol. 1 (Munich, 1989), 246; A. Micewski, *Ludzie i opcje* (Warsaw, 1993), 14–18.

DOBROWOLSKI, STANISŁAW RYSZARD (1907–85), poet, writer, and state official, whose poetry and fiction reflected a Party interpretation of history and politics. *Encyklopedyczny Słownik Sławynch Polaków* (Warsaw, 1996), 74.

DOŚWIADCZENIE I PRZYSZŁOŚĆ. See **"Experience and Future."**

DRAWICZ, ANDRZEJ (1932–97), historian of Polish and Russian literature, translator, and professor at Warsaw University* since 1993. In 1978–81 he was a lecturer of the Association of Scientific Courses*; during 1989–91 he served as president of the Radio and TV* Committee. *Nowa Encyklopedia Powszechna PWN*, vol. 2 (Warsaw, 1995); *Who's Who in the Socialist Countries of Europe*, ed. by J. Stroynowski, vol. 1 (Munich, 1989), 258.

DROBNER, BOLESŁAW (1883–1968), doctor of chemistry and socialist activist in the 1890s. A leader of the left wing of the Polish Socialist Party (PPS)* and its splinter parties, he belonged to the leaderships of the Union of Polish Patriots in the USSR during 1943–44 and the Polish Committee of National Liberation (PKWN) in 1944. During 1944–68 he was a member of the Polish Parliament; in 1948 he joined the Polish United Workers' Party (PZPR),* becoming one of its minor officials. Communist propaganda used his name and life story to show that the Soviet-sponsored post-1942 communist movement was a direct continuation of the prewar Polish socialist movement. After the ''Polish October'' of 1956,* Drobner served shortly as Party First Secretary in Cracow,* but he had to leave because his approach was too reformist. T. Mołdawa, *Ludzie Władzy 1944–1991. Władze państwowe i polityczne Polski według stanu na dzień 28 II 1991* (Warsaw, 1991), 346.

DRZEWIECKI, ZBIGNIEW (1890–1971), pianist and music professor, longtime president of conservatories in Cracow* and Warsaw,* expert on the music of F. Chopin and K. Szymanowski. M. Dąbrowska, *Dzienniki Powojenne 1945–1965*, vol. 1, ed. by T. Drewnowski (Warsaw, 1996), 216.

DRZYCIMSKI, ANDRZEJ J. (1942–   ), journalist and L. Wałęsa's* press secretary during 1989–94. A historian by profession, he worked for many years as a journalist and editor. In 1980 he participated in the Gdańsk* Lenin Shipyard strike and became a close collaborator of Wałęsa. Interned during Martial Law,* he later wrote many works on Polish history and Solidarity.* A ghost writer of Wałęsa's first autobiography, he served loyally as Wałęsa's personal and presidential spokesperson until he was unexpectedly fired. G. Sanford and A. Gozdecka-Sanford, *Historical Dictionary of Poland* (Metuchen, N.J., 1994), 61; *Kto jest kim w polityce polskiej*, ed. by R. Ignasiak (Warsaw, 1993), 67.

DUDA, EDWARD (1922–   ), activist and leader of the communist-sponsored Polish Peasant Movement; during 1976–80 a member and, during 1980–83, a secretary of the State Council (Rada Państwa).* T. Mołdawa, *Ludzie Władzy 1944–1991. Władze państwowe i polityczne Polski według stanu na dzień 28 II 1991* (Warsaw, 1991), 347.

DUNIKOWSKI, XAWERY (1875–1964), leading Polish sculptor, painter, art professor, and author of numerous historical monuments. He started his teaching career in 1904 in Warsaw.* Imprisoned by the Germans, he spent five years in Auschwitz. After the war he taught at the art academies of Cracow,* Warsaw, and Wrocław.* G. Sanford and A. Gozdecka-Sanford, *Historical Dictionary of Poland* (Metuchen, N.J., 1994), 61.

DWORAKOWSKI, WŁADYSŁAW (1908–76), Deputy Premier from November 1952 to March 1954 and chairman of the governmental Public Security

Committee (Komitet do Spraw Bezpieczeństwa Publicznego przy Radzie Ministrów) from December 1954 to March 1956. A member of the Communist Party of Poland (KPP) since 1934, he joined the Polish Workers' Party (PPR)* in 1942; he became a member of its Central Committee* in December 1945. In 1952 he became a deputy member of the Politburo,* and in March 1954, its full member. In the late 1940s he lead the party organization in Gdańsk* and Łódź.* His political career came to an end in 1956. He was later ill and returned to his initial job as locksmith. T. Mołdawa, *Ludzie Władzy 1944–1991. Władze państwowe i polityczne Polski według stanu na dzień 28 II 1991* (Warsaw, 1991), 347.

DYGAT, STANISŁAW (1914–78), writer, translator, and author of nostalgic-poetic works devoted to contemporary existential problems. *Dictionary of Polish Literature*, ed. by E. J. Czerwinski (Westport, Conn., 1994), 102–103; *Encyklopedyczny Słownik Sławynch Polaków* (Warsaw, 1996), 81.

DYKA, ZBIGNIEW S. J. (1928–   ), lawyer, Minister of Justice and attorney general in the governments of J. Olszewski* and H. Suchocka* from December 1991 to February 1993, member of the Christian-National Union (ZChN).* *Kto jest kim w polityce polskiej*, ed. by R. Ignasiak (Warsaw, 1993), 68.

DZIADY, actually *Dziady, Część III* (''Forefathers' Eve, Part III''), drama written by the most important national romantic bard of Poland, Adam Mickiewicz, in 1833. Inspired by the poet's experience in Russian-occupied Vilna, the drama describes Polish-Russian relations in the 1820s and presents Poland as the Messiah of nations, who would redeem Western civilization by Polish self-sacrifice and martyrdom. The drama belongs to the most sacred canon of Polish literature and national tradition. On November 25, 1967, *Dziady* opened at the National Theater to an enthusiastic reception. At once an illustration of important historical events and contemporary experiences, the drama prompted popular support but provoked the communist authorities. Its anti-Russian undertones led the authorities to instruct the theater to limit the number of performances and then to discontinue them. After the last performance, on January 30, 1968, a protest demonstration took place around Mickiewicz's statue in Warsaw. Authorities arrested some participants, which triggered the ''March events'' of 1968.* J. Karpiński, *Poland since 1944: A Portrait of Years* (Boulder, Colo., 1995), 143–146; J. Karpiński, *Polska, Komunizm, Opozycja* (London, 1985), 46.

DZIEWANOWSKI, KAZIMIERZ (1930–   ), journalist and Polish ambassador to the United States in 1990–94. He worked for several popular Polish papers such as *Życie Warszawy* (''Warsaw Life'')* and *Literatura*. In 1980–81 he participated in the DiP forum (''Experience and Future''*); in 1981 he was a deputy editor-in-chief of *Tygodnik Solidarność* (''The Solidarity Weekly'').* Later he served on the Solidarity Citizens' Committee* and took part in the

Round Table Negotiations.* *Kto jest kim w polityce polskiej*, ed. by R. Ignasiak (Warsaw, 1993), 59.

DZIŚ I JUTRO (''Today and Tomorrow''). See **PAX Association.**

DZIWISZ, STANISŁAW (1939–   ), priest and since 1978 personal secretary of John Paul II.* G. Polak, *Kto jest kim w Kościele katolickim* (Warsaw, 1996), 86.

EASTERN ARCHIVES (Archiwum Wschodnie), independent clandestine organization created in November 1987 to collect and edit documents on the fate of the Polish people in the USSR after 1939. Besides its main office in Warsaw,* it had several branches in provincial Polish towns. After 1989 it became a large, state-sponsored scientific, publishing, and documentation institution. D. Cecuda, *Leksykon opozycji politycznej 1976–1989* (Warsaw, 1989), 9.

ECOLOGICAL UNION OF DEMOCRATS (Ekologiczna Unia Demokratów), small and loose political organization established in Cracow,* Gorzów, and Łódź* in February 1991 with no parliamentary representation. *Partie Polityczne w Polsce*, ed. by A. Gargas and M. Wojciechowski (Gdańsk, 1991), 19.

ECOLOGY. Communist authorities neglected ecological protection. The post-communist Polish state inherited a highly polluted environment: A large part of the forests was dying, and industrial waste and untreated sewage poisoned most Polish rivers and lakes and the Baltic Sea. Compared with West European standards, conditions in some Polish regions, especially Silesia, are ecologically unacceptable; the populations living in such areas suffer various rare diseases and degenerate physically. In addition, much of Poland was affected by the 1986 Chernobyl nuclear explosion. The Association Agreement, signed by Poland with the European Community (EC) in 1991, obliged Polish authorities to introduce environmental protection measures used in the EC countries. The Sejm* passed new laws and established the State Bureau for Environmental Protection and Control. About 1% of the Polish GNP was assigned to this protection and environmental cleanup campaign. The most dangerous enterprises, like the Skawina Aluminum Plant near Cracow,* were either closed or modernized. The newly established National Fund for Environmental Protection coordinates and supports these operations. Its costs, however, make the plan to achieve West

European environmental standards questionable. G. Sanford and A. Gozdecka-Sanford, *Historical Dictionary of Poland* (Metuchen, N.J., 1994), 65–66.

ECONOMIC CRIMES, swindles and secret deals committed by directors or employees of industry, who used state-owned objects or equipment to do private business. This activity was so widespread and assumed such large dimensions that the authorities began to punish it severely. At least two fraudulent directors, one from the leather industry, another from the meat industry, were sentenced to death in 1956–89. J. Karpiński, *Polska, Komunizm, Opozycja* (London, 1985), 9.

ECONOMIC PLANS, one of the main pillars and character features of the communist economic system. The Sejm* passed the first long-term plan on July 2, 1947. Called the "Plan of Economic Reconstruction," or the Three-Year Plan, it was devoted to the period 1947–49. The First Congress of the Polish United Workers' Party (PZPR)* prepared the Six-Year Plan for 1950–55. Passed by the Sejm on July 21, 1950, it was called the "Plan of Economic Development and Construction of the Foundations of Socialism in Poland." The next plans were prepared for the following five-year periods: 1956–60, "a period of the most proportionate development of the national economy and rise in living standards"; 1961–65, an "initial phase of the long-term plan"; 1966–70, and so on. Z. Landau and J. Tomaszewski, *The Polish Economy in the Twentieth Century* (London, 1985); *Twenty Years of the Polish People's Republic*, ed. by E. Szyr (Warsaw, 1964), 95–97; J. Karpiński, *Polska, Komunizm, Opozycja* (London, 1985), 181–182.

ECONOMY. The post-1945 Polish economy has been shaped by three factors: the calamitous effects of World War II, the policies pursued by the communists, and the re-democratization of Poland after 1989. During World War II most Polish towns and cities were damaged or destroyed, with destruction reaching over 80% in many places. Approximately 42% of all Polish farms were destroyed, and most farms lost part of their livestock. Banks and finances* did not exist. The Polish population was reduced from 35 million to 24 million and did not return to its prewar level until 1975. Members of the Polish intelligentsia,* including the technical and managerial cadres, were deliberately exterminated by the Germans and the Soviets. Poland's borders* were moved westward, and Poland lost almost one-half of its prewar territory. The new "Recovered Territories"* Poland received in the west were economically far more attractive than the lost eastern areas. Yet the newly acquired regions were initially treated by the Russians as occupied territories and were heavily looted. The Soviets also looted the central regions of Poland, exploited by the Germans during 1939–45. All in all, Poland was among the most damaged territories of postwar Europe and, in contrast with the western part of the European continent, received only very limited help, far outweighed by the Soviet exploitation of Poland after 1945.

Initially, Polish communists did not present a program of radical economic transformation. The manifesto of the Polish Committee of National Liberation (PKWN) of July 22, 1944, announced that the new authorities would start a land reform* and would confiscate all German property. The property taken by the German occupational authorities, according to the manifesto, would be returned to its legal owners. The manifesto did not proclaim the construction of a socialist system but paved the way for it. At first the state organs managed most industrial plants. Their original owners had been killed or deported during the war or were West European entrepreneurs unable to control their businesses in Poland during the first months after the war. Prewar owners recovered their property slowly. On January 3, 1946, the National Home Council (KRN)* passed a radical nationalization* bill. Only small enterprises would remain in private hands. Thus in 1947 the private sector was responsible for only 20% of industrial production and engaged about 10% of labor. About 4% of labor was engaged by cooperatives and about 86% by nationalized industries. Agriculture,* however, was dominated by individual farmers. Repairs of war damage began quickly and were completed, in most industrial branches, during the Three-Year Plan of postwar reconstruction (1947–49). Within a year industrial production reached 70% of the prewar level, and in 1947 the output of large- and medium-sized industrial plants almost reached prewar production levels. Agriculture recovered even faster. Before 1948 Poland had been able to export foodstuffs; its per capita agriculture production achieved the prewar output. Western assistance and credits facilitated recovery. The Polish economic system during the communists' seizure of power* in 1945–48 roughly resembled the Soviet New Economic Policy of 1921–28.

The government's economic policy changed after 1948 during the Stalinist period.* In 1948 the collectivization* of agriculture started. As a consequence, Poland experienced serious problems with food supply and ceased to export foodstuffs. Under Soviet pressure, Poland's communist government rejected Western aid and credits. In 1949 Poland joined the Council of Mutual Economic Assistance (Comecon),* became tied to the USSR, and suffered substantial losses by selling various commodities to its communist oppressor below market prices. The State Commission for Economic Planning, led by H. Minc,* was established. During the Six-Year Plan of 1950–55, Poland adopted the Soviet model of industrialization. The command economy* was associated with extensive bureaucratization. The Ministry of Industry, created in 1945, was transformed into 12 ministries at the height of the Stalinist period. Most investments were allocated in heavy industry and armaments production. Remnants of small private industry were almost liquidated. In spring 1947 the ruling Polish Workers' Party (PPR)* began the so-called battle for trade and substantially limited private trade. The original targets of the Six-Year Plan, which resembled the Soviet Five-Year Plan of 1928–32, increased several times under pressure generated by the Cold War* and the Korean conflict. The planning process was never based on adequate statistics, however, because managers on every level often falsified statistics to show production increases in their units. The consumer goods industry and services were neglected, independent artisan production was stifled, and the housing situation deteriorated. The result was deteriorating living conditions* and failing per capita consumption. The mismanaged, accelerated industrial development and the burden imposed on the people by it resulted in the quasi-revolutionary outburst of the "Polish October"* of 1956.

There was no question of rejecting socialism altogether in 1956, but the "Polish October" brought deep economic changes. The collectivization of agriculture was abandoned. Peasants earlier forced to join collective farms were now given the right to withdraw and to revert to individual farming. With compulsory deliveries reduced and the resumption of individual farming, agricultural production began to grow again. The 1956–60 Five-Year Plan allocated more investments in the consumer goods industry, services, and construction. In 1957 the Central Economic Council was created. It was led by such outstanding economists as O. Lange,* E. Lipiński,* and Michał Kalecki. Central state administration of industry was simplified and decentralized, and workers' councils were established as a form of self-management. Planning and management reforms were initiated, and 1958 brought yet more changes in the general economic strategy. Only some changes—those introduced after 1956—remained. With the so-called Polish economic model abandoned, investments in heavy industry were increased again. Planning and management experiments were given up, and workers' self-management was reduced to a minimum. By the early 1960s Poland faced new problems. Demographic explosion, modernization of industry, and a gap between Western and communist technologies became pressing problems. Labor productivity was growing too slowly. Various strains in the economy, including insufficient reserves, supply shortages, mismanagement, insufficient investment control, and lack of balance between wages and price increases, forced the Gomułka* regime to look for a new program of development. In 1969 preparations began for economic changes. Yet Gomułka's economists had no long-term strategy, showed no social confidence, and neglected the sociopolitical implications of their program. Their "retail price reform" triggered the December events of 1970,* one of the most serious political crises in Poland.

The new Gierek* regime, which emerged from the crisis, withdrew price increases and promised to reform the planning and management systems. The Five-Year Plan for 1971–75 gave preferential treatment to the consumer goods industry and housing, and it managed to improve the standard of living. Real wages increased. Several spectacular projects, such as a new coal-mining region in Lublin* Province, the Gdańsk* Northern Port, a huge Huta Katowice* steel plant, and the development of the car industry, were constructed. National income and per capita incomes increased sixfold between 1945 and 1975, and thus the early 1970s constituted the period of least suffering in the history of communist Poland. But the Gierek economic strategy was based on large-scale borrowing from the West. New investments extended planned investments by about 31%. In 1971–80 Poland bought 452 licenses, 416 of which were imported from the West; not all of them were applied in practice. The authorities intended to discharge the involved credits by selling the licensed products to the West. However, many of these projects required more time and tied up a larger amount of capital than originally planned. Some purchased licenses were of no economic importance and in fact, were sometimes even useless. Eventually, Polish industries produced commodities that were worse than their equivalents in the West and were losing to international competition. These problems were worsened by the recession in the West, which influenced Poland's foreign trade and its repayments of its debts. This challenge the Gierek regime answered by borrowing more money from Western banks. Accelerated investments coupled with a fast increase in wages, but industrial output was growing slower than either. In 1976 it appeared impossible to continue this trend. To restore market equilibrium, the authorities decided to raise prices of basic foodstuffs—a move that triggered the June events of 1976.* As a consequence, the government had to give up the price-increase project and instead changed its economic policy. The new strategy consisted of attempts to curb imports and the rate of investments. The economy began to decline. Acute shortages of raw materials and foodstuffs appeared. The Poles developed an impressive second, or black market, economy based on Western currency. Although the government tried to develop economic experiments, such as Great Economic Organizations (WOG),* it was not able to change its general economic policy. Deteriorating living standards led to yet another crisis and the establishment of Solidarity* in 1980. Industrial stoppages, rising wages, and a shortened work week contributed to the economic deterioration caused by the mistakes of the Gierek era. Attempts to modify or reform the economy made under the Jaruzelski* regime had little effect. In the late 1980s output was falling and inflation exceeded 100%.

The first non-communist government, formed by T. Mazowiecki* in August 1989, began to transform the Polish economy from the central command system to a free market economy based on private ownership. In January 1990 economic shock therapy, known as the Balcerowicz* Plan, came into effect. It intended to promote Western investment, to make the Polish złoty convertible to Western currencies, to free prices, and to end government subsidies. Many bankrupt plants closed, and state and Party enterprises were redistributed to private investors. Poles also turned to the West for reduction of the crippling debt. On February 5, 1990, an agreement between Poland and the International Monetary Fund was approved. Poland received special credits for structural adjustment purposes. The Polish economy began to improve, although Poland's population had to pay a high price for the post-communist transformation. Real incomes declined dramatically, at least 50% during the first three months of 1990. Hundreds of thousands of people lost their jobs; additional thousands worked without pay. In spring 1990 prices stabilized and the złoty was made convertible. In June 1990 90% of prices were free, although retail prices of consumer goods and services rose by 560% and 780%, respectively, until the end of 1990. The rate of inflation began falling in 1991; it reached 60.4% in 1991, 44.3% in 1992,

37.6% in 1994, and 21.6% in 1995. In 1992 the fall in the GNP halted as Poland entered on the path of economic growth. Whereas in 1990 and 1991 the GNP had fallen by 11.6% and 7.6%, respectively, in the years 1992 to 1994 it increased by 1.5%, 3.8%, and 5%. During 1990–93 Poland's economy transformed into an open market system. The share of the GNP originating in the private sector grew from 28.6% in 1989 to 52% in 1993. The percentage of registered unemployed from 1990 to 1994 was as follows: 6.3% in 1990, 11.8% in 1991, 13.6% in 1992, 15.5% in 1993, 16.2% in 1994, 14.9% in 1995, and 13.5% in 1996. In addition, unemployment varied in different regions—from 28% in Suwałki, Koszalin, and Osztyn to 10% in Cracow,* Warsaw,* Poznań,* and Katowice.* Z. Landau and J. Tomaszewski, *The Polish Economy in the Twentieth Century* (London, 1985); *Eastern Europe and Commonwealth of Independent States, 1944* (London, 1994), 475–479; H. Kierzkowski, M. Okolski, and S. Wellisz, *Stabilization and Adjustment in Poland* (London, 1993); R. Frydman, A. Rapaczyński, and J. S. Earle, *The Privatization Process in Central Europe* (Budapest, 1993); *Keesing's Record of World Events*, Feb. 1990, p. 37254.

EDELMAN, MAREK (1923–   ), a leader of the 1943 Warsaw Ghetto Uprising. After the war he became a renowned cardiologist. An activist of the political opposition, he was harassed by the communist authorities. In 1980–81 Edelman was a member of the leadership of the Solidarity* Łódź* region. Arrested in 1981, he later joined Lech Wałęsa's* Civic Committee, chaired its National Minorities Commission, and participated in the Round Table Negotiations.* G. Lerski, *Historical Dictionary of Poland, 966–1945*, with special editing and emendations by P. Wróbel and R. J. Kozicki (Westport, Conn., 1996), 128; *Who's Who in the Socialist Countries of Europe*, ed. by J. Stroynowski, vol. 1 (Munich, 1989), 276.

EDUCATION. The Polish educational system, created after World War II and reshaped slightly in the late 1980s and the early 1990s, consists of three levels: primary, secondary, and university. Children start an eight-year-long (until 1966 seven-year-long) primary education at the age of seven. At 15 years of age, young people go the general grammar (liceum) or various technical and vocational schools, consisting mostly of four or five grades. Graduates of general grammar and technical schools must pass a final exam, called the *matura*. Only with the *matura* certificate can they take university admission exams. If they pass, they study for four or five years and graduate with a degree of *magister*. They can receive a doctorate (Ph.D.) after several additional years of postgraduate studies. To receive the Ph.D., candidates must pass a doctoral examination and present a doctoral thesis, "defended" during a public debate. The Ministry of Education supervises the structure, curriculum, and staff of the primary and secondary schools. The Ministry of Science, Higher Education, and Technology supervises the activities of schools of academic rank.

Primary education is obligatory and free. Immediately after World War II and the political changes in Poland, free education was of special importance. It eradicated illiteracy, filled the educational gap created by the war, and became instrumental in the social and professional advancement of the workers and rural population migrating to the cities. Primary schools were heavily subsidized and assisted in the indoctrination of the society. Religious instruction was removed from school in the late 1940s and restored for only four years in the late 1950s. Curricula were unified, and all the schools were state-controlled and secular. The communist authorities encouraged Polish women to work outside the home and organized a network of nursery schools to facilitate their doing so. In the 1980s a new compulsory kindergarten year for six-year-olds was introduced. After the fall of communism in Poland, new private or ''social'' schools—those controlled by a local community—appeared. Curricula were differentiated and religious instruction was returned to schools in 1991. The Law of September 7, 1991, confirmed this educational restructuring. Teachers in postwar Poland were always underpaid, but in the 1980s and during the post-communist transition, the Polish educational system entered a stage of permanent crisis. Many nursery and provincial schools closed. In all, in the 1990–91 school year there were 25,873 nurseries and kindergartens in Poland, with 1,230,000 pupils. There were also 17,554 primary schools, with 317,474 teachers and 5,120,000 children.

Approximately 96% of primary school students continue their education in secondary schools. About 20% of secondary school students, usually the best ones, attend the general grammar (liceum) schools. After the fall of communism, their number grew (from 931 in 1989 to 1,164 in 1991) and non-state schools appeared. A large percentage of primary school graduates continue their education in the secondary technical schools (technikum), whose curricula are specialized. Technical school graduates go directly to industry to work as technicians. Most students used to go to vocational schools (szkoła zawodowa), which did not award the *matura* but prepared skilled workers.

In 1990 there were 96 institutions of higher learning in Poland, including 18 politechnical universities (politechnika), 17 academies of art, 11 universities, 11 medical academies, 10 teachers' training colleges, 9 agricultural higher schools, 7 theological academies, 6 economic academies, 6 physical training academies, and 2 maritime-training schools. The quality of education varies from school to school, but two of them, Warsaw University* and Jagiellonian University* in Cracow,* undoubtedly provide a world-class education, and several others, such as Gdańsk,* Poznań,* and Wrocław* Universities, can easily compete with good West European and U.S. institutions of higher learning. *The International Encyclopedia of Education*, vol. 7, ed. by T. Husen and T. N. Postlethwaite (Oxford, 1985), 3951–3955; G. Sanford and A. Gozdecka-Sanford, *Historical Dictionary of Poland* (Metuchen, N.J., 1994), 63–65.

ELBLĄG (German Elbing), capital city of Elbląg Province in northern Poland close to the Vistula* lagoon. Incorporated into Poland after World War II, it was rebuilt and developed into an important rail junction, port, and industrial center of 119,000 inhabitants in 1987. During the 1970 and 1980 revolts in

Poland, Elbląg was a main strike center. G. Lerski, *Historical Dictionary of Poland, 966–1945*, with special editing and emendations by P. Wróbel and R. J. Kozicki (Westport, Conn., 1996), 128–129.

ELECTIONS OF JANUARY 19, 1947, first parliamentary elections in communist-controlled Poland. According to the declaration at Yalta,* the Provisional Government of National Unity (TRJN)*—a compromise between the Soviets and the Western Allies—was obliged to organize, as soon as possible, "free and unfettered elections" based on a general and secret ballot. After the war Poland had no regular Parliament. It was supplemented by the National Home Council (KRN),* organized by the communists during the war and joined by some non-communist politicians after 1945. The ruling Polish Workers' Party (PPR)* was afraid, however, that it would lose the elections, like its sister communist party in Hungary in November 1945. Also, Stalin knew that if free elections took place, Poland's government would be anti-Soviet. The PPR proposed, therefore, that instead of traditional elections the people of Poland would vote for the single list of the Bloc of Democratic Parties, comprised of all the legal parties in Poland. Parliamentary seats would be given in equal number to deputies of the PPR, the Polish Socialist Party (PPS),* the Polish Peasant Party (PSL),* and the communist-sponsored Peasant Party (SL)*; the Democratic Party (SD)* and the Labor Party (SP)* would have less deputies. Multiparty participation in government and administration would reflect this allocation. The largest opposition party, the PSL, rejected the plan because the division of the Sejm seats as proposed by the PPR was far from fair and failed to reflect the preferences of the Polish public. The PSL demanded 75% of Sejm* seats and governmental positions for the "representatives of the countryside." There was strong opposition to the common list among leaders of the PPS as well. They did not want the SL and the SD to participate in the Democratic Bloc as equal entities because they were, in fact, controlled by the PPR. Eventually, only the PPS, the SD, and the SL agreed to join the Democratic Bloc. Given this situation PPR leaders and their Soviet sponsors decided to delay the elections. They hoped that the repopulation of the "Recovered Territories,"* the rebuilding of the Polish economy, and political and economic reforms would make the ruling PPR more popular. They also hoped to eliminate or diminish the competition of the "fascist-reactionary" PSL before the planned elections. Gradually, the PPR policy evolved into a "strong arm" policy, prompted by the growing tension of the Cold War* and the increasing worsening of the Polish economic situation, followed by strikes and other forms of worker resistance. The PSL's popularity was growing. Under such circumstances the communist authorities had to prepare the elections most carefully and decided to precede them with a rehearsal. Called the People's Referendum, or just the referendum,* it took place on June 30, 1946, and, in spite of communist political terror and manipulations, brought negative results for the PPR. Only 25% of the vote supported the ruling party. The official, falsified results raised this rate to 68%.

The PPR and the Soviets decided to prepare the elections "better" than the referendum. Six weeks before the elections, 2,600 communist propaganda groups organized 67,000 pro-communist mass meetings attended by 6.5 million people. Over 61,000 soldiers were sent to the Polish countryside and towns to support this propaganda, which showed the alleged PSL's connection with the "reaction" and the "bands." The communist secret police recruited about 22,000 members of local electoral commissions and 81 candidates of the opposition parties (49 of them were eventually elected). Thousands of non-communist politicians and political activists were arrested, among them 1,800 activists of the opposition PSL and 149 of its candidates. In some provinces entire leading bodies of the PSL went to jail. In all, according to PSL estimates, about 80,000 of its activists were arrested or interned. The PSL press was harassed and refused paper. Official PSL activities were partially paralyzed; as a result, the PSL's election preparation assumed a semi-conspiratorial character. The Polish Army and the Citizens' Militia, supported by NKVD units, organized about 120 actions against the anti-communist underground and guerrillas, killed some 600 and arrested about 6,000 of them. The electoral campaign was paralleled by several widely publicized political trials. The Security Office (UB) eliminated approximately 410,000 persons from the lists of voters, mostly in those regions where the referendum results were bad for the PPR. Members of the PSL were removed from all electoral commissions. In 10 of 52 electoral districts, populated by 5.3 million persons, or 22% of all inhabitants of Poland, the candidate lists of the PSL were declared invalid and suspended. Electoral districts were so arranged that large regions known to be more anti-communist elected less Sejm deputies than smaller, less anti-communist areas. An NKVD team specializing in the falsification of official documents came from Moscow to assist the PPR leadership, which decided the official results of the elections before they took place.

Eventually, the 1947 Sejm elections saw the highest level of repression and terror imposed by communist authorities in the entire history of communist-controlled Poland. The true results of the elections remain unknown. Officially, the Democratic Bloc received 80.1% of the vote and the PSL 10.3%. The PSL estimated that it was supported by about 63% of the voting population, the Democratic Bloc by 28%. The only known official document gives the outcomes from Kielce* Province: 54% for the PSL and 44% for the Bloc. After the elections, W. Gomułka,* the Secretary General of the PPR, announced that the communist electoral victory opened a new chapter in the history of Poland.

K. Kersten, *The Establishment of Communist Rule in Poland, 1943–1948* (Berkeley, Calif., 1991), 232–341; M. K. Dziewanowski, *Poland in the Twentieth Century* (New York, 1977), 153; A. Paczkowski, "Styczeń 1947: jak sfałszowano wybory. Wolne i nieskrępowane?" *Polityka*, Jan. 18, 1997, pp. 69–71; J. Coutouvidis and J. Reynolds, *Poland, 1939–1947* (Leicester, 1986); *The History of Poland since 1863*, ed. by R. F. Leslie (Cambridge, 1980); N. Davies, *God's Playground: A History of Poland*, vol. 2 (New York, 1984).

ELECTIONS OF JUNE 4 AND 18, 1989. According to the Round Table Agreement* of February 5, 1989, only 35% of seats in the Sejm* were to be contested during the elections of June 1989. The communists expected Solidarity* to have insufficient time to prepare the electoral campaign and thus a portion of the contested seats would be taken by the PZPR and its two allies, the United Peasant Party (ZSL)* and the Democratic Party (SD).* The PZPR was to take 38% of the uncontested parliamentary seats, leaving the rest (up to 65%) to its satellite parties. In addition, the names of 35 principal leaders of the communist-dominated coalition were placed on an uncontested national list. The Round Table Agreement also stipulated that a 100-member Senate* would be established and all its seats would be contested as well. The communist plan failed totally. Of 35 candidates of the uncontested list, 33 failed to gain the required 50% of the vote; special arrangements made ad hoc allowed less-known and less important Party candidates to receive those 33 seats. Candidates sponsored by Solidarity gained all 35% of the contested seats (161) and 99 seats in the Senate, leaving a seat to a rich businessman who had a fancy to start a political career. In the shock caused by this landslide, L. Wałęsa* managed to convince ZSL and SD leaders that abandoning the losing PZPR and creating a new coalition with Solidarity would be better for them and for Poland. At the same time, however, Solidarity made another compromise with the communists by accepting Gen. W Jaruzelski* as President* of Poland. Jaruzelski nominated Gen. C. Kiszczak* Premier,* but the latter did not manage to form a government. B. Szajkowski (ed.), *Political Parties of Eastern Europe, Russia, and the Successor States* (London, 1994), 314; A. Dudek, *Pierwsze lata III Rzeczpospolitej, 1989–1995* (Cracow, 1997), 35–50.

ELECTIONS OF 1990. See **Presidential Elections of 1990.**

ELECTIONS OF OCTOBER 27, 1991, first completely free parliamentary elections in Poland after the fall of communism. When the Polish United Workers' Party (PZPR)* ceased to exist in January 1990, the situation in the Sejm* changed. The Sejm of 1989–91 was elected through to a compromise reached with the communists during the Round Table Negotiations.* Therefore, much Polish public opinion considered the Sejm non-representative, called it the ''Contract Sejm,'' and believed that since the PZPR had disappeared, the compromise with it was no longer binding. President L. Wałęsa* did not manage to change a proportional electoral law, which had no minimum threshold required to obtain Sejm representation and was hypersensitive to the electoral support to small parties. As a consequence, the elections of October 27 produced a severely fragmented Sejm constituted of 29 parties. T. Mazowiecki's* Democratic Union (UD)* came in first with 12.3% of the vote and 62 Sejm seats out of 460. The Democratic Left Alliance (SLD)* of the former communists came in second with 12% of the vote and 60 seats. In third place, with 8.7% and 49 seats, was the Catholic Electoral Action (WAK), an alliance dominated by the Christian-

National Union (ZChN).* Next followed the Center Alliance (PC)* with 8.7% and 44 seats, the Polish Peasant Party (PSL)* with 8.7% and 48 seats, the Confederation for the Independent Poland (KPN)* with 7.5% and 46 seats, the Liberal Democratic Congress (KLD)* with 7.5% and 37 seats, the Peasant Alliance (PL) with 5.5% and 28 seats, Solidarity* with 5.1% and 27 seats, the Polish Beer Lovers' Party (PPPP) with 3.3% and 16 seats, and other small parties, which together received 11.9% and 43 seats. With so many parties in the Sejm, the coalition-building process proved extremely problematic and, when the third cabinet formed in the Sejm, received a no-confidence vote. President Wałęsa dissolved Parliament in May 1993. *Political Handbook of the World: 1995–1996*, ed. by A. S. Banks, A. J. Day, and T. C. Muller (Binghamton, N.Y., 1996), 759; H. Tworzecki, *Parties and Politics in Post-1989 Poland* (Boulder, Colo., 1996), 58–61; R. Taras, *Consolidating Democracy in Poland* (Boulder, Colo., 1995), 191–193; *Dzieje Sejmu Polskiego*, ed. by J. Bardach (Warsaw, 1993), 345; A. Dudek, *Pierwsze lata III Rzeczpospolitej, 1989–1995* (Cracow, 1997), 171–190.

ELECTIONS OF SEPTEMBER 19, 1993, second free parliamentary elections in Poland after the fall of communism. Surprisingly, the 1993 elections brought a landslide victory of the political left and closed the historical period of 1989–93, when Poland was ruled by parties related to Solidarity.* In May 1993 the cabinet of H. Suchocka* was overthrown by a no-confidence vote. President L. Wałęsa,* who wanted to save the Suchocka government, dissolved the parliament and called for new elections. Before it, the Sejm* managed to pass a new election law based on the d'Hont formula, which established the threshold of 5% for political parties and 8% for coalitions. Most Polish voters were frustrated with the economic hardships of the post-communist transitional period and with the performance of Solidarity-related parties, ruling between 1989 and 1993. As a result, only six parties plus representatives of the German minority (who did not have to receive at least 5% of the vote) entered the Sejm. The Democratic Left Alliance (SLD)* received 20.4% of the vote and 171 out of 460 seats; the Polish Peasant Party (PSL),* 15.4% and 132 seats; the Democratic Union (UD),* 10.6% and 74 seats; the Union of Labor (UP),* 7.3% and 41 seats; the Confederation for the Independent Poland (KPN),* 5.8% and 22 seats; the Non-Party Bloc for the Support of Reforms (BBWR),* 5.4% and 16 seats; and the Germans,* 0.6% and 4 seats. Over 34% of those participating in the elections voted for 27 political organizations that did not cross the threshold and did not receive any seats in the Sejm. Parliament became dominated by the political left, which formed a powerful coalition and a government. The former communists returned to power. The political right, divided and quarreling, lost its parliamentary representation. H. Tworzecki, *Parties and Politics in Post-1989 Poland* (Boulder, Colo., 1996), 61–64; R. Taras, *Consolidating Democracy in Poland* (Boulder, Colo., 1995), 195–198; J. J. Wiatr, *Wybory parlamentarne 19 września 1993: przyczyny i następstwa* (Warsaw, 1993); A. Dudek, *Pierwsze lata III Rzeczpospolitej, 1989–1995* (Cracow, 1997), 271–296.

ELECTIONS OF 1995. See Presidential Elections of 1995.

EMIGRATION. Poland has historically been among the most important sources of emigrants to Western Europe and the New World. In the second half of the 19th and the first half of the 20th century about 3 million people left Poland for Western Europe and the Americas for economic and political reasons. This process continued after World War II: About one-half million Polish soldiers, prisoners of Nazi concentration and labor camps in Germany, decided to stay in the West after 1945. They were joined by numerous people escaping from Poland during 1945–47. This postwar wave included Jews* and non-communist political leaders. After 1948 Poland's borders* were sealed, to be partially opened only after 1956. Among the emigrants of the late 1950s were representatives of national minorities, the Jews in particular; They also dominated the emigration triggered by the March events of 1968* and were encouraged by the Party faction of M. Moczar.* The next large emigration wave left Poland during the Solidarity* period and after imposition of Martial Law* in December 1981. Approximately 1 million Poles left their country between 1980 and 1991, including some 10,000 scientists and university professors. J. Karpiński, *Polska, Komunizm, Opozycja* (London, 1985), 50; *Nowa Encyklopedia Powszechna PWN*, vol. 2 (Warsaw, 1995), 243.

EPISCOPATE, all the bishops of a given country. Poland had 86 bishops of the Roman Catholic Church* in 1985. Three of them were Cardinals: J. Glemp,* Primate* of Poland; F. Macharski,* Archbishop of Cracow;* and H. Gulbinowicz,* Archbishop of Wrocław.* The Main Episcopate Council (Rada Główna Episkopatu) includes 29 specialized commissions, such as the Commission for the Mass Media, the Commission for the Monasteries, and the Common Commission, consisting of representatives of the Episcopate and the authorities. J. Karpiński, *Polska, Komunizm, Opozycja* (London, 1985), 51.

EUROPA, liberal periodical established in October 1956 as part of the de-Stalinization of Polish culture. Its editorial staff, including such outstanding Polish writers as J. Andrzejewski,* S. Dygat,* M. Jastrun,* and A. Ważyk,* prepared the first three issues of *Europa,* never published because of a governmental ban. In response, some editors left the Party. J. Karpiński, *Polska, Komunizm, Opozycja* (London, 1985), 52.

EUROPEAN COMMUNITY (EC), loose confederation of several West European states established by the 1957 Treaty of Rome and initially called the European Economic Community. Before 1989 the USSR and its satellites considered the EC a hostile, anti-communist, political and economic pact. After communism fell in Poland, the Polish government and population took the opposite attitude by announcing their willingness to join the EC. Frequently expressed as a "return to Europe," this turnaround was considered a great economic and political opportunity for Poland. Even in 1988 the EC had recognized Comecon* and promised concessions to reforming East European countries. In September 1989 the Mazowiecki* government signed a cooperation agreement with the EC and received various forms of assistance, including economic and technical aid and debt rescheduling. In December 1991 Poland signed the EC associate member agreement, which obliged Poland to reshape its financial institutions, change its numerous legal rules and economic procedures, and modernize and privatize its economy in order to be integrated into the EC framework during a 10-year transition period. In July 1992 the Sejm* ratified this agreement by 238 votes to 78, and the Senate* by 75 to 1.

Yet important changes took place in the EC and in Poland in the meantime. In the early 1990s EC leaders replaced the policy of widening with the strategy of deepening their organization. As several advanced West European countries joined the competition to enter the EC, a group of Polish politicians and economists claimed that several required adjustments would be disadvantageous to their country. Frequently, Polish industrial products could not compete with West European goods. The EC Common Agricultural Policy agreement closed the West European markets to strong Polish agricultural export. Similar EC trade barriers handicapped Polish textile and steel production. Further, Polish politicians feared that West European cultural influences could harm Polish national heritage and Polish culture. Economists pointed out that Poland should concentrate on easier markets in the Third World and Eastern Europe. Many claimed that the transitionary procedures and demands of international economic organizations made life in Poland too difficult and that a more gradual "third way" would be more bearable. Most Poles believe their country will eventually join the EC, but their initial enthusiasm has disappeared. G. Sanford and A. Gozdecka-Sanford, *Historical Dictionary of Poland* (Metuchen, N.J., 1994), 66–68.

EUROPEAN FEDERALIST PARTY, POLISH SECTION (Europejska Partia Federalistyczna Sekcja Polska), small section of the European Federalist Party established in 1991, supports the complete unification of Europe. *Partie Polityczne w Polsce*, ed. by A. Gargas and M. Wojciechowski (Gdańsk, 1991), 20.

"EXPERIENCE AND FUTURE" (Doświadczenie i Przyszłość [DiP]), discussion group of experts organized on the initiative of the Gierek* regime, but became independent and even oppositional. It produced four influential critical reports in 1980–82. G. Sanford and A. Gozdecka-Sanford, *Historical Dictionary of Poland* (Metuchen, N.J., 1994), 68; J. Karpiński, *Polska, Komunizm, Opozycja* (London, 1985), 40.

EYSYMONTT, JERZY (1937–), economist and politician. In the early 1980s he worked with L. Balcerowicz* on a plan of market reforms in Poland and co-authored the Solidarity* economic program. During the presidential elections of 1990,* he served as deputy chairman of L. Wałşa's* electoral committee. A member of the Center Alliance (PC)* leadership, he headed the Central Planning Office (Centralny Urząd Planowania) in the governments of J. K. Bielecki* and J. Olszewski.* In 1992 he left the PC and joined the Parliamentary Club Polish Liberal Program (Klub Parlamentarny Polski Program Liberalny). In May 1996 he became the president of the Republican Party (PR). *Wprost* (Warsaw), May 5, 1996.

FEJGIN, ANATOL (1909–), interwar communist, deputy chief of Military Information, and director of the Tenth Department of the Ministry of Public Security, which spied on leaders of the communist establishment in Poland. Famous for his sadistic interrogation methods, he was a close collaborator of J. Różański.* Fejgin was removed from the Party after the dissolution of the Ministry of Public Security in December 1954, arrested in April 1955, and sentenced to 12 years in prison. Z. Błażyński, *Mówi Józef Światło. Za kulisami bezpieki i partii 1940–1955* (London, 1985); B. Fijałkowska, *Borejsza i Różański. Przyczynek do dziejów stalinizmu w Polsce* (Olsztyn, 1995).

FICOWSKI, JERZY (1934–), Home Army (AK)* veteran, sociologist, writer, and poet, interested in Gypsy* folklore. *Who's Who in the Socialist Countries of Europe*, ed. by J. Stroynowski, vol. 1 (Munich, 1989), 303.

FIELDORF, AUGUST EMIL (1895–1953), general and important leader of the Polish underground during 1940–45, arrested, tried, and executed by the Polish communist authorities. An NCO in the Polish Legions during World War I, he later joined the Polish Army* and fought against the Ukrainians* and the Bolsheviks during 1918–20. During the interwar period he continued his military career and later participated in the September campaign of 1939 as a commander of the 51st Infantry Regiment (Strzelców Kresowych). After the campaign he left for France, where he joined the staff of Gen. K. Sosnkowski. In 1940 Fieldorf was sent back to Poland. There, he served as inspector in the Organizational Department of the Main Command of the Union of Armed Struggle (ZWZ), commander of the Northeastern Region of the Home Army (AK),* and commander of its directorate of diversion (''Kedyw''). In 1943 Fieldorf was appointed an organizer of the super-secret ''Niepodległość'' or ''Nie'' (''Independence'' or ''No'')* conspiracy, which aimed to continue underground activities should Poland be occupied by the Red Army.* After the 1944 Warsaw Uprising Fieldorf became deputy commander-in-chief of the Home Army. After its dissolution on January 19, 1945, he continued his service as deputy commander-in-chief of *"Nie."* On March 7, 1945, he was arrested by the NKVD. Unrecognized, he was sent to a Soviet Ural labor camp as a black marketeer—he had $100 on his person. There, he felled trees until the end of 1946. In 1947, still unrecognized, exhausted and gravely ill, he landed in a Gulag hospital and then was sent back to Poland. He probably participated in the underground anti-Soviet "Wolność i Niezawisłość" or "WiN" ("Freedom and Independence*") movement. In 1948 he tried to leave the underground, revealing his identity during a legalization action organized by the Polish communist authorities, but in 1950, during this procedure, he was arrested, tried in a grotesque trial, sentenced to death, and buried in an unknown place. Fieldorf, the embodiment of patriotism, is considered one of the bravest and most meritorious leaders of the Polish World War II resistance. K. Kersten, *The Establishment of Communist Rule in Poland, 1943–1948* (Berkeley, Calif., 1991); *Słownik Historii Polski 1939–1948*, ed. by A. Chwalba and T. Gąsowski (Cracow, 1994), 41–43; S. Marat, J. Snopkiewicz, *Zbrodnia. Sprawa generała Fieldorfa-Nila* (Warsaw, 1989).

FIGHTING SOLIDARITY (Solidarność Walcząca), clandestine anticommunist organization established in Wrocław* shortly after imposition of Martial Law* in December 1981. Later Fighting Solidarity, more radical than Solidarity,* became active in most other major Polish cities. It published several underground periodicals, and organized anti-governmental demonstrations and independent broadcasting. In the late 1980s Fighting Solidarity opposed any compromise with the authorities and rejected the idea of the Round Table Negotiations.* In 1990 it was reshaped into the Freedom Party (PW).* *Polskie Partie Polityczne. Charakterystyki, dokumenty*, ed. by K. A. Paszkiewicz (Wrocław, 1996), 100–107; J. Karpiński, *Polska, Komunizm, Opozycja* (London, 1985), 254.

FIGHTING YOUTH FEDERATION (Federacja Młodzieży Walczącej), small and loose youth organization established in 1984 in Warsaw.* Initially clandestine, the Federation supported a program for an independent and democratic Poland. *Partie Polityczne w Polsce*, ed. by A. Gargas and M. Wojciechowski (Gdańsk, 1991), 23–24.

FIKUS, DARIUSZ (1932–96), journalist; member and secretary of the editorial staff of the prestigious, liberal communist weekly *Polityka** from 1958. In 1980 he was elected the secretary general of the Association of Polish Journalists,* which rejected governmental control and was de-legalized after imposition of Martial Law.* In response Fikus, a defender of independent journalism, left the Polish United Workers' Party (PZPR)* and the editorial staff of *Polityka*. In the 1980s he was active in the clandestine Association of Polish Journalists. He participated in the 1989 Round Table Negotiations* and was appointed editor-in-chief of *Rzeczpospolita* ("The Republic"), initially the official organ of the post-communist governments. *Więź* ("The Link"), June 1996, p. 203.

FINANCE. In July 1944, when the Red Army* took the regions of Białystok,* Lublin,* and Rzeszów* and installed a Polish communist government-in-waiting there, the Polish Committee of National Liberation (PKWN), a Polish monetary and credit system did not exist. The PKWN and its treasury had neither means nor concepts to develop one. By the end of August 1944, new złoty banknotes arrived from a Moscow printing house. For several weeks they circulated along with occupation złotys, German marks, and Soviet rubles. The latter three currencies were slowly exchanged for the Polish złoty. According to the January 6, 1945, decree, this exchange was limited to 500 złotys per person, which drastically reduced the amount of money in circulation and curbed inflation.* On January 15, 1945, the National Polish Bank (Narodowy Bank Polski [NBP]) was established. At the same time, there opened three other government banks— Bank Gospodarstwa Krajowego, Państwowy Bank Rolny and Pocztowa Kasa Oszczędności. Various communal and cooperative banks and three joint-stock banks, controlled mostly by the state, also opened their doors. Other private banks were refused assistance and concessions and went out of business.

In 1944–46, revenues of the new Soviet-controlled state were increasing slowly, whereas the debt of the Treasury to the NBP was growing. By 1947– 48 the budget showed a surplus and the debt was slowly discharged. In 1946 a gradual transformation of the Polish banking network started. It was completed in 1948, when the Polish finance system was adjusted to the Soviet one. The NBP became the central financial institution. The newly established Bank Inwestycyjny financed investments, the Bank Rolny financed agriculture,* the Bank Komunalny (dissolved in 1952) financed local self-government, the Bank Rzemiosła i Handlu (dismantled in 1952) credited private enterprises, and stateowned joint-stock banks were engaged in foreign operations.

Massive investment in industry, especially heavy industry, brought increased wages without an adequate increase in market supply. When the danger of inflation loomed, the government decided to balance the budget through a sudden and secretly prepared monetary reform, possible only under the conditions of the Stalinist period.* On October 28, 1950, the Sejm* accepted the reform regulations. The exchange ratio of the new złoty to the old one was fixed at 1:300, cash at 1:100, and the exchange was limited to 100,000 złoty. Money in circulation and savings were drastically diminished and the budget was balanced, although the people were hard-hit economically. Soon, however, circulation was growing again, in the Stalinist period and then in the Gomułka* period. In 1957, 19,672 million złoty were in circulation, which reached 58,644 million in 1970. At the same time, prices grew relatively slowly; although savings increased rapidly, shortages of some goods and foodstuffs appeared. After the "Polish October" of 1956,* the banking system was further simplified: The NBP came to control practically all domestic financial matters, and the Warsaw Bank Handlowy was in charge of foreign operations.

After the fall of Gomułka, the Gierek* regime started a new economic policy that involved a rapid increase in the money supply, rising by 406% between 1970 and 1980. Earnings were growing faster than market supply, which accounted for 87% of earnings in 1980. Huge monetary reserves were accumulated; market shortages and speculation were growing, although many prices were fixed. Also, budget revenues and expenses were growing such that in 1980 a budget deficit was recorded for the first time since 1946. Growing investment and modernization of industry were based, to a large extent, on borrowing in the West. Credits facilitated increase of imports without a similar increase in exports. The entire Gierek period saw a trade deficit with the capitalist states. Debts were accumulated without coordination of payment dates, and their constant increase led to a situation in which debt service costs accounted for 82% of total export receipts in 1980. Polish indebtedness reached $US 589 million to socialist countries and $US 21,746 million to other countries in 1980.

Transformation of the Polish economy required development of a banking infrastructure suited to the realities of a market economy. In the communist centrally planned economy, the National Bank of Poland (NBP) had played a relatively passive role in shaping economic processes. In contrast, in 1989 the NBP suspended its commercial operations to take on the role of a central bank in the Polish economy. Its new role was similar to that played by central banks in countries with market economies. In accordance with the new banking law, nine branches of the NBP in the biggest cities of Poland, together with their network of branches in surrounding regions, were transformed into state commercial banks. Most of them have since developed their own network of branches outside their main areas of operation, and two of them, the Wielkopolski Credit Bank (WBK) and the Bank of Silesia (BS), have been privatized. The remaining banks are engaged in a program of developing a working relationship with renowned Western banks. Ninety institutions have been given licenses to carry out banking activities, but many of these banks offer a limited range of services. In addition to the banks mentioned, Poland has an extensive network of small cooperative banks joined since 1990 to the Bank for the Food Sector (BGZ); these mainly serve the inhabitants of rural areas and the agricultural sector. In 1994 Poland had seven banks heavily invested with foreign capital; the country also hosted 21 representative offices of foreign banks. Z. Landau and J. Tomaszewski, *The Polish Economy in the Twentieth Century* (London, 1985); General Information about Poland <http://bmb.ippt.gov.pl/poland/partone.html>

FISZBACH, TADEUSZ (1935–   ), First Secretary of Gdańsk* Province organization of the Polish United Workers' Party (PZPR)* during 1975–82, who established good working relationship with Solidarity* in 1980–81 and was considered by many a possible future Party leader. Sidetracked as a commercial attaché in Finland after the imposition of Martial Law* on December 13, 1981, he was elected to the Sejm* in 1989 and became its Vice-Speaker. After the dissolution of the PZPR in January 1990, Fiszbach co-founded the Polish Socialist Union (PUS). This party was ready to cooperate with the political camp of L. Wałęsa* but was unable to take any Sejm seats during the 1991 election and faded away. *Who's Who in the Socialist Countries of Europe*, ed. by J. Stroynowski, vol. 1 (Munich, 1989), 310; T. Mołdawa, *Ludzie Władzy 1944–1991. Władze państwowe i polityczne Polski według stanu na dzień 28 II 1991* (Warsaw, 1991), 349.

FJN (Front Jedności Narodu [Front of National Unity]), political organization established before the 1952 parliamentary election as the National Front and reshaped into the FJN in late 1956, before the 1957 election. The FJN, in fact a window-dressing or ghost organization, was a creation and a tool of the communist authorities. According to their plan, it was established to represent all Polish citizens regardless of their party affiliation. The committees of the FJN— before 1956, of the National Front—drew lists of candidates for the national elections. Until 1957 voters were not offered a choice and were supposed to approve the single list drafted by the FJN. During the 1957 by-election, following the January election, voters could, for the first time, choose between opposing candidates. However, their selection remained controlled by the FJN. During 1952–56 the National Front was presided over by B. Bierut,* from August 1956 by A. Zawadzki,* and from April 1965 by E. Ochab.* The latter resigned in April 1968 in protest against the "March event."* He was replaced by M. Spychalski.* Until 1971 all FJN presidents were members of the Polish United Workers' Party (PZPR)* and their deputies usually represented the United Peasant Party (ZSL)* and the Democratic Party (SD).* One deputy did not belong to any party, and the Presidium of the FJN All-Polish Committee included representatives of various social groups and Christian organizations. This composition was supposed to show that all of Polish society was indeed represented in the FJN and participated in governing. In 1971, for the first time a non-Party personality, J. Groszkowski,* became president of the FJN. In 1976, he was replaced by the PZPR official, H. Jabłoński.* In July 1983 the FJN was dissolved and replaced by the Patriotic Movement of National Revival (PRON).* *Poland: Its People, Its Society, Its Culture*, ed. by C. R. Barnett (New York, 1958), 134; T. Mołdawa, *Ludzie Władzy 1944–1991. Władze państwowe i polityczne Polski według stanu na dzień 28 II 1991* (Warsaw, 1991), 306–309.

FLYING UNIVERSITY (Latający Uniwersytet), clandestine university established in Russian-occupied Poland in the last decade of the 19th century. It became a model for independent educational activities in communist Poland. In October 1977, on the initiative of the Workers' Defense Committee (KOR),* a group of Polish dissident* intellectuals began to organize lectures and courses beyond the control of the communist state educational institutions. This uncensored teaching was held mostly in private houses and churches and was popularly called the Flying University. In 1978 it was shaped into the more systematized Association of Scientific Courses (Towarzystwo Kursów Naukowych [TKN]).* G. Sanford and A. Gozdecka-Sanford, *Historical Dictionary of Poland* (Metuchen, N.J., 1994), 69; D. Cecuda, *Leksykon opozycji politycznej 1976–1989* (Warsaw, 1989), 115.

FORD, ALEKSANDER (1908–80), film director. He worked in documentary film production establishments both before World War II and in the communist-controlled First Polish Army* in the USSR. After 1945 he became a major organizers of the film industry in Poland and directed the "Polish Film" production enterprise. He directed *Ulica Graniczna* ("Border Street") in 1948, *Młodość Szopena* ("Chopin's Youth") in 1952, *Ósmy dzień tygodnia* ("The Seventh Day of the Week") in 1957, *Krzyżacy* ("Teutonic Knights") in 1960, and *Pierwszy dzień wolności* ("The First Day of Freedom"). M. Dąbrowska, *Dzienniki powojenne 1945–49*, vol. 1, ed. by T. Drewnowski (Warsaw, 1996), 375.

FOREIGN AFFAIRS. Polish foreign policy after 1945 was directly dependent on Soviet diplomatic priorities. As a Soviet satellite and a member of the Warsaw Treaty Organization,* communist Poland was not a sovereign state; its foreign relations had to be endorsed in advance by the Kremlin. This situation changed after 1989. Poland had to redefine its national interests and play a new role in Europe. Poland shaped a new sovereign foreign policy whose three main objectives are orientation toward the West and integration with Europe, regional cooperation in East-Central Europe, and good relations with all its neighbors, including Russia. To achieve these goals Poland had to dismantle the system of dependencies in which it had been confined until 1989; then Poland had to develop new ties with the West. Poland's quest for integration with Western Europe is an ancient one. For centuries Poland looked West for protection against its powerful neighbors, Germany and Russia, usually in vain. Today, the protective arm of the West can help Poland become "the eastern border of the Western block." To achieve this balanced and stable position, normalized relations with Russia are essential. The most important elements of this new approach were set during 1989–93, when Poland's foreign policy was dominated by its Foreign Minister, K. Skubiszewski,* and there was no visible change in Polish international policy after the defeat of Solidarity*-related parties and the return of ex-communists to power. *Polish Foreign Policy Reconsidered: Challenges of Independence*, ed. by I. Prizel and A. A. Michta (London, 1995); R. Taras, *Consolidating Democracy in Poland* (Boulder, Colo., 1995); T. Sasińska-Klas, "Aspects of Polish Security Policy in the Post–Cold War Era," *Beyond Solidarność: Essays on Poland's Past and Present*, ed. by G. C. Boehnert and T. Sasińska-Klas (Guelph, 1992), 194; K. Skubiszewski, *Pozycja Polski w Europie* (Warsaw, 1994).

FOREIGN DEBT. See **Finance.**

FRASYNIUK, WŁADYSŁAW (1954–   ), auto technician and chairman of the Solidarity* region of Silesia in 1981. After imposition of Martial Law,* he hid underground. Arrested, he spent the years 1982–84 and 1985–86 in prison. During 1988–89 he was a member of the Civic Committee* and participated in the Round Table Negotiations.* In 1990 he co-founded with Z. Bujak* the Citizens' Movement for Democratic Action (ROAD).* Later he helped to organize the Democratic Union (UD)* and became its vice-president. He kept this position in the Freedom Union (UW).* G. Sanford and A. Gozdecka-Sanford, *Historical Dictionary of Poland* (Metuchen, N.J., 1994), 71; *Who's Who in the Socialist Countries of Europe*, ed. by J. Stroynowski, vol. 1 (Munich, 1989), 320; *Kto jest kim w polityce polskiej*, ed. by R. Ignasiak (Warsaw, 1993), 84.

FREEDOM AND INDEPENDENCE (Wolność i Niezawisłość [WiN]), one of the largest underground organizations participating in the anti-Soviet resistance in Poland after World War II. Established on September 2, 1945, in Warsaw,* WiN fought against the totalitarian dictatorship in Poland and for free elections and democracy of a West European style. Soon after its organization, WiN controlled between 20,000 and 30,000 guerrillas out of about 80,000 members of the former Home Army (AK)* units that remained in the woods and continued military operations against the communist authorities. WiN based its strategy on the assumption that sooner or later a war would break out between the USSR and the Western Allies. In November and December 1945 First Headquarters of WiN was arrested, but in January 1946 Second Headquarters was established. The latter developed propaganda and intelligence operations, supported the Polish Peasant Party (PSL),* and signed agreements with the Ukrainian Insurgent Army (UPA)* in southeastern Poland. In spring 1946 guerrilla activities reached the intensity of the anti-communist military operations seen in the first half of 1945. WiN was especially active before the referendum* of June 30, 1946. In summer and fall 1946 the communist authorities liquidated WiN's Second Headquarters. The third one, created in December 1946, was destroyed at the beginning of 1947. Between February and March 1947 about 23,000 WiN members came out of the woods in response to the government amnesty.* The response meant the end of large-scale guerrilla activities, but at the same time, Fourth WiN Headquarters was organized. It rebuilt an organizational network, developed contacts with Poles in the West, and supported those activists of the Polish Socialist Party (PPS)* who opposed unification with the Polish Workers' Party (PPR).* In September and October 1947 Fourth Headquarters was arrested and the fifth one was already controlled by communist secret police and intelligence. Thousands of WiN soldiers were arrested by the communist authorities, and many were sentenced to death and executed. The last unit of WiN, its Delegacy Abroad (Delegatura Zagraniczna), dissolved itself in January 1953. J. Coutouvidis and J. Reynolds, *Poland, 1939–1947* (Leicester, 1986), 219–220; K. Kersten, *The Establishment of Communist Rule in Poland, 1943–1948* (Berkeley, Calif., 1991), 226–227, 310–313; *Słownik Historii Polski 1939–1948*, ed. by A. Chwalba and T. Gąsowski (Cracow, 1994), 218–219.

FREEDOM AND PEACE (Wolność i Pokój [WiP]), radical organization established in 1984 in Cracow* to change the contents of the oath taken by military conscripts, to gain the release of those imprisoned for refusing to take the military oath, and to introduce an alternative to military service. When all these aims were achieved in 1988, the WiP added to its program environmental issues, human rights, including ethnic minority rights, and total disarmament. The WiP had only 500–600 members, but its sympathizers were much more numerous. They supported Solidarity* but opposed the introduction of religious education into schools by the Mazowiecki* government and considered the presidential elections of 1990* an "historical anachronism." *Revolutionary and Dissident Movements: An International Guide* (London, 1991), 277.

FREEDOM PARTY (Partia Wolności [PW]), small party established in Wrocław* on July 7, 1990. It was based on the infrastructure of Fighting Solidarity* and was organized by its activists, among them K. Morawiecki,* who wanted to be a candidate in the 1990 presidential election but failed to collect the 100,000 required signatures. The PW opposed the Round Table Negotiations,* L. Wałęsa's* policies, and the Balcerowicz* Plan. G. Sanford and A. Gozdecka-Sanford, *Historical Dictionary of Poland* (Metuchen, N.J., 1994), 71; *Polskie Partie Polityczne. Charakterystyki, dokumenty*, ed. by K. A. Paszkiewicz (Wrocław, 1996), 100–107.

FREEDOM UNION (Unia Wolności [UW]), major political party established by a merger of the Democratic Union (UD)* and the Liberal Democratic Congress (KLD)* on April 23, 1994. The organizational congress elected T. Mazowiecki* president of the UW and D. Tusk* its deputy president. Stimulated by their failure in the elections of September 1993,* the UD and the KLD decided to form a "strong party of the center," which would be able to defend the reforms of 1989–93 against the triumphant post-communists on the one side and the frustrated political right on the other side. The UW presents itself as a party committed to market-oriented reforms and democratic social order, but not insensitive to social justice. Yet from its beginning the UW was divided into several factions: Social-Democratic left, Christian-Democratic right, and compromise-oriented center. They were unable to agree on a common candidate during the presidential elections of 1995.* In April 1995 T. Mazowiecki was replaced as the party chairman by L. Balcerowicz,* a move questioned by many party activists. *Political Handbook of the World: 1995–1996*, ed. by A. S. Banks, A. J. Day, and T. C. Muller (New York, 1996), 763; *Polskie partie polityczne*, ed. by K. A. Paszkiewicz (Warsaw, 1996), 298–312.

FREEMASONRY. All freemasonry organizations in Poland were dissolved by presidential decree in 1938. Faint efforts to revive them in 1945–46 and before the 1960s failed. In 1961, however, veterans of the National Polish Grand Lodge secretly revived the prewar lodge "Kopernik." Soon the lodge was joined by such prominent intellectuals as J. J. Lipski,* L. Cohn,* E. Lipiński,* A. Słonimski,* and J. Kielanowski,* but overall membership in 1961–89 was limited. Since 1990, emissaries of the Grand East of France organized several new lodges in Poland. The number of freemasons there is estimated at about 500 persons. In 1993 the Polish National Grand Lodge was officially registered by the court in Warsaw.* L. Hass, "Adepci sztuki królewskiej," *Polityka* (Warsaw, April 12, 1997); E. Wilk, "Powrót masonów," *Polityka* (Warsaw, Feb. 15, 1997); *Nowa Encyklopedia Powszechna PWN*, vol. 6 (Warsaw, 1995), 880.

FRELEK, RYSZARD (1929–), communist official, journalist, specialist in foreign affairs, and ideologue. An activist of communist-sponsored youth organizations, he was a member of the Polish United Workers' Party (PZPR)* since 1950 and a member of its Central Committee* during 1971–81. He was also a director of the Polish Press Agency (PAP),* headed the Polish Institute of International Affairs (PISM) from 1969, and presided over the Foreign Department of the Central Committee during 1971–77. Author of numerous politically correct works on history and political science subjects, he was considered a lively and representative spokesperson of the Gierek* regime. After the fall of Gierek, Frelek was marginalized and went to New York as a Polish representative to the United Nations in 1980–81. G. Sanford and A. Gozdecka-Sanford, *Historical Dictionary of Poland* (Metuchen, N.J., 1994), 72; *Who's Who in the Socialist Countries of Europe*, ed. by J. Stroynowski, vol. 1 (Munich, 1989), 320.

G

GAŁAJ, DYZMA (1915–), agricultural economist, member of the State Council (Rada Państwa)* during 1972–76, Speaker of the Sejm* in 1971–72, and one of the key leaders of the United Peasant Party (ZSL).* *Who's Who in the Socialist Countries of Europe*, ed. by J. Stroynowski, vol. 1 (Munich, 1989), 333.

GAŁCZYŃSKI, KONSTANTY ILDEFONS (1905–53), poet, writer, translator, satirist, and one of the greatest scoffers in the history of Polish literature. He participated in the September Campaign of 1939, spent the war in a POW camp in Germany, and devoted several beautiful patriotic poems to the Polish war experience. In 1946 he returned to Poland and tried to find a compromise with the political system installed there after 1945. He wrote for many periodicals and several cabarets. G. Sanford and A. Gozdecka-Sanford, *Historical Dictionary of Poland* (Metuchen, N.J., 1994), 73; C. Miłosz, *The History of Polish Literature* (Berkeley, Calif., 1983), 409–411; *Dictionary of Polish Literature*, ed. by E. J. Czerwinski (Westport, Conn., 1994), 122–125; *Encyklopedyczny Słownik Sławnych Polaków* (Warsaw, 1996), 94.

GAZETA LUDOWA ("The People's Gazette"), daily organ of the Polish Peasant Party (PSL)* published from 1944. When most members of its editorial staff were arrested in 1946–47, the newspaper lost its oppositional character and was taken over by those PSL leaders who agreed to cooperate with the communist authorities. J. Karpiński, *Polska, Komunizm, Opozycja* (London, 1985), 60.

GAZETA WYBORCZA ("The Electoral Gazette"), the largest newspaper in Poland, edited by A. Michnik.* *Gazeta* produces a national edition and 16 local editions, totalling 460,000 copies (the Sunday magazine, 760,000 copies). Every issue has between 16 and 75 pages. From the beginning *Gazeta* was an organ of the democratic opposition,* which took power in Poland after the Round Table Negotiations.* In July 1989 *Gazeta* made the first call for a government with a Solidarity*-backed Premier.* On its front page *Gazeta* wrote, in the familiar letters of the Solidarity logo, "There is no freedom without solidarity!" Along with the split taking place in the Solidarity camp during "the war at the top,"* *Gazeta*'s editorial board became divided as well, but eventually it sided with the Mazowiecki* camp. As a consequence, in September 1990 Solidarity's National Committee denied the newspaper the right to use the Solidarity logo. After Mazowiecki's defeat in the presidential elections of 1990,* *Gazeta* supported the new President, L. Wałęsa,* and the new government of J. K. Bielecki.* It opposed the Olszewski* government but refused to be an organ of any political party. *Gazeta Wyborcza* <http://soho-online.com/ppi/media/prasa/dzien_pl.htm>

GDAŃSK (German Danzig), capital city of Gdańsk Province and the region of eastern Pomerania, located at the mouth of the Vistula River * on the Baltic Sea. First mentioned as a Polish city in 997, it was alternately a capital of an independent Slavic Pomeranian principality or a part of Poland. Captured by the Teutonic Knights in 1308, it returned to Poland in 1466; it was incorporated into Prussia in 1792, during the Partition of the Polish-Lithuanian Commonwealth. After World War I Gdańsk became a free city. Ruined by as much as 55% during World War II and stripped of its industrial plants by the Soviets, it returned to Poland in 1945. Most of its German population had fled or was expelled by the end of the war, replaced by Poles, many from the Eastern Territories lost to the USSR. Fully reconstructed, Gdańsk developed into an important Polish center of industry, culture, education (Gdańsk University* opened in 1970), and politics; by 1991 it reached 465,000 inhabitants. Together with neighboring Sopot (46,000) and Gdynia * (251,000), Gdańsk constitutes a large metropolis, a "Three-City" (Trójmiasto) with two major ports and several shipyards. In December 1970 Gdańsk became a center of anti-regime demonstrations during which many people were killed by the army and the police. In August 1980 Gdańsk's shipyard, named after Lenin in the late 1960s, became the capital of the strike movement and the birthplace of Solidarity.* The Gdańsk Agreement* was signed there, and Solidarity headquarters remained in the city. In October 1988 Premier M. F. Rakowski* announced the closure of the Lenin Shipyard on economic grounds, although many interpreted his decision as an aggressive political move. A special Sejm* commission investigated Rakowski's policy toward the shipyard and in December 1989 concluded that the decision to close the shipyard was made with undue haste and insufficient consultation. In January 1990 the Mazowiecki* government announced its decision to save the shipyard, closed in 1997 by the government of W. Cimoszewicz.* *Political and Economic Encyclopedia of the Soviet Union and Eastern Europe*, ed. by S. White (London, 1990), 101; *International Dictionary of Historic Places*, ed. by T. Ring, vol. 2 (Chicago, 1995), 293.

GDAŃSK AGREEMENT (Porozumienie Gdańskie), agreement signed in the Lenin Shipyard of Gdańsk* on August 31, 1980, by M. Jagielski,* chairman of

the Governmental Commission, and L. Wałęsa,* who headed the Inter-Factory
Strike Committee.* Among other items, the agreement legalized the right to
strike and to organize free trade unions. Similar, although historically less im-
portant agreements, were signed in Szczecin* on August 30 and in Jastrzębie-
Zdrój* in Silesia on September 3, 1980. G. Sanford and A. Gozdecka-Sanford,
Historical Dictionary of Poland (Metuchen, N.J., 1994), 74; N. Ascherson, *The Polish
August: What Has Happened in Poland* (Penguin Books, 1981).

GDYNIA, large port on the Bay of Gdańsk, northwest of Gdańsk* city, center
of shipbuilding and maritime education and the home port of the Polish Navy.
Initially a tiny fishing settlement, Gdynia was constructed and developed from
1922 onward to bypass the German-controlled port of Gdańsk. Before World
War II Gdynia had been a large town and the major Baltic port, surpassing
Gdańsk and Szczecin.* Destroyed by the Germans during World War II, it was
quickly rebuilt, reaching 250,000 inhabitants by 1990. With Gdańsk and Sopot,
Gdynia constitutes a metropolis known as Three-City (Trójmiasto). Gdynia was
a scene of important historical events in 1970 and 1980. G. Sanford and A.
Gozdecka-Sanford, *Historical Dictionary of Poland* (Metuchen, N.J., 1994), 74.

GEOGRAPHY. Poland is situated on the North European Plain between the
Baltic Sea and the Carpathian Mountains, at the center of the European continent, approximately between the latitude 49° and 55° N and the longitude 14°
and 24° E. Poland's area is 120,727 square miles (312,683 km^2); its population
at last count was 38,521,000 (in 1993). Polish frontiers in the west run along
the Oder (Odra) River* and Lusatian Neisse, which border Germany. In the
north they run along the Baltic shore facing Sweden. In the south the frontiers
follow the Sudeten, Beskid, and Carpathian mountain ranges separating Poland
from Slovakia and the Czech Republic. In the northeast Poland borders Lithuania and Latvia, and in the east Belorussia and Ukraine. The territory of Poland
is a plain that slopes gently from the Carpathian Mountains to the shores of the
Baltic Sea. The average elevation of the whole country is 568 feet (173 m),
more than 75% of the land lies below 650 feet (200 m). Poland is naturally
divided into east-west zones. *The New Encyclopaedia Britannica*, vol. 25 (Chicago,
1990), 911.

GEREMEK, BRONISŁAW (1932–   ), prolific scholar of medieval history,
doctor *honoris causa* of several prestigious universities, leader of the democratic
opposition in communist Poland, and influential politician after 1989. A member
of the Polish United Workers' Party (PZPR)* in 1950–68, he worked at the
Institute of History of the Polish Academy of Sciences (PAN)* during 1955–
85 and after 1989. For a period he headed the Party organization in the Institute,
and during 1962–65 he directed the Polish Cultural Center in Paris. He left the
Party after the March events of 1968* to help organize the Flying University*
in 1978. In 1980 he served as an expert on the Inter-Factory Strike Committee*
in Gdańsk,* and during the First Solidarity* Congress he served as chairman of

the Program Committee. A major adviser to Solidarity and L. Wałęsa* in the 1980s, he was interned in 1981–82 and imprisoned in 1983. Later he helped to prepare and participated in the Round Table Negotiations.* He was elected as a Sejm* deputy in 1989. Considered a candidate for Premier,* he became chairman of the Citizens' Parliamentary Club.* During the "war at the top"* he supported T. Mazowiecki* against Wałęsa, co-organized the Democratic Union (UD),* and became its Parliamentary Club chairman. *Rok 1989. Bronisław Geremek opowiada Jacek Żakowski pyta* (Warsaw, 1990); G. Sanford and A. Gozdecka-Sanford, *Historical Dictionary of Poland* (Metuchen, N.J., 1994), 76; *Kto jest kim w polityce polskiej*, ed. by R. Ignasiak (Warsaw, 1993), 86.

GERHARD, JAN (1921–71), political writer and journalist. His writing explores the World War II experiences of the Poles. One of these books, *Łuny w Bieszczadach* ("Glows in the Bieszczady Mountains"), provides a biased anti-Ukrainian depiction of the fighting between the Polish People's Army* and the Ukrainian Insurgent Army (UPA)* after the war. P. Kuncewicz, *Agonia i nadzieja. Proza polska od 1956*, vol. 4 (Warsaw, 1994), 226–229.

GERMANS. The first Germans came to Poland in the 10th century. In the 12th and the 13th centuries, German colonization of Poland was especially intensive. Later smaller groups of German settlers immigrated to Poland in waves until the 20th century. A great portion of medieval Polish lands was Germanized and incorporated into Germany. German ethnic islands also existed in eastern Poland, for example, in Volhynia. Before 1939 about 1 million Germans lived in Poland, with about 9.5 million in the East German territories incorporated into Poland as the "Recovered Territories"* in 1945. During the last months of World War II, over 4 million Germans escaped from the East German provinces. According to German sources, about 1.2 million of these escapees returned to their towns and villages immediately after war's end. Yet before the end of 1945, between 730,000 and 780,000 Germans emigrated or were deported by the Poles. Mass deportations ejected about 3 million Germans from Poland until the end of 1947. The next group of 144,000 Germans was deported from Poland in the years 1948–50. By 1950 Poland's German population was about 150,000, according to Polish sources, but between 430,000 and 800,000 according to German statistics. Beginning in June 1952 ethnic Germans living in Poland could receive Polish citizenship, although many of them preferred to emigrate. Immigration to Germany had started in 1951 and also included those persons who had declared after the war their were of Slavic "autochtonous" background. In 1952–55 about 11,500 persons emigrated to Germany, in 1956–59 about 271,000, in 1960–70 about 100,000, in 1971–75 about 59,000, in 1976–79 about 120,000, in 1980–81 about 46,000, in 1983–87 about 59,000, in 1988 about 140,000, and in 1989 about 250,000. Altogether, between 1950 and 1989, about 1.1 million former German citizens and their relatives left Poland for Germany.

The German national minority in Poland was controlled, like all other national minorities,* by the Ministry of the Interior, although the Germans were treated more harshly than the others. First, in 1951 ethnic Germans received equal rights to work and to receive fair wage for their work. In 1952 there were 137 elementary schools providing German language instruction in Poland to 7677 students. In 1957 the German Social-Cultural Association (Niemieckie Towarzystwo Społeczno-Kulturalne [NTSK]) was established. The authorities refused to legalize any other German organizations, and the NTSK, strictly controlled by the police, was not too active. This situation changed in the mid-1980s when the German Friendship Circles began to appear. Initially, they were not recognized by Polish authorities, whose policy was changed after the fall of communism and the visit of the German Chancellor, H. Kohl, to Poland. The number of German ethnic organizations began to grow, reaching about 58 in 1994. According to Polish sources, between 500,000 and 550,000 ethnic Germans live in Poland as of 1997; according to German statistics, over 1 million. Concentrated mainly in the province of Opole,* but also near Katowice,* Bielsk, and Częstochowa,* the Germans have their own parliamentary representation, with seven Sejm* deputies and one senator in 1991–93 and four deputies and one senator after 1993. *Nowa Encyklopedia Powszechna PWN*, vol. 4 (Warsaw, 1995), 475–476; J. Bugajski, *Ethnic Politics in Eastern Europe: A Guide to Nationality Policies, Organizations, and Parties* (Armonk, N.Y., 1994), 359–395; Z. Kurcz, "Mniejszość niemiecka w wyborach parlamentarnych, samorządowych i prezydenckich—w latach 1989–1991," *Przegląd Zachodni*, no. 1 (Poznań, 1993), 145–163; K. Cordell, "Politics and Society in Upper Silesia Today: The German Minority since 1945," *Nationalities Papers*, vol. 24, no. 2 (1996), 269–285.

GERTYCH, ZBIGNIEW (1922–   ), economist, agronomist, Deputy Speaker of the Sejm* in 1982–85 and Deputy Premier in 1985–87. T. Mołdawa, *Ludzie Władzy 1944–1991. Władze państwowe i polityczne Polski według stanu na dzień 28 II 1991* (Warsaw, 1991), 352.

GESING, FRANCISZEK (1904–1982), member of the State Council (Rada Państwa)* in 1965–69 and 1971–72, and one of the main leaders of the United Peasant Party (ZSL).* T. Mołdawa, *Ludzie Władzy 1944–1991. Władze państwowe i polityczne Polski według stanu na dzień 28 II 1991* (Warsaw, 1991), 352.

GIEDROYC, JERZY (1906–   ), editor, publisher of the Paris *Kultura*,* an outstanding émigré journal. He graduated from Law School at Warsaw University* and held, successively, clerical positions at the Polish Telegraph Agency (1927–29), Ministry of Agriculture (1929–35), and Ministry of Industry and Commerce (1935–39). In 1930–39 he was the editor and the publisher of *Bunt Młodych* ("Rebellion of the Youth") biweekly and its successor, the weekly *Polityka* (its last issue appeared on September 4. 1939). Giedroyc left Poland in September 1939 and served as the secretary to the Polish ambassador in

Romania until November 1940. After liquidation of the Polish Embassy in Romania, he became the head of the Polish Department at the Chilean Legacy in Bucharest and collaborated with English Legacy. In 1941 he left Bucharest for Istanbul and Palestine, where he enlisted in the Polish Independent Brigade of Carpathian Fusiliers and fought at Tobruk. Later he served in Gen. W. Anders's* Second Corps as head of the department in the Propaganda Bureau. In 1945 Giedroyc became chief of the European Department of the Ministry of Information in the Polish Government-in-Exile* in London. After over a year he left London for Rome, where he and his friends started the Literary Institute (*Instytut Literacki**). The first issue of *Kultura* was published in Rome. In 1947 the Literary Institute moved to Maissons-Laffitte in France. As an editor and publisher of *Kultura* and *Zeszyty Historyczne* ("Historical Notebooks"), Giedroyc created a strong center of Polish political and cultural thought outside of Poland. He influenced many generations of Polish intelligentsia both at home and in diaspora. *Who's Who in the Socialist Countries of Europe*, ed. by J. Stroynowski, vol. 1 (Munich, 1989), 352; E. Berberyusz, *Książę z Maisons-Laffitte* (Gdańsk, 1995).

GIEREK, EDWARD (1913–   ), First Secretary of the Polish United Workers' Party (PZPR)* from December 20, 1970, to September 5, 1980. Born into a Silesian mining family, he immigrated to France in 1923 after his father was killed in a mine disaster. In France he worked as a miner and in 1931 joined the Communist Party. Deported to Poland for his participation in a strike in 1934, he emigrated again in 1937. This time he immigrated to Belgium. There he was active in the Communist Party of Belgium and in the anti-German resistance during World War II. In 1948 he returned to Poland to work in the Party apparatus. In 1954 he became a member of the Party Central Committee,* where he served as chairman of the Heavy Industry Department. He became a Politburo* member in 1956 and served as first secretary of the Katowice* provincial Party organization in 1957. He was considered one the most powerful provincial Party secretaries. Silesia, the most industrialized province of Poland, provided him with real political opportunities. Gierek became the head of a powerful Party faction known as "the technocrats."* He supported a Western-oriented modernization program for Poland. With his West European experience and distance from the Moscow faction, he was extremely popular within the Party apparatus, which also disliked the Soviets and detested W. Gomułka's* ascetic attitude. Gierek's popularity was striking as early as the March events of 1968,* when his name was shouted out during the Party-organized manifestations of support for Gomułka and the Party leadership. During the December events of 1970,* after Gomułka had a stroke, the Seventh Plenum of the Party Central Committee elected Gierek First Secretary. Gierek promised to improve the "material situation" of the Polish people and to reevaluate the government's economic policy. He went to the striking workers, asked them for help, received a positive answer, and managed to calm down the people. The Gierek regime received large loans from the West—in 1978, they reached $14 billion—and the first years of his decade became the most successful period of the communist era in Poland. Nonetheless, the essential elements of the communist system remained unchanged, and in the mid-1970s his government lost control over the Polish economy and had to introduce visible price increases, especially on food. This was answered by the workers' rebellion of 1976. The regime suppressed the rebellion but was unable to change its course and was crushed by the next revolt of 1980. Gierek was replaced by S. Kania,* temporarily imprisoned, interrogated by the Grabski* Commission, and removed from the Party in 1981. Retired, Gierek wrote several books and argued that his policy, except for some secondary mistakes, was right. He accused his former assistants and friends of conspiring against him. M. D. Simon and R. E. Kanet (eds.), *Background to Crisis* (Boulder, Colo., 1981); A. Bromke and J. W. Strong (eds.), *Gierek's Poland* (New York, 1973); K. J. Lepak, *Prelude to Solidarity: Poland and the Politics of the Gierek Regime* (New York, 1988); *Political and Economic Encyclopedia of the Soviet Union and Eastern Europe*, ed. by S. White (London, 1990), 109; *The Cold War, 1945–1991*, vol. 2, "Leaders and Other Important Figures in the Soviet Union, Eastern Europe, China, and the Third World," ed. by B. Frankel (Detroit, 1992), 107.

GIERTYCH, MACIEJ MARIAN (1936–   ), geneticist, physiologist, and son of the national émigré conservative politician Jędrzej Giertych. He returned to Poland in 1962, served as deputy president of the Primate's Council in 1988–91, as a member of the Consultative Council by the Chairman of the State Council (Rada Państwa)* in 1986–89, and as president of the National Party (SN)* since 1991. *Who's Who in the Socialist Countries of Europe*, ed. by J. Stroynowski, vol. 1 (Munich, 1989), 353; *Kto jest kim w polityce polskiej*, ed. by R. Ignasiak (Warsaw, 1993), 87.

GIEYSZTOR, ALEKSANDER (1916–   ), distinguished scholar of medieval history, member of several prestigious international academies of sciences, director of the Historical Institute of Warsaw University* during 1955–75, director of the Royal Castle Museum in Warsaw* during 1980–91, and chairman of the Polish Academy of Sciences (PAN)* during 1980–84 and after 1990. A veteran of the September Campaign of 1939 and the Home Army (AK),* he was not active in politics until the 1970s, when he participated in several mediating and consultative bodies and was generally respected by representatives of various political orientations. In 1989 he led the Round Table Negotiations.* *Who's Who in the Socialist Countries of Europe*, ed. by J. Stroynowski, vol. 1 (Munich, 1989), 353.

GIL, MIECZYSŁAW (1944–   ), steel worker and journalist, leader of several strikes in Nowa Huta,* and a main leader of Solidarity * in southern Poland. In 1989 he participated in the Round Table Negotiations* and was elected to the Sejm,* where he chaired the Citizens' Parliamentary Club (OKP)* in 1990–91. *Kto jest kim w polityce polskiej*, ed. by R. Ignasiak (Warsaw, 1993), 89.

GLAPIŃSKI, ADAM (1950–   ), politician and economics expert of the Center Alliance (PC),* Minister of Construction in the cabinet of J. K. Bielecki* in 1991, and holder of the portfolio of economic cooperation with foreign countries in the government of J. Olszewski* in 1991–92. *Kto jest kim w polityce polskiej*, ed. by R. Ignasiak (Warsaw, 1993), 88.

GLEMP, JÓZEF (1929–   ), Archbishop of Gniezno and Warsaw,* Cardinal, and Primate* of Poland. Born into a peasant family, he was ordained a priest in 1956 and studied at Lateran and Georgian Universities in Rome during 1958–64. He returned to Poland with doctorates in canon and civil law and began to work at the secretariats for Higher Priests' Seminary and for the metropolitan Curia. During 1967–79 Glemp served as a personal secretary to Cardinal S. Wyszyński,* who became his mentor. In 1979 Glemp was appointed bishop of Warmia. He had also been teaching at Warsaw's Catholic theological seminary. After the death of Wyszyński in 1981, Glemp succeeded him as Primate of Poland. In 1983 the Pope made him a Cardinal. During the Solidarity period* he tried to mediate between the Jaruzelski* regime and Solidarity and urged both to temper their attitudes and end their conflict. After the imposition of Martial Law,* Glemp condemned the arrests of Solidarity leaders and activists, but he tried to revive talks between the workers and the regime. A growing number of priests criticized Glemp for being too compromising in his attitude toward the regime. His policy, however, proved to be instrumental in the organization of the 1989 Round Table Negotiations.* Later Glemp had to distance himself from politics because of his increasingly poor health. R. C. Monticone, *The Catholic Church in Communist Poland, 1945–1985: Forty Years of Church-State Relations* (Boulder, Colo., 1986); P. Ramet, *Religion and Nationalism in the Soviet Union and Eastern Europe* (New York, 1991); G. Polak, *Kto jest kim w Kościele katolickim* (Warsaw, 1996), 104.

GŁOS ("The Voice"), underground monthly established in 1977 and published initially by J. Karpiński,* J. Kuroń,* A. Macierewicz,* J. J. Lipski,* Z. Romaszewski,* and P. Naimski* in 3,000 to 5,000 copies. Initially, *Głos* was intended to serve as an theoretical organ of the democratic movement, and its first issue included the *Declaration of the Democratic Movement*. Soon the editorial board split, and *Głos* became an organ of a group gathered around Macierewicz and Naimski. Thirty-five issues were published until December 1981. After the imposition of Martial Law,* the monthly appeared irregularly. *Dictionary of Polish Literature*, ed. by E. J. Czerwinski (Westport, Conn., 1994), 87; D. Cecuda, *Leksykon Opozycji Politycznaj 1976–1989* (Warsaw, 1989), 159.

GŁOWACKI, JANUSZ (1938–   ), prose writer, playwright, and journalist; master of irony and the grotesque. After the imposition of Martial Law* in December 1981, he stayed in the West, first in London and then in New York, where his play *Polowanie na Karaluchy* ("Hunting Cockroaches") was proclaimed one of the 10 best plays of the year. *Dictionary of Polish Literature*, ed. by E. J. Czerwinski (Westport, Conn., 1994), 126–129.

GŁÓDŹ, SŁAWOJ LESZEK (1945–   ), field bishop of the Polish Army* since 1991. G. Polak, *Kto jest kim w Kościele katolickim* (Warsaw, 1996), 107.

GŁÓWCZYK, JAN (1927–   ), member of the Politburo* of the Polish United Workers' Party (PZPR)* in 1986–88, deputy member in 1981–86. *Who's Who in the Socialist Countries of Europe*, ed. by J. Stroynowski, vol. 1 (Munich, 1989), 357.

GOCŁOWSKI, TADEUSZ (1931–   ), Archbishop of Gdańsk* since 1992. During his 1984–92 tenure as bishop of Gdańsk, he defended the rights of Gdańsk workers and members of Solidarity.* In 1994 he served as mediator in a conflict between employers and employees of the Lucchini Steelworks (former Warsaw Steelworks). G. Polak, *Kto jest kim w Kościele katolickim* (Warsaw, 1996), 108.

GOMBROWICZ, WITOLD (1904–69), writer who lived in Argentina from 1939 and in France from 1964, considered by many to be the most original and unusual writer of Polish literature. His satirical and grotesque novels and plays, such as his best-known work *Ferdydurke*, became very popular among Polish intellectuals. His works were banned in Poland during the Stalinist and Gomułka periods.* Until the 1970s, Gombrowicz published mostly outside Poland. His analytical and profound *Diaries* appeared in installments in Paris *Kultura*.* *Dictionary of Polish Literature*, ed. by E. J. Czerwinski (Westport, Conn., 1994), 129–131; *Encyklopedyczny Słownik Sławnych Polaków* (Warsaw, 1996), 100.

GOMULICKI, JULIUSZ WIKTOR (1909–   ), literary historian and editor. A Home Army (AK)* soldier during World War II and a participant of the Warsaw Uprising, he was editor-in-chief of Nowe Książki (New Books) Publishing House in 1949–53. He edited numerous treasures of Polish literature and worked on the editorial staffs of many periodicals. M. Dąbrowska, *Dzienniki Powojenne 1945–1965*, vol. 1, ed. by T. Drewnowski (Warsaw, 1996), 349; *Encyklopedyczny Słownik Sławnych Polaków* (Warsaw, 1996), 101.

GOMUŁKA, WŁADYSŁAW (1905–82), Secretary General of the Polish Workers' Party (PPR)* in 1943–48, First Secretary of the Polish United Workers' Party (PZPR)* during 1956–70, member of the State Council (Rada Państwa)* during 1957–71, and politician whose attitudes and activities influenced the development of the Polish People's Republic and several other Soviet satellites. Born to worker émigré parents who had returned from the United States disillusioned by their experience, he was trained as a locksmith. In the early 1920s he joined the Polish Socialist Party (PPS)*; later he moved farther to the left and, in 1926, became a member of the Communist Party of Poland (KPP).

In the late 1920s he was temporarily sent to Moscow. After his return to Poland, he was elected national secretary of the radical Chemical Workers Union in 1930. Arrested and imprisoned several times, he was shot in the leg by a police officer in 1932 during an arrest. In 1934–35 Gomułka studied in Moscow at the International Lenin School. In 1936 he was arrested again by the Polish police and sentenced to seven years in prison. The term saved his life, since in the late 1930s he could not follow his comrades to the Soviet Union, where almost all of them were executed by Stalin.

In September 1939, after the outbreak of World War II, Gomułka was released from prison and, according to communist historians, volunteered to participate in the defense of Warsaw. Later he moved to Soviet-occupied eastern Poland, where he worked as a minor factory official in a paper mill in Lvov and joined the Soviet Communist Party. When Lvov was occupied by the Germans after the outbreak of the German-Soviet war in 1941, Gomułka returned to his native town of Krosno and started organizing the communist underground there. In July 1942 he moved to Warsaw,* where he became a district secretary and a member of the Central Committee of the newly created Polish Workers' Party (PPR). Then in November 1943, after his predecessor was arrested by the Germans,* he became Secretary General of the PPR. He helped to write the party's ideological manifesto; in December 1943 he co-organized and joined the National Home Council (KRN).* In July 1944 he was appointed a member of the Polish Committee of National Liberation (PKWN) in Lublin.*

In January 1945 Gomułka became a Deputy Premier of the Soviet-sponsored Provisional Government.* He occupied the same position in the Provisional Government of National Unity (TRJN),* established in June 1945. He also became a minister of the "Recovered Territories."* A ruthless communist, he was instrumental in crushing the Polish Peasant Party (PSL)* and eliminating all opposition to the regime. He presided over the fraudulent 1946 referendum* and the sham 1947 elections.* Yet he opposed the rapid forced collectivization* of agriculture,* expressed reservations about the Cominform,* believed in an individual Polish approach to communism, and thought it possible to be a communist and a Polish patriot at the same time. As a consequence, he was accused of "rightist-nationalistic deviation" and was removed from his positions in the party, arrested in August 1951, and ejected from the Party in fall 1951. In December 1954 he was released, and in 1956 the new Party First Secretary, E. Ochab,* admitted that Gomułka, who had achieved considerable public popularity as a result of his persecution, should not have been arrested. After the June 1956 riots in Poznań,* the Party leadership came to the conclusion that Gomułka's return to power would restore stability in Poland. Thus in October 1956 he was appointed First Secretary of the Party and approved by Nikita Khrushchev, who flew to Warsaw and, after a dangerous confrontation, made an agreement with Gomułka.

The new First Secretary approved the dissolution of most collective farms, reached a modus vivendi with the Roman Catholic Church,* tolerated more freedom in culture and private life, and made several compromises with Poland's traditions. Many Poles were enthusiastic about the new leader and almost considered him a savior of Poland. They were soon disappointed, however. Gomułka did not change essential elements of communism. No major economic and political reforms were undertaken. Censorship* and almost total police control were quickly rebuilt. The standard of living was kept low; Gomułka, an unsophisticated and ascetic person, did not understand the people's complaints in this respect. On the contrary, he supported the idea of constructing cheap apartments with common washrooms and opposed the development of an auto industry as a bourgeois fancy. Discontent, especially among the intelligentsia and professionals, began to grow. Party factions fought for power and plotted against Gomułka. A net result of these conspiracies and a major crackdown on intellectual opposition were in the March events of 1968,* with their vitriolous anti-Semitic campaign and extensive purges. Gomułka saved his position and, in August 1968, joined in the aggression of Czechoslovakia. In 1970 he managed to normalize relations with the West German government, which accepted the post-1945 Oder-Neisse border.

Yet Gomułka's credibility was lost. Poland's economic situation was growing worse. To improve it and to import technology, the Gomułka regime decided to raise money; it announced drastic increases in the prices of food just before Christmas 1970. Riots broke out in the Baltic Coast shipyards and several Polish cities. Police and army units massacred dozens of demonstrators. In the atmosphere of outrage and near civil war, Gomułka had a heart attack and was forced to resign as First Secretary. Replaced by E. Gierek,* the leader of a "technocratic" Party faction, he retired into private life and disappeared completely from the public eye. In 1980 the Party recognized his contribution and published a tribute to him on his 75th birthday. He died of cancer in Warsaw on September 1, 1982. N. Bethell, *Gomułka: His Poland, His Communism* (Holt, 1969); P. Raina, *Władysław Gomułka* (London, 1969); M. K. Dziewanowski, *Poland in the Twentieth Century* (New York, 1977); *The Cold War, 1945–1991*, vol. 2, "Leaders and Other Important Figures in the Soviet Union, Eastern Europe, China, and the Third World," ed. by B. Frankel (Detroit, 1992), 109.

GORYSZEWSKI, HENRYK J. (1941–   ), Deputy Premier in charge of economic matters and president of the Economic Committee in the cabinet of H. Suchocka* in 1992–93. A Solidarity* activist in 1980 and a leader of Christian-National Union (ZChN),* he was elected to the Sejm* in 1989. *Kto jest kim w polityce polskiej*, ed. by R. Ignasiak (Warsaw, 1993), 90.

GORYWODA, MANFRED (1942–   ), Deputy Premier and president of a governmental Planning Commission in 1983–87. T. Mołdawa, *Ludzie Władzy 1944–1991. Władze państwowe i polityczne Polski według stanu na dzień 28 II 1991* (Warsaw, 1991), 355; A. Kępiński and Z. Kilar, *Kto jest kim w Polsce inaczej* (Warsaw, 1985), 111–122.

GOVERNMENT DELEGACY. See **Delegacy of the Government of the Republic of Poland.**

GOVERNMENT-IN-EXILE, Polish government based on the Constitution of 1935 and established in Paris after the German invasion of Poland in September 1939. In November 1939 the government was moved to the city of Angers, and in June 1940, after the defeat of France, it was evacuated to London. In April 1943 the USSR discontinued its relations with the Government-in-Exile; then on July 5, 1945, the Western Allies withdrew their recognition, in its place recognizing the Provisional Government of National Unity (TRJN),* established in Warsaw* on June 28, 1945. In 1947 the Government-in-Exile began losing popularity among Poles abroad. In 1954, when President A. Zaleski* failed to step down after seven years in office, the Council of Three (Rada Trzech)* was established to substitute for the government. Then in 1972, after Zaleski's death, his successor, S. Ostrowski, created a new government as a compromise between the Council of Three and Zaleski's supporters. In 1978 the Fund for Defense of Freedom of Speech and Human Rights in Poland and, in 1980, the Fund for Help to the Homeland were established by the government. The Government-in-Exile ceased to exist after the fall of communism when Poland again became a sovereign state. J. Lerski, *Historical Dictionary of Poland, 966–1945*, with special editing and emendations by P. Wróbel and R. J. Kozicki (Westport, Conn., 1996), 170–172; T. Radzik, *Z dziejów społeczności polskiej w Wielkiej Brytanii po drugiej wojnie światowej, 1945–1990* (Lublin, 1991); *Warszawa nad Tamizą,* ed. by A. Friszke (Warsaw, 1994); J. Karpiński, *Polska, Komunizm, Opozycja* (London, 1985), 240–241.

GOŹDZIK, LECHOSŁAW (1931–   ), First Secretary of the Party organization at the Żerań Car Factory, who became a spontaneous leader of the workers' movement in 1956 and contributed significantly to the changes brought about by the "Polish October."* Harassed by the authorities after 1956, he was expelled from the Polish United Workers' Party (PZPR)* in 1959, left Warsaw,* and settled in Pomerania, where he worked as a fisherman. *Nowa Encyklopedia Powszechna PWN*, vol. 2 (Warsaw, 1995), 585.

GÓRECKI, HENRYK (1933–   ), outstanding Polish contemporary composer and professor at Katowice* Conservatory. *Nowa Encyklopedia Powszechna PWN*, vol. 2 (Warsaw, 1995), 588.

GÓRNICKI, WIESŁAW (1931–96), journalist, communist official, apologist for Martial Law* and the Jaruzelski* regime. A member of the editorial staff of several important Polish newspapers, Górnicki joined the Polish United Workers' Party (PZPR)* in 1953. In 1968 he protested against the anti-Semitic purge in Poland. In 1981, unexpectedly, he became a top adviser to Gen. W. Jaruzelski. In 1989–90 Górnicki served as Secretary of State in the presidential chancellery of Jaruzelski, at that time President* of Poland. *Więź* ("The Link"), Feb. 1997, p. 203.

GRABSKI, STANISŁAW (1871–1949), economist and politician, professor at Lvov and Warsaw Universities* in 1910–39 and 1947–49, respectively. An important National-Democratic leader during 1918–26, he served as a parliamentary deputy of the National-Democratic Party and as the Minister of Religious and Public Education in 1923 and 1925–26. He retired from politics after the 1926 Piłsudski coup d'état. In 1939 he was arrested in Lvov and deported by the Soviets. Released in 1941, he left for England, where he presided over the National Council (Rada Narodowa), the Polish Parliament-in-Exile. In July 1945, following the Yalta* Agreement, he returned to Poland with S. Mikołajczyk* and was appointed deputy president of the National Home Council (KRN).* After its dissolution, he retired to scholarly life. A. Polonsky and B. Drukier, *The Beginnings of Communist Rule in Poland* (London, 1980).

GRABSKI, TADEUSZ (1929–), Deputy Premier from August to October 1980, member of the Politburo* in 1980–81 and the Central Committee* of the Polish United Workers' Party (PZPR)* during 1975–81. A leader of a conservative party faction, he was appointed chairman of a special commission that investigated corruption among the close collaborators of E. Gierek.* The committee produced fascinating material, published partly in Poland, partly abroad. *Who's Who in the Socialist Countries of Europe*, ed. by J. Stroynowski, vol. 1 (Munich, 1989), 369.

GREAT ECONOMIC ORGANIZATIONS (Wielkie Organizacje Gospodarcze [WOG]), great multienterprise corporations established as part of the new economic policy of the Gierek* regime. Similar factories were grouped as horizontal branches, acquiring relative independence from the institutions of central planning. In 1973 there were 24 WOGs; by 1975 the number rose to 110. The WOGs employed over 60% of the labor force and soon established a dangerous monopolistic position. *The History of Poland since 1863*, ed. by R. F. Leslic (Cambridge, 1980), 419.

GREEKS, group of Greek and Macedonian exiles from the Greek Civil War of the 1940s. About 10,000 of them lives mostly in several small pockets of Lower Silesia. S. M. Horak, *Eastern European National Minorities, 1919–1980: A Handbook* (Littleton, Col., 1985), 59; J. Bugajski, *Ethnic Politics in Eastern Europe: A Guide to Nationality Policies, Organizations, and Parties* (London, 1994), 359.

GROCHOWIAK, STANISŁAW (1939–76), rebellious poet and editor of several literary periodicals. C. Miłosz, *The History of Polish Literature* (Berkeley, Calif., 1983), 482; *Dictionary of Polish Literature*, ed. by E. J. Czerwinski (Westport, Conn., 1994), 134–136; *Encyklopedyczny Słownik Sławnych Polaków* (Warsaw, 1996), 105.

GRONKIEWICZ-WALTZ, HANNA (1952–), president of the Polish National Bank since 1992. A specialist on bank law, she taught at Warsaw University* from 1975. In 1995 she was one of the most popular, although eventually unsuccessful, candidates in the presidential elections. *Kto jest kim w polityce polskiej*, ed. by R. Ignasiak (Warsaw, 1993), 92.

GROSSFELD, LUDWIK (1889–1955), prewar leader of the Polish Socialist Party (PPS).* Grossfeld spent World War II in France and England, becoming an official and Minister of Finances in the Polish Government-in-Exile.* In September 1945 he returned to Poland, serving as Deputy Minister and Minister of the Merchant Navy in 1945–47 and of Trade in 1947–49. T. Mołdawa, *Ludzie Władzy 1944–1991. Władze państwowe i polityczne Polski według stanu na dzień 28 II 1991* (Warsaw, 1991), 357.

GROSZKOWSKI, JANUSZ (1898–1984), Deputy President of the State Council (Rada Państwa)* in 1972–76 and president of the National Unity Front (FJN)* during 1971–76. A professor of electronics, he also served as deputy president and president of the Polish Academy of Sciences (PAN)* in 1957–62 and 1963–71, respectively. T. Mołdawa, *Ludzie Władzy 1944–1991. Władze państwowe i polityczne Polski według stanu na dzień 28 II 1991* (Warsaw, 1991), 357.

GROTOWSKI, JERZY (1933–), founder and director of the experimental Theater Laboratory in Wrocław* during 1961–84, who greatly influenced Polish and world theater. G. Sanford and A. Gozdecka-Sanford, *Historical Dictionary of Poland* (Metuchen, N.J., 1994), 80; *Encyklopedyczny Słownik Sławnych Polaków* (Warsaw, 1996), 106.

GRUDZIEŃ, ZDZISŁAW (1924–82), First Secretary of the provincial Party organization in Katowice* during 1970–80 and a close assistant to E. Gierek.* Born into a Polish émigré family in France, he spent his entire youth there and in Belgium. During World War II he worked in the Belgian and French coal mines, joined the Communist Party of France in 1942, and participated in the anti-German resistance. In 1946 he returned to Poland and began to work in the Party apparatus. In 1971 he joined its Politburo,* first as a deputy member and, from 1975, as a member. In 1981 he was ejected from the Party. T. Mołdawa, *Ludzie Władzy 1944–1991. Władze państwowe i polityczne Polski według stanu na dzień 28 II 1991* (Warsaw, 1991), 358.

"GRUNWALD." See **Patriotic Association "Grunwald."**

GRYDZEWSKI, MIECZYSŁAW (1894–1970), editor, publisher, and literary critic, editor of the Warsaw* prewar weekly *Wiadomości Literackie* ("The Literary News"), which continued in Paris as *Wiadomości Polskie* ("The Polish News") and in London as *Wiadomości*. Thanks to Grydzewski's editorial skills,

Wiadomości became an institution in "Polish London." C. Miłosz, *The History of Polish Literature* (Berkeley, Calif., 1983), 522; J. Zieliński, *Leksykon polskiej literatury emigracyjnej* (Lublin, 1989), 52.

GRYNBERG, HENRYK (1936–), actor of Ida Kamińska's Jewish State Theater in Warsaw,* he asked for asylum in the United States in December 1967 as a protest against the anti-Semitic campaign in Poland. His writing explores the life of Polish Jews* after the Holocaust. C. Miłosz, *The History of Polish Literature* (Berkeley, Calif., 1983), 534; *Dictionary of Polish Literature*, ed. by E. J. Czerwinski (Westport, Conn., 1994), 136–137; P. Kuncewicz, *Agonia i nadzieja. Proza polska od 1956*, vol. 4 (Warsaw, 1994), 399–402; J. Zieliński, *Leksykon polskiej literatury emigracyjnej* (Lublin, 1989), 53–55.

GRZYB, ZOFIA (1928–), worker from Radom* who was suddenly promoted to the Central Committee* of the Polish United Workers' Party (PZPR)* in 1980 and to its Politburo* in 1981 as political "window dressing" and proof that the PZPR was still a workers' party. Grzyb appeared to be totally confused and did not play any role. A. Kępiński and Z. Kilar, *Kto jest kim w Polsce inaczej* (Warsaw, 1985), 111–122.

GUCWA, STANISŁAW (1919–94), Deputy President of the State Council (Rada Państwa)* in 1971–72 and Speaker of the Sejm* during 1972–85. A leader of the United Peasant Party (ZSL)* between 1959 and 1984, he held several important state positions, such as Minister of the Food Industry in 1968–71. T. Mołdawa, *Ludzie Władzy 1944–1991. Władze państwowe i polityczne Polski według stanu na dzień 28 II 1991* (Warsaw, 1991), 359; A. Kępiński and Z. Kilar, *Kto jest kim w Polsce inaczej* (Warsaw, 1985), 123–136.

GULBINOWICZ, HENRYK (1928–), since 1975 Archbishop of Wrocław* and one of the most respected and influential figures in the Polish Episcopate.* From 1970 he served as a bishop-administrator of the Białystok* diocese. In 1985 he was appointed Cardinal. G. Polak, *Kto jest kim w Kościele katolickim* (Warsaw, 1996), 122.

GWIAZDA, ANDRZEJ (1935–), veteran of the anti-communist democratic opposition in Poland and co-founder of the Free Trade Unions of the Coast in 1978 and of Solidarity* in 1980. An engineer by profession, he was a leader of the Gdańsk* Lenin Shipyard strike and played an important role in the negotiations leading to the Gdańsk Agreement* of August 1980. More radical than L. Wałęsa,* he lost to him in the election for national chairman at the 1981 Solidarity Congress but was elected vice-chairman. Several weeks later he resigned from this post in protest and issued an open letter to Wałęsa calling for more internal democracy in Solidarity. Marginalized by Wałęsa and harassed by the authorities, Gwiazda opposed the Round Table Negotiations* and allied himself with M. Jurczyk* and "Solidarity 1980." *Who's Who in the Socialist Countries of Europe*, ed. by J. Stroynowski, vol. 1 (Munich, 1989), 389.

GYPSIES (Roma), one of the smallest national minorities* in Poland, consisting of about 18,000 people. They are divided into four groups: Polish Highland Gypsies, Polish Lowland Gypsies, Kelderasze, and Lovari. The latter two groups are mainly newcomers from the former Soviet Union, Romania, and Hungary. In 1964 the Polish authorities forced the Gypsies to settle. Most of them are now concentrated in main industrial centers; however, the Roma people are also scattered throughout the Polish provinces. In June 1991 an anti-Gypsy pogrom took place in Mława, in northern Mazovia, and some Romani residents left Poland for Western Europe, especially Germany. They were soon replaced by a wave of Romanian Gypsies, migrating to Poland. S. M. Horak, *Eastern European National Minorities, 1919–1980: A Handbook* (Littleton, Colo., 1985), 59; J. Bugajski, *Ethnic Politics in Eastern Europe: A Guide to Nationality Policies, Organizations, and Parties* (London, 1994), 359; K. Kłosińska, "Mniejszości narodowe w Polsce," *Barometr kultury*, ed. by M. Grabowska (Warsaw, 1992), 53–63; J. Ficowski, *Cyganie na polskich drogach* (Warsaw, 1964).

HAGMAJER, JERZY (1913–   ), physician and PAX Association* official. A member of the National Radical Group *Falanga* before 1939, he participated in the anti-German resistance and the 1944 Warsaw Uprising during World War II. He then became a major collaborator of B. Piasecki,* helped to organize the PAX Association, and served as its deputy chairman from 1958 and its Sejm* deputy during 1961–80. *Who's Who in the Socialist Countries of Europe*, ed. by J. Stroynowski, vol. 1 (Munich, 1989), 396.

HALECKI, OSKAR (1891–1973), historian who popularized the notion East-Central Europe. He taught at Jagiellonian University* in Cracow* in 1916–18 and at the University of Warsaw* during 1918–39. Caught in Switzerland at the outbreak of World War II, he went to France; in 1940 he settled in the United States, where he organized the Polish Scientific Institute in New York and taught at several universities. An expert on modern Polish history and the history of Lithuania and East-Central Europe, he was one of the most prolific and interesting Polish historians of the 20th century. *Great Historians of the Modern Age: An International Dictionary*, ed. by L. Boia (New York, 1991), 479–480.

HALL, ALEKSANDER (1953–   ), historian, opposition activist, and politician. A leader and co-founder of the Young Poland Movement,* he was also active in the Movement for the Defense of Human and Civil Rights (ROPCiO)* and Solidarity.* Hall spent three years in hiding after the imposition of Martial Law.* In 1986 he was invited to the Primate's Social Council (Prymasowska Rada Społeczna). Later, in 1989, he participated in the Round Table Negotiations* and became a minister in charge of collaboration with political parties in the Mazowiecki* government. He left his post in October 1990 to organize Mazowiecki's electoral campaign before the presidential election of 1990.* During 1990–91 he led the Forum of the Democratic Right (FPD). Later, together with the Forum, he joined the Democratic Union (UD)* and became its deputy president. Member of the Sejm* from 1991, he split the UD, rebuilt an independent Forum of the Democratic Right, and united it with some other small parties to form the Conservative Party* in 1992. G. Sanford and A. Gozdecka-Sanford, *Historical Dictionary of Poland* (Metuchen, N.J., 1994), 82; *Kto jest kim w polityce polskiej*, ed. by R. Ignasiak (Warsaw, 1993), 98.

HANUSZKIEWICZ, ADAM (1924–), actor and theater director. *Encyklopedyczny Słownik Sławnych Polaków* (Warsaw, 1996), 111.

HASIOR, WŁADYSŁAW (1928–), sculptor and author of provocative poetic and philosophical assemblages. *Encyklopedyczny Słownik Sławnych Polaków* (Warsaw, 1996), 112.

HELSINKI COMMITTEE, unofficial watch group organized in Poland during Martial Law.* The Committee inspected the observance of civil rights in Poland and prepared four reports on *The Rights of Men and Citizens in the People's Republic of Poland* in 1982, 1983, 1984, and 1985. The Committee also produced several smaller documents for the United Nations, Amnesty International, and other international humanitarian organizations. J. Karpiński, *Polska, Komunizm, Opozycja* (London, 1985), 95.

HEMAR, MARIAN (1901–72), poet and satirist. Active in several cabarets in the early 1920s, he fought in the Carpathian Brigade in 1939 and immigrated to England in 1942. After the war he cooperated with Radio Free Europe* and wrote over 3,000 satiric political songs. *Encyklopedyczny Słownik Sławnych Polaków* (Warsaw, 1996), 112; J. Zieliński, *Leksykon polskiej literatury emigracyjnej* (Lublin, 1989), 57–58.

HERBERT, ZBIGNIEW (1924–), poet who made his debut in 1956. Fascinated with the civilization of the Mediterranean and extensively educated in humanism, Herbert wrote "crystalline, intellectual, and ironic poetry," "counterbalanced by his reflections on historical situations." Well-known for his high moral standards, he was at odds with the communist authorities in Poland but was widely translated into English and published abroad. C. Miłosz, *The History of Polish Literature* (Berkeley, Calif., 1983), 470–475; *Dictionary of Polish Literature*, ed. by E. J. Czerwinski (Westport, Conn., 1994), 140–142; *Encyklopedyczny Słownik Sławnych Polaków* (Warsaw, 1996), 114.

HERBST, STANISŁAW (1907–73), historian, professor at Warsaw University* from 1954, and a specialist on military, cultural, and urban history. E. Kridl Valkenier, "The Rise and Decline of Official Marxist Historiography in Poland, 1945–1983," *Slavic Review*, vol. 44, no. 4 (winter 1985), 661–680.

HERLING-GRUDZIŃSKI, GUSTAW (1919–), writer. He participated in the September Campaign of 1939 and the anti-German resistance. Threatened by the *Gestapo*, he escaped to the Soviet-occupied Polish Eastern Territories and was caught by the NKVD in 1940. Imprisoned in a camp near Archangel, he was released in 1942, joined the Anders* Army, left the USSR with it, and fought at Monte Cassino. After the war, he stayed in Italy, co-founded and contributed to the Paris *Kultura*,* and authored many works that, like his best-known *Inny świat* ("A World Apart"), criticized Stalinism and totalitarianism. His *Dziennik* ("Diary"), published systematically in *Kultura* from 1971 and his *Dziennik pisany nocą* ("A Journal Written by Night") strengthened his position as a major author of the important literary documents of our times. *Dictionary of Polish Literature*, ed. by E. J. Czerwinski (Westport, Conn., 1994), 142–143; M. Dąbrowska, *Dzienniki powojenne 1945–49*, vol. 1, ed. by T. Drewnowski (Warsaw, 1996), 394; *Encyklopedyczny Słownik Sławnych Polaków* (Warsaw, 1996), 115; J. Zieliński, *Leksykon polskiej literatury emigracyjnej* (Lublin, 1989), 58–59.

HERMASZEWSKI, MIROSŁAW (1941–), first Polish cosmonaut and member of the 1978 Soviet *Soyuz 30* expedition. He became a regime celebrity. Promoted to the rank of general, he was used by the Gierek* regime's "propaganda of success." After the imposition of Martial Law,* he became a member of the Military Council of National Salvation (WRON).* G. Sanford and A. Gozdecka-Sanford, *Historical Dictionary of Poland* (Metuchen, N.J., 1994), 82; *Who's Who in the Socialist Countries of Europe*, ed. by J. Stroynowski, vol. 1 (Munich, 1989), 428.

HERTZ, PAWEŁ (1918–93), Catholic poet, writer, translator, editor, and literary critic. During 1945–48 he contributed to the communist-sponsored weekly *Kuźnica* ("The Forge"), but later he joined the milieu of the prestigious *Tygodnik Powszechny* ("The Universal Weekly"),* was involved in the political opposition in Poland, and supported L. Wałęsa* during the presidential elections of 1990.* C. Miłosz, *The History of Polish Literature* (Berkeley, Calif., 1983), 456; *Dictionary of Polish Literature*, ed. by E. J. Czerwinski (Westport, Conn., 1994), 143–144; A. Micewski, *Ludzie i opcje* (Warsaw, 1993), 153–158.

HEXAGONALE. See **Pentagonale.**

HIMILSBACH, JAN (1931–88), stonecutter, hobo, and writer. Master of irony and black humor, he wrote mostly about the "social margin" and vagabonds like himself. P. Kuncewicz, *Agonia i nadzieja. Proza polska od 1956*, vol. 5 (Warsaw, 1994), 24–26.

HIRSZFELD, LUDWIK (1884–1954), professor of medicine, microbiologist, and co-founder of immunology and serology. He fought against the typhus epidemics in Serbia and built its health service during World War I. Later he organized and headed the Polish State Hygienic Institute and taught at the Free University (Wolna Wszechnica) in Warsaw.* During World War II he escaped from the Warsaw Ghetto and lived in hiding. He helped to establish the Maria Curie-Skłodowska University in Lublin* in 1944. The next year he organized the Immunology Institute at Wrocław University.* He founded the Polish school of immunology. M. Dąbrowska, *Dzienniki powojenne 1945–49*, vol. 1, ed. by T. Drewnowski (Warsaw, 1996), 138; *Encyklopedyczny Słownik Sławnych Polaków* (Warsaw, 1996), 117.

HLOND, AUGUST (1881–1948), Primate* of Poland and Archbishop of Poznań* and Gniezno* from 1926, Gniezno and Warsaw* after 1946, and Cardinal from 1927. Through the Vatican, Hlond became instrumental in recognizing the dioceses of the "Recovered Territories,"* received by Poland after World War II. G. Sanford and A. Gozdecka-Sanford, *Historical Dictionary of Poland* (Metuchen, N.J., 1994), 83; *Encyklopedyczny Słownik Sławnych Polaków* (Warsaw, 1996), 117.

HŁASKO, MAREK (1934–69), writer, idol of Poland's young generation, and enfant terrible of Warsaw's* literary milieu after 1956. Author of short stories, he left Poland in 1958 to live in Israel (on a temporary visa as a non-Jew), Western Europe, and the United States. One of the most original postwar writers, he became a legend. C. Miłosz, *The History of Polish Literature* (Berkeley, Calif., 1983), 526; *Dictionary of Polish Literature*, ed. by E. J. Czerwinski (Westport, Conn., 1994), 144–146; P. Kuncewicz, *Agonia i nadzieja. Proza polska od 1956*, vol. 5 (Warsaw, 1994), 8–14; J. Zieliński, *Leksykon polskiej literatury emigracyjnej* (Lublin, 1989), 60–61.

HOCHFELD, JULIAN (1911–66), lawyer, economist, sociologist, professor at several Polish universities, and socialist ideologue. A member of the Polish Socialist Party (PPS)* since 1930, he belonged to its leadership in the late 1940s. He joined the Polish United Workers' Party (PZPR)* in 1948 and served in several secondary apparatus positions but soon was marginalized by more obedient or radical activists. G. Sanford and A. Gozdecka-Sanford, *Historical Dictionary of Poland* (Metuchen, N.J., 1994), 83; T. Mołdawa, *Ludzie Władzy 1944–1991. Władze państwowe i polityczne Polski według stanu na dzień 28 II 1991* (Warsaw, 1991), 360.

HOLLAND, AGNIESZKA (1948–   ), film director who worked mostly outside Poland. Among her best-known productions is *Europa, Europa*. *Encyklopedyczny Słownik Sławnych Polaków* (Warsaw, 1996), 118.

HOLLAND, HENRYK (1920–61), prewar communist, soldier of the Polish People's Army* during World War II, editor-in-chief of the communist weekly *Walka Młodych* ("The Struggle of the Young"), and father of A. Holland.* Labeled a revisionist after 1956, he allegedly passed N. Khrushchev's story detailing the brutal killing of L. Beria to the French corespondent of *Le Monde*. Persecuted by secret police, Holland is said to have jumped out of a window during a police search in his apartment. Most people believed that he was killed by the secret police; his burial turned into an anti-regime demonstration. A. Michnik, J. Tischner and J. Żakowski, *Między Panem a Plebanem* (Cracow, 1995), 88–89; J. Nowak, *Polska z oddali* (London, 1988), 225, 283; *Gomułka i inni. Dokumenty z archiwum KC 1948–1982*, ed. by J. Andrzejewski (Warsaw, 1986), 179.

HOLOUBEK, GUSTAW (1923–   ) actor, theater director, and Solidarity* senator after 1991. G. Sanford and A. Gozdecka-Sanford, *Historical Dictionary of Poland* (Metuchen, N.J., 1994), 84; *Kto jest kim w polityce polskiej*, ed. by R. Ignasiak (Warsaw, 1993), 103.

HOME ARMY (Armia Krajowa [AK]), all-Polish resistance army established in occupied Poland in February 1942 as a successor of the Service for Polish Victory and the Union of Armed Struggle. The AK was active in the entire territory of Poland and constituted the armed force of the Polish underground state, directed by the Polish Government-in-Exile.* At its peak the AK had about 350,000 soldiers and was the largest and possibly the best-organized clandestine army in the whole of occupied Europe. Home Army guerrilla and intelligence activities contributed significantly to the victory over the Third Reich. The decline of the AK started after the Red Army* entered prewar Polish territories at the beginning of 1944. The Soviets imprisoned most AK officers and forcibly incorporated its soldiers into the Polish communist army. The organization and the leadership of the AK were seriously weakened after the fall of the Warsaw Uprising in October 1944. On January 12, 1945, the Red Army started a new offensive and occupied all Polish territories. The Soviets, supported by the Polish communist forces, started military operations and mass arrests against the AK. Commander-in-Chief Gen. L. Okulicki* and leaders of the underground Polish state decided to dissolve the AK on January 19, 1945. Many AK units did not follow this order; instead, they remained in the forests and continued to fight against the Soviets. Former members of the AK were persecuted and harassed until 1956. G. Sanford and A. Gozdecka-Sanford, *Historical Dictionary of Poland* (Metuchen, N.J., 1994), 84; J. Lerski, *Historical Dictionary of Poland, 966–1945*, with special editing and emendations by P. Wróbel and R. J. Kozicki (Westport, Conn., 1996), 8; *Słownik Historii Polski 1939–1948*, ed. by A. Chwalba and T. Gąsowski (Cracow, 1994), 246–253; J. Karpiński, *Polska, Komunizm, Opozycja* (London, 1985), 19–21.

HOOLIGANISM (chuligaństwo). Real hooliganism was indeed a plague in communist Poland, but the authorities also used it to explain and punish political opposition, especially among young people. In 1958 a decree was issued that made "hooliganism" a severely punishable offense. Simultaneously, law tribunals, controlled completely by the state authorities, decided what activities were of a hooligan character. J. Karpiński, *Polska, Komunizm, Opozycja* (London, 1985), 33.

HUPAŁOWSKI, TADEUSZ (1922–), general, member of the Military Council of National Salvation (WRON)* and Minister of Administration in 1981–83, and chairman of the Supreme Control Chamber (NIK)* during 1983– 91. *Who's Who in the Socialist Countries of Europe*, ed. by J. Stroynowski, vol. 1 (Munich, 1989), 459.

IDEOLOGY, systematic body of beliefs about society, economy, and history. Marxism-Leninism, practiced in the Soviet Union and its satellites, departed from classical Marxism. It constituted a fusion of the pragmatic policies of the Bolsheviks, especially their leaders V. I. Lenin and J. Stalin and, frequently, was modified in surprising and drastic ways. For example, it did not restrain the USSR from cooperation with Nazi Germany, and it was designed in a specific way during the Cold War.* In Poland, occupied by the Red Army* in 1945, a small fraction of the Polish intelligentsia and intellectuals became fascinated with Marxism and supported political changes introduced to Polish society by the Soviet Union. In the early 1950s most of these people became bitterly disappointed; some of them, such as L. Kołakowski,* became ardent critics of Marxism-Leninism. The ideological defectors of the 1950s were followed by another group in the 1960s. Especially after the purges and the anti-Semitic campaign of 1968, almost everyone in Poland agreed that the ideology was dead; by the 1970s it was difficult to meet a real supporter of Marxism, which had been replaced by opportunism and the ''common sense'' ideology of power and pragmatism. B. P. McCrea, J. C. Plano, and G. Klein, *The Soviet and East European Dictionary* (Oxford, 1984), 48–58; G. Lichtheim, *The Concept of Ideology* (New York, 1967); L. Kołakowski, *The Main Currents of Marxism* (many editions); J. Karpiński, *Polska, Komunizm, Opozycja* (London, 1985), 72.

IGNAR, STEFAN (1908–), professor of economics, member of the Polish Academy of Sciences (PAN),* Deputy President of the State Council (Rada Państwa)* during 1952–56, member of the Council in 1959–72, and Deputy Premier from 1956 to 1969. The son of a peasant family, he graduated from Poznań University* in 1931, joined the Peasant Party (SL)* in the same year, and was a member of the Leading Council of his party in 1935–39. During World War II he was among the activists of the anti-German peasant resistance.

After the war he joined the leadership of the communist-controlled United Peasant Party (ZSL),* serving as deputy president of its governing council during 1949–56 and as its president from 1956 to 1962. He was also active in the communist and peasant youth movements and occupied several less important positions in the communist apparatus, although during the political "thaw"* in Poland Ignar expressed the ZSL membership's desire for greater autonomy from the ruling Polish United Workers' Party (PZPR).* T. Mołdawa, *Ludzie Władzy 1944–1991. Władze państwowe i polityczne Polski według stanu na dzień 28 II 1991* (Warsaw, 1991), 361; G. Sanford and A. Gozdecka-Sanford, *Historical Dictionary of Poland* (Metuchen, N.J., 1994), 85; *Who's Who in the Socialist Countries of Europe*, ed. by J. Stroynowski, vol. 2 (Munich, 1989), 464.

IKONOWICZ, PIOTR I. (1956–   ), journalist, translator, and politician. A member of the Solidarity* Information Bureau in 1980–81, he was arrested and then interned in 1981. During 1983–87 he was a leader of the Worker Political Group. From 1987 he edited an underground periodical, *Robotnik* ("The Worker"), helped to rebuild the Polish Socialist Party (PPS),* and became one of its leaders. Elected to the Sejm* in 1989, he belonged to the Parliamentary Club of the Democratic Left Alliance (SLD)* and, in February 1994, helped to form a Club of the PPS. *Kto jest kim w Polsce* (Warsaw, 1993), 228.

INDEPENDENT STUDENTS' ASSOCIATION (Niezależne Zrzeszenie Studentów [NZS]), student organization established in 1981 in Warsaw* and active in the underground after imposition of Martial Law.* The NZS considered itself a continuation of the Students' Solidarity Committees (Studenckie Komitety Solidarności [SKS]) and the Polish Students' Association (ZSP) dissolved by the communists in the 1970s. Less active in the mid-1980s the NZS was revived in 1987 in all Polish academic centers. The NZS fought for an independent Poland, freedom of speech, autonomy of Polish universities, political pluralism, and the modernization of programs of study. D. Cecuda, *Leksykon Opozycji Politycznej 1976–1989* (Warsaw, 1989), 64; *Nowa Encyklopedia Powszechna PWN*, vol. 6 (Warsaw, 1996), 90.

INDUSTRY. Before World War II Poland had been a predominantly agricultural country. During the communist period of 1945–89, a shift from an agricultural to an industrial economy* took place. By 1989 about 56% of the GNP was generated by manufacturing, mining, and power production. Less than 15% was derived from agriculture.* Accelerated industrialization started during the Stalinist period* of 1948–56. Large investments helped to develop mining, hydroelectric plants, and iron and steel production. Poland became the second largest producer of coal, was among the world's largest producers of sulfur, and produced significant amounts of copper, zinc, and lead. Huge iron-smelting and steel plants were opened in Nowa Huta* near Cracow,* in Warsaw,* and near Częstochowa.* Poland also developed its mechanical, textile, chemical, shipbuilding, car, electrical, and food industries. Yet industrial development varies in different parts of Poland. The most industrialized area, Upper Silesia—or the Katowice* province—generated almost 20% of the entire Polish GNP in the 1980s. Z. Landau and J. Tomaszewski, *The Polish Economy in the Twentieth Century* (London, 1985); *Eastern Europe and Commonwealth of Independent States, 1944* (London, 1994), 475–479; R. H. Osborne, *East-Central Europe: An Introductory Geography* (New York, 1967); J. Szczepański (ed.), *Przemysł i społeczeństwo w Polsce Ludowej* (Wrocław, 1969).

INFELD, LEOPOLD (1898–1968), prominent Polish nuclear scientist and from 1950 professor at Warsaw University* who worked together with A. Einstein. An ardent communist, he was active in the World Peace Council and, in 1956, was among those in the guard of honor at B. Bierut's* bier. *Nowa Encyklopedia Powszechna PWN*, vol. 3 (Warsaw, 1995), 52.

INFLATION. High inflation constituted an inseparable part of the communist economic system in Poland. It was caused by budget deficit, industrialization, and mistakes of the central planning institutions. However, the authorities were able to stop or hide inflation, using some unconventional methods. In 1945 and 1950 a non-equivalent exchange of money took place. The latter exchange was arranged such that the Polish population lost about 66% of its savings and cash. From 1953 the authorities were constantly changing relations between prices and wages; the former were growing faster than the latter. In the Gomułka* period, inflation was limited by relatively cautious investment and spending. Visible growth of inflation started in the Gierek* period. By the 1980s inflation reached 112.4% and contributed decisively to the collapse of the system. In 1990 the rate of inflation increased to almost 250%. After the implementation of the Balecerowicz* Plan, inflation began to fall, dropping 60.4% in 1991, 37% in 1993, and 21.6% in 1995. *Nowa Encyklopedia Powszechna PWN*, vol. 3 (Warsaw, 1995), 53.

INGARDEN, ROMAN (1893–1970), outstanding Polish philosophers of the 20th century, founder of the "second phenomenology," professor at Jagiellonian University* in Cracow* during 1946–52 and from 1957, and member of the Polish Academy of Sciences (PAN)* from 1957. His works, written in Polish and German, dealt mainly with aesthetics, metaphysics, and epistemology. A. T. Tymieniecka, *Essence et existence: Essai sur la philosophie de N. Hartman et R. Ingarden* (1957).

INSTYTUT LITERACKI (Literary Institute), publishing institution created by J. Giedroyc* and his assistants in Rome in 1946. In 1947 the Institute moved to Paris. It publishes a monthly, *Kultura,** and, since 1962, *Zeszyty Historyczne* ("Historical Notebooks"). The Institute has also published about 500 books. Before the fall of communism in Poland in 1989, Instytut Literacki was one of the most important centers of independent Polish culture; it is therefore difficult to overestimate its influence on the thinking of Polish intellectuals. J. Karpiński, *Polska, Komunizm, Opozycja* (London, 1985), 73; J. Giedroyc, *Autobiografia na cztery ręcę* (Warsaw, 1994); E. Berberyusz, *Książę z Maisons-Lafitte* (Gdańsk, 1995).

INTELLIGENTSIA, term depicting social phenomenon endemic to 19th and 20th century Russia and East-Central Europe. The term describes both a social group and a state of mind. In Poland members of the intelligentsia were usually from the gentry, had a modern education, and were passionately involved in the political and social problems of their country. In the 20th century, the Polish intelligentsia suffered significant losses as its members became an ongoing target for extermination by both the Soviets and the Nazis. After 1945 the survivors of the prewar intelligentsia, together with the next generation, carried on with their mission, pursuing the dream of a sovereign Poland. Persecuted and often humiliated by the communists, they managed to remain visible during major crises in postwar Poland. The intelligentsia's contribution to the abolition of communism in Poland cannot be underestimated. Ironically, after 1989 the group's influence diminished. R. Zuzowski, "KOR after KOR: The Intelligentsia and Dissent in Poland, 1981–1987," *The Polish Review*, vol. 33, no. 2 (New York, 1988), 167–190; *Inteligencja polska w XIX i XX wieku*, ed. by R. Czepulis-Rastenis, vols. 1–5 (Warsaw, 1978–86); J. Babiuch-Luxmoore, *Portrety i autoportrety inteligencji polskiej* (Warsaw, 1989); B. Cywiński, *Rodowody niepokornych* (Paris, 1985).

INTER-FACTORY STRIKE COMMITTEE (Międzyzakładowy Komitet Strajkowy [MKS]), committee established on August 17, 1980, in the Lenin Shipyard in Gdańsk.* Originally, it represented the striking factories of the cities of the Baltic Coast, but soon it became representative of striking factories and institutions in all the regions of Poland. After two weeks of negotiations, on August 31, 1980, it signed the Gdańsk Agreement* with the communist authorities of Poland. In the late 1970s a group of Gdańsk workers and intelligentsia, among them L. Wałęsa,* began to form free trade unions. By early August 1980 their members helped to organize a strike in the Lenin Shipyard when the government announced sudden price increases for food. At that time the government faced various serious problems, was unable to start a political confrontation with the workers, and admitted that the price increase was implemented improperly. The striking shipyard workers presented mostly economic demands. On August 16 both sides were ready to sign an agreement. Workers of other factories in Gdańsk, Gdynia,* and Sopot, however, complained that their situation was bad as well and that they had not even begun to negotiate with their management. Wałęsa convinced part of the Lenin Shipyard crew to continue the strike together with the other factories and to add to the economic postulates some demands made by the democratic opposition in Poland. Its representatives, members of the Workers' Defense Committee (KOR)* and the Young Poland Movement,* and intellectuals such as T. Mazowiecki* and B.

Geremek* joined and supported the striking workers. The MKS initially presented a list of 16, and later 21, demands. The authorities made further concessions to striking workers and continued negotiations with the MKS, but simultaneously it started to arrest so-called anti-socialist forces. By then the strike had been joined by most factories on the Baltic Coast and the main industrial centers in Poland. The authorities, threatened with a general strike, decided to sign the Gdańsk Agreement. N. G. Andrews, *Poland, 1980–1981: Solidarity versus the Party* (Washington, D.C., 1985); N. Ascherson, *The Polish August: What Has Happened in Poland* (New York, 1981).

INTERNAL SECURITY TROOPS (Korpus Bezpieczeństwa Wewnętrznego [KBW]), special military formation established in 1945 and supervised by the Ministry of Public Security (Ministerstwo Bezpieczeństwa Publicznego). The KBW fought against Polish anti-communist guerrillas and the Ukrainian Insurgent Army (UPA)* until 1948. In October 1956 the KBW was put on alert and a portion of the public expected troops to be used against demonstrators, as had occurred in Poznań* in June 1956. Yet the KBW, commanded at that time by Gen. W. Komar,* was prepared to defend Warsaw* against possible intervention by the Soviet Army* and the Polish Army* units controlled by the Soviets. On July 1, 1965, the KBW was transferred to the competencies of the Defense Ministry and became a part of the territorial defense system. J. Karpiński, *Polska, Komunizm, Opozycja* (London, 1985), 109.

INTERNMENT, form of imprisonment used by the communist authorities of Poland as a mild and convenient kind of arrest. During 1953–56 Cardinal S. Wyszyński* was interned. The State Council's (Rada Państwa)* decree about the imposition of Martial Law* on December 13, 1981, included a chapter devoted to internment. It was to be applied to all adult citizens of Poland who were suspected of future activities against the rules of Martial Law. According to an official statement of Gen. C. Kiszczak,* the Minister of the Interior, on February 28, 1982, the authorities interned 6,647 persons between December 13, 1981, and February 26, 1982. On December 9, 1982, a Deputy Minister of the Interior gave the number of internees as 10, 131, although, allegedly, there were never more than 5,300 persons interned at the same time. Kept in several dozen camps, the internees had to fight for their rights; the internment experience created a bond among them: They became a veteran group and a political legend. On March 3, 1982, the authorities announced that internees could leave Poland. This decision started a large ''Solidarity emigration.'' On December 31, 1982, Martial Law was suspended and most internees were released. Yet a relatively large group of people was arrested and moved to regular prisons. J. Karpiński, *Polska, Komunizm, Opozycja* (London, 1985), 75.

INTERPRESS (Polska Agencja Interpress), Polish press agency established on January 1, 1967, to inform international public opinion about Poland. The agency created by the merger of the Western Press Agency (Zachodnia Agencja Prasowa) and "Polonia" Publishing Institute publishes books and periodicals in foreign languages and distributes them in Western Europe and the United States. J. Karpiński, *Polska, Komunizm, Opozycja* (London, 1985), 76.

IRANEK OSMECKI, KAZIMIERZ (1897–1984), a leader of the anti-German resistance during World War II, later a political activist in the Polish émigré community in England; also a writer and a historian. *Encyklopedyczny Słownik Sławnych Polaków* (Warsaw, 1996), 122.

IREDYŃSKI, IRENEUSZ (1939–86), rebellious and provocative poet and playwright. *Dictionary of Polish Literature*, ed. by E. J. Czerwinski (Westport, Conn., 1994), 150–151; *Encyklopedyczny Słownik Sławnych Polaków* (Warsaw, 1996), 123.

IWASZKIEWICZ, JAROSŁAW (1894–1980), prolific and outstanding Polish poet and writer of the 20th century. He studied law and music in Kiev from 1912, and in 1918 he settled in Warsaw,* where he helped to found *Skamander*, a group of lyrical poets. A private secretary to the Sejm* Speaker Maciej Rataj during 1923–25, Iwaszkiewicz later joined the Ministry of Foreign Affairs and served as a member of the Polish legations to Copenhagen and Brussels during 1932–36. In the late 1930s he was already a well-known poet. During World War II and the early postwar years he lived a private life, concentrating on writing. In 1953 he was appointed chairman of the Polish Committee to Defend Peace and a Sejm deputy. During 1943–49 and 1959–72 Iwaszkiewicz presided over the Union of Polish Writers (ZLP)*; from 1955 he edited the monthly literary periodical *Twórczość* ("Creation"). He published several collections of poems and numerous essays, plays, biographies, short stories, translations, and novels. The largest of these novels, *Sława i Chwała* ("Fame and Glory"), published in the 1956–63, is devoted to the Polish fate between 1914 and 1945. *Dictionary of Polish Literature*, ed. by E. J. Czerwinski (Westport, Conn., 1994), 153–158; *Encyklopedyczny Słownik Sławnych Polaków* (Warsaw, 1996), 124.

JABŁOŃSKI, HENRYK (1909–   ), historian and President of the State Council (Rada Państwa)* from March 28, 1972, to November 1985. A graduate of Warsaw University* and a member of the Polish Socialist Party (PPS)* from 1931, he participated in the September Campaign of 1939, in the Battle of Narvik in 1940, and in the Polish resistance in southern France. In 1945 he returned to Poland, becoming a member of the National Home Council (KRN)* and a faculty member (from 1950 a full professor) of Warsaw University. A leader of the postwar PPS, he supported ''unification'' with the Polish Workers' Party (PPR)* and joined the leadership of the Polish United Workers' Party (PZPR).* During 1947–53 he served as a Deputy Minister of Education, and during 1965–72 as Minister of Education. As history professor, minister, secretary of the Polish Academy of Sciences* (1955–65), and deputy president of the Academy, Jabłoński was one of those responsible for the communist indoctrination of Polish society, the 1968 purges, and the *Gleichschaltung* of the Polish educational system. During 1948–81 and 1986–90 he was a member of the Party Central Committee,* and during 1971–81 of the Politburo.* Appointed President of the State Council in 1972, he showed surprising political ambitions that resulted in a conflict with E. Gierek* over the presidency of Poland. *Who's Who in the Socialist Countries of Europe*, ed. by J. Stroynowski, vol. 2 (Munich, 1989), 481; T. Mołdawa, *Ludzie Władzy 1944–1991. Władze państwowe i polityczne Polski według stanu na dzień 28 II 1991* (Warsaw, 1991), 362.

JAGIELIŃSKI, ROMAN (1947–   ), Deputy Premier and Minister of Agriculture in the governments of J. Oleksy* and W. Cimoszewicz* between March 1995 and March 1997. A farmer and a graduate of the Agricultural Academy, he belonged to the United Peasant Party (ZSL)* and, from 1990, to the Polish Peasant Party (PSL).* Elected to the Sejm* in 1991, he served there on the

Agriculture Committee and as the head of the PSL caucus. *Kto jest kim w polityce polskiej*, ed. by R. Ignasiak (Warsaw, 1993), 109.

JAGIELLONIAN UNIVERSITY (Uniwersytet Jagielloński), the oldest and the most prestigious Polish university, established in Cracow* in 1364, the second oldest university of Northern and Eastern Europe. Germanized in 1847–48, it resumed using the Polish language in 1870. In 1939 it was closed by the Germans, who imprisoned 183 of its professors in Sachsenhausen concentration camp. The university became active underground in 1942; in 1945 it started regular classes. Then in the late 1940s and the 1950s, like all other Polish universities,* it accommodated to the communist system. It was nonetheless an important center of independent thought and political opposition.* In 1995 it had 19,400 students and 2,800 faculty members. *Dictionary of Polish Literature*, ed. by E. J. Czerwinski (Westport, Conn., 1994), 159–160; *Nowa Encyklopedia Powszechna PWN*, vol. 6 (Warsaw, 1995), 564.

JAGIELSKI, MIECZYSŁAW (1924–97), Deputy Premier from December 1970 to July 1980, negotiated the agreement with Solidarity* in Gdańsk* in August 1980. A member of the Polish Workers' Party (PPR)* from 1946, he worked in various state institutions dealing with agriculture.* From 1959 he served as the Minister of Agriculture. Member of the Party Central Committee* from 1959 and the Politburo* from 1964, Jagielski became one of the most important officials of the Gierek* decade; he was not only Deputy Premier but also chairman of the governmental Planning Committee (from October 26, 1971) and Polish representative to Comecon* (from 1971). Considered a main author of the Gierek team's economic program, he was severely criticized in 1976. In 1980–81 he was removed from all his positions and interrogated by the Grabski* Commission. *Who's Who in the Socialist Countries of Europe*, ed. by J. Stroynowski, vol. 2 (Munich, 1989), 479; T. Mołdawa, *Ludzie Władzy 1944–1991. Władze państwowe i polityczne Polski według stanu na dzień 28 II 1991* (Warsaw, 1991), 362; Z. Błażyński, *Towarzysze zeznają. Z tajnych archiwów Komitetu Centralnego* (London, 1987), 144–156.

JANAS, ZBIGNIEW P. (1953–   ), electrician from Tractor Factory Ursus* near Warsaw.* A friend of Z. Bujak,* Janas was involved in the activities of the democratic opposition* in the late 1970s. He cooperated with the Workers' Defense Committee (KOR),* helped to establish Solidarity* in his factory, and after the imposition of Martial Law* distinguished himself as a member of the underground Executive Committee of the Mazovian region of Solidarity. Elected to the Sejm* in 1989, he represented the Democratic Union (UD)* and then the Freedom Union (UW).* *Who's Who in the Socialist Countries of Europe*, ed. by J. Stroynowski, vol. 2 (Munich, 1989), 483; *Kto jest kim w polityce polskiej*, ed. by R. Ignasiak (Warsaw, 1993), 111.

JANKOWSKI, HENRYK (1936–   ), parish priest of St. Brigida parish in Gdańsk* and personal friend of L. Wałęsa.* Jankowski served as chaplain of the Lenin Shipyard in Gdańsk during the 1980 strike and, later, as chaplain of Gdańsk Solidarity,* but his way of life prompted criticism and his anti-Semitic remarks in June 1995 caused an international outrage. *Who's Who in the Socialist Countries of Europe*, ed. by J. Stroynowski, vol. 2 (Munich, 1989), 487; *Rodem z Solidarności*, ed. by B. Kopka and R. Żelichowski (Warsaw, 1997), 55–79.

JANOWICZ, SOKRAT (1936–   ), prolific writer and Belorussian activist in Poland. A member of, and later a leader of, the Belorussian Social-Cultural Association (BTSK), he was involved in several independent initiatives and was persecuted by state authorities. President of the Belorussian Democratic Association since 1990, he is one of the most important leader of the Belorussian national minority in Poland. *Kto jest kim w Polsce* (Warsaw, 1993), 243.

JANOWSKI, GABRIEL (1941–   ), activist of Rural Solidarity* and member of the Civic Committee,* he was elected to the Senate* in 1989 and served as Minister of Agriculture in the government of H. Suchocka.* G. Sanford and A. Gozdecka-Sanford, *Historical Dictionary of Poland* (Metuchen, N.J., 1994), 86.

JAROSZEWICZ, PIOTR (1909–92), Premier* from December 23, 1970, to February 18, 1980. A teacher and a director of an elementary school in interwar Poland, he volunteered to the communist-controlled First Polish Army* in the USSR in 1943. In 1944 he became a deputy commander and the head political officer of this army. A member of the Polish Workers' Party (PPR)* from 1944, he was appointed a deputy chief of the Political-Educational Direction of the Polish Army in 1945; soon after he became Deputy Minister of Defense. A member of the Party Central Committee* from 1948 and the Politburo* from 1964, he served as a deputy chairman of the State Planning Committee from 1950 and, during 1952–70, as a Deputy Premier. In addition, during 1954–56 he was the Minister of Coal Mining. During 1955–70 he served in Moscow as Polish representative to Comecon* and as a member of its Executive Committee. During the December 1970 events,* Jaroszewicz became a full Politburo member and the Premier. Considered an autocratic soviet viceroy in Poland—Moscow did not trust Gierek completely—he became one of the most controversial politicians even among the ruling communists as early as his prime ministerial tenure. In 1980–81 he was removed from his positions and the Party and was interrogated by the Grabski* Commission. Declared one of those responsible for the 1976 events, for discrediting communism in Poland, and disliked by even his former colleagues, he was accused before the State Tribunal* in February 1984. Due to the July 1984 amnesty, the case against him was closed. Jaroszewicz and his wife were brutally killed in their villa, allegedly by robbers. *Who's Who in the Socialist Countries of Europe*, ed. by J. Stroynowski, vol. 2 (Munich, 1989), 490; T. Mołdawa, *Ludzie Władzy 1944–1991. Władze państwowe i polityczne*

Polski według stanu na dzień 28 II 1991 (Warsaw, 1991), 364; Z. Błażyński, *Towarzysze zeznają. Z tajnych archiwów Komitetu Centralnego* (London, 1987), 46–60.

JARUZELSKI, WOJCIECH (1923–   ), general and politician, known for imposing Martial Law* in Poland on December 13, 1981. Born to a noble landowner in the Lublin* region, he received primary and secondary education at a Jesuit school in Warsaw.* In 1939, after the outbreak of war, he moved with his family to Lithuania. In 1940, following the Soviet occupation of Lithuania, he was deported to Siberia with his entire family. His parents perished in a labor camp, and he worked as a lumberman and as a coal miner in Soviet Kazakhstan. In 1943 he joined the communist-controlled Polish Army* and participated in all its campaigns, including the liberation of Warsaw and the conquest of Berlin. After the war he fought the anti-communist guerrillas in Poland, and in 1947 he joined the Polish Workers' Party (PPR).* Educated in military academies in the Soviet Union and in Poland, he was appointed Poland's youngest general in 1956. He advanced steadily in the military becoming head of the Main Political Department (1960–65), Deputy Minister of Defense (1962–68), chief of staff (1965–68), and Minister of Defense (1968–83). Throughout his career he maintained a strong position both in the Polish Army and in the Communist Party of Poland (KPP). He was a member of the PPR in 1947–48 and the Polish United Workers' Party (PZPR)* during 1948–90. After the December 1970 events he was given full membership in the Politburo* (1971–89). Facing a deep political and economic crisis in Poland in 1980, Polish ruling circles chose Jaruzelski as the best candidate to stop the erosion of the communist system. On February 11, 1981, he became Premier,* a position he held until November 6, 1985; in October 1981 he replaced S. Kania* as First Secretary of the Central Committee* until 1989. Holding these posts, Jaruzelski became the most powerful person in Poland. He was considered the strong man of its communist regime; his fierce ambition, personal abilities, and long years of experience as the chief of the Polish Army contributed to that opinion. Yet he was not able to ease the confrontation with Solidarity,* and it appears that he did not control those segments of the state-Party apparatus hostile to the democratic opposition* in Poland. On December 13, 1981, Jaruzelski announced imposition of Martial Law and became head of the Military Council of National Salvation (WRON)* until July 1983. He remained commander-in-chief and chairman of the National Defense Committee (KOK) until 1990. After 1983 Jaruzelski tried to initiate a dialogue with moderate members of the opposition.* When M. Gorbachev declared his *perestroika* policy in the mid 1980s, Jaruzelski obtained more freedom for political maneuvers. He was instrumental in bringing to life the Round Table Negotiations* in 1989 and participated in the peaceful transformation from communism to democracy. Chairman of the State Council (Rada Państwa)* since 1985, he became President* of Poland (July 1989–December 1990). Later he retired from politics to concentrate on writing. Jaruzelski's historical role remains controversial. G. Sanford and A. Gozdecka-Sanford, *Historical Dictionary of*

Poland (Metuchen, N.J., 1994), 87; *Who's Who in the Socialist Countries of Europe*, ed. by J. Stroynowski, vol. 2 (Munich, 1989), 491; *The Cold War, 1945–1991*, vol. 2, "Leaders and Other Important Figures in the Soviet Union, Eastern Europe, China, and the Third World," ed. by B. Frankel (Detroit, 1992), 161; *Research Guide to European Historical Biography, 1450–Present*, vol. 2, ed. by J. A. Moncure (Washington, D.C., 1992), 1017–1022.

JASIENICA, PAWEŁ (1909–70), pen name of Leon Lech Beynar, journalist, historical writer, and outstanding Polish popularizer of history, whose books cover almost the entire Polish past. A Pole of remote Tatar* background, he graduated from the University of Vilna. During and World War II he was part of the anti-German resistance; after, he took part in in the anti-Soviet resistance. Eventually, he left his guerrilla group and contributed to the prestigious *Tygodnik Powszechny* ("The Universal Weekly")* as a publicist. In 1948 he was arrested and sentenced to death for his underground activities. Unexpectedly released, Jasienica was pressed to work for B. Piasecki's* group. Jasienica left the PAX Association* in the early 1950s to concentrate on writing, becoming a major activist of the Crooked Circle Club.* For his independence and his creative, non-Marxist writing, he was punished during the March events of 1968* when he publicly condemned the policies of the regime. W. Gomułka,* who disliked intellectuals and considered Jasienica the embodiment of this class, announced that Jasienica was released from prison in return for being a police informer. Jasienica, broken and depressed, died two years later. *Dictionary of Polish Literature*, ed. by E. J. Czerwinski (Westport, Conn., 1994), 161–162; A. Micewski, *Ludzie i opcje* (Warsaw, 1993), 64–67; P. Kuncewicz, *Agonia i nadzieja. Proza polska od 1956*, vol. 4 (Warsaw, 1994), 347.

JASKIERNIA, JERZY (1950–   ), Minister of Justice in the government of J. Oleksy.* A graduate and a faculty member of the Warsaw University* Law Department, Jaskiernia served as president of the the Union of Socialist Polish Youth (ZSMP)* during 1981–84 and as secretary general of the Patriotic Movement of National Revival (PRON)* in 1984–87. In 1989 and 1991 he was elected to the Sejm* as a representative of the Social-Democracy of the Republic of Poland (SdRP).* *Kto jest kim w polityce polskiej*, ed. by R. Ignasiak (Warsaw, 1993), 121.

JASTRUN, MIECZYSŁAW (1903–83), poet, writer, and translator. He made his poetic debut in 1924. He spent World War II in Lvov and Warsaw,* where he taught in clandestine schools and was a member of the communist underground. After the war he became an editor of the communist cultural periodical *Kuźnica* ("The Forge"). His best poems were written after the 1956 "thaw."* He also authored several biographical novels on great Polish poets. C. Miłosz, *The History of Polish Literature* (Berkeley, Calif., 1983),408; *Dictionary of Polish Literature*, ed. by E. J. Czerwinski (Westport, Conn., 1994), 164–165; *Encyklopedyczny Słownik Sławnych Polaków* (Warsaw, 1996), 135.

JASTRZĘBIE-ZDRÓJ, important coal mining center south of Katowice.* Originally a spa popular for its iodobromite waters, it grew rapidly in the 1970s, when large coking-coal deposits were discovered there. In summer 1980 Jastrzębie became a center of strikes and the venue for an important agreement between striking workers and the communist authorities. *Nowa Encyklopedia Powszechna PWN*, vol. 3 (Warsaw, 1995), 153.

JASZCZUK, BOLESŁAW (1913–90), Minister of Power Engineering Industry in 1952–56 and Machine Industry in 1957–59, ambassador to the USSR during 1959–63. He joined the Polish Workers' Party (PPR)* in 1942 and was elected to the Central Committee* in 1948 and to the Politburo* in 1964. After the March events of 1968,* Jaszczuk was promoted to top leadership of the Party and was responsible for economic reforms, which involved food price increases and provoked the December 1970 events* and the fall of W. Gomułka.* On February 7, 1971, Jaszczuk was removed from the Central Committee and retired. T. Mołdawa, *Ludzie Władzy 1944–1991. Władze państwowe i polityczne Polski według stanu na dzień 28 II 1991* (Warsaw, 1991), 365.

JAWORSKI, SEWERYN (1931–   ), worker and opposition* activist. Expelled from the Polish United Workers' Party (PZPR)* in 1956, he helped to organize Solidarity* in Warsaw* in 1980 and was a delegate to the First Solidarity Congress in Gdańsk* in September 1981. Interned after the imposition of Martial Law,* he continued his political activities and was arrested several times during the Jaruzelski* administration. *Who's Who in the Socialist Countries of Europe*, ed. by J. Stroynowski, vol. 2 (Munich, 1989), 493.

JEDYNAK, ANDRZEJ (1932–   ), communist manager and Deputy Premier in 1981–82. T. Mołdawa, *Ludzie Władzy 1944–1991. Władze państwowe i polityczne Polski według stanu na dzień 28 II 1991* (Warsaw, 1991), 365.

JEWS, national minority of approximately 30,000 people in the mid-1990s. Before World War II over 3 million Jews lived in Poland. Only between 380,000 and 500,000 of them survived the war, including 250,000–300,000 in the USSR, 20,000–40,000 in the German camps, 30,000–60,000 hidden among the Polish population, 10,000–15,000 in the woods, and several thousand outside Germany and Eastern Europe. About 2,500 Polish Jews managed to reach Palestine during the war. In 1944, when the Red Army* took eastern Poland, about 8,000 Jews gathered in the Lublin* and Białystok* regions. The Central Committee of the Polish Jews (Centralny Komitet Żydów Polskich [CKZP]) was created there. In January 1945 over 13,000 Jews fought in the Polish Army,* and many more fought in the Red Army. Between November 1944 and the end of 1948, about 54,000 Jews came to Poland from the prewar Polish Eastern Territories incorporated into the USSR in 1945. The Jewish population gathered mainly in large cities and the western "Recovered Territories,"* where civil war was absent and life safer. The communist authorities wanted to settle millions of people there to replace the original German population. Most Jewish survivors felt unsafe in Poland and did not want to live "on the graveyard" of their families. Before the end of 1945, about 25,000 Jews left mostly for Western Europe. Yet about 136,000 Jews returned to Poland from the USSR with the repatriation* of 1945–46. In summer 1946 over 250,000 Jews lived in Poland. A large number of them left with the emigration triggered by the Kielce pogrom* of July 4, 1946. By 1948 the Polish Jewish community numbered only about 100,000 people. During the Stalinist period* the borders* of Poland were almost totally sealed. In the late 1940s, many Jews joined the state-Party apparatus. However, the Israeli-Soviet conflict contributed to the worsening of the Jewish situation in Poland. At the beginning of the 1950s, a slow anti-Jewish purge started. The "Polish October" of 1956* opened the borders to the Jews. At the same time, about 25,000 Jews returned to Poland from the USSR. As a result of these migrations, about 35,000 Jews lived in Poland in the early 1960s, when the Jewish issue seemed to disappear from public attention. "The Jewish problem" was revived by M. Moczar* and his supporters in 1967, though, and during the March events of 1968.* In response to this "anti-Zionist" campaign, about 25,000 people of Jewish background left Poland. Only a small Jewish community of between 5,000 and 15,000 persons remained in Poland. In the 1980s and the 1990s this group began to grow as people returned to their Jewish roots, revived Jewish organizations, and restored synagogues.* I. Hurwic-Nowakowska, *A Social Analysis of Postwar Polish Jewry* (Jerusalem, 1986); K. Kersten, *Polacy, Żydzi Komunizm* (Warsaw, 1992); M. Chęciński, *Poland: Communism, Nationalism, Anti-Semitism* (New York, 1982); *Najnowsze dzieje Żydów w Polsce*, ed. by J. Tomaszewski (Warsaw, 1990).

JĘDRYCHOWSKI, STEFAN (1919–96), communist official. A graduate of Vilna University and a member of leftist organizations close to the Communist Party of Poland (KPP) in the 1930s, he spent World War II in the Soviet Union, where he was a member of the Supreme Soviet from 1941. In 1943 he became active in the Union of Polish Patriots (ZPP) and helped to organize the First Division of the communist-controlled Polish Army.* He joined the Polish Workers' Party (PPR)* in 1944—which became the Polish United Workers' Party (PZPR)* in 1948—and was a member of its Central Committee* during 1945–75 and its Politburo* during 1956–71. Until the mid-1970s he occupied several important positions. He represented the Polish Committee of National Liberation (PKWN) in Moscow in 1944 and the Provisional Government* in France in 1945. He also served as Minister of Foreign Trade in 1945–47, of Foreign Affairs in 1968–71, and of Finances during 1971–74. He chaired or co-chaired central state planning institutions several times and, from December 1951 to October 1956, was Deputy Premier. He retired in 1978 after three years as Polish ambassador in Budapest. *Who's Who in the Socialist Countries of Europe*, ed. by J.

Stroynowski, vol. 2 (Munich, 1989), 495; T. Mołdawa, *Ludzie Władzy 1944–1991. Władze państwowe i polityczne Polski według stanu na dzień 28 II 1991* (Warsaw, 1991), 365.

JOHN PAUL II (1920–), born Karol Wojtyła, Pope since October 16, 1978 (the first non-Italian Pope in 456 years), theologian, poet, and playwright. Born into the family of a professional military officer in the small town of Wadowice, southwest of Cracow,* he began to study philosophy at Jagiellonian University* in 1938. The outbreak of World War II interrupted his studies. During 1940–44 he labored as an ordinary worker in a chemical "Solvay" Factory in Borek Fałęcki near Cracow. Simultaneously, he began studies at Cracow's Archbishopric Seminar in 1942 and, on November 1, 1946, was ordained a priest. In 1945–48 he was a teaching assistant in the Department of Theology at Jagiellonian University, also studying at the Angelicum University in Rome and the Catholic University of Lublin (KUL).* In June 1948 he received his Ph.D. degree. During 1949–51 he served as vicar in a Cracow parish, going on leave in 1951–53 to write his *Habilitazionschrift*. Appointed docent in 1956, he later taught philosophy at the Universities of Lublin and Cracow. In 1958 he became an auxiliary bishop, and in 1963 the Archbishop of Cracow. Then in May 1967 he was made a Cardinal.

Elected the 264th Pope, the first Polish and Slavic Pope in the Church's history, he assumed the name John Paul II to emphasize that he would continue the policy of his predecessors. Fluent in a number of modern languages, he paid official visits to numerous countries and considerably strengthened the position of the Roman Catholic Church* in the Third World, where he appointed many bishops and beatified local historical figures who had distinguished themselves as Christians and martyrs. Involved in the anti-totalitarian democratic opposition* in Poland, on May 13, 1981, he was wounded by a Turkish assassin who was probably sponsored by communist secret services. Conservative on several issues, including abortion,* family planning, divorce, celibacy, and ordination of women to priesthood, John Paul II remains progressive in regard to social justice, democracy, and policies toward the Third World. T. Szulc, *Pope John Paul II* (New York, 1995); *The Cold War, 1945–1991*, vol. 2, "Leaders and Other Important Figures in the Soviet Union, Eastern Europe, China, and the Third World," ed. by B. Frankel (Detroit, 1992), 164.

JÓŹWIAK, FRANCISZEK (1895–1966), commander-in-chief of the Citizens' Militia (MO)* during 1944–49, member of the State Council (Rada Państwa),* and President of the Supreme Control Chamber (NIK)* during 1949–52. A worker and a peasant's son, Jóźwiak joined the Polish Socialist Party (PPS)* in 1912 and fought in the Piłsudski Legions during World War I. An activist of the Communist Party of Poland (KPP) from 1921, he spent several years in Polish prisons. After 1939 he lived in the Polish territories occupied by the Soviet Union, and in 1941 he joined the Bolshevik Party. In March 1942 Jóźwiak came to German-occupied Warsaw,* joined the Polish Workers' Party (PPR),* sat on its Central Committee,* and became the chief of staff of its People's Guard. In 1944 he took the same position in the People's Army. From October 1944 he commanded the MO and beginning in March 1945 also served as a Deputy Minister of Public Security. Later he went to the NIK and the State Council, served as Minister of State Control in 1952–55, and eventually served as a Deputy Premier. He retired after the "Polish October" of 1956.* T. Mołdawa, *Ludzie Władzy 1944–1991. Władze państwowe i polityczne Polski według stanu na dzień 28 II 1991* (Warsaw, 1991), 366; A. K. Kunert, *Ilustrowany przewodnik po Polsce podziemnej, 1939–1945* (Warsaw, 1996), 495.

JUNE EVENTS OF 1976, political crisis that contributed to the fall of E. Gierek.* Gierek's economic maneuvering failed in the mid-1970s. In 1976 Poland's economic situation became so difficult that communist leaders decided to raise prices. On June 24, without any warning or consultation with the population, Premier P. Jaroszewicz* announced in the Sejm* that food prices would be increased on average by 60% as of June 27. In response, on June 25 workers all over Poland stopped work in protest. A large demonstration by employees of the petrochemical complex in Płock was dispersed by police. In Ursus* near Warsaw,* workers at a local tractor factory tore up a railway track and stopped traffic on the Moscow-Warsaw-Berlin railway. In Radom* large-scale demonstrations developed into clashes with police. The Party's provincial committee building was set on fire, and many shops were looted. That evening Jaroszewicz announced withdrawal of increases and promised to consult with workers. The police nonetheless started an extremely brutal campaign against demonstrators and entire communities where demonstrations had taken place. Thousands of people were arrested and sentenced to imprisonment. Some were brutally beaten. Numerous persons were dismissed from their jobs and harassed. Police brutalities outraged Polish public opinion, and the Workers' Defense Committee (KOR)* was established to help the workers and their families. The June crisis of 1976 signaled that the Gierek regime was out of touch with the population; as a result of the events, the regime lost credibility and the approbation it had received from the workers in 1970–71. J. J. Lipski, *KOR: A History of the Workers' Defense Committee in Poland, 1976–81* (Berkeley, Calif., 1985), 30–42; *The History of Poland since 1863*, ed. by R. F. Leslie (Cambridge, 1980); J. Leftwich Curry and L. Fajfer, *Poland's Permanent Revolution: People vs. Elites, 1956 to the Present* (Washington, D.C., 1996), 109–166.

JURCZYK, MARIAN (1935–   ), right-wing Solidarity* leader. A worker and a participant in the 1970 strikes, he chaired the Inter-Factory Strike Committee in Szczecin* and signed the agreement with the government on August 30, 1980. Later he became the head of Solidarity, West Pomerania Region. During the 1981 Solidarity Congress, Jurczyk was a candidate for the union's national chairman but lost to L. Wałęsa.* Criticizing Wałęsa for his authoritarian methods and concessions to the communist regime, Jurczyk supported the extreme "Fighting Solidarity"* faction as early as 1980. After imposition of Martial Law,* Jurczyk was interned. Released in 1982, he was immediately rearrested and remained in prison until 1984. In 1989 he co-organized "Solidarity 80" and opposed the Round Table Negotiations* as an unnecessary and harmful deal with the communists. He also criticized the post-1989 reforms in Poland as a sellout of the country to Western capitalism. G. Sanford and A. Gozdecka-Sanford, *Historical Dictionary of Poland* (Metuchen, N.J., 1994), 95; *Who's Who in the Socialist Countries of Europe*, ed. by J. Stroynowski, vol. 2 (Munich, 1989), 506; *Kto jest kim w polityce polskiej*, ed. by R. Ignasiak (Warsaw, 1993), 121.

JUREK, MAREK (1960–   ), Christian-National politician. A graduate of the Poznań University History Department, he was active in the Movement for the Defense of Human and Civil Rights (ROPCiO),* the Young Poland Movement,* and the Independent Students' Association (NZS).* Jurek also contributed to several Catholic and underground periodicals. In 1989 he was elected to the Sejm* and became a deputy president of the Christian-National Union (ZChN).* Elected to the Sejm again in 1991, he was a leader of the ZChN caucus and a deputy chairman of the Parliamentary Commission for Foreign Affairs. *Kto jest kim w polityce polskiej*, ed. by R. Ignasiak (Warsaw, 1993), 121.

KACZMAREK, WIESŁAW W. (1958–), Minister of Privatization in the governments of W. Pawlak,* J. Oleksy,* and W. Cimoszewicz.*He became a member of the Polish United Workers' Party (PZPR)* in 1979, and later, in 1989, also joined the Social Democracy of the Republic of Poland (SdRP),* representing it in the Sejm.* A co-author of the economic program of the Democratic Left Alliance (SLD),* he was appointed a minister when former communists returned to power in 1993. A portion of Polish public opinion considered his performance inefficient and harmful; even the Polish Peasant Party (PSL),* the coalition ally of the former communists, wanted Kaczmarek to step down. *Kto jest kim w polityce polskiej*, ed. by R. Ignasiak (Warsaw, 1993), 124.

KACZOROWSKI, RYSZARD (1919–), last President* of the Polish Government-in-Exile* in London during 1989–91. T. Radzik, *Z dziejów społeczności polskiej w Wielkiej Brytanii po drugiej wojnie światowej* (Lublin, 1991).

KACZYŃSKI, JAROSŁAW A. (1949–), lawyer, politician, founder and leader of the Center Alliance (PC),* and twin brother of L. A. Kaczyński.* A graduate and faculty member of Warsaw University,* he joined the Workers' Defense Committee (KOR)* in 1976. Later he became an important activist in the Solidarity* movement. He headed a law section of the Social Research Center of Solidarity, Mazowsze Region, edited the underground paper *Głos* ("The Voice"),* joined the clandestine Solidarity leadership after imposition of Martial Law,* worked on the Polish Helsinki Committee, and was a member of the Solidarity Civic Committee.* He participated in the Round Table Negotiations* in 1989; that same year, L. Wałęsa* appointed him editor-in-chief of *Tygodnik Solidarność* ("Solidarity Weekly"),* an influential organ of Solidarity. In December 1990 he joined the presidential chancellery, became its Minister-Chief, co-organized the Center Alliance, and was a main player in the "war on the top."* He was elected to the Senate* in 1989, and in 1991 to the Sejm,* where he worked on the Justice and Constitutional Committees. One of Poland's most powerful and efficient politicians and a close assistant to Wałęsa, he was unexpectedly fired by the President* in October 1991. The Alliance received no seats in the 1993 parliamentary elections, and Kaczyński became a half-forgotten, second-rate politician. *Kto jest kim w polityce polskiej*, ed. by R. Ignasiak (Warsaw, 1993), 125; T. Torańska, *My* (Warsaw, 1994), 89–169; *Rodem z Solidarności*, ed. by B. Kopka and R. Żelichowski (Warsaw, 1997), 81–112.

KACZYŃSKI, LECH A. (1949–), lawyer, politician, President of the Supreme Control Chamber (NIK),* and twin brother of J. A. Kaczyński.* A graduate and faculty member at Warsaw and Gdańsk Universities, he cooperated with the Workers' Defense Committee (KOR)* from 1977. Later he joined Solidarity,* was interned after imposition of Martial Law,* and became a leader of clandestine Solidarity in 1986. He participated in the Round Table Negotiations* in 1989 and was deputy president of the Solidarity Country Committee during 1990–91. Elected to the Senate* in 1989 and to the Sejm* in 1991, he represented the Center Alliance* and served on the Administration and Internal Affairs, Social Policy, and Constitutional Committees. In March 1991 he became Minister of State in the presidential chancellery responsible for national security affairs. After a conflict with President L. Wałęsa,* he left the chancellery in October 1991 and during 1992–95 presided over the NIK. *Kto jest kim w polityce polskiej*, ed. by R. Ignasiak (Warsaw, 1993), 125.

KAIM, FRANCISZEK (1919–), Minister of Industry in 1967–70 and of Metallurgy in 1976–80, and Deputy Premier from December 1970 to February 1979. A member of the Gierek* team, he was removed from all his positions and the Party in 1980–81. T. Mołdawa, *Ludzie Władzy 1944–1991. Władze państwowe i polityczne Polski według stanu na dzień 28 II 1991* (Warsaw, 1991), 368.

KAMIŃSKI, ALEKSANDER (1903–78), activist of Polish scouting* in the 1930s, co-organizer of the underground Gray Ranks (Szare Szeregi) during 1939–40, important member of the anti-German resistance during World War II, and deputy president and president of the Union of Polish Scouting (Związek Harcerstwa Polskiego [ZHP]) during 1945–58. *Encyklopedyczny Słownik Sławnych Polaków* (Warsaw, 1996), 143; A. K. Kunert, *Ilustrowany przewodnik po Polsce podziemnej, 1939–1945* (Warsaw, 1996), 498.

KANIA, STANISŁAW (1927–), First Secretary of the Polish United Workers' Party (PZPR)* from September 6, 1980, to October 18, 1981. A son of a poor peasant family, he began to work for a blacksmith at the age of 15. In 1944 he became active in the resistance as a member of the Peasant Battalions. In April 1945 he joined the Polish Workers' Party (PPR)* and worked for many years in the communist-controlled rural youth movement and in the Party apparatus. In 1952 he graduated from the Party central school. In 1964 he was elected to the Party Central Committee* and in 1968 became its full member and head of its administration department. Elected a Central Committee secretary in April 1971, he helped E. Gierek* to consolidate his leadership. In 1975 Kania joined the Politburo,* where he was responsible for the Polish Army* and security affairs. He was first elected to the Sejm* in 1972. In September 1980, at the beginning of the Solidarity* era and after Gierek had a heart attack, the hastily arranged Central Committee Plenum elected Kania First Secretary of the PZPR. Kania supported a compromise with Solidarity, which provoked internal Party opposition to him. During the Extraordinary Congress of the Party in July 1981, Kania was re-elected First Secretary, but the growing conflict with Solidarity worsened his position. During a Plenum in October 1981, the leader of the hard-line opposition, T. Grabski,* stated that the Party led by Kania was unable to control the situation in Poland. Kania resigned and was replaced by Gen. W. Jaruzelski.* During 1982–85 Kania was a member of the State Council (Rada Państwa).* He left the Central Committee in 1986 and lost his parliamentary seat in 1989, when he failed to get elected as the candidate on the Party national list. *Who's Who in the Socialist Countries of Europe*, ed. by J. Stroynowski, vol. 2 (Munich, 1989), 524; T. Mołdawa, *Ludzie Władzy 1944–1991. Władze państwowe i polityczne Polski według stanu na dzień 28 II 1991* (Warsaw, 1991), 369; *Political and Economic Encyclopedia of the Soviet Union and Eastern Europe*, ed. by S. White (London, 1990), 148.

KANTOR, TADEUSZ (1915–90), theater director, stenographer, and painter. Founder of the experimental theaters Cricot 1 and Cricot 2, he significantly influenced the development of Polish and world theater. *Who's Who in the Socialist Countries of Europe*, ed. by J. Stroynowski, vol. 2 (Munich, 1989), 525; *Encyklopedyczny Słownik Sławnych Polaków* (Warsaw, 1996), 143.

KAPUŚCIŃSKI, RYSZARD (1932–   ), journalist, writer, and famous reporter who visited numerous remote parts of the globe and described them in many fascinating books translated into several foreign languages. His *Imperium* (''Empire''), *Wojna futbolowa* (''Soccer War''), and *Szachinszach* (''Shakhinshakh'') became instant best-sellers in the West. *Encyklopedyczny Słownik Sławnych Polaków* (Warsaw, 1996), 144.

KARKOSZKA, ALOJZY (1929–   ), Deputy Premier from May 1975 to December 1976 and Politburo* member from February 1980. He occupied several important apparatus positions, such as First Secretary of provincial Party organizations in Gdańsk* (1970–71) and Warsaw* (1976–80) but in November 1980 he was removed from all his posts. *Who's Who in the Socialist Countries of Europe*, ed. by J. Stroynowski, vol. 2 (Munich, 1989), 531; T. Mołdawa, *Ludzie Władzy 1944– 1991. Władze państwowe i polityczne Polski według stanu na dzień 28 II 1991* (Warsaw, 1991), 370.

KARNY, ALFONS (1901–89), sculptor and member of the Powiśle group. He specialized in portrait sculptures. *Who's Who in the Socialist Countries of Europe*, ed. by J. Stroynowski, vol. 2 (Munich, 1989), 532.

KARPIŃSKI, JAKUB (1940–), sociologist, political dissident,* and writer (pen-name Marek Tarniewski), wrote several important books about communism in Poland. *Who's Who in the Socialist Countries of Europe*, ed. by J. Stroynowski, vol. 2 (Munich, 1989), 533.

KASMAN, LEON (1905–84), activist of the Communist Party of Poland (KPP) before World War II, member of the Central Committee* of the Polish United Workers' Party (PZPR)* between 1948 and 1968, and editor-in-chief of *Trybuna Ludu* ("The Tribune of the People")* in 1951–54 and 1957–67. Z. Błażyński, *Mówi Józef Światło* (London, 1985).

KATOWICE (German Kattowitz), capital city of Katowice Province (województwo), covers the region of Upper Silesia. Located in the heart of large black coal deposits, the city has been an important center of heavy industry since the mid-19th century and an industrial capital (coal mining, iron and steel works, zinc and electromechanical manufacturing) of the People's Republic of Poland after 1945. It is also an important cultural center with five institutions of higher learning. Renamed Stalinogród in the early 1950s, it was not only the site of one of the Poland's largest concentration of workers but also the capital of the richest part of the country and, during 1957–70, the seat of a powerful Party faction, "the technocrats,"* led by E. Gierek.* In the 1970s the Huta-Katowice metal complex, one of the largest industrial projects of postwar Poland, was built there. In 1990 the city had 367,000 inhabitants and constituted a fragment of the large Upper Silesian metropolis, also including the towns of Sosnowiec (259,000 inhabitants in 1990), Bytom (231,000), Gliwice (214,000), Zabrze (205,000), Tychy (191,000), Ruda Śląska (171,000), and Rybnik (144,000). However, the entire region stood on the edge of an ecological catastrophe. In addition, several disadvantageous changes affected Katowice after 1989. Coal lost its importance as a source of energy. At the same time, Poland entered a free market economy and its government ceased to subsidize mining. Silesian industry lost some of its markets in the former Soviet Union, lacked financial means to renovate its installations, and was unable to compete with Western producers. As a consequence, Katowice and its region experienced a crisis. A large segment of frustrated workers supports the Confederation for an Independent Poland (KPN),* the Social Democracy of the Republic of Poland (SdRP),* and S. Tymiński's* Party X.* G. Sanford and A. Gozdecka-Sanford, *Historical Dictionary of Poland* (Metuchen, N.J. 1994), 97; K. Ullmann, *Schlesien-Lexikon* (Munich, 1979); *Kattowitz: seine Geschichte und Gegenwart*, ed. by H. Kostorz et al. (Dulmen, 1985); *The New Encyclopaedia Britannica*, vol. 6 (Chicago, 1990), 763.

KATYŃ, name of a village near Smolensk. In May 1940, in a forest outside the village, the NKVD executed over 4,000 Polish officers taken as POWs during the September Campaign of 1939. The Katyń massacre became an important political issue and a symbol of Soviet oppression in postwar Poland. Mass graves of killed officers were discovered by the Germans* in April 1943. The discovery was used by Goebbels's propaganda to compromise the USSR and to sow discord among the Allies. The Soviets blamed the Germans, and when the Polish Government-in-Exile* asked the International Red Cross to investigate the case, the Soviet government accused the Poles in London of collaboration with the Third Reich and broke off diplomatic relations with them. The Katyń affair was a convenient pretext. The Soviets had already begun to prepare Polish communist forces, who would take power in Poland after the war. The International Red Cross investigation and subsequent research showed beyond any doubt that the Soviets were responsible for the crime. Yet the Western Allies were not interested in pursuing the issue because they wanted to keep the anti-Nazi coalition strong. Soviet authorities held to their explanation, which was accepted by many scholars and public figures in the West after the war. In Poland, Katyń became the symbol of the Soviet lie, violence, and oppression. Communist censorship* prevented publicity about Soviet responsibility for Katyń. Indeed, the case was presented by the Polish communist mass media and educational institutions as a blatant example of malicious anti-Soviet propaganda. As late as 1985 the Soviets erected a monument at Katyń with an inscription referring to the victims of Nazi crime. Throughout the communist era private individuals tried to inscribe the date May 1940 on the symbolic graves of their family members and friends killed in Katyń; the authorities, however, persecuted those responsible for this "provocation" and changed the date to summer 1941, when the Smolensk area had already been occupied by the Nazis. In the late 1980s the Katyń crime became the subject of public discussion, and by October 1990 the Polish Prosecutor-General asked Soviet authorities for further investigation. In March and April 1990 they admitted that it was the NKVD who murdered the Polish officers. This admission came on the eve of a visit to Katyń by President Jaruzelski.* Then in June 1990 the Soviet authorities disclosed that more mass graves, containing the remains of Polish officers and civil servants, were located near Kharkov and at Mednoye near Kalinin (Tver). On October 14, 1992, the Russian President, B. Yeltsin, gave to the President* of Poland, L. Wałęsa,* a collection of documents concerning the Katyń massacre. Among the collection is a decree issued by the Political Bureau of the Bolshevik Party in March 1940, specifying the decision to kill Polish officers. U.S. House of Representatives. Selected Committee of the Katyn Forest Massacre, *The Katyń Forest Massacre: Hearings before the Selected Committee* (U.S. Government Printing Office, Washington, D.C., 1952); J. K. Zawodny, *Death in the Forest* (South Bend, Ind., 1962); L. Fitz Gibbon, *The Katyń Cover-Up* (London, 1972); *Keesing's Record of World Events*, April 1990, p. 37383.

KAWALEROWICZ, JERZY (1922–   ), film director whose films received many international prizes. His *Faraon* (Pharaoh) was nominated for the Oscar in 1965. *Who's Who in the Socialist Countries of Europe*, ed. by J. Stroynowski, vol. 2 (Munich, 1989), 538; *Encyklopedyczny Słownik Sławnych Polaków* (Warsaw, 1996), 147.

KĄKOL, KAZIMIERZ (1920–   ), Home Army (AK)* veteran, journalist, professor at the Journalistic Institute of Warsaw University,* and Minister of Religious Affairs in 1974–80. Although the communists' policy toward the Roman Catholic Church* was more pragmatic during his tenure, Kąkol was considered by the Catholics a symbol of the petty annoyances of the communists against the Church. *Who's Who in the Socialist Countries of Europe*, ed. by J. Stroynowski, vol. 2 (Munich, 1989), 515; T. Mołdawa, *Ludzie Władzy 1944–1991. Władze państwowe i polityczne Polski według stanu na dzień 28 II 1991* (Warsaw, 1991), 370.

KBW. See **Internal Security Troops.**

KC. See **Central Committee.**

KERN, ANDRZEJ P. (1937–), lawyer and Solidarity* expert in 1980–81. In 1989 he was elected to the Sejm.* Re-elected in 1991, he became its Deputy Speaker. He also helped to organize the Center Alliance (PC).* *Kto jest kim w polityce polskiej*, ed. by R. Ignasiak (Warsaw, 1993), 133.

KERSTEN, KRYSTYNA (1931–   ) historian and one of the best authorities on the communist period in Polish history. She has authored many articles and books, including her seminal *The Establishment of Communist Rule in Poland, 1943–1948* (Berkeley, Calif., 1991). P. S. Wandycz, "Historiography of the Countries of Eastern Europe: Poland," *American Historical Review*, Oct. 1992, p. 1023; E. Kridl Valkenier, "The Rise and Decline of Official Marxist Historiography in Poland, 1945–1983," *Slavic Review*, vol. 44, no. 4 (winter 1985), 661–680.

KĘPA, JÓZEF (1928–   ), Deputy Premier during 1976–79, member of the Politburo* of the Polish United Workers' Party (PZPR)* in 1970–80 (full member from 1975). Initially an activist of the communist youth movement, he later occupied several important apparatus positions, such as First Secretary of the Warsaw* Party organization during 1967–76 and Minister of Administration in 1979–81. A member of the Gierek* team, he retired from politics in 1981. *Who's Who in the Socialist Countries of Europe*, ed. by J. Stroynowski, vol. 2 (Munich, 1989), 543; T. Mołdawa, *Ludzie Władzy 1944–1991. Władze państwowe i polityczne Polski według stanu na dzień 28 II 1991* (Warsaw, 1991), 371.

KIELANOWSKI, JAN (1910–   ), zoologist, member of the Polish Academy of Sciences (PAN)* and the Workers' Defense Committee (KOR).* *Who's Who in the Socialist Countries of Europe*, ed. by J. Stroynowski, vol. 2 (Munich, 1989), 550.

KIELCE, capital of Kielce Province (województwo) in central Poland in the region of the Świętokrzyskie Mountains. A medium-sized industrial center (metal, chemical, and mechanical machinery industries), the town is located on the Warsaw*-Cracow* railroad. During 1950–89 the number of the town's inhabitants grew by three times, reaching 214,000 by 1992. On August 7, 1945, a guerrilla unit of Freedom and Independence (WiN)* organized a spectacular operation against a local prison and freed 300 political prisoners. On July 4, 1946, the infamous anti-Jewish Kielce pogrom* took place in the town. G. Sanford and A. Gozdecka-Sanford, *Historical Dictionary of Poland* (Metuchen, N.J., 1994), 100; *Nowa Encyklopedia Powszechna PWN*, vol. 3 (Warsaw, 1995), 345.

KIELCE POGROM, anti-Jewish riots on July 4, 1946. The pogrom remains one of the most controversial topics in Polish post–World War II history and is described in many books and articles. On July 4, 1946, a rumor spread in Kielce* that the Jewish survivors, living in a "Jewish House" in Planty Street, had kidnapped a boy. The boy was found later, but the mob attacked the Jews* and killed 42 of them. Among the murderers were members of the Citizens' Militia (MO)* and the Polish Army.* One theory suggests that the riots were provoked by the communist secret police. M. Chęciński, *Poland: Communism, Nationalism, Anti-Semitism* (New York, 1982); B. Szaynok, *Pogrom Żydów w Kielcach 4 lipca 1946 (Wrocław, 1992); S. Meducki and Z. Wrona, Antyżydowskie wydarzenia kieleleckie 4 lipca 1946 roku: dokumenty i materiały*, vols. 1–2 (Kielce, 1992–94).

KIENIEWICZ, STEFAN (1907–92), historian, veteran of the anti-German resistance during World War II, professor at the Historical Institute of Warsaw University* from 1949, and member of the Polish Academy of Sciences (PAN).* He authored many important works on the 19th century. *Who's Who in the Socialist Countries of Europe*, ed. by J. Stroynowski, vol. 2 (Munich, 1989), 551; P. S. Wandycz, "Historiography of the Countries of Eastern Europe: Poland," *American Historical Review*, Oct. 1992, p. 1021; E. Kridl Valkenier, "The Rise and Decline of Official Marxist Historiography in Poland, 1945–1983," *Slavic Review*, vol. 44, no. 4 (winter 1985), 661–680.

KIERNIK, WŁADYSŁAW (1879–1971), one of the most important leaders of the Polish peasant movement. He joined the Polish Peasant Party (PSL)* in 1903 and served in several crucial Party and state positions during 1918–26. After the Piłsudski coup d'état, Kiernik remained a leader of the democratic opposition in Poland. Tried in the 1933 Brest Litovsk trial, he spent the years 1933–39 in political exile in Czechoslovakia. During World War II he was active in the anti-German resistance. After the war he became an important PSL organizer and leader. During 1945–46, he was deputy president of its Main Executive Committee, and during 1946–48, of its Main Council (Rada Naczelna). Between 1945 and 1952 he represented the anti-communist opposition in the Sejm.* T. Mołdawa, *Ludzie Władzy 1944–1991. Władze państwowe i polityczne Polski według stanu na dzień 28 II 1991* (Warsaw, 1991), 371.

KIEŚLOWSKI, KRZYSZTOF (1941–96), film director who gained the attention of an international audience with his poetic trilogy *Three Colors* and *The Double Life of Veronique*. He earned a place among the most acclaimed contemporary European filmmakers with his biblically inspired *Decalogue*. *Current Biography Yearbook, 1995* (New York, 1995), 301–305.

KIJOWSKI, ANDRZEJ (1928–85), writer, literary critic, and author of brilliant philosophical and historical essays. He published in many periodicals, including the prestigious *Tygodnik Powszechny* ("The Universal Weekly").* In the 1970s and 1980s he was active in the anti-communist civic movement, became a member of the Citizens' Commission of the Workers' Defense Committee (KOR),* and later participated in the Commission of Experts, during the 1980 strike in Szczecin.* J. J. Lipski, KOR: *A History of the Workers' Defense Committee in Poland, 1976–81* (Berkeley, Calif., 1985); P. Kuncewicz, *Agonia i nadzieja. Proza polska od 1956*, vol. 4 (Warsaw, 1994), 277–280.

KIK. See **Clubs of Catholic Intelligentsia.**

KIRCHMAYER, JERZY (1885–1959), general and military historian. He served in the Polish Army* from 1918 and, during World War II, was one of the leaders of the Home Army (AK).* He joined the Polish People's Army in September 1944 but was arrested in 1948 and sentenced to life in prison in 1950. Released in 1956, he became a research fellow at the History Institute of the Polish Academy of Sciences (PAN).* *System represji w Polsce, 1947–1955* (Warsaw, 1987), 188.

KISIELEWSKI, STEFAN (1911–91), composer, writer, publicist, and an outstanding contributor to the prestigious Paris *Kultura** and the Cracow* *Tygodnik Powszechny* ("The Universal Weekly").* A graduate of the Warsaw Conservatory in 1937, he participated in the September Campaign of 1939, the anti-German resistance, and the 1944 Warsaw Uprising. After the war Kisielewski moved to Cracow, where he edited *Ruch Muzyczny* ("Musical Movement"), taught at a conservatory, and contributed to *Tygodnik Powszechny*. In 1949 he was fired from all his positions and silenced for his critique of Socialist Realism.* He returned to work in 1955, and in 1957 he became a Sejm* deputy and a member of the Catholic Club *Znak* ("The Sign").* In 1965 Kisielewski resigned from his seat in protest against the policies of the communist authorities. When he called them a "dictatorship of the dumb" (dyktatura ciemniaków), in 1968, he was severely beaten by the police in retaliation. After 1989 Kisielewski enthusiastically supported the free market reforms and the Balcerowicz* Plan. During his lifetime he wrote more than 10 novels, thousands of essays, and several dozen musical works, including four symphonies. He was one of the most outstanding Polish intellectuals of the 20th century. C. Miłosz, *The History of Polish Literature* (Berkeley, Calif., 1983), 497–498; *Dictionary of Polish Literature*, ed. by E. J. Czerwinski (Westport, Conn., 1994), 176–178; *Who's Who in the Socialist Countries of Europe*, ed. by J. Stroynowski, vol. 2 (Munich, 1989), 557; A. Micewski, *Ludzie i opcje* (Warsaw, 1993), 29–33; J. Waldorff, *Słowo o Kisielu* (Warsaw, 1994).

KISZCZAK, CZESŁAW (1925–), a close collaborator and personal friend of Gen. W. Jaruzelski,* Minister of Internal Affairs from 1981 to 1989 and from September 1989 to July 1990, when he also served as Deputy Premier. One of the four communist ministers of the Mazowiecki* government, he left it with his three colleagues in July 1990. A son of a peasant family, he joined the Polish People's Army* and the Party in 1945. He graduated from the Polish General Staff Academy and the Soviet Voroshilov Academy. After serving mostly in the Department of Military Intelligence and Counterintelligence, he was appointed its chief in 1972. In July 1981 Kiszczak became a Deputy Minister and, in August 1981, Minister of Internal Affairs. In the same period, which came shortly before and immediately after the imposition of Martial Law,* he was included in the Party Central Committee* and the Politburo,* becoming a full member in 1986. Kiszczak was, like his chief, a controversial figure instrumental in organizing Martial Law and the entire Jaruzelski policy. A flexible and informal deputy of General Jaruzelski, Kiszczak contributed decisively to the arrangement of the Round Table Negotiations* and served as their vice-president. Immediately after the June 1989 elections* he was nominated as Premier,* but he failed to create a cabinet. *Political and Economic Encyclopedia of the Soviet Union and Eastern Europe*, ed. by S. White (London, 1990), 150; G. Sanford and A. Gozdecka-Sanford, *Historical Dictionary of Poland* (Metuchen, N.J., 1994), 100; *Who's Who in the Socialist Countries of Europe*, ed. by J. Stroynowski, vol. 2 (Munich, 1989), 559.

KLASA, JÓZEF (1931–), Party official and diplomat. A Polish ambassador to several countries and a member of the Central Committee* of the Polish United Workers' Party (PZPR),* he served as the secretary general of *Polonia*'s Association for Liaison with Poles Abroad. *Who's Who in the Socialist Countries of Europe*, ed. by J. Stroynowski, vol. 2 (Munich, 1989), 560.

KLD. See **Liberal-Democratic Congress.**

KLIMASZEWSKI, MIECZYSŁAW (1908–), professor of geography, rector of Jagiellonian University* during 1964–72, and Deputy President of the State Council (Rada Państwa)* from 1965 to 1972. T. Mołdawa, *Ludzie Władzy 1944–1991. Władze państwowe i polityczne Polski według stanu na dzień 28 II 1991* (Warsaw, 1991), 372.

KLISZKO, ZENON (1908–90), Sejm* Deputy Speaker during 1957–71, Secretary of the Central Committee* of the Polish United Workers' Party (PZPR)* in 1957–70, and Politburo* member during 1959–70. Kliszko was a close collaborator of W. Gomułka* during 1956–70 and shared his fate over several decades of their collaboration. A son of a worker family, Kliszko graduated from Warsaw University,* joined the Communist Party of Poland (KPP) in 1931, and worked for periodicals of the radical left. During 1939–41 he lived in the Soviet-occupied Eastern Territories of Poland. In 1941 he moved to Warsaw and co-organized the Polish Workers' Party (PPR)* and its People's Guard. From October 1944, Kliszko chaired the Personnel Department of the PPR Central Committee, and from April 1945 he served in its secretariat. Accused of ''rightist'' and ''national deviation,'' he was removed from these institutions together with Gomułka in September 1948 and, later, imprisoned. Kliszko returned to Party leadership and an active political life in summer 1956 as a man of revival and reform. He became the main Party ideologue and quickly proved to be a ruthless and conservative communist. After the fall of Gomułka, Kliszko, responsible in part for the 1970 massacre in Gdańsk,* retired from all his posts. T. Mołdawa, *Ludzie Władzy 1944–1991. Władze państwowe i polityczne Polski według stanu na dzień 28 II 1991* (Warsaw, 1991), 373; A. Micewski, *Ludzie i opcje* (Warsaw, 1993), 83–86.

KŁOCZOWSKI, JERZY (1924–   ), professor of history at the Catholic University of Lublin (KUL)* and an outstanding contemporary Polish historian. An activist in Solidarity,* he was elected to the Senate* in the June 1989 elections.* He represented Poland in several important international institutions, including the Council of Europe in Strasbourg. *Kto jest kim w polityce polskiej*, ed. by R. Ignasiak (Warsaw, 1993), 136.

KŁOSIEWICZ, WIKTOR (1907–   ), hard-line communist, member of the State Council (Rada Państwa)* during 1952–56, and chairman of the Central Council of the Trade Unions (CRZZ*) during 1950–56. A bricklayer and a member of the Communist Party of Poland (KPP) since 1928, he immigrated to France in 1938, joining the Polish forces in the West, to fight the Germans and after five years in German POW camps returned to Poland in 1945. In Poland he joined the Polish Workers' Party (PPR)* and served as First Secretary of its provincial organizations in Cracow* (1945–46) and Szczecin* (1946–49). During the Stalinist period* Kłosiewicz was an important Party leader. Excluded from the Central Committee in 1958, he occupied secondary positions until his retirement in 1976. T. Mołdawa, *Ludzie Władzy 1944–1991. Władze państwowe i polityczne Polski według stanu na dzień 28 II 1991* (Warsaw, 1991), 373.

KOCIOŁEK, STANISŁAW (1933–   ), Deputy Premier between June and December 1970 responsible, in part, for the massacre of workers in Gdańsk* and Gdynia* in the same year. An activist in the communist youth movement and a member of the Polish United Workers' Party (PZPR)* from 1953, Kociołek was considered by his bosses to be especially energetic and intelligent; he served as First Secretary of the Party's provincial organizations in Warsaw* (1964–67) and Gdańsk (1967–70). The 1970 premiership was the pinnacle of his career. Disliked by the public, he was sent abroad as ambassador to Belgium and Luxembourg (1971–78) and to Tunisia (1980). In 1980–82 he was again First Secretary in Warsaw; but later, during 1982–85, he served as ambassador to the USSR. *Who's Who in the Socialist Countries of Europe*, ed. by J. Stroynowski, vol. 2 (Munich, 1989), 574; T. Mołdawa, *Ludzie Władzy 1944–1991. Władze państwowe i polityczne Polski według stanu na dzień 28 II 1991* (Warsaw, 1991), 374.

KOŁAKOWSKI, LESZEK (1927–   ), philosopher, essayist, and contemporary specialist on Marxism. He joined the Polish United Workers' Party (PZPR)* in 1948, worked in its Institute of Social Sciences in 1953–55, and became an important party theoretician. Bitterly disappointed with communism, he began to criticize Party policies in the mid-1950s. In 1966 he was expelled from the Party, an immediate result of a speech at a students' meeting: Kołakowski declared on that occasion that he saw no reason to celebrate the anniversary of the "Polish October" of 1956:* "There is still no genuine democratic freedom in Poland, [and the existing conditions] make for a ruling group that is inefficient and devoid of a sense of responsibility to the people." In November 1966, twenty-two prominent Polish writers, all Party members, protested Kołakowski's expulsion in a letter to the Party leadership, and many of them returned their party cards. After the March events of 1968,* Kołakowski was removed from his university professorship and left Poland. Since 1970 he has been teaching and continuing his research at Oxford University. A prolific writer, he has authored many classic works on philosophy, theology, and Marxism, including *The Main Trends of Marxism. Who's Who in the Socialist Countries of Europe*, ed. by J. Stroynowski, vol. 2 (Munich, 1989), 579; *Who's Who, 1996* (London, 1996), 1100; C. Miłosz, *The History of Polish Literature* (Berkeley, Calif., 1983), 517–519; *Dictionary of Polish Literature*, ed. by E. J. Czerwinski (Westport, Conn., 1994), 186–187; *Yearbook of International Communist Affairs, 1966* (Stanford, Calif., 1967), 67.

KOŁODKO, GRZEGORZ (1950–   ), economist, professor at the Main Trade School (Szkoła Główna Handlowa), and Deputy Premier* and Minister of Finance in the cabinets of W. Pawlak,* J. Oleksy,* and W. Cimoszewicz* during 1994–97. A member of the Polish United Workers' Party (PZPR)* since 1969, he served as adviser to the president of the Polish National Bank during 1982–88 and studied in the United States as a Fullbright Foundation scholar in 1985–86. He participated in the Round Table Negotiations* on the communist side. In 1991–92 he worked for the International Monetary Fund as an adviser. He authored *Strategia dla Polski* ("A Strategy for Poland"), a comprehensive but controversial program of economic development, as well as many other books and articles. *Wprost* (Warsaw), April 28, 1996.

KOŁODZIEJ, EMIL (1917–   ), peasant politician and member of the State Council (Rada Państwa)* in 1980–85. T. Mołdawa, *Ludzie Władzy 1944–1991. Władze państwowe i polityczne Polski według stanu na dzień 28 II 1991* (Warsaw, 1991), 374.

KOŁODZIEJCZYK, PIOTR (1939–   ), admiral and Minister of Defense in the cabinets of T. Mazowiecki,* J. K. Bielecki,* and W. Pawlak* in 1990–91 and 1993–94. In November 1994, after a conflict with the chief of general staff, Gen. T. Wilecki, Kołodziejczyk retired from his post and from politics to serve as the chairman of the Sailing Association Poland. T. Mołdawa, *Ludzie Władzy 1944–1991. Władze państwowe i polityczne Polski według stanu na dzień 28 II 1991* (Warsaw, 1991), 374; *Kto jest kim w polityce polskiej*, ed. by R. Ignasiak (Warsaw, 1993), 138.

"KOMANDOSI," group of politically obstreperous young people who began to set the tone of the intellectual and political life of the Warsaw* student milieu before 1968. The name was chosen by the leaders of the Party organization at Warsaw University,* because the "commandos" used to participate in student meetings and ask politically "inappropriate" questions. Among its members were A. Michnik,* S. Blumsztajn,* and Jan T. Gross. J. J. Lipski, *KOR: A History of the Workers' Defense Committee in Poland, 1976–81* (Berkeley, Calif., 1985), 12–13.

KOMAR, WACŁAW (1909–72), general in charge of the Internal Security Troops (KBW)* since 1947, prepared the defense of Warsaw* against the Red Army* and Soviet-controlled Polish units in October 1956. A member of the communist youth movement during the interwar period, he was active as an executioner in the Communist Party of Poland (KPP), killing several persons sentenced as provocateurs by the Party leadership. In 1927 he left Poland for the USSR, joined the Bolshevik Party, went through military training in the Red Army, and operated as a Soviet agent in the West. He then returned to Poland and, in 1937, went to Spain to command several international units in the Civil War. He participated in the French Campaign of 1940 as a soldier of the Polish Army in France and was taken a POW by the Germans. Liberated by the Americans in 1945, he served as deputy chief of the communist Polish Military Mission in Paris; in December 1945 he was appointed chief of the second (Intelligence) Department of the Polish Army. In 1951 he was transferred to the position of the general quartermaster. Arrested in 1952, he was kept in prison without a trial until 1956. When released, he was appointed commander of the KBW. Then in 1960 he was transferred to the position of the director general of the Ministry of Internal Affairs, where he worked until his retirement in 1972. J. Leftwich Curry and L. Fajfer, *Poland's Permanent Revolution: People vs. Elites, 1956 to the Present* (Washington, D.C., 1996), 39; Z. Błażyński, *Mówi Józef Światło. Za kulisami bezpieki i partii* (London, 1985); J. Poksiński, *"TUN." Tatar—Utnik—Nowicki* (Warsaw, 1992).

KOMENDER, ZENON (1923–   ), leader of the PAX Association,* close assistant to B. Piasecki,* Deputy Premier in 1982–85, Deputy Chairman of the State Council (Rada Państwa)* in 1985–89, and member of the Patriotic Movement of National Revival (PRON)* from 1983. *Who's Who in the Socialist Countries of Europe*, ed. by J. Stroynowski, vol. 2 (Munich, 1989), 584; A. Kępiński and Z. Kilar, *Kto jest kim w Polsce inaczej* (Warsaw, 1985), 171–184.

KOMOROWSKI, BRONISŁAW M. (1952–   ), historian. Active in the Workers' Defense Committee (KOR)* and the Movement of the Defense of Human and Civil Rights (ROPCiO)* in the 1970s, Deputy Minister of Defense in 1990–1992, and member of the Parliamentary Club of the Democratic Union (UD).* *Kto jest kim w polityce polskiej*, ed. by R. Ignasiak (Warsaw, 1993), 139.

KOMOROWSKI, TADEUSZ. See **Bór-Komorowski, Tadeusz.**

KONWERSATORIUM "DOŚWIADCZENIE I PRZYSZŁOŚĆ." See **"Experience and Future."**

KONWICKI, TADEUSZ (1926–   ), writer, screenwriter, and film director. A member of Polish anti-German and then anti-Soviet resistance in his native Vilna region during World War II, he joined the Polish United Workers' Party (PZPR)* in 1949 and contributed to the development of Socialist Realism* in the early 1950s. Disillusioned with communism, he left the Party in the late 1960s to become one of the most outspoken critics of the corrupted and repressive system of "real socialism." His first film, *Ostatni dzień lata* ("The Last Day of Summer"), made in 1956, won the Venice Film Festival Grand Prix in 1958. Most of his books are devoted to Poland's cataclysms, the devastation of war, and the ideology of the second half of the 20th century. *Merriam-Webster Encyclopedia of Literature* (Springfield, Mass., 1995), 643; C. Miłosz, *The History of Polish Literature* (Berkeley, Calif., 1983), 499–501; *Dictionary of Polish Literature*, ed. by E. J. Czerwinski (Westport, Conn., 1994), 192–196.

KOR. See **Workers' Defense Committee.**

KORBOŃSKI, STEFAN (1901–89), lawyer, politician, and writer. A veteran of the 1919 defense of Lvov, the 1919–20 Polish-Soviet War, and the 1921 third Silesian Uprising, he was active in the Polish Peasant Movement during the interwar period. In 1940 he joined the leadership of the Polish underground state, and in March and April 1945 he served as the delegate of the Polish Government-in-Exile.* Temporarily imprisoned, he continued his political activities in the Polish Peasant Party (PSL)* after his release in 1946. He participated in the elections of 1947* and became a Sejm* deputy but had to leave Poland when threatened by the communist secret police. He immigrated to the United States, where he was active in the Polish community and wrote several important books about World War II and the postwar period in Poland. *Encyklopedyczny Słownik Sławnych Polaków* (Warsaw, 1996), 166; A. K. Kunert, *Ilustrowany przewodnik po Polsce podziemnej, 1939–1945* (Warsaw, 1996), 510.

KORCZYŃSKI, GRZEGORZ (1915–71), general, Deputy Minister of Defense in 1965–71, and member of the "Partisans Group" of M. Moczar.* Korczyński fought in the Spanish Civil War in 1936–38 and in the Polish Army in France in 1940. Later he returned to Poland, joined the Polish Workers' Party (PPR),* and helped to organize its guerrilla units. After the war he worked at the Ministry of Public Security. Arrested in 1951 as a member of W. Gomułka's* faction, he was rehabilitated in 1956 and joined the Party Central Committee* in 1959, only to be sidetracked at the beginning of the Gierek* period. *Encyklopedyczny Słownik Sławnych Polaków* (Warsaw, 1996), 167; Z. Błażyński, *Mówi Józef Światło* (London, 1985).

KOROTYŃSKI, HENRYK (1913–86), journalist and Party official. Editor-in-chief of the daily *Życie Warszawy* ("Warsaw Life")* in 1951–71, he served as a Sejm* deputy during 1952–80 and as a vice-chairman of the Union of Fighters for Freedom and Democracy (ZBoWiD)* in 1979–86. *Who's Who in the Socialist Countries of Europe*, ed. by J. Stroynowski, vol. 2 (Munich, 1989), 596.

KORWIN-MIKKE, JANUSZ R. (1942–   ), president of the Conservative-Liberal Party "Union of Realistic Policy" and, previously, of the Union of Political Realism (UPR).* Mathematician and philosopher by education, he was arrested for the first time in 1965 for signing the "Letter of 34."* Expelled from Warsaw University* in 1968, he was arrested again. He was a candidate during the presidential election of 1995* and received 2.4% of the vote. *Kto jest kim w polityce polskiej*, ed. by R. Ignasiak (Warsaw, 1993), 142.

KOSTRZEWSKI, JÓZEF (1885–1969), an outstanding Polish archeologist and founder of the "neo-autochtonous school," which claims that the Slavs were indigenous people in the basins of the Vistula* and Oder* Rivers. *Great Historians of the Modern Age: An International Dictionary*, ed. by L. Boia (New York, 1991), 485–486; *Encyklopedyczny Słownik Sławnych Polaków* (Warsaw, 1996), 171.

KOTARBIŃSKI, TADEUSZ (1886–1981), philosopher and logician, author of many textbooks, and creator of radically nominalist epistemology. Regarded by many as a moral authority, he signed the 1964 "Letter of 34,"* protesting against the cultural policy of the communist authorities in Poland. He taught at several Polish universities* and presided over the Polish Academy of Sciences (PAN)* in 1957–62. H. Skolimowski, *Polish Analytical Philosophy* (London, 1967).

KOTT, JAN (1914–   ), historian and critic of literature. He participated in the September Campaign of 1939, spent the years 1939–41 in Soviet-occupied

Lvov, and then served as an officer in the communist resistance. During 1945–48 Kott was an important contributor to *Kuźnica* ("The Forge"), a communist cultural and ideological periodical. A research director and a co-founder of the Institute of Literary Studies (IBL) during 1953–55, he taught at Wrocław University in 1949–51 and Warsaw University* from 1951. In 1967 he moved to the United States, where he is a professor at the State University of New York at Stony Brook. *Dictionary of Polish Literature*, ed. by E. J. Czerwinski (Westport, Conn., 1994), 202–204; *Encyklopedyczny Słownik Sławnych Polaków* (Warsaw, 1996), 174; C. Miłosz, *The History of Polish Literature* (Berkeley, Calif., 1983), 516–517.

KOWALCZYK, EDWARD (1924–), Democratic Party (SD)* politician and Deputy Premier in 1981–85. T. Mołdawa, *Ludzie Władzy 1944–1991. Władze państwowe i polityczne Polski według stanu na dzień 28 II 1991* (Warsaw, 1991), 377; A. Kępiński and Z. Kilar, *Kto jest kim w Polsce inaczej* (Warsaw, 1985), 185–196.

KOWALCZYK, STANISŁAW (1924–), member of the Politburo* of the Polish United Workers' Party (PZPR)* from 1973, Minister of Internal Affairs during 1973–80, and Deputy Premier in 1980–81. He was responsible, in part, for the brutal suppression of the revolt of 1976. T. Mołdawa, *Ludzie Władzy 1944–1991. Władze państwowe i polityczne Polski według stanu na dzień 28 II 1991* (Warsaw, 1991), 377.

KOWALSKA, ANKA (1932–), writer, dissident,* and founding member of the Workers' Defense Committee (KOR).* *Who's Who in the Socialist Countries of Europe*, ed. by J. Stroynowski, vol. 2 (Munich, 1989), 611; J. J. Lipski, *KOR: A History of the Workers' Defense Committee in Poland, 1976–1981* (Berkeley, Calif., 1985).

KOWALSKA, ANNA (1903–69), writer whose literary interests covered a wide spectrum. She wrote about 17th-century Poland, ancient Greece, the history of Wrocław,* and contemporary Poland. She is also remembered as a close friend and intellectual partner of M. Dąbrowska.* P. Kuncewicz, *Agonia i nadzieja. Literatura polska od 1939*, vol. 2 (Warsaw, 1994), 381–384.

KOWALSKI, WŁADYSŁAW (1894–1958), writer, veteran of the Polish Peasant Movement, Speaker of the 1947–52 Sejm,* and member of the State Council (Rada Państwa)* in 1947–56. T. Mołdawa, *Ludzie Władzy 1944–1991. Władze państwowe i polityczne Polski według stanu na dzień 28 II 1991* (Warsaw, 1991), 378.

KOZAKIEWICZ, MIKOŁAJ (1923–), sociologist, leader of the Polish Peasant Movement, and politically influential Speaker of the Sejm* in 1989–91. *Who's Who in the Socialist Countries of Europe*, ed. by J. Stroynowski, vol. 2 (Munich, 1989), 612; G. Sanford and A. Gozdecka-Sanford, *Historical Dictionary of Poland* (Metuchen, N.J., 1994), 104; *Kto jest kim w polityce polskiej*, ed. by R. Ignasiak (Warsaw, 1993), 147.

KOZŁOWSKI, KRZYSZTOF J. (1931–), senator and Minister of Internal Affairs. A graduate of the Catholic University of Lublin (KUL)* and a doctor of philosophy, he co-edited *Tygodnik Powszechny* ("The Universal Weekly")* from 1956. He participated in the Round Table Negotiations* and served first as Deputy Minister and then as Minister of Internal Affairs in the Mazowiecki* government between July and December 1990. He also represented the Polish Sejm* in the Parliamentary Assembly of the European Council in Strasbourg. He became a member of the Senate* in 1989. *Kto jest kim w polityce polskiej*, ed. by R. Ignasiak (Warsaw, 1993), 148; *Wprost* (Warsaw), June 16, 1996.

KOŹNIEWSKI, KAZIMIERZ (1919–), writer and journalist, who spent most of his career on the editorial staff of *Polityka** and, during 1982–85, served as editor-in-chief of *Tu i Teraz* ("Here and Now"), a regime periodical that tried to legitimize the policies of Gen. W. Jaruzelski.* *Who's Who in the Socialist Countries of Europe*, ed. by J. Stroynowski, vol. 2 (Munich, 1989), 615.

KPN. See **Confederation for an Independent Poland.**

KRAKÓW. See **Cracow.**

KRAŚKO, WINCENTY (1916–76), journalist, communist official, member (1959–76) and Secretary (1974–76) of the Central Committee* of the Polish United Workers' Party (PZPR).* He served as director of the Culture Department of the Central Committee during 1960–71, Deputy Premier in 1971–72, and member of the State Council (Rada Państwa)* during 1972–76. T. Mołdawa, *Ludzie Władzy 1944–1991. Władze państwowe i polityczne Polski według stanu na dzień 28 II 1991* (Warsaw, 1991), 379.

KRAWCZUK, ALEKSANDER (1922–), Home Army (AK)* veteran, professor of ancient history at Jagiellonian University* in Cracow,* prolific writer, and Minister of Culture and Art in 1986–89. *Who's Who in the Socialist Countries of Europe*, ed. by J. Stroynowski, vol. 2 (Munich, 1989), 623; T. Mołdawa, *Ludzie Władzy 1944–1991. Władze państwowe i polityczne Polski według stanu na dzień 28 II 1991* (Warsaw, 1991), 380.

KRĄG ("Circle"), independent publishing house established in Warsaw* in February 1981. It broke away from *Głos* ("The Voice").* It published several underground periodicals and books by such authors as K. Kersten,* Stanisław Swianiewicz, B. Cywiński,* and Jerzy Holzer, whose *Solidarność 1980–1981, geneza i historia* ("Solidarity, 1980–1981: Genesis and History") sold 10,000 copies. *Dictionary of Polish Literature*, ed. by E. J. Czerwinski (Westport, Conn., 1994), 89; D. Cecuda, *Leksykon opozycji politycznej 1976–1989* (Warsaw, 1989), 132; J. Karpiński, *Polska, Komunizm, Opozycja* (London, 1985), 115.

KRĄPIEC, MIECZYSŁAW (1921–), clergyman and philosopher, professor at the Catholic University of Lublin (KUL)* from 1954, and its rector during 1970–83. *Who's Who in the Socialist Countries of Europe*, ed. by J. Stroynowski, vol. 2 (Munich, 1989), 619.

KRN. See **National Home Council.**

KROPIWNICKI, JERZY J. (1945–), economist, Solidarity* leader, Minister of Labor in the government of J. Olszewski* in 1990–91, and Minister-Chief of the Central Planning Bureau in the cabinet of H. Suchocka* in 1991–92. A faculty member of Łódź* University, he was a founder and leader of Solidarity in Łódź. In 1981 he was elected to the Solidarity National Committee (Komisja Krajowa) and was imprisoned after imposition of Martial Law* in December 1981. In 1990 he helped to organize the Christian-National Union (ZChN),* becoming its deputy president. He was elected to the Sejm* in 1991. *Kto jest kim w polityce polskiej*, ed. by R. Ignasiak (Warsaw, 1993), 151.

KRÓL, KRZYSZTOF (1963–), a leader of the Confederation for an Independent Poland (KPN),* veteran of democratic opposition* in the late 1970s and the 1980s, and chairman of KPN's Parliamentary Club from 1989. *Kto jest kim w polityce polskiej*, ed. by R. Ignasiak (Warsaw, 1993), 151.

KRÓL, MARCIN (1944–), historian, writer, and translator. An editorial staff member of the prestigious *Tygodnik Powszechny* ("The Universal Weekly"),* he edited *Res Publica*,* underground in 1979–81, legally beginning in 1987 and as *Nowa Res Publica* in October 1992. Król authored many important works on Polish history and contemporary politics and distinguished himself as an animator of cultural and intellectual life. *Who's Who in the Socialist Countries of Europe*, ed. by J. Stroynowski, vol. 2 (Munich, 1989), 628.

KRUCZEK, WŁADYSŁAW (1910–), communist official. A member of the communist movement from 1929, he spent several years in the prisons of interwar Poland. From 1941 he fought in the Red Army.* Taken a POW by the Germans, he escaped, moved to his native Rzeszów* region, joined the Polish Workers' Party (PPR)* in 1942, and helped to build its apparatus in southern Poland. Arrested by the Germans, he went through Auschwitz, Oranienburg, and Sachsenhausen. In 1945 he returned to Poland, where he served as a local Party secretary in Poznań,* Bydgoszcz,* and Rzeszów. During 1954–81 he was on the Central Committee* of the Polish United Workers' Party (PZPR)* and, in 1968–80, in the Politburo.* A leader of the communist-controlled trade unions,* he served as chairman of the Central Council of Trade Unions (CRZZ)* in 1971–80 and Deputy President of the State Council (Rada Państwa)* in 1972–80. T. Mołdawa, *Ludzie Władzy 1944–1991. Władze państwowe i polityczne Polski według stanu na dzień 28 II 1991* (Warsaw, 1991), 380.

KRUCZKOWSKI, LEON (1900–62), writer, socialist activist, and communist official. He participated in the September Campaign of 1939, spent the war in a German POW camp, and returned to Poland in 1945 to serve as Deputy Minister of Culture (till 1948) and member of the National Home Council (KRN).* A member of the Central Committee* of the Polish United Workers' Party (PZPR),* he presided over the Union of Polish Writers (ZLP)* during 1949–56. His *Kordian i Cham* ("Kordian and the Boor"), published in 1932, showed the different fates of the nobility and the peasantry during the 1830–31 November Uprising; the work became a communist literary classic. C. Miłosz, *The History of Polish Literature* (Berkeley, Calif., 1983), 427; *Dictionary of Polish Literature*, ed. by E. J. Czerwinski (Westport, Conn., 1994), 219–221; *Polski Słownik Biograficzny*, vol. 15, 384–387.

KRYTYKA ("The Critique"), underground political quarterly of the democratic opposition* in Poland, published continuously from 1978 to the present. The first issues sold between 2,000 and 3,000 copies, were about 200 pages in length, represented a social-democratic orientation—in the West European sense— and were edited by S. Barańczak,* K. Bieliński,* M. Haraszti, S. Starczewski, V. Havel, J. Kuroń,* J. Lityński,* A. Michnik,* J. Walc,* and R. Wojciechowski. *Krytyka* was reprinted in the West by *Aneks*￼* Publishing House. At present *Krytyka* is among the most sophisticated political and social journals in Poland. *Dictionary of Polish Literature*, ed. by E. J. Czerwinski (Westport, Conn., 1994), 87; D. Cecuda, *Leksykon Opozycji Politycznej, 1976–1989* (Warsaw, 1989), 170.

KRZAK, MARIAN (1931–   ), economist and Minister of Finance in 1980–82. T. Mołdawa, *Ludzie Władzy 1944–1991. Władze państwowe i polityczne Polski według stanu na dzień 28 II 1991* (Warsaw, 1991), 381.

KRZAKLEWSKI, MARIAN (1950–   ), union leader. With a Ph.D. in computer science, he joined Solidarity* in 1980 and was active in underground organizations after imposition of Martial Law.* In 1989 he became a deputy head of the Regional Executive Committee of Solidarity in Katowice.* In 1991 he became national chairman of Solidarity, and in 1996 he was elected chairman of the National Council of the Election Action Solidarity. *Kto jest kim w polityce polskiej*, ed. by R. Ignasiak (Warsaw, 1993), 148.

KRZYWE KOŁO. See **Crooked Circle Club.**

KRZYŻANOWSKA, OLGA (1929–   ), medical doctor active in Solidarity* since 1980. After the June 1989 elections* she joined the Sejm* and became its Deputy Speaker. T. Mołdawa, *Ludzie Władzy 1944–1991. Władze państwowe i polityczne Polski według stanu na dzień 28 II 1991* (Warsaw, 1991), 381.

KRZYŻANOWSKI, JULIAN (1892–1976), literary historian, author of many textbooks and monographs, and member of the Polish Academy of Sciences (PAN).* *Dictionary of Polish Literature*, ed. by E. J. Czerwinski (Westport, Conn., 1994), 222–223; *Encyklopedyczny Słownik Sławnych Polaków* (Warsaw, 1996), 187.

KUBIAK, HIERONIM (1934–), professor of sociology at Jagiellonian University,* co-founder and director of the Polonia Research Institute (Instytut Badań Polonijnych). A member (1981–90) and a secretary (1981–82) of the Central Committee* of the Polish United Workers' Party (PZPR),* he also served in its Politburo* (1981–86) and directed an extraordinary Party committee, whose mission was to explain the course and the causes of the social crises of communist Poland. T. Mołdawa, *Ludzie Władzy 1944–1991. Władze państwowe i polityczne Polski według stanu na dzień 28 II 1991* (Warsaw, 1991), 382; A. Kępiński and Z. Kilar, *Kto jest kim w Polsce inaczej* (Warsaw, 1985), 211–234.

KUCZYŃSKI, STEFAN (1904–), historian, expert on the Middle Ages in Poland, and author of historical novels. *Who's Who in the Socialist Countries of Europe*, ed. by J. Stroynowski, vol. 2 (Munich, 1989), 640.

KUCZYŃSKI, WALDEMAR (1939–), economist, activist in Solidarity,* and adviser to T. Mazowiecki* and Minister of Privatization in his government between September and December 1990. Since 1991 he has been a leader of the Democratic Union (UD)* and its successor, the Union of Freedom (UW).* *Who's Who in the Socialist Countries of Europe*, ed. by J. Stroynowski, vol. 2 (Munich, 1989), 640; *Kto jest kim w polityce polskiej*, ed. by R. Ignasiak (Warsaw, 1993), 157.

KUKLIŃSKI, RYSZARD (1930–), colonel of the Polish People's Army* and U.S. intelligence agent. He joined the Polish People's Army in 1947 and, from 1963, worked in the General Staff. During 1976–81 he was the chief of its Strategic Planning Division, a liaison officer to the Soviet General Staff, and a close assistant to Gen. W. Jaruzelski.* He was also a CIA agent, from 1970, and on several occasions transferred crucial secret information to the United States, leaking the plans of a Soviet military intervention in Poland in 1980, for example, and of Martial Law* in 1981. Evacuated by the Americans from Poland in November 1981, he was tried in absentia and sentenced to death. The sentence was revoked in May 1995 by the Polish Supreme Court. R. Pipes, "Introduction to Ryszard Kukliński," *Orbis: A Journal of World Affairs*, vol. 32, no. 1 (winter 1988), 6–31; R. Kukliński, "The Suppression of Solidarity," *Between East and West: Writings from Kultura*, ed. by R. Kostrzewa (New York, 1990), 72–98; *Nowa Encyklopedia Powszechna PWN*, vol. 3 (Warsaw, 1995), 614.

KUKOŁOWICZ, ROMUALD (1922–), veteran of anti-German resistance during World War II, economist, sociologist, personal adviser to Primate S.

Wyszyński* and to L. Wałęsa.* He participated in the 1980 strike in Gdańsk* as a representative of the Polish Episcopate* and joined the Solidarity* leadership of the Mazovia region. *Who's Who in the Socialist Countries of Europe*, ed. by J. Stroynowski, vol. 2 (Munich, 1989), 643.

KUL. See Catholic University of Lublin.

KULA, WITOLD (1916–88), historian of international fame, prolific writer, and specialist in economic history. *Who's Who in the Socialist Countries of Europe*, ed. by J. Stroynowski, vol. 2 (Munich, 1989), 643.

KULCZYŃSKI, STANISŁAW (1895–1975), professor of biology, one of the leaders of the Democratic Party (SD),* and Deputy President of the State Council (Rada Państwa)* in 1956–69. T. Mołdawa, *Ludzie Władzy 1944–1991. Władze państwowe i polityczne Polski według stanu na dzień 28 II 1991* (Warsaw, 1991), 383.

KULERSKI, WIKTOR (1935–   ), teacher and one of the leaders of Solidarity* in the 1980s. Active in the Workers' Defense Committee (KOR)* and the democratic opposition* in the late 1970s, he served as Deputy Minister of Education in the cabinet of T. Mazowiecki.* T. Torańska, *My* (Warsaw, 1994), 171–215; *Kto jest kim w polityce polskiej*, ed. by R. Ignasiak (Warsaw, 1993), 159.

KULTURA ("Culture"), weekly devoted to literature and politics, published in Warsaw* during 1963–81 and edited by J. Wilhelmi* in 1963–73 and Dominik Horodyński in 1973–81. It resulted from a merger of *Przegląd Kulturalny* ("The Cultural Review") and *Nowa Kultura* ("The New Culture"). Sympathetic to Solidarity,* *Kultura* was dissolved after imposition of Martial Law* in December 1981. J. Karpiński, *Polska, Komunizm, Opozycja* (London, 1985), 122.

KULTURA ("Culture"), Polish émigré monthly published in Rome in 1947, since 1948 in Paris (Maisson-Laffitte). Created by J. Giedroyc,* *Kultura* has been a forum of free thought for several generations of Poles both in Poland and abroad. Since 1956 the library of *Kultura* began publishing books and documents and, since 1962, *Zeszyty Historyczne* ("Historical Notebooks"). Fiercely fought by the communists, *Kultura* was smuggled into Poland and managed to influence Polish political and cultural life by introducing Poles to new subjects and points of view forbidden by censorship.* J. Karpiński, *Polska, Komunizm, Opozycja* (London, 1985), 122; *Zostało tylko słowo . . . Wybór tekstów o "Kulturze" Paryskiej i jej twórcach* (Lublin, 1990).

KUŁAJ, JAN (1950–   ), farmer, member of the United Peasant Party (ZSL)* from 1979, co-founder and leader of Rural Solidarity.* *Who's Who in the Socialist Countries of Europe*, ed. by J. Stroynowski, vol. 2 (Munich, 1989), 643.

KUNCEWICZOWA, MARIA (1899–1989), writer and essayist, leading representative of feminist literature in Poland, author of penetrating psychological works, such as her best-known novel *Cudzoziemka* ("The Stranger"). In 1939 she escaped to Paris; during 1940–56 she lived in London, and later in Poland and the United States, where she taught at the University of Chicago in 1961–64. *Dictionary of Polish Literature*, ed. by E. J. Czerwinski (Westport, Conn., 1994), 224–225; *Encyklopedyczny Słownik Sławnych Polaków* (Warsaw, 1996), 193; C. Miłosz, *The History of Polish Literature* (Berkeley, Calif., 1983), 430–431.

KUNICKI-GOLDFINGER, WŁADYSŁAW (1916–96), microbiologist, professor at Warsaw University,* and member of the Polish Academy of Sciences (PAN).* He belonged to the Polish Socialist Party (PPS)* before 1948. In the 1970s, he engaged in activities of the democratic opposition.* He signed the 1976 protest against constitutional changes, co-founded the Flying University* in 1978, and participated in numerous actions defending intellectual and human rights in Poland. Interned after imposition of Martial Law,* he helped to reestablish the PPS in November 1987. *Who's Who in the Socialist Countries of Europe*, ed. by J. Stroynowski, vol. 2 (Munich, 1989), 647.

KURATOWSKA, ZOFIA (1931–   ), professor of medicine and leader of a liberal wing of the Democratic Union (UD),* later the Freedom Union (UW).* During 1980–81 she chaired a Solidarity* organization of the employees of the health system of Warsaw's* Ochota district. After imposition of Martial Law,* she continued her Solidarity activities underground. Persecuted for her political involvement, she participated in the Round Table Negotiations* as a Solidarity expert on health system problems. Elected to the Senate* in 1989, she represented Warsaw Province and served as Deputy Speaker during the first and third terms. T. Mołdawa, *Ludzie Władzy 1944–1991. Władze państwowe i polityczne Polski według stanu na dzień 28 II 1991* (Warsaw, 1991), 384; *Kto jest kim w polityce polskiej*, ed. by R. Ignasiak (Warsaw, 1993), 161.

KUROŃ, JACEK J. (1934–   ), important leader of the democratic opposition* in communist Poland and deputy president of the Democratic Union (UD),* later the Freedom Union (UW).* Born into an intelligentsia family in Lvov, he joined the communist Union of Polish Youth (ZMP)* in 1949 and the Polish United Workers' Party (PZPR)* in 1953. Several months later he was expelled from the Party for ideological reasons and for his refusal to write a self-criticism. In 1954 he became involved in communist scouting* and formed the General Walter Teams. During the "Polish October" of 1956,* he was readmitted to the Party. In 1957 he graduated from History Department of Warsaw University* and helped to establish an independent political discussion club. By the early 1960s, when de-Stalinization was over, Kuroń was bitterly disappointed with the Polish communist system. In 1964, together with K. Modzelewski,* he published an open letter to the Party leadership. In consequence, both authors

were arrested and sentenced to three years in prison. Soon after they were released, they helped to organize student protests in Warsaw; arrested on March
8, 1968, they were sentenced to a three-and-one-half-year prison term. Later
Kuroń reacted to the Constitution crisis of 1975 and with other intellectuals
signed an open letter protesting anti-democratic amendments to the Constitution.
In 1976 he co-organized the Workers' Defense Committee (KOR),* and in 1978
he helped to form the Flying University.* (In 1979 KOR was reshaped into the
Committee for Social Self-Defense (KSS-KOR) and helped to form first independent trade unions.) Involved in the strike campaign of Polish workers in
summer 1980, Kuroń became adviser to the Inter-factory Strike Committee
(MKS);* later he also advised the regional Solidarity branch in Gdańsk* and
the National Coordinating Committee. Interned after imposition of Martial Law*
on December 13, 1981, he was tried nine months later. Eventually, he was
released from prison under the amnesty* of August 1984. Altogether he spent
nine years in the prisons of communist Poland; his wife, also interned, died
when he was behind bars. Released, Kuroń continued his political activities: He
served as adviser to the underground Interim Coordinating Committee of Solidarity; in 1988 he joined the Solidarity Citizens' Committee.* In 1989 he participated in the Round Table Negotiations* in the Section for Political Reforms
and was elected to the Sejm.* In 1989–91 and 1992–93 he served as Minister
of Labor and Social Policy in the cabinets of T. Mazowiecki* and H. Suchocka.*
A prolific writer, he is one of the most popular politicians in Poland. J. Kuroń,
K. Modzelewski et al., *Revolutionary Marxist Students in Poland Speak Out, 1964–68*
(New York, 1968); J. J. Lipski, *KOR: A History of the Workers Defense Committee,
1976–81* (Berkeley, 1985); J. Staniszkis, *Poland's Self-Limiting Revolution* (Princeton,
N.J., 1984); *The Cold War, 1945–1991*, vol. 2, "Leaders and Other Important Figures
in the Soviet Union, Eastern Europe, China, and the Third World," ed. by B. Frankel
(Detroit, 1992), 189; *Who's Who in the Socialist Countries of Europe*, ed. by J. Stroy-
nowski, vol. 2 (Munich, 1989), 650; *Rodem z Solidarności*, ed. by B. Kopka and R.
Żelichowski (Warsaw, 1997), 113–134.

KUROWSKI, STEFAN (1923–   ), professor of economics at the Catholic
University of Lublin (KUL).* Persecuted for his scientific theories and ideas,
he served as adviser to Solidarity* in 1980–81, member of the Solidarity Civic
Committee,* and adviser to the President* of Poland in 1991 and to the Premier*
in 1992. *Who's Who in the Socialist Countries of Europe*, ed. by J. Stroynowski, vol.
2 (Munich, 1989), 650; G. Polak, *Kto jest kim w Kościele katolickim* (Warsaw, 1996),
198.

KUROWSKI, ZDZISŁAW (1937–   ), economist, leader of the communist-
controlled youth movement, and secretary of the Central Committee* of the
Polish United Workers' Party (PZPR)* in 1980–81. T. Mołdawa, *Ludzie Władzy
1944–1991. Władze państwowe i polityczne Polski według stanu na dzień 28 II 1991*
(Warsaw, 1991), 384.

KURYŁOWICZ, JERZY (1895–1978), historical linguist, 20th-century specialist on Indo-European languages, professor at universities in Lvov and, after World War II, in Wrocław* and Cracow.* *Nowa Encyklopedia Powszechna PWN,* vol. 3 (Warsaw, 1995), 634.

KUŚNIEWICZ, ANDRZEJ (1904–93), writer, poet, diplomat, and author of many subtle psychological and historical novels, including works devoted to the lost world of Habsburg Galicia. *Encyklopedyczny Słownik Sławnych Polaków* (Warsaw, 1996), 195; P. Kuncewicz, *Agonia i nadzieja. Proza polska od 1956,* vol. 4 (Warsaw, 1994), 36–41.

KWAŚNIEWSKI, ALEKSANDER (1954–   ), President* of Poland since December 23, 1995. A communist youth activist and a member of the Polish United Workers' Party (PZPR)* from 1977, he was involved in leadership of the Union of Socialist Polish Students (SZSP)* in 1979–81 and an editor-in-chief of two periodicals sponsored by the youth movement: *Itd* ("Etc.") during 1981–84 and *Sztandar Młodych* ("The Banner of Youth") in 1984–85. In 1985 he was appointed Minister without Portfolio in the cabinet of Z. Messner* and became president of the Committee for the Youth and Sport. In October 1987 he became Minister for Youth. In 1988 he held the same position in the government of M. Rakowski* and presided over its Social-Political Committee. He participated in the Round Table Negotiations* of 1989, representing the communist authorities in the section for trade union pluralism. After dissolution of the PZPR in January 1990, he joined the newly formed Social Democracy of the Republic of Poland (SdRP)* and was elected president of its Main Council. In March 1993, during the Second Congress of the SdRP, he was re-elected to the same position. In December 1995 he defeated L. Wałęsa* in the second round of the elections, received 51.72% of the vote, became President* of Poland, and left the SdRP. In addition, he chaired the Polish Olympic Committee in 1988–91, was elected to the Sejm* in October 1991, and headed the Parliamentary Club of the Democratic Left Alliance (SLD)* until December 1995. *Kto jest kim w polityce polskiej,* ed. by R. Ignasiak (Warsaw, 1993), 163.

KWIATKOWSKI, EUGENIUSZ (1888–1974), Vice-Premier and Minister of Finance before World War II, he served as the director of the Governmental Delegation for the Reconstruction of the Polish Baltic Coastal Region in 1945–47. J. Lerski, *Historical Dictionary of Poland, 966–1945,* with special editing and emendations by P. Wróbel and R. J. Kozicki (Westport, Conn., 1996), 286.

L

LABOR PARTY (Stronnictwo Pracy [SP]), political party established in 1937, opposed to the authoritarian regime in Poland. During World War II, the party was active in the West, in both the National Council (Rada Narodowa) and the Government-in-Exile,* and in occupied Poland, specifically, in the underground state. Two delegates of the Government-in-Exile, Cyryl Ratajski and Jan Stanisław Jankowski, were members of the SP. During the last months of the war, the party divided into two groups in Poland. One of these, led by F. Widy-Wirski* and known as Zryw (from the title of their periodical), cooperated with the communists. Its leaders received several attractive state positions, among them provincial governorships (wojewoda). On July 6, 1945, K. Popiel,* the president of the party, returned to Poland from London. He tried to rebuild the SP, but the communist authorities allowed him to do this only on one condition: that the pro-communist Zryw group become part of the re-established party. Popiel and his supporters accepted this ultimatum; the party was officially recognized by the authorities and received several seats in the National Home Council (KRN).* In July 1946 the pro-communist group, supported by the authorities, organized an interparty coup d'état to eliminate Popiel and his collaborators from the SP. On July 18, 1946, Popiel declared the party dissolved and, together with his supporters, resigned from the KRN. An attempt to establish a new Christian Labor Party failed. In October 1947, Popiel, threatened by communist secret police, left Poland. Leaders of the communist-dominated rump SP dissolved it in 1950 and asked its members to join the Democratic Party (SD).* *Słownik Historii Polski 1939–1948*, ed. by A. Chwalba and T. Gąsowski (Cracow, 1994), 210–213.

LABUDA, BARBARA (1946–), literary historian, faculty member of the Romance Languages Department of Wrocław University (1973–81), and politician. She helped to organize the Workers' Defense Committee (KOR)* and

served as an adviser and important activist of Silesian Solidarity.* After imposition of Martial Law,* she hid in the underground but was arrested and imprisoned (1982–83). In 1989 she was elected to the Sejm* as a representative
of the Solidarity Civic Committee.* In 1990 she helped to organize the Citizens'
Movement for Democratic Action (ROAD)* and, in 1991, the Democratic Union
(UD).* One of its most energetic leaders, she was reelected to the Sejm in 1993.
Later she distanced herself from her party, and in January 1996 she was nominated undersecretary of state in the chancellery of President* A. Kwaśniewski.*
Kto jest kim w polityce polskiej, ed. by R. Ignasiak (Warsaw, 1993), 165.

LABUDA, GERARD (1916–   ), historian, member of the Polish Academy of
Sciences (PAN),* and expert on medieval history and Polish-German relations.
Who's Who in the Socialist Countries of Europe, ed. by J. Stroynowski, vol. 2 (Munich,
1989), 659.

LAND REFORM. Property structure of Polish agriculture* constitutes one of
the most complicated problems of 20th-century Polish economy.* Several unsuccessful attempts were made to change this structure before 1939, when every
political party in Poland had its program of land reform. During World War II
the Polish Government-in-Exile* and the Polish underground state in occupied
Poland accepted the program of the Peasant Party (SL).* It proposed to expro-
priate without indemnities all land over 50 hectares belonging to a given person
and to use this land to create strong farms between 6 and 25 hectares large. The
communists, in contrast, intended to confiscate estates belonging to Germans*
and ''traitors of the nation'' (collaborators), to take surpluses over 50 hectares,
and to create smaller farms of about 5 hectares. On September 6, 1944, the
Polish Committee of National Liberation (PKWN) decreed implementation of
the communist system of land reform. The distribution of land went slowly.
Peasants did not trust the communists, nor did they consider their new masters
a legitimate power; they were afraid that reform was a temporary tactic, since
communist ideology supported collective farming. The first stage of communist-
organized land reform took place in the eastern and southeastern provinces of
post-1945 Poland, where the countryside was heavily overpopulated and land
was insufficient to create larger farms. As a result, new farms were often two
or three hectares large—too little to produce for the market. The second stage
of the land reform took place in central Poland in spring 1945, and the third in
western Poland (Greater Poland and Pomerania) in summer 1945. Only in western Poland were land estates over 50 or even up to 100 hectares allowed; there,
newly created farms frequently measured over 10 hectares. Very often, though,
the land reform progressed chaotically, directed primarily against the former
gentry, whose estates were confiscated even if they were smaller than 50 hectares. Numerous manors were devastated, and considerable cultural treasures
were looted or destroyed. The entire land-owning class disappeared, but the
structure of Polish agriculture was not improved. To the contrary, in eastern and

southern Poland arable land was even more atomized. The new structure was criticized by the Polish Peasant Party (PSL)* and other organizations of the democratic opposition* established in Poland in summer 1945. The communist program was based not on economic arguments but on political ones. The communists needed support in the countryside and received it, at least temporarily, by giving out land. For several months the Polish Workers' Party (PPR)* was of a predominantly peasant character in many regions. This support disappeared when the PSL became active, but the atomization of Polish agriculture became a fact. The collectivization* attempt of the late 1940s and the early 1950s failed, and the crippled communist land reform shaped the Polish agriculture for the second half of the 20th century. Z. Landau and J. Tomaszewski, *The Polish Economy in the Twentieth Century* (London, 1985), 187–189; *Słownik Historii Polski 1939–1948*, ed. by A. Chwalba and T. Gąsowski (Cracow, 1994), 174–179.

LANGE, OSKAR (1904–65), professor of economics, member of the Polish Academy of Sciences (PAN),* and chairman of the Economic Council during 1957–63. He joined the Polish Socialist Party (PPS)* in 1927 and belonged to its leadership after World War II. During 1938–45, he taught at the University of Chicago; in 1945–47 he represented communist Poland as its ambassador to the United States and, in 1947, as a delegate to the United Nations. In 1948 he became a member of the Central Committee* of the Polish United Workers' Party (PZPR).* He joined the State Council (Rada Państwa)* in 1955. During 1957–65 he was its deputy chairman. Serving as an economics adviser to many international organizations and governments, Lange developed an innovative theory of economic planning; but in Poland his reforms were stopped by W. Gomułka.* G. Sanford and A. Gozdecka-Sanford, *Historical Dictionary of Poland* (Metuchen, N.J., 1994), 108; T. Mołdawa, *Ludzie Władzy 1944–1991. Władze państwowe i polityczne Polski według stanu na dzień 28 II 1991* (Warsaw, 1991), 385–386.

LASKI, village near Warsaw* where Franciscan nuns maintain an excellent school for blind children. Since the 1920s Laski has been an important center of Catholic thought, where several outstanding Polish intellectuals lived and worked. *Nowa Encyklopedia Powszechna PWN*, vol. 3 (Warsaw, 1995), 675.

LASOTA, ELIGIUSZ (1929–   ), journalist and chief editor of *Po Prostu* ("Plainly Speaking"),* who distinguished himself during the de-Stalinization process and was elected to the Sejm* in 1957. *Who's Who in the Socialist Countries of Europe*, ed. by J. Stroynowski, vol. 2 (Munich, 1989), 668.

LEAGUE FOR THE DEFENSE OF THE COUNTRY (Liga Obrony Kraju [LOK]), government and army-sponsored organization popularizing military sports to improve Poland's defensive capacities. G. Sanford and A. Gozdecka-Sanford, *Historical Dictionary of Poland* (Metuchen, N.J., 1994), 108.

LEC, STANISŁAW JERZY (1909–66), poet and satirist, author of popular ironic and lyrical aphorisms. He went through a Nazi extermination camp in 1941–43, escaped, and joined the communist People's Army (AL). After the war he served in the Polish Political Mission to Vienna. In 1950 he left for Israel, but in 1952 he returned and settled in Poland. C. Miłosz, *The History of Polish Literature* (Berkeley, Calif., 1983), 519–521; *Dictionary of Polish Literature*, ed. by E. J. Czerwinski (Westport, Conn., 1994), 229–230.

LECHOŃ, JAN (1899–1956), poet and member of the Skamander group. In 1940 he settled in New York, where he co-organized the Polish Scientific Institute and co-edited *Tygodnik Polski* ("The Polish Weekly"). From 1952 he cooperated with Radio Free Europe.* He committed suicide in New York. *Dictionary of Polish Literature*, ed. by E. J. Czerwinski (Westport, Conn., 1994), 231–232; *Encyklopedyczny Słownik Sławnych Polaków* (Warsaw, 1996), 198; C. Miłosz, *The History of Polish Literature* (Berkeley, Calif., 1983), 397–398.

LECHOWICZ, WŁODZIMIERZ (1911–86), economist and one of the main leaders of the Democratic Party (SD)* during 1942–73. After World War II he served in several important positions, such as Minister of Food Supplies in 1947–48. Imprisoned by the Stalinist regime in 1948, he returned to the Sejm* and SD activities after 1956. T. Mołdawa, *Ludzie Władzy 1944–1991. Władze państwowe i polityczne Polski według stanu na dzień 28 II 1991* (Warsaw, 1991), 386.

LEJCZAK, WŁODZIMIERZ (1924–   ), miner, Party official, and Minister of Heavy Industry (1970–76) and Mining (1977–80). A member of the Gierek* team, he was expelled from the Party in 1981. *Who's Who in the Socialist Countries of Europe*, ed. by J. Stroynowski, vol. 2 (Munich, 1989), 676; T. Mołdawa, *Ludzie Władzy 1944–1991. Władze państwowe i polityczne Polski według stanu na dzień 28 II 1991* (Warsaw, 1991), 386.

LEM, STANISŁAW (1921–   ), an outstanding science fiction writer. The author of many books translated into numerous languages and made into films, Lem lives and works in Cracow.* *Dictionary of Polish Literature*, ed. by E. J. Czerwinski (Westport, Conn., 1994), 234–237; G. Sanford and A. Gozdecka-Sanford, *Historical Dictionary of Poland* (Metuchen, N.J., 1994), 109; C. Miłosz, *The History of Polish Literature* (Berkeley, Calif., 1983), 501–502.

LEMKO (Łemkowie), small ethnic group related to Ukrainians.* In post–World War II Poland the Lemko people lived in the Carpathian Mountains along the Polish-Slovak border. In 1947, during the Action Wisła,* most Lemkos were deported to the former German "Recovered Territories."* In the 1980s and 1990s a national and cultural revival started among the Lemko people. G. Lerski, *Historical Dictionary of Poland, 966–1945*, with special editing and emendations by P. Wróbel and R. J. Kozicki (Westport, Conn., 1996), 296; *Łemkowie w historii i kulturze Karpat*, vols. 1–2, ed. by J. Czajkowski (Rzeszów, 1992–94).

LEPPER, ANDRZEJ (1954–), radical populist politician and organizer of several independent peasant organizations since the late 1970s. His controversial "Self-Defense" (Samoobrona),* organized in 1989, twice occupied a building of the Agriculture Ministry in 1992, blocked freeways, threatened the Sejm,* and offended senior Polish state officials. Lepper, an owner of a heavily indebted farm, was a candidate in the 1995 presidential elections,* but he gained minimal support. *Kto jest kim w polityce polskiej*, ed. by R. Ignasiak (Warsaw, 1993), 166.

LETTER OF THE POLISH BISHOPS TO THE BISHOPS OF GERMANY, conciliatory letter published by the Polish Episcopate* on November 18, 1965. In 1965 the Polish bishops attended the Vatican Council and made an unofficial contact with the German hierarchy. The Poles decided to make a gesture of reconciliation toward the German bishops and invited them to participate in the 1966 millennium celebration.* They also proposed mutual forgiveness for wrongs suffered by both nations at each other's hand. The communist authorities of Poland were furious about the proposals. The letter, a long text of nine printed pages, describing the history of the Roman Catholic Church* in Poland and Polish-German relations, was never published. Communist-controlled mass media printed only one short fragment out of context: "We [the Polish bishops] are extending our hands to you, sitting in the chairs of the council which is drawing to an end, granting forgiveness and asking for forgiveness." The bishops, accused of high treason, bad taste, and interference in Polish foreign policy, were condemned during a virulent propaganda campaign, supported zealously by the PAX Association.* Primate S. Wyszyński* was denied a passport for some years, as a result. The incident constituted the worst conflict between the Roman Catholic Church and the state since 1956, and it negatively affected the millennium celebration. *Poland since 1956*, ed. by T. N. Cieplak (New York, 1972), 150–158; *The History of Poland since 1863*, ed. by R. F. Leslie (Cambridge, 1980),

LETTER OF 34, letter of 34 intellectuals delivered to the Premier* of Poland, J. Cyrankiewicz,* on March 14, 1964, by A. Słonimski.* The letter consisted of only two sentences: "Restrictions in allocation of paper for printing books and periodicals, as well as tightening of press censorship* are creating a situation which is endangering the development of Polish national culture. The undersigned, recognizing that the existence of public opinion, the right to criticize, the freedom of discussion and access to reliable information are necessary factors to progress, and, being motivated by civic concern, demand that Polish cultural policy be changed to conform the spirit of the rights guaranteed by the Polish Constitution and the national good." The letter was signed by J. Andrzejewski,* M. Dąbrowska,* S. Dygat,* Karol Estreicher, Marian Falski, A. Gieysztor,* Konrad Górski, P. Hertz,* L. Infeld,* P. Jasienica,* S. Kisielewski,* T. Kotarbiński,* A. Kowalska,* J. Krżyzanowski,* Z. Kossak-Szczucka, J. Kott,* Kazimierz Kumaniecki, E. Lipiński,* S. Cat-Mackiewicz,* J. Parandowski,* Stanisław Pigoń, M. Ossowska,* A. Rudnicki,* A. Słonimski, A. Sandauer,* Wacław Sierpiński, J. Szczepański,* W. Tatarkiewicz,* J. Turowicz,* M. Wańkowicz,* A. Ważyk,* K. Wyka,* and Jerzy Zagórski. These signatories were concerned about the drop in the number of literary fiction and criticism titles and were dissatisfied with W. Gomułka's* repressive cultural policies. The Letter of 34 was the first protest of this kind and provoked a furious reaction by the authorities, who persecuted, or at least harassed, the signatories. M. K. Dziewanowski, *Poland in the Twentieth Century* (New York, 1977), 189; *The History of Poland since 1863*, ed. by R. F. Leslie (Cambridge, 1980), 387; *Poland since 1956*, ed. by T. N. Cieplak (New York, 1972), 130–133; *Kultura*, no. 5 (199) and 12 (206) (Paris, 1964).

LEWANDOWSKI, JANUSZ (1951–   ), economist, a leader and co-organizer of the Liberal-Democratic Congress (KLD),* and Minister of Reprivatization (przekształceń własnościowych) in the governments of J. K. Bielecki* and H. Suchocka* in 1991–93. T. Moldawa, *Ludzie Władzy 1944–1991. Władze państwowe i polityczne Polski według stanu na dzień 28 II 1991* (Warsaw, 1991), 387.

LIBERAL-DEMOCRATIC CONGRESS (Kongres Liberalno-Demokratyczny [KLD]), liberal and centrist party dedicated to building a capitalist market democracy, established in February 1990. Among its leaders were J. K. Bielecki,* D. Tusk,* J. Lewandowski,* A. Glapiński,* and other liberals associated with the journal *Przegląd Polski* ("The Polish Review") and the organizers of the Congress of Liberals held in Gdańsk* in December 1988. During the presidential elections of 1990,* the tiny KLD supported L. Wałęsa,* who after his victory nominated one of the Party's leaders, J. K. Bielecki, Premier.* Bielecki's tenure helped KLD to gain recognition and popularity. During the elections of October 1991,* the party won 7.48% of the vote and received 37 seats in the Sejm* and 6 in the Senate.* Between December 1991 and June 1992 KLD remained in opposition to the Olszewski* government; in July 1992 the party joined the coalition that formed the Suchocka* government. Bielecki became Minister for Liaison with the European Community, and Lewandowski received the privatization portfolio. Public opinion began to associate KLD with the negative sides of the economic "shock therapy" and privatization. During the 1993 elections* the party gained only 3.99% of the vote, did not cross the electoral threshold, and received no seats in Parliament. In spring 1994 KLD merged with its long-time ally, the Democratic Union (UD),* to form the Union of Freedom (UW).* G. Sanford and A. Gozdecka-Sanford, *Historical Dictionary of Poland* (Metuchen, N.J., 1994), 109; B. Szajkowski (ed.), *Political Parties of Eastern Europe, Russia, and the Successor States* (London, 1994), 333.

LIBERALS. The liberals had never played an important role in Polish politics, although they were active in Poland before both world wars. The contemporary Polish liberal movement was rebuilt in the 1980s. In the early 1990s it split into two trends: The first one, represented by the Union of Political Realism (UPR),* stressed traditional moral values and based its program on the writings of F. Hayek and M. Friedman. The second, led by the Liberal Democratic Congress (KLD),* supported the separation of Church and state and emphasized the importance of privatization and the limitation of state involvement in economic and social life. *Nowa Encyklopedia Powszechna PWN*, vol. 3 (Warsaw, 1995), 729.

LINKE, BRONISŁAW WOJCIECH (1906–62), painter, sculptor, and illustrator who frequently took on contemporary political and social subjects. He devoted many of his works to the subject of the destruction of Poland during World War II. M. Dąbrowska, *Dzienniki powojenne 1945–49*, vol. 1, ed. by T. Drewnowski (Warsaw, 1996), 102.

LIPIŃSKI, EDWARD (1888–1986), outstanding Polish economist, member of the Polish Academy of Sciences (PAN),* and veteran of the socialist movement. In 1975 he left the Polish United Workers' Party (PZPR)* to help organize public protests against a new constitution proposed by the Party. In 1976 he joined the Workers' Defense Committee (KOR).* He was also active in the Movement for Defense of Human and Civil Rights (ROPCiO)* and other initiatives of the democratic opposition* in Poland. *Who's Who in the Socialist Countries of Europe*, ed. by J. Stroynowski, vol. 2 (Munich, 1989), 690; J. J. Lipski, *KOR: A History of the Workers' Defense Committee in Poland, 1976–81* (Berkeley, Calif., 1985).

LIPSKI, JAN JÓZEF (1926–91), literary historian and critic, veteran of the Home Army (AK)* and the 1944 Warsaw Uprising, political dissident,* and journalist. An organizer, activist, and chronicler of the Workers' Defense Committee (KOR),* he also contributed decisively to the development of Solidarity,* helped to rebuild the Polish Socialist Party (PPS)* in 1987, and was elected senator in 1989. *Who's Who in the Socialist Countries of Europe*, ed. by J. Stroynowski, vol. 2 (Munich, 1989), 691; G. Sanford and A. Gozdecka-Sanford, *Historical Dictionary of Poland* (Metuchen, N.J., 1994), 111; J. J. Lipski, *KOR: A History of the Workers' Defense Committee in Poland, 1976–81* (Berkeley, Calif., 1985).

LIS, BOGDAN J. (1952–   ), Solidarity* activist. Employee of the Gdańsk* port and various state enterprises in this city and a friend of A. Gwiazda,* he helped to organize free trade unions in the late 1970s, served as deputy chairman of the Strike Committee in the Lenin Shipyard, and participated in the negotiations between striking workers and communist authorities in August 1980. He then served on the Presidium of the Solidarity National Coordinating Committee. After imposition of Martial Law,* he went underground, becoming one of the most wanted political fugitives. He was instrumental in the activities of the underground Solidarity Provisional Coordinating Committee. A member of L. Wałęsa's Civic Committee,* he was elected to the Senate* in 1991. *Who's Who* *in the Socialist Countries of Europe*, ed. by J. Stroynowski, vol. 2 (Munich, 1989), 692; *Kto jest kim w polityce polskiej*, ed. by R. Ignasiak (Warsaw, 1993), 170.

LITERATURE. Writers have always played an important role in Polish life. They frequently substituted as political leaders and persons of state. Sometimes they were considered national spiritual leaders. Thus, literature is more important to most Poles than fine arts or music and reflects the complicated history of their country. After the catastrophe of World War II, most Polish writers wrote on subjects related to the disaster, often about their own traumatic experiences. Among such writers were J. Iwaszkiewicz,* Z. Nałkowska,* J. Andrzejewski,* A. Rudnicki,* J. Putrament,* J. J. Szczepański,* and T. Borowski,* who wrote about the war. Some writers, like T. Breza,* M. Dąbrowska,* K. Wyka,* and E. Osmańczyk,* put the war themes into a broader philosophical and historical context. Dealing with the memory of the war, or escaping from it, contributed to the spectacular development of Polish poetry (see, for example, K. I. Gałczyński,* L. Staff,* J. Tuwim,* A. Słonimski,* C. Miłosz,* or T. Różewicz*) and drama (see L. Kruczkowski,* J. Szaniawski, and J. Zawieyski*). Together with their cities and factories, the Poles were rebuilding their literary life after the war. As many writers returned from abroad, various literary groups and periodicals appeared. Yet this development was not totally free and spontaneous. Writers were initially left free to write in their own way; but the communists, who understood well the educational and propaganda importance of literature, gradually tightened their control over the "engineers of the souls" in Poland and, later, molded Polish literature in the "ideologically proper way." In 1949 Polish writers were forced to accept Socialist Realism,* the only accepted style of writing during the Stalinist period.* Works written in a different way had no chance of publication. Some writers, such as Stanisław Rembek, practically disappeared from public view. Literature became sterile, dull, and gray.

After the "Polish October" of 1956,* Poland's literary life entered a new phase. Writers began to settle accounts with Stalinism and, frequently, their own fascination with communism. Some émigré writers, such as W. Gombrowicz,* were allowed to publish in Poland or, like M. Wańkowicz* and S. Cat-Mackiewicz,* to return to Poland. In 1956 and 1957, censorship* was less oppressive, periodicals were full of interesting articles, and many books were published, written in a way unseen in Poland for a long time. New literary forms appeared at the hand of writers such as S. Lem,* an outstanding science fiction writer, and L. Kołakowski,* a master of the philosophical essay. Poetry developed rapidly with such leading poets as Z. Herbert* and W. Szymborska* and later S. Barańczak,* T. Różewicz, and A. Zagajewski.* The early 1960s also brought the golden age of Polish drama, developed by S. Mrożek,* S. Grochowiak,* T. Różewicz, and others. Yet the end of the Gomułka* regime and later the Gierek* period were not good to the literature. Censorship became once again oppressive, and several writers were forbidden to publish at all. The March events of 1968* decimated the literary milieu. In the late 1970s many writers published their works through underground publications.* Imposition of Martial Law* created deep divisions within literary society. Polish literature recovered partially from the crisis in the late 1980s, but it faced new challenges after the fall of communism. *Dictionary of Polish Literature*, ed. by E. J. Czerwinski (Westport, Conn., 1994), 62–71; C. Miłosz, *The History of Polish Literature* (Berkeley, Calif., 1983), 453–540; G. Sanford and A. Gozdecka-Sanford, *Historical Dictionary of Poland* (Metuchen, N.J., 1994), 116–118.

LITHUANIANS, national minority of about 10,000 people concentrated in the northern part of the Suwałki region around the small town of Sejny. The former county (powiat) of Sejny was 40% Lithuanian. In 1956 the Lithuanian Social-Cultural Association (Litewskie Towarzystwo Społeczno-Kulturalne [LTSK]), was established and attracted about 1,300 members. It publishes a Lithuanian-language quarterly, *Aušra*. Small colonies of Lithuanians also live in western Poland, near Gorzów, Wrocław,* and Słupsk. In 1990 the Lithuanian Society of Saint Casimir (Litewskie Towarzystwo Św. Kazimierza [LTSK]) was established; it continues the tradition of an interwar organization by the same name and concentrates on religious and national work among Polish Lithuanians. In March 1992 the LTSK was reshaped into the Association of Lithuanians in Poland (Stowarzyszenie Litwinów w Polsce). It continues to finance the Lithuanian language biweekly *Aušra* and the House of Lithuanian Culture in Puńsk. It calls for guaranteed Lithuanian representation in the Sejm,* for a nomination of a Lithuanian as deputy governor of Suwałki Province and governor of the Sejny district, and for bilingualism in administration in the Sejny and Puńsk districts, where Lithuanians have several representatives on local councils. S. M. Horak (ed.), *Eastern European National Minorities, 1919–1980: A Handbook* (Littleton, Colo., 1985), 59; J. Bugajski, *Ethnic Politics in Eastern Europe: A Guide to Nationality Policies, Organizations, and Parties* (New York, 1994), 359, 384; K. Podlaski, *Białorusini, Litwini, Ukraińcy* (London, 1985); K. Kłosińska, ''Mniejszości narodowe w Polsce,'' *Barometr kultury*, ed. by M. Grabowska (Warsaw, 1992), 53–63.

LITTLE CONSTITUTION. See Constitution of the Polish People's Republic.

LITYŃSKI, JAN (1946–   ), dissident and leader of the Democratic Union (UD).* Participant in the March events of 1968,* he was arrested and sentenced to two and one-half years in prison. A member of the Workers' Defense Committee (KOR),* editor of the underground papers *Robotnik* (''The Worker'')* and *Krytyka* (''The Critique''),* he was one of the most energetic Solidarity* activists during 1980–89. Interned and imprisoned in 1981–83, he was elected to the Sejm* in 1989 and served as adviser in charge of cooperation with the trade unions in the Ministry of Labor and Social Policy. A co-organizer and leader of the Citizens' Movement for Democratic Action (ROAD),* the Democratic Union (UD), and the Freedom Union (UW),* he was reelected to the Sejm in 1993. *Who's Who in the Socialist Countries of Europe*, ed. by J. Stroynowski, vol. 2 (Munich, 1989), 694; J. J. Lipski, *KOR: A History of the Workers' Defense Committee in Poland*, 1976–81 (Berkeley, Calif., 1985).

LIVING STANDARDS. As a result of several factors, such as concealed inflation, the standard of living in Poland is difficult to measure and to compare with that of Western countries. A large proportion of goods supplied to the Polish population would be unsaleable in the West. Many items considered bare necessities in Western Europe or the United States were unavailable to communist Poland. People had to spend a large proportion of their time queuing and spent large sums of money on the black market. The Polish authorities, ideologically motivated and pressed by the Soviet Union, used to invest most financial resources in heavy industry and neglected the food and light industries and the service sector. In 1948 Poland ceased to export food. During the Stalinist period* and later, during every political crisis, Poland experienced food shortages. Each new Party faction that came to power in 1956, 1970, and 1981 promised improved living standards and temporarily redirected a part of investments to the food and light industries. As a consequence, after 1956, and especially after 1970, real incomes and the standard of living rose in Poland. Yet very soon the authorities returned to their former policies, and both in the 1960s and the late 1970s life in Poland became difficult again. By 1980 the Polish economy reached a stage of permanent crisis; living standards deteriorated quickly in the early 1980s and later again in 1987. *Political and Economic Encyclopedia of the Soviet Union and Eastern Europe*, ed. by S. White (London, 1990), 156; *Słownik Historii Polski 1939–1948*, ed. by A. Chwalba and T. Gąsowski (Cracow, 1994).

LOGA-SOWIŃSKI, IGNACY (1914–92), close collaborator of W. Gomułka,* member of the Politburo* of the Polish United Workers' Party (PZPR),* chairman of the communist trade unions (CRZZ*) between 1956 and 1971, and member of the State Council (Rada Państwa)* during 1957–65 and its deputy chairman in 1965–71. Initially a construction worker, Loga-Sowiński joined the Communist Party of Poland (KPP) in 1935 and was active in its youth movement. In 1942 he helped to organize the Polish Workers' Party (PPR)* and became a member of its Central Committee* in 1943. He was sidetracked as a collaborator of Gomułka in 1948, but in 1956 Loga-Sowiński returned with him as one of the most powerful men in Poland. After the fall of the Gomułka regime in 1970, Loga-Sowiński was sidetracked again and sent as ambassador to Turkey. G. Sanford and A. Gozdecka-Sanford, *Historical Dictionary of Poland* (Metuchen, N.J., 1994), 119; T. Mołdawa, *Ludzie Władzy 1944–1991. Władze państwowe i polityczne Polski według stanu na dzień 28 II 1991* (Warsaw, 1991), 385–386.

LORANC, WŁADYSŁAW (1930–   ), minister in charge of religions in 1987–88. A member of the Party from 1952, he worked in its various organizations responsible for ideology and propaganda and chaired the Radio and TV* Committee in 1981–82. *Who's Who in the Socialist Countries of Europe*, ed. by J. Stroynowski, vol. 2 (Munich, 1989), 698; T. Mołdawa, *Ludzie Władzy 1944–1991. Władze państwowe i polityczne Polski według stanu na dzień 28 II 1991* (Warsaw, 1991), 388.

LORENTZ, STANISŁAW (1899–1991), historian of art and museologist. A graduate and a faculty member of Vilna University, he became a deputy director of the National Museum in Warsaw* in 1935. The following year he was appointed director of the National Museum, serving in this position until 1982 (with a break during World War II). During the war he participated in the anti-German resistance and was in charge of salvaging Polish historical and art treasures. During 1945–51 he chaired the Main Directorate of Museums and Conservation of Historical Monuments. A member of the Polish Academy of Sciences (PAN)* and several similar foreign institutions, he was a professor at Warsaw University* from 1947, specializing in art history with a concentration on the Enlightenment. Beginning in 1971 he served as a deputy chairman of the Citizens' Committee for Reconstruction of the Royal Castle in Warsaw. *Who's Who in the Socialist Countries of Europe*, ed. by J. Stroynowski, vol. 2 (Munich, 1989), 698; M. Dąbrowska, *Dzienniki powojenne 1945–49*, ed. by T. Drewnowski (Warsaw, 1996), 60.

LOS, Warsaw underground publishing house active in 1984–86. D. Cecuda, *Leksykon Opozycji Politycznej 1976–1989* (Warsaw, 1989), 133.

LUBIN, town in Lower Silesia in the Legnica region, major center of copper mining and industry. After World War II Lubin, 70% of which was destroyed, was returned to Poland. Rebuilt, it reached a population of 83,000 in 1992. An important Solidarity* stronghold, Lubin became well known to Polish public opinion under Martial Law.* During the anti-communist demonstrations of August 31–September 2, 1982, the Citizens' Militia (MO)* killed several workers. *Nowa Encyklopedia Powszechna PWN*, vol. 3 (Warsaw, 1995), 809.

LUBLIN, city in eastern Poland, capital of Lublin Province (województwo), and one of the oldest and historically most important cities in Poland. In 1944 Lublin was the seat of the Polish Committee of National Liberation (PKWN) and briefly in 1945, of the Provisional Government.* During World War II the Germans killed hundreds of thousands of people in the Lublin-Majdanek camp and in the prison at the castle of Lublin. After the war both these sites were used by the Soviets and the Polish communist authorities to incarcerate and kill members of the Polish non-communist underground and people who did not support communism. The city is a center for farm machinery, chemical, and auto production and the foodstuff industry. Several important cultural and educational institutions, such as the Catholic University of Lublin (KUL)* and the Maria Skłodowska-Curie University, are located there. In 1990 Lublin had

350,000 inhabitants. *Dzieje Lublina*, ed. by J. Dobrzański (Lublin, 1975); *Historia Lublina w zarysie*, ed. by H. Zins (Lublin, 1972); *Nowa Encyklopedia Powszechna PWN*, vol. 3 (Warsaw, 1995), 809.

LUTHERANS, members of the autonomous Evangelical-Augsburg Church, the largest Protestant denomination in Poland. In 1989 about 91,000 Lutherans lived in 122 parishes, grouped in six dioceses. Most were concentrated in the Cieszyn* and Mazury regions. W. Sienkiewicz, *Mały słownik historii Polski* (Warsaw, 1991), 95.

LUTOSŁAWSKI, WITOLD (1913–94), world-famous composer and conductor, best known for his orchestral works. He ranged from a conservative style to music influenced by Polish folklore and aleatory operations in combination with conventional effects. *Who's Who in the Socialist Countries of Europe*, ed. by J. Stroynowski, vol. 2 (Munich, 1989), 709; *Encyklopedyczny Słownik Sławnych Polaków* (Warsaw, 1996), 211.

ŁĄCZKOWSKI, PAWEŁ J. (1942–   ), professor of sociology, founder and primary leader of the Christian Democratic Party (PChD)* since 1991. A member of Solidarity* since 1980, he served as Deputy Premier in the Suchocka* government during 1992–93 and deputy chairman of the Civic Political Committee (Obywatelski Komitet Polityczny [OKP]). *Kto jest kim w polityce polskiej*, ed. by R. Ignasiak (Warsaw, 1993), 173.

ŁAMBINOWICE (German Lambsdorf), village in Opole* Province. During World War II a complex of POW camps was located there. About 390,000 POWs, including 74,000 Poles, went through the complex, and 57,000 of all its prisoners died there. After the war Polish and Soviet security organizations established their own camp in Łambinowice. Officially, it contained only former Nazi Party members, but in fact about 5,000 ordinary Germans* and Silesians of Polish ethnic background were imprisoned there, with some even killed. Presently, there is a Central Museum of War Prisoners in Łambinowice. *Nowa Encyklopedia Powszechna PWN*, vol. 3 (Warsaw, 1995), 840.

ŁAPICKI, ANDRZEJ (1924–   ), popular theatrical actor, professor of the State Drama School (PWST); activist of Solidarity,* the Citizens' Movement for Democratic Action (ROAD),* the Democratic Union (UD),* and numerous professional associations; elected to the Sejm* in 1989. *Kto jest kim w polityce polskiej*, ed. by R. Ignasiak (Warsaw, 1993), 173.

ŁAPOT, STANISŁAW (1914–72), Deputy Premier during 1954–56. He joined the Communist Party of Poland (KPP) in 1937 and the Polish Workers' Party (PPR)* in 1944. In the 1940s and 1950s he occupied several important positions in the Party-state apparatus. T. Mołdawa, *Ludzie Władzy 1944–1991. Władze państwowe i polityczne Polski według stanu na dzień 28 II 1991* (Warsaw, 1991), 389.

ŁATYŃSKI, MAREK (1930–), director of the Polish Section of Radio Free Europe* from 1987 and author of *Nie paść na kolana* ("Not to Fall on Our Knees"), a book about the Mikołajczyk* opposition* in 1945–47. J. Nowak, *Polska z oddali*, vol. 2 (London, 1988), 215.

ŁĘTOWSKA, EWA (1940–), professor of law and highly acclaimed first Polish ombudsman—Spokesperson for Civic Rights (Rzecznik Praw Obywatelskich)— during 1987–92. In 1992 the Parliament of Europe and the Committee of European Unions awarded her the title Woman of the Year. *Kto jest kim w polityce polskiej*, ed. by R. Ignasiak (Warsaw, 1993), 174.

ŁOMNICKI, TADEUSZ (1927–92), very popular postwar Polish actor, immortalized in a film version of Henryk Sienkiewicz's *Pan Wołodyjowski*. G. Sanford and A. Gozdecka-Sanford, *Historical Dictionary of Poland* (Metuchen, N.J., 1994), 1119.

ŁOPATKA, ADAM (1928–), professor of law and Minister-Chairman of Religious Affairs during 1982–87. T. Mołdawa, *Ludzie Władzy 1944–1991. Władze państwowe i polityczne Polski według stanu na dzień 28 II 1991* (Warsaw, 1991), 389.

ŁOPUSZAŃSKI, JAN E. (1955–), leader of the Christian-National Union (ZChN).* Solidarity* activist during 1980–89 and a member of the Citizens Committee (Komitet Obywatelski [KO]),* he was elected to the Sejm* in 1989 and helped to establish the ZChN. Reelected to Parliament in 1993, he became an outspoken popularizer of his party's program and ideology. *Kto jest kim w polityce polskiej*, ed. by R. Ignasiak (Warsaw, 1993), 175.

ŁOWMIAŃSKI, HENRYK (1898–1984), historian, professor at the universities of Vilna (1932–39) and Poznań* (1945–68), and an expert on the ancient and medieval history of Baltic and Slavonic societies and states. *Great Historians of the Modern Age: An International Dictionary*, ed. by L. Boia (New York, 1991), 489–490.

ŁÓDŹ, city of 848,200 inhabitants (1990), located in central Poland, and the largest Polish textile center. Hastily built in the late 19th and early 20th centuries, the city is one of the worst-polluted and most uninhabitable places in Poland. The living conditions improved in Łódź at the beginning of the Gierek* period in the early 1970s, but only for a short of time. The economic changes that followed the fall of communism took a heavy toll on the city. G. Sanford and A. Gozdecka-Sanford, *Historical Dictionary of Poland* (Metuchen, N.J., 1994), 119; A. Szram, *Łódź* (Łódź, 1987); *Łódź: dzieje miasta*, ed. by R. Rosin (Warsaw, 1980).

ŁUBIEŃSKI, KONSTANTY (1910–77), Catholic writer, economist, lawyer, member of the State Council (Rada Państwa)* in 1976–77, and Sejm* deputy from 1952. During 1945–56 he was active in the PAX Association.* After 1956 he became a leader of the Clubs of Catholic Intelligentsia (KIK).* In 1976–77 he served as chairman of the *Znak** Parliamentary Club, and during 1971–77 as deputy president of the National Unity Front (FJN*). G. Sanford and A. Gozdecka-Sanford, *Historical Dictionary of Poland* (Metuchen, N.J., 1994), 119.

ŁUCZAK, ALEKSANDER P. (1943–   ), professor of history and political science at Warsaw University,* Deputy Premier and Minister of Education since October 1993. A member of the United Peasant Party (ZSL)* from 1968 and one of its leaders in the 1980s, he was among the organizers and leaders of the Polish Peasant Party ''Revival'' (PSL Odrodzenie) in 1989–90 and of the Polish Peasant Party (PSL)* since 1990. Undersecretary of state in the Ministry of Education in 1987–88, he became Minister-Chief of the Office of the Minister Council in 1993 in the government of W. Pawlak.* In October 1992 he was promoted to Deputy Premier, a position he kept in the cabinet of J. Oleksy* until February 1996. *Who's Who in the Socialist Countries of Europe*, ed. by J. Stroynowski, vol. 2 (Munich, 1989), 712; T. Mołdawa, *Ludzie Władzy 1944–1991. Władze państwowe i polityczne Polski według stanu na dzień 28 II 1991* (Warsaw, 1991), 390.

ŁUKASZEWICZ, JERZY (1931–83), Politburo* member during 1975–80, responsible for propaganda and mass media. An activist of the communist youth movement, he joined the Polish United Workers' Party (PZPR)* in 1951 and became a member of its Central Committee* in 1968. Responsible for the Gierek* team's irritating ''success propaganda'' and an overlord of the Polish mass media, he was interrogated by the Grabski* Commission, accused of ''mistakes in the leading of Party ideological activities,'' and removed from all his positions and the Party in 1980–81. T. Mołdawa, *Ludzie Władzy 1944–1991. Władze państwowe i polityczne Polski według stanu na dzień 28 II 1991* (Warsaw, 1991), 390; Z. Błażyński, *Towarzysze zeznają. Z tajnych archiwów Komitetu Centralnego* (London, 1987), 106–119.

M

MACHARSKI, FRANCISZEK (1927–), Cardinal and Archbishop of Cracow* since 1978. Ordained in 1950, he is one of the most respected priests in Poland. He taught theology in several church institutions of higher learning, worked closely with K. Wojtyła* and replaced him as Archbishop of Cracow, and served as a deputy president of the Conference of the Polish Episcopate* in 1979–94 and as the president of its Commission of Catholic Science in 1981–94. After the death of S. Wyszyński,* the majority of Poles expected Macharski to become the next Primate* of Poland. *Who's Who in the Socialist Countries of Europe*, ed. by J. Stroynowski, vol. 2 (Munich, 1989), 712; G. Polak, *Kto jest kim w Kościele katolickim* (Warsaw, 1996), 217.

MACHEJEK, WŁADYSŁAW (1920–91), writer, journalist, and Party official. Active in the communist movement before the war, he co-organized the communist People's Guard and then the People's Army in the Cracow* region during the war. After 1945 he helped to establish the communist system in Poland as an activist and a writer and served as chief editor of several literary and cultural periodicals. *Who's Who in the Socialist Countries of Europe*, ed. by J. Stroynowski, vol. 2 (Munich, 1989), 712; P. Kuncewicz, *Agonia i nadzieja. Literatura polska od 1939*, vol. 2 (Warsaw, 1994), 201, 277–280.

MACIEREWICZ, ANTONI (1948–), historian, dissident,* and politician. Imprisoned for his participation in the March events of 1968,* he was active in Polish scouting,* where he supported an anti-communist orientation. In 1976 he helped to establish the Workers' Defense Committee (KOR)* and became a leader of its right wing. He also co-organized and edited *Głos* ("The Voice"),* an important underground monthly. In 1980–81 he helped to create and lead Solidarity's* Social Research Center. After imposition of Martial Law,* he continued his Solidarity involvement in the underground, joined Solidarity's Civic

Committee,* participated in the elections of June 1989,* and became a Sejm* deputy. He also helped to form the Christian-National Union (ZChN)* in 1989 and became its deputy president. In December 1991 Macierewicz received the portfolio of internal affairs in the newly formed cabinet of J. Olszewski.* A strong supporter of the lustration of leading politicians, Macierewicz began lustration procedures in a way that caused the fall of the Olszewski government. On the list of communist police informers and secret collaborators made public by Macierewicz were the names of L. Wałęsa* and numerous leaders of the pre-1989 democratic opposition,* including ZChN president, W. Chrzanowski.* As a consequence, Macierewicz was ejected from his party, established a small Christian-National Movement for Polish Action (Ruch Chrześcijańsko-Narodowy Akcja Polska), and later joined the Movement for Reconstruction of Poland (ROP).* *Who's Who in the Socialist Countries of Europe*, ed. by J. Stroynowski, vol. 2 (Munich, 1989), 714; J. J. Lipski, *KOR: A History of the Workers' Defense Committee in Poland, 1976–81* (Berkeley, Calif., 1985); *Kto jest kim w polityce polskiej*, ed. by R. Ignasiak (Warsaw, 1993), 178.

MACISZEWSKI, JAREMA (1930–   ), historian and member of the Central Committee* of the Polish United Workers' Party (PZPR)* and since 1972 chairman of its Department of Education and Upbringing. *Who's Who in the Socialist Countries of Europe*, ed. by J. Stroynowski, vol. 2 (Munich, 1989), 714.

MACKIEWICZ, JÓZEF (1902–85), prolific writer and brother of S. Mackiewicz.* A volunteer during the Polish-Soviet War of 1919–20, he worked as an editor and a journalist for several conservative periodicals during the interwar period. During World War II he contributed to the German-sponsored *Goniec Codzienny* ("The Daily Messenger"). Sentenced by the Home Army (AK)* to death for collaboration, he escaped with the Germans in 1945, eventually settling in Munich. Most of his books, described as "powerful, traditionally realistic novels," are devoted to anti-communist subjects and describe the Soviet occupation of eastern Poland after 1939. As a consequence, communist censorship* made him an "un-person" in Poland. C. Miłosz, *The History of Polish Literature* (Berkeley, Calif., 1983), 524–525; *Dictionary of Polish Literature*, ed. by E. J. Czerwinski (Westport, Conn., 1994), 245–247; *Encyklopedyczny Słownik Sławnych Polaków* (Warsaw, 1996), 216; J. Zieliński, *Leksykon polskiej literatury emigracyjnej* (Lublin, 1989), 86–88.

MACKIEWICZ, STANISŁAW (1896–1966), journalist, conservative politician, and prolific writer, who used the pen name "Cat." A member of the Polish Military Organization (POW) in 1916–17, he founded and edited a conservative newspaper, *Słowo* ("The Word"), in Vilna during 1922–39. An activist in a conservative group known as Żubry ("The Bisons"), he helped to reconcile this group with J. Piłsudski after the 1926 coup d'état. In 1934 he was instrumental in the signing of the Polish-German non-aggression treaty. During 1928–35 he served as a deputy in the Sejm, and in 1940–41 on the National Council (Rada Narodowa), the Polish Parliament-in-Exile in London. During 1954–55 Mackiewicz was premier of the Polish émigré government. In June 1956 he returned to Poland. Close to the PAX Association,* he published historical essays in its journal, *Słowo Powszechne* (''Universal Word''). In March 1964 Mackiewicz was among the signatories of the open Letter of 34* concerning censorship and freedom of speech. He also contributed to the Paris *Kultura** and published many popular books on the history of Poland. J. Jaruzelski, *Stanisław Cat-Mackiewicz 1896–1966. Wilno-Londyn-Warszawa* (Warsaw, 1987); A. Micewski, *Ludzie i opcje* (Warsaw, 1993), 68–72.

MAIN STATISTICAL OFFICE (Główny Urząd Statystyczny [GUS]), the main statistical bureau of Poland established in 1918 and recognized for the quality of its work. G. Sanford and A. Gozdecka-Sanford, *Historical Dictionary of Poland* (Metuchen, N.J., 1994), 121.

MALINOWSKI, ROMAN (1935–   ), economist, state official, and United Peasant Party (ZSL)* politician. Joining the ZSL in 1956, he rose to become its president during 1981–89. During 1980–85 he served as Deputy Premier and Minister of the Food Industry, and during 1985–89 he was Speaker of the Sejm.* A supporter and an assistant close to Gen. W. Jaruzelski,* he was considered a possible candidate for Premier* in summer 1989, but after the June 1989 elections* he unexpectedly accepted L. Wałęsa's* proposal to reverse political alliances and to form a non-communist government based on a coalition of the ZSL, the Democratic Party (SD),* and Solidarity.* Eventually, as a person deeply involved in the communist system, he was eliminated from the leadership of the peasant movement. G. Sanford and A. Gozdecka-Sanford, *Historical Dictionary of Poland* (Metuchen, N.J., 1994), 121; A. Kępiński and Z. Kilar, *Kto jest kim w Polsce inaczej* (Warsaw, 1985), 235–248.

MAŁACHOWSKI, ALEKSANDER (1924–   ), journalist and politician. A Home Army (AK)* veteran, he was arrested by the NKVD in 1940 and 1944 and was deported to a labor camp in the Soviet Union. Between the early 1950s and the late 1980s he was a member of several periodical editorial staffs and worked in Polish TV,* where he produced 75 documentary films. During 1958–61 he presided over the Crooked Circle Club.* After 1978 he was a member of the ''Experience and Future'' discussion club (DiP).* In 1980 he was elected to the leadership of Solidarity,* Mazowsze Region. Interned after imposition of Martial Law* and arrested in 1983, he was elected to the Sejm* in 1989. Initially a member of the Civic Parliamentary Club (OKP),* he was a primary organizer of the Union of Labor (UP).* *Kto jest kim w polityce polskiej*, ed. by R. Ignasiak (Warsaw, 1993), 183.

MARCH EVENTS OF 1968, political crisis partially staged by M. Moczar's* ''Partisans'' faction of the Polish United Workers' Party (PZPR).* The crisis was triggered by several factors. After the Six-Day War between Israel and Arab states in June 1967, members of the Warsaw Treaty Organization* discontinued their diplomatic relations with Tel-Aviv. In Poland many people, not only of Jewish background, expressed their satisfaction with the outcome of the war. They understood this conflict as a war by proxies between the Western world, supporting Israel, and the Soviet Union, using the Arab states to extend its influences in the Middle East. The Arabic defeat was considered to be a Soviet fiasco and was celebrated by many Poles. This prompted W. Gomułka* to make a widely broadcasted speech on June 19, 1967, including "anti-Zionist" remarks and calling the Jews* of Poland the "fifth column." Taking this as a signal, Moczar's "Partisans" started an anti-Semitic campaign. As a consequence, about 500 persons left Poland by the end of 1967.

In January 1968 the authorities banned the performance of a play by A. Mickiewicz, *Dziady* ("Forefather's Eve"),* staged by K. Dejmek* in the National Theater. This prompted students to organize a demonstration in front of the Mickiewicz monument after the last performance of the play. Two students, A. Michnik* and H. Szlajfer,* who co-organized the demonstration and informed a Warsaw corespondent of *Le Monde* about it, were arrested and expelled from the University of Warsaw.* On March 8 and 9, 1968, serious disturbances occurred on the university campus when hundreds of police and "workers-activists" attacked demonstrating students, who demanded the release and the reinstatement of Michnik and Szlajfer. The demonstrations at Warsaw University were followed by similar occurrences at other institutions of higher learning in Warsaw and the major Polish cities and by street riots. The events were partially provoked and used by Moczar, who wanted to oust W. Gomułka and to crush the reformist wing of the Party. As a Minister of Interior, Moczar controlled the Citizens' Militia (MO)* and other security forces, which acted extremely brutally during and after the demonstrations. Moczar's faction used the crisis to purge the Party, the state apparatus, and the intellectual circles, combining the purge with the earlier anti-Semitic campaign. Several senior government officials, most of them of Jewish background, were dismissed after their children were alleged to be ringleaders in the student demonstrations. A concerted campaign in the Polish press blamed the "Zionists" and "Zionist sympathizers" for the unrests. The same theory was presented during staged pro-governmental demonstrations in most large enterprises. Poland's leading writers, scholars, and intellectuals, among them numerous people of Jewish origin, were accused of inspiring the demonstrations. Many persons were expelled from the Party, and several professors and many students from Warsaw University, where some departments were closed. On March 19 Gomułka made a vitriolic speech to a Party rally in Warsaw. He stated that between March 8 and 15 only 1,208 persons, including 367 students, had been arrested for participation in the demonstrations. The campaign continued in April. About 60 prominent officials were removed from their posts, and over 6,000 people from the Party. Several leading politicians, such as E. Ochab* and A. Rapacki,* were forced to retire because they refused to support the campaign.

The victims of the purge were allowed to emigrate. About 25,000 people of Jewish background, mostly professionals, left the country. The purge poisoned Polish intellectual life and affected the structure of the Party's leadership and the national economy. Party hard-liners eliminated plans of economic reform similar to the Hungarian New Economic Model. The "Partisans" did not manage to topple Gomułka, who neutralized Moczar and promoted new Party leaders, such as K. Olszewski,* J. Tejchma,* and B. Jaszczuk.* G. Sanford and A. Gozdecka-Sanford, *Historical Dictionary of Poland* (Metuchen, N.J., 1994), 122; *Keesing's Contemporary Archives*, April 27–March 4, 1968, pp. 22664–22667, and May 4–11, 1978, p. 22684; M. K. Dziewanowski, *Poland in the Twentieth Century* (New York, 1977), 198–206; J. Eisler, *Marzec 1968* (Warsaw, 1991).

MARTIAL LAW, also known as a State of War. Martial Law was declared in Poland by Gen. W. Jaruzelski* in the early hours of December 13, 1981. Power was taken over by the Military Council of National Salvation (WRON),* which declared that Solidarity* activities constituted a counter-revolution, destabilized Poland, pushed it toward the edge of bankruptcy, and threatened it with a Soviet invasion. WRON announced that it would rule for an unspecified time to protect legal order and restore social discipline. Thousands of Solidarity activists were interned, civil rights and most social organizations were suspended, and a curfew and rigorous discipline were imposed. The Polish United Workers' Party (PZPR)* removed almost 100,000 members from its lists. Thousands of outraged members returned their Party cards to protest against Martial Law. The full rigors of Martial Law were lifted after several weeks, and on December 31, 1982, Martial Law was suspended. It was fully revoked in July 1983. The Jaruzelski regime managed to restore political order but was unable to stop completely the growing economic decline of the country. *Political and Economic Encyclopedia of the Soviet Union and Eastern Europe*, ed. by S. White (London, 1990), 247; J. Leftwich Curry and L. Fajfer, *Poland's Permanent Revolution: People vs. Elites, 1956 to the Present* (Washington, D.C., 1996), 187–199; D. Ost, *Solidarity and the Politics of Anti-Politics: Opposition and Reform in Poland since 1968* (Philadelphia, 1990), 149–165; A. Świdlicki, "Mechanisms of Repression in Poland during Martial Law," *The Polish Review*, vol. 29, nos. 1–2 (1984), 97–126.

MARXISM-LENINISM. See Ideology.

MASS FOR THE FATHERLAND, church service held once a month from the beginning of 1982 by J. Popiełuszko* in his church of St. Stanisław Kostka in the Żoliborz district in Warsaw.* The communist authorities considered the mass dangerous anti-communist propaganda, and Popiełuszko was killed by secret police in 1984. *Encyklopedyczny Słownik Sławnych Polaków* (Warsaw, 1996), 299.

MATUSZEWSKI, STEFAN (1905–85), member of the State Council (Rada Państwa)* during 1952–57 and Propaganda Minister in 1944–46. A son of a peasant, he graduated from the Warsaw University* Theology Department and became a Catholic priest. He soon resigned, though, and joined the Polish Socialist Party (PPS).* He spent World War II in the USSR, where he volunteered in the communist-controlled Polish Army.* After the war he continued his activities in the PPS and supported its "unification" with the Polish Workers' Party (PPR).* After the 1948 "unification" he became a member of the Central Committee* and the Politburo* of the Polish United Workers' Party (PZPR),* where he served in several important apparatus positions, such as First Secretary of the Party provincial organization in Warsaw* in 1948–49. In 1958 he retired from politics to become a professor at Warsaw University. T. Mołdawa, *Ludzie Władzy 1944–1991. Władze państwowe i polityczne Polski według stanu na dzień 28 II 1991* (Warsaw, 1991), 392.

MATWIN, WŁADYSŁAW (1916–   ), Secretary of the Central Committee* of the Polish United Workers' Party (PZPR).* He joined the Communist Party of Poland (KPP) and was active in its youth movement in the 1930s. Matwin spent the war in the USSR, where he was active in the Union of Polish Patriots (ZPP) and served as Polish ambassador in 1945–46. Later he occupied several important positions in the communist apparatus, such as First Secretary of the Party provincial organization in Wrocław* (1947–49 and 1957–63) and in Warsaw* (1952–54), and editor-in-chief of the main Party organ, *Trybuna Ludu* ("Tribune of the People")* (1954–57). During the "Polish October"* of 1956 Matwin belonged to the so-called group of young secretaries supporting political changes in Poland, but he was eliminated from the Central Committee in 1964. T. Mołdawa, *Ludzie Władzy 1944–1991. Władze państwowe i polityczne Polski według stanu na dzień 28 II 1991* (Warsaw, 1991), 393; A. Micewski, *Ludzie i opcje* (Warsaw, 1993), 61–62.

MAZOWIECKI, TADEUSZ (1927–   ), journalist, Social-Catholic and Solidarity* activist, and Premier* of Poland from August 1989 to December 1990. He studied at the Warsaw University* Law Department. He joined the PAX Association,* became the head of its youth division, and edited its *Wrocławski Tygodnik Katolików* ("Wrocław Catholics' Weekly") in the early 1950s. In 1955 Mazowiecki left PAX and, in 1956, became an activist in the Clubs of Catholic Intelligentsia (KIK).* Between 1961 and 1972, he was a Sejm* deputy and a member of the *Znak* ("The Sign")* caucus. During 1958–81 he edited the monthly *Więź* ("The Link").* From 1977 to 1980, he was a member of the Program Council of the Association of Scientific Courses (TKN)* and cooperated with the Workers' Defense Committee (KOR).* In August 1980 Mazowiecki chaired a committee of experts helping the Gdańsk* shipyard strike. Later he became an important Solidarity adviser and edited its *Tygodnik Solidarność* ("The Solidarity Weekly")* in 1981. Interned from December 1981 to December 1982, he served as adviser to the Solidarity National Executive Committee (KKW) again from 1987 and as editor-in-chief of *Tygodnik Solidarność* from 1989. A principal architect of the Round Table Negotiations* and Premier from August 1989, Mazowiecki provoked various reactions. Initially, his government enjoyed nearly total public support. Later the population began to feel the effects of the Balcerowicz* Plan, and Mazowiecki's policies began to be criticized. Especially controversial was his policy of a "thick line" ("gruba kreska"), which suggested that an individual's communist involvement should be disregarded in the new Poland. Mazowiecki did not consult L. Wałęsa* about the composition of his cabinet and excluded from it several individuals close to the president of Solidarity. Wałęsa accused Mazowiecki of retaining former communists in the cabinet. To rebut this criticism, Mazowiecki dismissed three former communists from his cabinet and appointed three new ministers on July 6, 1990. The Interior Minister, Gen. C. Kiszczak,* was replaced by K. Kozłowski,* a former Vice-Minister of Interior and well-known Solidarity journalist; Defense Minister Gen. F. Siwicki* was replaced by Vice-Admiral P. Kołodziejczyk;* and Transportation Minister Adam Wielądek was replaced by Ewaryst Waligórski, a Solidarity economist. On September 14, Communications Minister Marek Kucharski was replaced by his peer from the Democratic Party (SD),* Jan Wiktor Ślęzak. At the same time, a Ministry of Ownership Transformation was formed and given to W. Kuczyński,* a Solidarity economist; Janusz Byliński from Rural Solidarity* took the portfolio of Agriculture and Food Industry, vacant since July 5, when the previous minister, Czesław Janicki, resigned in protest against the government's unwillingness to make economic concessions to farmers. Mazowiecki's decision to participate in the 1990 presidential elections* contributed to the start of the "war at the top."* On November 25, 1990, he received 18.08% of the vote and lost to L. Wałęsa and S. Tymiński.* In December 1990 he was elected the president of the Democratic Union (UD).* From fall 1993 to April 1995 Mazowiecki headed a new party—the Union of Freedom (UW),* established by a merger of the Democratic Union and the Liberal Democratic Congress.* Between August 1992 and July 1995 he served as a special envoy of the U.N. Human Rights Committee to the former Yugoslavia. *The Cold War, 1945–1991*, vol. 2, "Leaders and Other Important Figures in the Soviet Union, Eastern Europe, China, and the Third World," ed. by B. Frankel (Detroit, 1992), 214; A. Micewski, *Ludzie i opcje* (Warsaw, 1993), 25–28; *Political and Economic Encyclopedia of the Soviet Union and Eastern Europe*, ed. by S. White (London, 1990), 159; H. Tworzecki, *Parties and Politics in Post-1989 Poland* (Boulder, Colo., 1996); *Rodem z Solidarności*, ed. by B. Kopka and R. Żelichowski (Warsaw, 1997), 135–156; A. Dudek, *Pierwsze lata III Rzeczpospolitej, 1989–1995* (Cracow, 1997), 51–94.

MAZUR, FRANCISZEK (1895–1975), Deputy Speaker of the Sejm* during 1952–56 and Deputy President of the State Council (Rada Państwa)* during 1952–57. A son of an agricultural worker, he joined the Polish Socialist Party (PPS)* in 1917. Two years later he became a member of the Bolshevik Party and participated in the Civil War in Russia. In 1930 he returned to Poland from the USSR, joined the Communist Party of Poland (KPP) and its Central Committee, and headed the autonomous Communist Party of Western Ukraine. He spent World War II in the Soviet Union and returned to Poland in 1945 to join the leadership of the Polish Workers' Party (PPR).* Until 1956 he chaired several important Central Committee* institutions. After the "Polish October"* of 1956, he was removed from the Party Central Committee and retired as the Polish ambassador to Czechoslovakia. As a Politburo* member, he was responsible for, among other things, the Party's Church policy. T. Mołdawa, *Ludzie Władzy 1944–1991. Władze państwowe i polityczne Polski według stanu na dzień 28 II 1991* (Warsaw, 1991), 393; A. Micewski, *Ludzie i opcje* (Warsaw, 1993), 55–56.

MAZURKIEWICZ, JAN (1896–1988), war veterans' leader. He fought in the Piłsudski Legions during World War I and in the Polish Army during the 1919–20 Polish-Soviet War, participated in the September Campaign of 1939, and became one of the most important commanders of the Home Army (AK)* during World War II (nom de guerre Radosław). Arrested by the communist police in 1949, he was kept in prison without trial during 1949–56. Once released, he became a symbol of the Polish patriot persecuted by the Stalinist regime. In 1956 he was elected vice-president of the Warsaw Board of the Union of Fighters for Liberty and Democracy (ZBoWiD)*; in 1964 he became vice-president of its Main Board. His involvement was criticized by many, since ZBoWiD was part of the communist state's establishment. *Who's Who in the Socialist Countries of Europe*, ed. by J. Stroynowski, vol. 2 (Munich, 1989), 755; A. Kunert, *Ilustrowany Przewodnik po Polsce Podziemnej 1939–1945* (Warsaw, 1996), 525–526.

MERKEL, JACEK (1954–), Solidarity* activist and state official. An engineer employed at Gdańsk's* Lenin Shipyard, he helped to organize the August 1980 strike. Interned after imposition of Martial Law* on December 13, 1981, he was released in December 1982 and returned to independent trade union activities. In August 1988 he co-organized another strike in the shipyard and was elected to the Sejm* in 1989. In fall 1990 he served as director of L. Wałęsa's* presidential campaign. In December 1990, after the electoral victory, Merkel was appointed head of the presidential office and Minister of State in charge of national security. Dismissed by Wałęsa in March 1991, he became involved in the activities of the Liberal Democratic Congress (KLD).* T. Mołdawa, *Ludzie Władzy 1944–1991. Władze państwowe i polityczne Polski według stanu na dzień 28 II 1991* (Warsaw, 1991), 394; T. Torańska, *My* (Warsaw, 1994), 217–242.

MESSNER, ZBIGNIEW (1929–), professor of economics, Deputy Premier during 1983–85, Premier* in 1985–88, and member of the State Council (Rada Państwa)* in 1988–89. In 1953 he joined the Polish United Workers' Party (PZPR)* and July 1981 became a member of its Central Committee,* holding office until the dissolution of the Party in January 1990, and a member of its Politburo,* until December 1988. Rector of Katowice* Academy of Economics, he became one of the main economic experts of the Jaruzelski* regime, but he did not manage to implement the reforms intended to save the Polish economy.* After 1988 he retired from politics and returned to the Academy of Economics. *Who's Who in the Socialist Countries of Europe*, ed. by J. Stroynowski, vol. 2 (Munich, 1989), 762; T. Mołdawa, *Ludzie Władzy 1944–1991. Władze państwowe i polityczne Polski według stanu na dzień 28 II 1991* (Warsaw, 1991), 394; A. Kępiński and Z. Kilar, *Kto jest kim w Polsce inaczej* (Warsaw, 1985), 251–264.

MICEWSKI, ANDRZEJ (1926–   ), historian, Catholic journalist, and writer. Initially a member of the PAX Association,* he co-edited the prestigious *Tygodnik Powszechny* ("The Universal Weekly")* from 1974, *Więź* ("The Link")* during 1960–70, and *Znaki Czasu* ("The Signs of Time"), published under the guidance of Poland's Primate,* J. Glemp,* in Vienna since 1986. Micewski was active in the Clubs of Catholic Intelligentsia* from 1957, served on the Social Council of the Primate* of Poland, and authored several important books on the history of the Roman Catholic Church,* such as a biography of Cardinal S. Wyszyński.* *Who's Who in the Socialist Countries of Europe*, ed. by J. Stroynowski, vol. 2 (Munich, 1989), 766.

MICHNIK, ADAM (1946–   ), political dissident,* leader of the democratic opposition* in communist Poland, journalist, writer, and politician. A member of the "Red Scouts," he was strongly influenced by J. Kuroń* and communist ideology.* During 1965–68 he studied history at Warsaw University,* but he was suspended twice and eventually expelled for political reasons. During the March events of 1968,* he was arrested for protesting against the communist ban of the play *Dziady* ("Forefathers' Eve"),* tried, and sentenced to three years in prison. Released after two years he could only obtain a job as welder in the Rosa Luxemburg plant in Warsaw, where he worked in 1971–73. Later he became personal secretary to the poet A. Słonimski.* Michnik completed his history degree as an external student at Poznań University in 1975. From 1976 he was increasingly involved in the activities of the Workers' Defense Committee (KOR),* of the Flying University,* and the editorial staffs of such underground periodicals as *Zapis* ("The Record"),* *Biuletyn Informacyjny* ("Information Bulletin"),* and *Krytyka* ("The Critique").* In the late 1960s and the 1970s he was arrested and detained over 100 times. The communist authorities would imprison him every time the regime was in danger. They did it again in August 1980, at the beginning of the Solidarity* crisis. Striking workers demanded the release of political prisoners, who, including Michnik, were soon freed. Michnik became a key adviser to Solidarity. On December 13, 1981, he was interned, and in September 1982 he was arrested and accused of conspiracy against the political system. Released after the amnesty* of 1984, he was imprisoned again in February 1985, sentenced to three years in prison, and granted amnesty in August 1986. He returned to his activities in the underground mass media, especially in the publishing house NOWa,* and became a member of the Solidarity Civic Committee.* He participated in the Round Table Negotiations* and was elected to the Sejm* in June 1989. In May 1989 he became editor-in-chief of *Gazeta Wyborcza* ("The Electoral Gazette")* and, during the next years, transformed it into the largest newspaper of Central and Eastern Europe. One of his programmatic articles, published in the gazette, "Your President—Our Premier," helped to solve a political crisis that arose after the elections of June 1989.* In 1990 Michnik participated in the "war at the top"* and helped to organize the Citizens' Movement for Democratic Action (ROAD)* and, later, the Democratic Union (UD).* At the same time, Michnik began his return to the ideological left. As a consequence of the transformation of his worldview and his anti-Wałęsa involvement, Solidarity withdrew its logo from the vignette of *Gazeta Wyborcza*. An outstanding and prolific essayist and writer, Michnik received several important international awards, such as the Robert Kennedy Award for Human Rights and the French PEN Club's Prix de la Liberté. Michnik is one of those persons most instrumental in the democratic transformation of Poland. P. Raina, *Independent Movements in Poland* (London, 1981); J. J. Lipski, *KOR: A History of the Workers' Defense Committee in Poland, 1976–81* (Berkeley, Calif., 1985); *The Cold War, 1945–1991*, vol. 2, "Leaders and Other Important Figures in the Soviet Union, Eastern Europe, China, and the Third World," ed. by B. Frankel (Detroit, 1992), 220; *Kto jest kim w polityce polskiej*, ed. by R. Ignasiak (Warsaw, 1993), 191; *Who's Who in the Socialist Countries of Europe*, ed. by J. Stroynowski, vol. 2 (Munich, 1989), 770; *Rodem z Solidarności*, ed. by B. Kopka and R. Żelichowski (Warsaw, 1997), 159–178.

MIĘDZYRZECKI, ARTUR (1922–96), poet and writer. A deportee in the Soviet Union during 1940–42, he left this country with the Anders* Army and fought in the Battle of Monte Cassino in 1944. Later he studied journalism in Bologna and Paris; in 1949 he returned to Poland. Editor of several periodicals, he also taught in New York in 1971–74 and was active in the Union of Polish Writers (ZLP).* In 1991 he became president of the Polish PEN Club and deputy president of the World Union of PEN Clubs. His works, philosophical and frequently ironic, reflect problems of the war generation in Poland. *Who's Who in the Socialist Countries of Europe*, ed. by J. Stroynowski, vol. 2 (Munich, 1989), 772; *Encyklopedyczny Słownik Sławnych Polaków* (Warsaw, 1996), 235.

MIJAL, KAZIMIERZ (1910–), economist and Minister-Head of the Office of the Council of Ministers during 1952–56. A bank clerk before the war, he joined the Polish Workers' Party (PPR)* in 1942 and played an active role in the communist anti-German resistance. From 1945 to 1959, he was a member of the Party Central Committee,* a full member from 1948, and occupied several important apparatus positions, such as secretary of the National Home Council (KRN)* Presidium in 1944–45, director of the Civil Chancellery of the President* of Poland during 1947–50, and Minister of Communal Administration in 1950–52 and 1956–57. In 1966 he secretly left Poland to establish the so-called Communist Party of Poland in Albania and China. He returned to Poland in 1984. *Who's Who in the Socialist Countries of Europe*, ed. by J. Stroynowski, vol. 2 (Munich, 1989), 775; *Yearbook of International Communist Affairs 1966* (Stanford, Calif., 1967), 68; T. Mołdawa, *Ludzie Władzy 1944–1991. Władze państwowe i polityczne Polski według stanu na dzień 28 II 1991* (Warsaw, 1991), 395.

MIKOŁAJCZYK, STANISŁAW (1901–66), Peasant Party (SL) politician, Premier* of the Polish Government-in-Exile,* and Deputy Premier of the Provisional Government of National Unity (TRJN)* between June 1945 and February 1947. An activist of the peasant movement from the early 1920s, he belonged to the SL leadership in 1931–39 and served as a Sejm* deputy in 1930–35. He fought in the 1939 September Campaign and was interned in Hungary, but he escaped to the West, where he became president of the SL Abroad Committee. In January 1940 he was elected Deputy President of the National Council (Rada Narodowa), a form of Parliament-in-Exile, and in September 1941 he joined the Polish émigré government as Deputy Premier and Minister of the Interior. In July 1943, after the death of Gen. W. Sikorski, Mikołajczyk became Prime Minister. In November 1944 he resigned, and on June 27, 1945, he returned to Poland to become Deputy Premier and Minister of Agriculture and Land Reform in the communist-dominated government. After his return Mikołajczyk helped to build, and presided over, the large Polish Peasant Party (PSL),* the main political force opposed to the establishment of communist power that tried to create a democratic non-Soviet authority in Poland. In 1946, especially during the propaganda campaigns preceding the referendum* and the elections of January 1947,* the PSL was decimated by the communist terror and failed to prevent electoral manipulations. In October 1947 Mikołajczyk, facing imminent arrest, fled Poland for England; later he settled in the United States, where he presided over the émigré PSL and the Peasant International and wrote several important works on contemporary Polish history. S. Mikołajczyk, *Pattern of Soviet Domination* (London, 1948); A. Paczkowski, *Stanisław Mikołajczyk* (Warsaw, 1994).

MIKOŁAJSKA, HALINA (1925–89), actress and dissident. Wife of M. Brandys,* she was one of the most active and the most persecuted members of the Workers' Defense Committee (KOR)* and the Polish democratic opposition.* During 1976–81 she was forbidden to perform in state theaters and on TV,* which almost led to her professional death because the communists controlled entertainment and the arts. *Who's Who in the Socialist Countries of Europe*, ed. by J. Stroynowski, vol. 2 (Munich, 1989), 778; J. J. Lipski, *KOR: A History of the Workers' Defense Committee in Poland, 1976–81* (Berkeley, Calif., 1985); *Nowa Encyklopedia Powszechna PWN*, vol. 4 (Warsaw, 1995), 217.

MILCZANOWSKI, ANDRZEJ (1939–   ), lawyer and Minister of Internal Affairs in the cabinets of H. Suchocka,* W. Pawlak,* and J. Oleksy.* Before 1980 he served as public prosecutor in Szczecin,* where he participated in Solidarity* activities in 1980–81. Sentenced to five years in prison for underground activities during Martial Law,* he joined Solidarity's Civic Committee* in 1988 and participated in the Round Table Negotiations* in 1989. Between July 1990 and January 1992 he was chief of the newly established Bureau for State Protection (UOP) and helped to rebuild the secret police. Next, he was appointed Minister of the Interior. He resigned on November 28, following A. Kwaśniewski's* victory in the presidential elections of 1995.* On December 19 he presented documentary evidence that he said proved that the Premier,* J. Oleksy, had collaborated with the Soviet and Russian intelligence since 1983. The announcement started a scandal that toppled Oleksy's government. *Who's Who in the Socialist Countries of Europe*, ed. by J. Stroynowski, vol. 2 (Munich, 1989), 780; *Kto jest kim w polityce polskiej*, ed. by R. Ignasiak (Warsaw, 1993), 192.

MILEWSKI, JERZY J. (1935–97), Solidarity* activist. In 1981 he helped to establish the "Network of Leading Factory Workplaces" ("Sieć"). During 1982–90 he directed the Solidarity Coordinating Bureau Abroad in Brussels. In 1991 he became a presidential adviser and head of the National Security Council. *Kto jest kim w polityce polskiej*, ed. by R. Ignasiak (Warsaw, 1993), 193.

MILEWSKI, MIROSŁAW (1928–   ), Interior Minister from October 1980 to July 1981 and member of the Politburo* of the Polish United Workers' Party (PZPR)* during 1981–85. A lifetime member of the communist police, he started his career with the Security Forces at the age of 16 in 1944. In 1971 he was promoted to general of the Citizens' Militia* and Deputy Minister of Interior. He lost all his positions after his subordinates murdered Father J. Popiełuszko.* *Who's Who in the Socialist Countries of Europe*, ed. by J. Stroynowski, vol. 2 (Munich, 1989), 781; T. Mołdawa, *Ludzie Władzy 1944–1991. Władze państwowe i polityczne Polski według stanu na dzień 28 II 1991* (Warsaw, 1991), 396.

MILITARY COUNCIL OF NATIONAL SALVATION (Wojskowa Rada Ocalenia Narodowego [WRON]), emergency extra-constitutional committee, a form of junta, established on the night of December 12–13, 1981, to rule Poland during Martial Law.* Headed by Gen. W. Jaruzelski,* it consisted of 22 persons, including all top generals in the Polish People's Army,* such as C. Kiszczak,* F. Siwicki,* T. Tuczapski, J. Baryła, T. Hupałowski,* M. Janiszewski, T. Molczyk, and C. Piotrowski, as well as, Admiral Janczyszyn and M. Hermaszewski,* Poland's only astronaut. Disliked by most Poles, it was called a "crow," because its acronym sounds almost like that bird's name in Polish. WRON was dissolved on July 22, 1983, the day Martial Law officially ended. G. Sanford and A. Gozdecka-Sanford, *Historical Dictionary of Poland* (Metuchen, N.J., 1994), 126.

MILITIA (Milicja Obywatelska [MO]), police formation established by the decree of the Polish Committee of National Liberation (PKWN) of October 7, 1944, to maintain public order and enforce the law. In addition, the MO was involved in military operations and other activities against the anti-Soviet resistance, operating in Poland until the end of the 1940s. Later the MO helped to suppress popular revolts against the communist regime. In 1945–54 the MO was supervised by the Ministry of Public Security.* After its liquidation in 1954, the MO was transferred to the Ministry of Internal Affairs.* The MO worked closely with the Security Service (SB),* harassed and persecuted independent intellectuals, political opposition,* and the Roman Catholic Church,* and was supported by additional specialized units such as the Motorized Units of the People's Militia (ZOMO)* and the Volunteer Reserves of the Citizens' Militia (ORMO).* A symbol of oppression, the MO was dissolved in 1990. *Nowa Encyklopedia Powszechna PWN*, vol. 4 (Warsaw, 1995), 225.

MILLENNIUM CELEBRATIONS. A few years after the "Polish October" of 1956,* the communist authorities of Poland began a new campaign against the Roman Catholic Church.* In 1959 the government decreed the end of the Church's tax exemption. In 1961 religious instruction in schools was abolished. Controversy over birth control was growing. In 1965 the letter of the Polish bishops to the bishops of Germany* triggered a governmental propaganda offensive against the Church. This became an introduction to the activities arranged in 1966, when the country was celebrating the millennium of Christianity in Poland. Polish press published vitriolic comments against the Church. Primate S. Wyszyński* was denied a passport to attend millennial ceremonies at the Vatican. In March 1966 Polish Embassies abroad began refusing visas for pilgrims who wanted to attend the celebrations in Poland. The Pope was told that his visit would be "inopportune." The religious millennial festivities were initiated on April 9 as authorities intensified their attempts to split the Episcopate.* The bishops traveled through Poland, visiting every diocese. Meanwhile, the authorities tried to interrupt this travel, declared a boycott of Church festivities, tried to draw people away from them, and staged counter-celebrations, military parades, political meetings, soccer matches, bicycle races, and other events. On April 17 W. Gomułka* and Cardinal Wyszyński spoke at separate ceremonies in Poznań.* On May 2–3 hundreds of thousands of the faithful attended liturgy, sermons, and processions at Częstochowa,* participating in the largest open-air demonstration in Poland since October 1956. At the same time, the authorities organized a mass gathering to lay a cornerstone of a monument dedicated to the memory of Silesian Insurrections of 1919–21. An open-air sermon by Wyszyński on June 4, in Lublin,* was paralelled by public entertainment arranged nearby. Party newspapers accused the Church of abusing the millennial celebrations for political purposes. The entire governmental operation failed, but anti-Church activities were continued. In the same year, the authorities closed four Catholic seminars. M. K. Dziewanowski, *Poland in the Twentieth Century* (New

York, 1977), 191; *The History of Poland since 1863*, ed. by R. F. Leslie (Cambridge, 1980), 388; *Yearbook of International Communist Affairs*, 1966 (Stanford, Calif., 1967), 65–66.

MILLER, LESZEK (1946–   ), post-communist politician and deputy president of the Social Democracy of the Republic of Poland (SdRP),* nicknamed the "Chancellor." A worker in a textile factory in Żyrardów, he joined the Polish United Workers' Party (PZPR)* in 1969; in 1977 he began to work in the apparatus of its Central Committee.* During 1986–89 he served as the First Secretary of the Party organization in Skierniewice Province, and during 1988– 90, as Secretary of the Party Central Committee. In January 1990 he was instrumental in the establishment of the SdRP and became its secretary general. He served as Minister of Labor and Social Affairs in the governments of W. Pawlak* and J. Oleksy* in 1994–96. In the cabinet of W. Cimoszewicz,* Miller worked as Minister-Head of the Office of the Council of Ministers. He was appointed Minister of Internal Affairs and Administration on January 1, 1997. Tadeusz Mołdawa, *Ludzie Władzy 1944–1991. Władze państwowe i polityczne Polski według stanu na dzień 28 II 1991* (Warsaw, 1991), 396; *Kto jest kim w polityce polskiej*, ed. by R. Ignasiak (Warsaw, 1993), 194.

MIŁOSZ, CZESŁAW (1911–   ), poet and writer who won the 1980 Nobel Prize in Literature. He graduated from Vilna University, where he belonged to a circle of young liberal intellectuals and poets. During the war he was active in the anti-German resistance. His first postwar books were widely published in communist Poland, where Miłosz served as a diplomat. In 1951, however, he sought political asylum in Paris; nine years later he moved to the United States, where he joined the faculty of the University of California in Berkeley. Born in the ethnically mixed territories of northeastern prewar Poland and later involved in the political transformation of his country, he was interested in identity and worldview problems and devoted several of his best books to these issues (see, for example, *The Captive Mind* and *Native Realm*). He also authored numerous volumes of poems and a history of Polish literature. *Who's Who in the Socialist Countries of Europe*, ed. by J. Stroynowski, vol. 2 (Munich, 1989), 783; *Dictionary of Polish Literature*, ed. by E. J. Czerwinski (Westport, Conn., 1994), 268– 273; M. Dąbrowska, *Dzienniki powojenne 1945–49*, vol. 2, ed. by T. Drewnowski (Warsaw, 1996), 90.

MINC, HILARY (1905–74), one of three prominent Polish Stalinists and the creator of Poland's Stalinist economic system. Born into a Jewish family in Kazimierz Dolny, he joined the Communist Party of Poland (KPP) in 1922 and then, during his studies in Paris and Toulouse, became active in the Communist Party of France. In 1928 he returned to Poland and started working in the Main Statistical Office (GUS)* in Warsaw.* He spent World War II in the Soviet Union, where he taught economics at the University of Samarkand in 1939–43;

he also worked in the Union of Polish Patriots (ZPP) and the political apparatus of the communist-controlled Polish Army* in 1943–44. In 1944 he joined the Polish Workers' Party (PPR)* and its Politburo.* Between July and December 1944 he directed the Polish Committee of National Liberation (PKWN) the Office of Economics. Later he served as Minister of Industry (1945–49), as president of the government's Economic Committee (1945–50), as member of the secretariat of the Central Committee of the Polish United Workers' Party (PZPR)* (1948–54), as chairman of the Planning Committee (1949–54), and as Deputy Premier (1949–56). An architect of Stalinism in Poland and responsible for economic affairs, he led the "battle for trade" ("bitwa o handel"), tried to collectivize agriculture,* and (mis)developed heavy industry. As a result of de-Stalinization, Minc was dismissed from all his posts after October 1956 and, in 1957, retired. T. Mołdawa, *Ludzie Władzy 1944–1991. Władze państwowe i polityczne Polski według stanu na dzień 28 II 1991* (Warsaw, 1991), 396; *Encyklopedyczny Słownik Sławnych Polaków* (Warsaw, 1996), 237.

MINISTRY OF INTERNAL AFFAIRS (Ministerstwo Spraw Wewnętrznych [MSW]), continuation of the Ministry of Public Security* after its restructuring in 1954. MSW is in charge of the Citizens' Militia (MO)* and the political police—the Security Service.* MSW was directed, in succession, by W. Wicha* in 1954–64, M. Moczar* in 1964–68, K. Świtała in 1968–71, F. Szlachcic* in 1971, W. Ociepka in 1971–73, S. Kowalczyk* in 1973–80, M. Milewski* in 1980–81, and C. Kiszczak* in 1981–90. J. Karpiński, *Polska, Komunizm, Opozycja* (London, 1985), 148.

MINISTRY OF PUBLIC SECURITY (Ministerstwo Bezpieczeństwa Publicznego), institution established by the Polish Committee of National Liberation (PKWN) as a Department of Public Security to maintain order and defend the newly installed communist system in Poland. On December 31, 1944, the department, headed by S. Radkiewicz,* became one of the ministries of the Provisional Government.* Responsible for gross violations of the law and crimes against humanity, the Ministry of Public Security was dissolved in December 1954 and replaced by the Public Security Office, headed by W. Dworakowski,* and the Ministry of Internal Affairs, directed by W. Wicha.* Z. Błażyński, *Mówi Józef Światło. Za kulisami bezpieki i partii* (London, 1985).

MIODOWICZ, ALFRED (1929–   ), trade union activist and opponent of Solidarity.* A blast furnace worker in the Lenin Metallurgical Works in Nowa Huta* from 1952, he was active in the Polish Youth Movement (ZMP),* in government-controlled trade unions, and in the Polish United Workers' Party (PZPR).* During Martial Law,* in June 1983, he became chairman of the government-sponsored Federation of Metalworkers' Trade Union. From November 25, 1984, he served as chairman of the All-Poland Alliance of Trade Unions (OPZZ),* which according to the regime's plans was to replace Solidarity. Some members of the Jaruzelski* regime believed Miodowicz, being a true workers' leader, would be able to replace L. Wałęsa.* Indeed, in the mid-1980s Miodowicz's government-sponsored union became stronger than the persecuted Solidarity. Between November 1985 and July 1986 Miodowicz was a member of the State Council (Rada Państwa).* He joined both the Central Committee* and the Politburo* of the Party in July 1986 and stayed there until the end of the PZPR. He resisted re-legalization of Solidarity, trade union pluralism, the Round Table Negotiations,* and later the Balcerowicz* Plan. On November 30, 1988, Miodowicz lost his television debate with Wałęsa, and in the elections of June 1989,* he was defeated on the national list. In summer 1990 he helped to establish the Movement of the Working People (RLP) as a political platform for the OPZZ. A. T. Lane (ed.), *Biographical Dictionary of European Labor Leaders* (Westport, Conn., 1995), 654; *Who's Who in the Socialist Countries of Europe*, ed. by J. Stroynowski, vol. 2 (Munich, 1989), 787; *Kto jest kim w polityce polskiej*, ed. by R. Ignasiak (Warsaw, 1993), 195.

MIREWICZ, JERZY (1909–96), Jesuit, writer, one of the spiritual leaders of the Polish émigré community in England during 1963–93. T. Radzik, *Z dziejów społeczności polskiej w Wielkiej Brytanii po drugiej wojnie światowej* (Lublin, 1991), 85; J. Mirewicz, *Życie wewnętrzne emigracji* (London, 1978).

MIŚKIEWICZ, BENON (1930–), Minister of Science and Higher Education during 1982–87, responsible for implementation of Martial Law* rules at Polish universities* and other scientific institutions. T. Mołdawa, *Ludzie Władzy 1944–1991. Władze państwowe i polityczne Polski według stanu na dzień 28 II 1991* (Warsaw, 1991), 397.

MKS. See **Inter-Factory Strike Committee.**

MŁYŃCZAK, TADEUSZ WITOLD (1934–), leader of the Democratic Party (SD)* and Deputy President of the State Council (Rada Państwa)* between 1976 and 1989. *Who's Who in the Socialist Countries of Europe*, ed. by J. Stroynowski, vol. 2 (Munich, 1989), 792; A. Kępiński and Z. Kilar, *Kto jest kim w Polsce inaczej* (Warsaw, 1985), 265–283.

MO. See **Militia.**

MOCZAR, MIECZYSŁAW (1913–86), communist-nationalist politician and a main architect of the March events of 1968.* Born Mikołaj Demko into the family of a textile worker in Łódź,* he joined the Communist Party of Poland (KPP) in 1937. During 1939–41 he worked for Soviet intelligence in the Soviet-occupied territories of eastern Poland. In 1942 he joined the Polish Workers' Party (PPR)* and helped to organize communist guerrilla movements, the People's Guard (GL), and later the People's Army (AL). He served as commander-

in-chief of several of its districts and became a member of the Party Central
Committee.* During 1945–48 he was the chief of the Security Office (UB)* in
Łódź. Then, he occupied various important state apparatus positions. In 1956
he became Deputy Minister, and in 1964, the Minister of Interior. Simultaneously, he led the so-called Partisan faction within the Polish United Workers'
Party (PZPR).* The faction created its own "ideology," which combined basic
elements of "real socialism" with Polish chauvinism and based its power on
the war veterans' organization—the Union of Fighters for Independence and
Democracy (ZBoWiD)*—headed by Moczar. Most "Partisans" spent the war
in the communist underground in Poland and disliked their colleagues, who
"came from Moscow" after the war. Moczar and his friends accused W.
Gomułka* of being old and inefficient; they wanted to oust him and to intensify
communist control over Polish society. In his political manipulations Moczar
tried to use the anti-revisionist and anti-Jewish attitudes of the Soviet leaders
and the frustrations of Polish intellectuals and students in the mid-1960s. The
"Partisans" managed to provoke the March 1968 events and started a vitriolic
anti-Semitic campaign, which prompted the emigration from Poland of about
25,000 people of remote Jewish background. The Moczar faction purged the
Party and terrorized intellectuals, but it failed to oust Gomułka or to win the
support of the Soviets, who distrusted Moczar's authoritarian and chauvinist
tendencies. After the March events Moczar was "kicked upwards"; he lost his
ministerial post but became a deputy member and, then, full member of the
Politburo* and a member of the State Council (Rada Państwa).* Later he was
sidetracked by E. Gierek,* who in 1971 removed Moczar from the Politburo
and made him chairman of the Supreme Control Chamber (NIK).* In 1972,
Moczar was also dismissed from the post of president of the ZBoWiD; in 1976
he left the State Council. In 1980, during the Solidarity crisis,* he returned to
the Politburo and his ZBoWiD presidency, continued his anti-revisionist policy,
and made his last bid for power. Some Party leaders believed he would be able
to replace S. Kania,* but in July 1981 he left the Politburo again, and in 1983
he lost his NIK chairmanship and the leadership of ZBoWiD. Moczar's activities
are frequently considered a shameful chapter in the history of communist Poland.
Who's Who in the Socialist Countries of Europe, ed. by J. Stroynowski, vol. 2 (Munich,
1989), 794; G. Sanford and A. Gozdecka-Sanford, *Historical Dictionary of Poland* (Metuchen, N.J., 1994), 127; *The New York Times*, Nov. 2, 1986; T. Mołdawa, *Ludzie Władzy
1944–1991. Władze państwowe i polityczne Polski według stanu na dzień 28 II 1991*
(Warsaw, 1991), 398.

MOCZARSKI, KAZIMIERZ (1907–75), journalist. An important leader of
the underground Bureau of Information and Propaganda of the Home Army
(AK),* he was arrested by the communists in 1945 and sentenced to death for
alleged collaboration with the Gestapo. He spent 225 days in a prison cell with
SS General Jürgen Stroop, who commanded the final operation against the Warsaw Ghetto. In 1956 Moczarski, whose sentence was changed to life impris-

onment, left the prison and was rehabilitated. He authored *Conversations with the Executioner*, an important portrayal of Stroop, translated into several languages. *Encyklopedyczny Słownik Sławnych Polaków* (Warsaw, 1996), 240.

MOCZULSKI, LESZEK (1930–   ), politician, historian, and journalist. Between the early 1950s and the late 1970s he worked for several of Warsaw's periodicals, including the main organ of the Polish United Workers' Party (PZPR),* *Trybuna Ludu* ("The Tribune of the People").* Simultaneously, from the mid-1950s he headed a clandestine group that was transformed into the Confederation for an Independent Poland (KPN)* in 1979. Its program, based on the political heritage of Piłsudski, sought full sovereignty for Poland under a strong presidential system. Moczulski also helped to organize the Movement for the Defense of Human and Civil Rights (ROPCiO)* in 1977. In the 1980s Moczulski, the unquestioned autocratic leader of his party, was imprisoned many times and gained considerable prestige in select segments of Polish society. Yet during the presidential elections of 1990,* he received only 2.5% of the vote. His popularity grew due to the popular frustration of the post-communist period of transition in Poland. In the 1991 elections* the KPN received 8.7% of the vote and 44 seats in the Sejm.* During the September 1993 elections* the KPN did not manage to receive any seats, however, and the party gradually disintegrated. Moczulski lost his political position. *Who's Who in the Socialist Countries of Europe*, ed. by J. Stroynowski, vol. 2 (Munich, 1989), 794; *Kto jest kim w polityce polskiej*, ed. by R. Ignasiak (Warsaw, 1993), 196.

MODZELEWSKI, KAROL (1937–   ), historian, leader of the democratic opposition* in communist Poland, important politician after 1989, and son of Z. Modzelewski.* He gained fame in 1964 when, together with J. Kuroń,* he authored the "Open Letter to the Party," for which he was sentenced to three years in prison, removed from the Polish United Workers' Party (PZPR),* and expelled from his assistantship at Warsaw University.* Released in 1967, he was arrested again after the March events of 1968.* He stayed in prison until 1971. During the 1980–81 Solidarity* crisis he served as the spokesperson of Solidarity and as a member of its National Committee, but he resigned in April 1981 in protest against the autocratic leadership of L. Wałęsa.* Interned and imprisoned after imposition of Martial Law,* he joined the Solidarity Civic Committee* and was elected senator in 1989. During Solidarity's decomposition, known as the "war at the top,"* Modzelewski helped to form Labor Solidarity (Solidarność Pracy) and, in 1991, the Union of Labor (UP).* *Who's Who in the Socialist Countries of Europe*, ed. by J. Stroynowski, vol. 2 (Munich, 1989), 795; *Kto jest kim w polityce polskiej*, ed. by R. Ignasiak (Warsaw, 1993), 196; *Rodem z Solidarności*, ed. by B. Kopka and R. Żelichowski (Warsaw, 1997), 179–202.

MODZELEWSKI, ZYGMUNT (1900–54), economist and influential figure of the communist regime in postwar Poland. A member of the Social-Democracy of the Polish Kingdom and Lithuania (SDKPiL) from 1917 and of the Communist Party of Poland (KPP) from 1918, he emigrated to France in 1923, joined the Communist Party of France in the same year, and was elected to its Central Committee in the next year. In 1937 he moved to the Soviet Union, where he was active in the Union of Polish Patriots (ZPP) and the Bureau of Polish Communists in 1944. In 1945 he was appointed ambassador of communist Poland to Moscow. In 1945–47 he served as Deputy Minister and, during 1947–51, as Minister of Foreign Affairs. In 1952–54 he was also a member of the State Council (Rada Państwa),* and in 1951–54, Director of the Party's Institute of Social Sciences. T. Mołdawa, *Ludzie Władzy 1944–1991. Władze państwowe i polityczne Polski według stanu na dzień 28 II 1991* (Warsaw, 1991), 399.

MORAWIECKI, KORNEL (1941–   ), radical anti-communist activist. A veteran of the March events of 1968,* he helped to organize strikes in Wrocław* in 1980. Arrested and released in 1980, he was active in the underground after imposition of Martial Law* and, in 1982, established Fighting Solidarity.* Arrested in 1987, he was deported from Poland in 1988 but returned through the "green border" in the same year. He opposed the Round Table Negotiations,* continued his radical crusade against elements of the old system in post-1989 Poland, and formed the Freedom Party (Partia Wolności)* in 1990. He intended to participate in the presidential elections of 1990,* but he failed to collect the necessary number of his supporters. *Kto jest kim w polityce polskiej*, ed. by R. Ignasiak (Warsaw, 1993), 197.

MORAWSKI, JERZY (1918–   ), economist and journalist. He joined the Polish Workers' Party (PPR)* in 1942 and, until the end of the 1940s, was one of the main Party organizers of the communist youth movement. In the early 1950s he became a supervisor of the Party's propaganda apparatus. In 1955 he became Secretary of the Central Committee* of the Polish United Workers' Party (PZPR),* and in 1956 he joined the Party Politburo.* In 1960 he was removed from these two positions and sidetracked. T. Mołdawa, *Ludzie Władzy 1944–1991. Władze państwowe i polityczne Polski według stanu na dzień 28 II 1991* (Warsaw, 1991), 399.

MOSKWA, ZYGMUNT (1908–75), engineer and communist state official. A leader of the Democratic Party (SD),* he occupied several ministerial positions in the 1950s and 1960s and served as Deputy President of the State Council (Rada Państwa)* in 1969–75. T. Mołdawa, *Ludzie Władzy 1944–1991. Władze państwowe i polityczne Polski według stanu na dzień 28 II 1991* (Warsaw, 1991), 400.

MOTYKA, LUCJAN (1915–   ), driver by training. He was one of those leaders of the Polish Socialist Party (PPS)* who supported "unification" with the Polish Workers' Party (PPR).* In the late 1940s he was active in the communist youth movement and, in 1948–49, served as secretary general of the Union of

Polish Youth (ZMP).* Promoted from one state position to another, he reached the post of Minister of Culture in 1964. In 1971 he was dismissed and side-tracked as ambassador to several countries. *Who's Who in the Socialist Countries of Europe*, ed. by J. Stroynowski, vol. 2 (Munich, 1989), 805; T. Mołdawa, *Ludzie Władzy 1944–1991. Władze państwowe i polityczne Polski według stanu na dzień 28 II 1991* (Warsaw, 1991), 400.

MOVEMENT FOR THE DEFENSE OF HUMAN AND CIVIL RIGHTS
(Ruch Obrony Praw Człowieka i Obywatela [ROPCiO]), loose, independent organization established in March 1977 in Warsaw.* Among its founders were such experienced dissidents as L. Moczulski,* A. Czuma,* A. Pajdak,* J. Zieja,* and W. Ziembiński.* ROPCiO published several underground periodicals and mobilized public opinion against the communist regime. Its activities were sometimes considered competition with the Workers' Defense Committee (KOR).* Ideologically, ROPCiO was closer to the right than KOR and based its program on the Piłsudski tradition. In 1978 ROPCiO was divided into several groups. Their activities were crucial to the establishment of Solidarity* in 1980. J. J. Lipski, *KOR: A History of the Workers' Defense Committee in Poland, 1976–81* (Berkeley, Calif., 1985); J. Karpiński, *Polska, Komunizm, Opozycja* (London, 1985), 237; D. Cecuda, *Leksykon opozycji politycznej 1976–1989* (Warsaw, 1989), 99–101.

MOVEMENT FOR THE RECONSTRUCTION OF POLAND (Ruch Odbudowy Polski [ROP]), political organization established by supporters of J. Olszewski* after the first round of the presidential elections of 1995* on November 18. Soon ROP was joined by several right-oriented or small populist organizations and splinter groups from other parties; in 1996 it became one of the largest political blocs in Poland. Among its leaders are such experienced politicians as S. Jaworski,* K. Morawiecki,* P. Naimski,* Zygmunt Wrzodak, and J. Parys. *Polskie Partie Polityczne*, ed. by K. A. Paszkiewicz (Wrocław, 1996), 198–200.

MOVEMENT FOR THE REPUBLIC (Ruch dla Rzeczpospolitej [RdR]), small right-wing party organized in July 1992 by J. Olszewski* and a group of his supporters, who withdrew from the Center Alliance (PC)* after the fall of his government. The Olszewski group was joined by R. Szeremietiew's* tiny Polish Independence Party* and radical splinters from other ''center-right'' or right-oriented parties, such as the Christian-Democratic Labor Party (ChDSP)* or the Movement of the Third Republic (RTR). During the September 1993 elections* the RdR formed a coalition, called the Coalition for the Republic (KdR),* with A. Macierewicz's* Polish Action (AP) and K. Morawiecki's* Freedom Party (Partia Wolności, formerly Fighting Solidarity).* The KdR won only 2.7% of the vote and split after the elections in December 1993. The RdR considered itself a Christian, ''patriotic and pro-independence force,'' supported lustration, fundamental de-communization, and accession to NATO. Simulta-

neously, RdR supported economic interventionism and criticized "corrupt" privatization of the Mazowiecki* and Bielecki* governments. B. Szajkowski (ed.), *Political Parties of Eastern Europe, Russia, and the Successor States* (London, 1994), 334; *Polskie Partie Polityczne*, ed. by K. A. Paszkiewicz (Wrocław, 1996), 186–188.

MROZOWSKA, ZOFIA (1922–83), actress and professor at Warsaw's* State Drama School. She made her debut in 1945 and spent most of her career in the *Teatr Współczesny* ("Contemporary Theater") in Warsaw. *Nowa Encyklopedia Powszechna PWN*, vol. 3 (Warsaw, 1995), 324.

MROŻEK, SŁAWOMIR (1930–   ), prolific playwright and writer, whose satirical plays, such as *Tango, The Police*, and *The Ambassador*, gained him international fame. From 1963 Mrożek lived in France and Mexico, but in 1996 he returned to Poland. A master of the grotesque and the absurd, he caricatured primitive, cut-and-dry routines of contemporary life. *Dictionary of Polish Literature*, ed. by E. J. Czerwinski (Westport, Conn., 1994), 283–287; *Encyklopedyczny Słownik Sławnych Polaków* (Warsaw, 1996), 246.

MUNK, ANDRZEJ (1921–61), film director and representative of the early Polish postwar cinematographers, whose movies, such as *Pasażerka* ("The Female Passenger") and *Człowiek na torze* ("A Man of the Railwaytrack"), won several international awards. *Encyklopedyczny Słownik Sławnych Polaków* (Warsaw, 1996), 247.

MUSIC. The history of Polish music after 1945 reflects the general Polish situation after World War II. The entire structure of Poland's musical life had to be rebuilt after the destruction caused by the war. New orchestras and new song and dance ensembles were organized. Music-publishing houses were established, and the collection and classification of folklore began on a large scale. Polish music education was revitalized. Neoclassicism continued as the main compositional trend, reaching its peak in the early postwar years. In 1949 the first postwar Chopin Competition was held. Yet in the same year the era of Socialist Realism* began. Its doctrine, together with official hostility toward innovation and Western influences, separated Poland from contemporary trends in world music. During the entire Stalinist period* only a few outstanding works were produced on the margins of official musical life. The "thaw"* and the "Polish October" of 1956* brought a dramatic change in music as well. Outstanding new composers, such as K. Penderecki* and H. Górecki,* appeared and by the 1960s gained worldwide fame. The important music festival "Warsaw Autumn" was organized every year since 1956. Avant-garde music began to flourish in Poland to a higher degree than in any other East European state. *The New Grove Dictionary of Music and Musicians*, ed. by S. Sadie, vol. 15 (New York, 1980), 28–29; J. M. Chomiński, *Muzyka Polski Ludowej* (Warsaw, 1968).

NAIMSKI, PIOTR (1951–), member of the Workers' Defense Committee (KOR)* from 1976 and Solidarity* activist from 1980. He co-edited the underground periodical *Głos* ("Voice")* from 1977 and directed the *Głos* Publishing House in 1989–92. In 1992 he became chief of the State Protection Bureau (UOP). *Kto jest kim w polityce polskiej*, ed. by R. Ignasiak (Warsaw, 1993), 190; J. J. Lipski, *KOR: A History of the Workers' Defense Committee in Poland, 1976–81* (Berkeley, Calif., 1985).

NAJDER, ZDZISŁAW (1930–), literary historian, who taught at Warsaw University* but was removed for political reasons in 1960. In the 1970s Najder was active in the clandestine Polish Independence Agreement (PPN).* Later he was a visiting professor at many U.S. and West European universities. A director of the Polish section of Radio Free Europe* during 1981–87, he was sentenced to death *in absentia* by the communist authorities in 1983. After his return to Poland in 1990, Najder ran the Citizens' Committees, and in February 1990 he became chairman of the National Citizens' Committee.* He also served as adviser to President L. Wałęsa* and Premier J. Olszewski.* He retired from politics in 1992, when it became known that he had in the past maintained vague contacts with communist secret police. G. Sanford and A. Gozdecka-Sanford, *Historical Dictionary of Poland* (Metuchen, N.J., 1994), 132; *Kto jest kim w polityce polskiej*, ed. by R. Ignasiak (Warsaw, 1993), 190; T. Mołdawa, *Ludzie Władzy 1944–1991. Władze państwowe i polityczne Polski według stanu na dzień 28 II 1991* (Warsaw, 1991), 401; A. Micewski, *Ludzie i opcje* (Warsaw, 1993), 130–135.

NAŁKOWSKA, ZOFIA (1884–1954), prolific writer active mostly in the interwar period. After the war she served as the director of the Main Committee for Research of German [later Nazi] Crimes in Poland and accepted a seat in the National Home Council (KRN)* and the Sejm.* She was also a member of the *Kuźnica* ("The Forge") editorial staff. *Dictionary of Polish Literature*, ed. by E. J. Czerwinski (Westport, Conn., 1994), 289–291; *Encyklopedyczny Słownik Sławnych Polaków* (Warsaw, 1996), 249.

NAMIOTKIEWICZ, WALERY (1931–), Party official. A personal secretary of W. Gomułka* during 1956–71, he continued his career as deputy chief editor of the monthly *Nowe Drogi* ("New Ways"),* the main theoretical organ of the Polish United Workers' Party (PZPR),* in 1971–74, and as the head of the Ideological Department of the Central Committee* of the PZPR. *Who's Who in the Socialist Countries of Europe*, ed. by J. Stroynowski, vol. 2 (Munich, 1989), 825.

NAROŻNIAK, JAN (1950–), Solidarity* activist. After imposition of Martial Law,* he continued his activities in the underground. Wounded and arrested by secret police, he was carried away from a hospital in a spectacular action by the underground Solidarity. J. Holzer, K. Leski, *Solidarność w podziemiu* (Łódź, 1990), 53.

NASZKOWSKI, MARIAN (1912–), Party official. Active in the communist movement before the war, he served in the communist-controlled Polish Army* in the USSR, headed the Polish Military Mission to Paris in 1945–47, directed the Main Political Board of the Polish Army in 1950–52, and was a Deputy Foreign Minister in 1952–65. *Who's Who in the Socialist Countries of Europe*, ed. by J. Stroynowski, vol. 2 (Munich, 1989), 828.

NATIONAL ARMED FORCES (Narodowe Siły Zbrojne [NSZ]), underground guerrilla organization established in German-occupied Poland in August–September 1942 by part of the clandestine National Party (SN). The SN and its National Military Organization (NOW) split in mid-1942, when nearly half their members refused to join the Home Army (AK)* or recognize the underground Delegacy of the Polish Government-in-Exile.* The radicals united with the Rampart Group (Szaniec), the Union of Salamander (Związek Jaszczurczy), and several other groups previously organized by the leaders of the prewar National-Radical Camp (ONR) and founded the NSZ, subject to the Provisional National Political Council. Although the NSZ numbered about 70,000 people in 1943, it remained internally divided into two factions. The less radical faction eventually joined the AK in March 1944, whereas the more radical faction remained independent. The radicals claimed that of the two enemies of Poland—Germany and the USSR—the latter was more dangerous; they fought with leftist guerrilla groups to cleanse Poland of Soviet agents before the Red Army* entered the country. As a consequence of this policy, the NSZ murdered several communist guerrilla groups and Jews* hiding in the forests. During its anti-Jewish action the NSZ killed several AK members of Jewish background, including two officers from the High Command of the AK in June 1943. In 1944 the NSZ tried to mobilize its forces to evacuate them from Poland to the Allied-controlled West. In January 1945 the NSZ Świętokrzyska Brigade, in agreement with the Germans, left Poland for Czechoslovakia to join the U.S. Army. In May 1945 the NSZ commander-in-chief, Gen. Zygmunt Broniewski, "Bogucki," ordered the guerrilla units dissolved. Yet many units continued their activities and participated in the anti-Soviet resistance until 1948 despite lack of a NSZ central political and military command, which had either immigrated to the West or been caught and frequently sentenced to death by the communist authorities. Service in the NSZ was not recognized by the Government-in-Exile as service in the Polish armed forces. S. Korboński, *The Polish Underground State: A Guide to the Underground, 1939–1945* (New York, 1978), 104–108; K. Kersten, *The Establishment of Communist Rule in Poland, 1943–1948* (Berkeley, Calif., 1991), 21, 126, 229; *Słownik Historii Polski 1939–1948*, ed. by A. Chwalba and T. Gąsowski (Cracow, 1994), 78–80.

NATIONAL BANK OF POLAND (Narodowy Bank Polski [NBP]). See **Finance.**

NATIONAL DEMOCRATS, traditional trend in Polish politics. The name is derived from the National Democratic Party established by Roman Dmowski at the end of the 19th century. Later the party assumed several different names and existed in Poland until the end of World War II. After 1989 numerous political groups built their programs upon the National Democratic heritage. G. Sanford and A. Gozdecka-Sanford, *Historical Dictionary of Poland* (Metuchen, N.J., 1994), 132.

NATIONAL FRONT. See **FJN.**

NATIONAL HOME COUNCIL (Krajowa Rada Narodowa [KRN]), underground representative body established by the Polish Workers' Party (PPR)* in Warsaw* on December 31, 1943–January 1, 1944. It consisted of 31 representatives of the PPR and several small left-oriented groups, such as a faction of the Workers' Party of Polish Socialists and the peasant "People's Will." The KRN rejected the authority of the Polish Government-in-Exile,* its delegates,* and its structures in Poland. It aimed to seize power in Poland and establish a communist system with the help of the Red Army.* The KRN developed the communist guerrilla movement, transforming the People's Guard (GL) into the People's Army (AL), and sent a KRN delegation to Moscow. It reached the capital of the USSR in May 1944 and, in the next month, was recognized by Soviet leaders as the only legal representation of the Polish nation. In July 1944 KRN members helped establish the Polish Committee of National Liberation (PKWN), and beginning in 1945 the KRN served as a provisional parliament. Presided by B. Bierut,* it had 444 co-opted members and, during eight sessions, passed 44 laws and endorsed 435 decrees of the PKWN, the Provisional Government,* and the Provisional Government of National Unity (TRJN).* The last session of the KRN took place in September 1946. On January 19, 1947, the

KRN was replaced by the Sejm,* a move arranged after the elections of January 1947.* M. K. Dziewanowski, *The Communist Party of Poland: An Outline of History* (Cambridge, Mass., 1976), 170–174; J. Coutouvidis and J. Reynolds, *Poland, 1939–1947* (Leicester, 1986); K. Kersten, *The Establishment of Communist Rule in Poland, 1943–1948* (Berkeley, Calif., 1991); *Dzieje Sejmu Polskiego*, ed. by J. Bardach (Warsaw, 1993).

NATIONAL MINORITIES. Throughout its history, but especially between the 13th century and World War II, Poland was a multinational country. In the interwar Polish state, national minorities constituted 31% of the whole population. During World War II most Jews* were killed; the postwar territorial and population shift completely changed the ethnic makeup of Poland. It lost its Eastern Territories (Kresy Wschodnie), which, before the war, contained a majority of its non-Polish citizens. In exchange Poland received the "Recovered Territories" (Ziemie Odzyskane),* formerly German. In 1944–45 about 6 million Germans* emigrated or were expelled from these areas and were followed next by large groups of German migrants after the war. As a consequence of several repatriation agreements with the Soviet Union, about 3 million Poles moved to Poland from the east. Simultaneously, hundreds of thousands of non-Polish people left for the Soviet Union. Between 1946 and 1949 about 2.5 million Germans, Ukrainians,* Belorussians,* and Jews emigrated from Poland. In the 1950s and 1960s several new waves of German and Jewish migrations left Poland. By 1950 the Polish authorities estimated that only 450,000 citizens of Poland (1.5%) were ethnically non-Polish. In the mid-1960s the official estimate placed the size of the non-Polish population at 440,000, including about 180,000 Ukrainians, 160,000 Belorussians, 25,000 Jews, 20,000 Slovaks, 2,000 Czechs, 10,000 Russians, 10,000 Lithuanians,* 4,000 Germans, 18,000 Gypsies,* 10,000 Greeks* and Macedonians, and 1,000 others. In reality all these numbers, especially those concerning the German, Ukrainian, and Belorussian minorities, were higher. West German sources estimated the non-Polish population at 2.5 million, or 8% of the population, which also appears too high. Credible sources to confirm the estimates do not exist. Since the 1950s, Polish censuses did not include questions concerning national consciousness of Polish citizens. According to the Constitution of 1952,* all citizens, "independently of nationality, race or religion," possess "equal rights in all spheres of governmental, political, economic, social and cultural life." Further, the same Constitution stated: "The violation of these principles through direct or indirect expansion or restriction of the law with regard to nationality, race or religion is punishable," and "The dissemination of hatred or indifference, the instigation of discord, or the humiliation of any person of different nationality, race or religion is forbidden." In fact, however, the state authorities tried to "Polonize" and to territorially disperse national minorities. The official theory that Poland was practically an ethnically homogenous state constituted an important part of an attempt to legitimize the communist system, which had allegedly given Poland new, improved borders.* After the war most Poles were not interested in

national-minority problems, and it was only in the Solidarity* era that Polish
mass media began to publish more about national minorities. S. M. Horak (ed.),
Eastern European National Minorities, 1919–1980: A Handbook (Littleton, Colo., 1985),
52–55.

NATIONAL SYMBOLS. Polish national emblem or coat of arms, flag, and
anthem. The traditional, 1,000-year-old coat of arms is the white eagle with
golden beak and talons, turned to its right on a red field. The white eagle of the
Polish People's Republic had no crown. In 1989 the eagle's head was crowned
again, as during the interwar period. The flag, made up of the national colors,
is divided into two symmetric horizontal stripes, the white one on the top, the
red one on the bottom. The present national anthem has been developed from
the "Song of the Legions," written by Józef Wybicki in 1797 for Polish le-
gionnaires fighting under Napoleon in Italy. The anthem symbolizes the hope
and belief of Poles in the recovery and success of their state and starts with the
words: "Poland has not yet perished while we are still alive! What foreign
aggression has deprived us of we will recover with our own sabers!" G. Sanford
and A. Gozdecka-Sanford, *Historical Dictionary of Poland* (Metuchen, N.J., 1994), 132.

NATIONAL UNITY FRONT. See **FJN.**

NATIONALIZATION, communist state assumption of ownership of economic
enterprises in Poland. The communist state apparatus, through a series of governmental decrees, parliamentary votes, and administrative procedures during
1944–52, took over an absolute majority of all Polish enterprises.
Nationalization, consistent with the Soviet policy in East-Central Europe, had
numerous far-reaching consequences for the development of Poland. The country's political left traditionally supported nationalization, and after 1944 there
was no force left in Poland to oppose this procedure. Although the Manifesto
of the Polish Committee of National Liberation (PKWN) did not mention it, the
entire economic policy of the PKWN, and later of the communist-controlled
governments, led to complete nationalization. Already on December 14, 1944,
the National Home Council (KRN)* had decreed the nationalization of some
categories of forests.

During World War II the Germans controlled all Polish economic enterprises
and killed or deported most of their owners. Only a few owners remained to
direct their businesses in early 1945, immediately after the Germans left Poland.
Most economic establishments were led by their crews. On May 20, 1945, the
KRN issued a decree limiting the prerogatives of Workers' Councils. Meanwhile, the Ministry of Industry gradually developed an apparatus that controlled
most enterprises. The decrees of March 2 and May 6, 1945, introduced vague
categories of "abandoned" (opuszczony) and "left" (porzucony) enterprises.
A new institution, the Provisional State Administration (Tymczasowy Zarząd
Państwowy), was responsible for them and was also in charge of re-privatization

when original owners returned from abroad, hiding, and concentration camps. The state administration used many pretexts to slow down the re-privatization process. Owners were accused of collaboration with the Germans or of the inability to start new production. Frequently, according to governmental decisions, the disputed enterprises were substantially developed during the war, their production profile was changed, and as a consequence, their values and character were different from those of the properties "abandoned" before 1945. Often, however, the original owners' rights were indisputable. A visible part of Polish industry was recovered by private entrepreneurs, and Poland went through a period comparable to the Soviet New Economic Policy. Nonetheless, on January 3, 1946, the KRN passed a law to nationalize enterprises with more than 50 workers employed on one shift. This law stipulated that in special cases smaller establishments should be nationalized too. All the parties represented in the KRN voted for this law, although the Polish Peasant Party (PSL)* voiced several reservations. The PSL was afraid that early nationalization would slow down the rebuilding of war-damaged Poland and believed that nationalization should follow a successful rebuilding of the country. The PSL also wanted enterprises of up to 100 workers to stay in private hands and was against the stipulation that in special cases the government would be able to nationalize a given enterprise by a simple decree. These reservations were rejected, and the nationalization law was accepted in its original radical form. Fast and efficient nationalization procedures followed, supported by a portion of Polish workers. Already by 1947 over 70% of them were employed in the nationalized enterprises. In 1947 and 1948 most shops and restaurants were taken over by the state. In 1951 private pharmacies were nationalized, and in 1952, foundations' properties. Only land owned by peasants remained in private hands, but the government hoped that collectivization* would solve this problem automatically. The whole of Polish industry became highly centralized and Sovietized to be compatible with the economy of the USSR. K. Kersten, *The Establishment of Communist Rule in Poland, 1943–1948* (Berkeley, Calif., 1991), 62–63, 165–166, 202–203; *Słownik Historii Polski 1939–1948*, ed. by A. Chwalba and T. Gąsowski (Cracow, 1994), 73–78.

NATOLIN. See **Polish October of 1956.**

NATURAL ENVIRONMENT. See **Ecology.**

NAWROCKI, JERZY (1926–90), member of the State Council (Rada Państwa)* during 1985–89. T. Mołdawa, *Ludzie Władzy 1944–1991. Władze państwowe i polityczne Polski według stanu na dzień 28 II 1991* (Warsaw, 1991), 401.

NEGATIVE SELECTION, selection of leaders of the Party and all state institutions based not on their meritorious qualities but, primarily, on their obedience toward the Party-state apparatus. This process proved to be detrimental to Poland and to the communist system itself because it eliminated numerous intelligent people who opposed communism and did not want to compromise their integrity by accepting a Party card. M. K. Dziewanowski, *The Communist Party of Poland: An Outline of History* (Cambridge, Mass., 1976), 253–257.

NEWERLY, IGOR (1903–87), writer whose works, such as *Pamiątka z celulozy* ("Remembrance of Cellulose Works"), became standards of Polish socialist literature. *Who's Who in the Socialist Countries of Europe*, ed. by J. Stroynowski, vol. 2 (Munich, 1989), 842; P. Kuncewicz, *Agonia i nadzieja. Literatura polska od 1939*, vol. 2 (Warsaw, 1993), 416–420.

NEWSPEAK, word coined by G. Orwell in his novel *1984* to name the ambiguous and deceptive talk of the government to influence, indoctrinate, and control public opinion. Newspeak became the language of communist ideology, changed the meaning of numerous old words, primitivized the exchange of thoughts, and contributed to the lie of the "real socialism" ideology. J. Karpiński, *Polska, Komunizm, Opozycja* (London, 1985), 161.

NEY, ROMAN (1931–   ), professor of geology, member of the Central Committee* of the Polish United Workers' Party (PZPR)* during 1980–81 and 1986–90, and vice-president of the Polish Academy of Sciences (PAN)* from 1990. *Who's Who in the Socialist Countries of Europe*, ed. by J. Stroynowski, vol. 2 (Munich, 1989), 843; T. Mołdawa, *Ludzie Władzy 1944–1991. Władze państwowe i polityczne Polski według stanu na dzień 28 II 1991* (Warsaw, 1991), 402.

NIE OR NIEPODLEGŁOŚĆ ("Independence"), underground organization established by the Home Army (AK)* in spring 1944 to continue resistance during the Red Army* occupation of Poland. Nie was maintained as a skeleton organization, dissolved after the arrest of the 16 leaders of the Polish underground state by the Soviets in March 1945. A. Chwalba and T. Gąsowski, *Słownik historii Polski 1939–1948* (Cracow, 1994), 80–85.

NIEĆKO, JÓZEF (1891–1953), journalist and peasant politician. From 1938 he became a leader of the Peasant Party in 1938 and edited, or contributed to, its numerous periodicals during the interwar period. A leader of the clandestine Peasant Party and its guerrilla units during the war, he served as a deputy president of the Main Executive Committee of the Polish Peasant Party (PSL)* in 1945–47. A supporter of a compromise with the communists, he was expelled from the PSL in March 1947, presided over the PSL-Left and, in 1947–49, was president of a new communist-sponsored PSL. From 1948 to his death in 1953, he served as a member of the State Council (Rada Państwa).* T. Mołdawa, *Ludzie Władzy 1944–1991. Władze państwowe i polityczne Polski według stanu na dzień 28 II 1991* (Warsaw, 1991), 402; A. K. Kunert, *Ilustrowany przewodnik po Polsce podziemnej, 1939–1945* (Warsaw, 1996), 534.

NIEPODLEGŁOŚĆ ("Independence"), underground monthly established and published by a group gathered around Józef Darski from 1982. In 1984 it became the main organ of the Liberal-Democratic Party "Independence," but after a split in the party, two periodicals of the same title appeared until the late 1980s. D. Cecuda, *Leksykon opozycji politycznej 1976–1989* (Warsaw, 1989), 176; J. Karpiński, *Polska, Komunizm, Opozycja* (London, 1985), 159.

NIESIOŁOWSKI, STEFAN K. (1944–   ), activist of anti-communist opposition, co-organizer and leader of the Christian-National Union (ZChN).* A graduate and faculty member of Łódź University, he participated in clandestine opposition groups from the mid-1960s. Deeply involved in Solidarity* and interned in 1981, he became a leader of Solidarity, Łódź Region. A member of the Solidarity Civic Committee,* he was elected in 1989 to the Sejm,* where he became one of the most active representatives of the ZChN. *Kto jest kim w polityce polskiej*, ed. by R. Ignasiak (Warsaw, 1993), 200.

NIEZABITOWSKA, MAŁGORZATA (1948–   ), journalist and spokesperson of the Mazowiecki* government. *Kto jest kim w polityce polskiej*, ed. by R. Ignasiak (Warsaw, 1993), 204.

NIK. See **Supreme Control Chamber.**

NOMENKLATURA, list of important state positions that could be occupied exclusively by persons accepted by the Party leadership. *Nomenklatura* is also understood as a specific social class or group of people regarded by communist authorities as suitably qualified to fill top positions in state apparatus, industry, administration, culture, and so on. The institution of *nomenklatura* reduced all elections in communist states to a show of acceptance of decisions made by the top party leaders. The word "nomenklatura" was taken from the Russian language and became a part of the "newspeak,"* a communist lingo. In Poland the *nomenklatura* was especially strengthened during the Gierek* period, when it reached about 130,000 members. After imposition of Martial Law,* Gen. W. Jaruzelski* tried to curb the *nomenklatura*, but he failed and the group actually doubled. After communism fell in Poland, the *nomenklatura* initially lost its political significance, although it survived as a group of interest and frequently managed to transform previous political control over state property into private ownership. After former communists returned to power in Poland in 1993, the old *nomenklatura* liaisons became relevant again. *Political and Economic Encyclopedia of the Soviet Union and Eastern Europe*, ed. by S. White (London, 1990), 185; J. Karpiński, *Polska, Komunizm, Opozycja* (London, 1985), 160.

NON-PARTY BLOC FOR THE SUPPORT OF REFORM (Bezpartyjny Blok Wspierania Reform [BBWR]), party founded under L. Wałęsa's* patronage in June 1993. After the fall of the Suchocka* government and before the elections of 1993,* Wałęsa tried to unite all the parties of the Suchocka cabinet into an electoral alliance. When his effort failed, Wałęsa decided to organize a "presidential" party that would resemble the interwar Non-Party Bloc of the Cooperation with Government. The latter had the same role and acronym, BBWR, and was formed by J. Piłsudski, with whom Wałęsa immodestly, if not grotesquely, identified. Wałęsa expected Solidarity,* the business community, the peasantry, and local government bodies to support BBWR, but he grossly miscalculated their response. The party did not have well-known leaders, except for A. Olechowski,* and gained only 5.4% of the vote, which gave it 16 seats in the Sejm* and two in the Senate.* BBRW postulated the strengthening of the president's role and powers for local government. The party's electoral manifesto of 1993 amazed Polish public opinion, promising credit of 300 million złoty (about $US 15,000) for all. Splits and internal conflicts soon turned the party into a third-rate political group. B. Szajkowski (ed.), *Political Parties of Eastern Europe, Russia, and the Successor States* (London, 1994), 335.

NOSSOL, ALFONS (1932–   ), bishop of Opole* since 1977 and professor of theology, active in the field of dialogue with the Lutherans. *Who's Who in the Socialist Countries of Europe*, ed. by J. Stroynowski, vol. 2 (Munich, 1989), 850; G. Polak, *Kto jest kim w Kościele katolickim* (Warsaw, 1996), 260.

NOWa (Niezależna Oficyna Wydawnicza [Independent Publishing House]), one of the largest underground publishing houses in communist Poland. Established in 1977 by J. Krupski, A. Macierewicz,* M. Chojecki,* B. Borusewicz,* and P. Jegliński, it survived into the post-communist period and published several periodicals and numerous books by Polish and foreign authors forbidden by censorship.* *Dictionary of Polish Literature*, ed. by E. J. Czerwinski (Westport, Conn., 1994), 88; D. Cecuda, *Leksykon opozycji politycznej 1976–1989* (Warsaw, 1989), 136; J. Karpiński, *Polska, Komunizm, Opozycja* (London, 1985), 159.

NOWA HUTA, industrial district of Cracow* and site of a large Lenin (now Sędzimir) iron and steel complex founded in the late 1940s. The decision to locate the Lenin Works there was strictly political, aimed at making conservative and primarily anti-communist Cracow more "proletarian." From the economic and ecological point of view, the location was wrong, even disastrous. Nowa Huta, initially a symbol of the communist transformation of Poland, became an important center of political opposition in the 1970s and 1980s. New workers coming from the countryside fought to build a church and demanded better living conditions. With 216,000 inhabitants in 1982, Nowa Huta witnessed bloody skirmishes between the workers and the Citizens' Militia* several times. *Nowa Encyklopedia Powszechna PWN*, vol. 4 (Warsaw, 1995), 537.

NOWA KULTURA ("The New Culture"), weekly published in Warsaw* during 1950–63 and organ of the Polish Writers' Union in 1952–56. Initially, the weekly served as an important means of indoctrination. It popularized Socialist Realism* and criticized the "American way of life" and "Atlantic culture." In the mid-1950s *Nowa Kultura* gradually changed, becoming involved in the political and cultural "thaw."* It published A. Ważyk's* *Poem for Adults* and articles by L. Kołakowski,* W. Woroszylski,* and K. T. Toeplitz.* Identified with the revisionist forces by the Party leadership, the weekly was dissolved in 1963 and replaced by *Kultura*. J. Karpiński, *Polska, Komunizm, Opozycja* (London, 1985), 161.

NOWAK, ROMAN (1900–80), member of the State Council (Rada Państwa)* during 1957–69 and the First Secretary of the provincial Party organization in Opole* in 1950–56. T. Mołdawa, *Ludzie Władzy 1944–1991. Władze państwowe i polityczne Polski według stanu na dzień 28 II 1991* (Warsaw, 1991), 403.

NOWAK, ZENON (1905–80), important communist official and spokesperson of the hard-line Party faction "Natolin" in 1954–56. A member of the Communist Party of Poland (KPP) from 1924 and its Central Committee* from 1932, he spent World War II in German labor camps and served in the Red Army* in 1945–47. Later he returned to Poland, joined the Polish Workers' Party (PPR, after 1948 the Polish United Workers' Party [PZPR])* and occupied several key positions in its apparatus. During 1948–80 he was a member of the Party Central Committee, and in 1954–56, of the Politburo.* In 1948 he headed the Party organization in Katowice* Province, in 1948–50 he directed a Personnel Department of the Central Committee, and during 1952–68 he was Deputy Premier. Despite his being a main leader of the "Natolin" faction, he was removed from the top Party and state leadership after 1956. He lost his position as Deputy Premier and served in secondary posts such as President of the Supreme Control Chamber (NIK)* in 1969–71 and ambassador to the USSR in 1971–78. G. Sanford and A. Gozdecka-Sanford, *Historical Dictionary of Poland* (Metuchen, N.J., 1994), 135; T. Mołdawa, *Ludzie Władzy 1944–1991. Władze państwowe i polityczne Polski według stanu na dzień 28 II 1991* (Warsaw, 1991), 403.

NOWAK-JEZIORAŃSKI, JAN (1913–   ), soldier and courier of the Home Army (AK)* during World War II, staff member of the Polish section of the BBC in 1948–52, and director of the Polish section of Radio Free Europe* in 1952–75. He arranged the J. Światło* broadcasts in the 1950s and other broadcasts unmasking the communist regime in Poland. After his retirement from Radio Free Europe, he became an important leader of the Polish lobby and community in the United States. He also authored several important books. A. Micewski, *Ludzie i opcje* (Warsaw, 1993), 117–122; *Nowa Encyklopedia Powszechna PWN*, vol. 4 (Warsaw, 1995), 53; J. Nowak, *Wojna w eterze* (London, 1985); J. Nowak, *Polska z oddali* (London, 1988).

NOWAKOWSKI, MAREK (1935–   ), writer and activist of political opposition* persecuted for his opinions. His short stories and novellas mostly describe everyday life of "gray people," the social margin, and the criminal underground. Communist critics accused Nowakowski of tendentiousness and seeing reality in black. P. Kuncewicz, *Agonia i nadzieja. Proza polska od 1956*, vol. 5 (Warsaw, 1994), 14–20.

NOWE DROGI ("New Ways"), theoretical organ of the Central Committee* of the Polish Workers' Party (PPR)* and then the Polish United Workers' Party (PZPR),* published as a monthly during 1947–89. Some issues, including, for example, protocols of the Central Committee plenary sessions, constitute an important primary source. *Nowa Encyklopedia Powszechna PWN*, vol. 4 (Warsaw, 1995), 539.

NOWINA-KONOPKA, PIOTR (1949–   ), economist and Solidarity* spokesperson in 1988–89. A graduate and faculty member of Gdańsk University, he served as a secretary of the Gdańsk* Club of Catholic Intelligentsia* in 1980–84 and collaborated closely with L. Wałęsa* from 1982. From November 1989 to November 1990, he was Minister of State and unofficial Solidarity representative in the chancellery of the President* of Poland, Gen. W. Jaruzelski.* During the "war at the top"* he joined the political camp of T. Mazowiecki.* From December 1990 he served as the secretary general of the Democratic Union (UD).* T. Mołdawa, *Ludzie Władzy 1944–1991. Władze państwowe i polityczne Polski według stanu na dzień 28 II 1991* (Warsaw, 1991), 404.

NSZ. See **National Armed Forces.**

NSZZIRS. See **Artisans' Solidarity.**

NSZZR. See **Rural Solidarity.**

NZS. See **Independent Students' Association**.

O

OASIS MOVEMENT, Polish religious youth movement. It began in 1954, when only 60 persons participated in its activities. In spite of harassment by communist authorities, the movement grew rapidly, reaching 64,000 members in 1994. Since 1976 Oasis is known as the Light-Life Movement (Ruch Światło-Życie). Its initial name was derived from summer camps, called oases, where members participated in religious recollections. *Nowa Encyklopedia Powszechna PWN*, vol. 6 (Warsaw, 1996), 261; J. Karpiński, *Polska, Komunizm, Opozycja* (London, 1985), 239.

OBODOWSKI, JANUSZ (1930–), economist, Minister of Labor in 1980–81, and Deputy Premier during 1981–85. *Who's Who in the Socialist Countries of Europe*, ed. by J. Stroynowski, vol. 2 (Munich, 1989), 859; A. Kępiński and Z. Kilar, *Kto jest kim w Polsce inaczej* (Warsaw, 1985), 283–300.

OCHAB, EDWARD (1906–89), economist, First Secretary of the Polish United Workers' Party (PZPR)* from March to October 1956, Deputy President of the State Council (Rada Państwa)* in 1961–64, and its Chairman during 1964–68. A member of the Communist Party of Poland (KPP) from 1929, he was considered a truly "believing" communist. He spent World War II in the USSR, where he volunteered in the Red Army* and an organizer and leader of the Union of Polish Patriots (ZPP). In 1943 Ochab was transferred to the Polish Army* and soon became its political deputy commander. In 1944 he joined the Polish Workers' Party (PPR)* and its Central Committee.* After the war he occupied several important apparatus positions, such as a Deputy Minister and Minister of Public Administration in 1944–45, First Secretary of the Katowice* provincial Party organization in 1946–48, and Deputy Minister of Defense in 1949–50. From 1948 he was a Politburo* member in charge of ideology; after the death of B. Bierut,* he became the Party First Secretary. Yet in October

1956 he peacefully retired from this position to make room for W. Gomułka.*
Resigning during the March events of 1968* as a protest against the anti-Semitic
policies of the regime, he joined the opposition within the communist establishment. G. Sanford and A. Gozdecka-Sanford, *Historical Dictionary of Poland* (Metuchen,
N.J., 1994), 136; *Who's Who in the Socialist Countries of Europe*, ed. by J. Stroynowski,
vol. 2 (Munich, 1989), 861; T. Mołdawa, *Ludzie Władzy 1944–1991. Władze państwowe
i polityczne Polski według stanu na dzień 28 II 1991* (Warsaw, 1991), 404; Z. Błażyński,
Mówi Józef Światło. Za kulisami bezpieki i partii (London, 1985), 44–46.

ODER RIVER (Polish and Czech Odra), the second largest river in Poland;
also the second river (after the Vistula*) emptying into the Baltic, flowing 531
miles (854 km) from its source in the Oder Mountains to the Baltic Sea. Since
the origin of the Polish state in the 10th century the river has formed Poland's
border with the Germanic states. From the 14th century to 1945, the Oder ran
through German-controlled territories; later, as the Oder-Neisse Line, it became
a part of the Polish-German border again. The longest navigable river in Poland,
connected by canals with the Vistula and the Western European waterway system, the Oder is of major economic importance, especially as a connection
between Silesia and the ports of the Baltic. *The New Encyclopaedia Britannica*, vol.
8 (Chicago, 1990), 872–873.

ODER-NEISSE LINE, western border of Poland on the Rivers Oder (Odra)*
and Neisse (Nysa) established after World War II and recognized de facto by
the Allies at the Yalta* and Potsdam* Conferences as a compensation for the
territories lost by Poland to the Soviet Union. This transfer caused mass migrations of Poles and Germans* and became a bone of contention between Germany
and Poland. In Yalta the United States and Great Britain accepted the Oder as
a border but wanted to extend the line along the Eastern Neisse (Glatzer Neisse
or Nysa Kłodzka). It joins the Oder between Wrocław* and Opole* and is
located about 100 kilometers east of the Western Neisse (Nysa Łużycka). Yet
the Soviets transferred administration of the whole of Silesia to Poland, including the territories between the Western and Eastern Neisse. In Potsdam this
border was recognized de facto by the Western Allies. On July 6, 1950, the
German Democratic Republic signed the Zgorzelec (Gorlitz) Treaty with Poland,
recognizing the Oder-(Western) Neisse Line as a permanent boundary between
both states. On December 7, 1970, West Germany signed a treaty with Poland
and fully recognized *de iure* the Oder-Neisse border. The latter agreement was
reconfirmed after the reunification of Germany in 1990. G. Sanford and A.
Gozdecka-Sanford, *Historical Dictionary of Poland* (Metuchen, N.J., 1994), 137; *The
New Encyclopaedia Britannica*, vol. 8 (Chicago, 1990), 872–873.

ODOJEWSKI, WŁODZIMIERZ (1930–   ), writer and journalist who defected from Poland in 1971 and joined the staff of Radio Free Europe.* Most
of his works are devoted to World War II and the postwar years in southeastern

parts of prewar Poland. *Dictionary of Polish Literature*, ed. by E. J. Czerwinski (Westport, Conn., 1994), 303–304; *Who's Who in the Socialist Countries of Europe*, ed. by J. Stroynowski, vol. 2 (Munich, 1989), 862.

OKP. See **Citizens' Parliamentary Club.**

OKULICKI, LEOPOLD (1898–1946), general, one of the most important leaders of the Polish underground state during World War II, arrested by the Soviets on March 27, 1945, in Pruszków, and tried in Moscow in the "Trial of the Sixteen"* all leaders of the Polish resistance. A. K. Kunert, *Ilustrowany przewodnik po Polsce podziemnej, 1939–1945* (Warsaw, 1996), 540–541.

OLBRYCHSKI, DANIEL (1945–   ), popular film and theater actor who played several major roles in the films by A. Wajda.* *Who's Who in the Socialist Countries of Europe*, ed. by J. Stroynowski, vol. 2 (Munich, 1989), 865; *Nowa Encyklopedia Powszechna PWN*, vol. 4 (Warsaw, 1995), 625.

OLECHOWSKI, ANDRZEJ (1947–   ), economist, Minister of Finance in the government of J. Olszewski* in 1992 and Minister of Foreign Affairs in the cabinet of W. Pawlak.* He worked for several international and U.N. institutions, served as adviser to the President* (1987), and became first deputy president of the National Polish Bank (1989–91). *Kto jest kim w polityce polskiej*, ed. by R. Ignasiak (Warsaw, 1993), 209.

OLECHOWSKI, TADEUSZ (1926–   ), diplomat and Minister of Foreign Affairs in 1988–89. T. Mołdawa, *Ludzie Władzy 1944–1991. Władze państwowe i polityczne Polski według stanu na dzień 28 II 1991* (Warsaw, 1991), 405.

OLEKSY, JÓZEF (1946–   ), economist and Premier* during 1995–96. He graduated from Warsaw's Main School of Planning and Statistics in 1966, taught there, and completed his doctorate there in 1977. Oleksy joined the Polish United Workers' Party (PZPR)* in 1968 and gradually climbed the Party-state apparatus ladder. During 1987–89 he served as First Secretary of the provincial Party organization in Biała Podlaska, and in 1989, as the minister in charge of cooperation with the trade unions* in M. Rakowski's* government. In 1989 Oleksy participated in the Round Table Negotiations* on the communist side and was elected to the Sejm.* He was elected again in 1991, serving on several important parliamentary committees, as deputy chairman of the Democratic Left Alliance's (SLD)* Parliamentary Club, and as Speaker of the Sejm. On March 3, 1995, he retired from this position and became Premier on the next day. On January 25, 1996, he resigned, having been accused of being a Soviet intelligence agent. Two days later he was elected president of the Social Democracy of the Republic of Poland (SdRP).* T. Mołdawa, *Ludzie Władzy 1944–1991. Władze*

państwowe i polityczne Polski według stanu na dzień 28 II 1991 (Warsaw, 1991), 405;
Kto jest kim w polityce polskiej, ed. by R. Ignasiak (Warsaw, 1993), 210.

OLEWIŃSKI, MARIAN (1912–82), Deputy Premier in 1969–70. T. Mołdawa,
*Ludzie Władzy 1944–1991. Władze państwowe i polityczne Polski według stanu na dzień
28 II 1991* (Warsaw, 1991), 406.

OLSZEWSKI, JAN F. (1930–   ), lawyer and Premier* from December 23,
1991, to June 5, 1992. He became a well-known figure as a defender of opposition activists persecuted by the communist authorities. Olszewski graduated
from Warsaw University* Law Department in 1953 and subsequently worked
in the Ministry of Justice, in the Polish Academy of Sciences (PAN),* and for
the reformist weekly *Po Prostu* ("Plainly Speaking").* In the 1960s he defended such well-known figures as J. Kuroń,* K. Modzelewski,* Nina Karsov,
and J. Szpotański.* Because of this involvement he was persecuted by the communist authorities and temporarily deprived of his attorney's license. A member
of the Crooked Circle Club* during 1956–62, in 1975 he participated in the
protests against the new Polish Constitution, which included articles establishing
a leading role for the Party and a permanent alliance with the USSR. In the late
1970s he collaborated with the Workers' Defense Committee (KOR)* and the
Social Self-Defense Committee of KOR. Olszewski co-organized the Polish Independence Agreement (PPN)* and was active in the Movement for Defense of
Human and Civil Rights (ROPCiO).* A Solidarity* adviser in 1980–81, he
continued this role during the underground Solidarity period. He participated in
the Round Table Negotiations* and was a member and then deputy president
of the Civic Committee.* In 1989 Olszewski was appointed deputy chairman of
the State Tribunal and was elected to the Sejm* in 1991. A leader of the Center
Alliance (PC),* he was asked by President L. Wałęsa* to form a new cabinet
in December 1990, but eventually it was J. K. Bielecki* who managed to do
this. After the fall of the Bielecki government in December 1991, Olszewski
became Premier of Poland. His cabinet was based on a broad but shaky party
coalition, deprived of the support of the Democratic Union (UD)* and the Confederation for an Independent Poland (KPN).* Soon several acts of this government antagonized large segments of the public, including major political forces
in Poland. The government tried to criminalize abortion.* Its Minister of Defense, J. Parys, lost his fight for control over the Polish Army* and had to resign
when he accused Wałęsa of preparing a military coup d'état. The government
eventually collapsed when its Minister of the Interior, A. Macierewicz,* revealed
secret security files and issued a list of alleged secret police collaborators, which
included not only the names of Wałęsa and centrist and leftist leaders but also
the name of W. Chrzanowski,* the leader of the ZChN. After the fall of his
government, Olszewski was removed from the Center Alliance. In 1994 he
formed his own small party, the Movement for the Republic (RdR),* and in
1995, the Movement for Reconstruction of Poland (ROP).* G. Sanford and A.

Gozdecka-Sanford, *Historical Dictionary of Poland* (Metuchen, N.J., 1994), 137–138; *Who's Who in the Socialist Countries of Europe*, ed. by J. Stroynowski, vol. 2 (Munich, 1989), 867; J. Olszewski, *Przerwana premiera* (Warsaw, 1992); *Kto jest kim w polityce polskiej*, ed. by R. Ignasiak (Warsaw, 1993), 240; A. Micewski, *Ludzie i opcje* (Warsaw, 1993), 136–139; *Rodem z Solidarności*, ed. by B. Kopka and R. Żelichowski (Warsaw, 1997), 203–216; A. Dudek, *Pierwsze lata III Rzeczpospolitej, 1989–1995* (Cracow, 1997), 192–223.

OLSZEWSKI, KAZIMIERZ (1917–   ), Party official and Deputy Premier in 1972–77. *Who's Who in the Socialist Countries of Europe*, ed. by J. Stroynowski, vol. 2 (Munich, 1989), 868.

OLSZOWSKI, STEFAN (1931–   ), Minister of Foreign Affairs during 1971–76 and 1982–85 and Politburo* member from December 1970 to February 1980 and from August 1980 to November 1985. A leader of communist youth organizations, he joined the Polish United Workers' Party (PZPR)* in 1952 and occupied several important positions in its apparatus. During 1963–68 he served as director of the Party Press Bureau; later he was responsible for propaganda in the Politburo. He was considered by many to be the main inter-Party competitor to E. Gierek,* who eventually eliminated Olszowski. The latter managed to return to the Politburo after the fall of Gierek, but he was removed from his posts by Gen. W. Jaruzelski* in 1985. In 1986 he unexpectedly left Poland for the United States and retired to private life. *Who's Who in the Socialist Countries of Europe*, ed. by J. Stroynowski, vol. 2 (Munich, 1989), 868; T. Mołdawa, *Ludzie Władzy 1944–1991. Władze państwowe i polityczne Polski według stanu na dzień 28 II 1991* (Warsaw, 1991), 426.

OLSZTYN (German Allenstein), provincial capital on the Łyna River in the Masurian district of northeastern Poland. Incorporated into Poland in 1945, Olsztyn is a local industrial and cultural center. Its population was 161,000 inhabitants in 1989. *The New Encyclopaedia Britannica*, vol. 8 (Chicago, 1990), 922.

ONE HUNDREDS' MOVEMENT (Ruch STU), political movement established as the "One Hundreds' Committee" ("Komitet Stu") on April 8, 1995, by 100 outstanding personalities from Polish politics, arts, and sciences who could not fit into any existing political parties. On October 21–22, 1995, the central One Hundreds' Committee and its local branches were transformed into a liberal-conservative party called the Ruch STU and led by C. Bielecki* and A. Olechowski.* Ruch STU placed itself on the liberal-conservative side of the Polish political scene and attempted to reinforce its views, namely, its advocacy of private ownership and the free market system, independence of the individual, effectiveness of the state, and international atmosphere for the country's development and independence. Ruch STU believed that these goals could be achieved through increasing private ownership, lowering taxes, making the government open and accessible to the people, participating in the pan-European debate, restating traditional national values, and putting an emphasis on local activities. During the presidential elections of 1995,* Ruch STU was skeptical about L. Wałęsa's* candidacy; but during the second round of the elections, the party voted for him. General Information about Poland <http://bmb.ippt.gov.pl/poland/partone.html>; *Polskie partie polityczne. Charakterystyki, dokumenty,* ed. by K. A. Paszkiewicz (Wrocław, 1996), 202–204.

ONYSZKIEWICZ, JANUSZ (1937–   ), alpinist, mathematician, and politician. He participated in the March events of 1968* and the 1980 strike in the Szczecin* shipyard. A Solidarity* press spokesperson, he was interned during 1981–82 and imprisoned in 1983. A spokesperson of the underground Solidarity, he participated in the Round Table Negotiations,* was elected to the Sejm* in 1989, and was reelected to the Democratic Union (UD)* in 1991. Deputy Minister of Defense during 1990–91, he served as full minister in the 1992–93 Suchocka* government. He married the granddaughter of Marshal Piłsudski, Joanna Jaraczewska, in a prison in 1983. G. Sanford and A. Gozdecka-Sanford, *Historical Dictionary of Poland* (Metuchen, N.J., 1994), 139; *Who's Who in the Socialist Countries of Europe*, ed. by J. Stroynowski, vol. 2 (Munich, 1989), 869; *Kto jest kim w polityce polskiej*, ed. by R. Ignasiak (Warsaw, 1993), 211.

OPOLE, capital of Opole Province (województwo) on the Oder River* with a population of 128,400 in 1990. Heavily damaged during World War II, it was incorporated into the Polish state, rebuilt, and transformed into an important economic and cultural center as well as a major river port and rail link. The Opole region hosts the main concentration of the German minority in Poland. The resident Germans* demand autonomy for Silesia, and since 1989 they have been represented by their own Parliamentary Club in the Sejm.* G. Sanford and A. Gozdecka-Sanford, *Historical Dictionary of Poland* (Metuchen, N.J., 1994), 139; L. Straszewicz, *Opole Silesia: Outline of Economic Geography* (Warsaw, 1965).

OPPOSITION, political parties, social organizations, and loose groups that tried to reform or abolish communism in Poland during 1945–89. Their activities and the response of the communist authorities differed in character and intensity during the discussed period. In 1945–48 a civil war took place in Poland. Underground armed forces and clandestine political organizations as well as legal political parties participated in the anti-Soviet resistance. Among the guerrilla units were such groups as the remnants of the Home Army (AK),* Delegacy of the Armed Forces,* Nie,* "Freedom and Independence" (WiN),* and National Armed Forces (NSZ).* Among legal organizations, the most important were the Polish Peasant Party (PSL),* the Labor Party (SP),* and groups of Catholics gathered around *Tygodnik Powszechny* ("The Universal Weekly")* and *Tygodnik Warszawski* ("The Warsaw Weekly").* All these groups, backed by the Poles in exile, rejected communism; most of them supported a program for a democratic Poland and expected that, sooner or later, the Western Allies would help them eject the Soviet Army* from East-Central Europe. The communist authorities answered with mass terror, intimidation, pacifications of entire regions and social groups, and political show trials, especially during the referendum* of June 1946 and the elections of January 1947.* The communists continued these methods between 1948 and 1956, when legal opposition ceased to exist and guerrilla units gradually disappeared. Polish society was paralyzed by fear during the Stalinist period.* The barrier of fear was broken during the "Polish October" of 1956,* however. An opposition group within the Polish United Workers' Party (PZPR),* known as the revisionists, appeared. Some politicians tried to rebuilt parties dissolved in the 1940s. Independent initiatives, such as the Crooked Circle Club* and the Clubs of Catholic Intelligentsia,* began to use new methods to oppose communism. In the mid-1960s Polish students and intellectuals, disappointed with communism, protested against state cultural policies. All these initiatives were destroyed during the March events of 1968,* but soon, during the December events of 1970,* the workers rebelled against the regime. Workers and intellectuals in the opposition united after the June events of 1976.* In the late 1970s several opposition organizations were created. The most important among them were the Polish Independence Agreement (PPN),* the Workers' Defense Committee (KOR),* the Movement for the Defense of Human and Civil Rights (ROPCiO),* the Young Poland Movement (RMP),* and the Confederation for an Independent Poland (KPN).* Aside from the political organizations *sensu stricto*, the democratic opposition included numerous cultural and educational institutions such as the Flying University* and its continuation, the Association of Scientific Courses (TKN),* as well as home theaters, independent producers of video films, and underground publications.* This entire sphere was called in Polish *drugi obieg*, which was usually translated as "second circulation," "second estate," or "independent culture." The activities of these groups contributed to the establishment of Solidarity* in 1980. Undergoing a deep crisis in 1980–81, Poland's communist party was unable to answer the challenge of the opposition. After imposition of Martial Law* in December 1981, the Party regime was replaced by the military regime of the Polish People's Army* led by Gen. W. Jaruzelski.* Despite arrests and internment of thousands of people, Solidarity was rebuilt in the underground and took power in 1989, when the communists faced complete disintegration of their system and agreed to start the Round Table Negotiations.* P. Raina, *Political Opposition in Poland, 1954–1977* (London, 1978); T. G. Ash, *The Polish Revolution, 1980–82* (London, 1983); A. Friszke, *Opozycja polityczna w PRL 1945–80* (London, 1993); *Nowa Encyklopedia Powszechna PWN*, vol. 4 (Warsaw, 1995), 657; *Dictionary of Polish Literature*, ed. by E. J. Czerwinski (Westport, Conn., 1994), 83–85.

OPZZ. See **All-Poland Alliance of Trade Unions.**

ORANGE ALTERNATIVE (Pomarańczowa Alternatywa), movement organized by a young art historian, Waldemar Fydrych, in Wrocław* after imposition of Martial Law* in December 1981. The Orange Alternative abandoned traditional protest demonstrations, in their place organizing spectacular and colorful peaceful happenings, which turned the tense atmosphere of Martial Law into grotesque and absurd situations. *Polityka*, April 19, 1997, pp. 61–62.

ORMO (Ochotnicza Rezerwa Milicji Obywatelskiej [Volunteer Reserves of the Citizens' Militia]), paramilitary organization established on the initiative of the Polish Workers' Party (PPR)* in 1946. The ORMO units participated in military operations against anti-communist guerrillas in the late 1940s and in the collectivization* of agriculture* in the early 1950s. Later they were used in such operations as attacks against students demonstrations during the March events of 1968* and police activities after imposition of Martial Law* in December 1981. In 1980 ORMO had over 460,000 members. It was dissolved in 1989. *Nowa Encyklopedia Powszechna PWN*, vol. 4 (Warsaw, 1996), 580.

ORSZULIK, ALOJZY (1928–   ), Catholic priest, bishop, director of the Episcopal Press Bureau of the Polish Episcopate* in the 1960s, close collaborator of Primate S. Wyszyński* in the 1970s, and assistant secretary general of the Episcopate. He was instrumental in political negotiations between the communist authorities and the opposition* in 1980–81 and 1988–89. G. Sanford and A. Gozdecka-Sanford, *Historical Dictionary of Poland* (Metuchen, N.J., 1994), 141; A. Micewski, *Ludzie i opcje* (Warsaw, 1993), 112–116.

ORTHODOX CHURCH IN POLAND. It was formed after World War I, when some 4 million Orthodox Ukrainians,* Belorussians,* and Russians found themselves within the borders* of Poland. In 1924 Poland's Orthodox Church was granted autocephaly by Constantinople. After World War II only about 400,000 Orthodox faithful remained within the new Poland. In 1948 the head of the Polish Orthodox Church, Metropolitan Dionysius, was arrested and his Church was forced to come under the jurisdiction of the Patriarch of Moscow. Polish Uniates were forcibly included into Orthodoxy. The Patriarchate of Moscow reconferred the autocephaly to the Polish Orthodox Church, but it did not regain full independence until the fall of communism in 1989. In 1991 the Polish Orthodox Church had one archbishopric of Warsaw*—Bielsk—and five bishoprics of Białystok*—Gdańsk,* Łódź*–Poznań,* Wrocław*–Szczecin,* Przemyśl–Nowy Sącz, and Lublin*–Chełm.* The Orthodox Episcopate had 12 Metropolitans, Archbishops, and bishops; and 254 priests. They work in 410 Orthodox churches attended by 900,000 faithful. The Church also has three monasteries and three seminaries, and it publishes several periodicals. In the 1990s a vibrant youth movement developed among the Orthodox of Poland. M. Prokurat, A. Golitzyn, and M. D. Peterson, *Historical Dictionary of the Orthodox Church* (Lanham, Md., 1996), 266–267; *New Catholic Encyclopedia*, vol. 10 (New York, 1967), 793; K. Urban, *Mniejszości religijne w Polsce 1945–1991* (Cracow, 1994), 134.

ORZECHOWSKI, MARIAN (1931–), historian, professor of political sciences, and Minister of Foreign Affairs during 1985–88. He joined the Polish United Workers' Party (PZPR)* in 1952. During 1981–90 he was a member of its Central Committee,* and during 1983–90, of the Politburo,* gaining full membership in 1986. During 1982–84 Orzechowski served as the secretary general of the Patriotic Movement of National Revival (PRON).* Elected to the Sejm* in 1989, he chaired the PZPR Parliamentary Club and, in 1990, the Democratic Left Alliance's (SLD)* caucus. G. Sanford and A. Gozdecka-Sanford, *Historical Dictionary of Poland* (Metuchen, N.J., 1994), 141; T. Mołdawa, *Ludzie Władzy 1944–1991. Władze państwowe i polityczne Polski według stanu na dzień 28 II 1991* (Warsaw, 1991), 408; A. Kępiński and Z. Kilar, *Kto jest kim w Polsce inaczej* (Warsaw, 1985), 301–316.

OSIATYŃSKI, JERZY (1941–), professor of economics, leader of the Democratic Union (UD),* and UD deputy to the Sejm* since 1989. A member of the Polish United Workers' Party (PZPR)* during 1963–67, he later became an important Solidarity* activist. He served as Minister-Chief of the Central Planning Bureau in the government of T. Mazowiecki* in 1989–90 and as Minister of Finance in the cabinet of H. Suchocka* in 1992–93. Reaching a compromise with the International Monetary Fund, he managed to reduce the Polish foreign debt. T. Mołdawa, *Ludzie Władzy 1944–1991. Władze państwowe i polityczne Polski według stanu na dzień 28 II 1991* (Warsaw, 1991), 408.

OSIECKA, AGNIESZKA (1936–97), poet, writer, and journalist who authored numerous satirical works, lyrics for popular songs, plays, children's books, and memoirs. Her poems reflect the taste and sense of humor of the generation of Poles who were about 20 years old in 1956. P. Kuncewicz, *Agonia i nadzieja. Poezja polska od 1956*, vol. 3 (Warsaw, 1993), 127–128; *Polityka*, no. 11 (Warsaw, March 15, 1997).

OSMAŃCZYK, EDMUND JAN (1913–89), prolific journalist and member of the State Council (Rada Państwa)* in 1979–80. Born in the Opole* region, he became an important activist of the Polish minority in Germany. A resistance member during World War II, he served as a war correspondent and in 1945 became a foreign correspondent, covering the Nuremberg Trials and the Potsdam Conference.* T. Mołdawa, *Ludzie Władzy 1944–1991. Władze państwowe i polityczne Polski według stanu na dzień 28 II 1991* (Warsaw, 1991), 408; *Nowa Encyklopedia Powszechna PWN*, vol. 4 (Warsaw, 1995), 696.

OSÓBKA-MORAWSKI, EDWARD (1909–97), socialist, instrumental in Sovietization of Poland after World War II. Osóbka joined the Polish Socialist Party (PPS)* in 1928 and was active in its cooperative and educational institutions. During the war he was a leader of the left wing of the clandestine socialist movement. On December 31, 1943, he became deputy president of the

National Home Council (KRN).* In July 1944 Osóbka was made president of the Polish Committee of National Liberation (PKWN), the chief of its Foreign Affairs Department, and then of its Agricultural Department. His position, decorative and concealed, was designed to show that the PKWN was not an exclusively communist arrangement. In the same character, he served as Premier* in 1945–47, Minister of Foreign Affairs in 1944–45, and Minister of Administration in 1947–49. He was, at the same time, a leader of the PPS faction that supported unification with the Polish Workers' Party (PPR).* Once this was done, Osóbka was sidelined and became a director of state resorts. In 1970 he left the Party to join the political opposition.* In 1990 he became president of the reborn PPS Executive Committee. *Who's Who in the Socialist Countries of Europe*, ed. by J. Stroynowski, vol. 2 (Munich, 1989), 874; T. Mołdawa, *Ludzie Władzy 1944–1991. Władze państwowe i polityczne Polski według stanu na dzień 28 II 1991* (Warsaw, 1991), 408.

OSSOWSKA, MARIA (1896–1974), sociologist, wife of S. Ossowski,* student of T. Kotarbiński,* and expert on the sociology of morality. *Nowa Encyklopedia Powszechna PWN*, vol. 4 (Warsaw, 1996), 698; J. Karpiński, *Nie być w myśleniu posłusznym. Ossowscy, socjologia, filozofia* (London, 1989).

OSSOWSKI, STANISŁAW (1897–1963), sociologist whose first major books, such as *On the Foundations of Aesthetics*, were written during the interwar period, when he was close to left-oriented intellectual circles. During the war he was active in the anti-German resistance and taught at the underground Warsaw University.* After 1945 he taught first in Łódź* and later in Warsaw.* During the Stalinist period* in Poland, he was deprived of contacts with students, but he continued his research. Restored to his chair of sociology at Warsaw University in 1956, he helped to rebuild sociology in Poland. S. M. Lipset, "Stanisław Ossowski (1897–1963)," *American Sociological Review*, vol. 29: 748–751; J. Karpiński, *Nie być w myśleniu posłusznym. Ossowscy, socjologia, filozofia* (London, 1989).

OZDOWSKI, JERZY (1925–94), professor of economics, member of the State Council (Rada Państwa)* in 1980, Deputy Premier in 1980–82, Deputy Speaker of the Sejm* during 1982–89, member and deputy president of the Patriotic Movement of National Revival (PRON)* from 1982 to 1987. During 1956–80 he was a deputy chairman and chairman of the Club of Catholic Intelligentsia* in Poznań.* A non-party politician, he was co-opted to the Jaruzelski* ruling establishment to represent and engage Catholic organizations. *Who's Who in the Socialist Countries of Europe*, ed. by J. Stroynowski, vol. 2 (Munich, 1989), 877; T. Mołdawa, *Ludzie Władzy 1944–1991. Władze państwowe i polityczne Polski według stanu na dzień 28 II 1991* (Warsaw, 1991), 409.

OZGA-MICHALSKI, JÓZEF (1919–), writer, peasant politician, Deputy Speaker of the Sejm* during 1952–56, member of the State Council (Rada Państwa)* in 1957–72, its Deputy Chairman in 1972–76 and its member again during 1976–85. From the late 1930s he was active in the peasant movement. During the war he fought in the peasant wing of the anti-German resistance, and after 1944 he was among the most important leaders of the Peasant Party (SL)* and United Peasant Party (ZSL).* He sat in the Sejm from 1944 to 1989.

Who's Who in the Socialist Countries of Europe, ed. by J. Stroynowski, vol. 2 (Munich, 1989), 877; T. Mołdawa, *Ludzie Władzy 1944–1991. Władze państwowe i polityczne Polski według stanu na dzień 28 II 1991* (Warsaw, 1991), 409.

PACZKOWSKI, ANDRZEJ (1938–), historian specializing in the contemporary history of Poland and former president of the Polish Mountaineering Association. *Who's Who in the Socialist Countries of Europe*, ed. by J. Stroynowski, vol. 3 (Munich, 1989), 881.

PAJDAK, ANTONI (1894–1988), lawyer, activist of the Polish Socialist Party (PPS),* and since 1943 a Polish Government-in-Exile* deputy delegate to Poland. Arrested with the 16 leaders of the Polish underground state by the NKVD in Pruszków in March 1945 and abducted to Moscow, he refused to talk during the interrogation and was tried separately. Sentenced to five years in prison and lifetime deportation to Siberia, he returned to Poland in 1955. In 1976 he was a founder and then an active member of the Workers' Defense Committee (KOR).* J. J. Lipski, *KOR: A History of the Workers' Defense Committee in Poland, 1976–81* (Berkeley, Calif., 1985); A. Pajdak, Z *Pruszkowa na Łubianki* (Warsaw, 1986); A. K. Kunert, *Ilustrowany przewodnik po Polsce podziemnej, 1939–1945* (Warsaw, 1996), 547.

PAJESTKA, JÓZEF (1924–94), economist and deputy chairman of the Planning Commission of the Council of Ministers between 1968 and 1981. *Who's Who in the Socialist Countries of Europe*, ed. by J. Stroynowski, vol. 3 (Munich, 1989), 882.

PAJEWSKI, JANUSZ (1907–), veteran of the Home Army (AK)* and outstanding historian specializing in modern Polish history. *Who's Who in the Socialist Countries of Europe*, ed. by J. Stroynowski, vol. 3 (Munich, 1989), 882.

PAŁKA, GRZEGORZ (1950–), co-founder of Solidarity* in Łódź,* member of its Regional Board, and delegate to the First National Solidarity Congress.

Who's Who in the Socialist Countries of Europe, ed. by J. Stroynowski, vol. 3 (Munich, 1989), 885.

PAŁUBICKI, JANUSZ (1948–   ), dissident,* founder, and leader of Solidarity,* Poznań* Region. *Who's Who in the Socialist Countries of Europe*, ed. by J. Stroynowski, vol. 3 (Munich, 1989), 886.

PANUFNIK, ANDRZEJ (1914–91), internationally recognized pianist, composer, and conductor. An author of numerous innovative compositions, Panufnik lived in England since 1954. *Who's Who in the Socialist Countries of Europe*, ed. by J. Stroynowski, vol. 3 (Munich, 1989), 889; *Encyklopedyczny Słownik Sławnych Polaków* (Warsaw, 1996), 281.

PAPAL VISITS. John Paul II* visited his homeland, Poland, six times since becoming Pontiff in 1978. The first visit, which took place on June 2–10, 1979, greatly influenced the Solidarity* and anti-communist movements in 1980. The following visits—June 16–23, 1983; June 8–14, 1987; June 1–9 and August 13–15, 1991; and May 22, 1995—were always considered important events in Poland, with John Paul II referring in his homilies to the most crucial spiritual, political, and social issues. His most recent visit of May 31–June 10, 1997, drew the attention of millions of Poles eager to listen to papal teachings and looking for comfort in a difficult time of change. J. J. Lipski, *KOR: A History of the Workers' Defense Committee in Poland, 1976–81* (Berkeley, Calif., 1985), 331–339; T. Szulc, *Pope John Paul II* (New York, 1995).

PARANDOWSKI, JAN (1895–1978), writer, translator, and president of the Polish PEN Club from 1933 to his death. An expert in the culture of ancient Greece and Rome, he published a dozen books on this subject, although his *Niebo w płomieniach* (''Heaven in Flames'') deals with the experiences of a young man going through a religious crisis. *Dictionary of Polish Literature*, ed. by E. J. Czerwinski (Westport, Conn., 1994), 311–313; *Encyklopedyczny Słownik Sławnych Polaków* (Warsaw, 1996), 282.

PARLIAMENT. See **Sejm** and **Senate**.

PARNICKI, TEODOR (1908–88), writer specializing in great historical and political subjects. *Dictionary of Polish Literature*, ed. by E. J. Czerwinski (Westport, Conn., 1994), 313–315; *Encyklopedyczny Słownik Sławnych Polaków* (Warsaw, 1996), 283.

''PARTISANS.'' See **Moczar, Mieczysław**.

PARTY X (Partia X), populist party formed by a maverick businessman from Canada, S. Tymiński,* after the first ballot of the 1990 presidential elections* when he unexpectedly came second after L. Wałęsa* and before third-place finisher T. Mazowiecki.* Party X attracted much publicity but made little significant impact on political life in Poland. Several Party X activists proved to be former secret security agents, and the leadership, with no positive program, was often troubled with splits. During the 1991 elections* Party X gained only three seats in the Sejm.* During the 1993 elections* it gained only 2.79% of the vote, did not cross the electoral 5%, threshold, and did not receive any seats in Parliament. B. Szajkowski (ed.), *Political Parties of Eastern Europe, Russia, and the Successor States* (London, 1994), 335; *Polskie Partie Polityczna. Charakterystyki, dokumenty*, ed. by K. A. Paszkiewicz (Wrocław, 1996), 107–111.

PASSENDORFER, JERZY (1923–   ), film director, manager of several state film-producing units, and TV* director. Among his films are such standards of socialist cinematography as *Skąpani w ogniu* ("Baptized by Fire"), *Kierunek Berlin* ("Destination Berlin"), and *Barwy walki* ("The Colors of Battle"). *Who's Who in the Socialist Countries of Europe*, ed. by J. Stroynowski, vol. 3 (Munich, 1989), 895.

PASSENT, DANIEL (1938–   ), journalist in the Party weekly *Polityka** and popular essayst. *Who's Who in the Socialist Countries of Europe*, ed. by J. Stroynowski, vol. 3 (Munich, 1989), 895.

PASTUSIAK, LONGIN (1935–   ), political scientist specializing in the United States and politician of the Polish United Workers' Party (PZPR)* and its successor, the Social Democracy of the Republic of Poland (SdRP).* *Who's Who in the Socialist Countries of Europe*, ed. by J. Stroynowski, vol. 3 (Munich, 1989), 895.

PASZYŃSKI, ALEKSANDER (1928–   ), journalist and Solidarity* activist who wrote extensively on the problems of housing and became Minister of Construction in the Mazowiecki* government. *Kto jest kim w polityce polskiej*, ed. by R. Ignasiak (Warsaw, 1993), 220.

PATRIOTIC ASSOCIATION "GRUNWALD," unofficial organization established in February–March 1981 on the initiative of the Warsaw* Party Committee to counter Solidarity* activities. Its Warsaw University* branch planned to arrange a large demonstration on March 8, 1981, in order to commemorate the March events of 1968.* On March 6, 1981, flyers and posters appeared in Warsaw asking the city population to participate in a demonstration that would honor the memory of all Polish victims of the Zionist members of the communist secret police after World War II. The text had a clearly anti-Semitic character and was signed by "Grunwald." Among its leaders were some old anti-communists, but the tone of Grunwald's activities was set by a small group of communist nationalists headed by a film director, B. Poręba.* The Association tried unsuccessfully to spread its activities to other cities in Poland. Anti-

Semitism was not popular during the Solidarity period, and "Grunwald" was weakened by its internal conflicts and divisions. J. Holzer, *Solidarność, 1980–1981. Geneza i Historia* (Warsaw, 1983), 97.

PATRIOTIC MOVEMENT OF NATIONAL REVIVAL. See PRON.

PAWLAK, WALDEMAR (1959–   ), peasant politician and Premier* from June 5 to July 11, 1992, and from October 18, 1993, to March 3, 1995. A farmer in his native village of Kamionka in Płock Province, he belonged to the United Peasant Party (ZSL)* during 1985–90. Later he was an activist in the Polish Peasant Party (PSL),* becoming its president in June 1991. In 1992 he was designated by the President* of Poland, L. Wałęsa,* to create a cabinet and became the youngest Premier in the history of 20th-century Europe. Yet he failed to form a government and returned to his position after the elections of October 1993,* when, in a new political situation, he created a government in coalition with the Democratic Left Alliance (SLD).* Under pressure from Wałęsa and the SLD, he resigned. He managed to defend his strong position as president of his party and chairman of its Parliamentary Club. *Wprost* (Warsaw, May 19, 1996); *Kto jest kim w polityce polskiej*, ed. by R. Ignasiak (Warsaw, 1993), 221.

PAX ASSOCIATION, Catholic lay organization established by a prewar right-wing radical, B. Piasecki,* in 1945. The history of PAX, especially of its beginning, has not yet been satisfactorily researched. In 1944 Piasecki, the leader of a radical rightist underground organization, was arrested by the NKVD but soon re-emerged and was allowed to establish the weekly *Dziś i Jutro* ("Today and Tomorrow") in November 1945. A group of Catholics gathered around the periodical and, from 1947, used the name "PAX." According to rumors and sources difficult to verify, Piasecki made a deal with the Soviets and promised, to quote J. Światło,* to "subvert the Catholic Church from within." It appears that Piasecki, who had a strong drive to gain power, believed that some form of cooperation with the communists was inevitable, that Marxism was directed not against God but against the traditional social role of religion and the Church, and that socialism and Christianity were not mutually exclusive. The communist authorities badly needed a Catholic ally against the well-organized and strongly anti-communist Roman Catholic Church* in Poland. During initial conflicts between the communists and the Church, PAX sided with the authorities and opposed the Episcopate.* Soon PAX developed into a form of capitalist enterprise involved in commercial activities and industrial production. It created a publishing empire with its own publishing house and several periodicals. PAX tried to mediate between the state and the Church but did it such that public opinion accused PAX leaders of full collaboration with the regime. In 1953 PAX reached the zenith of its influence and took over the prestigious weekly *Tygodnik Powszechny* ("The Universal Weekly").* In 1954 Piasecki published

a book, *Zagadnienia istotne* ("Essential Problems"), which presented his theological arguments supporting his policy of cooperation with the communists.
The book, together with *Dziś i Jutro*, was condemned in 1955 by the Holy
Office in Rome. During the "Polish October" of 1956,* Piasecki declared that
force should be used to prevent democratization. Yet W. Gomułka* returned to
power, Primate S. Wyszyński* was released from internment, *Tygodnik Powszechny* was returned to its legitimate editors, open allegations appeared about
the connections between Piasecki and the secret police, and PAX found itself
on the edge of destruction. Disliked both by communist officials and the Episcopate, PAX survived and continued its activities into the 1960s, when it received several seats in the Sejm.* In 1964 PAX condemned the Polish bishops
for their letter to the German bishops, and during the March events of 1968* it
assumed an anti-liberal position. In the late 1960s PAX was more Stalinist than
the Politburo* and was losing its political influence. In 1979 Piasecki died and
was replaced as PAX president first by R. Reiff* and then, from 1982, by Z.
Komender.* The PAX Association supported the Jaruzelski* regime, but its best
period was over. In 1980 PAX had about 20,000 members, in 1983 about
17,000. After 1989 PAX disintegrated and its members were divided between
the Christian Democratic and the Christian-National Parties. J. Held, *Dictionary
of East European History since 1945* (Westport, Conn., 1994), 354–356; R. Taras, *Consolidating Democracy in Poland* (Boulder, Colo., 1995), 97; J. Karpiński, *Polska, Komunizm, Opozycja* (London, 1985), 177–178; A. Micewski, *Współrządzić czy nie
kłamać? Pax i Znak w Polsce 1945–1976* (Paris, 1978).

PEASANT ACCORD (Polskie Stronnictwo Ludowe [Porozumienie Ludowe]),
party formed during the October 1991 elections* as a merger of the Polish
Peasant Party–Solidarity and Rural Solidarity.* The party participated in the
Olszewski* government and then in the cabinet of H. Suchocka,* when a party
leader, G. Janowski,* served as the Minister of Agriculture. Janowski, however,
left the government in spring of 1993 to protest the government's lack of support
for agriculture.* Due to splits and internal conflicts, the strongly anti-communist
and pro-Christian Peasant Accord received only 2.37% of the vote in the September 1993 elections,* did not cross the 5% electoral threshold, received no
parliamentary seats, and practically disintegrated. B. Szajkowski (ed.), *Political
Parties of Eastern Europe, Russia, and the Successor States* (London, 1994), 336.

PEASANT PARTY (Stronnictwo Ludowe [SL]), traditional name of Polish
peasants' political organizations. The first Peasant Party was established in 1895
in Galicia; and the next one, in the Congress Poland in 1915. After the unification of the Polish peasant movement in 1931, the newly established organization was called the Peasant Party as well. During World War II it was active
in the underground as the Peasant Party "Roch" (SL "Roch"). It constituted
a pillar of the Polish underground state and the Polish Government-in-Exile* in
London. At the beginning of 1944, a group of left-oriented leaders of the SL

Roch established their half-independent faction called the Peasant Party "People's Will" (SL "Wola Ludu"). It cooperated with the Polish Workers' Party (PPR)* and participated in the National Home Council (KRN)* and the Soviet-sponsored government-in-waiting, the Polish Committee of National Liberation (PKWN). In September 1944 in Lublin,* which had already been taken by the Soviets, the SL People's Will activists established their Peasant Party (SL). Its leadership cooperated closely with the Polish communists and the Soviets, joined the Bloc of Democratic Parties,* and opposed the activities of the Polish Peasant Party (PSL)* of S. Mikołajczyk.* Nonetheless, most provincial SL organizations joined the PSL in 1945 and 1946. After the Referendum* of 1946 and the elections of 1947,* when the communists destroyed the PSL by police methods, the SL began to cooperate with those few PSL activists ready to follow the communists. In 1949 the SL and the PSL were merged into the United Peasant Party (ZSL),* completely controlled by the communist authorities. K. Kersten, *The Establishment of Communist Rule in Poland, 1943–1948* (Berkeley, Calif., 1991); J. Coutouvidis and J. Reynolds, *Poland, 1939–1947* (Leicester, 1986).

PENDERECKI, KRZYSZTOF (1933–   ), composer, conductor, and professor who gained worldwide acclaim for his orchestral symphonies, concertos, and vocal-instrumental compositions. Among his best works are such compositions as *Threnody for the Victims of Hiroshima, Stabat Mater*, and *The Devils of Loudun*. *Who's Who in the Socialist Countries of Europe*, ed. by J. Stroynowski, vol. 3 (Munich, 1989), 907; G. Sanford and A. Gozdecka-Sanford, *Historical Dictionary of Poland* (Metuchen, N.J., 1994), 146.

PENTAGONALE (Central European Initiative), loose intergovernmental structure established on the initiative of Italy at a meeting on July 31–August 1, 1990, to develop cooperation in South-Central Europe across the West-East divide, increase Italian influence in this region, and limit German economic and political expansion. Originally, the Pentagonale included Italy, Austria, Czechoslovakia, Hungary, and Yugoslavia. In 1991 it was joined by Poland and renamed Hexagonale. In 1992 the membership of the rump Yugoslavia was suspended because of its involvement in the war in Bosnia. In October 1995 the Hexagonale foreign ministers met in Warsaw* and agreed to further extend their organization and to accept Albania, Bulgaria, Romania, Ukraine, and Belarus in the future. R. East and J. Pontin, *Revolution and Change in Central and Eastern Europe* (London, 1997), 330.

PETELSKI, CZESŁAW (1922–96) and **EWA** (1920–   ), film directors and representatives of a "politically correct" socialist trend in Polish cinematography who based most of their films on contemporary Polish literature. *Więź* ("The Link"), Nov. 1996, p. 232; *Nowa Encyklopedia Powszechna PWN*, vol. 4 (Warsaw, 1995), 845.

PGR (Państwowe Gospodarstwo Rolne [State Agricultural Farm]), state farms organized on the grounds taken from larger landowners and, in the "Recovered Territories,"* from the Germans* after World War II. In the 1950s, the PGRs covered 13% of all arable land in Poland but produced less than 13% of food and needed extensive subsidies. Initially called the State Land Estates (Państwowe Nieruchomości Ziemskie), they were renamed PGRs in 1949. During 1951–56 there was a special PGR Ministry. In 1954–56 S. Radkiewicz,* formerly Minister of Public Security, served as the PGR Minister. In 1956 he was followed in this position by another member of the police, M. Moczar.* In December 1956, however, the PGR Ministry was dissolved and the PGRs were supervised by the Ministry of Agriculture. Since 1989 the PGRs have been sold to private agricultural entrepreneurs. J. Karpiński, *Polska, Komunizm, Opozycja* (London, 1985), 174.

PIASECKI, BOLESŁAW (1915–79), leader of the extremist nationalist ONR-Falanga during 1935–39, head and ideologue of the PAX Association* from 1952, and member of the State Council (Rada Państwa)* during 1971–79. A graduate of Warsaw University* Law Department in 1935, he was very active in several organizations of the nationalist movement before the war, which led to his imprisonment in the concentration camp of Bereza Kartuska by the Piłsudski regime in 1934. After eight months in a Gestapo prison in 1939–40, Piasecki joined the anti-German resistance and created and commanded a dynamic clandestine group, the Confederation of the Nation (Konfederacja Narodu), which later became the right wing of the Home Army (AK).* From November 1944 to July 1945, he was kept in a prison by the Soviets, who allegedly made a deal with Piasecki and allowed him to create a "progressive" Catholic group that would support the communist authorities and oppose the organized Roman Catholic Church* in Poland. Initially, the group gathered around the weekly *Dziś i Jutro* ("Today and Tomorrow"), established by Piasecki in 1945, and later it accepted the name PAX. During the Stalinist period* it was instrumental in the communist actions against the Polish Episcopate.* After 1956 PAX lost its previous role but became a publishing empire, tried to build a new strong position in cooperation with communist nationalist M. Moczar,* and supported the hard-line pro-Soviet policy. After 1973 PAX lost any political importance and, after Pisaecki's death, evolved in a more reformist direction under the leadership of R. Reiff.* G. Sanford and A. Gozdecka-Sanford, *Historical Dictionary of Poland* (Metuchen, N.J., 1994), 146; A. Micewski, *Ludzie i opcje* (Warsaw, 1993), 19–24; L. Blit, *The Eastern Pretender: Bolesław Piasecki, His Life and Times* (London, 1965); A. Micewski, *Współrządzić czy nie kłamać* (Paris, 1978).

PIEŃKOWSKA, ALINA (1952–   ), nurse, senator after 1991, and Solidarity* activist who played an important role during the 1980 strike in the Gdańsk* Lenin Shipyard. *Kto jest kim w polityce polskiej*, ed. by R. Ignasiak (Warsaw, 1993), 232.

PIERONEK, TADEUSZ (1934–), secretary general of the Conference of Polish Episcopate* since 1993, professor of canonical law, and auxiliary bishop of Sosnowiec since 1992. G. Polak, *Kto jest kim w Kościele katolickim* (Warsaw, 1996), 285.

PIETRUSZKA, ADAM. See **Popiełuszko, Jerzy.**

PINIOR, JÓZEF (1955–), Solidarity* activist. In 1980 he helped to organize the Solidarity movement in Lower Silesia and was elected to the Solidarity Regional Board there. As a banking law specialist, he served as Solidarity treasurer and, on December 3, 1981, several days before imposition of Martial Law,* he managed to withdraw $80 million from the Solidarity account in Wrocław.* The money was used by the underground National Provisional Commission of Solidarity. Pinior, arrested several times in the 1980s, helped to rebuild the Polish Socialist Party (PPS)* in 1987. *Who's Who in the Socialist Countries of Europe*, ed. by J. Stroynowski, vol. 3 (Munich, 1989), 924.

PIŃKOWSKI, JÓZEF (1929–), member of the Central Committee* of the Polish United Workers' Party (PZPR)* from 1971, Secretary of the Central Committee from 1974, and a leading economist of E. Gierek's* administration. A Party and state apparatus staffer for many years, he served as the first deputy chairman of the governmental Planning Committee from 1971. On August 24, 1980, during the Solidarity crisis,* he replaced E. Babiuch* as Premier* and, in the same months, he became a Politburo* member. His colorless tenure as Premier came to its end in February 1981, when Gen. W. Jaruzelski* took the premiership. In April 1981 Pińkowski was removed from the Politburo, interrogated by the Grabski* Commission, and accused of mismanagement. *Who's Who in the Socialist Countries of Europe*, ed. by J. Stroynowski, vol. 3 (Munich, 1989), 924; Z. Błażyński, *Towarzysze zeznają. Z tajnych archiwów Komitetu Centralnego* (London, 1987), 157–169; T. Mołdawa, *Ludzie Władzy 1944–1991. Władze państwowe i polityczne Polski według stanu na dzień 28 II 1991* (Warsaw, 1991), 411.

PIOTROWSKI, GRZEGORZ. See **Popiełuszko, Jerzy.**

PO PROSTU ("Plainly Speaking"), student periodical established in September 1955. It published articles about provincial life, crime, the difficult situation of young people, and various aspects of Polish life previously ignored or censored by the communist-controlled mass media. *Po Prostu* popularized clubs of young intelligentsia and criticized the activities of the Union of Polish Youth (ZMP).* In 1956 the periodical radicalized itself even further and in summer 1957 was closed by censorship.* On September 3, 1957, the students of Warsaw* organized a protest demonstration, which developed into a scuffle with the Citizens' Militia (MO)* and was followed by persecutions of the participants. The closing of the journal was seen as a signal that the authorities were eliminating the achievements of the "Polish October" of 1956.* J. Karpiński, *Polska, Komunizm, Opozycja* (London, 1985), 200.

PODEDWORNY, BOLESŁAW (1898–1972), state official, one of the main leaders of the United Peasant Party (ZSL)* during 1949–72, and Deputy Chairman of the State Council (Rada Państwa)* in 1957–71. T. Mołdawa, *Ludzie Władzy 1944–1991. Władze państwowe i polityczne Polski według stanu na dzień 28 II 1991* (Warsaw, 1991), 412.

POLISH ACADEMY OF SCIENCES (Polska Akademia Nauk [PAN]), all-Polish scientific institution established during the First Congress of Polish Science between June 29 and July 2, 1951. The PAN replaced the Polish Academy of Knowledge (Polska Akademia Umiejętności) and Warsaw's Scientific Association (Towarzystwo Naukowe Warszawskie), both dissolved during the same Congress. The communist authorities restructured Polish science in order to better control it and to promote new methodologies. In 1952 PAN had 148 members; in the 1960s, over 200; and in the 1980s about 400. Divided into six departments, PAN was presided over by J. Dembowski (1952–56), T. Kotarbiński* (1957–62), J. Groszkowski* (1963–71), W. Trzebiatowski (1972–77), W. Nowacki (1978–80), and A. Gieysztor* (1980–84 and after 1990). J. Karpiński, *Polska, Komunizm, Opozycja* (London, 1985), 190.

POLISH-AMERICAN CONGRESS, umbrella organization established in 1944 at the congress in Buffalo, New York. The Congress unites several associations of American *Polonia** and considers itself the representative of Polish people living in the United States. J. Karpiński, *Polska, Komunizm, Opozycja* (London, 1985), 105.

POLISH CATHOLIC-SOCIAL UNION (Polski Związek Katolicko-Społeczny [PZKS]), organization established in January 1981 by J. Zabłocki* and his supporters, who had originally belonged to the Znak* group. In 1976 they voted in the Sejm* for communist constitutional amendments. As a consequence, they lost the support of their constituency. For some years they still used the old name Znak, but eventually they formed a new group, the PZKS. It had its own periodical, the weekly *Ład* ("The Order"), and was led by Zabłocki and, after 1984, successively by Andrzej Horodecki and Zbigniew Zieliński. In 1983 the organization numbered 5,000 members, who tried to constitute an organization that would be Catholic, independent, and on a peaceful footing with the communist authorities. J. Karpiński, *Polska, Komunizm, Opozycja* (London, 1985), 199, 322.

POLISH HELSINKI COMMISSION. See Helsinki Committee.

POLISH INDEPENDENCE AGREEMENT. See PPN.

POLISH INDEPENDENCE PARTY (Polska Partia Wolności), small party led by R. Szeremietiew* that merged with J. Olszewski's* group and formed the Movement for the Republic (RdR)* in July 1992. B. Szajkowski (ed.), *Political Parties of Eastern Europe, Russia, and the Successor States* (London, 1994), 334.

"POLISH OCTOBER" OF 1956, symbolic name for the culmination of the de-Stalinization process in Poland, which led to the establishment of W. Gomułka's* regime and took place in October 1956. The death of J. Stalin in March 1953 triggered a cultural and intellectual "thaw"* and an erosion of the totalitarian Stalinist system. The tyrannical Ministry of Public Security* was abolished in Poland, many of its officials were arrested, and over 100,000 political prisoners were amnestied. Two factions fought for power within the Polish United Workers' Party (PZPR).* The "Natolin" faction, named after its headquarters, a governmental palace residence near Warsaw,* supported a traditional Stalinist policy mixed with a chauvinist Polish orientation. The outcome of this mixture and the general appearance of the faction were so repulsive that "Natolin" was frequently called "the boors" ("Chamy"). They were opposed by the "Puławska group," named after an elegant street in Warsaw where some members of the group had their apartments. This faction stressed the importance of structural reforms to the communist system in Poland. The "reformists" of the "Puławska group," some of whom had been hard-line communists before 1953, supported more flexible methods of rule and the loosening of Polish-Soviet links. It happened that there were numerous communists of Jewish background in this group, and sometimes popular public opinion called the group "the Jews" ("Żydy"). The changes started by Stalin's death stimulated a popular desire for more reforms, but the authorities acted slowly. On June 28, 1956, the workers of the Cegielski factory organized a strike and a large demonstration in the center of Poznań.* A crowd of 50,000 marched through the city and attacked several governmental buildings. The authorities sent Polish People's Army* units to the city, and regular fighting started. According to official data, 53 people were killed and over 300 wounded during a few days. The Poznań uprising, together with a series of lesser provincial strikes, riots, and demonstrations, destructed the Stalinist myth and convinced the authorities that significant changes had to be undertaken. Yet, the Party and its leadership were divided. "Dogmatists" believed that the political "thaw" and relaxation had to end, and the old Stalinist ruling methods should be used to discipline and mobilize Polish society. "Reformists," "liberals," and frustrated youth were convinced that further modification of the regime and its reforms was inevitable. They also wanted a higher standard of living,* the end of collectivization,* more religious freedom, and more independence from the Soviet Union. All these desired changes were impossible without at least partial rearrangement of the Party and state leadership. The Seventh Plenum of the Party Central Committee, which started on July 18, 1956, accepted a resolution criticizing "economic neglect," "abandonment of the inner party democracy," and "personality cult

and bureaucratization." The Plenum rehabilitated Gomułka, M. Spychalski,*
and Z. Kliszko,* and it elected a new Central Committee that included a group
of young communists without any Moscow training. The Stalinists opposed
democratization and defeated their positions in the Party-state apparatus, but
political ferment and the mood of dissatisfaction continued growing in Poland.
Riots and demonstrations spread, workers organized workers' councils independent of the bureaucracy and the Party. In August the government-controlled
Central Council of Trade Unions* demanded a complete change of its former
policies. That same month Gomułka, Spychalski, and Kliszko rejoined the Party.
W. Komar,* a personal friend of Gomułka, was appointed commander of the
Internal Security Corps (KBW),* which was not supervised by Marshal Rokos-
sowski.* In September a new session of the Sejm* opened in a stormy way.
The press sharply criticized collectivization and the economic performance of
the authorities. On October 9 H. Minc,* chief of the State Economic Planning
Commission, resigned from the Commission and the Politburo.* The situation
in Poland became very tense. On October 19 the Eighth Plenum of the Central
Committee met in Warsaw and co-opted Gomułka and his supporters. It appeared that Gomułka would be reelected First Secretary and Rokossowski would
be ejected from the Polish Party and state leadership. Moscow came to the
conclusion that a coup d'état had started in Poland. Soviet military units stationed in Poland began to move toward Warsaw. Warsaw workers and the Internal Security Corps began to prepare a defense of the city, and many Polish
units refused to obey Rokossowski's orders. That same day, October 19, a Soviet
delegation led by N. Khrushchev unexpectedly flew to Warsaw, started negotiations with Gomułka and Ochab, and threatened armed intervention. The atmosphere in Warsaw resembled the first days of September 1939 or the
beginning of the 1944 Warsaw Uprising. After many hours of negotiations,
Soviet leaders accepted a compromise; they left for Moscow on October 20,
realizing that armed intervention in Poland would be too risky and, in fact,
unnecessary. Gomułka and his assistants appeared to be reliable communists.
That day Gomułka addressed the Central Committee, criticized the mistakes of
the Polish Stalinist leadership, and presented his version of the "Polish road to
socialism." On Sunday, October 21, Gomułka was elected First Secretary of
the Central Committee. A new Politburo was formed. Dominated by supporters
of the changes, it excluded most Stalinists. Gomułka's triumph was accepted by
the Polish masses with enthusiasm.

The Eighth Plenum was followed by far-reaching changes in many fields of
national life. Yet the initial enthusiasm was over soon. Gomułka's return to
power was not followed by structural, democratic, and economic reforms. The
most energetic supporters of political and economic liberalization were eliminated from the leadership during the following few years. New strikes took place
as early as 1957, and control over the Polish society was dramatically tightened.
The "Polish October," so optimistic at first, became a symbol of Gomułka's
betrayal. G. Sanford and A. Gozdecka-Sanford, *Historical Dictionary of Poland* (Me-

tuchen, N.J., 1994), 136; M. K. Dziewanowski, *The Communist Party of Poland: An Outline of History* (Cambridge, Mass., 1976); M. K. Dziewanowski, *Poland in the Twentieth Century* (New York, 1977); R. F. Leslie (ed.), *The History of Poland since 1863* (Cambridge, 1980); J. C. Curry and L. Fajfer, *Poland's Permanent Revolution: People vs. Elites, 1956 to the Present* (Washington, D.C., 1996).

POLISH PARTY OF THE FRIENDS OF BEER (Polska Partia Przyjaciół Piwa [PPPP]), small party founded in December 1990 by an actor and satirist, J. Rewiński, supported a common-sense liberal program. During the 1991 elections* the party won 3.27% of the vote and 16 seats in the Sejm.* Later it split into two groups, known as "Large Beer" and "Small Beer," and lost political significance. G. Sanford and A. Gozdecka-Sanford, *Historical Dictionary of Poland* (Metuchen, N.J., 1994), 149.

POLISH PEASANT PARTY (Polskie Stronnictwo Ludowe [PSL]), **(1)** major peasant party that between 1945 and 1949 opposed growing communist domination in Poland. During World War II two peasant parties were active in the underground: a pro-communist "Lublin" Peasant Party and the Peasant Party "Roch," cooperating with the Polish Government-in-Exile.* On June 27, 1945, S. Mikołajczyk,* its Premier until November 1944 and a prewar peasant leader, returned to Poland and started organizing a new party. On July 8, 1945, representatives of the clandestine Peasant Party "Roch" and the prewar peasant movement established a Provisional Main Executive Committee. On July 11 it initiated activities of the new Polish Peasant Party (PSL). It was led by President W. Witos and three deputy presidents: S. Mikołajczyk, J. Niećko,* and W. Kiernik.* Since Witos was ill, the Party was headed by Mikołajczyk. Soon the PSL became the largest and the most popular party in Poland. It had 200,000 members in November 1945, about 500,000 in January 1946, and about 800,000 in May 1946. Yet, it received only three portfolios in the Provisional Government of National Unity (TRJN).* Mikołajczyk became Deputy Premier and Minister of Agriculture and Land Reform, C. Wycech* Minister of Education, and Kiernik Minister of Public Administration. The PSL aimed at quick elections and hoped to gain a majority vote, like the Smallholders in Hungary in November 1945. During its First Congress in January 1946, the PSL accepted a new program based on agrarism and, in the area of foreign policy, on friendship with the USSR and close ties with Western powers. The alarmed Polish Workers' Party (PPR)* tried to weaken the PSL, accusing it of collaboration with the anticommunist underground, terrorizing and killing its activists, and isolating PSL politicians and state officials. The communists delayed parliamentary elections. To neutralize the PSL, the PPR leaders proposed to create an electoral "Democratic Bloc," which would go to the elections together and would divide the seats in the Sejm* such that the PPR, PSL, and PPS would each receive 20% of the seats and the Democratic Party (SD)* and the Labor Party (SP)* each 10%. The PSL rejected this offer; it wanted 75% of all the seats for "the countryside,'' which meant the PSL and the rump ''Lublin'' Peasant Party. The communists intensified their anti-PSL campaign; instead of the elections, they organized the referendum* on June 30, 1946. According to official data, the PSL lost the referendum. The PSL was obviously unable to defend itself against the communist terror. During the elections of January 1947,* the PSL was decimated by secret police and received only 28 seats in the newly established Sejm. Within the PSL appeared several factions that wanted to turn from the policy of uncompromising resistance against communism to cooperation. A splinter group led by Niećko and Wycech formed the ''Left'' Polish Peasant Party (''Lewica'' PSL). On October 26, 1947, Mikołajczyk, threatened by secret police, escaped abroad, followed by another PSL leader, S. Korboński.* A group of their colleagues from the PSL leadership and numerous party activists were arrested by the secret police. The PSL was paralyzed. The ''Left'' PSL took over PSL facilities and, in November 1949, merged with the ''Lublin'' Peasant Party into the United Peasant Party (ZSL),* fully controlled by the communist authorities. S. Mikołajczyk, *The Pattern of Soviet Domination* (London, 1948); K. Kersten, *The Establishment of Communist Rule in Poland, 1943–1948* (Berkeley, Calif., 1991); *Słownik Historii Polski 1939–1948*, ed. by A. Chwalba and T. Gąsowski (Cracow, 1994), 134–142.

(2), successor to the United Peasant Party (ZSL).* Formed in May 1990, the PSL united the Polish Peasant Party–Rebirth (Polskie Stronnictwo Ludowe–Odrodzenie), a product of evolutionary changes in the ZSL and the smaller PSL Wilanów Group, which included activists of the 1945–49 PSL and stressed its links with this party. The new PSL wanted to be a ''third force'' in Polish politics. In September 1990 it left the governmental coalition of T. Mazowiecki* as a protest against its agricultural policy. The PSL leader, R. Bartoszcze,* participated in the presidential elections of 1990* but gained only 7.2% of the vote. This defeat triggered interparty tensions and conflicts aggravated in spring 1991. In June 1991 Bartoszcze was replaced by W. Pawlak.* During the elections of October 1991* the PSL won 8.67% of the vote and 48 parliamentary seats, which was a decline compared to 69 deputies it had had in the 1989–91 Sejm. In early 1992, the party supported the ruling coalition of J. Olszewski* and was ready to join it when the lustration affair of June 1992 toppled the government. The PSL opposed lustration and supported the vote of no confidence in Olszewski. On June 5, 1992, President L. Wałęsa* nominated Pawlak Premier. Although he failed to form a government, he gained considerable respect from his 33 days in office. The PSL opposed the Balcerowicz* ''shock therapy,'' privatization, and some elements of ''de-communization'' and demanded special support for and protection of Polish agriculture. During the elections of September 1993* the PSL—with 200,000 members, the largest party in Poland—gained 46% of the vote and 132 seats in the Sejm. The party thus became the second largest Parliamentary Club after the Democratic Left Alliance (SLD).* In October 1993 Pawlak formed the PSL-SLD coalition. The

1989–93 period, when Poland was governed by Solidarity's successor parties, was closed. B. Szajkowski (ed.), *Political Parties of Eastern Europe, Russia, and the Successor States* (London, 1994), 336–338.

POLISH PEASANT PARTY–SOLIDARITY (Polskie Stronnictwo Ludowe–Solidarność PSL-S), small party formed by a splinter group of Rural Solidarity.* B. Szajkowski (ed.), *Political Parties of Eastern Europe, Russia, and the Successor States* (London, 1994), 330.

POLISH PEOPLE'S ARMY. See **Army.**

POLISH PRESS AGENCY (Polska Agencja Prasowa [PAP]), communist official state agency founded after World War II. G. Sanford and A. Gozdecka-Sanford, *Historical Dictionary of Poland* (Metuchen, N.J., 1994), 149.

POLISH SOCIALIST PARTY (Polska Partia Socjalistyczna [PPS]), Polish democratic socialist party, founded in 1892. One of the largest parties in Poland during the interwar period, it continued its activities in the underground during World War II. Rebuilt after the war, the PPS consisted of two factions. The larger one wanted to continue its prewar tradition and to remain independent of communist domination. The smaller one, led by J. Cyrankiewicz,* supported collaboration with the Soviet-sponsored Polish Workers' Party (PPR).* Forced to merge with the PPR into the Polish United Workers' Party (PZPR),* in 1948 the PPS ceased to exist. Some PPS activists in exile, such as Z. Zaremba* and A. and L. Ciołkosz,* continued their activities abroad. In the late 1980s, the PPS was re-established in Poland; however, it was divided into several factions and has never gained real importance. Especially after the death of J. J. Lipski,* the leading PPS activist in Poland, the demise of the party was evident. G. Sanford and A. Gozdecka-Sanford, *Historical Dictionary of Poland* (Metuchen, N.J., 1994), 149; J. Coutouvidis and J. Reynolds, *Poland, 1939–1947* (Leicester, 1986); W. Pański (J. Holzer), *Z dziejów PPS 1944–1948* (Warsaw, 1980); J. Tomicki, *Polska Partia Socjalistyczna 1892–1948* (Warsaw, 1983); R. Stefanowski, PPS 1892–1992 (Warsaw, 1992).

POLISH UNITED WORKERS' PARTY (Polska Zjednoczona Partia Robotnicza [PZPR]), communist party established in December 1948 and ruling in Poland until summer 1989. Formed by a unification of the Polish Workers' Party (PPR)* and the Polish Socialist Party (PPS),* the PZPR was supervised by the Soviets, modeled on their Communist Party, and enjoyed a monopoly of power in Poland. After 1948 the PZPR helped to transform Polish economic and political systems into copies of the Soviet systems. By 1956 the PZPR managed to gain a certain independence, accommodated itself to Polish national tradition and to the popular influence of the Roman Catholic Church,* and developed its own "Polish Road to Socialism." In the 1960s and 1970s the PZPR proved unable to answer economic and political challenges. Dissatisfied Polish society, especially the disappointed workers who theoretically constituted the ruling class, rebelled several times against the Party, which reached about 3 million members by 1980 but failed to solve Poland's growing social and economic problems. Its authority was reduced by a military dictatorship established in 1981 by the Jaruzelski* regime. In 1989 the PZPR disintegrated, formally dissolving itself during its last congress in January 1990. Its activists formed two new successor parties: the Social Democracy of the Republic of Poland (SdRP)* and the Polish Socialist Union (PUS). The PZPR was directed by First (or General) Secretaries: B. Bierut* (1945–56), E. Ochab* (March–October 1956), W. Gomułka* (1956–70), E. Gierek* (1970–80), S. Kania* (1980–81), W. Jaruzelski* (1981–89), and M. F. Rakowski* (1989–90). G. Sanford and A. Gozdecka-Sanford, *Historical Dictionary of Poland* (Metuchen, N.J., 1994), 154; J. de Weydenthal, *The Communists of Poland: An Historical Outline* (Stanford, Calif., 1986); M. K. Dziewanowski, *The Communist Party of Poland* (Cambridge, 1976).

POLISH WORKERS' PARTY (Polska Partia Robotnicza [PPR]), communist party formed in Warsaw* on January 5, 1942, by a group of agents of the International sent to Poland from Moscow in December 1941. The PPR party replaced the Communist Party of Poland (KPP), dissolved by J. Stalin in 1938. Until 1944 the PPR was active in the underground; however, it did not join the Polish underground state, did not cooperate with the Polish Government-in-Exile* in London, and frequently fought against the Home Army (AK).* In July 1944 the PPR, led by its First Secretary, W. Gomułka,* joined the Soviet-sponsored communist government-in-waiting, the Polish Committee of National Liberation (PKWN), and later became instrumental in the establishment of the communist system in Poland. In August 1944 the PPR had about 20,000 members directed by a Central Committee* consisting of 18 persons. All of them were prewar communists, although the members of the KPP constituted only a small minority in provincial Party organizations. In August 1944 the Party's Politburo* was formed. It included J. Berman,* H. Minc,* A. Zawadzki* (all of them from the Central Bureau of the Polish Communists* in the USSR), W. Gomułka, and B. Bierut.* In May 1945 the Politburo was joined by M. Spychalski* and R. Zambrowski* and, during the First Congress of the Party in December 1945, by S. Radkiewicz.* In the central leadership of the Party, those communists who spent the war in the USSR always had a majority over "homeland" communists. The latter constituted a clear majority in provincial and local organizations and frequently disliked its central apparatus, which included a significant percentage of Jews.* Competing against the Polish Socialist Party (PPS)* and other parties, the PPR tried to gain as many members as possible. In December 1945 their number grew to 250,000; in December 1946, to 550,000; and in December 1948, to almost 1 million. After the Yalta* Agreement, the PPR shared power with the Polish Peasant Party (PSL),* the partially independent PPS, and other democratic groups. Most members of the Party elite supported Gomułka, who believed that the Party policy should be adequate for the internal situation of Poland and that the opposition should be eliminated with political and police methods. The elimination process was accelerated after the elections of 1947.* In summer 1948 Stalin came to the conclusion that the Sovietization of Poland should be intensified, he thus supported the "Moscovites" against the "homeland" faction. During the July 1948 Plenum of the Central Committee, Gomułka was sharply criticized for "national" and "rightist" deviation, and during the August-September 1948 Plenum, he was removed as Secretary General and replaced by Bierut. Gomułka's supporters were sidetracked or removed. Altogether about 30,000 people were purged from the Party. In December 1948 the PPS was forced to unite with the PPR. The newly established Polish United Workers' Party (PZPR)* monopolized power and Sovietized Poland during the Stalinist period.* G. Sanford and A. Gozdecka-Sanford, *Historical Dictionary of Poland* (Metuchen, N.J., 1994), 155; M. K. Dziewanowski, *The Communist Party of Poland* (Cambridge, 1976); K. Kersten, *The Establishment of Communist Rule in Poland, 1943–1948* (Berkeley, Calif., 1991); J. de Weydenthal, *The Communists of Poland: An Historical Outline* (Stanford, Calif., 1986); *Słownik Historii Polski 1939–1948*, ed. by A. Chwalba and T. Gąsowski (Cracow, 1994), 108–114.

POLITBUREAU, political bureau of a communist party Central Committee* and the decision-making body of communist regimes. The Soviet Politburo was formed in 1917, but in the late 1920s its influence was reduced by Stalin's dictatorial rule. In 1952 the Politburo was replaced by a Presidium of the Central Committee, but in 1966 L. Brezhnev reinstated the original name. Communist regimes of the Soviet satellite states adopted a similar institution. Also, in Poland the Politbureau occupied the most powerful position inside the Polish Workers' Party (PPR)* and, from 1948, the Polish United Workers' Party (PZPR).* Yet Article 33 of the PZPR statute merely stated that the "Central Committee elects [from among its own membership] a Political Bureau for directing the work of the Central Committee during the period between plenary sessions." The composition of the Politburo and its changes reflected the political situation in the country. The most thorough alternations of the Polish Polibureau took place in 1948, 1956, 1970, and 1980–81 and constituted turning points in Polish postwar history. R. F. Staar, *Poland, 1944–1962: The Sovietization of a Captive People* (New Orleans, 1962), 18, 157–159; J. L. Curry and L. Fajfer, *Poland's Permanent Revolution: People vs. Elites, 1956 to the Present* (Washington, D.C., 1996); B. P. McCrea, J. C. Plano, and G. Klein, *The Soviet and East European Dictionary* (Oxford, 1984), 118.

POLITYKA ("Politics"), weekly established in 1957 in Warsaw* to replace the dissolved *Po Prostu* ("Plainly Speaking").* Devoted mainly to contemporary Polish political, social, economic, and cultural issues, it represented the mildly reformist milieu in the leadership of the Polish United Workers' Party (PZPR).* Edited in succession by S. Żółkiewski,* M. F. Rakowski* from 1958, J. Bijak from 1982, and J. Baczyński since 1994, *Polityka* survived the fall of communism, changed its profile, and became one of the most popular periodicals in Poland. Series of anniversary articles in *Polityka* in March 1997.

POLITYKA POLSKA ("Polish Politics"), political quarterly published by the Young Poland Movement (RMP)* from 1982 in the underground and, during 1990–91, legally. D. Cecuda, *Leksykon opozycji politycznej 1976–1989* (Warsaw, 1989), 181.

POLONIA, traditional name for Polish communities abroad. Polonia includes all the people who consider themselves Polish, regardless of their place of birth and language. Polonia, or Polish Diaspora, appeared as a consequence of emigration* and changes to Polish borders.* Emigration from Poland started as early as the 18th century, when the first Polish communities in the United States were established. After the Partitions of Poland, a large part of Polish territory was incorporated into Russia. Most of these lands were never returned to Poland and their Polish population was forced to live in Russia. The same thing happened after World War II, when the USSR annexed almost one-half of the prewar Polish state. Presently, between 14 and 17 million Poles live outside Poland. Quite frequently they stay in touch with Polish political and economic life. The division of the contemporary Polonia is shown in the following table:

Country	Number of Poles	Main centers of Polonia
United States	from 6 to 10 million	Chicago, New York, Detroit, Cleveland, Buffalo
Germany	1.5 million	Berlin
Brazil	from 800,000 to 1 million	Curitiba
France	from 800,000 to 1 million	Paris
Canada	600,000	Toronto, Winnipeg, Montreal
Belorussia	from 400,000 to 1 million	Grodno, Minsk
Ukraine	from 300,000 to 500,000	Lvov, Zhitomir
Lithuania	from 250,000 to 300,000	region of Vilna
Great Britain	150,000	London, Manchester
Australia	from 130,000 to 180,000	Melbourne, Sydney
Argentina	from 100,000 to 170,000	Buenos Aires
Russia	100,000	Moscow, Petersburg, Siberia
Czech Republic	from 70,000 to 100,000	Cieszyn, Silesia
Latvia	from 70,000 to 80,000	Riga, Daugapilis
Kazakhstan	from 60,000 to 100,000	Alma Ata, Karaganda
Belgium	55,000	Antwerp, Liege

Sweden	from 40,000 to 60,000	Stockholm, Malmö
Austria	from 30,000 to 40,000	Vienna, Graz, Linz
Italy	30,000	Rome
South Africa	15,000	Johannesburg, Capetown
The Netherlands	13,000	Rotterdam, Amsterdam
Denmark	12,000	Copenhagen
Switzerland	from 5,000 to 10,000	Zurich, Geneva
Hungary	from 5,000 to 7,000	Budapest
Romania	from 5,000 to 7,000	Bucharest
New Zealand	from 3,000 to 5,000	Wellington, Auckland
Norway	from 1,500 to 5,000	Oslo, Moss, Halden
Finland	1,500	Helsinki

Nowa Encyklopedia Powszechna PWN, vol. 4 (Warsaw, 1995), 967.

POPIEL, KAROL (1887–1977), minister in the Polish Government-in-Exile*
during World War II and politician who returned to Poland and rebuilt and
headed the Labor Party (SP)* in 1945. In 1946 he suspended the activities of
his party in protest against its infiltration by communists. In 1947, threatened
by the authorities, he left Poland. *Encyklopedyczny Słownik Sławnych Polaków* (Warsaw, 1996), 298; T. Mołdawa, *Ludzie Władzy 1944–1991. Władze państwowe i polityczne
Polski według stanu na dzień 28 II 1991* (Warsaw, 1991), 412.

POPIEŁUSZKO, JERZY (1947–84), Catholic priest whose church and parish
of St. Stanisław Kostka in the northern Warsaw* district of Żoliborz became a
center of Solidarity* and anti-communist resistance during Martial Law.* "Father Jerzy," as Popiełuszko was known, was a fiery and radical preacher; his
sermons became famous throughout all of Poland. He worked closely with the
Solidarity activists of the nearby Huta Warszawa iron-and-steel works, supported
the banned Solidarity, and regularly served a patriotic "Mass for the Fatherland."* Considered a major enemy and harassed by the communist authorities
and the political police, he was abducted by three secret police officers, G.
Piotrowski, J. Pękała, and W. Chmielewski, on October 19, 1984. He was tortured and murdered, and his body was thrown into the Vistula River.* The
murder aroused widespread anger and contributed to the political crisis of the
1980s and the fall of communism in Poland. In February 1985, the perpetrators,
working in the Surveillance Department of the Ministry of Interior, were tried
and sentenced, together with Col. A. Pietruszka, who headed the department. In
1990 the case was reopened after one of the convicted men accused senior
government officials of being involved in the affair. Two former Security Service generals were charged with planning Popiełuszko's murder, but they were
acquitted in August 1994. Yet there was no thorough investigation, and the

mystery of the secret plotting remained unsolved. Whether the murder was an isolated initiative of Piotrowski or a provocation against the Jaruzelski* regime, which was seen by many communists as too mild, cannot be determined definitively. Popiełuszko became a popularly acclaimed saint and martyr, his church a national shrine, and his murder a symbol of communist bestiality. G. Sanford and A. Gozdecka-Sanford, *Historical Dictionary of Poland* (Metuchen, N.J., 1994), 156; *Encyklopedyczny Słownik Sławnych Polaków* (Warsaw, 1996), 229.

POPŁAWSKI, STANISŁAW (1902–73), general and Deputy Minister of Defense during 1949–56, contributed to Stalinization of the Polish People's Army* and to the destruction of the military underground after 1945. An officer of the Red Army* from 1920, he was transferred to the Polish communist forces in September 1944. He served initially as deputy commander-in-chief of the Second Army; from December 1944 he was deputy commander-in-chief of the First Army. During 1945–47 he commanded the Silesian Military District. In 1956 he returned to the USSR. *Encyklopedyczny Słownik Sławnych Polaków* (Warsaw, 1996), 299.

POPULATION. Before World War II Poland had 35.1 million citizens. Over 6 million of them were killed during the war. Millions more were deported to the USSR and Germany, and part of the Polish population found itself in the territories incorporated into the Soviet Union after 1945. In 1946 about 24.3 million people lived in Poland (only 31.8% in towns). Hundreds of thousands left Poland in the late 1940s, but another large group of people came to Poland through the repatriations.* After the war Poland showed a very high rate of demographic growth, with 1.7% increase during 1951–60. As a result of this growth, the number of Polish citizens increased to 30 million in 1960, over 32.5 million in 1970, and 37 million in 1984. Most Polish citizens are Polish-speaking Roman Catholics. National minorities* constitute less than 4% of the entire population. At the beginning of 1994, the population grew to 38.5 million, of whom 61.8% lived in towns. The average population density was 123 people per square kilometer. For every 100 men there were 105 women. About 29% of the population was younger than productive age (below 18), 58% was of productive age (18–64 for men, 18–59 for women), and 13% was over productive age. According to forecasts by the Main Statistical Office (GUS),* the population of Poland will reach 39.54 in the year 2000. *Eastern Europe and the Commonwealth of Independent States, 1994* (London, 1994), 466; M. Okolski, "Demographic Anomalies in Poland," *Poland: The Economy in the 1980s*, ed. by R. A. Clarke (London, 1989), 88–102.

PORĘBA, BOGDAN (1934–   ), film director and the president of the Patriotic Association "Grunwald."* *Who's Who in Poland* (Warsaw, 1983), 684.

POTSDAM CONFERENCE, the last Allied conference of World War II held in the town of Potsdam, near Berlin, between July 17 and August 2, 1945. The chief participants representing the three Great Powers—the President of the United States, H. S. Truman, the Soviet dictator, J. Stalin, and the British Prime Minister, W. Churchill (replaced by C. Attlee, who became Prime Minister during the conference)—met to settle conditions that would guarantee lasting peace in Europe. Yet they failed to reach agreement or sign a peace treaty with Germany and its allies. The conference was closed with several contracts, and the participants decided that negotiations would be continued through the Council of Foreign Ministers. The central issues debated in Potsdam concerned the administration of defeated Germany, the western borders* of Poland, the occupation of Austria, Soviet policy toward Eastern Europe, reparations, the United Nations, and the war against Japan. The debate in Potsdam was much cooler and less friendly than during the earlier war conferences and was clearly affected by the beginning of the Cold War.* Truman told Stalin about a "new weapon" that was to be used against Japan. The Soviet Union rejected any Western interference in Eastern Europe and presented several demands reaching beyond it, such as permission to establish a Red Army* base on the Dardanelles. Several Polish issues, discussed during the conference, contributed to the growing tension between the Allies. Since the Provisional Government of National Unity (TRJN)* had been established in June 1945, according to the agreement made in Yalta,* Stalin demanded that the Western Allies discontinue any relations with the Polish Government-in-Exile* and dissolve all Polish wartime institutions in the West. Churchill and Truman wanted the Soviets to guarantee the rights of those Poles who would return to Poland from the West. The Allies also discussed the issue of the Oder-Neisse Line.* The Americans and the British were afraid that the frontier located on the Western Neisse (Nysa Łużycka) would further weaken the German economy and would make the administration of Germany and reparation problems more difficult. Eventually, the Western Allies recognized de facto the Oder-Neisse Line as the western border of Poland. As a result, the radical westward shift of Poland's borders strengthened the protectorate character of Soviet-controlled Poland and allowed the USSR to take more reparations from Germany and former German territories incorporated into Poland. The Soviet delegation and representatives of the Polish government, invited to Potsdam, promised to organize "free and unfettered elections" as soon as possible and to guarantee their unrestricted monitoring by foreign press. The Polish communists showed their "participation" in the conference as proof of the true success of Poland and confirmation of the right course of their Soviet-oriented policy. K. Kersten, *The Establishment of Communist Rule in Poland, 1943–1948* (Berkeley, Calif., 1991); A. B. Lane, *I Saw Poland Betrayed* (Indianapolis, 1948).

POWIAT, administrative unit introduced in pre-Partitions Poland, equivalent of an Anglo-Saxon county. During the interwar period and in 1944–50, the chief executive officer of a powiat was called *starosta* (elder). In 1950 the post was abolished; and almost 400 powiats were eliminated during the administration reform of 1975.* J. Karpiński, *Polska, Komunizm, Opozycja* (London, 1985), 202.

POZNAŃ, capital city of Poznań Province (województwo) and medieval capital of Poland, located on the River Warta in the heart of Greater Poland (Wielkopolska). The city reached 590,000 inhabitants in 1990 and is an important industrial, transportation, and cultural center of western Poland with several institutions of higher learning, including Adam Mickiewicz University. One of the places of the epochal "Polish October" events in 1956,* Poznań entered the history chronicles of communist Poland. G. Sanford and A. Gozdecka-Sanford, *Historical Dictionary of Poland* (Metuchen, N.J., 1994), 158; J. E. Nalepa, *Pacyfikacja zbuntowanego miasta: Wojsko Polskie w czerwcu 1956 roku w Poznaniu* (Warsaw, 1992); *Poznański czerwiec 1956*, ed. by J. Maciejewski and Z. Trojanowiczowa (Poznań, 1990); *Dzieje Poznania*, ed. by J. Topolski, vols. 1–3 (Warsaw, 1988).

POZNAŃ EVENTS or POZNAŃ UPRISING. See "Polish October" of 1956.

PPN (Polish Independence Agreement [Polskie Porozumienie Niepodległościowe]), loose group of independent intellectuals and opposition activists who published their program in the London *Tygodnik Polski* ("The Polish Weekly") and the Paris *Kultura** in May 1976. Later they published reports and information on political, economic, and social problems in Poland. They acted anonymously, but G. Herling-Grudziński,* L. Kołakowski,* J. Lerski, and M. Winowska served as their delegates and confirmed the authenticity of their texts. One of the most active members of the group was Z. Najder.* The PPN supported the vision of an independent and democratic Poland, maintaining good relations with free Ukraine, Lithuania, Belorussia, and a united Germany. The group stressed civilization-in-common as the link between Poland and Western Europe. After the emergence of Solidarity* in 1980, the PPN discontinued its activities. J. J. Lipski, *KOR: A History of the Workers Defense Committee in Poland, 1976–81* (Berkeley, Calif., 1985), 120–121; J. Karpiński, *Polska, Komunizm, Opozycja* (London, 1985), 197; D. Cecuda, *Leksykon opozycji politycznej 1976–1989* (Warsaw, 1989), 81.

PREMIER (Prime Minister or President of the Council of Ministers), chief executive officer in Poland. The position was introduced on January 1, 1945, when the Provisional Government* replaced the Polish Committee of National Liberation (PKWN). It was occupied by the following politicians: E. Osóbka-Morawski,* a member of the Polish Socialist Party* (initially as chairman of the PKWN), from July 21, 1944, to February 5, 1947; J. Cyrankiewicz,* first a member of the PPS and later of the Polish United Workers' Party (PZPR),* from February 6, 1947, to November 20, 1952; B. Bierut* (PZPR), November 20, 1952, to March 18, 1954; J. Cyrankiewicz, March 18, 1954, to

December 23, 1970; P. Jaroszewicz* (PZPR), December 23, 1970, to February 18, 1980; E. Babiuch* (PZPR), February 18, 1980, to August 24, 1980; J. Pińkowski* (PZPR), August 24, 1980, to September 5, 1980, and as acting Premier, September 5, 1980, to February 11, 1981; W. Jaruzelski* (PZPR), February 11, 1981, to November 6, 1985; Z. Messner* (PZPR), November 6, 1985, to September 19, 1988; M. F. Rakowski* (PZPR), September 27, 1988, to August 1, 1989; C. Kiszczak* (PZPR), August 2, 1989, to August 24, 1989; T. Mazowiecki* (Solidarity*), August 24, 1989, to December 14, 1990; J. K. Bielecki* (Liberal-Democratic Congress*), January 4, 1991, to December 23, 1991; J. Olszewski* (ZChN), December 23, 1991, to June 5, 1992; W. Pawlak* (the Polish Peasant Party*), June 6, 1992, to July 11, 1992; H. Suchocka* (Democratic Union*), July 11, 1992, to October 18, 1993; W. Pawlak, October 18, 1993, to March 4, 1995; J. Oleksy* (Social Democracy of the Republic of Poland [SdRP]*), March 4, 1995, to January 25, 1996; W. Cimoszewicz* (SdRP), from January 25, 1996. T. Mołdawa, *Ludzie Władzy 1944–1991. Władze państwowe i polityczne Polski według stanu na dzień 28 II 1991* (Warsaw, 1991), 174.

PRESIDENT OF POLAND, post of head of state established by the 1921 Constitution. Before World War II Poland had three Presidents: G. Narutowicz (in 1922), S. Wojciechowski (1922–26), and I. Mościcki (1926–39). During and after the war there were Presidents in exile: W. Raczkiewicz* (1939–47), A. Zaleski* (1947–72), S. Ostrowski (1972–79), and E. Raczyński* (1979–90). In communist Poland the post of President of the National Home Council (KRN),* occupied by B. Bierut,* was considered the equivalent of the post of President of the state. After the fake elections of 1947,* the new Sejm* gave Bierut the title of President of state. Between 1952 and 1989, according to the Constitution of 1952,* the President was replaced by the Chairman of the collegial State Council (Rada Państwa).* In July 1989 as a part of a deal between his regime and the democratic opposition,* Gen. W. Jaruzelski* was elected President by both chambers of Parliament. In December 1990 he was replaced by L. Wałęsa,* who, after the presidential election of 1995,* was followed by A. Kwaśniewski.* G. Sanford and A. Gozdecka Sanford, *Historical Dictionary of Poland* (Metuchen, N.J., 1994), 159.

PRESIDENTIAL ELECTIONS OF 1990. Following the Round Table Agreement,* Gen. W. Jaruzelski,* the outgoing Chairman of the State Council (Rada Państwa),* was elected by the National Assembly to the new office of President* for a six-year term on July 19, 1989. His election and the Round Table Negotiations were bitterly criticized by much of Polish society. Many people claimed that with the fall of communism and the advent of new political conditions, the Round Table Agreement had become invalid and inapplicable. On July 27, 1990, one hundred deputies and senators from the Center Alliance (PC)* petitioned Jaruzelski to step down so that L. Wałęsa* could be named President.* On October 2 M. Kozakiewicz,* Speaker of the Sejm,* set November 25 as the

date for the presidential election by popular vote. On October 4 T. Mazowiecki*
announced his candidacy and stated his wish to be President in order to safeguard the reforms his government had initiated. Wałęsa assailed Mazowiecki's
candidacy as divisive and formally launched his own campaign at a large rally
in a Warsaw* steel plant on October 9. He asserted that Poland's intellectuals
and mass media did not believe him, a blue-collar worker, and that they would
consider it embarrassing to have an electrician as their President. In addition to
Wałęsa and Mazowiecki, leaders of several small parties announced their inten-
tions to participate in the election, although under the electoral law signed by
President Jaruzelski on October 1, they had to collect the signatures of at least
100,000 supporters. On November 25 only 60.6% of the 27 million eligible
voters participated in the election. Wałęsa received 39.9% of the vote. Surprisingly, S. Tymiński,* a Polish-born entrepreneur from Canada, nicknamed "the
man from Mars" by the Polish press, received 23.1% of the vote. Mazowiecki
came third with 18.1%. Three other candidates, W. Cimoszewicz,* R. Bartoszcze,* and L. Moczulski,* shared the remainder of the vote. This result proved
to be a shock to many. Mazowiecki, humiliated and disappointed, resigned as
Premier* on November 26, (though he indicated that he and his cabinet would
remain in office until a new Premier was appointed by the next President. *Gazeta
Wyborcza* ("The Electoral Gazette")* announced that Tymiński's second place
was "an embarrassment for the whole nation." Wałęsa and B. Geremek,* a
leader of Solidarity's* anti-Wałęsa faction, called post-Solidarity organizations
to unite behind Wałęsa for the December 9 runoff. The turnout was, again,
relatively low—55%. Wałęsa gained a landslide victory and received 74.3% of
the vote, compared to 25.7% for Tymiński. As in the first-round campaign,
Wałęsa claimed he would be the best guarantee for reforms and democratization
in Poland. Tymiński's campaign was weakened by allegations about his links
with former communists and the secret police. On December 12 Wałęsa resigned
as chairman of Solidarity and, on December 22, was sworn in as President for
a five-year term. General Jaruzelski was excluded from all the inaugural events,
and Wałęsa accepted his office not from him but, symbolically, from R. Kaczorowski,* the last President of the Polish Government-in-Exile.* On December
29 Wałęsa nominated J. K. Bielecki* to the post of Premier.* *Keesing's Record
of World Events*, July 1990, p. 37621; Dec. 1990, p. 37921; *Facts on File*, Oct. 19, 1990,
p. 780; H. Tworzecki, *Parties and Politics in Post-1989 Poland* (Boulder, Colo., 1996),
55; A. Dudek, *Pierwsze lata III Rzeczpospolitej, 1989–1995* (Cracow, 1997), 111–134.

PRESIDENTIAL ELECTIONS OF 1995. A. Kwaśniewski,* chairman of the
Democratic Left Alliance (SLD)* and former communist, defeated the incum-
bent President,* Solidarity* leader L. Wałęsa.* On September 6, 1995, the
Speaker of the Sejm,* J. Zych,* announced that elections would be held on
November 5, with a second round on November 19 if no candidate gained an
absolute majority of votes. On September 28, at the close of registration, 18
candidates were registered, among them Wałęsa, Kwaśniewski, the president of

the Polish National Bank,* H. Gronkiewicz-Waltz,* a former Minister of Labor and Solidarity activist, J. Kuroń,* and the Premier* until February 1995 and the chairman of the Polish Peasant Party (PSL),* W. Pawlak.* During the first round of the elections, the turnout was 64.7%: Kwaśniewski gained 35.1% of the vote, Wałęsa 33.1%, Kuroń 9.2%, J. Olszewski* 6.9%, Pawlak 4.3%, T. Zieliński* 3.5%, Gronkiewicz-Waltz 2.8%, J. Korwin-Mikke* 2.4%, and others 2.7%. Wałęsa presented himself as the only candidate able to safeguard the reforms and counterbalance the left-wing government. Kwaśniewski stressed his commitment to the reforms and European integration, played down his communist past, and campaigned under the slogan "Let's elect the future." In the second round Wałęsa received the support of most of the other candidates from the center and right-wing parties and from the Roman Catholic Church.* Yet 51.7% voted for Kwaśniewski, Wałęsa received 48.3%, and the turnout was 68.2%. Wałęsa's supporters submitted 598,000 protests to the Supreme Court, claiming that the elections should be declared invalid because Kwaśniewski had wrongly claimed to have a university degree and had suppressed information on his wife's financial assets. On November 28, W. Bartoszewski,* A. Milczanowski,* and Z. Okoński, the Foreign, Interior, and Defense Ministers, respectively, resigned because their portfolios were appointed after consultation with the former President. On December 9 the Supreme Court rejected the application that the election of Kwaśniewski should be annulled on the grounds of electoral impropriety. On December 23 Kwaśniewski was sworn in as President for a five-year term. In his inauguration speech he promised to seek a broader national consensus, to promote reforms, and to work for the integration of Poland with the European Union* and NATO. *Keesing's Record of World Events*, Sept.–Dec. 1995; H. Tworzecki, *Parties and Politics in Post-1989 Poland* (Boulder, Colo., 1996), 64–68; A. Dudek, *Pierwsze lata III Rzeczpospolitej, 1989–1995* (Cracow, 1997), 338–364.

PRICES. The invisible hand of the market did not exist in centrally controlled economies or in Poland where prices were regulated according to the beliefs of the leaders and the imperfect expertise of communist economists. Three times, in December 1970, June 1976, and July 1980, sudden price changes triggered workers' rebellions. As a consequence, communist leaders were afraid of price increases, subsidized several branches of the economy, manipulated inflation, and used propaganda tricks. In the early 1980s prices in Poland started increasing quickly, ideological limitations stopped real reforms, and the Polish economy was heading toward major crisis. J. Karpiński, *Polska, Komunizm, Opozycja* (London, 1985), 31.

PRIMATE OF POLAND, head of the Roman Catholic Church* in Poland, a position of great political importance. Before the Partitions of Poland, a Primate ruled as interrex after the death of a King, and before a subsequent election. In post–World War II Poland, Primates, invariably Cardinals, headed the Episco-

pate* and, to most Poles, constituted the superior spiritual authority in the country. During 1926–48 A, Hlond* served as Primate, followed by S. Wyszyński*
in 1948–81 and J. Glemp* after 1981. G. Sanford and A. Gozdecka-Sanford,
Historical Dictionary of Poland (Metuchen, N.J., 1994), 159.

PRIVATIZATION. One of the most important elements of economic transformation after the fall of communism in Poland. The process was started by the
Mazowiecki* government, which planned to sell one-half of some 8,000 state
enterprises within five years. Initial privatization legislation was passed by the
Sejm* in July 1990, and a Ministry of Privatization was established. In November 1990 the first five large firms were offered for privatization. Yet the process
went slowly as a result of indecision over legal, administrative, and political
details. Frequently disputed was which enterprises to privatize first. In February
1993 an Enterprise Pact was signed between the authorities and the trade unions.* In April 1993 a mass privatization scheme was approved by the Sejm. In
fall 1993 the enterprises selected for privatization were grouped and managed
by about 20 investment trusts, called National Investment Funds. They issued
shares of their companies, distributed for a small fee. By the end of 1993, most
small firms, especially trade and artisan enterprises, were already privatized.
After the victory of the Democratic Left Alliance (SLD)* and the Polish Peasant
Party (PSL)* in the elections of 1993,* however, the privatization process
slowed down. *Eastern Europe and the Commonwealth of Independent States, 1994*
(London, 1994), 479; R. Frydman, A. Rapaczyński, J. S. Earle et al., *The Privatization
Process in Central Europe* (Budapest, 1993), 148–210; *Constraints and Impacts of Privatization*, ed. by V. V. Ramanadham (London, 1993), 102–115; I. Major, *Privatization
in Eastern Europe* (Edward Elgar, 1993), 31.

PRO-AMERICAN FORUM (Forum Proamerykańskie), small and loose organization established in May 1991. It supports close Polish-American relations
and the implementation of U.S. economic and political patterns in Poland. It
was competitive with the American-Polish Union (Unia Amerykańsko-Polska).
Partie Polityczne w Polsce, ed. by A. Gargas and M. Wojciechowski (Gdańsk, 1991),
25.

PRON (Patriotyczny Ruch Odrodzenia Narodowego [Patriotic Movement of
National Revival]), organization formed by the Jaruzelski* regime after the imposition of Martial Law* in December 1981. On July 1982 Gen. W. Jaruzelski,
the representatives of the Polish United Workers' Party (PZPR),* the United
Peasant Party (ZSL),* the Democratic Party (SD),* and the pro-governmental
Christian associations announced that a new, broad all-Polish organization supporting the regime would be established. In fall 1982 the Citizens' Committees
of National Salvation (later Revival), formed during the first weeks of Martial
Law under the auspices of the Military Council of National Salvation (WRON),*
were reshaped into local PRON cells. On December 17, 1982, the first meeting

of the PRON Provisional Council was arranged. In July 1983, the PRON replaced the Front of National Unity (FJN).* J. Karpiński, *Polska, Komunizm, Opozycja* (London, 1985), 176.

PRONASZKO, ANDRZEJ (1881–1961), "formist" artist, stage director, and professor of the State Drama School. *Encyklopedyczny Słownik Sławnych Polaków* (Warsaw, 1996), 304.

PRONASZKO, ZBIGNIEW (1885–1958), "formist" painter, stage director, and sculptor. *Encyklopedyczny Słownik Sławnych Polaków* (Warsaw, 1996), 304.

PROVISIONAL COORDINATING COMMITTEE OF SOLIDARITY (Tymczasowa Komisja Koordynacyjna Solidarności [TKK]), provisional governing body of Solidarity* established underground in April 1982 by a group of Solidarity activists who managed to escape and hide after imposition of Martial Law* on December 13, 1981. Initially, the TKK was led by four representatives of the largest regions of Solidarity: Z. Bujak* from Mazovia (Mazowsze), W. Frasyniuk* from Lower Silesia, W. Hardek from Little Poland, and B. Lis* from Gdańsk.* The TKK fought for the cancellation of Martial Law, the release of all interned and arrested activists, the re-establishment of civil rights, and the rebuilding of Solidarity. The TKK organized and coordinated numerous strikes and protest actions. Its members were hunted and arrested by police, and its composition changed several times. J. Karpiński, *Polska, Komunizm, Opozycja* (London, 1985), 279.

PROVISIONAL GOVERNMENT OF NATIONAL UNITY (Tymczasowy Rząd Jedności Narodowej [TRJN]), coalition government formed on June 28, 1945, on the basis of two agreements, one between the Western Allies and the USSR made at the Yalta Conference,* and the other between the communist Provisional Government of the Republic of Poland* on one side and several Polish émigré politicians from London and the London-oriented underground on the other side at a meeting in Moscow on June 17–21, 1945. Initially, five parties joined the coalition government: the Polish Workers' Party (PPR)* with seven members; the Polish Socialist Party (PPS),* with six members; the Polish Peasant Party (PSL),* with three members; the Peasant Party (SL),* with three members; and the Democratic Party (SD),* with two members. The TRJN consisted of 21 persons, 18 of whom belonged to the communist-controlled National Home Council (KRN).* The most important portfolios were held by the following politicians: Premier,* E. Osóbka-Morawski* from the PPS (previously Premier of the Provisional Government of the Republic of Poland* and Chairman of the Polish Committee of National Libaration [PKWN]); First Deputy Premier, W. Gomułka* from the PPR; Second Deputy Premier, S. Mikołajczyk* from the PSL; Minister of Public Security, S. Radkiewicz* from the PPR; Minister of Information and Propaganda, S. Matuszewski* from the PPS; National Defense, M. Żymierski* from the PPR; Industry, H. Minc* from the PPR; Foreign Affairs, W. Rzymowski* from the SD. On November 13, 1945, the powerful Ministry of Recovered Territories was established and given to W. Gomułka. In September 1946 S. Matuszewski was replaced as Minister of Information and Propaganda by F. Widy-Wirski* from the Labor Party (SP),* a new member of the coalition, although at that time the group of Widy-Wirski was controlled by the PPR. On July 5, 1945, the government was recognized by the United States and Great Britain, who simultaneously withdrew their recognition of the Polish Government-in-Exile.* The TRJN was dissolved on February 6, 1947, after the elections of Jan. 1947.* T. Mołdawa, *Ludzie Władzy 1944–1991. Władze państwowe i polityczne Polski według stanu na dzień 28 II 1991* (Warsaw, 1991), 95.

PROVISIONAL GOVERNMENT OF THE REPUBLIC OF POLAND (Rząd Tymczasowy Rzeczpospolitej Polskiej), government formed by the communist-controlled National Home Council (KRN)* on December 31, 1944, as a continuation of the Polish Committee of National Liberation (PKWN). Initially, it resided in Lublin,* and from Feb. 1, 1945, in Warsaw.* The government was established despite the pleas of the Western Allies and was not recognized by them. Yet the USSR recognized the government on January 4, 1945, and signed a treaty of friendship and collaboration with it. Initially, the government consisted of 17 persons. Sixteen of them belonged to the KRN, five were from the Polish Workers' Party (PPR),* five from the Polish Socialist Party (PPS),* five from the Peasant Party (SL),* and two from the Democratic Party (SD).* The most important governmental posts were held by E. Osóbka-Morawski* from the PPS (previously the Chairman of the Polish Committee of National Liberation [PKWN]), Premier* and Minister of Foreign Affairs; W. Gomułka* from the PPR, First Deputy Premier; S. Janusz from the SL, Second Deputy Premier; S. Radkiewicz* from the PPR, Minister of Public Security; S. Matuszewski* from PPS, Minister of Information and Propaganda; and M. Żymierski* from the PPR, Minister of Defense. The government was reshaped into the Provisional Government of National Unity on June 28, 1945. T. Mołdawa, *Ludzie Władzy 1944–1991. Władze państwowe i polityczne Polski według stanu na dzień 28 II 1991* (Warsaw, 1991), 93.

PRUSZYŃSKI, KSAWERY (1907–1950), prolific writer and journalist. Before World War II he contributed to several major periodicals. During the war he fought in the Polish Army in the West and was in the diplomacy wing of the Polish Government-in-Exile.* After the war he represented the communist Polish authorities in the United States and Holland. Most of his journalistic pieces and stories are devoted to historical turning points and World War II. *Dictionary of Polish Literature*, ed. by E. J. Czerwinski (Westport, Conn., 1994), 330–331; M. Dąbrowska, *Dzienniki powojenne 1945–49*, vol. 1, ed. by T. Drewnowski (Warsaw, 1996), 73.

PRZEDŚWIT ("The Dawn"), underground publishing house established in November 1982. One of the largest institutions of this kind, it published more than 100 books. D. Cecuda, *Leksykon opozycji politycznej 1976–1989* (Warsaw, 1989), 138.

PRZEGLĄD KATOLICKI ("The Catholic Review"), cultural, religious, and social weekly published by Warsaw* archbishopric during 1863–1915, 1922–39, and from 1984. J. Karpiński, *Polska, Komunizm, Opozycja* (London, 1985), 218.

PRZEGLĄD POWSZECHNY ("The Universal Review"), cultural, religious, and social monthly published by the Jesuits in Poland during 1884–1914, 1916–39, 1947–53, and from 1982. J. Karpiński, *Polska, Komunizm, Opozycja* (London, 1985), 219.

PRZYBOŚ, JULIAN (1901–70), poet and essayist, member of the Skamander and Cracow's Awangarda groups. He spent World War II in Lvov and in his native village. After the war he was the first president of the Union of Polish Writers (ZLP)* and a deputy of the National Home Council (KRN).* Polish envoy to Bern in 1947–51 and director of the Jagiellonian Library during 1952–55, he later worked as an editor and wrote poetry and literary essays. C. Miłosz, *The History of Polish Literature* (Berkeley, Calif., 1983), 402–404; *Dictionary of Polish Literature*, ed. by E. J. Czerwinski (Westport, Conn., 1994), 331–333; P. Kuncewicz, *Agonia i nadzieja. Literatura polska od 1939*, vol. 2 (Warsaw, 1993), 80–84.

PRZYGOŃSKI, ANTONI (1924–   ), Party historian and expert on the Polish communist movement during World War II. *Who's Who in the Socialist Countries of Europe*, ed. by J. Stroynowski, vol. 3 (Munich, 1989), 954.

PSL-PL. See **Peasant Accord.**

PSTROWSKI, WINCENTY (1904–48), miner and highly publicized Polish Stakhanovite. He returned to Poland from Belgium in 1946 and worked in a mine in Zabrze. In 1947 he reached 273% of the individual miner productivity quota and appealed to other miners to start a work competition. A year later he died, officially of leukemia. R. F. Staar, *Poland, 1944–1962: The Sovietization of a Captive People* (New Orleans, 1962), 104.

PSZCZÓŁKOWSKI, EDMUND (1904–   ), economist, state official, cooperative activist, and chairman of the Public Security Committee of the Council of Ministers from March to November 1956. T. Mołdawa, *Ludzie Władzy 1944–1991. Władze państwowe i polityczne Polski według stanu na dzień 28 II 1991* (Warsaw, 1991), 413.

PTASIŃSKI, JAN (1921–), communist official. A mason by profession, he joined the Polish Workers' Party (PPR)* in 1942 and fought in its People's Guard and its successor, the People's Army. After the war he served as the Party provincial First Secretary in several provinces and as a Deputy Minister of Public Security in 1953–56. *Who's Who in the Socialist Countries of Europe*, ed. by J. Stroynowski, vol. 3 (Munich, 1989), 955.

PULS ("The Pulse"), underground literary quarterly published in Poland from fall 1977. Initially reprinted in London, it was published there after imposition of Martial Law* in Poland. At that time, a publishing house, Puls Publication, was also established in London. *Dictionary of Polish Literature*, ed. by E. J. Czerwinski (Westport, Conn., 1994), 88; J. Karpiński, *Polska, Komunizm, Opozycja* (London, 1985), 221.

PUŁAWY GROUP (OR PUŁAWSKA GROUP). See **"Polish October" of 1956.**

PUTRAMENT, JERZY (1910–86), writer and politician. He made his literary debut in 1930 and later was a member of the Żagary ("Fire-brands") poetic group. During World War II he was a leader of the Union of Polish Patriots (ZPP) and an organizer of the First Division of the communist-controlled Polish Army* in the USSR. In 1945 he was appointed envoy to Switzerland, and during 1947–50 he served as Polish ambassador in Paris. A member of the Sejm* in 1952–56 and of the Central Committee* of the Polish United Workers' Party (PZPR)* during 1952–81, he was a highly influential communist writer of postwar Poland who published numerous novels, autobiographical works, and essay collections. *Dictionary of Polish Literature*, ed. by E. J. Czerwinski (Westport, Conn., 1994), 336–338; P. Kuncewicz, *Agonia i nadzieja. Literatura polska od 1939*, vol. 2 (Warsaw, 1993), 294–299.

PUŻAK, KAZIMIERZ (1883–1950), important leader of the pre–World War II Polish Socialist Party (PPS),* he belonged among the main founders and leaders of the resistance in German-occupied Poland. From 1944 served as president of the Council of National Unity (Rada Jedności Narodowej [RJN]). The NKVD arrested Pużak together with fifteen other leaders of the Polish underground state in March 1945. Pużak was abducted to Moscow, tried, and sentenced to ten years in prison. Released after a year and a half, he returned to Poland in 1946 and in 1948 was rearrested by the Polish communist authorities in connection with the trial of the clandestine Polish Socialist Party "Freedom, Equality, Independence" (PPS Wolność, Równość, Niepodległość). He died in the Rawicz prison. During his short stay outside Polish and Soviet prisons, he wrote fascinating memoirs, smuggled out of Poland and published abroad. G. J. Lerski, *Historical Dictionary of Poland 966–1945*, with special editing and emendations by P. Wróbel and R. J. Kozicki (Westport, Conn., 1996), 485–486; A. K. Kunert, *Illustrowany przewodnik po Polsce podziemnej, 1939–1945* (Warsaw, 1996), 564.

PYJAS, STANISŁAW (1953–77), student at Jagiellonian University* and early associate of the Workers' Defense Committee (KOR)* in Cracow,* most probably killed by secret police on May 7, 1977. The murder triggered mass student demonstrations and initiated the establishment of the Students' Solidarity Committees (SKS)* in 1977–79. J. J. Lipski, *KOR: A History of the Workers' Defense Committee in Poland, 1976–81* (Berkeley, Calif., 1985).

PYKA, TADEUSZ (1930–   ), assistant of E. Gierek,* economy professor, member of the Central Committee* of the Polish United Workers' Party (PZPR)* from 1971, deputy member of the Politburo* from February 1980, and Deputy Premier during 1975–80. On August 17, 1980, Pyka was appointed head of a governmental delegation that started negotiations with the striking workers in the Gdańsk* Lenin Shipyard. Inflexible and inefficient, he was replaced by M. Jagielski* after four days. In October 1980 Pyka was removed from the Central Committee, and in July 1981, from the Party. Interrogated by the Grabski* Committee, he was accused of mismanagement and stripped of the People's Poland Builder order. *Who's Who in the Socialist Countries of Europe*, ed. by J. Stroynowski, vol. 3 (Munich, 1989), 959; Z. Błażyński, *Towarzysze zeznają. Z tajnych archiwów Komitetu Centralnego* (London, 1987), 131–143; T. Mołdawa, *Ludzie Władzy 1944–1991. Władze państwowe i polityczne Polski według stanu na dzień 28 II 1991*, (Warsaw, 1991), 414.

RACZKIEWICZ, WŁADYSŁAW (1885–1947), statesman and President* of Poland during 1939–47. Before World War II he occupied several important state posts, such as Minister of the Interior and the Speaker of the Senate.* After the outbreak of the war, he was nominated by President I. Mościcki, who was interned in Romania, his successor. Unwilling to recognize the Yalta* Agreement and the Provisional Government of National Unity (TRJN),* established in Warsaw* in June 1945, Raczkiewicz held his office until his death, even though the Allies withdrew their recognition of the Polish Government-in-Exile* in July 1945. J. Lerski, *Historical Dictionary of Poland, 966–1945*, with special editing and emendations by P. Wróbel and R. J. Kozicki (Westport, Conn., 1996), 170–172; T. Radzik, Z *dziejów społeczności polskiej w Wielkiej Brytanii po drugiej wojnie światowej, 1945–1990* (Lublin, 1991); *Warszawa nad Tamizą*, ed. by A. Friszke (Warsaw, 1994); G. V. Kacewicz, *Great Britain, the Soviet Union, and the Polish Government in Exile, 1939–45* (London, 1979).

RACZYŃSKI, EDWARD (1891–1993), diplomat and statesman. From 1919 he served as a diplomat and official in the Ministry of Foreign Affairs. From 1934 to 1945, when the Western Allies withdrew their recognition of the Polish Government-in-Exile,* he was Poland's ambassador to London. In 1940 his mediation was crucial to the establishment of the Government-in-Exile and the Polish forces in Great Britain. In 1941–43 Raczyński also served as the Polish Foreign Minister. During 1954–72 he belonged, with Generals Anders* and Bór-Komorowski,* to the Council of Three (Rada Trzech),* a leading body of the Polish emigration in England. Between 1979 and 1986 he was President of the Republic of Poland in Exile. G. V. Kacewicz, *Great Britain, the Soviet Union, and the Polish Government in Exile, 1939–45* (London, 1979); E. Raczyński, *In Allied London* (London, 1962).

RADIO, aside from its traditional role, radio constituted an important element of communist propaganda and its indoctrination system. The Polish Committee of National Liberation (PKWN) established an institution called "Polskie Radio" (Polish Radio) as early as November 1944. In 1944–45 several local radio stations appeared. Listening to foreign broadcasting was severely punished during the postwar years. In 1949 the Central Office for Radio Broadcasting (Centralny Urząd Radiofonii) was established, and in 1960 the Committee for Radio and TV was created to control both institutions. More than 9 million people had a radio in Poland by 1983. J. Karpiński, *Polska, Komunizm, Opozycja* (London, 1985), 225; *Wielka Encyklopedia Powszechna PWN*, vol. 9 (Warsaw, 1969).

RADIO FREE EUROPE, radio station in Munich, established in 1950, financed by the U.S. government to provide the populations of the Soviet European satellites with news, opinions, music, and religious programs. It broadcasted in six languages and was extremely popular. To most people in Poland it was the only source of uncensored information. In 1976 it merged with Radio Liberty, broadcasting in several languages of the former Soviet Union. The Polish section of Radio Free Europe was directed by J. Nowak* in 1952–76, Zygmunt Michałowski in 1976–82, Z. Najder* in 1982–87, and M. Łatyński* after 1987. *The Cold War, 1945–1991*, ed. by B. Frankel, vol. 3 (Detroit, 1992), 241–242; R. T. Holt, *Radio Free Europe* (Minneapolis, 1958); J. Nowak, *Wojna w eterze* (London, 1985); J. Nowak, *Polska z oddali* (London, 1988).

RADKIEWICZ, STANISŁAW (1903–87), Minister of Public Security during 1944–54 and one of the most hated and ruthless Stalinists of Poland. He joined the Communist Party of Poland (KPP) in 1925 and spent World War II in the USSR, where he belonged to the leadership of the Union of Polish Patriots (ZPP) and served as Secretary of the Central Bureau of Polish Communists. In 1944 he joined the Polish Workers' Party (PPR)* and, in July, was made chief of the Security Department of the Polish Committee of National Liberation (PKWN). He occupied the same ministerial position in all communist governments from December 1944 to December 1954, when he became Minister of State Farms (PGR*). This transfer constituted one of the first signs of de-Stalinization in Poland. Radkiewicz belonged to the Party Politburo* from 1945; however, in August 1955 he had to leave it, and in May 1957 he was removed from the Party. Reaccepted in 1960, he was appointed director of the State Reserves Office (Urząd Rezerw Państwowych) and served in this position until his retirement in 1968. M. K. Dziewanowski, *The Communist Party of Poland: An Outline of History* (Cambridge, Mass., 1976); K. Kersten, *The Establishment of Communist Rule in Poland, 1943–1948* (Berkeley, Calif., 1991); Z. Błażyński, *Mówi Józef Światło. Za kulisami bezpieki i partii* (London, 1985).

RADOM, town in central Poland, 100 kilometers south of Warsaw.* Established in the 10th century, it developed into an administrative and industrial center, with a population of 228,500 in 1990. After World War II the town's economy was based on metal, radio, television, telephone, shoe, cigarette, building materials, porcelain, glass, and food production. On June 25, 1976, Radom workers started mass demonstrations against a substantial increase in food prices. G. Sanford and A. Gozdecka-Sanford, *Historical Dictionary of Poland* (Metuchen, N.J., 1994), 161.

RADZIWIŁŁ, ANNA M. (1939–   ), teacher, dissident, Solidarity* activist, and Deputy Minister of Education in the government of T. Mazowiecki* in 1989–91. In 1989 she participated in the Round Table Negotiations* and was elected to the Senate.* *Kto jest kim w polityce polskiej*, ed. by R. Ignasiak (Warsaw, 1993), 235.

RAKOWSKI, MIECZYSŁAW FRANCISZEK (1926–   ), prominent journalist, Deputy Premier from February 1981 to November 1985, Deputy Speaker of the Sejm* during 1985–88, Premier* from September 1988 to August 1989, and First Secretary of the Party from July 1989 to its end in January 1990. A peasant son from the Bydgoszcz* region, he volunteered for the communist-controlled Polish Army* in 1945, went through the Łódź* training school for political officers, and served in the military until 1949. In 1946 he joined the Polish Workers' Party (PPR).* When he left the Polish People's Army, he studied journalism and then received a post as an instructor in the Press and Publishing Department of the Central Committee* of the Polish United Workers' Party (PZPR).* In 1955 he moved to the Central Committee Propaganda Department, and in 1956 he defended his doctorate at the Warsaw Institute of Social Sciences. When the authorities established the weekly *Polityka*,* after closing down the outspoken and reformist *Po Prostu* (''Plainly Speaking'')* in 1957, Rakowski joined the editorial staff of the new periodical; the following year, in May 1958, he became its editor-in-chief. *Polityka* was considered by many a relatively independent and high-quality periodical that supported a reformist line. Rakowski, the chairman of the Association of Polish Journalists* from 1958, was considered a liberal and reasonable person who, nevertheless, enjoyed the confidence of the PZPR leadership and maintained close links with the political establishment. In 1964 he became a deputy member of the Central Committee, in 1972 a deputy to the Sejm,* and in 1975 a full member of the Central Committee. Rakowski reached the pinnacle of his career in the 1980s, when he became a main collaborator of Gen. W. Jaruzelski.* The latter expected Rakowski to negotiate with the political opposition and promoted him to Deputy Premier in 1981. Yet after his elevation Rakowski showed a different face, failed to reach a compromise with Solidarity, and came to be disliked by many Poles, who considered him intelligent but a cynical and overambitious player. In 1985 Rakowski left the government, sidelined as a Deputy Speaker of the Sejm. In December 1987 he was elected to the Politburo,* and in June 1988 he became a Central Committee secretary. In September 1988, after new strikes, he returned to power as the last Premier of communist Poland.

As Premier he tried to implement moderate market reforms. Rakowski's political plan was to give Solidarity limited access to power in return for shared responsibility for the regime's performance. Therefore, he supported the Round Table Negotiations* and the partially free election of June 1989.* But he underestimated popular support for Solidarity and failed to foresee its spectacular landslide victory in the 1989 election. Along with the names of many other prominent figures put on the communists' uncontested national list, his name was crossed off by a majority of voters, and he failed to gain election to the Sejm. Instead, on July 29 he was elected to replace Jaruzelski as First Secretary of the PZPR. On August 2, 1989, the newly elected Sejm established an extraordinary commission to examine the records of the Rakowski government. In December 1989 the commission concluded that Rakowski's decision to close the Lenin Shipyard in Gdańsk had been taken hastily and without proper consultation; it asked the Constitutional Tribunal for further deliberations. In January 1990 Rakowski presided over the last congress of the PZPR. He refused to stand for election to the leadership of the PZPR successor party, the Social Democracy of the Republic of Poland (SdRP),* but he remained its influential member and an editor-in-chief of his own periodical, *Dziś* ("Today"). *Political and Economic Encyclopedia of the Soviet Union and Eastern Europe*, ed. by S. White (London, 1990), 204; G. Sanford and A. Gozdecka-Sanford, *Historical Dictionary of Poland* (Metuchen, N.J., 1994), 163; *Who's Who in the Socialist Countries of Europe*, ed. by J. Stroynowski, vol. 3 (Munich, 1989), 972; A. Micewski, *Ludzie i opcje* (Warsaw, 1993), 87–93; A. Kępiński and Z. Kilar, *Kto jest kim w Polsce inaczej* (Warsaw, 1985), 335–350.

RAPACKI, ADAM (1909–70), economist, Minister of Foreign Affairs during 1956–68, and author of the 1957 Rapacki Plan.* He participated in the September Campaign of 1939 and spent the war in a POW camp in Germany. In 1945 he joined the Polish Socialist Party (PPS),* becoming one of its leaders. After the 1948 forced unification of the PPS and the Polish Workers' Party (PPR),* Rapacki became a member of the Polish United Workers' Party (PZPR)* Central Committee* and the Politburo* (full member from 1956). He served in several ministerial positions. He gained international prominence when, on October 2, 1957, he presented his plan to the U.N. General Assembly. In December 1968 Rapacki was removed from his post as minister of Foreign Affairs for his refusal to support the anti-Semitic campaign of the Polish communist authorities. G. Sanford and A. Gozdecka-Sanford, *Historical Dictionary of Poland* (Metuchen, N.J., 1994), 164; *The New Encyclopaedia Britannica*, vol. 9 (Chicago, 1990), 940; T. Mołdawa, *Ludzie Władzy 1944–1991. Władze państwowe i polityczne Polski według stanu na dzień 28 II 1991* (Warsaw, 1991), 416.

RAPACKI PLAN, proposal designed by the Polish Minister of Foreign Affairs, A. Rapacki,* and presented to the U.N. General Assembly on October 2, 1957.

The plan recommended the establishment of a nuclear-free zone in East-Central Europe. The Western Powers rejected the plan. G. Sanford and A. Gozdecka-Sanford, *Historical Dictionary of Poland* (Metuchen, N.J., 1994), 164; *The New Encyclopaedia Britannica*, vol. 9 (Chicago, 1990), 940.

RECHOWICZ, HENRYK (1929–   ), rector of Silesian University in Katowice* in 1972–82 and Party historian, specializing in the "ideologically proper" interpretation of the contemporary history of Poland. *Who's Who in the Socialist Countries of Europe*, ed. by J. Stroynowski, vol. 3 (Munich, 1989), 981.

RECOVERED TERRITORIES, several prewar provinces of Germany, located between the 1937 eastern border of the Third Reich and the Oder-Neisse Line,* incorporated into Poland after 1945 in accordance with the agreements made by the Allies in Yalta* and Potsdam.* The "Recovered Territories," or "Western Lands," include 103,000 square kilometers. Most of these territories belonged to the Polish state in the Middle Ages but were separated from Poland and Germanized after the 14th century. Two of them, Silesia and the southern part of East Prussia, included a significant Polish-speaking minority. Looking for a presentable explanation for the changes to Polish borders after 1945, the communist authorities called the shift of Poland to the west a return to the Polish lands of the Piast dynasty. The name "Recovered Territories" was generally accepted, because the non-communist Polish political movement also considered the transfer of Silesia and Pomerania to Poland a just "return" of the land seized by the Germans during their *Drang nach Osten*. Immediately after the war the Recovered Territories were devastated and treated as occupied country by the Red Army.* In September 1945 Polish authorities established the Ministry of Recovered Territories, headed by W. Gomułka.* Between 1945 and 1949 over 4.5 million Poles settled in the Recovered Territories. In the 1990s, some 50 years after the war, they constitute an integral part of Poland. N. Davies, *God's Playground: A History of Poland*, vol. 2 (New York, 1984), 489, 501, 526–535.

RECZEK, WŁODZIMIERZ (1911–   ), party official responsible for sport and tourism* in 1950–81. *Who's Who in the Socialist Countries of Europe*, ed. by J. Stroynowski, vol. 3 (Munich, 1989), 981.

RED ARMY (since 1946, Soviet Army). The Red Army seized the prewar Polish territories during 1944–45. After the war most Soviet forces withdrew from Poland; however, in fall 1946 about 300,000 Soviet soldiers remained. After the Polish communist authorities and the remnants of the Polish World War II underground state, the Soviet Army constituted the third power in Poland and realized its own policy there. On November 6, 1949, on the grounds of an "agreement" between the Polish and the Soviet governments, Soviet Marshal K. Rokossowski,* the 1945–49 commander-in-chief of the Soviet Northern Red Army Group, which was stationed in Poland, became the Polish Minister of

Defense. Soon he was also nominated a Marshal of Poland and a member of the Central Committee* of the Polish United Workers' Party (PZPR).* In 1950 he joined its Politburo,* and in 1952 he was appointed Deputy Premier of Poland. The Warsaw Treaty* of 1955, renewed in 1985 for the next 20 years, constituted the official grounds for the presence of the Soviet Army in Poland and created a unified military command with political and military structures totally dominated by the Soviet Union.

The Soviet garrisons in Poland constituted an important element of the Soviet military security system. They were used during the "Polish October" of 1956* to influence the political situation in Poland. Polish and Soviet forces invaded Czechoslovakia from Poland in 1968. The most important transportation routes to Soviet-controlled East Germany went from the USSR through Poland. After the fall of communism in Poland and in other states of East-Central Europe, the Soviet Army presence in Eastern Europe became an intensively discussed and negotiated issue. In December 1989 Soviet authorities announced that they would bring home all foreign-based Soviet troops by the year 2000. In February and March 1990 the Soviets agreed to withdraw their forces from Czechoslovakia and Hungary by mid-1991 and offered to begin negotiations on the withdrawal of the Soviet Army from Poland. At that time, about 40,000 Soviet soldiers were stationed in Poland. In early 1990 negotiations started between Poland and the USSR on the withdrawal of the Soviet Army. In January 1990 L. Wałęsa* demanded the forces to be evacuated from Poland that same year, but disagreements over Soviet property in Poland and mutual compensations slowed down the evacuation process. The last units of the Soviet Army withdrew from Poland on the day before the elections of September 19, 1993.* The last noncombatant troops that facilitated the transit of Russian forces across Poland from their bases in Germany left Polish soil on September 8, 1994. *Eastern Europe and the Commonwealth of Independent States, 1994* (London, 1994), 474; *Keesing's Record of World Events*, Feb. 1990, p. 37258 and Sept. 1994, p. 40198.

REFERENDUM OF JUNE 30, 1946, political test organized by the ruling Polish Workers' Party (PPR)* before the elections of January 19, 1947,* as part of communist preparations for these elections. The idea of a "Referendum of the People" appeared in March 1946, when the PPR and its allies from the Bloc of Democratic Parties* faced increasing problems and growing political competition from the opposition Polish Peasant Party (PSL),* which refused to join the Bloc. The referendum aimed to demonstrate that in spite of political differences between the ruling PPR and the opposition, most people in Poland supported the essential elements of the PPR program. The referendum was also intended to verify popular support for the Democratic Bloc and test the methods the communists intended to use during the electoral campaign. Some leaders of the Polish Socialist Party (PPS)* hoped that the outcomes of the referendum would prompt the PSL to cooperate with the Democratic Bloc and that Poland would not have to go through dangerous political polarization and conflict. The parties of the Bloc agreed that the referendum questions would be as follows: (1) Do you support the abolition of the Senate?* (2) Do you want the new constitution to safeguard the economic system introduced by the land reform* and the nationalization* of the basic branches of the national economy* while preserving the rights of private initiative? (3) Do you wish to keep Poland's western borders on the Baltic, Oder,* and Western Neisse? The questions were cleverly composed. Affirmative answers to all of them were to be taken as a support for the PPR; at the same time, they reflected the traditional demands of the peasant movement in Poland.

PSL leader could not reject the Referendum; they asked only that it should be followed by parliamentary elections relatively quickly, namely, by the end of July 1946. However, the PPR and its helpers started a general attack on the PSL. Censorship* of its publications was tightened; growing numbers of its members were killed, arrested, threatened, blackmailed, or dismissed from administrative and economic posts. A faction hostile to S. Mikołajczyk* was sponsored within the PSL, many of its country boards were dissolved, and the Party was harassed in many ways by the Security Office (UB).* Nobody felt safe. Meanwhile, a propaganda campaign started throughout the country. The Bloc parties accused the PSL of ties to the underground, especially the National Armed Forces (NSZ),* and asked for an affirmative response to all three questions, which were published by the press on May 11, 1946. The PSL encouraged its supporters to answer negatively to the first question, deciding to treat it as a national plebiscite for or against communism. Some anti-communist underground organizations endorsed a "no" response to the first two questions. The anti-communist camp also included the legal Labor Party (SP)* and the Roman Catholic Church.* In June 1946 the pre-referendum propaganda reached its zenith. Over 84 million posters, leaflets, and brochures were issued. Propaganda teams agitated everywhere. State-controlled radio* began a psychological offensive. Manipulating strong anti-German Polish sentiments, the communists argued that every "no" vote is a "yes" to Germany. On Sunday June 30, 1946, over 11,857,000 people—85.3% of those entitled to vote—participated in the referendum. In most electoral districts the principle of secrecy had been violated. Under pressure, many people were afraid to go behind the curtain to vote. The true results of the referendum are unknown. Very frequently the ballots were not counted, and the urns were destroyed or remained unopened. Frequently, the ballots marked "no" were replaced by "yes" votes produced by referendum commissions. On July 12 the official results of the referendum were announced: 68.2% (7,844,522) voted "yes" on the first question; 77.3% (8,896,105), on the second question; and 91.4% (10,435,697), on the third. According to the PSL estimates, 83.3% of those voting answered "no" to the first question. Indeed, it appears that about 80% responded negatively to the first question. The communists presented the official outcome of the referendum as their spectacular victory, but they drew several conclusions from the real results: They were weak, the anti-communist resistance was still strong, the referendum was prepared badly, and the coming elections needed more terror and intimidation. For PSL leaders, the referendum proved that a one-party system could not be introduced in Poland. K. Kersten, *The Establishment of Communist Rule in Poland, 1943–1948* (Berkeley, Calif., 1991), 232–285; J. Coutouvidis and J. Reynolds, *Poland, 1939–1947* (Leicester, 1986); M. K. Dziewanowski, *Poland in the Twentieth Century* (New York, 1977); *The History of Poland since 1863*, ed. by R. F. Leslie (Cambridge, 1980); N. Davies, *God's Playground: A History of Poland*, vol. 2 (New York, 1984).

REFERENDUM ON NOVEMBER 29, 1987. Organized by the Messner* government to ease the tense political situation in Poland and to show social support for the government's economic reforms. The referendum ''Further Reformation of the State and the National Economy'' was decided by the Sejm* on October 12. On Oct. 23 the two questions for the referendum were made public: (1) ''Are you in favor of the full implementation of the program of radical improvement of the national economy, submitted to the Sejm and intended to improve markedly living conditions, even though you realize that this requires a difficult transition period of two to three years during which rapid changes will take place?'' (2) ''Are you for the Polish model of a profound democratization of political life, intended to strengthen self-government, to extend civil rights, and to increase citizens' participation in the government of the country?'' Only about 40% of those qualified to vote participated in the referendum, preceded by an intensive Solidarity* propaganda action against this political manoeuvre. According to the official data, 67.3% of those qualified voted; 44.3% of them supported the economic reform, whereas 46.3% voted for political reform. Most Poles considered the event a government failure. The political position of Premier Messner was seriously weakened. In October 1988 Gen. W. Jaruzelski* replaced Messner with M. F. Rakowski.* J. Karpiński, *Poland since 1944: A Portrait of Years* (Boulder, Colo., 1995), 266–267; A. Micewski, *Ludzie i opcje* (Warsaw, 1993), 248.

REIFF, RYSZARD (1923–   ), right hand of B. Piasecki,* one of the 16 founding members of the PAX Association,* its deputy president during 1976–79 and, after Piasecki's death, president of PAX in 1979–82. During 1981–82 he served as a member of the State Council (Rada Państwa)* and was its only member who voted against Martial Law* in December 1981. Known for his pro-Solidarity sympathies, he was elected to the Senate* in 1989. *Who's Who in the Socialist Countries of Europe*, ed. by J. Stroynowski, vol. 3 (Munich, 1989), 983; G. Sanford and A. Gozdecka-Sanford, *Historical Dictionary of Poland* (Metuchen, N.J., 1994) 164; T. Mołdawa, *Ludzie Władzy 1944–1991. Władze państwowe i polityczne Polski według stanu na dzień 28 II 1991* (Warsaw, 1991), 416.

RELIGA, ZBIGNIEW (1938–   ), cardiologist and politician. After a long and successful medical career, he became the leader of the Non-Party Bloc for Support of Reform (BBWR),* a political party established by L. Wałęsa* and mod-

eled on the interwar BBWR (Non-Party Bloc for Cooperation with the
Government) of Józef Piłsudski. Religa represented the BBWR in the Senate,*
but in winter 1995 he left his party to create a new one—the Republican Party
(Partia Republikanie), pro-Western and independent of Wałęsa. *Wprost* (Warsaw),
Feb. 12, 1995.

RELIGIONS. Poland has always been a religiously diverse country. After 1945,
when Poland "was moved" westward and lost most of its national minorities,*
Polish society became almost homogeneously Roman Catholic. The communist
regime started an intensive atheization of society and an energetic campaign
against the Roman Catholic Church.* As a part of this campaign, the authorities
supported non-Catholic denominations. As a consequence of this support, in
addition to the sudden opening to the West after 1989 and the controversial
politicization of the Polish Church, over 40 religious associations are now active
in Poland. The Jehovah's Witnesses reached about 97,000 members in 1990.
The Zen Buddhists are energetically developing their community. There are also
several denominations traditionally present in Poland: about 900,000 Orthodox
Christians, 300,000 Greek Catholics, 115,000 Protestants, mostly Augsburg-
Evangelicals with some Reformed Calvinists, 8,000 Moslems, mostly Polish
Tatars,* 3,000 Jews,* and other smaller groups. G. Sanford and A. Gozdecka-
Sanford, *Historical Dictionary of Poland* (Metuchen, N.J., 1994), 165; K. Urban, *Mniej-
szości religijne w Polsce 1945–1991* (Cracow, 1994).

REPATRIATION, transfer of the Polish population from prewar eastern Polish
lands, incorporated into the USSR in 1945, to new postwar Poland. Most "re-
patriates" were sent to the formerly German "Recovered Territories"* in the
northwest. Initially, the repatriation was led by the Union of Polish Patriots
(ZPP) in the USSR. During 1944–50, the State Repatriation Office was in charge
of all population transfers inside Poland and from outside the state. During
1944–48 about 1.5 million Poles came to Poland from the USSR and about 0.5
million from Western Europe and Germany. The second repatriation wave took
place in 1957–58 when about 200,000 Poles arrived from the Soviet Union. N.
Davies, *God's Playground: A History of Poland*, vol. 2 (New York, 1984), 566; P. R.
Magocsi, *Historical Atlas of East Central Europe* (Seattle, 1993), 164–168; J. Karpiński,
Polska, Komunizm, Opozycja (London, 1985), 232.

RES PUBLICA, sophisticated liberal-conservative quarterly published in the
underground in 1979–81 and devoted to politics, social issues, history of ideas,
fine arts, and books. The first issues were edited by M. Król,* Wojciech Karpiński, and Barbara Toruńczyk. In May 1981, the editors of *Res Publica* began
to negotiate with the communist authorities to legalize their periodical. The
negotiations were interrupted by imposition of Martial Law* in December 1981.
The first issue of the new series, published legally, appeared in June 1987. In
1992 *Res Publica* was discontinued, probably for financial reasons, but it reap-

peared in 1993 as *Nowa Res Publica*. D. Cecuda, *Leksykon opozycji politycznej 1976–1989* (Warsaw, 1989), 185.

ROAD (Ruch Obywatelski Akcja Demokratyczna [Citizens' Movement for Democratic Action]), loose political organization established at the July 1990 congress after the beginning of the ''war at the top,''* which contributed to the disintegration of Solidarity.* The organization was formed on the initiative of two leading Solidarity activists, Z. Bujak* and W. Frasyniuk,* who left the Civic Committee* in June. They stated that they helped to organize ROAD to defend the Mazowiecki* government against L. Wałęsa's* attacks and to provide a credible alternative to the Center Alliance (PC),* which supported Wałęsa and escalated the ''war at the top.'' ROAD played an important role in the presidential elections of 1990* by opposing Wałęsa and supporting T. Mazowiecki. After the defeat of Mazowiecki, the ROAD was rebuilt into the Democratic Union (UD),* however, Bujak did not join the UD and attempted, unsuccessfully, to establish a more leftist Democratic-Social Movement (Ruch Demokratyczno-Społeczny [RD-S]).* G. Sanford and A. Gozdecka-Sanford, *Historical Dictionary of Poland* (Metuchen, N.J., 1994), 58; *Keesing's Record of World Events*, July 1990, p. 37620.

ROBOTNIK (''The Worker''), traditional title of the press organs of the Polish Socialist Party (PPS).* The first *Robotnik* was published in 1894, and during the interwar period it constituted the most important newspaper of the political left. During 1944–48 *Robotnik* appeared as the organ of the PPS but was discontinued after the PPS was forced to unify with the Polish Workers' Party (PPR).* The PPS-in-Exile edited its own *Robotnik* after the war until the late 1980s. In September 1977 *Robotnik* was re-established in Poland in the underground as a biweekly, edited by a group of people working with, or close to, the Workers' Defense Committee (KOR).* The most important members of this group were B. Borusewicz,* J. Lityński,* W. Onyszkiewicz, H. Łuczywo, and H. Wujec.* In 1980–81 their periodical cooperated with Solidarity* and reached 60,000 copies. After imposition of Martial Law* in December 1981, most *Robotnik* editors were interned and the periodical was discontinued. However, several underground periodicals by this title appeared, although none was affiliated with either the PPS, which did not exist in Poland at that time, or with the Borusewicz-Lityński group. *Dictionary of Polish Literature*, ed. by E. J. Czerwinski (Westport, Conn., 1994), 87; J. Karpiński, *Polska, Komunizm, Opozycja* (London, 1985), 235; D. Cecuda, *Leksykon Opozycji Politycznej 1976–1989* (Warsaw, 1989), 186.

ROKITA, JAN MARIA (1959–   ), politician. The president of the Independent Students' Union (NZS)* at Jagiellonian University* in Cracow* in 1980–83, he was active in the Freedom and Peace (WiP)* movement in 1985–89 and the underground Solidarity Intervention and Law Committee in 1986–89. He participated in the Round Table Negotiations* in 1989 and was a founding

member and leader of the Citizens' Movement for Democratic Action (ROAD)*
in 1990 and the Democratic Union (UD)* in 1991. Elected to the Sejm* in
1989, he was reelected in 1991 and 1993. In 1992–93 he served as Minister-
Chief of the Office of the Minister Council of H. Suchocka.* *Sejm Reczpospolitej
Polskiej. II Kadencja. Przewodnik* (Warsaw, 1994), 145.

ROKOSSOWSKI, KONSTANTY (1896–1964), Red Army* Marshal from
1944, Polish Minister of Defense, and member of the Politburo* of the Polish
United Workers' Party (PZPR).* A Pole born in eastern Belorussia, he volunteered for the Russian cavalry during World War I. In 1919 he joined the Bolsheviks and the Red Army and fought in the Russian Civil War. He continued
his military career during the interwar period until 1937, when he was arrested
and sent to the Gulag. Released in March 1940, he returned to the Red Army.
During the 1941–42 defense of Moscow, he commanded an army, and during
the Battle of Stalingrad, the Don Front. Later he commanded the Belorussian
Front, which included the communist-controlled First Polish Army,* and was
instrumental in the liberation of Poland. During 1945–49 Rokossowski served
as commander-in-chief of the Soviet Northern Red Army Group, stationed in
Poland. On November 6, 1949, based on an "agreement" between the Polish
and the Soviet governments, he became the Polish Minister of Defense. Soon
he was also nominated Marshal of Poland and a member of the Central Committee* and, from 1950, a member of the Politburo of the PZPR. In addition,
in 1952 he was appointed Deputy Premier of Poland. During his service in the
Polish Army, it was modernized and substantially enlarged. In November 1956
Rokossowski returned to the Soviet Union, where he became a Deputy Minister
of Defense, a deputy member of the Central Committee of the Communist Party
of the Soviet Union, and a member of the Supreme Soviet. *The Cold War, 1945–
1991*, vol. 2, "Leaders and Other Important Figures in the Soviet Union, Eastern Europe,
China, and the Third World," ed. by B. Frankel (Detroit, 1992), 286.

ROMAN CATHOLIC CHURCH. The Church has always had a unique position in Polish society. Several times, when Poland was partitioned by its neighbors, the Church constituted a vital link that maintained a sense of national unity
and shielded Polish national identity from Russification and Germanization. During World War II no Polish bishops or priests collaborated with the Nazis. After
the war the Church represented the most serious resistance to the Sovietization
of Poland. From the late 1950s it constituted the most powerful social organization in Poland, checked only by the sheer force of the Polish communist state
apparatus backed by the Soviet Union. The Catholic Church had its strongest
base, among all the communist states, in Poland, where 95% of the entire population is Catholic and where Catholicism is frequently understood as synony-
mous with Polish national identity.

The Polish Catholic Church emerged from World War II with an authority
greater than ever, but it simultaneously suffered enormous losses. Out of 12,000

priests and members of religious orders, almost 2,500 were murdered by the Nazis. Some dioceses lost almost 50% of their priests. Immediately after the war the Polish Episcopate* and Primate,* A. Hlond,* who received special powers and prerogatives from Pope Pius XII, began to reconstruct the Polish Episcopal structure. Several bishops were consecrated, seminaries and religious instruction at school were restored, some new bishoprics were created, and Catholic press, economic, social, and cultural organizations reappeared. Soon the Church was well organized and powerful again. The communists did not intend to tolerate such competition, yet they knew that they could not go too far with their anti-Catholic policies because doing so would trigger unforseeable consequences. The manifesto issued by the Polish Committee of National Liberation (PKWN) on July 22, 1944, guaranteed, among other rights, freedom of conscience and respect for the rights of the Catholic Church. Initially, communist dignitaries participated in religious celebrations and left the Church relatively unmolested. Nonetheless, during the communist seizure of power* between 1944 and 1948, the Church faced its first difficulties and restrictions. On September 12, 1945, the Polish government abrogated the Concordat of 1925. In 1945 an organization of "progressive Catholics," the PAX Association,* was established to divide the Church and to weaken its integrity from within. Catholic Church property was nationalized, its youth associations and broadcasts were dissolved, its hospitals were taken over by the state health system, and its publications were controlled by censorship.*

The death of Primate Hlond in December 1948 coincided with the beginning of the Stalinist period.* When the communists won their quest for power in Poland in 1948, they came to the conclusion that they could start a complete transformation of Polish society according to the Soviet model. To do so they had to eliminate their most dangerous ideological adversary, the Catholic Church. The new Primate, S. Wyszyński,* the Vatican, and the entire ecclesiastical organization became objects of a vitriolous propaganda campaign. In addition to PAX, a group of "patriot priests" was organized. The clergy was intimidated and blackmailed in order to force it to collaborate with the communists. The Cold War* and Pope Pius XII's statement that all Catholics who collaborated with communists would be subjected to excommunication made the situation even more tense. Wyszyński was afraid the communists could use radical measures against the Church, as they had done in Hungary and Czechoslovakia. To avoid this, Wyszyński and the Episcopate signed an "understanding" with the authorities in April 1950. The "understanding" confirmed the dogmatic, liturgical, and catechetical prerogatives of the Church, which, in return, promised not to oppose a voluntary collectivization* of agriculture* and other structural changes of the Polish economic-political system. The "understanding" was criticized by many in Poland and was disapproved of by the Vatican, but it helped the Catholic Church in Poland survive the worst part of the Stalinist period. On February 9, 1953, the government decreed that the filling of all ecclesiastical offices had to be supervised and approved by the state, which was also empowered to remove the clergy from their posts. The bishop of Kielce,* Czesław Kaczmarek, had already been arrested in 1951, and the authorities intensified their campaign against the Church. Wyszyński decided to confront the regime. He rejected the decree of February 1953 and sent a protest letter to the Party's leader, B. Bierut.* Wyszyński listed all acts of persecution and defended the arrested priests and bishops. As a consequence, the Primate was arrested in September 1953. His arrest was followed with further infiltration and subversion of the clergy, dissolution of seminaries, measures against the Catholic University of Lublin (KUL),* abolition of the theological faculties at Polish universities,* banning of religious instruction from schools, and expropriation of monasteries. The number of churches and chapels declined by about 30%, and many parish posts were filled only temporarily.

The ''Polish October'' of 1956* brought improvement in the situation of the Church. Freed, Wyszyński returned to Warsaw on October 28, 1956. A mixed commission made up of representatives of the Church and the state was established to remove tensions. Also, the decree of February 1953 was withdrawn. All imprisoned bishops and clergy were released from prison and returned to their dioceses and parishes. The Church was allowed to conduct religious instruction at schools and to publish its periodicals. Clubs of Catholic Intelligentsia* were organized, and a small caucus of Catholic deputies, known as the Znak* group appeared in the Sejm.* In 1956, as happened later in 1970 and 1980, the Church urged moderation on the regime and the people and warned that direct confrontation could lead to Soviet intervention. Yet as soon as the Gomułka* regime regained full control of the situation in Poland, hostilities between the Church and the state resumed. On June 15, 1961, the government decreed to withdraw religion from schools again. The Church was overtaxed, and its publications were drastically limited under the pretext of paper shortages. The authorities used the 1965 ''Letter of the Polish Bishops to the Bishops of Germany''* to strengthen the anti-Church campaign. The millennium celebrations* were accompanied by a state-sponsored, anti-religious offensive as well. During the March events of 1968,* Wyszyński condemned police brutalities and repression against students and intellectuals. During the December events of 1970,* the Church defended workers' rights. In the early 1970s the Episcopate and the clergy engaged in defending human rights in Poland. By the late 1970s the Church became an umbrella for the democratic opposition* and began to cooperate with representatives of various worldviews, including former Marxists and other leftist intellectuals.

Under Pope John XXIII and Paul VI, the Vatican was afraid that the political status quo in Eastern Europe would not change for a long time and sought a modus vivendi with the communist regimes. This Ostpolitik changed after 1978, when Cardinal K. Wojtyła from Poland was elected Pope John Paul II.* He adopted an uncompromising policy toward the regime in Warsaw.* His visit to Poland in June 1979 strengthened the Catholic Church. Masses of Polish people realized that they could organize themselves independently of the state apparatus, which could be at least partially ignored. In 1980 the Church strongly supported Solidarity.* L. Wałęsa,* the leader of Solidarity, considered the Pope to be his ultimate spiritual guide and was reinforced by his deep Catholic piety. When Wyszyński died in 1981, he was called "the Primate of 1,000 years" by the people because he not only managed to save the Church from the Stalinist onslaught but also developed the Polish Roman Catholic Church considerably. Under Wyszyński, the number of priests and churches doubled and the Catholic Church gained prestige unprecedented in the contemporary world.

The Episcopate opposed the declaration of Martial Law* and asked Solidarity and the Jaruzelski* regime to negotiate. Again, the Church tried to serve as a mediator. This policy was supported by Cardinal J. Glemp,* the new Primate of Poland, and by Pope John Paul II, who visited Poland in 1983 and 1987. Some priests supported a more aggressive line against the regime, and one of them, Fr. J. Popiełuszko,* was murdered by security police in 1984. After 1989 the Church participated in the democratization of Poland. Several Christian-Democratic and Christian-National political parties emerged. Yet a portion of the Polish public was afraid that the Church's involvement in politics was too intense. Under new political and socioeconomic conditions, the Roman Catholic Church of Poland has had to face new challenges, has had to change its strategy, and like all of Polish society, has been going through an epochal transformation. *Political and Economic Encyclopedia of the Soviet Union and Eastern Europe*, ed. by S. White (London, 1990), 208; J. Nowak, "The Church in Poland," *Problems of Communism*, vol. 31, no. 1 (1982), 1–16; B. Szajkowski, *Next to God . . . Poland: Politics and Religion in Contemporary Poland* (London, 1983); *New Catholic Encyclopedia*, vol. 11 (New York, 1967), 483–485; A. Micewski, *Kościół—Państwo 1945–1989* (Warsaw, 1994); A. Dudek, *Państwo i Kościół w Polsce 1945–1970* (Cracow, 1995); J. Gowin, *Kościół po komunizmie* (Warsaw, 1995).

ROMASZEWSKA, ZOFIA. See **Romaszewski, Zbigniew.**

ROMASZEWSKI, ZBIGNIEW (1940–   ), physicist and dissident.* Together with his wife, Zofia, he joined the Workers' Defense Committee (KOR)* in 1976. As director of its Intervention Bureau, he signed several appeals protesting against the policies of the communist authorities in Poland and co-edited the underground monthly *Głos* ("The Voice").* Repeatedly harassed and detained by police, he was released from prison in September 1980, after the Gdańsk Agreement.* Member of the Presidium of Solidarity's* Mazowsze Regional Board and delegate to the Solidarity First National Congress in September-October 1981, he went (with his wife) into hiding after imposition of Martial Law* in December 1981. Four months later, in April 1982, he organized the underground radio transmitter in Warsaw known as Radio Solidarity. After this spectacular Solidarity success, he was arrested with his wife, in August 1982, and the authorities mounted a propaganda campaign against them. Released from prison after the 1984 amnesty,* he belonged among the most active leaders of the underground Solidarity. In 1989 he participated in the Round Table Negotiations* and was elected to the Senate.* After the disintegration of Solidarity, Romaszewski underwent political radicalization and eventually joined the Movement for the Republic (RdR).* *Who's Who in the Socialist Countries of Europe*, ed. by J. Stroynowski, vol. 3 (Munich, 1989), 996; *Kto jest kim w polityce polskiej*, ed. by R. Ignasiak (Warsaw, 1993), 241.

ROMKOWSKI, ROMAN (1907–68), Deputy Minister of Public Security in 1945–54. Born as Menashe Grynszpan, he joined the Communist Party of Poland (KPP) in his youth and spent the late 1930s in the USSR, where he was trained by the NKVD. Romkowski was instrumental in the establishment of the communist system in Poland, was active in fighting against the democratic opposition,* and helped to prepare the most important political trials after 1948. The revelations of J. Światło* disclosed the criminal activities of the Ministry of Public Security.* In January 1955 Romkowski was expelled from the Party; in April 1955 he was arrested. Tried in November 1957, he was sentenced to 15 years in prison for using "illegal" interrogation methods (tortures) during his tenure. A. Polonsky and B. Drukier, *The Beginnings of Communist Rule in Poland* (London, 1980); Z. Błażyński, *Mówi Józef Światło. Za kulisami bezpieki i partii* (London, 1985).

ROPCiO. See **Movement for the Defense of Human and Civil Rights.**

ROSATI, DARIUSZ (1946–   ), economist and Minister of Foreign Affairs in the Cimoszewicz* government. Graduate and professor at the Main School of Planning and Statistics (Szkoła Główna Planowania i Statystyki [SGPiS], he served as an adviser to the Rakowski* government. From 1991 he worked in the U.N. European Economic Committee in Geneva. In 1993 he was proposed as Minister of Finance. Since 1996 he has been serving as Minister of Foreign Affairs. *Wprost* (Warsaw), May 19, 1996.

ROUND TABLE AGREEMENT. See **Round Table Negotiations.**

ROUND TABLE NEGOTIATIONS, debate between representatives of the democratic opposition* and the communist authorities of Poland from February to April 5, 1989. Despite imposition of Martial Law* the Jaruzelski regime* failed to improve the communist system or stop the growing erosion of the command economy.* The referendum of November 1987* failed, and price increases in spring 1988 caused a new wave of industrial unrest and strikes. Some influential members of the opposition and the authorities concluded that neither side was able to win and that their conflict might destroy Poland. The Roman Catholic Church* urged a compromise. On August 31, L. Wałęsa* met Gen. C. Kiszczak.* They agreed that both sides engaged in the conflict should examine the questions of trade union pluralism, the recognition of Solidarity,* and a range of social, economic, and political issues together. This agreement led to the Round Table Negotiations. Originally scheduled for October 1988, the talks were repeatedly postponed. Radical members of the opposition rejected the idea of dialogue with the authorities, whereas hard-line communists preferred police methods in dealing with opposition. The inclusion of such opposition leaders as J. Kuroń* and A. Michnik* especially caused resistance to the Round Table idea. Eventually, the talks opened in February 1989. An initial agreement was reached on March 9, and a comprehensive agreement was signed on April 5 that provided for the re-legalization of Solidarity and freedom of association, not only for trade unions but also for political parties. The "contract" stipulated that partially free parliamentary elections would be organized in June 1989. The communists did not intend to relinquish power. They expected the arrangement to benefit them and hoped that Solidarity would take much of the responsibility for the situation in Poland without significant participation in government. However, they miscalculated. The elections of June 1989* dealt a mortal blow to the communist power in Poland. *Political and Economic Encyclopedia of the Soviet Union and Eastern Europe*, ed. by S. White (London, 1990), 220; B. Szajkowski (ed.), *Political Parties of Eastern Europe, Russia, and the Successor States* (London, 1994), 313; A. Dudek, *Pierwsze lata III Rzeczpospolitej, 1989–1995* (Cracow, 1997), 26–34.

ROZŁUBIRSKI, EDWIN (1926–), general of the People's Polish Army* from 1965. A veteran of the communist People's Guard and People's Army during World War II, he was one of the high-ranking officers who protested against the invasion of Czechoslovakia in 1968. Dismissed from the military and unemployed in the 1970s, he returned to active service after the imposition of Martial Law* in December 1981. *Who's Who in the Socialist Countries of Europe*, ed. by J. Stroynowski, vol. 3 (Munich, 1989), 1003.

ROZPŁOCHOWSKI, ANDRZEJ (1950–), Solidarity* activist who chaired the Strike Committee in Katowice* Ironworks (Huta Katowice) in August 1980 he signed an agreement with a government commission and joined the Solidarity National Committee. *Who's Who in the Socialist Countries of Europe*, ed. by J. Stroynowski, vol. 3 (Munich, 1989), 1004.

RÓG-ŚWIOSTEK, MIECZYSŁAW (1919–), member of the State Council (Rada Państwa)* during 1981–85 and the Party expert on agriculture.* *Who's Who in the Socialist Countries of Europe*, ed. by J. Stroynowski, vol. 3 (Munich, 1989), 994; T. Mołdawa, *Ludzie Władzy 1944–1991. Władze państwowe i polityczne i polityczne Polski według stanu na dzień 28 II 1991* (Warsaw, 1991), 418.

RÓŻAŃSKI, JACEK (1907–81), director of the Investigation Department at the Ministry of Public Security (MBP)* during 1945–54 and brother of J. Borejsza.* Born Józef Goldberg to a Zionist journalist in Warsaw,* he joined the communist movement in Poland in the late 1920s and began to work for Soviet intelligence. He spent World War II in the USSR, where he volunteered in the communist Polish Army* in February 1944. In August 1944 he was transferred to the security apparatus and changed his name. He distinguished himself with cruelty and was quickly promoted. In 1954, at the beginning of the political "thaw"* in Poland, he was removed from his post; arrested, he was tried in 1955. He stayed in prison until 1964. B. Fijałkowska, *Borejsza i Różański. Przyczynek do dziejów stalinizmu w Polsce* (Olsztyn, 1995).

RÓŻEWICZ, TADEUSZ (1921–   ), writer, poet, playwright, and veteran of the Home Army (AK).* His first postwar works, "contaminated by death," reflected the World War II experiences of his generation. His poetry rejects traditional metrics and rhyme, and his plays are often dark and tend toward the avant-garde and the "theater of the absurd." Translated into several languages, Różewicz is an outstanding representative of postwar Polish literature.* C. Miłosz, *The History of Polish Literature* (Berkeley, Calif., 1983), 462–471; *Dictionary of Polish Literature*, ed. by E. J. Czerwinski (Westport, Conn., 1994), 360–365; *Who's Who in the Socialist Countries of Europe*, ed. by J. Stroynowski, vol. 3 (Munich, 1989), 1003.

RUCH ("Movement"), clandestine opposition organization established in 1965 in Łódź* and active in several cities in the late 1960s. Led by such activists as A. Czuma* and W. Kęcik, Ruch was broken by the security police in 1971; its members later joined the Workers' Defense Committee (KOR)* and the Movement for Defense of Human and Civil Rights (ROPCiO).* J. J. Lipski, *KOR: A History of the Workers' Defense Committee in Poland, 1976–81* (Berkeley, 1985), 20; Stefan Niesiołowski, "Anty-komuniści," *Wprost*, Nov. 2, 1997, pp. 32–35.

RUCH MŁODEJ POLSKI. See Young Poland Movement.

RUDNICKI, ADOLF (1912–90), writer whose prose explores Jewish life in Poland and its destruction during World War II. He made his literary debut in 1932. He participated in the September Campaign of 1939, escaped from a German POW camp to Soviet-occupied Lvov, contributed to the communist paper *Nowe Widnokręgi* ("New Horizons"), and participated in the anti-German resistance after 1941. After the war he joined the Marxist literary group Kuźnica ("The Forge") and contributed to its weekly of the same title. His writing became a "testament to the Polish Jews." C. Miłosz, *The History of Polish Literature* (Berkeley, Calif., 1983), 493–495; *Who's Who in the Socialist Countries of Europe*, ed. by J. Stroynowski, vol. 3 (Munich, 1989), 1006.

RULEWSKI, JAN (1944–   ), dissident* and Solidarity* leader. Chairman of the Solidarity, Bydgoszcz* Region in 1980–82, he was also a member of the Solidarity Country Committee in 1980–81 and 1990, and its deputy president in 1991. Elected to the Sejm* in 1991, he was re-elected in 1993. *Sejm Rzeczpo-*

politej Polskiej. II Kadencja. Przewodnik (Warsaw, 1994), 145; T. Torańska, *My* (Warsaw, 1994), 243–275.

RUMIŃSKI, BOLESŁAW (1907–71), communist official and member of the State Council (Rada Państwa)* in 1969–71. T. Mołdawa, *Ludzie Władzy 1944–1991. Władze państwowe i polityczne Polski według stanu na dzień 28 II 1991* (Warsaw, 1991), 418.

RURAL SOLIDARITY, free trade union of individual farmers, established unofficially in March 1981 and led by J. Kułaj.* The authorities were afraid of an independent union of peasants, who delivered most of the food products available in Poland, and did not want to register Rural Solidarity. This led to rural unrest and protests. One protest, in Bydgoszcz,* turned into a serious conflict. Threatened with a general strike, the authorities registered the union in April 1981. De-legalized after imposition of Martial Law,* Rural Solidarity was active in the underground and was re-legalized together with Solidarity* in April 1989. Renamed the Polish Peasant Party ''Solidarity'' in September 1989, it was headed by J. Ślisz* and G. Janowski.* It did not join the reborn Polish Peasant Party (PSL).* During the elections of October 1991,* it formed the Polish Peasant Party–Peasant Agreement with some other small political groups and won 28 seats in the Sejm* and 5 in the Senate.* In 1993 the Party did not manage to enter Parliament. G. Sanford and A. Gozdecka-Sanford, *Historical Dictionary of Poland* (Metuchen, N.J., 1994), 176–177; *Polskie Partie Polityczne. Charakterystyki, dokumenty,* ed. by K. A. Paszkiewicz (Wrocław, 1996), 168–172; J. Karpiński, *Polska, Komunizm, Opozycja* (London, 1985), 254.

RURARZ, ZDZISŁAW (1930–   ), faculty member of the Main School of Planning and Statistics (SGPiS) in Warsaw* and diplomat. Polish ambassador to Japan from February 1981, he defected and asked for political asylum in the United States after imposition of Martial Law* in December 1981. Tried in absentia, he was accused of high treason and sentenced to death. *Who's Who in the Socialist Countries of Europe,* ed. by J. Stroynowski, vol. 3 (Munich, 1989), 1009; *Perfidna gra. Spotkania z prof. Rurarzem,* ed. by T. S. Pochron, vols. 1–2 (Chicago, 1993–94).

RUSINEK, KAZIMIERZ (1905–84), journalist and secretary general of the Central Commission of Trade Unions (CRZZ)* during 1945–47. A veteran and leader of the Polish Socialist Party (PPS),* he became a member of the Polish United Workers' Party (PZPR)* Central Committee* and occupied several important apparatus positions. T. Mołdawa, *Ludzie Władzy 1944–1991. Władze państwowe i polityczne Polski według stanu na dzień 28 II 1991* (Warsaw, 1991), 419.

RYBICKI, MARIAN (1915–87), professor of law, Secretary of the State Council (Rada Państwa)* during 1952–56, attorney general in 1956–57, and Minister of Justice during 1957–65. *Who's Who in the Socialist Countries of Europe*, ed. by J. Stroynowski, vol. 3 (Munich, 1989), 1013; T. Mołdawa, *Ludzie Władzy 1944–1991. Władze państwowe i polityczne Polski według stanu na dzień 28 II 1991* (Warsaw, 1991), 419.

RYBICKI, ZYGMUNT (1925–   ), professor of administrative law and rector of Warsaw University* in 1969–80. He ordered to dismiss several activists of the democratic opposition* from their positions. *Who's Who in the Socialist Countries of Europe*, ed. by J. Stroynowski, vol. 3 (Munich, 1989), 1014.

RYDZYK, TADEUSZ (1946–   ), Catholic priest who, in 1991, organized and has since directed a fundamentalist Christian-National radio station known as Radio Maryja. *Polityka*, April 19, 1997, p. 92.

RZEPECKI, JAN (1899–1982), army officer and historian. A soldier of the Polish Legions during World War I, he served in the Polish Army* after 1918, taught in the Higher War School in 1935–39, and participated in the September Campaign of 1939. During the war he was an important leader of the resistance; among other things he commanded the Bureau of Information and Propaganda of the Union of Armed Struggle (ZWZ) and then the Home Army (AK).* In 1945 he was appointed delegate for the Armed Forces* and tried to reshape military resistance into political resistance. Rzepecki co-founded the WiN (''Freedom and Independence'')* clandestine organization. Arrested, he was sentenced to eight years in prison. From 1955 he worked at the Institute of History of the Polish Academy of Sciences (PAN)* and authored many books and articles on military history. M. Dąbrowska, *Dzienniki powojenne 1945–49*, ed. by T. Drewnowski (Warsaw, 1996), 118.

RZESZÓW, capital city of Rzeszów Province in southeastern Poland, on the road and railway from Cracow* to Lvov. A small town before the war, it expanded greatly in the 1960s and 1970s, reaching 150,000 inhabitants in 1990. An important center in the food industry and the capital of an agricultural region, Rzeszów became a stronghold of Rural Solidarity* in 1981 and the Polish Peasant Party (PSL)* after 1989. *The New Encyclopaedia Britannica*, vol. 10 (Chicago, 1990), 272.

RZYMOWSKI, WINCENTY (1883–1950), writer, lawyer, economist, and Minister of Foreign Affairs during 1945–47. A member of the Polish Academy of Literature during 1933–37, he joined the Democratic Clubs in 1937, the Democratic Party (SD)* in 1939; after the war he became a main SD leader. He spent the war in the Soviet Union and was active in the Union of Polish

Patriots (ZPP). From July 1944 he headed the Culture Department of the Polish Committee of National Liberation (PKWN) and later served as Minister of Culture (1945) and of Foreign Affairs. T. Mołdawa, *Ludzie Władzy 1944–1991. Władze państwowe i polityczne Polski według stanu na dzień 28 II 1991* (Warsaw, 1991), 420.

S

SABBAT, KAZIMIERZ (1913–89), lawyer, veteran of World War II, activist of Polish émigré community in England, Premier of the Polish Government-in-Exile* from 1976, and President of the Republic of Poland in Exile between 1986–89. *Encyklopedyczny Słownik Sławnych Polaków* (Warsaw, 1996), 339; L. Ciołkoszowa, "Kazimierz Sabbat," *Kultura*, no. 9/509 (Paris, 1989), 140–146.

SADOWSKI, ZDZISŁAW (1925–   ), professor of economics and expert on economic reform for the Jaruzelski* regime. He taught economics at several Polish and foreign universities* and directed the Development Center in the U.N. secretariat in 1970–72. In October 1981 he was appointed undersecretary in the Office of the Council of Ministers to supervise economic reforms. In 1985 he became a deputy chairman, and in 1987, chairman of the Economic Con-sultation Council. In 1987–88 he served as Deputy Premier, as chairman of the Committee for the Implementation of Economic Reform, and as chairman of the Planning Committee. Sadowski authored several books and designed an economic program that led toward the marketization of the socialist system, but it was only partially put into place. *Who's Who in the Socialist Countries of Europe*, ed. by J. Stroynowski, vol. 3 (Munich, 1989), 1019; T. Mołdawa, *Ludzie Władzy 1944–1991. Władze państwowe i polityczne Polski według stanu na dzień 28 II 1991* (Warsaw, 1991), 420; A. Micewski, *Ludzie i opcje* (Warsaw, 1993), 245–250.

SALIJ, JACEK (1942–   ), Dominican friar, professor of theology, and popular writer involved in activities of the Club of Catholic Intelligentsia* in Warsaw.* G. Polak, *Kto jest kim w Kościele katolickim* (Warsaw, 1996), 321.

SAMBORSKI, ARTUR "NACHT-" (1898–1974), "kapist" artist and pro-fessor at the Warsaw Academy of Fine Arts in 1947–69. *Encyklopedyczny Słownik Sławnych Polaków* (Warsaw, 1996), 339.

SAMO-OBRONA. See **Self-Defense.**

SAMOZWANIEC, MAGDALENA (1894–1972), prolific satirist writer, daughter of the painter Wojciech Kossak, and sister of the poet Maria Jasnorzewska-Pawlikowska. *Encyklopedyczny Słownik Sławnych Polaków* (Warsaw, 1996), 339.

SAMSONOWICZ, HENRYK B. (1930–   ), professor of history and Minister of Education in the government of T. Mazowiecki* (September 1989–December 1990). From 1950, Samsonowicz taught at Warsaw University,* where he was rector in 1980–82. As supporter of Solidarity,* he was ejected from the Polish United Workers' Party (PZPR)* in 1982. During 1977–82 he presided over the Polish Historical Society. *Who's Who in the Socialist Countries of Europe*, ed. by J. Stroynowski, vol. 3 (Munich, 1989), 1023; T. Mołdawa, *Ludzie Władzy 1944–1991. Władze państwowe i polityczne Polski według stanu na dzień 28 II 1991* (Warsaw, 1991), 420; *Kto jest kim w polityce polskiej*, ed. by R. Ignasiak (Warsaw, 1993), 253.

SANDAUER, ARTUR (1913–89), prolific literary critic, translator, writer, and professor at Warsaw University,* known for his sometimes eccentric ideas. *Who's Who in the Socialist Countries of Europe*, ed. by J. Stroynowski, vol. 3 (Munich, 1989), 1024; *Encyklopedyczny Słownik Sławnych Polaków* (Warsaw, 1996), 340.

SAPIEHA, ADAM (1867–1951), Prince, bishop (from 1912) and Archbishop (from 1925) of Cracow,* and Cardinal (from 1946). He started a scandal when he ordered the mortal remains of J. Piłsudski be removed from the crypt of Polish Kings in the Cathedral on Wawel Hill in 1937. During World War II he was engaged in anti-German resistance and supplemented the Primate* of Poland, A. Hlond,* who spent the war abroad. In 1945 he helped to establish the prestigious *Tygodnik Powszechny* (''The Universal Weekly'')* and became an important spiritual leader of Soviet-occupied Poland. *Encyklopedyczny Słownik Sławnych Polaków* (Warsaw, 1996), 341.

SARP. See **Union of Polish Architects.**

SB (Służba Bezpieczeństwa). See **Security Service.**

SCHAFF, ADAM (1913–   ), sociologist, philosopher, and Party ideologue. Active in the communist movement before the war, he joined the Polish Workers' Party (PPR)* in 1944, occupied several positions in the Party apparatus, and served on its Central Committee* during 1957–68. Doctor *honoris causa* of several foreign universities and a member of the Polish Academy of Sciences (PAN)* and its Presidium in 1960–68, he taught Marxist philosophy at Warsaw University* in 1948–70. In 1984 he was expelled from the Party. *Who's Who in the Socialist Countries of Europe*, ed. by J. Stroynowski, vol. 3 (Munich, 1989), 1030.

SCHILLER, LEON (1887–1954), theater director active in the Polish theater life from 1917. He managed some of the most important Polish theaters and directed several performances that occupy a permanent place in the history of the Polish stage. M. Fik, *Leon Schiller: The 25th Anniversary of His Death* (Warsaw, 1978).

SCOUTING (harcerstwo), youth organization established in Poland in 1911 and shaped after the British scouting movement. From its beginning, Polish scouting had a strong national and patriotic character. Scouts participated in Polish freedom fighting, especially during World War II, when the organization constituted an integral part of the Polish resistance. In 1939 the Polish scouting organization ([ZHP] Związek Harcerstwa Polskiego, or Union of Polish Scouting) had about 200,000 members and constituted the third largest scouting organization in the world. After the war the communist authorities tried to accommodate Polish scouting to Soviet patterns. In 1948 ZHP was isolated from West European scouting, and in 1950 it was dissolved and incorporated into the Union of Polish Youth (ZMP)* as its scouting organization. In 1954–55 J. Kuroń* established the Walterite scout troops (Walterowcy), named after Gen. K. Świerczewski's* nom de guerre during the Spanish Civil War. The Walterites opposed the Baden-Powell scouting tradition and tried to raise their members as communist "new men." The formation, characterized by strong group bonding, anti-conformism, and almost fanatic idealistic ideological involvement, was eventually liquidated by the authorities. In 1956 ZHP was rebuilt and its traditional character partially revived. Yet the authorities attempted to secure the socialist character of the organization permanently, and in 1959 supporters of traditional Polish patriotic scouting left ZHP. In 1980 a serious crisis started within ZHP ranks. A semi-clandestine Movement of Scouting of the Polish Republic (Ruch Harcerstwa Rzeczpospolitej) was established in the early 1980s. In 1989 the movement created a new organization, the Union of Scouting of the Polish Republic (Związek Harcerstwa Rzeczpospolitej [ZHR]). In the same year, ZHP started a process of transformation and a return to the old models of scouting activities. J. J. Lipski, *KOR: A History of the Workers' Defense Committee in Poland, 1976–81* (Berkeley, Calif., 1985), 14–15; J. Karpiński, *Polska, Komunizm, Opozycja* (London, 1985), 69; *Nowa Encyklopedia Powszechna PWN*, vol. 6 (Warsaw, 1996), 1051.

SDP. See **Association of Polish Journalists.**

SDPRL. See **Association of Journalists of the People's Republic of Poland.**

SdRP. See **Social Democracy of the Republic of Poland.**

SECOMSKI, KAZIMIERZ (1910–   ), professor of economics, member of the Polish Academy of Sciences (PAN),* Deputy Premier during 1976–80, President of the State Council (Rada Państwa)* in 1980–85, and a State Council member in 1985–89. During the 1950s, 1960s, and 1970s he served as a member or a chairman of various governmental planning institutions. *Who's Who in the Socialist Countries of Europe*, ed. by J. Stroynowski, vol. 3 (Munich, 1989), 1052; T. Mołdawa, *Ludzie Władzy 1944–1991. Władze państwowe i polityczne Polski według stanu na dzień 28 II 1991* (Warsaw, 1991), 421.

SECURITY SERVICE (Służba Bezpieczeństwa [SB]), secret political police formally supervised by the Citizens' Militia (MO)* but, in practice, fully autonomous and directed by the leadership of the Polish United Workers' Party (PZPR).* The SB fought the political opposition* and any anti-communist activities. The SB was a direct continuation of the Security Office (Urząd Bezpieczeństwa [UB]), created by the Soviets and Polish communists in subjugated Poland in 1944–45. The SB and UB constituted the most important elements of the terror apparatus in Poland: They were active outside the law and committed many crimes against human and citizens' rights in Poland. A. Polonsky and B. Drukier, *The Beginnings of Communist Rule in Poland* (London, 1980); J. Karpiński, *Polska, Komunizm, Opozycja* (London, 1985), 247–248, 283–284; Z. Błażyński, *Mówi Józef Światło. Za kulisami bezpieki i partii* (London, 1985).

SEJM, historical name for the Polish Parliament formed at the beginning of the 16th century. After World War II the Sejm was reorganized in the election of January 1947* as the supreme organ of state power in Poland. According to the Little Constitution* of January 19, 1947, and the Constitution of 1952,* the Sejm passed or confirmed all legislation, controlled other state organs, appointed and recalled the government, and elected, from among its members, the State Council (Rada Państwa).* Sessions were held twice a year, and 460 members of the Sejm were chosen for terms of four years. In practice, however, the communist system gave more power to the ruling communist party. The major functions of the Sejm became ritualistic and legitimizing. Parliamentary elections were arranged such that they gave little effective choice to voters while ensuring the Polish United Workers' Party (PZPR)* a built-in majority.

The practice and formal status of the Sejm changed considerably in 1989. Solidarity* won the elections of June 1989.* Its candidates gained all 35% of the contested seats (161) in the Sejm and 99 seats in the Senate* (leaving one remaining seat to a rich businessman who fancied a political career). In the shock caused by this landslide, L. Wałęsa* convinced leaders of the United Peasant Party (ZSL)* and the Democratic Party (SD)* that it would be better for him and for Poland to abandon the losing PZPR and to create a new coalition with Solidarity. At the same time, however, Solidarity made another compromise with the communists and accepted Gen. W. Jaruzelski* as President* of Poland. Jaruzelski nominated Gen. C. Kiszczak* Premier,* but the latter failed to form a government. A new coalition of the Citizens' Parliamentary Club (OKP) of Solidarity, the ZSL, and the SD formed the first non-communist government after the war, led by T. Mazowiecki.* In January 1990 the PZPR ceased to exist, the communist system was disappearing. The composition of the Contract Sejm, with its large group of PZPR deputies, did not reflect the actual political situation in the country. A new Sejm was formed after the elections of October 1991* and after the elections of September 1993.* *Political and Economic Encyclopedia of the Soviet Union and Eastern Europe*, ed. by S. White (London, 1990), 226; *Dzieje Sejmu Polskiego*, ed. by J. Bardach (Warsaw, 1993); J. Lerski, *Historical Dictionary of Poland, 966–1945*, with special editing and emendations by P. Wróbel and R. J. Kozicki (Westport, Conn., 1996), 531–532.

SEKUŁA, IRENEUSZ L. (1943–   ), Deputy Premier* in 1988–89 and Minister of Labor in 1988. He joined the Polish United Workers' Party (PZPR)* in 1966 and worked in the Party apparatus. In January 1990 he became a leader of the newly established Social Democracy of the Republic of Poland (SdRP).* *Who's Who in the Socialist Countries of Europe*, ed. by J. Stroynowski, vol. 3 (Munich, 1989), 1057; T. Mołdawa, *Ludzie Władzy 1944–1991. Władze państwowe i polityczne Polski według stanu na dzień 28 II 1991* (Warsaw, 1991), 421.

SELF-DEFENSE (Samo-Obrona), political party and, simultaneously, a form of radical peasant trade union established at the beginning of 1992 as a consequence of demonstrations and hunger strikes on behalf of peasant debtors struggling with repayment. Led by A. Lepper,* the "peasant Tymiński,"* it occupied several state offices, including the Ministry of Agriculture, organized frequent road blockades, and blamed the banks, L. Balcerowicz,* the U.S. economist J. Sachs, the International Monetary Fund, Western governments, and the President* of Poland, L. Wałęsa,* for the difficult situation of the peasants. Self-Defense assumed the posture of a "party of working people, of the impoverished, of the injured" and attracted groups of frustrated people from various parties. During the elections of September 1993,* it gained 2.78% of the vote. B. Szajkowski (ed.), *Political Parties of Eastern Europe, Russia, and the Successor States* (London, 1994), 338.

SENATE, historical Royal Council transformed into an upper chamber of the Polish Sejm* in the 16th century. The Senate existed throughout the entire interwar period, did not meet after 1939, and was abolished by the communists in 1947. It was reestablished as a part of the Round Table Agreement* in 1989 as a traditional, parliamentary upper chamber with a four-year term. The Senate cannot initiate legislation, but it has the power of veto over the Sejm. The veto can be overturned by a two-thirds majority in the Sejm, with half the deputies present. During the elections of June 1989,* 99 of the Senate's 100 seats were taken by Solidarity*-sponsored candidates. The only other seat was won by a rich businessman. During the following elections of 1991* and 1993,* several parties won the seats in Senate. G. Sanford and A. Gozdecka-Sanford, *Historical Dictionary of Poland* (Metuchen, N.J., 1994), 184; *Dzieje Sejmu Polskiego*, ed. by J.

Bardach (Warsaw, 1993); J. Lerski, *Historical Dictionary of Poland, 966–1945*, with special editing and emendations by P. Wróbel and R. J. Kozicki (Westport, Conn., 1996), 534.

SEREJSKI, MARIAN HENRYK (1897–1975), historian, professor at the universities at Warsaw* and Łódź,* and an expert on the history of Polish historiography. *Great Historians of the Modern Age: An International Dictionary*, ed. by L. Boia (New York, 1991), 494–495.

SIEMIĄTKOWSKI, ZBIGNIEW (1957–   ), spokesperson of the Parliamentary Club of the Democratic Left Alliance (SLD),* one of the leaders and founding members of the Social Democracy of the Republic of Poland (SdRP).* *Sejm Rzeczpospolitej Polskiej. II Kadencja. Przewodnik* (Warsaw, 1994), 151.

SIŁA-NOWICKI, WŁADYSŁAW (1913–94), lawyer and politician who rebuilt the Labor Party (SP)* in 1989. He fought in the September Campaign of 1939 as a cavalry officer and then joined the resistance, was a leader of the Directorate of Diversion (''Kedyw''), and participated in the Warsaw Uprising. In 1945–46 he served as deputy president of the provincial SP organization in Lublin* and, simultaneously, as an inspector of the anti-communist conspiracy Freedom and Independence (WiN).* Arrested in 1947, he was sentenced to death and, thanks to the intercession of his aunt, Aldona Dzierżyńska (sister of Feliks), re-sentenced to lifetime in prison. Released in 1956, he worked as an attorney defending political prisoners. During 1980–81 and 1988–89 he served as a Solidarity* adviser. During 1987–89 he was a member of the Consultation Council by the President of the State Council (Rada Państwa),* Gen. W. Jaruzelski.* In 1989 Siła-Nowicki participated in the Round Table Negotiations.* He was a 1990 presidential elections candidate, but his campaign office failed to collect 100,000 supporting signatures. In 1992 he became a member of the State Tribunal. *Who's Who in the Socialist Countries of Europe*, ed. by J. Stroynowski, vol. 3 (Munich, 1989), 1068; T. Mołdawa, *Ludzie Władzy 1944–1991. Władze państwowe i polityczne Polski według stanu na dzień 28 II 1991* (Warsaw, 1991), 421; *Kto jest kim w polityce polskiej*, ed. by R. Ignasiak (Warsaw, 1993), 256.

SIWAK, ALBIN (1933–   ), construction worker, communist trade union activist, and member of the Politburo* and the Central Committee* of the Polish United Workers' Party (PZPR)* from 1981, known for his sometimes grotesque radicalism and uncompromising hard-line position. *Who's Who in the Socialist Countries of Europe*, ed. by J. Stroynowski, vol. 3 (Munich, 1989), 1076; A. Kępiński and Z. Kilar, *Kto jest kim w Polsce inaczej* (Warsaw, 1985), 351–366.

SIWEK, SŁAWOMIR A. (1950–   ), Catholic journalist and Solidarity* activist. A member of the Press Bureau of the Polish Episcopate* in

1982–89 and a leader of the Center Alliance (PC),* he served as Secretary of State in the chancellery of the President* of Poland in 1990 and as Sejm* deputy in 1991–93. *Kto jest kim w polityce polskiej*, ed. by R. Ignasiak (Warsaw, 1993), 262.

SIWICKI, FLORIAN (1925–   ), Polish Army general and a close collaborator of Gen. W. Jaruzelski.* Siwicki, a veteran of the Red Army* and the First Division of Polish People's Army* and a member of the Polish United Workers' Party (PZPR)* and its Politburo* from 1981, was considered a military technician rather than a politician. In 1968 he commanded the Polish Expedition Corps in Czechoslovakia and then served as chief of staff of the Polish Army during 1973–83, as a member of the Military Council of National Salvation (WRON)* in 1981–83, and as Minister of National Defense in 1983–90. *Who's Who in the Socialist Countries of Europe*, ed. by J. Stroynowski, vol. 3 (Munich, 1989), 1077; G. Sanford and A. Gozdecka-Sanford, *Historical Dictionary of Poland* (Metuchen, N.J., 1994), 187.

SKUBISZEWSKI, KRZYSZTOF (1926–   ), politician, Minister of Foreign Affairs during 1989–92, and professor of International Law at Poznań University and the Polish Academy of Sciences (PAN).* A member of the Primate's* Social Council and of Gen. W. Jaruzelski's* Consultative Council, he served as Minister of Foreign Affairs in the first four post-communist governments. A great supporter of unification with the European Union* and NATO, he rebuilt Polish-German relations and led Poland out of the Warsaw Treaty Organization* and the Comecon.* Yet it is widely believed that he neglected Polish eastern policy and failed to develop regional cooperation with Hungary and Czechoslovakia. *Who's Who in the Socialist Countries of Europe*, ed. by J. Stroynowski, vol. 3 (Munich, 1989), 1081; G. Sanford and A. Gozdecka-Sanford, *Historical Dictionary of Poland* (Metuchen, N.J., 1994), 187; *Kto jest kim w polityce polskiej*, ed. by R. Ignasiak (Warsaw, 1993), 270.

SKULBASZEWSKI, ANTONI (1915–   ), colonel of the Red Army* and Soviet Ukrainian adviser in Poland responsible in part for Stalinist terror. First, he served in the Main Military Prosecutor's Department (Naczelna Prokuratura Wojskowa), where he was in charge of several political cases, such as the trial of M. Rola-Żymierski.* In 1949 he was transferred to the post of deputy chief of the Main Information Office of the Polish People's Army* (counterintelligence), where he was in charge of political interrogations. He was dismissed from his position and left Poland in 1954. Z. Błażyński, *Mówi Józef Światło. Za kulisami bezpieki* (London, 1985), 59, 75; J. Poksiński, "TUN." *Tatar-Utnik-Nowicki* (Warsaw, 1992).

SLD. See **Democratic Left Alliance.**

SŁOMKA, ADAM (1964–   ), activist of the Confederation for an Independent Poland* since 1981 and President of its faction known as the Patriotic Camp. *Sejm Rzeczpospolitej Polskiej. II Kadencja. Przewodnik* (Warsaw, 1994), 155.

SŁONIMSKI, ANTONI (1895–76), poet and writer. He made his poetic debut in 1913. During the interwar period he was a member of the Skamander group, wrote intellectual, rationalist, and liberal works, and cooperated with *Wiadomości Literackie* ("The Literary News"). In 1939 he left Poland for Paris and London, where he edited *Nowa Polska* ("The New Poland") until 1946. Later he directed the Polish Cultural Institute in London, headed the UNESCO literature section of, and in 1951 returned to Poland as a supporter of Socialist Realism.* Disappointed with communism, he became part of an intellectual millieu that was later transformed into the democratic opposition* in Poland. During 1956–59 Słonimski presided over the Union of Polish Writers (ZLP).* The author of numerous volumes of poems and essays, he also wrote plays for the theater and satires. One of the most influential writers of the postwar Poland, he was active in politics and belonged among the initiators of the 1964 "Letter of 34"* protest petition. C. Miłosz, *The History of Polish Literature* (Berkeley, Calif., 1983), 393–395; *Dictionary of Polish Literature*, ed. by E. J. Czerwinski (Westport, Conn., 1994), 386–388; P. Kuncewicz, *Agonia i nadzieja. Literatura polska of 1939 roku*, vol. 2 (Warsaw, 1994), 102–107.

SŁOWIK, ANDRZEJ (1949–   ), co-founder and leader of Solidarity* in Łódź,* Deputy Minister of Labor in 1992. *Kto jest kim w Polsce* (Warsaw, 1993), 657.

SOCIAL DEMOCRACY OF THE REPUBLIC OF POLAND (Socjaldemokracja Rzeczpospolitej Polskiej [SdRP]), leftist party, organized after January 28, 1990, when the Polish United Workers' Party (PZPR)* dissolved itself. The SdRP succeeded the PZPR, taking its resources, experience, organizational network and skills, part of its leadership, relations with the Soviets, the daily newspaper, *Trybuna* (formerly *Trybuna Ludu*),* and about 47,000 members. The SdRP rejects Marxism and promotes pluralism and social democracy of the West European style. It supported the Mazowiecki* government, but went into opposition after the presidential elections of 1990.* The SdRP's presidential candidate was W. Cimoszewicz,* who received 9.2% of the vote in the first round. In 1991 the SdRP formed, with the All-Poland Alliance of Trade Unions (OPZZ),* the Democratic Left Alliance (SLD),* a broad leftist coalition. During the elections of October 1991* the coalition received 12% of the vote, which gave it 60 seats and made it the second strongest party in the Sejm* (first was the Democratic Union [UD],* which soon split and lost its primacy). This result shocked Polish public opinion, strengthened the SdRP's self-confidence, and made its activities even more energetic. In 1993 the SLD included part of the

Polish Socialist Party (PPS)* and about 20 other organizations. The coalition supported a "genuine social market economy" but, at the same time, capitalized on the insecurity of the post-communist transitory period, demanding greater social protection, the liquidation of unemployment, and the maintenance of the welfare-state; it also opposed re-privatization, defended state ownership, and promoted a secular state. In foreign policy it aimed at integration with the European Union* and NATO. In the elections of September 1993,* the SLD, benefitting from the fragmentation of the political right wing and a majority electoral law with a 5% threshold, received 20.4% of the vote—this, as a result of the electoral system, gave it 37.2% of the seats in the Sejm. After the elections the SLD formed a majority coalition with the Polish Peasant Party (PSL)* and created the three consecutive governments of W. Pawlak,* J. Oleksy,* and W. Cimoszewicz.* B. Szajkowski (ed.), *Political Parties of Eastern Europe, Russia, and the Successor States* (London, 1994), 338.

SOCIALIST REALISM, theory and method of literary composition established in the USSR in the early 1930s as the only proper way of writing. N. Ostrovsky's 1932 novel, *Kak zakalyalas stal* ("How the Steel Was Tempered"), became the classic representative of this style, related to the tradition of 19th-century Russian Realism and also accepted in fine arts. Socialist Realism was the only criterion for measuring literary and artistic works, which should represent "Party character," support communist ideology, and reflect typical scenes of everyday communist life. It portrayed positive heroes and an ideal communist society that never existed. In the late 1940s Polish writers and artists were pressed to accept Socialist Realism, and most of them did. Following a series of congresses, writers, architects, and artists decided to accept the new style, promoted by W. Sokorski* in literature, Zofia Lissa in music, Juliusz and Helena Krajewski in fine arts, and Edmund Goldzamzt in architecture. As a consequence, Polish literature* and fine arts* were isolated from contemporary Western trends and underwent a deep crisis during 1948–56. Socialist Realism was rejected in Poland after the "Polish October" of 1956.* B. Groys, *The Total Art of Stalin: Avant-Garde, Aesthetic, Dictatorship, and Beyond* (Princeton, N.J., 1988); J. Jodzewicz, *The Sovietization of Polish Culture* (Paris, 1952); C. Vaughan James, *Soviet Socialist Realism: Origins and Theory* (New York, 1973); *The New Encyclopaedia Britannica*, vol. 10 (Chicago, 1990), 927; J. Karpiński, *Polska, Komunizm, Opozycja* (London, 1985), 229–230.

SOCIALIST UNION OF POLISH STUDENTS (Socjalistyczny Związek Studentów Polskich [SZSP]), student organization established in 1973 after a forced merger of the Union of Socialist Youth (ZMS)* and the Union of Polish Students (ZSP).* The ZMS had never been popular at the Polish universities,* but it really lost steam after the March events of 1968* and was losing its competition with the ZSP, which functioned more like an apolitical student trade union. Therefore, the authorities decided to "simplify" the organizational life of students and "unify" their organizations. This decision provoked frustration among students. A group of them began to organize protests and joined the democratic opposition* in Poland. In 1980 and 1981 student activists at several universities demanded that the SZSP be dissolved. J. J. Lipski, *KOR: A History of the Workers' Defense Committee in Poland, 1976–81* (Berkeley, Calif., 1985), 21–22; M. H. Bernhard, *The Origins of Democratization in Poland: Workers, Intellectuals, and Oppositional Politics, 1976–1980* (New York, 1993), 115, 147.

SOKORSKI, WŁODZIMIERZ (1908–   ), communist official and writer. An activist of the Union of Independent Socialist Youth Życie ("Life"), the Polish Socialist Party–Left, and the Communist Party of Poland (KPP) in the interwar period, he spent World War II in the USSR, where he was active in the Union of Polish Patriots (ZPP) and served as a deputy political commander of the First Division of the Polish People's Army.* Sokorski was secretary of the Central Committee of Trade Unions* during 1945–48, Deputy Minister and then Minister of Culture during 1948–56, and chairman of the Radio and TV Committee during 1956–72. He had great literary ambitions and wrote novels, autobiographical works, and essays, which can be used as primary sources in studies on communism in Poland. *Who's Who in the Socialist Countries of Europe*, ed. by J. Stroynowski, vol. 3 (Munich, 1989), 1095; M. Dąbrowska, *Dzienniki Powojenne 1945–1965*, vol. 1, ed. by T. Drewnowski (Warsaw, 1996), 220.

SOLIDARITY (the Independent Self-Managing Trade Union Solidarity [Niezależny Samorządny Związek Zawodowy "Solidarność"]), existing social movement and trade union born in 1980. It became the first independent labor organization in a country belonging to the Soviet bloc. After a long political crisis of the Jaruzelski* period, Solidarity formed the first non-communist government within this bloc. Its formation was pivotal to the fall of communism. Its history, however, antedates 1980, beginning in 1976, when the Workers' Defense Committee (KOR)* formed and became active. In the late 1970s the first independent workers' committees, strike committees, and small trade unions emerged in various parts of Poland, including Gdańsk.* On December 18, 1979, in its Lenin Shipyard, a service of commemoration was held for workers killed by the communists during the December events of 1970.* The service was attended by some 4,000 people, including dissidents and members of KOR. Many participants were arrested and dismissed from their jobs. On January 25, 1980, a workers' committee, which included L. Wałęsa,* was established in one of Gdańsk's factories to campaign for the reinstatement of the fired employees. During the wave of strikes in summer 1980, Gdańsk's Lenin Shipyard became a center of anti-regime opposition.* In August about 17,000 workers staged a strike by barricading themselves in the shipyards. Initially, they presented mostly economic demands, but in mid-August the Inter-Factory Strike Committee (MKS)* was established in the shipyards calling for the legitimization of independent trade unions, the lifting of censorship, the release of political prisoners, the strengthening of the position of the Roman Catholic Church,* and changes in government priorities in social welfare. Led by L. Wałęsa, the MKS coordinated strikes in the northern part of Poland and started direct negotiations with the authorities. On August 31 the Gdańsk Agreement* was signed by the representatives of the communist government and Wałęsa. The Gdańsk Agreement sanctioned the right to strike, the right to form independent trade unions, and several other freedoms previously limited by the regime. The MKZ had to acknowledge the Polish United Workers' Party (PZPR)* as the undisputed "leading force." Similar agreements were signed in Szczecin* and Jastrzębie-Zdrój.*

On September 18, 1980, some 250 delegates of regional trade unions met in Gdańsk and several days later merged their organizations into an all-Polish union named Solidarity. They accepted Wałęsa as its chairman. On September 24, Solidarity applied for the registration of its statutes by the Warsaw* district court. A long conflict ensued over giving Solidarity a Party "leading role." On December 14, 1980, a separate union, named Rural Solidarity,* was formed by individual farmers. In spring 1981 Solidarity had about 10 million members (most adult citizens of Poland). The organization led a national social movement fusing all opposition trends and thus was seen as a threat by the authorities. Throughout 1981 conflict between Solidarity and the authorities intensified. The former radicalized and presented new political and economic demands; the latter, pressed by the Soviet leadership, tried to limit and control the development of the free trade union. On September 5–10 and September 20–October 7, 1981, Solidarity held its first national congress in Gdańsk. The congress re-elected L. Wałęsa as the trade union's chairman and approved a large number of resolutions, which intensified conflict with the government. In fall 1981 a strong faction, led by A. Gwiazda,* appeared within Solidarity and accused Wałęsa of an "excessively moderate" attitude toward the government.

On December 13, 1981, Gen. W. Jaruzelski imposed Martial Law* in Poland. Solidarity was suspended, and most of its leaders and activists, including L. Wałęsa, were interned. Those who managed to escape roundups hid underground, formed a provisional executive (the Provisional National Committee), and organized strikes, which were brutally suppressed before the end of December 1981. Yet a "Solidarity resistance committee" and the two Solidarity Presidium members still at large, Z. Bujak* and W. Frasyniuk,* called for continued public resistance. On April 12, 1982, an underground Solidarity radio began weekly broadcasts in Warsaw. On October 8, 1982, the Sejm* formally dissolved Solidarity and created a framework for new, more closely controlled trade unions. The first of them appeared on January 3, 1983, three days after the Jaruzelski regime suspended Martial Law. On November 14, 1982, L. Wałęsa was released and returned home, but he was still harassed, partially prevented from participating in political life, and forbidden to attend the award ceremony at which he received the 1983 Nobel Prize for Peace. In 1983 the authorities continued to arrest hundreds of activists of underground Solidarity. Its Provisional National Committee (TKK) led the weakening resistance throughout the following years and received a papal blessing during John Paul II's* visit in Poland in June 1987. On October 25, 1987, a national meeting of Solidarity activists in Gdańsk replaced the TKK by a 10-member National Executive Commission (KKW) chaired by L. Wałęsa. The authorities refused to register the KKW.

A new wave of strikes broke out in spring and summer 1988. Their leaders demanded, among other reforms, the re-legalization of Solidarity. Poland's economy was falling down at a threatening pace. On August 31, 1988, L. Wałęsa met Gen. C. Kiszczak,* Minister of the Interior, and brought about a cessation of most strikes. The negotiations with Kiszczak led to the Round Table Negotiations* in February 1989. They resulted in the re-legalization of Solidarity and Rural Solidarity on April 17, 1989, and the elections of June 1989.* After its landslide victory Solidarity formed a government in August 1989, led by T. Mazowiecki.* Simultaneously, internal divisions started inside Solidarity, accelerated by the "war at the top"* during the presidential elections of 1990.* Membership dropped to about 2.5 million dues-paying members. The Solidarity Parliamentary Club was split, and the most experienced and active leaders of the movement established several new parties: the Center Alliance (PC),* the Citizens' Movement for Democratic Action (ROAD),* the Democratic Right Forum (FPD), which merged later into the Democratic Union (UD),* the Democratic Social Movement,* and several smaller organizations. Solidarity survived as a trade union, but L. Wałęsa resigned as its leader after the 1990 elections and was replaced by M. Krzaklewski.* Wałęsa did not have close relations with him and was bitterly criticized by some segments of Solidarity, which received only 5.05% of the vote and 27 seats in the Sejm during the October 1991 elections.* Frustrated and disappointed, it evolved toward the political right and supported lustration, radical de-communization, and the increasingly politically active Roman Catholic Church. In July 1992 Solidarity helped to create the Suchocka* seven-party government* and later supported it without entering the coalition. A growing wave of strikes in late 1992 and early 1993 destroyed this agreement, and Solidarity parliamentary deputies tabled the successful vote of no confidence in Suchocka's cabinet in May 1993. At the same time, the Solidarity Parliamentary Club divided as groups of deputies left for other parties. During the September 1993 elections* Solidarity gained only 4.9% of the vote and did not enter the Sejm. *Revolutionary and Dissident Movements: An International Guide*, ed. by Henry W. Degenhardt (London, 1991), 269–276; N. G. Andrews, *Poland, 1980–81: Solidarity versus the Party* (Washington, D.C., 1985); T. G. Ash, *The Polish Revolution: Solidarity, 1980–1982* (London, 1983); J. Holzer, *Solidarność 1980–81* (Paris, 1984); A. Kemp-Welch, *The Birth of Solidarity: The Gdańsk Negotiations, 1980* (London, 1983); D. Ost, *Solidarity and the Politics of Anti-Politics: Opposition and Reform in Poland since 1968* (Philadelphia, 1990); B. Szajkowski (ed.), *Political Parties of Eastern Europe, Russia, and the Successor States* (London, 1994), 340.

SOLIDARITY EMIGRATION. See **Emigration.**

SOLIDARITY PRESS INFORMATION BUREAU (Biuro Informacji Prasowej "Solidarności" [BIPS]), institution cooperating with the Solidarity National Committee (Komisja Krajowa) and publishing the most important documents of, and information on, Solidarity and political life in Poland. J. Karpiński, *Polska, Komunizm, Opozycja* (London, 1985), 27.

SOLIDARNOŚĆ. See **Solidarity.**

SOLIDARNOŚĆ WALCZĄCA. See **Fighting Solidarity.**

SOLSKI, LUDWIK (1855–1954), actor, director of several theaters, and distinguished artist of the theater in Poland after World War II. *Wielka Encyklopedia Powszechna PWN*, vol. 10 (Warsaw, 1966), 661.

SOMMERSTEIN, EMIL (1883–1957), lawyer, Zionist activist before World War II, and head of the War Reparation Department of the Polish Committee of National Liberation (PKWN) and the Provisional Government.* T. Mołdawa, *Ludzie Władzy 1944–1991. Władze państwowe i polityczne Polski według stanu na dzień 28 II 1991* (Warsaw, 1991), 424.

SOSKA, JACEK (1954–   ), politician and farmer. Active in the peasant movement since 1980, he helped to reshape the United Peasant Party (ZSL)* into the Polish Peasant Party (PSL)* and has represented it in the Sejm* since 1989. *Sejm Rzeczpospolitej Polskiej. II Kadencja. Przewodnik* (Warsaw, 1994), 158.

SOVIET ARMY. See **Red Army.**

SPASOWSKI, ROMUALD (1920–   ), diplomat. A former Deputy Minister of Foreign Affairs, he served as Polish ambassador to the United States in 1955–60 and 1978–81. After imposition of Martial Law* in December 1981, he asked for political asylum in the United States and was sentenced to death *in absentia* by a Polish court. R. Spasowski, *The Liberation of One* (New York, 1986).

SPATiF (Union of Polish Artists of Theater and Film). See **ZASP.**

SPYCHALSKA-CZUMA, EWA T. (1949–   ), deputy president (1990–91) and president (1991–95) of the All-Poland Alliance of Trade Unions (OPZZ).* *Sejm Rzeczpospolitej Polskiej. II Kadencja. Przewodnik* (Warsaw, 1994), 158.

SPYCHALSKI, MARIAN (1906–80), Marshal of the Polish Army* and a close collaborator of W. Gomułka.* In 1931 he graduated from the Architecture Department of Warsaw Polytechnic University (Politechnika) and joined the Communist Party of Poland (KPP). Active in communist underground organizations from the beginning of World War II, he became a leader of the newly formed Polish Workers' Party (PPR)* and its People's Guard in January 1942. He also joined the National Home Council (KRN)* and went with its delegation to Moscow in spring 1944. During 1945–48 he was a Deputy Minister of Defense and a member of the PPR Politburo.* As an assistant close to Gomułka, Spychalski was sidetracked in 1948, removed from all his positions in 1949, and eventually imprisoned. In 1956 he returned to power with Gomułka and became Minister of Defense. He returned to the Politburo in 1959 and was promoted to Marshal in 1963. After the March events of 1968,* he was removed from the Polish Army* and sidelined again as Chairman of State Council (Rada Państwa)* and president of the Front of National Unity (FJN).* After the December events of 1970,* he was purged again and retired from politics to write his memoirs. G. Sanford and A. Gozdecka-Sanford, *Historical Dictionary of Poland* (Metuchen, N.J., 1994), 195; *Encyklopedyczny Słownik Sławnych Polaków* (Warsaw, 1996), 366.

STACHANOVITES, members of the movement named for A. Stachanov, the legendary Soviet coal miner who greatly increased his personal productivity and was used by Soviet propaganda as a role model for other workers to prompt them to work harder for communism. Polish communist authorities tried to start a similar movement in Poland, but with no real success. A Polish equivalent of Stachanov, a Silesian coal minor, W. Pstrowski,* died at the age of 44. R. F. Staar, *Poland, 1944–1962: The Sovietization of a Captive People* (New Orleans, 1962), 83, 104; J. Gunther, *Inside Russia Today* (New York, 1958), 372; *The New Encyclopaedia Britannica*, vol. 11 (Chicago, 1990), 204.

STACHURA, EDWARD (1937–79), poet and writer, existentialist and rebel. *Encyklopedyczny Słownik Sławnych Polaków* (Warsaw, 1996), 367.

STAFF, LEOPOLD (1878–1957), playwright, translator, and great "poet of three generations." He made his debut in 1898, was active during three epochs in the history of Polish literature:* "Young Polish," interwar, and post-1939. He wrote over 30 volumes of verse. He also did translations and wrote dramas. A member of the Polish Academy of Literature and a patron of the *Skamander* poetic group before World War II, Staff changed his poetics style and worldview several times. He started as a modernist, was later influenced by Nietzscheanism and Romanticism, and became the outstanding classicist of 20th-century Polish poetry. After World War II he was a celebrity of Polish literature. C. Miłosz, *The History of Polish Literature* (Berkeley, Calif. 1983), 343–347; *Dictionary of Polish Literature*, ed. by E. J. Czerwinski (Westport, Conn., 1994), 394–395; *Encyklopedyczny Słownik Sławnych Polaków* (Warsaw, 1996), 367.

STALINIST PERIOD, era when Poland was dominated by Stalinist methods of rule and subject to Soviet hegemony. During this time of terror and intense ideological indoctrination, Poland's political system quickly became totalitarian, comparable to the classic totalitarian regimes in the Stalinist Soviet Union, Nazi Germany, and Fascist Italy. In the USSR the Stalinist period started in 1929 and began to erode after Stalin's death in March 1953. According to most scholars, the Stalinist period in Poland began in 1948 and came to its end in 1956. Yet, some historians argue, the years 1944–48, when the communists seized power,* should also be considered part of the Stalinist period, since Poland was subjugated by the Stalinist Soviet Union in 1944–45 and underwent a process of structural accommodation to the USSR as early as 1944. Most historians believe, however, that 1944–48, as a time of relative political pluralism nurturing an incipient New Economic Policy, cannot be considered Stalinist; for them, the Stalinist period began in 1948, when all political parties not controlled by the communists disappeared, when the remnants of the democratic opposition* were imprisoned, forced to emigrate, and were intimidated, and when collectivization* of Polish agriculture* started. These events happened in the context of important international developments: the establishment of the Cominform* in September 1947, the communist coup d'état in Czechoslovakia in February 1948, the beginning of an open conflict between Yugoslavia and the USSR in June 1948, the absorption of socialist parties into communist parties in Romania, Hungary, and Czechoslovakia between February and December 1948, the Blockade of Berlin, the formation of the Comecon* in January 1949, and the creation of NATO after April 1949.

All these events, which constituted an escalation of the Cold War,* were paralleled by structural changes in Poland. During the plenum of the Central Committee* of the Polish Workers' Party (PPR)* on August 31–September 3, 1948, W. Gomułka* was accused of "nationalist deviation," a conciliatory attitude toward Tito of Yugoslavia, and slowing down the tempo of collectivization. In November 1948 he was removed as Secretary General of the Party and replaced with B. Bierut,* an obedient agent of the Kremlin. The elimination of Gomułka was followed by a purge of the Party. All Gomułka sympathizers were removed, and the PPR became a reliable tool of Soviet policies in Poland. Peasant movements merged into the United Peasant Party (ZSL),* and collectivization of Polish agriculture accelerated. Trade unions*were purged and their role changed from representation of the workers to their mobilization. In November 1949 Soviet Marshal, K. Rokossowski,* was installed in Poland, first as its Minister of Defense and commander-in-chief of its army and then as member of the Politburo* and Deputy Premier. He supervised the development of the Polish People's Army,* reorganizing it according to the Soviet pattern. The Army was purged: all prewar officers and people not trusted by the communists were eliminated from important military positions. During the Unification Congress* of December 15–21, 1948, the partially independent Polish Socialist Party (PPS)* incorporated into the PPR, and together they became the Polish United Workers' Party (PZPR).* The same congress accepted the Six-Year Plan for 1950–55. Called the "Plan of Economic Development and Construction of the Foundations of Socialism in Poland,'' it concentrated most investments in heavy and military industries. Poland's judicial system was recast on Soviet lines in 1950. Soviet control over Poland was complete. The Kremlin expected Poland's society, economy, and culture to mirror the Soviet system within several years. The new Constitution of the Polish People's Republic,* accepted by the Sejm* in 1952, was, therefore, a copy of the Stalinist Constitution of 1936.

In summer 1950, after the outbreak of the Korean War, the original targets of the Six-Year Plan significantly increased. Mobilization of the Polish workforce was extended, and control over Polish society was tightened. Thousands were arrested, and thousands more were sent to labor camps. Even the most meek forms of opposition against the system were cruelly punished. Total nationalization* of the economy became the target of the authorities. Soviet exploitation of the Polish economy increased: Polish coal, sugar, and other commodities were delivered to the USSR at "special prices" significantly lower than world market prices. At the same time, the communist authorities began a cultural revolution in Poland. Socialist Realism* became the only acceptable form of artistic expression. Ideological indoctrination assumed overwhelming proportions. An extensive campaign against the Roman Catholic Church* was started. In September 1953, half a year after Stalin's death, the Primate* of Poland, Cardinal S. Wyszyński,* was arrested.

As a result of a growing abyss between the Party leadership and the general population, a "new class" of *nomenklatura** emerged. Collectivization caused serious food shortages. Allocation of most investments in heavy and military industries was followed by problems in availability of consumer goods, housing, and community services. The development of Polish literature* was paralyzed by ideology* and the communist doublespeak. Fine arts* were choked by Socialist Realism. Universities* and scientific institutions degenerated. As overwhelming bureaucratization, police terror, and falling living standards contributed to an atmosphere of tension, alienation, hopelessness, and general misery for most people, some Party leaders realized that the system did not work properly. Tension grew within the Party, a mass organization of over 1 million members by the beginning of the 1950s. Systematic contradictions and political anxiety in Poland were intensified by the struggle for power in the USSR after Stalin's death. After liquidating L. Beria, the Soviet political police was discredited and partially disorganized, which also affected the Polish police apparatus. In December 1953 a well-informed insider of the secret police in Poland, J. Światło,* defected while in West Berlin. His revelations about the terror system in Poland, broadcasted by Radio Free Europe,* started an avalanche. In December 1954 the Ministry of Public Security was abolished. The most notorious torturers and persecutors working in the Ministry were arrested and tried. As secret police in Poland lost their self-confidence, in 1955 and 1956, the terror diminished. Gomułka was released from detention, and plans for his large political trial were abandoned. In February 1956 the Twentieth Congress of the Communist Party of the Soviet Union and the secret speech of N. Khrushchev condemned Stalinist terror and rehabilitated the Communist Party of Poland, liquidated by Stalin in 1938. With the Stalinist myth destroyed, the process of disillusionment of those Poles who had, after World War II, been fascinated with communism became complete. The political "thaw"* started: Ideology, Socialist Realism, and Stalinist economics were increasingly criticized openly. At the same time, the Polish economy* grew worse. In June 1956 Poznań* workers revolted and the "Polish October"* began. M. K. Dziewanowski, *Poland in the Twentieth Century* (New York, 1977), 165–180; R. F. Leslie (ed.), *The History of Poland since 1863* (Cambridge, 1980), 299–344; N. Davies, *God's Playground: A History of Poland*, vol. 2 (New York, 1984), 574–586; R. F. Staar, *Poland, 1944–1962: The Sovietization of a Captive People* (New Orleans, 1968); M. K. Dziewanowski, *The Communist Party of Poland: An Outline of History* (Cambridge, Mass., 1976), 208–252.

STAMM, FELIKS (1901–76), boxer and popular coach, the founder of Polish boxing. *Encyklopedyczny Słownik Sławnych Polaków* (Warsaw, 1996), 367, 368.

STAŃCZYK, JAN (1886–1953), activist of the Polish Socialist Party (PPS)* from 1904, Minister of Labor in the Polish Government-in-Exile* during 1940–44 and in the Provisional Government of National Unity (TRJN)* in 1945–46. T. Mołdawa, *Ludzie Władzy 1944–1991. Władze państwowe i polityczne Polski według stanu na dzień 28 II 1991* (Warsaw, 1991), 424.

STAREWICZ, ARTUR (1917–   ), Party official. An activist in the communist youth movement in the 1930s, he spent World War II in the USSR. In 1944 he returned to Poland, joined the Polish Workers' Party (PPR),* and started a Party career. He served as Party provincial First Secretary in several regions of Poland in 1945–48 and as a secretary of the Central Council of Trade Unions (CRZZ)* in 1954–56. In 1948–1954 he headed the Propaganda Department of the Central Committee,* and in 1956–63, its Press Bureau. T. Mołdawa, *Ludzie Władzy 1944–1991. Władze państwowe i polityczne Polski według stanu na dzień 28 II 1991* (Warsaw, 1991), 425.

STASIAK, LUDOMIR (1919–   ), economist, leader of the Peasant Party (SL)* and the United Peasant Party (ZSL)* during 1945–80, and Secretary of the State Council (Rada Państwa)* in 1969–80. T. Mołdawa, *Ludzie Władzy 1944–1991. Władze państwowe i polityczne Polski według stanu na dzień 28 II 1991* (Warsaw, 1991), 425.

STASZEWSKI, STEFAN (1906–   ), Party official. Engaged in the communist movement beginning in 1920, he studied at the International Lenin Higher School in Moscow and occupied several important positions in the Communist Party of Poland (KPP). Expelled from the Party in 1936, he went to the USSR and was deported to a forced labor camp in Kolyma. In 1945 he returned to

Poland and served, among other positions, in the Party-state apparatus as the head of the Press and Publications Department of the Central Committee* of the Polish Workers' Party (PPR).* During the "Polish October" of 1956,* he played an important role as First Secretary of the Warsaw* Party Committee (he held this post between September 1955 and February 1957). Later he was marginalized as an editor by W. Gomułka.* He resigned from the Party in protest against the March events of 1968* and sympathized with the Workers' Defense Committee (KOR)* and Solidarity.* *Who's Who in the Socialist Countries of Europe*, ed. by J. Stroynowski, vol. 3 (Munich, 1989), 1115.

STATE AGRICULTURAL FARM. See PGR.

STATE COUNCIL (Rada Państwa), executive body elected by the Sejm* and introduced by the Little Constitution* of February 11, 1947. According to this legislative act, the State Council consisted of the President of the Republic as its Chairman, a Speaker and two Deputy Speakers of the Sejm, a President of the Supreme Control Chamber (NIK),* and several additional members elected by the Sejm. During war a commander-in-chief of the Polish People's Army* was supposed to join the State Council. The Constitution of 1952* eliminated the post of President and reshaped the State Council, which then consisted of Chairman, who filled the representative functions of a chief of state, four deputies, a secretary, and several members. It possessed the authority to call elections, convoke the Sejm, exercise legislative initiative, interpret laws, issue decrees, appoint and recall diplomatic representatives, supervise local people's councils, and legislate during the intervals between sessions of the Sejm. In practice, however, the role of the State Council was limited. Before it was eliminated in 1989, it was chaired by the following members of the ruling Polish Workers' Party (PPR)* and, later, the Polish United Workers' Party (PZPR):* B. Bierut* (initially president of the National Home Council [KRN]*), January 1, 1944–November 20, 1952; A. Zawadzki,* November 20, 1952–August 7, 1964; E. Ochab,* August 12, 1964–April 11, 1968; M. Spychalski,* April 11, 1968–December 23, 1970; J. Cyrankiewicz,* December 23, 1970–March 28, 1972; H. Jabłoński,* March 28, 1972–November 6, 1985; and W. Jaruzelski,* November 6, 1985–July 19, 1989. T. Mołdawa, *Ludzie Władzy 1944–1991. Władze państwowe i polityczne Polski według stanu na dzień 28 II 1991* (Warsaw, 1991), 170; J. Karpiński, *Polska, Komunizm, Opozycja* (London, 1985), 223–224.

STATE OF WAR. See Martial Law.

STATE TRIBUNAL, the highest legal organ, elected by the Sejm* and chaired by the First President of the Supreme Court. The State Tribunal existed during the interwar period and was reestablished in 1982. It investigates parliamentary charges against the President,* the Premier,* ministers, and high state officials.

G. Sanford and A. Gozdecka-Sanford, *Historical Dictionary of Poland* (Metuchen, N.J., 1994), 195.

STEINSBERG, ANIELA (1896–1988), lawyer and dissident.* A member of the Polish Socialist Party (PPS)* before the war, she defended communists in the political trials of the 1930s. After the war she defended soldiers of the Home Army (AK)* charged, by communists, with treason and spying. In 1966 she defended J. Kuroń* and K. Modzelewski,* and later she participated in the political trials after the March events of 1968.* A member of the Crooked Circle Club* in Warsaw,* she was suspended as a barrister and then dismissed from the Bar* by the Minister of Justice in 1968. In 1976 she was a founding member of the Workers' Defense Committee (KOR).* *Who's Who in the Socialist Countries of Europe*, ed. by J. Stroynowski, vol. 3 (Munich, 1989), 1123.

STELMACHOWSKI, ANDRZEJ (1925–   ), professor of law at Warsaw University* and legal adviser to Solidarity* from 1980. Elected to the Senate* in 1989, he became its Speaker. G. Sanford and A. Gozdecka-Sanford, *Historical Dictionary of Poland* (Metuchen, N.J., 1994), 196.

STEMPOWSKI, JERZY (1894–1969), erudite literary critic. A "father" of the Polish school of essay writing, he contributed to the Paris *Kultura* ("Culture")* from 1946. *Dictionary of Polish Literature*. ed. by E. J. Czerwinski (Westport, Conn., 1994), 395–396; *Encyklopedyczny Słownik Sławnych Polaków* (Warsaw, 1996), 374.

STOCK EXCHANGE. Prior to 1939 there were six stock exchanges in Poland. The oldest one was founded in Warsaw* in 1817. The activities of these stock exchanges were not resumed after World War II. The Warsaw Stock Exchange opened again in April 1991, after the fall of communism in Poland. In a relatively short time it has developed a dynamic scale of activity. The Warsaw Stock Exchange is becoming the place to allocate capital and may thus come to have a strategic significance for the Polish economy as a whole. In January 1995 the Exchange listed 39 firms, with 8 more listed in the parallel market. General Information about Poland <http://bmb.ippt.gov.pl/poland/partone.html>

STOMMA, STANISŁAW (1908–   ), Catholic intellectual, politician, writer, and publicist. He co-edited the prestigious *Tygodnik Powszechny* ("The Universal Weekly")* from 1957, served as deputy chairman of the Club of Catholic Intelligentsia* from 1960 and as chairman of the Catholic *Znak* caucus in the Sejm* during 1957–76. A professor of law at Jagiellonian University* in Cracow,* he chaired the Primate's* Social Council in Warsaw* during 1981–84. *Who's Who in the Socialist Countries of Europe*, ed. by J. Stroynowski, vol. 3 (Munich, 1989), 1130; A. Micewski, *Ludzie i opcje* (Warsaw, 1993), 39–44.

STRIKES. According to the official Party line before 1989, strikes did not exist under socialism. The communist mass media referred instead to "work stoppages" and explained that they were caused by hooligans or arranged by foreign agents or anti-socialist forces.* Nevertheless, strikes took place in communist Poland and greatly affected its political life. Waves of strikes rippled through Poland in June 1956, during and after the December events of 1970,* in June 1976, during the Solidarity* period in 1980–81, and in spring and summer 1988. The strikes contributed to the erosion and eventually fall of communism in Poland. J. Karpiński, *Polska, Komunizm, Opozycja* (London, 1985), 265.

STRONNICTWO DEMOKRATYCZNE. See Democratic Party.

STRUŻEK, BOLESŁAW (1920–   ), Deputy President of the State Council (Rada Państwa)* from September 1984 to November 1985. T. Mołdawa, *Ludzie Władzy 1944–1991. Władze państwowe i polityczne Polski według stanu na dzień 28 II 1991* (Warsaw, 1991), 426.

STRYJKOWSKI, JULIAN (1905–96), writer who authored numerous novels on the Jews,* the Holocaust, communism, and biblical subjects. Initially a Zionist and, before World War II, a member of the Communist Party of Western Ukraine, he co-edited the daily *Czerwony Sztandar* ("The Red Banner") in Soviet-occupied Lvov after 1939 and the weekly organ of the Union of Polish Patriots (ZPP) in the USSR, *Wolna Polska* ("Free Poland"), during 1943–46. After the war he worked at the Polish News Agency and served on the editorial board of the *Twórczość* ("Creation"), a literary monthly. Disappointed with communism, he became active in the democratic opposition* in Poland in the 1960s and 1970s. His terrifying novel about communism, *Wielki strach* ("The Great Fear"), was published as *samizdat*. *Who's Who in the Socialist Countries of Europe*, ed. by J. Stroynowski, vol. 3 (Munich, 1989), 1139; *Dictionary of Polish Literature*, ed. by E. J. Czerwinski (Westport, Conn., 1994), 397–398; P. Kuncewicz, *Agonia i nadzieja. Proza polska od 1956*, vol. 4 (Warsaw, 1994), 42–48.

STRZELECKI, JAN (1918–88), veteran of the anti-German resistance during World War II, sociologist, and essayist. In the late 1970s he cooperated with the Workers' Defense Committee (KOR),* the Association of Scientific Courses (TKN),* and the "Experience and Future"* group. After his murder in Warsaw,* the public believed he was killed by the secret police. *Nowa Encyklopedia Powszechna PWN*, vol. 6 (Warsaw, 1996), 87.

STRZELECKI, RYSZARD (1907–88), member of the State Council (Rada Państwa)* during 1961–72. A heavy industry worker in interwar Poland, he joined the Polish Workers' Party (PPR)* and its military underground organizations in 1942. After the war he served in the communist apparatus in such positions as Transportation Minister and First Secretary of provincial Party organizations in Cracow* (1946–48) and Katowice* (1948–50). A close collaborator of W. Gomułka,* Strzelecki was removed from politics by the "Silesian group" of E. Gierek.* *Who's Who in the Socialist Countries of Europe*, ed. by J. Stroynowski, vol. 3 (Munich, 1989), 1140; T. Mołdawa, *Ludzie Władzy 1944–1991. Władze państwowe i polityczne Polski według stanu na dzień 28 II 1991* (Warsaw, 1991), 422.

STRZEMBOSZ, ADAM J. (1930–   ), law professor and Solidarity* activist. From September 1989 to June 1990, he served as Deputy Justice Minister and then became First President of the Supreme Court* and Chairman of the State Tribunal.* In 1995 he was a candidate in the presidential election, but he withdrew his candidacy shortly before the election. T. Mołdawa, *Ludzie Władzy 1944–1991. Władze państwowe i polityczne Polski według stanu na dzień 28 II 1991* (Warsaw, 1991), 427.

STS (Studencki Teatr Satyryków [Student's Satirical Theater]), amateur cabaret established on March 13, 1954, in Warsaw* as a part of the cultural "thaw"* and de-Stalinization. Located in the Zug Palace, which once housed a Masonic lodge, the STS specialized in political songs and sketches. A. Osiecka,* J. Abramow,* and Andrzej Jarecki belonged among the most prolific writers and Marek Lusztig, Edward Pałłasz, and Stanisław Młynarczyk among the most prolific composers working for the STS. Zofia Merle, Anna Prucnal, Krystyna Sienkiewicz, Leszek Biskup, and Sława Przybylska were the most active artists of the theater. In 1969 it was reshaped into a state theater. *Nowa Encyklopedia Powszechna PWN*, vol. 6 (Warsaw, 1996), 90, 333; *Wkład Polaków do kultury świata*, ed. by M. A. Krąpiec (Lublin, 1976), 726.

STUDENT SOLIDARITY COMMITTEES (Studenckie Komitety Solidarności [SKS]), independent student organizations established on the initiative of the Workers' Defense Committee (KOR)* and the Movement for the Defense of Human and Civil Rights (ROPCiO)* after the 1977 death of S. Pyjas,* killed in Cracow by secret police. The SKS formed the Independent Students' Association (NZS)* in 1980–81. *Nowa Encyklopedia Powszechna PWN*, vol. 6 (Warsaw, 1996), 90.

SUCHOCKA, HANNA (1946–   ), Premier* from July 11, 1992, to October 18, 1993. In 1968 she graduated from the Law Department of the University of Poznań,* where she continued her scholarly career. She also worked at Columbia University, the Catholic University of Lublin,* and several other scientific institutions in Leyden, Strasburg, Heidelberg, and Warsaw.* In 1980 she was elected to the Sejm* as a representative of the Democratic Party (SD).* Simultaneously, she was active in Solidarity* as an expert on constitutional law. She opposed the SD political line, voted against the imposition of Martial Law* in

1981, and left the SD in 1984. In 1989 she became a leader of the Citizens Committee (OK)* and was elected to the Sejm. She joined the Parliamentary Club of the Democratic Union (UD)* in 1991 and was elected to the next Parliament. She represented the conservative Christian wing of the UD and supported a restrictive anti-abortion law. In 1992 she served as Deputy President of the Parliamentary Assembly of the European Council. G. Sanford and A. Gozdecka-Sanford, *Historical Dictionary of Poland* (Metuchen, N.J., 1994), 196; *Kto jest kim w polityce polskiej*, ed. by R. Ignasiak (Warsaw, 1993), 278; A. Dudek, *Pierwsze lata III Rzeczpospolitej, 1989–1995* (Cracow, 1997), 228–270.

SUCHODOLSKI, BOHDAN (1903–92), philosopher, pedagogue, historian of science and culture, professor at Warsaw University,* member of the Polish Academy of Sciences (PAN)* and its Presidium during 1969–80, and a founder of socialist pedagogy in Poland. *Who's Who in the Socialist Countries of Europe*, ed. by J. Stroynowski, vol. 3 (Munich, 1989), 1142; *Encyklopedyczny Słownik Sławnych Polaków* (Warsaw, 1996), 380.

SUPREME CONTROL CHAMBER (Najwyższa Izba Kontroli [NIK]), theoretically independent body established in 1947 to control the activities of the most important state institutions and to investigate the most serious crimes. Having existed in the interwar Polish state, NIK was replaced during 1944–47 by Control Bureau (Biuro Kontroli) attached to the Presidium of the National Home Council (KRN).* NIK was replaced by the Ministry of State Control in 1952 and, rebuilt again in 1957. Until 1976 it was supervised by the Sejm,* during 1976–80 by the Premier,* and since 1980 by the Parliament again. Its importance grew during acute political crises, like the one in 1980, when NIK prepared a large report about corruption among the most important state officials. In 1983 NIK had about 1,400 employees. NIK was presided over by H. Kołodziejski (1947–49), Gen. F. Jóźwiak* (1949–52), K. Dąbrowski* (1957–69), Z. Nowak* (1969–71), Gen. M. Moczar* (1971–83), Gen. T. Hupałowski* (1983–91), W. Pańko (1991), and L. Kaczyński* (1992–95). G. Sanford and A. Gozdecka-Sanford, *Historical Dictionary of Poland* (Metuchen, N.J., 1994), 198; J. Karpiński, *Polska, Komunizm, Opozycja* (London, 1985), 153; General Information about Poland <http://bmb.ippt.gov.pl/poland/partone.htlm>

SUPREME COURT (Sąd Najwyższy), the highest court of appeal and institution supervising activities of all lower courts. It is composed of four chambers (Civil, Criminal, Administration, and Labor and Social Insurance) and headed by its First President, elected by the Sejm.* The First President appoints members of the Court nominated by the National Council for Judiciary (Krajowa Rada Sądownicza [KRS]). During 1945–56 the post of First President was held by W. Barcikowski; in 1956–67, by J. Wasilkowski; in 1967–72 by Z. Resich; in 1972–76 by J. Bafia*; in 1976–86 by W. Berutowicz; in 1987–90 by A.

Łopatka*; and since 1990 by A. Strzembosz.* G. Sanford and A. Gozdecka-Sanford, *Historical Dictionary of Poland* (Metuchen, N.J., 1994), 198.

SWINARSKI, KONRAD (1929–75), theater director, together with L. Schiller* an outstanding artist of the Polish theater in the second half of the 20th century. *Encyklopedyczny Słownik Sławnych Polaków* (Warsaw, 1996), 381.

SYGIETYŃSKI, TADEUSZ (1896–1955), composer, promoter of Polish folklore, and founder and director of the famous state song and dance ensemble *Mazowsze* ("Mazovia"). *Encyklopedyczny Słownik Sławnych Polaków* (Warsaw, 1996), 382.

SYNAGOGUES. Poland was home to several hundred synagogues before World War II, but only a few survived the war and remain the only evidence of the Jewish presence in Poland. Presently, there are 245 synagogues in Poland, but only 15 of them are open for prayer: 1 in Warsaw,* 2 in Cracow,* and 1 in Szczecin,* Wrocław,* Żary, Bytom, Gliwice, Katowice,* Łódź,* Legnica, Lublin,* Dzierżoniów, Wałbrzych, and Bielsko-Biała. The remaining temples are in ruins or serve as museums, art galleries, libraries, cinemas, archives, schools, clubs, or warehouses.

SYRYJCZYK, TADEUSZ A. (1948–), Solidarity* activist from Cracow* and Industry Minister in the government of T. Mazowiecki* in 1989–90. G. Sanford and A. Gozdecka-Sanford, *Historical Dictionary of Poland* (Metuchen, N.J., 1994), 198; *Kto jest kim w polityce polskiej*, ed. by R. Ignasiak (Warsaw, 1993), 279.

SZACKI, JERZY (1929–), outstanding contemporary sociologist and professor at Warsaw University.* *Who's Who in the Socialist Countries of Europe*, ed. by J. Stroynowski, vol. 3 (Munich, 1989), 1157.

SZAJNA, JÓZEF (1922–), artist, director, and co-founder of Polish avantgarde theater and director of overwhelmingly catastrophist theatrical performances. *Who's Who in the Socialist Countries of Europe*, ed. by J. Stroynowski, vol. 3 (Munich, 1989), 1158; *Encyklopedyczny Słownik Sławnych Polaków* (Warsaw, 1996), 384.

SZAŁAJDA, ZBIGNIEW (1934–), engineer, manager, Minister of Metallurgy in 1980–82, and Deputy Premier during 1982–88. *Who's Who in the Socialist Countries of Europe*, ed. by J. Stroynowski, vol. 3 (Munich, 1989), 1160; A. Kępiński and Z. Kilar, *Kto jest kim w Polsce inaczej* (Warsaw, 1985), 369–387.

SZANIAWSKI, JERZY (1886–1970), playwright and prose writer whose ironic and lyrical works explored the nature of theater and well-established stereotypes. *Dictionary of Polish Literature*, ed. by E. J. Czerwinski (Westport, Conn., 1994), 400–402.

SZANIAWSKI, KLEMENS (1925–90), philosopher, professor at Warsaw University,* and member of the Polish Academy of Sciences (PAN).* *Who's Who in the Socialist Countries of Europe*, ed. by J. Stroynowski, vol. 3 (Munich, 1989), 1160.

SZCZECIN (German Stettin), capital city of Szczecin Province (województwo) in the historical region of Western Pomerania. Situated on the mouth of the River Oder,* 40 miles (65 km) from the Baltic Sea, Szczecin is a major commercial port and a center of the shipbuilding industry. Originally a Slavic stronghold controlled by the first Polish rulers of the Piast dynasty, it became one of the principal Hanseatic towns and later a Brandenburg, Swedish, and Prussian city. Completely destroyed during World War II, it returned to Poland after 1945. Rebuilt and developed, it reached a population of 413,000 by 1990. In 1970 and 1980 Szczecin was one of the main centers of industrial unrest and strikes. The Inter-Factory Strike Committee led by M. Jurczyk* signed an important Szczecin agreement with the Government Commission headed by K. Barcikowski* on August 30, 1980. G. Sanford and A. Gozdecka-Sanford, *Historical Dictionary of Poland* (Metuchen, N.J., 1994), 199; C. Piskorski, *A Guide to Szczecin and Environs* (Warsaw, 1977); T. Białecki, *Historia Szczecina* (Wrocław, 1992); *Chronik der Stadt Stettin*, ed. by I. Gudden-Luddeke (Leer, 1993).

SZCZEPAŃSKI, JAN (1913–   ), member of the State Council* (Rada Państwa) during 1977–82 and prominent sociology professor. A member of the Polish Academy of Sciences (PAN)* from 1969 and its deputy president during 1972–80, he chaired the Extraordinary Sejm* Committee for Control of Gdańsk,* Szczecin,* and Jastrzębie-Zdrój* Agreements with Solidarity.* *Who's Who in the Socialist Countries of Europe*, ed. by J. Stroynowski, vol. 3 (Munich, 1989), 1163; T. Mołdawa, *Ludzie Władzy 1944–1991. Władze państwowe i polityczne Polski według stanu na dzień 28 II 1991* (Warsaw, 1991), 428.

SZCZEPAŃSKI, MACIEJ (1928–   ), journalist and Party official. After a long career in the Party propaganda apparatus, he headed the Polish Radio and TV* Committee during 1972–80. In 1980 he was expelled from the Polish United Workers' Party (PZPR),* arrested for corruption, and in January 1984 sentenced to eight years in prison. *Who's Who in the Socialist Countries of Europe*, ed. by J. Stroynowski, vol. 3 (Munich, 1989), 1163.

SZCZĘSNA, JOANNA, journalist, dissident,* and member of the Ruch* Movement. She joined the Workers' Defense Committee (KOR)* and co-edited its *Bulletin*. J. J. Lipski, KOR: *A History of the Workers' Defense Committee in Poland, 1976–81* (Berkeley, Calif., 1985), 20, 111, 126.

SZCZYPIORSKI, ANDRZEJ (1924–   ), writer and activist of the Democratic Union (UD).* A soldier of the anti-German resistance during World War II, he worked as a journalist and diplomat after the war. A leader of the Polish PEN Club and author of many books, among them *Msza za miasto Arras* ("Mass for Arras"), he was also active as a liberal publicist and stern critic of the political right. *Who's Who in the Socialist Countries of Europe*, ed. by J. Stroynowski, vol. 3 (Munich, 1989), 1164; *Kto jest kim w polityce polskiej*, ed. by R. Ignasiak (Warsaw, 1993), 279.

SZELACHOWSKI, TADEUSZ (1932–   ), physician, leader of the United Peasant Party (ZSL),* Minister of Health during 1981–85, and Deputy President of the State Council (Rada Państwa)* during 1985–89. T. Mołdawa, *Ludzie Władzy 1944–1991. Władze państwowe i polityczne Polski według stanu na dzień 28 II 1991* (Warsaw, 1991), 428.

SZEREMIETIEW, ROMUALD (1945–   ), Deputy Minister of National Defense in 1992 and activist of several independence organizations since the early 1970s. *Kto jest kim w polityce polskiej*, ed. by R. Ignasiak (Warsaw, 1993), 280.

SZLACHCIC, FRANCISZEK (1920–90), a trusted personal friend of E. Gierek,* Deputy Premier during 1974–76, member of the State Council (Rada Państwa)* during 1972–74, Minister of Internal Affairs during 1971–74, and, in 1971–75, Politburo* member responsible for security, intelligence, foreign affairs, and relations with other communist parties. A Silesian miner, he fought in the communist resistance during World War II and joined the Polish Workers' Party (PPR)* in 1943 and the Citizens' Militia (MO)* in 1945. Later, his entire career was tied to the security. In 1976 Szlachcic was suddenly and unexpectedly eliminated from all his positions and retired as chairman of the Polish Measures and Normalization Committee. Among many interpretations of this vicissitude, the most probable are that he became a victim of internal Party intrigues or that Gierek began to consider him dangerous competition. T. Mołdawa, *Ludzie Władzy 1944–1991. Władze państwowe i polityczne Polski według stanu na dzień 28 II 1991* (Warsaw, 1991), 429; Z. Błażyński, *Towarzysze zeznają. Z tajnych archiwów Komitetu Centralnego* (London, 1987), 77–98.

SZLAJFER, HENRYK (1947–   ), economist and dissident.* He participated in the March events of 1968,* was arrested, and spent a year in prison. In the 1980s he cooperated with the underground *Krytyka* ("The Critique"), and in 1989–90 he worked for the Civic Parliamentary Club (OKP).* H. Szlajfer, *Krajobraz po szoku* (Warsaw, 1989).

SZMAJDZIŃSKI, JERZY A. (1952–   ), leader of communist youth movement, member of the Central Committee* of the Polish United Workers' Party (PZPR)* in 1989–90 and of the Central Executive Committee of the Social

Democracy of the Republic of Poland (SdRP)* during 1990–92. *Who's Who in the Socialist Countries of Europe*, ed. by J. Stroynowski, vol. 3 (Munich, 1989), 1173; *Kto jest kim w polityce polskiej*, ed. by R. Ignasiak (Warsaw, 1993), 280.

SZPOTAŃSKI, JANUSZ (1934–), mathematician, chess player, and poet, wrote an opera, *Cisi i gęgacze* ("The Silent Ones and the Gabbers"), in 1964. The opera was based on the events following the protest known as the "Letter of 34,"* which criticized and ridiculed the Gomułka* regime. Published and recorded many times, the letter became very popular and made Gomułka furious. The author was arrested and sentenced to three years in prison, but he soon wrote his next satirical poem, "Ballada o Łupaszce" ("The Ballad about Łupaszko"). M. Fik, *Kultura polska po Jałcie. Konika lat 1944–1981* (London, 1989), 386, 416, 438.

SZTACHELSKI, JERZY (1911–75), physician and communist official. An activist of the communist youth movement in interwar Poland, he served in the Soviet administration of Vilna during 1939–41 and as a physician in the Red Army* during 1941–43. In 1943 he joined the communist-controlled Polish Army in the USSR, where he belonged among the leaders of the Union of Polish Patriots in the Soviet Union (ZPP). After the war he worked in the communist apparatus in such positions as Minister of Food Supplies during 1945–47, Minister of Health during 1951–56 and 1961–68, and Minister in Charge of State-Church Relations in 1956–61. T. Mołdawa, *Ludzie Władzy 1944–1991. Władze państwowe i polityczne Polski według stanu na dzień 28 II 1991* (Warsaw, 1991), 430.

SZTURM DE SZTREM, TADEUSZ (1892–1968), economist, leading Polish statistician, and activist of the Polish Socialist Party (PPS).* A leader of the clandestine PPS during World War II, he was arrested in 1947 and 1948 by the communist authorities and sentenced to ten years in prison for his independent socialist activities. Amnestied after five years, he worked as an editor. M. Dąbrowska, *Dzienniki powojenne 1945–49*, ed. by T. Drewnowski (Warsaw, 1996), 138; *System represji w Polsce, 1947–1955* (Warsaw, 1987), 191.

SZWALBE, STANISŁAW (1898–96), economist and leader of the Polish Socialist Party (PPS).* A member of the PPS from 1917 and an activist of the Polish cooperative movement during the interwar period, he belonged among the major leaders of the clandestine socialist organizations in German-occupied Poland. In 1943 he helped to established a new group, known as the Workers' Party of the Polish Socialists (Robotnicza Partia Polskich Socjalistów [RPPS]) and began to cooperate with the Polish Workers' Party (PPR).* In 1945 he served as State Secretary in the Presidium of the National Home Council (KRN)* and as director of its presidential office. From May 1945 to February 1947, Szwalbe was KRN Deputy President. An important member of the PPS leadership, he supported "unification" with the PPR and, in December 1948, became a member of the Central Committee* of the newly formed Polish United Workers' Party (PZPR).* During 1947–52 he served as Deputy Speaker of the Sejm* and member of the State Council (Rada Państwa).* Later he returned to the cooperative movement. *Who's Who in the Socialist Countries of Europe*, ed. by J. Stroynowski, vol. 3 (Munich, 1989), 1177; T. Mołdawa, *Ludzie Władzy 1944–1991. Władze państwowe i polityczne Polski według stanu na dzień 28 II 1991* (Warsaw, 1991), 430.

SZYDLAK, JAN (1925–97), Deputy Premier during 1976–80 and Politburo* member. One of three close collaborators of E. Gierek,* Szydlak was in charge of the economic policy of the Polish United Workers' Party (PZPR).* A son of a Silesian miner, he joined the Party in 1945 and worked in its apparatus and youth organizations. In 1954 he was elected to the Party Central Committee* (full member from 1964), and in 1968 to the Politburo (full member from 1970). In the 1950s he served as Party Secretary in Katowice,* and from 1960 to 1968 he was First Secretary of the provincial Party organization in Poznań.* Removed from the Central Committee in October 1980 and from the Party in July 1981, he was declared responsible for mistakes in the economic policy of the Gierek regime. *Who's Who in the Socialist Countries of Europe*, ed. by J. Stroynowski, vol. 3 (Munich, 1989), 1178; T. Mołdawa, *Ludzie Władzy 1944–1991. Władze państwowe i polityczne Polski według stanu na dzień 28 II 1991* (Warsaw, 1991), 430; Z. Błażyński, *Towarzysze zeznają. Z tajnych archiwów Komitetu Centralnego* (London, 1987), 169–185.

SZYFMAN, ARNOLD (1882–1967), theater director and one of the central figures of 20th-century Polish theater history. Szyfman founded and directed several outstanding Polish theaters, among them the Polish Theater, established in 1913 and led by Szyfman until 1957 (with breaks for World War II and Socialist Realism*). In 1945 he directed *Teatr Kameralny* and chaired the Ministry of Culture Theater Department. During 1950–65 he directed the state's reconstruction of the Great Theater in Warsaw.* M. Dąbrowska, *Dzienniki powojenne 1945–49*, ed. by T. Drewnowski (Warsaw, 1996), 72.

SZYMBORSKA, WISŁAWA (1923–   ), one of the best Polish postwar poets and winner of the 1996 Nobel Prize in Literature. She made her debut in 1945. Her early poems reflected a fascination with the new socialist order, but by the 1950s she turned to personal and philosophical reflections on the universal human condition. Her poems, written in a simple yet precise and warm, sometimes ironic and witty way, were translated into many languages. C. Miłosz, *The History of Polish Literature* (Berkeley, Calif., 1983), 485, 534; *Dictionary of Polish Literature*, ed. by E. J. Czerwinski (Westport, Conn., 1994), 403–404; P. Kuncewicz, *Agonia i nadzieja. Poezja polska od 1956*, vol. 3 (Warsaw, 1994), 227–232.

SZYR, EUGENIUSZ (1915–   ), Deputy Premier from October 1959 to March 1972. A member of the Communist Party of Poland (KPP) from 1934, he emigrated to France in 1936 and joined the Communist Party of France in the same year. During 1937–38 he participated in the Civil War in Spain, where he served as a deputy commander and political commissar in the Dąbrowski 13th International Brigade. After years in concentration camps in France and Algeria (1939–43), he moved to the USSR, where he was active in the Union of Polish Patriots (ZPP), joined the Polish Workers' Party (PPR),* and served as a political officer in the Polish People's Army.* After the war he worked in the Party and state apparatus in such positions as Deputy Minister of Industry in 1946–49; deputy chairman and chairman of the State Planning Committee during 1949–56, Minister of Construction in 1956, and Minister of Resources from 1976 to 1981, when he retired. *Who's Who in the Socialist Countries of Europe*, ed. by J. Stroynowski, vol. 3 (Munich, 1989), 1180; T. Mołdawa, *Ludzie Władzy 1944–1991. Władze państwowe i polityczne Polski według stanu na dzień 28 II 1991* (Warsaw, 1991), 431.

Ś

ŚCIBOR-RYLSKI, ALEKSANDER (1928–   ), film director and writer, author of several Social Realist novels. *Encyklopedyczny Słownik Sławnych Polaków* (Warsaw, 1966), 399.

ŚLĄSKA, ALEKSANDRA (1925–89), film and theater actress, best known for her role in *Ostatni etap* ("The Last Stage"). *Nowa Encyklopedia Powszechna PWN*, vol. 6 (Warsaw, 1995), 240.

ŚLISZ, JÓZEF (1934–   ), farmer and leader of Rural Solidarity* in 1980 and the Polish Peasant Party–Solidarity (PSL-Solidarność) since 1992. In 1989 he participated in the Round Table Negotiations,* was elected to the Senate,* and became its Deputy Speaker. G. Sanford and A. Gozdecka-Sanford, *Historical Dictionary of Poland* (Metuchen, N.J., 1994), 188; T. Mołdawa, *Ludzie Władzy 1944–1991. Władze państwowe i polityczne Polski według stanu na dzień 28 II 1991* (Warsaw, 1991), 431.

ŚWIATŁO, JÓZEF (1905–   ), deputy director of the X Department of the Ministry of Public Security, who defected in West Berlin on December 5, 1953, and started cooperating with U.S. intelligence. Światło's was the first defection of this caliber in communist Poland and gave the nation a shock. After long preparations, in September 1954, Radio Free Europe* began to broadcast 140 presentations by Światło in a program entitled *Za kulisami bezpieki i partii* ("Behind the Scenes of the Party and Security Office"). Światło presented more than 30 additional programs. They caused a thorough reorganization of security installations in Poland and had a disastrous effect on the "morale" of Poland's communist cadres and on the efficiency of regime propaganda. Later, brochures with a selection of Światło's revelations were dropped over Poland by balloons. A member of a Zionist communist youth organization and later of the Communist Youth Association, Światło served in the communist First Polish Army* in the USSR and, after the war, was transferred from the military to the Citizens' Militia (MO)* and then, in January 1945, to security. There, he occupied several important positions and participated in crucial operations, such as the arrest of the 16 leaders of the Polish underground state. Promoted to Department X, which spied on Poland's communist leaders, he was trusted by Moscow secret police in Poland. He personally arrested W. Gomułka,* M. Rola-Żymierski,* and Primate S. Wyszyński.* He defected three weeks before the death of Beria and was probably afraid of his future in Poland. In 1954 the X Department was dissolved, and after 1956 its employees became scapegoats accused of the worst Stalinist crimes in Poland. Światło received political asylum in the United States. Z. Błażyński, *Mówi Józef Światło* (London, 1985).

ŚWIDERSKI, JAN (1916–88), outstanding theater actor and director and professor of the State Theater High School (PWST). *Encyklopedyczny Słownik Sławnych Polaków* (Warsaw, 1966), 401.

ŚWIERCZEWSKI KAROL (1897–1947), general and revolutionary. Born in Warsaw,* he was evacuated with a factory staff to Russia in 1915. In 1917, he joined the Bolshevik Red Guard and participated in the revolution in Moscow. A member of the Bolshevik Party from 1918, he led Red Army* units against Denikin in Ukraine during 1918–20. He was a political commissar in a school of Polish revolutionaries in 1921; later, during 1924–27, he studied at Frunze Military Academy. In 1936–38 he fought in Spain, where under the pseudonym General Walter he commanded the 14th International Brigade and later the 35th International Division. From 1941 he served as a commander of a Red Army infantry division. Transferred to the communist-controlled Polish forces in 1943, he served first as deputy commander of their First Corps and then of the First Army. In fall 1944 he began to organize the Second Army, made a forced crossing of the Neisse River, and captured Dresden. A member of the Polish Workers' Party (PPR)* and its Central Committee* from 1944, he became a general inspector of military settlements after the war, was appointed a deputy minister of national defense in February 1946 and, in January 1947, was elected to the Sejm.* He reportedly was "killed by bandits" during operations against the Ukrainian Insurgent Army (UPA)* in southeastern Poland. *The Modern Encyclopedia of Russian and Soviet History*, ed. by J. L. Wieczynski, vol. 43 (Gulf Breeze, Fl., 1984), 141–142; S. L. Wadecka, *Generał Karol Świerczewski "Walter"* (Warsaw, 1976).

ŚWIĘCICKI, MARCIN (1947–   ), economist, member of the Polish United Workers' Party (PZPR)* in 1974–90 and of the Democratic Union (UD)* from 1991, and minister of economic cooperation with foreign countries in the government of T. Mazowiecki* between September 1989 and December 1990. *Kto jest kim w polityce polskiej*, ed. by R. Ignasiak (Warsaw, 1993), 291.

ŚWITOŃ, KAZIMIERZ (1931–   ), electrician and co-founder of free trade unions in Katowice* in 1978. A member of the Movement for the Defense of Human and Civil Rights (ROPCiO),* he participated in numerous hunger strikes and other actions against the communist authorities in Poland. He was also a leader of Silesian Solidarity* and Christian Democracy. He was elected a Sejm* deputy during 1989–93. *Kto jest kim w polityce polskiej*, ed. by R. Ignasiak (Warsaw, 1993), 293.

TATAR, STANISŁAW (1896–1980), general (from 1943) and one of the leaders of the Polish underground state during World War II. An officer in the Russian Army during World War I, he served in various commanding positions in the Polish Army* throughout the entire interwar period, participated in the September Campaign of 1939, and joined the anti-German resistance. In September 1943 he became deputy chief of staff in the Home Army (AK).* Tatar believed that a future Soviet occupation was inevitable and suggested that cooperation with Moscow would be necessary. As a consequence, in April 1944 he was transferred from Poland to London, where he served as a deputy chief of staff of the Polish commander-in-chief in exile. In July 1947 Tatar helped to smuggle to Poland 350 kilograms of gold from the prewar Fund of National Defense. In fall 1947 he returned to Poland and was appointed commander of the 12th Infantry Division. Arrested in 1950 and sentenced to life in prison, he was released from prison and rehabilitated in April 1956. *Słownik Historii Polski 1939–1948*, ed. by A. Chwalba and T. Gąsowski (Cracow, 1994), 213–216: J. Poksiński, "TUN." *Tatar—Utnik—Nowicki* (Warsaw, 1992).

TATARKIEWICZ, WŁADYSŁAW (1886–1980), philosopher, historian of philosophy and art, specialized in esthetics, ethics, and pedagogy. A member of many Polish and international scholarly organizations, including the Polish Academy of Sciences (PAN),* he taught at several universities, was an extraordinarily prolific writer, and significantly influenced the development of social sciences in 20th-century Poland. *Encyklopedyczny Słownik Sławnych Polaków* (Warsaw, 1996), 406.

TATARS, one of the smallest national minorities* in post-1945 Poland. The Tatars began to settle in the territories of Lithuania and Poland at the beginning of the 15th century. Most of their settlements were located in the eastern areas of the Polish-Lithuanian Commonwealth; after Poland's Partitions, they found themselves within the borders of Russia. During 1918–39 about 5,400 Tatars lived in Poland, mostly in the provinces of Białystok,* Nowogródek (Navahrudak), and Vilna. After 1945 only a small segment of the Tatarian community remained in Poland; today that population is shrinking as a result of Polonization and Belorussification. In 1985 the Moslem Religious Association, established by the Tatars before the war as their informal representation, had about 2,000 members. S. M. Horak, *Eastern European National Minorities, 1919–1980: A Handbook* (Littleton, Colo., 1985), 59; P. Borowski and A. Dubiński, *Tatarzy polscy* (Warsaw, 1986).

"TATERNICY." See **"Tatra Mountaineers."**

"TATRA MOUNTAINEERS," group of young people, among them the sociologist J. Karpiński* and the songwriter Jan Kelus, who in collaboration with their Czech friends organized the smuggling of copies of the Paris *Kultura** into Poland through Czechoslovakia and across the Tatra Mountains. They were arrested and sentenced in 1969, but by then had created a milieu that later contributed significantly to the Polish democratic opposition.* J. J. Lipski, *KOR: A History of the Workers' Defense Committee in Poland, 1976–81* (Berkeley, Calif., 1985), 20.

TAZBIR, JANUSZ (1927–   ), historian, member of several prestigious Polish and international scholarly associations, including the Polish Academy of Sciences (PAN),* and prolific author of such books as *A State without Stakes* and *Polish Religious Tolerance in the 16th and 17th Centuries. Who's Who in the Socialist Countries of Europe*, ed. by J. Stroynowski, vol. 3 (Munich, 1989), 1191.

"TECHNOCRATS," "enlightened" faction within the Polish United Workers' Party (PZPR)* formed in the 1960s and led by E. Gierek.* The faction supported the modernization of Poland, its opening to the West, and relative political relaxation. Concentrated mainly in Upper Silesia, where its leader occupied the post of provincial Party organization First Secretary, the "technocrats" fought against the faction of M. Moczar* and were increasingly popular during the last years of the Gomułka period.* A. Bromke, *Poland: The Protracted Crisis* (Oakville, Ont., 1983); J. Woodall, *The Socialist Corporation and Technocratic Power: The Polish United Workers' Party, Industrial Organization and Workforce Control, 1958–80* (Cambridge, 1982).

TEJCHMA, JÓZEF (1927–   ), Deputy Premier during 1972–79, Minister of Culture during 1974–78 and 1980–82, and Minister of Education in 1979–80. Born to a peasant family, he became a leader of the communist-sponsored youth movement and joined the Polish United Workers' Party (PZPR)* in 1952. After years of work in the Party-state apparatus, he was elected to the Party Central

Committee* in 1964. As a minister and Deputy Premier he was considered by many to be more liberal than his colleagues. He also served as Polish ambassador to Switzerland in 1980 and to Greece during 1984–88. *Who's Who in the Socialist Countries of Europe*, ed. by J. Stroynowski, vol. 3 (Munich, 1989), 1192; T. Mołdawa, *Ludzie Władzy 1944–1991. Władze państwowe i polityczne Polski według stanu na dzień 28 II 1991* (Warsaw, 1991), 433; G. Sanford and A. Gozdecka-Sanford, *Historical Dictionary of Poland* (Metuchen, N.J., 1994), 200.

TELEVISION. An element of Western popular culture, television played an important role in the communist system of information and propaganda. Television programs were strictly controlled and carefully planned by the communist authorities. The Roman Catholic Church* and political opposition fought for access to television but failed to gain it until the fall of communism. In 1954 the Experimental TV Center (Doświadczalny Ośrodek Telewizyjny) began to work in Warsaw.* Starting in 1956 a TV program about five hours long was broadcast five days a week in Warsaw and its region. In 1960 about 500,000 people in central Poland could watch TV: by 1981 about 8 million. In the early 1960s, provincial TV stations began to operate; in 1970 a second TV appeared, and in 1971 color TV made its debut. Broadcast were movies, entertainment, and educational programs, but TV's role in ideological indoctrination was crucial to the authorities. Everyday news was given a specific interpretation of contemporary and historical events in Poland and abroad. In some institutions, such as the Polish Army,* watching news was obligatory. During Martial Law* Polish actors and popular journalists tried to boycott TV. After the fall of communism, the governmental TV monopoly was broken and several independent TV stations appeared, which led to visible deterioration of state-owned public TV. J. Karpiński, *Polska, Komunizm, Opozycja* (London, 1985), 273.

TERLECKI, OLGIERD (1922–   ), veteran of the Battle of Monte Cassino, writer, and historian, who wrote extensively on World War II and contemporary history of Poland. *Who's Who in the Socialist Countries of Europe*, ed. by J. Stroynowski, vol. 3 (Munich, 1989), 1194; *Encyklopedyczny Słownik Sławnych Polaków* (Warsaw, 1996), 407.

TESCHEN. See **Cieszyn.**

"THAW," term usually applied to the period of political relaxation and liberalization in communist countries after the death of J. Stalin. In Poland the "thaw" came to an end soon after the "Polish October" of 1956,* in 1957. The term is derived from the title of Ilya G. Ehrenburg's novel *Otepel* ("The Thaw"), written shortly after Stalin's death and published in 1954. B. P. McCrea, J. C. Plano, and G. Klein, *The Soviet and East European Dictionary* (Oxford, 1984), 305.

TISCHNER, JÓZEF (1931–   ), priest, popular writer and essayist in *Tygodnik Powszechny* ("The Universal Weekly")* in Cracow,* and professor of philosophy. Considered one of the most liberal and sophisticated priests in Poland and a friend of many liberal dissidents,* such as A. Michnik,* Tischner has both numerous enthusiasts and numerous enemies. *Who's Who in the Socialist Countries of Europe*, ed. by J. Stroynowski, vol. 3 (Munich, 1989), 1201; G. Polak, *Kto jest kim w Kościele katolickim* (Warsaw, 1996), 380; A. Michnik, J. Tischner, and J. Żakowski, *Między Panem a Plebanem* (Cracow, 1995).

TOEPLITZ, KRZYSZTOF TEODOR (1933–   ), journalist and writer, literary manager of several state film production enterprises. From 1981 he served as an adviser to Gen. W. Jaruzelski.* *Who's Who in the Socialist Countries of Europe*, ed. by J. Stroynowski, vol. 3 (Munich, 1989), 1205.

TOKARCZUK, IGNACY MARCIN (1918–   ), Archbishop since 1992, bishop of Przemyśl from 1965, professor of theology at the Catholic University of Lublin (KUL).* Ordained in 1942, he is one of the leaders of the Roman Catholic Church* who defended it in the worst of the Stalinist period.* *Who's Who in the Socialist Countries of Europe*, ed. by J. Stroynowski, vol. 3 (Munich, 1989), 1205; G. Polak, *Kto jest kim w Kościele katolickim* (Warsaw, 1996), 381.

TOMASZEWSKI, BOGDAN (1921–   ), outstanding sports journalist and businessman. *Encyklopedyczny Słownik Sławnych Polaków* (Warsaw, 1996), 410.

TOMASZEWSKI, HENRYK (1914–   ), poster and stage designer, professor at Warsaw's Academy of Fine Arts, and graphic artist. He gained international renown. *Who's Who in the Socialist Countries of Europe*, ed. by J. Stroynowski, vol. 3 (Munich, 1989), 1208; *Encyklopedyczny Słownik Sławnych Polaków* (Warsaw, 1996), 410.

TOPOLSKI, JERZY (1928–   ), historian, professor at Poznań University,* member of the Polish Academy of Sciences (PAN),* and specialist in methodology and on the history of Poland. *Who's Who in the Socialist Countries of Europe*, ed. by J. Stroynowski, vol. 3 (Munich, 1989), 1212.

TORUŃ, city of 202,000 inhabitants in central Poland, capital of a province, and a tourist attraction because of its long history and medieval architecture. A seat of the renowned Nicholas Copernicus University, Toruń is also a center of the chemical, machine, and food industries. G. Sanford and A. Gozdecka-Sanford, *Historical Dictionary of Poland* (Metuchen, N.J., 1994), 200; *The New Encyclopaedia Britannica*, vol. 11 (Chicago, 1990), 861; *Thorn: Königin der Weichsel, 1291–1981*, ed. by B. Jahning and P. Letkemann (Göttingen, 1981); *Toruń dawny i dzisiejszy: zarys dziejów*, ed. by M. Biskup (Warsaw, 1983).

TORUŃCZYK, BARBARA, sociologist and activist of the Workers' Defense Committee (KOR)* and editor of its *Bulletin.* J. J. Lipski, *KOR: A History of the Workers' Defense Committee in Poland, 1976–81* (Berkeley, Calif., 1985), 163, 168, 314.

TOURISM, initially neglected, but since the 1970s an increasingly important branch of the Polish economy* and recreation. Although Poland offers numerous spectacular tourist attractions, its tourist infrastructure is less impressive than that of Western Europe. A few international hotels were erected in Poland in the 1970s. The number of Western tourists to Poland peaked in 1980, then decreased in 1981 and declined very sharply during Martial Law* in 1982. In 1983 and 1984 visitors began to return, but after the Chernobyl catastrophe, the number of foreign tourists declined once again. After the fall of communism in 1989, tourism began to develop quickly. In 1990 about 18 million people, mostly from Germany, Czechoslovakia, and the former USSR, visited Poland. In 1994 this number grew to over 74 million. Integration of Poland with the European Community* opens new opportunities in this field. *Poland: Country Profile, 1989–1990,* ed. by The Economist Intelligence Unit (London, 1990), 29.

TOWARZYSTWO KURSÓW NAUKOWYCH. See **Association of Scientific Courses.**

TRADE UNIONS. Trade union activities have a long tradition in Poland, where unions have existed since the end of the 19th century. During the interwar period over 1,000 union branches were active in Poland. This activity was interrupted by World War II but resumed in July 1944 in the territories taken from the Germans by the Red Army.* During the Lublin* congress of November 1944, a Provisional Central Commission of Trade Unions was formed as the executive of the Trade Unions Federation (Zrzeszenie Związków Zawodowych [ZZZ]). Beginning in 1947, all unions active in Poland had to belong to the ZZZ, whose executive organ was named the Central Council of Trade Unions (Centralna Rada Związków Zawodowych [CRZZ])* in 1949. Unions—a ''transmission belt'' between the Party and the workers—were committed to building socialism in Poland under Party leadership. The unions were totally controlled by *nomenklatura,* overburdened with administrative and auxiliary functions, and unable to negotiate collective labor agreements, which were one-sidedly and authoritatively regulated by the regime. During de-Stalinization, in fall 1956, Workers' Councils (Rady Robotnicze) were established; an act of December 1958 instituted workers' self-government. Yet the councils and the unions were still subjugated to the Party, since all the unions belonged to, and were supervised by, the CRZZ chaired by Politburo* members. Unions were unable to stop deterioration of workers' living conditions* and growth of their frustration. By the 1970s unions became practically irrelevant. Then in 1980 the CRZZ lost about 85%–90% of its members to Solidarity* and dissolved itself in October of that year. It was replaced by the Coordinating Commission of Branch Trade Unions (Komisja Porozumiewawcza Branżowych Związków Zawodowych), which never gained any real importance and was dissolved by a Martial Law* law passed by the Sejm* on October 8, 1982. The law also banned the Independent Self-Managing Trade Union Solidarity (NSZZ "Solidarność") established in September 1980. Solidarity gained the right to organize strikes and free trade unions; together with Rural Solidarity,* it soon gathered some 10 million members—most adult citizens of Poland. After imposition of Martial Law, Solidarity was suspended and, on October 8, 1982, dissolved by the Sejm. The Jaruzelski* regime replaced Solidarity and the old trade unions with the All-Poland Alliance of Trade Unions (Ogólnopolskie Porozumienie Związków Zawodowych [OPZZ]* formed in November 1984. It developed considerably, survived the fall of communism, and with its 5 million members, in June 1990 joined the Democratic Left Alliance (SLD).* In the meantime a decision had been made during the Round Table Negotiations* to make Solidarity legal again. On April 17, 1989, it was re-registered, but soon the "war at the top"* and the elitist policies of the Mazowiecki* government divided Solidarity into several parties. Whereas in October 1990 Solidarity had 2.3 million members, that number declined to 1.6 million in summer 1993. In 1990 L. Wałęsa* was elected President* of Poland, replaced as the Solidarity chairman by M. Krzaklewski.* During the October 1991 elections* Solidarity gained 5% of the vote, which meant 27 seats in the Sejm* and 11 in the Senate.* Solidarity was supported by Rural Solidarity, re-established in April 1989, and gathered about 300,000 members in December 1990. After imposition of Martial Law, a very radical and anti-communist Solidarity faction transformed itself into "Solidarity 80," which survived into the post-communist period. J. Campbell, *European Trade Unions* (Westport, Conn., 1992), 343–350; G. Sanford and A. Gozdecka-Sanford, *Historical Dictionary of Poland* (Metuchen, N.J., 1994), 201.

TRIAL OF THE SIXTEEN, political trial against 16 leaders of the Polish World War II resistance on June 18–21, 1945, in Moscow, organized to discredit and weaken the Polish underground state, which was led by the Government-in-Exile.* The trial was intended to prepare a situation convenient for the installation of left-oriented, Soviet-sponsored authorities in Poland. The time of the trial coincided with the Moscow negotiations that led to the creation of the Provisional Government of National Unity.* In March 1945 the leadership of the Polish secret state was invited by the Soviets through an intermediary to a meeting to discuss the question of emerging from the underground. The Poles hesitated, but they realized that they had been identified by the NKVD. In addition, they were told that if they refused, the Soviets would negotiate with someone else. After they received a promise of inviolability, the 16 leaders met "General Ivanow," in reality the NKVD Gen. Ivan Serov, in a local NKVD headquarters in Pruszków on March 27, 1947. There, they were arrested and abducted to Moscow. After long interrogations (these documents were collected in 36 thick volumes), the indictment was ready on June 14, 1945. It stated that the Home Army (AK)* and its successor organization Nie* formed guerrilla units operating behind the German-Russian front against the Red Army and were involved with the Germans in the preparation of an anti-Soviet uprising. The trial was well prepared and took place in the House of the Soviets in Moscow, where the great political trials of the 1930s had been organized. The Poles were accused by Prosecutor General Vasili Ulrich, who had been in charge of the trials against Zinovev, Pyatakov, Bukharin, and others. Some British and U.S. diplomats and journalists were allowed to watch the trial, for the Soviets wanted to demonstrate their "good will." The grotesque trial ended with "liberal" sentences: The commander of the armed forces in Poland, Gen. L. Okulicki,* was sentenced to ten years in prison; Deputy Premier of the Government-in-Exile and its delegate to Poland J. S. Jankowski, to eight years; members of the Home Council of Ministers A. Bień,* S. Jasiukowicz, and A. Pajdak,* to five years; the chairman of the Council of National Unity, K. Pużak,* to eighteen months; leaders of the Peasant Party K. Bagiński* and S. Mierzwa to one year to four months, respectively; leaders of the National Party Z. Stypułkowski and A. Zwierzyński to four months to eight months, respectively; J. Chaciński and F. Urbański from the Labor Party* to four months; E. Czarnowski from the Democratic Party* to six months. K. Kobylański from the National Party, S. Michałowski from the Democratic Party, and their translator, J. Stemler-Dąbski, were found not guilty. Jasiukowicz, Okulicki, and Jankowski died in Soviet prisons. In October 1989 the Prosecutor General of the Republic of Poland asked the Soviet authorities to start a rehabilitation procedure, and in April 1990 the Soviet Supreme Court rehabilitated all 16 leaders. Z. Stypułkowski, *Invitation to Moscow* (London, 1951); K. Kersten, *The Establishment of Communist Rule in Poland, 1943–1948* (Berkeley, Calif., 1991), 134, 153; A. Chmielarz and A. K. Kunert, *Sprawa 16-tu. Protokoły przesłuchań gen. Leopolda Okulickiego i współoskarżonych* (Warsaw, 1993); *Proces szesnastu. Dokumenty NKVD*, ed. by A. Chmielarz and A. K. Kunert (Warsaw, 1995).

TRYBUNA ("The Tribune"), everyday newspaper and organ of the Social Democracy of the Republic of Poland (SdRP)* published as a continuation of *Trybuna Ludu* ("The Tribune of the People"),* the organ of the Polish United Workers' Party (PZPR).* *Trybuna* has appeared since January 1990, when the PZPR ceased to exist and was replaced by the SdPR. H. Palska, "Stylistyka Przemiany. *O Trybunie* w początkach 1990 r." *Kultura i Społeczeństwo*, vol. II, no. 2, pp. 183–194.

TRYBUNA LUDU ("The Tribune of the People"), organ of the Central Committee* of the Polish United Workers' Party (PZPR).* Its first issue appeared on December 16, 1948, when, after the unification of the Polish Workers' Party (PPR)* and the Polish Socialist Party (PPS),* their organs, *Głos Ludu* ("The Voice of the People") and *Robotnik* ("The Worker"),* respectively, were merged into one new newspaper. In 1984 *Trybuna Ludu* published 700,000 copies daily. The paper presented the official policy of the ruling Party and was edited in a rather dull way. J. Karpiński, *Polska, Komunizm, Opozycja* (London, 1985), 276.

TRZECIAKOWSKI, WITOLD M. (1926–   ), professor of economics at Łódź University (1969–80) and at the Polish Academy of Sciences (PAN).* A veteran of the Home Army (AK),* he joined Solidarity,* served as its adviser, and participated in the Round Table Negotiations.* Minister without Portfolio in the Mazowiecki* government (August 1989–December 1990), a chairman of its Economic Committee, and a senator (1989–93), he returned to scholarly work at PAN after 1993. *Życie Gospodarcze*, Nov. 29, 1996.

TURLEJSKA, MARIA (1918–   ), historian and expert on the contemporary history of Poland. After World War II she directed the Department of the History of the Party by the Central Committee* of the Polish Workers' Party (PPR).* In 1955 she was expelled from the Party, and from 1978 she helped to publish the underground periodical *Krytyka* ("The Critique").* She has authored several important books on Polish history. P. S. Wandycz, "Historiography of the Countries of Eastern Europe: Poland," *American Historical Review*, Oct. 1992, pp. 1011–1025; *Nowa Encyklopedia Powszechma PWN*, vol. 6 (Warsaw, 1995), 501.

TUROWICZ, JERZY (1912–   ), editor-in-chief of the most important and prestigious periodical of lay Catholics in Poland, *Tygodnik Powszechny* ("The Universal Weekly"),* in 1945–53 and from 1956. In 1953, after the death of J. Stalin, Turowicz refused to publish a special obituary devoted to the Soviet dictator. As a consequence, the communist authorities took *Tygodnik Powszechny* from him and gave it to PAX Association.* An expert on Western Catholicism, Turowicz supported changes introduced by the Second Vatican Council. A member of the Commission of the Polish Episcopate* for Dialogue with Judaism, he was also a co-founder of the Clubs of Catholic Intelligentsia* in Cracow* and Warsaw,* the President of the publishing institute Znak ("The Sign"),* during 1960–90, and a leader of the Democratic Union (UD)* in 1991–93. *Who's Who in the Socialist Countries of Europe*, ed. by J. Stroynowski, vol. 3 (Munich, 1989), 1228; G. Polak, *Kto jest kim w Kościele katolickim* (Warsaw, 1996), 385; A. Micewski, *Ludzie i opcje* (Warsaw, 1993), 34–38.

TURSKI, STANISŁAW (1906–86), mathematician and professor at several Polish universities. Between 1952 and 1969 he served as rector of Warsaw University* and tried to defend its students against the brutal police assault during the March events of 1968.* *Who's Who in the Socialist Countries of Europe*, ed. by J. Stroynowski, vol. 3 (Munich, 1989), 1229.

TUSK, DONALD (1957–   ), historian, journalist, and politician. An activist of Solidarity* and the Independent Students' Union (NZS)* in Gdańsk* in 1980,

he joined the anti-communist underground after imposition of Martial Law,*
became a member of L. Wałęsa's* Civic Committee, and helped to organize
and beginning in 1991 presided over the Liberal Democratic Congress (KLD).*
Kto jest kim w polityce polskiej, ed. by R. Ignasiak (Warsaw, 1993), 300.

TUWIM, JULIAN (1894–1953), outstanding poet of interwar Poland, translator, and author of delightful poems for children. Born to a middle-class Jewish
family in Łódź,* he was a co-founder and chief representative of the Skamander
poetic group in the 1920s. He also contributed to several cultural and satirical
magazines and various cabarets before World War II. After its outbreak he left
for Romania, France, South America, and eventually the United States, where
he worked for the Polish émigré press and wrote his great book in verse, *Kwiaty
Polskie* ("Polish Flowers"). In 1946 he returned to Poland, joined a pro-
communist literary milieu, and became a celebrity, but he wrote nothing else of
value. *Dictionary of Polish Literature*, ed. by E. J. Czerwinski (Westport, Conn., 1994),
410–412; C. Miłosz, *The History of Polish Literature* (Berkeley, Calif., 1983), 387–389.

TWARDOWSKI, JAN (1915–   ), priest and poet, veteran of the Home Army
(AK)* and the 1944 Warsaw Uprising. *Dictionary of Polish Literature*, ed. by E. J.
Czerwinski (Westport, Conn., 1994), 412; *Encyklopedyczny Słownik Sławnych Polaków*
(Warsaw, 1996), 416; *Nowe Książki*, no. 12 (Warsaw, 1996).

TYGODNIK MAZOWSZE ("The Mazovia Weekly"), underground organ of
Solidarity,* Mazowsze (Mazovia) Region, initially printed by NOWa* Publishing House. Its first issue appeared on February 11, 1982. Soon the weekly
became an all-Polish organ of the central Solidarity leadership. *Tygodnik Mazowsze* published official Solidarity documents and announcements, essays, de-
bates, and news. Its last issue appeared on April 12, 1989. J. Karpiński, *Polska,
Komunizm, Opozycja* (London, 1985), 277; D. Cecuda, *Leksykon opozycji politycznej
1976–1989* (Warsaw, 1989), 194.

TYGODNIK POWSZECHNY ("The Universal Weekly"), prestigious Catholic
weekly devoted to social and cultural issues, published in Cracow* since March
24, 1945. Since October 30, 1945, J. Turowicz* has been serving as its editor-in-
chief, although the authorities suspended *Tygodnik Powszechny* in March 1953,
when its editorial staff refused to publish a large and hagiographic obituary of
J. Stalin. This came as a good pretext, because the authorities had for some time
been irritated by the independent character of the weekly. In June 1953 its
publishing facilities were given to the government-sponsored PAX Association,*
which published its own version of *Tygodnik Powszechny*. On December 25,
1956, the weekly was returned to its original staff and continued its traditional
policy. After imposition of Martial Law* on December 13, 1981, the weekly
was suspended again, this time together with almost all other Polish newspapers
and periodicals. Its first issue after this break appeared on May 23, 1982. *Ty-*

godnik Powszechny has been close to the Znak* group; as a consequence, it has been criticized both by the political left and by the Catholic-nationalistic right. In 1995 it was published in 37,000 copies. J. Karpiński, *Polska, Komunizm, Opozycja* (London, 1985), 278.

TYGODNIK SOLIDARNOŚĆ ("The Solidarity Weekly"), the most important periodical of Solidarity* published between March 31 and December 11, 1981, and re-established in 1989. In 1981 the weekly sold 500,000 copies; during the September 1981 Solidarity congress, 1 million copies. *Tygodnik Solidarność* gathered around it a group of outstanding journalists: T. Mazowiecki* served as its editor-in-chief; B. Cywiński* and W. Kuczyński* were his deputies. Partially beyond the reach of censorship,* the periodical published official Solidarity documents and announcements, news, and essays, among which were numerous articles on the contemporary history of Poland devoted to important themes previously forbidden by censorship. After 1989 the weekly became less important. It became involved in the "war at the top,"* assumed a partial character, and bitterly criticized the enemies of L. Wałęsa.* J. Karpiński, *Polska, Komunizm, Opozycja* (London, 1985), 278.

TYGODNIK WARSZAWSKI ("The Warsaw Weekly"), Catholic weekly published in Warsaw* during 1945–48 by Warsaw's archbishopric. The weekly was far from enthusiastic toward the new political system in Poland; as a consequence, the authorities arrested several of its editors and collaborators and disbanded the periodical. J. Karpiński, *Polska, Komunizm, Opozycja* (London, 1985), 279.

TYMIŃSKI, STANISŁAW (1948–), maverick politician. He emigrated from Poland to Canada and Peru in 1969 and started successful enterprises there. In 1990 he owned a small computer systems company in Canada and a cable TV company in Peru. He held Canadian and Peruvian citizenships in addition to his Polish citizenship. He was the head of the Libertarian Party of Canada, which had about 3,500 members, but did not manage to elect anyone to a major public office. During the presidential campaign of 1990,* Tymiński appeared in Poland purportedly to promote his self-financed autobiography, *Sacred Dogs*; however, he entered the political competition. His financial resources enabled him to create an image of himself as a rich self-made man able to overcome any difficulty. He promised to use his business skills to bring quick and widespread prosperity—a "democracy of money." He accused Premier T. Mazowiecki* and his government of "betraying the nation" by selling Polish industry to foreigners at bargain prices. A large part of the electorate, frustrated and tired with the transition period in Poland, voted for Tymiński, who came in second with 23.1% of the vote, eliminating Premier Mazowiecki. In the runoff Tymiński lost to L. Wałęsa.* Tymiński then organized his own "Party X,"* which managed to win three seats during the elections of 1993.* G. Sanford and A. Gozdecka-Sanford,

Historical Dictionary of Poland (Metuchen, N.J., 1994), 203; *Kto jest kim w polityce polskiej*, ed. by R. Ignasiak (Warsaw, 1993), 302; *Facts on File*, Nov. 30, 1990, p. 895.

TYRMAND, LEOPOLD (1920–85), writer, journalist, and music critic. He spent World War II in Vilna and Germany. In 1946 he returned to Poland and started a journalism career. Harassed by communists, he became one of the most spectacular dissidents.* He described his experiences in his famous *Dziennik 1954* ("The 1954 Diary"). In 1965 he left Poland and settled in the United States, where he became associated with the neoconservative movement and published in U.S. and Polish émigré periodicals. *Dictionary of Polish Literature*, ed. by E. J. Czerwinski (Westport, Conn., 1994), 413–415; J. Zieliński, *Leksykon polskiej literatury emigracyjnej* (Lublin, 1989), 128–129; L. Tyrmand, *Dziennik 1954, wersja oryginalna*, introduction by H. Dasko (Warsaw, 1995), 5–39.

UB (Urząd Bezpieczeństwa). See **Security Service.**

UJAZDOWSKI, KAZIMIERZ MICHAŁ (1964–), secretary general of the Forum of Democratic Right in 1990, leader of the Democratic Union (UD)* in 1991, co-organizer of the Conservative Party (PK)* in 1992 and of the Conservative Coalition (KK)* in 1994. *Kto jest kim w polityce polskiej*, ed. by R. Ignasiak (Warsaw, 1993), 303; *Polskie partie polityczne*, ed. by K. A. Paszkiewicz (Warsaw, 1996), 37–42.

UKRAINIAN INSURGENT ARMY (Ukrainska Povstanska Armiia [UPA]), Ukrainian guerrilla organization active in Volhynia, eastern Galicia, and the Carpathian Mountains in 1943–54. Its first units appeared in Volhynia in 1942. After the unification of 1943, the UPA fought as one, centrally commanded underground army, supervised by the Ukrainian Supreme Liberation Council from July 1944. To establish an independent Ukrainian state, which was its main goal, the UPA fought against the Germans, the Soviets, the Polish population of Volhynia and, to a lesser extent of eastern Galicia. First, the UPA attacked Red Army* units dispersed over western Ukraine after the 1941 German aggression. Then, the UPA tried to eject Soviet guerrillas operating there and organized actions against the Germans. In spring 1943 the UPA turned against the Poles of Volhynia and exterminated thousands of them during a cruel ethnic cleansing. When the UPA reached its zenith, in 1944, and had about 40,000 soldiers, it began to fight with the Red Army, entering western Ukraine. In late 1944 and in 1945, the NKVD started large military operations against the UPA. In spring 1946 its Supreme Command decided to demobilize most of its units. The demobilization order did not apply to the UPA San (Sian) Division—the units operating in the Ukrainian ethnic territories of the postwar southeastern Poland; they were ordered to defend the Ukrainian population from deportations to the USSR. The UPA reached an understanding with Polish anti-communist guerrillas in those territories and organized several successful actions against the Polish communist authorities. On March 28, 1947, a Polish Deputy Minister of Defense, Gen. K. Świerczewski,* was killed in a UPA ambush. The Polish authorities answered with Action Wisła* and deported about 140,000 Ukrainians from southeastern to northwestern Poland. Some UPA units managed to escape to the West, however. The last UPA groups fought in the USSR until 1954. *Encyclopedia of Ukraine,* vol. 5, ed. by D. Husar Struk (Toronto, 1993), 392–395; *Nowa Encyklopedia Powszechna PWN,* vol. 6 (Warsaw, 1996), 545; A. B. Szczęśniak and W. Z. Szota, *Droga do nikąd: Działalność Organizacji Ukraińskich Nacjonalistów i jej likwidacja w Polsce* (Warsaw, 1973); R. Torzecki, *Polacy i Ukraińcy. Sprawa ukraińska w czasie II wojny światowej na terenie II Rzeczpospolitej* (Warsaw, 1993).

UKRAINIANS, largest or second-largest national minority in Poland, with 300,000 to 400,000 people. Before World War II over 5 million Ukrainians lived in Poland; they comprised over 15% of all Polish citizens. During the war a number of Ukrainians moved to Poland from prewar Soviet-controlled Ukrainian territories; sizeable Ukrainian communities appeared in such cities as Warsaw* and Cracow.* Most Ukrainians left for the West before the Red Army* occupied central Poland. Most prewar Polish Ukrainians found themselves within Soviet borders when the prewar Polish Eastern Borderlands (*Kresy wschodnie*) were incorporated into the Soviet Union. In addition, about 500,000 Ukrainians from post-1945 southeastern Poland were ''repatriated'' to the Soviet Union as part of the Polish-Soviet postwar exchange of population. Yet a substantial Ukrainian minority—in some regions actually a majority—remained in the eastern and southern parts of Lublin* Province, in the Przemyśl (Peremyshl) and San (Sian) regions, and in the Carpathians in the Lemko* region. Most of this population was deported from its native territories during the Action Wisła* in April–July 1947. The deportees were divided into small groups and scattered throughout the northern and western ''Recovered Territories,''* where they were mixed with the Polish population in order to Polonize them. Not recognized as a national minority, they were not allowed to organize. In 1956, after political liberalization in Poland, the Ukrainians were allowed to establish the Ukrainian Social and Cultural Society (Ukraińskie Towarzystwo Społeczno-Kulturalne). In 1957–58 about 11,000 Ukrainians requested permission to return to their native regions, but only less than 3,000 (mostly Lemkos) managed to resettle, although their native territories remained sparsely settled or depopulated. At present, between 50,000 and 60,000 Ukrainians live in Olsztyn* Province, about 30,000 in Koszalin Province, 20,000 in Wrocław* Province, 10,000 in Szczecin* Province, and almost 10,000 in Zielona Góra Province. About 20,000 Ukrainians lived throughout the communist period in their native regions of Zamość, Chełm* (Kholm), and Włodawa (Volodova). Now, about 90% of Ukrainians live in the countryside. After the fall of communism in Poland in 1989, a revival of Ukrainian political and cultural life started, although new conflicts also appeared, especially in the ethnically mixed Polish-Ukrainian regions of southeastern Poland. *Encyclopedia of Ukraine*, vol. 4, ed. by D. Husar Struk (Toronto, 1993), 81–84; J. Bugajski, *Ethnic Politics in Eastern Europe: A Guide to Nationality Policies, Organizations, and Parties* (Armonk, N.Y., 1994), 359–395; S. M. Horak, *Eastern European Minorities, 1919–1980: A Handbook* (Littleton, Colo., 1985), 57; M. Truhan, *Ukraintsi v Pol'shchi pislia druhoi svitivoi viyni* (New York, 1990); M. Czech, "Kwestia ukraińska w III Rzeczpospolitej," *Zeszyty Historyczne*, no. 103 (Paris, 1993); *Nowa Encyklopedia Powszechna PWN*, vol. 6 (Warsaw, 1996), 543–545; K. Podlaski, *Białorusini, Litwini, Ukraińcy* (London, 1985).

UNDERGROUND. See Opposition.

UNDERGROUND PUBLICATIONS. Poland's system of underground publishing institutions constituted an important part of the political opposition.* Uncensored publications were first issued under the auspices of the Workers' Defense Committee (KOR)* in 1976. Soon KOR publications included such well-known titles as *Robotnik* ("The Worker"),* *Głos* ("The Voice"),* and *Krytyka* ("The Critique").* Other opposition groups followed KOR, and in August 1980 thirty-five publishing houses worked in the underground. After the Gdańsk Agreement* this number increased to 160. Between 1981 and 1986 about 25,000 issues of various periodicals were published underground. Such independent publishing houses as CDN,* Oficyna Literacka (Literary Publishing House), and the Student Publishing House of Cracow (Krakowska Oficyna Studentów [KOS]), also published novels, textbooks, and scholarly works. Underground publishing houses existed in every large town. Even national minorities* had their own clandestine publishing institutions. The Party monopoly of information was broken. *Dictionary of Polish Literature*, ed. by E. J. Czerwinski (Westport, Conn., 1994), 83–102; *Polish Dissident Publications: An Annotated Bibliography*, ed. by J. M. Preibisz (New York, 1982); D. Cecuda, *Leksykon opozycji politycznej 1976– 1989* (Warsaw, 1989).

UNEMPLOYMENT. Unemployment appeared in Poland, together with industrialization, by the end of the 19th century. During the interwar period of 1918– 39 and particularly during the Great Depression in Poland in 1929–34, unemployment was among the worst problems of the Polish economy. Under communism, unemployment did not exist in Poland, at least not in the form known in the capitalist economies. As in other centrally planned economies, labor in Poland was in short supply as a result of various policies. Wages and the general standard of living were low. A relatively large segment of the productive population served in the Polish Army,* police, and other divisions of the state apparatus. Bureaucracy was heavily overstaffed, and enterprise managers usually hoarded labor as a safeguard to meet unexpected increases. All these factors contributed to so-called hidden unemployment, which became visible after the fall of communism and the beginning of Poland's economic transformation in 1989–90. In 1990 the unemployment rate amounted to 6.3% of people of active working age. In 1994 it reached 16%, or about 3 million persons. In 1995 it fell to 14.9%, or about 2.6 million. *Poland: Country Profile 1989–90*, ed. by The Economist Intelligence Unit (London, 1990), 18; *Poland, 1996: The Economic Situation*, ed. by Embassy of the Republic of Poland to Canada (Ottawa, 1996), 8; *Facts on File*, July 13, 1990, p. 518; Oct. 19, p. 781; Nov. 30, p. 895.

UNIFICATION CONGRESS OF 1948, joint congress of the Polish Workers' Party (PPR)* and the Polish Socialist Party (PPS)* held December 15–21, 1948, in the main hall of Warsaw Politechnical University. The congress was attended by over 1,500 delegates. Nearly two-thirds of delegates represented about 1.0 million members of the PPR, and less than one-third represented about 0.5 million PPS members. This proportion reflected the composition of the Politburo* of the newly created Polish United Workers' Party (PZPR)*—eight out of eleven members of the PZPR Politburo previously belonged to the PPR. The Unification Congress was preceded by long preparations. Many PPS activists were against unification, which meant domination by the communists and establishment of the Soviet system in Poland. Opponents of unification were harassed by the secret police and administration, were forced to leave Poland, or were intimidated. The 28th Congress of the PPS, held on December 14, adopted a resolution on the merger by acclamation. That same day the Second Congress of the PPR unanimously adopted a similar resolution. Later the Jewish Bund* was incorporated into the PZPR. The *Gleichschaltung* of the Polish left constituted the symbolic beginning of the Stalinist period* in Poland. J. Karpiński, *Poland since 1944: A Portrait of Years* (Boulder, Colo., 1995), 29; K. Kersten, *The Establishment of Communist Rule in Poland, 1943–1948* (Berkeley, Calif., 1991), 466–467.

UNION OF DEMOCRATIC YOUTH (Związek Młodzieży Demokratycznej), youth organization of the Democratic Party (SD),* established in 1945, and incorporated into the Union of Polish Youth (ZMP)* in 1948. *Nowa Encyklopedia Powszechna PWN*, vol. 6 (Warsaw, 1996), 1052.

UNION OF LABOR (Unia Pracy [UP]), left-wing party created in June 1992 by a merger of Labor Solidarity,* the Democratic-Social Movement,* elements of the Polish Socialist Party (PPS),* and the Great Poland Social Democratic Union. The UP, led from its beginning by R. Bugaj,* criticized the liberal economic policies of L. Balcerowicz,* attacked his "shock therapy" as too rapid and insensitive to the interests of the population, favored a mixed economy and a strong welfare state, opposed the "degradation and commercialization of health and education," and advocated the separation of church and state. In foreign policy the UP supported integration with the European Union* and NATO. The Union was the first political party of the post-1989 period to gather former members of both the democratic opposition and the Polish United Workers' Party (PZPR).* During the September 1993 elections* the UP achieved a spectacular success, gaining 7.3% of the vote and 41 seats in the Sejm. B. Szajkowski (ed.), *Political Parties of Eastern Europe, Russia, and the Successor States* (London, 1994), 340.

UNION OF POLISH ARCHITECTS (Stowarzyszenie Architektów Polskich [SARP]), professional organization established as Cracow Technical Association in 1877. Rebuilt in 1944, it protects the rights of its members, publishes several periodicals, and founds prizes for the best projects. *Nowa Encyklopedia Powszechna PWN*, vol. 6 (Warsaw, 1996), 62.

UNION OF POLISH STUDENTS (Związek Studentów Polskich [ZSP]), student association established in 1950. It conducted "ideological and educational work among students in the spirit of the program of the Front of National Unity."* The ZSP, to continue the official contemporary description of its activities, "is becoming increasingly active in strengthening the ties of students with industrial and agricultural workers, in deepening their consciousness of the role and tasks of the intelligentsia* in developing the national economy* and culture and in fashioning the socialist outlook of Poland." Yet most ZSP members did not care about communism; their organization was controlled less strictly than the Union of Polish Youth* and, then, the Union of Socialist Youth.* The ZSP became a student trade union in charge of financial and material issues and the organization of cultural life, sports, and tourism.* The authorities did not tolerate this. In 1973 the ZSP was forced to unite with the Union of Socialist Youth, active at the universities,* into the Socialist Union of Polish Students (SZSP),* which provoked frustration and protests among students. *Twenty Years of the Polish People's Republic*, ed. by E. Szyr et al. (Warsaw, 1964), 71; J. J. Lipski, *KOR: A History of the Workers' Defense Committee in Poland, 1976–81* (Berkeley, Calif., 1985), 21–22; M. H. Bernhard, *The Origins of Democratization in Poland: Workers, Intellectuals, and Oppositional Politics, 1976–1980* (New York, 1993), 115, 147.

UNION OF POLISH TEACHERS (Związek Nauczycielstwa Polskiego [ZNP]), one of the largest Polish trade unions* and the largest one active in education. Established in 1930 by a merger of several organizations, some dating from the beginning of the 20th century, it was active in the underground during World War II. Rebuilt in 1945, the ZNP became the only professional organization of Polish teachers and university professors after 1948. Suspended after introduction of Martial Law* in December 1981, it resumed its activities in 1983. In 1984 the ZNP joined the All-Poland Alliance of Trade Unions (OPZZ).* Many people left the ZNP for Solidarity* and other organizations, but it still dominates education in Poland. *Nowa Encyklopedia Powszechna PWN*, vol. 6 (Warsaw, 1995), 1054.

UNION OF POLISH WRITERS (Związek Literatów Polskich [ZLP]), trade union* of Polish writers established in 1920 by Stefan Żeromski. After 1945 its independence was limited by the communist authorities, and during its Szczecin* congress in January 1949, the ZLP totally embraced Socialist Realism.* After the "Polish October" of 1956,* the ZLP regained partial independence, but it was curbed again in the late 1950s. After years of bitter compromise, a new ZLP leadership, elected in December 1980, started a new independent policy. After imposition of Martial Law* in December 1981, however, the ZLP was suspended and, in 1983, dissolved. That same year the Jaruzelski* regime established a new ZLP, headed by such obedient writers as H. Auderska* and W. Żukrowski.* *Nowa Encyklopedia Powszechna PWN*, vol. 6 (Warsaw, 1996), 1052; J. Trznadel, *Hańba domowa* (Warsaw, 1986); J. J. Szczepański, *Kadencja* (Cracow, 1989); M. Fik, *Kultura polska po Jałcie. Kronika lat 1944–1981* (London, 1989).

UNION OF POLISH YOUTH (Związek Młodzieży Polskiej [ZMP]), communist youth organization established in July 1948 by a forced merger of several youth associations. The ZMP, controlled by the Polish Workers' Party (PPR)* and then by the Polish United Workers' Party (PZPR),* organized an intense political indoctrination aimed at completely transforming the worldview of Polish youth. The organization also mobilized young people to work, participated in the collectivization* of agriculture,* supported the "great constructions of socialism" like Nowa Huta,* shaped the cultural life of the young people, and controlled their specialized organizations. In 1955 the ZMP reached 2 million members, but after the "Polish October" of 1956,* it disintegrated and, in January 1957, was formally dissolved. R. F. Staar, *Poland, 1944–1962: The Sovietization of a Captive People* (New Orleans, 1962), 56–57, 211–214; *Nowa Encyklopedia Powszechna PWN*, vol. 6 (Warsaw, 1996), 1052.

UNION OF POLITICAL REALISM (Unia Polityki Realnej [UPR]), small radical laissez-faire party organized as a group of eccentric "conservative liberals" in 1987 but registered in April 1989 and led, from its beginning, by J. Korwin-Mikke.* The UPR advocates wholesale privatization, a dramatic reduction of the state apparatus, and taxes only to support a strong police and a professional army.* The party endorses Christian and "family" values and a strong presidency. During the October 1991 elections* the UPR gained 2.25% of the vote and three seats in the Sejm* One seat was occupied by J. Korwin-Mikke himself, who introduced into Parliament the lustration resolution of June 1992. During the September 1993 elections* the UPR received 3.18% of the vote but no seats, because it failed to cross the necessary threshold. B. Szajkowski (ed.), *Political Parties of Eastern Europe, Russia, and the Successor States* (London, 1994), 341.

UNION OF RURAL YOUTH (Związek Młodzieży Wiejskiej [ZMW]), organization of countryside youth established in 1957 by a forced merger of several rural associations. The ZMW appeared after the disintegration of the Union of Polish Youth (ZMP).* Renamed Union of Socialist Rural Youth (Związek Socjalistycznej Młodzieży Wiejskiej [ZSMW]), it was controlled by the Polish United Workers' Party (PZPR)* and the United Peasant Party (ZSL).* It organized cultural and political activities for rural youth and prepared young people in the countryside to join the PZPR or ZSL. In 1970, ZMW had about 1 million members. In 1976 it was forced to join the Union of Socialist Polish Youth (ZSMP),* but in 1990 it resumed independent activities. *Nowa Encyklopedia Powszechna PWN*, vol. 6 (Warsaw, 1996), 1053; R. F. Staar, *Poland, 1944–1962: The Sovietization of a Captive People* (New Orleans, 1962), 217–219; *Twenty Years of the Polish People's Republic*, ed. by E. Szyr et al. (Warsaw, 1964), 71.

UNION OF SOCIALIST POLISH YOUTH (Związek Socjalistycznej Młodzieży Polskiej [ZSMP]), organization established in 1976 by a merger of the Union of Socialist Youth (ZMS),* the Union of Rural Youth (ZMW),* and the Socialist Youth of the Army (Związek Młodzieży Wojskowej). Controlled by the Polish United Workers' Party (PZPR),* the organization indoctrinated young people and prepared them to join the Party. The ZSMP changed its program in 1990 and joined the Democratic Left Alliance (SLD)* in 1991. *Nowa Encyklopedia Powszechna PWN*, vol. 4 (Warsaw, 1995), 1056.

UNION OF SOCIALIST YOUTH (Związek Młodzieży Socjalistycznej [ZMS]), youth organization established in 1957 by a forced merger of several youth associations, which appeared after the disintegration of the Union of Polish Youth (ZMP).* The ZMS was totally controlled by the Polish United Workers' Party (PZPR)* and had as its main goal indoctrination of young people to prepare them to join the Party. The ZMS was active in all milieus, but it was not very popular at the universities,* where it competed poorly with the Union of Polish Students (ZSP).* The ZMS grew from about 70,000 members in 1957 to 1.3 million in 1973. In 1976 the ZMS was incorporated into the Union of Socialist Polish Youth (ZSMP).* *Nowa Encyklopedia Powszechna PWN*, vol. 6 (Warsaw, 1996), 1053; R. F. Staar, *Poland, 1944–1962: The Sovietization of a Captive People* (New Orleans, 1962), 214–217; *Twenty Years of the Polish People's Republic*, ed. by E. Szyr et al. (Warsaw, 1964), 71.

UNITED PEASANT PARTY (Zjednoczone Stronnictwo Ludowe [ZSL]), party founded in 1949 by a merger of the small pro-communist Peasant Party (SL),* also called the "Lublin" Peasant Party, and the Polish Peasant Party (PSL),* decimated and terrorized by the communist secret services. The ZSL served as an auxiliary institution to the ruling Polish United Workers' Party (PZPR)* to secure its agrarian policy. After the June 1989* elections the ZSL changed alliances, created a coalition with Solidarity,* gained independence, and reconstituted itself as the Polish Peasant Party–Revival (Polskie Stronnictwo Ludowe–Odrodzenie). O. Narkiewicz, *The Green Flag: Polish Populist Politics, 1867–1970*

(London, 1976); R. F. Staar, *Poland, 1944–1962: The Sovietization of a Captive People* (New Orleans, 1962); C. R. Barnett, *Poland: Its People, Its Society, Its Culture* (New York, 1958); Z. Mikołajczyk and E. Patryn, "The Place of the United Peasant Party in the Polish Party System," *Poland since 1956*, ed. by T. N. Cieplak (New York, 1972), 68–76; M. Nadolski, *Komuniści wobec chłopów w Polsce 1941–1956* (Warsaw, 1993).

UNIVERSITIES. Before the war Poland had six universities, one each in Warsaw,* Cracow,* Vilna, Lvov, Poznań,* and Lublin* (the Catholic University of Lublin [KUL]).* After the war two universities, those in Lvov and Vilna, found themselves in the territories incorporated into the USSR. Four new universities were therefore established: in Wrocław* (existed before the war in Germany), Maria Curie-Skłodowska University in Lublin (in 1944), Copernicus University in Toruń* (1945), and in Łódź* (1945). Toruń absorbed scholars from Vilna, and Wrocław invited the faculty from Lvov. In 1968–84, new universities in Silesia, Gdańsk,* and Szczecin* were organized. Initially, most Polish university scholars were prewar graduates and opposed, or were accused of opposing, communism. In the early 1950s, the communist authorities replaced most old professors with a new Marxist or obedient faculty, which staffed the universities until the fall of communism in Poland. After 1989 Polish universities entered a transformation period. Initial reforms have been introduced to accommodate Polish universities to the West European and U.S. academic systems. In 1990 Poland had 97 institutions of higher learning of all kinds and 378,000 students. L. Jilek, *Historical Compendium of European Universities* (Geneva, 1984); Z. Tokarski, *Uniwersytety w Polsce* (Warszawa, 1972); J. Karpiński, *Polska, Komunizm, Opozycja* (London, 1985), 287.

UNIVERSITY OF ŁÓDŹ. Established in 1945 in the town of Łódź,* which was not destroyed during the war, the university played an important role during the postwar period when most other universities were in ruins. Many intellectuals of communist Poland studied in Łódź in the late 1940s. *Dictionary of Polish Literature*, ed. by E. J. Czerwinski (Westport, Conn., 1994), 419–421.

UNIVERSITY OF POZNAŃ, one of the largest and best Polish universities, established in 1919 and renamed Adam Mickiewicz University (UAM) in 1955. Among many outstanding scholars, its faculty included historians such as H. Łowmiański,* G. Labuda,* and J. Topolski.* *Dictionary of Polish Literature*, ed. by E. J. Czerwinski (Westport, Conn., 1994), 421.

UNIVERSITY OF WARSAW, largest Polish university with 45,700 students and 2,800 faculty members in 1995. The university was established in 1816. In 1831 Russian authorities dissolved it as repression for the 1830–31 November Insurrection. In 1862 the university was reopened as the Main School (Szkoła Główna). Then 1869 it was closed again and shaped into a Russian university. In 1915 the university resumed teaching in Polish. Closed by the Germans during 1939–45, it was active underground and constituted a part of the Polish resistance. In 1945 it re-established normal courses, although the communist authorities accommodated them to the new political system. The faculty changed; the prewar professors who survived were replaced with a new communist faculty. Traditional academic autonomy disappeared. The University of Warsaw was controlled by the authorities and by the Party. In the mid-1950s the Theological, Medical, and Veterinary Departments were separated from the university proper. Many independent scholars were expelled from work in the 1960s and 1970s. Nonetheless, the university remained an important center of independent thought and politics and constituted a problem for all the regimes ruling Poland between 1945 and 1989. The March events of 1968* started there, a powerful Solidarity* organization and a local branch of the Independent Students' Union (NZS)* were established there in 1980–81, and numerous students and faculty members participated in the democratic opposition* and eventually helped to topple the communist system in Poland. After 1989 the University of Warsaw, like all other Polish institutions, entered a period of transformation to catch up with world standards and trends. *Dictionary of Polish Literature*, ed. by E. J. Czerwinski (Westport, Conn., 1994), 423–425; *Nowa Encyklopedia Powszechna PWN*, vol. 6 (Warsaw, 1996), 567.

UNIVERSITY OF WROCŁAW, established in 1811 by the Prussians, it was shaped into a Polish university in August 1945. Its faculty was joined by many scholars repatriated from the prewar eastern Polish territories incorporated into the USSR after 1945. *Dictionary of Polish Literature*, ed. by E. J. Czerwinski (Westport, Conn., 1994), 425.

UPA. See **Ukrainian Insurgent Army.**

URBAN, JERZY (1933–   ), journalist. An editorial staff member of the reformist *Po Prostu* ("Plainly Speaking")* and a supporter of the "Polish October" of 1956,* he was expelled from work and blacklisted by the Gomułka* regime. Disappointed, Urban went through a deep ideological transformation to become one of the most cynical regime journalists in the entire history of communist Poland. During 1961–81 he directed the National Affairs Department of the prestigious government weekly *Polityka.** In August 1981 he was appointed spokesperson of the Jaruzelski* regime and became hated by most Poles for his ultra-cynical attitude. In 1989 he was made chairman of the Radio and TV Committee and a director of a large publishing house. After the fall of communism, he founded a very successful tabloid, *Nie* ("No"), becoming one of the wealthiest people in Poland and a sponsor of the post-communist Democratic Left Alliance (SLD).* *Who's Who in the Socialist Countries of Europe*, ed. by J. Stroynowski, vol. 3 (Munich, 1989), 1238; A. Kępiński and Z. Kilar, *Kto jest kim w Polsce inaczej* (Warsaw, 1985), 389–408.

URSUS, district of Warsaw,* home to a large tractor factory, and center of workers' opposition* against the communist regime in the 1970s and 1980s. In 1924–28 a large metallurgic and car-producing shop called Ursus was established in the village of Czechowice at the outskirts of Warsaw. Incorporated into the State Engineering Factory in 1930 the plant became one of the largest Polish military plants. It contained a German forced labor camp during 1939–44 and was destroyed in 1945. Rebuilt after the war, the plant was extended as a tractor factory. In 1952 the settlement, already named Ursus, received city rights, and in 1977 it was incorporated into Warsaw. The workers of the plant participated in the June events of 1976.* They organized a strike; during which they blocked and cut the tracks of the international railway line leading from Warsaw to Berlin and Paris and from Warsaw to Katowice* and Vienna. The workers' protest was followed by an extremely brutal police action, and Ursus became a terrain of the Workers' Defense Committee's (KOR)* activities. In 1980 the factory was an important strike and Solidarity* center. The Ursus Solidarity organization occupies an important position in the political scene of Poland. J. J. Lipski, *KOR: A History of the Workers' Defense Committee in Poland, 1976–81* (Berkeley, Calif., 1985); *Nowa Encyklopedia Powszechna PWN*, vol. 6 (Warsaw, 1996), 576.

UZIĘBŁO, JERZY (1942–   ), captain in the merchant marine, member of the State Council (Rada Państwa)* during 1986–1989, deputy president of the All-Poland Alliance of Trade Unions (OPZZ),* and a leader of the Social Democracy of the Polish Republic (SdRP).* T. Mołdawa, *Ludzie Władzy 1944–1991. Władze państwowe i polityczne Polski według stanu na dzień 28 II 1991* (Warsaw, 1991), 435.

V

VIRION, TADEUSZ JÓZEF DE (1926–), attorney who defended dissidents* in the 1970s and 1980s. A veteran of the Home Army (AK)* and the 1944 Warsaw Uprising, he joined the Polish Bar* in 1950. From 1980 he was a member of the Legal Commission of the Polish Episcopate.* In 1990 he was appointed Polish ambassador to the United Kingdom. *Who's Who in the Socialist Countries of Europe*, ed. by J. Stroynowski, vol. 3 (Munich, 1989), 1264; *Kto jest kim w polityce polskiej*, ed. by R. Ignasiak (Warsaw, 1993), 306.

VISTULA ACTION. See **Action Wisła.**

VISTULA RIVER (Wisła), largest river of Poland and in the Baltic Sea's drainage basin. It rises in the Beskidy Mountains close to the southern border of Poland and flows east and then north 1,069 kilometers (664 mi) to its delta and the Gulf of Gdańsk.* Several important Polish towns and cities, such as Cracow,* Sandomierz, Warsaw,* Płock, Włocławek, Toruń,* Malbork, Tczew, and Gdańsk, are located on this river. It is navigable from the San River, northeast of Cracow, and is linked by canals with the Oder* and the Dnieper Rivers. The Vistula drainage area covers two thirds of Polish territory, and the river is a Polish national symbol. *The New Encyclopaedia Britannica*, vol. 12 (Chicago, 1990), 399.

WACHOWICZ, BARBARA (1937–   ), journalist and author of popular works about Polish literature and history. *Encyklopedyczny Słownik Sławnych Polaków* (Warsaw, 1996), 420; P. Kuncewicz, *Agonia i nadzieja. Proza polska*, vol. 5 (Warsaw, 1994), 108.

WACHOWSKI, MIECZYSŁAW (1950–   ), personal secretary of L. Wałęsa* and Secretary of State in his presidential chancellery. Sailor, car mechanic, and taxi driver, he was hired by Solidarity* as Wałęsa's chauffeur in 1981 and became his friend. After Wałęsa was elected President* of Poland, Wachowski became *eminence grise* of his chancellery. Hated by many, he was accused of being a KGB agent and the President's "evil spirit." In summer 1995 Wachowski was fired by Wałęsa, who wanted to improve his image before the presidential election of 1995.* P. Rabiej and I. Rosińska, *Kim Pan jest Panie Wachowski?* (Warsaw, 1993).

WAJDA, ANDRZEJ (1926–   ), film and theater director. He made his debut with the film *Pokolenie* ("Generation") in 1955. Later he worked with the best theaters in Poland and directed over 30 films, such as *Kanał* ("Sewers") in 1956, *Popiół i diament* ("Ash and Diamond") in 1958, and *Człowiek z marmuru* ("Man of Marble") in 1977. His *Człowiek z żelaza* ("Man of Iron"), made in 1981, became an illustration of the Solidarity* period. Chairman of the Association of Polish Filmmakers during 1978–83, Wajda had always been politically involved; in 1989 he was elected a Solidarity senator and was active on various committees and political bodies close to Solidarity as an expert on culture. *Who's Who in the Socialist Countries of Europe*, ed. by J. Stroynowski, vol. 3 (Munich, 1989), 1278; *Encyklopedyczny Słownik Sławnych Polaków* (Warsaw, 1996), 420.

WALC, JAN (1948–93), dissident,* scientist, and specialist in Polish literature. He participated in student protests during the March events of 1968* and was arrested for the first time for his political involvement. Later he was detained many times and signed numerous letters to the Polish authorities in protest against their policies. An activist of the Workers' Defense Committee (KOR),* he was also a prolific essayist and scholar at the Institute of Literary Research of the Polish Academy of Sciences (PAN).* *Who's Who in the Socialist Countries of Europe*, ed. by J. Stroynowski, vol. 3 (Munich, 1989), 1278; J. J. Lipski, *KOR: A History of the Workers' Defense Committee in Poland, 1976–81* (Berkeley, Calif., 1985).

WALDORFF, JERZY (1910–   ), prolific writer, music critic and columnist of several Polish periodicals, contributor to Polish TV* and Radio, animator of cultural life and organizer of numerous associations, such as the Civic Commission for Conservation of Old Powązki Cemetery in Warsaw.* *Who's Who in the Socialist Countries of Europe*, ed. by J. Stroynowski, vol. 3 (Munich, 1989), 1279; P. Kuncewicz, *Agonia i nadzieja. Literatura polska od 1939*, vol. 2 (Warsaw, 1994), 250.

WALENTYNOWICZ, ANNA (1929–   ), Solidarity* activist. A farmhand in the Gdańsk* region after the war, she began to work at the Lenin Shipyard in Gdańsk in 1950. In 1968 she was dismissed from work for attempting to disclose abuses in the government-sponsored trade unions.* She participated in the December events of 1970* and then returned to work as a crane operator at the shipyard. She also engaged herself in organizing anniversaries of the December events and, in the late 1970s, became a member of the Founding Committee of Free Trade Unions of the Baltic Coast. She also cooperated with the Workers' Defense Committee (KOR)* and contributed to underground publications. Harassed and kept under surveillance by the police, she was dismissed from work on August 8, 1980, which triggered the strike in the Lenin Shipyard. After the Gdańsk Agreement* had been signed, Walentynowicz became a member of Solidarity's Executive Board, although her disagreement with L. Wałęsa* over the structure and leadership of Solidarity had already started at that time. She helped to organize a strike in the shipyard after imposition of Martial Law,* was interned, released, rearrested, and put into a mental hospital in November 1982. *Who's Who in the Socialist Countries of Europe*, ed. by J. Stroynowski, vol. 3 (Munich, 1989), 1280.

WALTER, pseudonym of Gen. K. Świerczewski* during the Spanish Civil War.

WALICHNOWSKI, TADEUSZ (1928–   ), rector of the Academy of Internal Affairs after 1982, chief director of the State Archives during 1978–81, staff member of the Ministry of Internal Affairs (Intelligence Service), head of the Jewish section (renamed Anti-Zionist section) of the Ministry of Internal Affairs

in 1965–69, and communist specialist on the "Jewish and German questions."
Who's Who in the Socialist Countries of Europe, ed. by J. Stroynowski, vol. 3 (Munich, 1989), 1280.

"WALTEROWCY." See **Scouting.**

WAŁĘSA, LECH (1943–   ), President* of Poland during 1990–95 and founder of Solidarity.* Born to a poor peasant family in a village in central Poland, he graduated from a secondary vocational school. In 1961 he began to work as an electrician for a state agriculture machinery center but was drafted into the army in 1963. In 1967 he moved to Gdańsk* and was hired at the Lenin Shipyard. He participated in the December events of 1970,* was elected chairman of a workshop strike committee, and was arrested for several days. In 1976 he was dismissed from the shipyard for criticizing the management, had to change jobs several times, and was unemployed from February 1980 until the August 1980 strike. In the late 1970s he came into contact with the publishers of the underground paper *Robotnik* ("The Worker")* and the Workers' Defense Committee (KOR).* In 1978 he became a member of the Founding Committee of the Free Trade Unions of the Baltic Coast. In December 1978 and December 1979 Wałęsa was fined and dismissed from work for organizing commemorative ceremonies for workers killed during the December events of 1970. In January 1980 he became a member of an independent workers' commission set up to fight dismissal and harassment by police and Lenin Shipyard management. The commission became instrumental in the shipyard strike of August 1980. Shipyard workers demanded the reinstatement of Wałęsa and A. Walentynowicz.* On August 14 Wałęsa showed up at the shipyard, became leader of the strike, and managed to convince his colleagues to form the Inter-Factory Strike Committee (MKS),* and to fight for trade union pluralism and the rights of the workers outside the shipyard as well. On August 22 the MKS presented a historic manifesto of 21 demands, including the rights to form free trade unions and to strike. Wałęsa led negotiations with Poland's Deputy Premier, M. Jagielski,* and became the "hero of the hour." On August 31 Wałęsa signed the Gdańsk Agreement* with the authorities, and in September 1980 he was elected chairman of a new National Coordinating Commission of Solidarity.

   Wałęsa developed Solidarity's national organization and his own prestige as a symbolic leader of the opposition, * although he was criticized by many for his authoritarian rule of the union. He was nonetheless unable to control the more radical members of Solidarity; as a result, its relationship with the communist government worsened dramatically throughout 1981. Interned after imposition of Martial Law* in December 1981, Wałęsa was released in November 1982 and returned to work in the shipyard in 1983. In October 1983 he received the Nobel Peace Prize. He maintained contacts with the underground Solidarity network and the Roman Catholic Church* and, in 1988, reemerged as one of the most important politicians in Poland. In December 1988 the Citizens' Committee of the Chairman of Solidarity* was organized, and in spring 1989 Wałęsa was a dominating figure during the Round Table Negotiations.* The elections of June 1989* were his personal triumph. He reached the height of his popularity and became a symbol and embodiment of the Polish revolt against communism. After the elections Wałęsa managed to convince the leaders of the United Peasant Party (ZSL)* and the Democratic Party (SD)* that a coalition with Solidarity would be better for them than their old alliance with the Polish United Workers' Party (PZPR).* As a consequence, the first postwar non-communist government was formed in Poland, led by Wałęsa's closest adviser, T. Mazowiecki.* Several months later, however, a disagreement between Mazowiecki and Wałęsa developed into the "war at the top"* and poisoned the electoral campaign before the presidential election of 1990.* Wałęsa won the presidency, but his election was hardly a triumph. During the first ballot, he received 39.9% of the vote, whereas an unknown outsider, S. Tymiński,* received 23.1% of the vote in the first ballot and 25.7% in the second. Wałęsa never regained his earlier popularity. His presidency was not perfect either. He lost a conflict with the Sejm* over the Constitution and the electoral law before the parliamentary elections of 1991.* In spring 1992 he got involved in a new conflict with J. Parys, Minister of Defense in the government of J. Olszewski,* over the control of the Polish Army.* Wałęsa maintained good relations with Premier H. Suchocka* and dissolved the Sejm when she received a no-confidence vote in May 1993. Wałęsa hoped that the elections of September 1993* would limit the number of parties in Parliament and thereby produce a more solid Solidarity-based coalition. Yet the elections gave a clear parliamentary majority to the Democratic Left Alliance (SLD):* 171 seats in the Sejm (out of 460) and 37 seats in the Senate (out of 100), and to the Polish Peasant Party (PSL):* 132 seats in the Sejm and 36 seats in the Senate. Wałęsa's own newly formed Non-Party Bloc for Supporting the Reforms (BBWR)* received only 16 seats in the Sejm and 2 seats in the Senate. The newly formed governmental coalition of the SLD and the PSL was critical of Wałęsa, who, in response, accused the cabinet of corruption and mismanagement. During the presidential elections of November 1995,* Wałęsa was defeated by A. Kwaśniewski* and became a second-rate politician. A devout Roman Catholic, Wałęsa is married to Mirosława "Danuta" Gołos, with whom he has eight children. *The Cold War, 1945–1991*, vol. 2 "Leaders and Other Important Figures in the Soviet Union, Eastern Europe, China, and the Third World," ed. by B. Frankel (Detroit, 1992), 350; L. Wałęsa, *The Struggle and the Triumph* (New York, 1992); M. Craig, *Lech Wałęsa and His Poland* (London, 1987); *Current Biography Yearbook, 1996*, ed. by J. Graham (New York, 1996), 613–617; *Rodem z Solidarności*, ed. by B. Kopka and R. Żelichowski (Warsaw, 1997), 217–256.

WANIOŁKA, FRANCISZEK (1912–71), member of the Politburo* of the Polish United Workers' Party (PZPR)* in 1964–68, Deputy Premier in 1962–68, and holder of several ministerial portfolios of mining and heavy industry between 1954 and 1962. T. Mołdawa, *Ludzie Władzy 1944–1991. Władze państwowe i polityczne Polski według stanu na dzień 28 II 1991* (Warsaw, 1991), 436.

WAŃKOWICZ, MELCHIOR (1892–1974), journalist, writer, and pillar of Polish 20th-century nonfiction literature.* A soldier in the Polish Corps in Russia in 1917–18 and later of the Polish Army,* he graduated from Warsaw's School of Political Sciences in 1922 and worked for several journals and publishing houses. He spent World War II in Romania, the Middle East, Italy, France, Germany, and England. During 1943–45 he served as a war correspondent. In 1949 he moved to the United States; in 1958 he returned to Poland. A master of *rapportage*, he wrote several collections, including his famous *Bitwa o Monte Casino* ("The Battle of Monte Casino"). He also wrote essays, novels, and popular historical works. Independent and outspoken, he was at odds with the communist authorities and was harassed by them. *Dictionary of Polish Literature*, ed. by E. J. Czerwinski (Westport, Conn., 1994), 429–431; P. Kuncewicz, *Leksykon polskich pisarzy współczesnych*, vol. 2 (Warsaw, 1995), 393–396.

"WAR AT THE TOP," popular name of a conflict that split Solidarity* in 1990, when L. Wałęsa* and T. Mazowiecki* competed for the office of President* of Poland. Political differences inside Solidarity came to the fore as early as 1989. Mazowiecki did not consult Wałęsa about the composition of his cabinet and excluded from it several individuals close to Wałęsa. Animosities deepened at the Solidarity congress in April 1990. In June a political dispute arose between Wałęsa and Mazowiecki sympathizers over the structure of Solidarity. Simultaneously, Wałęsa accused the Mazowiecki government of delaying economic and political reforms and retaining former communists in the cabinet. Several Solidarity leaders accused Wałęsa of populism, of dictatorial tendencies, and of exploiting the dispute with the government to further his own presidential ambitions. A. Michnik,* editor-in-chief of Solidarity newspaper *Gazeta Wyborcza* ("The Electoral Gazette"),* wrote on June 7 that Wałęsa was behaving "like a Caesar." On June 24 Michnik, Z. Bujak,* and H. Wujec* resigned from Solidarity's Civic Committee* in protest. In May 1990 Wałęsa supporters established the Center Alliance* and petitioned President Jaruzelski* to step down so that Wałęsa could be named President. On July 7 Mazowiecki and Wałęsa were brought together through the mediation of the Roman Catholic Church* to settle the dispute. They agreed to accelerate reforms and work together, but on the next day Wałęsa accused Solidarity's Sejm* deputies of losing touch with ordinary people in Poland. On July 16 the Citizens' Movement for Democratic Action (ROAD)* was established to provide support for Mazowiecki. The Mazowiecki-Wałęsa conflict overshadowed the August 31 celebrations of the 10th anniversary of the Gdańsk Agreement. On September 5, 1990, by a narrow majority Solidarity's National Commission voted to ban use of the Solidarity logo on the masthead of *Gazeta Wyborcza* and accused it of publishing articles "aimed at discrediting and ridiculing Chairman Wałęsa." After Wałęsa's victory in the presidential elections of 1990,* the Citizens' Parliamentary Club (OKP)* formally split on January 4, 1991, and new, smaller parliamentary clubs appeared. Solidarity disintegrated. *Keesing's Record of World Events*,

June 1990, p. 37546; July 1990, 37620; H. Tworzecki, *Parties and Politics in Post-1989 Poland* (Boulder, Colo., 1996), 52–55; *Revolutionary and Dissident Movements: An International Guide*, ed by Henry W. Degenhardt (London, 1991), 276; A. Dudek, *Pierwsze lata III Rzeczpospolitej, 1989–1995* (Cracow, 1997), 95–110.

WARSAW, capital of Poland since 1611 and its largest city (1.7 million inhabitants in 1990), located on the Vistula River* in east-central Poland at the junction of important routes across the European Plain. Destroyed by as much as 84% during World War II, Warsaw lost 782 out of its 957 prewar historic sites and 850,000 inhabitants. Out of almost 400,000 Jews* living in the city before the war, only several hundred survived. By war's end the Germans deported the remaining population, and on January 15–17, 1945, the Red Army* liberated a sea of empty ruins. Intense reconstruction began as early as 1945, and Warsaw soon became the center of administration and government of Poland and its artistic and cultural capital, with many museums, galleries, libraries, theaters, and universities.* Among the historic sites rebuilt were the Royal Castle and the Krakowskie Przedmieście Boulevard, lined with churches and palaces. In one site, the Radziwiłł Palace, the 1955 Warsaw Treaty* was signed.

Warsaw hosts many important international cultural events, such as the Chopin pianists' competition, and is headquarters to the Polish Academy of Sciences (PAN).* Warsaw is also the second largest Poland's industrial center, after Silesia, with large enterprises specializing in electrical engineering, metallurgy, printing, machine products, chemicals, textiles, clothing, and food. A large group of Warsaw's inhabitants participated in most political events of postwar Poland, but especially in the "Polish October" of 1956,* the March events of 1968,* and Solidarity* activities. In the decades following the war, the city was completely rebuilt and expanded beyond its prewar size, but under the communist regime it remained gray and rather unattractive. After 1989, Warsaw changed its image dramatically to become one of the most vibrant cities in Central Europe. *International Dictionary of Historic Places*, ed. by T. Ring, vol. 2 (Chicago, 1995), 783; *The New Encyclopaedia Britannica*, Macropaedia, vol. 29 (Chicago, 1990), 696; M. Baranowska, *Warszawa. Miesiące, lata, wieki* (Wrocław, 1996).

WARSAW PACT. See **Warsaw Treaty Organization.**

WARSAW TREATY ORGANIZATION, military organization controlled by the USSR and established on its initiative on May 14, 1955, officially established as a response to the admission of West Germany into the North Atlantic Treaty Organization. The Warsaw Treaty was joined by all European communist countries except Yugoslavia. Finland declined the invitation but assured the USSR of its neutrality. Albania withdrew from the organization unofficially in 1961 but formally in 1968. The Treaty created a unified military command with political and military structures totally dominated by the Soviet Union. The Treaty's headquarters, located in Moscow, was a departmental section of the

Soviet High Command; all senior positions were occupied by the Soviets, and non-Soviet forces were linked to particular Soviet commands and prepared to support Red Army military operations. Besides frequent joint maneuvers, Warsaw Treaty Organization armed forces were used only once—during the 1968 intervention in Czechoslovakia. After M. Gorbachev's accession to power in 1985, the cohesion of the Treaty began to erode. At its summit in July 1989, Gorbachev rejected the Brezhnev Doctrine,* stating that the USSR would not intervene in internal affairs of other states. At the 1990 summit, representatives of non-communist governments of East-Central European states and the Soviet Union agreed to dismantle the military structure of the Treaty in April 1991 and the political organization by March 1992. By 1994 all Red Army troops had been withdrawn from former Treaty territories. B. P. McCrea, J. C. Plano, and G. Klein, *The Soviet and East European Dictionary* (Oxford, 1984), 341.

WARSAW UNIVERSITY. See University of Warsaw.

WASILEWSKA, WANDA (1905–64), writer and leftist politician instrumental in the establishment of communism in Poland. A daughter of Leon Wasilewski, an important leader of the Polish Socialist Party (PPS),* she belonged to its leadership in the interwar period and wrote for its periodicals. In the 1930s she moved further to the political left, beyond the PPS ideology. After the outbreak of World War II in 1939, she settled in Lvov, accepted Soviet citizenship, and became a member of the Supreme Soviet in Moscow. From 1941 she served in the Red Army* as a propagandist and war correspondent. That year she helped to establish *Nowe Widnokręgi* ("New Horizons"), a communist journal that became a gathering point for Polish communists in Soviet Russia. In 1943 she contributed greatly to the organization of the communist Polish Army* in the USSR and became the president of the Union of Polish Patriots (ZPP). In 1944 she was appointed deputy chairman of the Polish Committee of National Liberation (PKWN). Retiring from politics, in 1945 she settled in Kiev with her husband, O. Korneychuk, a former Soviet Deputy Minister of Foreign Affairs and a Ukrainian writer. She published about 20 novels, which preceded and, later contributed to, the development of Socialist Realism.* As leader of the ZPP, she saved many human lives in the USSR, but to many Poles she is a symbol of national treason. K. Kresten, *The Establishment of Communist Rule in Poland, 1943–1948* (Berkeley, Calif., 1991); A. Ciołkosz, *Wanda Wasilewska* (London, 1977); P. Kuncewicz, *Agonia i nadzieja. Literatura polska od 1918 roku*, vol. 1 (Warsaw, 1994), 238.

WASILEWSKI, ANDRZEJ (1928–   ), editor, literary critic, and Party official. A member of several editorial boards of major Polish periodicals, a program director of the Polish TV,* and a member of the Politburo,* he was responsible with others for shaping Polish culture under communism. *Who's Who in the Socialist Countries of Europe*, ed. by J. Stroynowski, vol. 3 (Munich, 1989), 1284.

WAT, ALEKSANDER (1900–67), poet, writer, and co-founder of Futurism in Poland. An editor of the communist *Miesięcznik Literacki* ("The Literary Monthly") before World War II, after the outbreak of war he escaped from the Nazis to Soviet-occupied Lvov. Arrested in 1940, he was deported to Kazakhstan. He returned to Poland in 1946 and re-entered literary life but was silenced as a political deviationist during the Stalinist period.* In 1956 he began to publish his poetry again and became relatively popular. In 1963 he defected and settled in the West. His memoir, *Mój wiek* ("My Century"), is a document about Soviet communism. C. Miłosz, *The History of Polish Literature* (Berkeley, Calif., 1983), 475–478; *Dictionary of Polish Literature*, ed. by E. J. Czerwinski (Westport, Conn., 1994), 431–432; J. Zieliński, *Leksykon polskiej literatury emigracyjnej* (Lublin, 1989), 131–133; P. Kuncewicz, *Leksykon polskich pisarzy współczesnych*, vol. 2 (Warsaw, 1995), 399.

WAŻYK, ADAM (1905–82), poet, writer, and theoretician of Socialist Realism* in Poland. During 1939–41 he lived in Soviet-occupied Lvov; after the outbreak of the German-Soviet war, he escaped to the East. Active in a group of Polish communists gathered around a journal, *Nowe Widnokręgi* ("New Horizons"), he joined the communist Polish Army* in 1943 and returned to Poland as an officer. After the war he contributed to the Stalinization of Polish culture as an editor of the communist literary journals *Kuźnica* ("The Forge") and *Twórczość* ("Creation") during 1946–49 and 1950–54, respectively. Disappointed with Stalinism, he rebelled in 1955 and published the famous *Poemat dla dorosłych* ("A Poem for the Adults"). In 1964 he signed the "Letter of 34,"* protesting against the cultural policy of the communist authorities in Poland. Later, in 1968, he tried to defend students persecuted by police. He authored numerous collections of poems and essays, novels, and works on the history of Polish literature. C. Miłosz, *The History of Polish Literature* (Berkeley, Calif., 1983), 405–408; *Dictionary of Polish Literature*, ed. by E. J. Czerwinski (Westport, Conn., 1994), 432–433; P. Kuncewicz, *Agonia i nadzieja. Literatura polska od 1939 roku*, vol. 2 (Warsaw, 1994), 96.

WENDE, JAN KAROL (1910–86), writer, one of the main leaders of the Democratic Party (SD)* in 1944–73, and Deputy Speaker of the Sejm* in 1961–71. T. Mołdawa, *Ludzie Władzy 1944–1991. Władze państwowe i polityczne Polski według stanu na dzień 28 II 1991* (Warsaw, 1991), 437.

WERBLAN, ANDRZEJ (1924–   ), communist ideologue and propagandist, member of the Central Committee* of the Polish United Workers' Party (PZPR)* from 1956 and its Secretary from 1974, member of the Politburo* from February to December 1980, and Deputy Speaker of the Sejm* during 1971–82. He also occupied several less important apparatus positions, such as the head of the Propaganda Department at the Central Committee in 1956–60. His Party career came to an end during the Solidarity* period, when he retired to become a political science professor at Silesian University. *Who's Who in the Socialist Countries of Europe*, ed. by J. Stroynowski, vol. 3 (Munich, 1989), 1293; T. Mołdawa, *Ludzie Władzy 1944–1991. Władze państwowe i polityczne Polski według stanu na dzień 28 II 1991* (Warsaw, 1991), 438.

WERESZYCKI, HENRYK (1898–   ), outstanding historian and specialist on modern Polish history. He did not accept Marxism and was silenced by communist censors in the 1950s and 1960s. *Who's Who in the Socialist Countries of Europe*, ed. by J. Stroynowski, vol. 3 (Munich, 1989), 1293.

WERFEL, ROMAN (1906–   ), communist ideologue and propagandist. He joined the communist movement in 1921 and occupied several important positions in it before he was expelled from the Communist Party of Poland (KPP) in 1936. After the occupation of Lvov by the Soviets in 1939, he joined the Bolshevik Party, edited a communist daily, *Czerwony Sztandar* ("The Red Banner"), and contributed to the journal *Nowe Widnokręgi* ("New Horizons"). From 1942 he edited the latter periodical in Moscow. In 1944 he joined the Polish Workers' Party (PPR)* and returned to Poland to serve as chief editor of the Party organs *Głos Ludu* ("The Voice of the People"), *Nowe Drogi* ("New Ways"),* and during 1952–59 *Trybuna Ludu* ("The Tribune of the People").* During 1963–68 he directed the History of Polish-Soviet Relations Research Center of the Polish Academy of Sciences (PAN).* Expelled from the Polish United Workers' Party (PZPR)* in 1968, he retired and his family emigrated from Poland. In 1983 he received his Party card again. *Who's Who in the Socialist Countries of Europe*, ed. by J. Stroynowski, vol. 3 (Munich, 1989), 1293.

WIADOMOŚCI ("News"), underground Solidarity,* Mazowsze Region weekly published from December 17, 1981; initially published as *Wiadomości Dnia* ("News of the Day"). The periodical informed about Solidarity activities and commented on international and Polish events. D. Cecuda, *Leksykon opozycji politycznej 1976–1989* (Warsaw, 1989), 197.

WIATR, JERZY (1931–   ), Party ideologue and professor of sociology. He joined the Polish United Workers' Party (PZPR)* in 1949 and graduated from Warsaw University* in 1954, where he taught until 1959. He then moved to Jagiellonian University* in Cracow,* where from 1958 he taught at the Military Political Academy. He returned to Warsaw University in 1969. During 1981–84 he directed the Institute of the Basic Problems of Marxism-Leninism of the Party Central Committee.* In 1989 he participated in the Round Table Negotiations* on the communist side. In 1991 he was a founder of the Social Democracy of the Republic of Poland (SdRP),* which he represented in the Sejm* during 1991–93. In February 1996 he received the portfolio of Education Minister in the government of W. Cimoszewicz.* Many Poles considered him partly responsible for communist indoctrination before 1989 and believed that his ministerial appointment was unfortunate. *Who's Who in the Socialist Countries of Europe*, ed. by J. Stroynowski, vol. 3 (Munich, 1989), 1296.

WICHA, WŁADYSŁAW (1904–84), Minister of Internal Affairs in 1954–64 instrumental in de-Stalinization of the communist police apparatus in Poland. A member of the Communist Party of Poland (KPP) before the war, he served in various important Party and governmental positions after 1945. A member of the State Council (Rada Państwa)* in 1965–69, he was purged during the campaign of M. Moczar.* T. Mołdawa, *Ludzie Władzy 1944–1991. Władze państwowe i polityczne Polski według stanu na dzień 28 II 1991* (Warsaw, 1991), 438.

WIDY-WIRSKI, FELIKS (1907–82), professor of medicine and leader of the Labor Party (SP).* He cooperated with the communists and helped to split his party. A state official during the early postwar years, he was imprisoned in 1950–54 and was later politically sidetracked. T. Mołdawa, *Ludzie Władzy 1944–1991. Władze państwowe i polityczne Polski według stanu na dzień 28 II 1991* (Warsaw, 1991), 438.

WIELOWIEYSKI, ANDRZEJ (1927–   ), Catholic journalist and politician. A member of the editorial staff of *Więź* ("The Link")* in 1961–78 and a secretary of Warsaw's Club of Catholic Intelligentsia* in 1972–80 and 1984–89, he served as an adviser to the strike committee in Gdańsk* in 1980 and to L. Wałęsa* from 1984. He was also a member of the "Experience and Future" inquiry (DiP)* and of the Primate's* Social Council in 1981–84. He participated in the Round Table Negotiations,* was elected to the Senate,* and became its Deputy Speaker. *Who's Who in the Socialist Countries of Europe*, ed. by J. Stroynowski, vol. 3 (Munich, 1989), 1299; T. Mołdawa, *Ludzie Władzy 1944–1991). Władze państwowe i polityczne Polski według stanu na dzień 28 II 1991* (Warsaw, 1991), 439.

WIERBŁOWSKI, STEFAN (1904–   ), communist official. A member of the Communist Party of Poland (KPP) from 1925, he spent World War II in the Soviet Union, where he belonged to the Central Bureau of the Polish Communists.* After the war he occupied several important posts in the Party-state apparatus, including the position of Deputy Minister of Foreign Affairs in the early 1950s. R. F. Staar, *Poland, 1944–1962: The Sovietization of a Captive People* (New Orleans, 1962), 121, 156; A. Albert, *Najnowsza historia Polski 1918–1920* (London, 1989), 424, 628.

WIERZYŃSKI, KAZIMIERZ (1894–1969), poet and translator. A founder of the poetic group Skamander, he belonged among the most notable Polish poets of the interwar period. In September 1939 Polish authorities evacuated him with the staff of *Gazeta Polska* ("The Polish Gazette") from Warsaw* to Lvov. He was able to escape through Romania to France and, in 1941, to New York. Until his death in London, he was one of the most outstanding Polish émigré artists.

C. Miłosz, *The History of Polish Literature* (Berkeley, Calif., 1983), 395–397; *Dictionary of Polish Literature*, ed. by E. J. Czerwinski (Westport, Conn., 1994), 434–435; J. Zieliński, *Leksykon polskiej literatury emigracyjnej* (Lublin, 1989), 133–135.

WIĘŹ ("The Link"), monthly published in Warsaw* since 1958 by a group of progressive Catholics associated with the Club of Catholic Intelligentsia.* *Więź* was devoted to cultural and social matters, to the contemporary history of Poland and its Roman Catholic Church,* and to the problems of sociology and philosophy. It was edited by T. Mazowiecki* in 1958–81. The monthly, which supported Solidarity,* was suspended after imposition of Martial Law* in December 1981. One of the most sophisticated Polish periodicals, *Więź* was harassed by the communist authorities and has always had its enemies among fundamentalist Catholics. *Nowa Encyklopedia Powszechna PWN*, vol. 6 (Warsaw, 1996), 779.

WILCZEK, MIECZYSŁAW (1932–), communist manager and, from 1974, private entrepreneur who made a fortune in the chemistry and foodstuffs industries. He was unexpectedly appointed the last communist Minister of Industry in M. Rakowski's* government in 1988–89. T. Mołdawa, *Ludzie Władzy 1944–1991. Władze państwowe i polityczne Polski według stanu na dzień 28 II 1991* (Warsaw, 1991), 439.

WILHELMI, JANUSZ (1927–78), journalist, editor-in-chief of *Kultura*,* director of Polish TV* in 1972–76, and Deputy Minister of Culture in 1977–78. Wilhelmi died in an airplane accident in Bulgaria. T. Mołdawa, *Ludzie Władzy 1944–1991. Władze państwowe i polityczne Polski według stanu na dzień 28 II 1991* (Warsaw, 1991), 440.

WIŁKOMIRSKI, KAZIMIERZ (1901–95), composer, cellist, conductor, and educator. After 1945 he was instrumental in rebuilding of conservatories of music in Poland. *Nowa Encyklopedia Powszechna PWN*, vol. 6 (Warsaw, 1996), 793.

WIN. See **Freedom and Independence.**

WINIEWICZ, JÓZEF (1905–84), diplomat and publicist, Deputy Minister of Foreign Affairs in 1957–72. *Nowa Encyklopedia Powszechna PWN*, vol. 6 (Warsaw, 1996), 796.

WIP (Wolność i Pokój). See **Freedom and Peace.**

WITASZEWSKI, KAZIMIERZ (1906–), general, Deputy Minister of Defense in 1952–56, and director of the Administration Department of the Central Committee* of the Polish United Workers' Party (PZPR)* in 1960–68. T. Mołdawa, *Ludzie Władzy 1944–1991. Władze państwowe i polityczne Polski według stanu na dzień 28 II 1991* (Warsaw, 1991), 440.

WITOS, ANDRZEJ (1878–1973), farmer and politician used by the communists because of his famous last name (he was Wincenty Witos's brother). An activist of the Polish peasant movement from 1907 and one of its leaders in the interwar period, he was deported to northern Russia in 1940. In 1943 he was co-opted to the leadership of the Union of the Polish Patriots (ZPP) in the USSR, and in 1944 he became its deputy president. In July 1944 he was appointed a Deputy Chairman of the Polish Committee of National Liberation (PKWN) and, later, occupied several less important positions in the state apparatus. He retired from politics in 1950, although, in 1956–59, he chaired a district (powiatowy) committee of the United Peasant Party (ZSL).* T. Mołdawa, *Ludzie Władzy 1944– 1991. Władze państwowe i polityczne Polski według stanu na dzień 28 II 1991* (Warsaw, 1991), 440.

WOG. See **Great Economic Organizations.**

WOJTASZEK, EMIL (1927–   ), Minister of Foreign Affairs during 1976–80. T. Mołdawa, *Ludzie Władzy 1944–1991. Władze państwowe i polityczne Polski według stanu na dzień 28 II 1991* (Warsaw, 1991), 441.

WOJTYŁA, KAROL. See **John Paul II.**

WOLA, industrial district of Warsaw* and important center of workers' movement and anti-communist opposition.* In 1982 the clandestine Political Group "Wola" was established there. The organization published an underground weekly, *Wola. Nowa Encyklopedia Powszechna PWN*, vol. 6 (Warsaw, 1996), 875.

WORKERS' DEFENSE COMMITTEE (Komitet Obrony Robotników [KOR]), organization established in September 1976 to assist workers persecuted by the communist authorities for their participation in the June events of 1976* and other forms of opposition. The KOR composed an appeal to Polish society and the authorities, initially signed by only 14 persons, although others joined later. Among the most important leaders and members of the KOR were J. Kuroń,* A. Michnik,* J. Andrzejewski,* E. Lipiński,* J. J. Lipski,* and Z. Romaszewski.* The KOR provided lawyers, who defended workers accused of crimes against the state, organized financial support for families of the arrested workers, demanded a general amnesty* for the demonstrators and dismissal of corrupt officials, and informed foreign journalists of the abuses of human rights in Poland. After Poland signed the Helsinki Final Act of the Conference on Security and Cooperation in Europe, the KOR was transformed into the Committee for Society's Self-Defense KOR (Komitet Samoobrony Społecznej KOR). The committee triggered a rapid growth of underground press and opposition groups. It was formally dissolved at the First Congress of Solidarity* in September 1981. J. J. Lipski, *KOR: A History of the Workers' Defense Committee in Po-*

land, 1976–1981 (Berkeley, Calif., 1985); J. Held, *Dictionary of East European History since 1945* (Westport, Conn., 1994), 312.

WOROSZYLSKI, WIKTOR (1927–96), prolific writer, poet, and journalist. He graduated from the Gorky Institute of Literature in Moscow and, in 1957–58, served as editor-in-chief of *Nowa Kultura* ("The New Culture"),* where he was previously on the editorial staff. His worldview was changed completely when he witnessed the 1956 Hungarian revolution in Budapest. Attacked by W. Gomułka* and Radio Moscow for "extreme pessimism and lack of perspective," he was expelled from the Party in connection with the 1966 Kołakowski* case. In the 1970s he signed several open letters, protesting against the government, especially its cultural policies in Poland. As a consequence, his writing was forbidden to be published and he began to cooperate with underground periodicals, especially *Zapis* ("The Record"). *Who's Who in the Socialist Countries of Europe*, ed. by J. Stroynowski, vol. 3 (Munich, 1989), 1319.

WOŹNIAKOWSKI, JACEK (1920–   ), Catholic intellectual, professor of history of art, co-founder and president of Cracow's Znak Publishing Institute (Instytut Wydawniczy Znak),* and mayor of Cracow* after 1989. A veteran of the September Campaign of 1939 and the Home Army (AK),* he served on the editorial board of the prestigious *Tygodnik Powszechny* ("The Universal Weekly")* from its inception. Very active in Cracow's social and cultural life, he co-founded the Cracow branch of the Clubs of Catholic Intelligentsia.* *Who's Who in the Socialist Countries of Europe*, ed. by J. Stroynowski, vol. 3 (Munich, 1989), 1320.

WOZNIESIENSKI, DYMITR (1905–   ), colonel of the Red Army* and Soviet adviser co-responsible for Stalinist terror and crimes in Poland. He came to Poland in 1944, where he helped to organize and directed the Main Information Office of the Polish People's Army* (counter-intelligence, Polish equivalent of the Soviet "SMERSH") until 1954. J. Poksiński, *"TUN." Tatar-Utnik-Nowicki* (Warsaw, 1992).

WROCŁAW (German Breslau), major city of Lower Silesia. Initially part of Poland or a capital of an independent principality, it fell into Habsburg hands in 1526 and was annexed by Prussia in 1741. Destroyed by as much as 70% during World War II, it was transferred to Poland in 1945 and became an important cultural, industrial, and administrative center. In 1990 it reached 643,000 inhabitants. In 1948 Wrocław hosted the Congress of Intellectuals for Peace.* In the 1980s the city was an important Solidarity* stronghold. *The New Encyclopaedia Britannica*, vol. 12 (Chicago, 1990), 775; *Nowa Encyklopedia Powszechna PWN*, vol. 6 (Warsaw, 1996), 894–896; G. Scheuermann, *Das Breslau-Lexikon*, vols. 1–2 (Laumann, 1994).

WRON. See **Military Council of National Salvation.**

WROŃSKI, STANISŁAW (1916–), historian, member of the Central Committee* of the Polish United Workers' Party (PZPR)* in 1968–81 and of the State Council (Rada Państwa)* in 1974–85. *Who's Who in the Socialist Countries of Europe,* ed. by J. Stroynowski, vol. 3 (Munich, 1989), 1322; T. Mołdawa, *Ludzie Władzy 1944–1991. Władze państwowe i polityczne Polski według stanu na dzień 28 II 1991* (Warsaw, 1991), 443.

WRZASZCZYK, TADEUSZ (1932–), Deputy Premier from October 1975 to August 24, 1980, member of the Party Central Committee* from December 1971, deputy member of the Politburo* from December 1975 and full member from February 1980. An engineer by profession, he served as director of Warsaw's Car Factory (Fabryka Samochodów Osobowych) from 1962; in 1965, he was charged with modernizing the Polish auto industry. He made his name as a skillful manager, instrumental in the opening of Polish Fiat production. As such, he became a member of the Gierek* team and was considered one of its most intelligent managers. In December 1970 he was appointed Minister of the Machine Industry. During the changes of the mid-1970s, he became Deputy Premier, chairman of the Planning Committee, and member of a special commission in charge of modernization and the improvement of the Polish centralized management system. Removed from his positions in 1980, he was ejected from the Party on April 28, 1981 for "mistakes in central planning" and "using his position for personal advantages." *Who's Who in the Socialist Countries of Europe,* ed. by J. Stroynowski, vol. 3 (Munich, 1989), 1322; Z. Błażyński, *Towarzysze zeznają. Z tajnych archiwów Komitetu Centralnego* (London, 1987), 186–204.

WUJEC, HENRYK (1941–), dissident,* Solidarity* leader, and physicist. An activist of the Warsaw* Club of Catholic Intelligentsia* in the 1960s, in 1975 he signed a letter to the Polish authorities protesting changes in the Polish Constitution. In 1976 he joined the Workers' Defense Committee (KOR)* and, in 1977, was dismissed from work. He co-edited the underground paper *Robotnik* ("The Worker")* in 1977–81 and was detained by the police over 100 times. In 1980 he co-founded Solidarity, Mazowsze (Mazovia) Region and became one of its main leaders. Interned after imposition of Martial Law* on December 13, 1981, he was released and rearrested several times in the 1980s. In 1989 he participated in the Round Table Negotiations* and was elected to the Sejm,* where he belonged to the Civic Parliamentary Club (OKP).* During the "war at the top,"* he joined the Citizens' Movement for Democratic Action (ROAD).* Later he was a member of the Democratic Union (UD).* As one of its leaders, he was re-elected to the Sejm in 1991 and 1993. *Who's Who in the Socialist Countries of Europe,* ed. by J. Stroynowski, vol. 3 (Munich, 1989), 1322; *Kto jest kim w polityce polskiej,* ed. by R. Ignasiak (Warsaw, 1993), 322.

"WUJEK" COAL WORKS, Silesian coal mine where miners protested against imposition of Martial Law* on December 13, 1981, by organizing an occupational strike. Many similar strikes were organized in Poland at that time, and troops and riot police attacked and occupied striking enterprises. The miners of "Wujek" tried to defend themselves on December 16. When the attackers opened fire, nine miners died on the spot or were fatally wounded. J. Karpiński, *Poland since 1944: A Portrait of Years* (Boulder, Colo., 1995), 231.

WYCECH, CZESŁAW (1899–1977), Deputy Chairman of the State Council (Rada Państwa)* in 1956–57 and Speaker of the Sejm* in 1957–71. A Polish peasant movement activist in the interwar period, he worked underground for the Delegacy of the Government-in-Exile* in occupied Poland during World War II. In 1945 he joined the Polish Peasant Party (PSL),* and in 1946 he became a member of its leadership, where he supported a policy of cooperation with the communists. After the dissolution of the PSL in 1949, he joined the United Peasant Party (ZSL)* and was one of its leaders until 1973. T. Mołdawa, *Ludzie Władzy 1944–1991. Władze państwowe i polityczne Polski według stanu na dzień 28 II 1991* (Warsaw, 1991), 443.

WYKA, KAZIMIERZ (1910–75), critic and historian of literature, professor at Warsaw University,* and director of the Institute of Literary Studies (IBL). His *Życie na niby* ("Life as If"), a diary written during the war and the early postwar period, is a master analysis of everyday life in Nazi-occupied Poland. C. Miłosz, *The History of Polish Literature* (Berkeley, Calif., 1983), 515; *Dictionary of Polish Literature*, ed. by E. J. Czerwinski (Westport, Conn., 1994), 442–443; M. Dąbrowska, *Dzienniki powojenne 1945–49*, ed. by T. Drewnowski (Warsaw, 1996), 68; *Encyklopedyczny Słownik Sławnych Polaków* (Warsaw, 1996), 444.

WYSZKOWSKI, KRZYSZTOF (1947–   ), democratic opposition* activist who initiated the Free Trade Unions committee in Gdańsk* and drafted their original statement in 1978. He accompanied L. Wałęsa* during his official visit to France, participated in the 1980 strike in the Lenin Shipyard, and became associate editor of the *Tygodnik Solidarność* ("The Solidarity Weekly")* in 1981. D. Ost, *Solidarity and the Politics of Anti-Politics* (Philadelphia, 1990), 12–13.

WYSZYŃSKI, STEFAN (1901–81), Cardinal, Archbishop of Gniezno and Warsaw,* and Primate* of Poland, instrumental in protecting the Polish Roman Catholic Church* during the Stalinist period* and considered by many the greatest Pole of the postwar period. A son of a country organist, he was ordained a priest in 1924, earned a doctorate in sociology and ecclesiastical law at the Catholic University of Lublin (KUL),* and completed his versatile education in France, Italy, and Belgium. In 1935 he founded Christian Workers University and directed it until World War II. From March 1945 he taught at a religious seminary in Włocławek, and in 1946 he was appointed bishop of Lublin.* Two years later, on November 12, 1948, he became Archbishop and Primate. During the Stalinist period Wyszyński tried to preserve the Church's independence by signing an agreement with the communist authorities in April 1950. He was sharply criticized for this compromise. Yet he had not intended to legitimize the communist regime. When the communists broke the agreement, Wyszyński issued a categorical memorandum protesting the government's anti-religious policy. As a consequence, in 1953 he was arrested and imprisoned in remote monasteries. Released during the "Polish October" of 1956,* he reached another compromise with the new Party First Secretary, W. Gomułka.* The latter started a new anti-religious crusade culminating in 1966, when Wyszyński organized a nationwide religious celebration of the 1,000th anniversary of Christianity in Poland. In the 1970s Wyszyński supported Polish human rights and opposition* movements, became a mediator between the eroding communist system and Polish society, and enjoyed tremendous popularity, although some accused him of being too nationalistic. Wyszyński's policy contributed to the selection of Karol Wojtyła, the bishop of Cracow,* as Pope John Paul II* and to the fall of communism in Poland. After his death Wyszyński was called "the Primate of the Millennium."*The Cold War, 1945–1991*, vol. 2, "Leaders and Other Important Figures in the Soviet Union, Eastern Europe, China, and the Third World," ed. by B. Frankel (Detroit, 1992), 352–353; A. Micewski, *Cardinal Wyszyński: A Biography* (New York, 1984); H. Stehle, *The Eastern Policies of the Vatican, 1917–1979* (Athens, Ohio, 1981).

YALTA CONFERENCE, meeting of Allied leaders, Joseph Stalin, Winston Churchill, and Franklin D. Roosevelt, at Yalta in the Crimea, February 4–11, 1945. There, the leaders agreed on their goals and policies during the last stages of the war. Poland was a major subject of the Yalta talks. The Allies decided that the Curzon Line would be Poland's eastern border and the Oder-Neisse Line* its western frontier, that the Provisional Government* would be extended with the inclusion of a group of democratic émigré Polish politicians from London, especially S. Mikołajczyk,* and that a free parliamentary election would be organized in Poland as soon as possible. It appears that Stalin, who already controlled Polish territories, did not take this agreement seriously. The first Polish postwar election, organized in January 1947, was neither free nor fair. There was no free election in Poland until 1989 or even 1990. Poland became a part of the Soviet "outer empire," and the Polish public believed the country had been sold by the Western powers in exchange for Soviet help against Japan and other minor concessions. Yalta became a code word for treason and immoral bargaining in international politics. Poles felt betrayed by their own allies. Phrases such as "we were sold at Yalta," "the order of Yalta," "victims of Yalta," and "betrayal of Yalta" became basic to Polish political vocabulary. The myth of Yalta became an important element in the political programs of most anti-communist organizations in Poland. G. Lerski, *Historical Dictionary of Poland, 966–1945*, with special editing and emendations by P. Wróbel and R. J. Kozicki (Westport, Conn., 1996), 671–672; K. Kersten, *Jałta w polskiej perspektywie* (London, 1989); J. Coutouvidis and J. Reynolds, *Poland, 1939–1947* (Leicester, 1986), 173–174, 194; A. Polonsky (ed.), *The Great Powers and the Polish Question, 1941–45* (London, 1976), 235–251; B. P. McCrea, J. C. Plano, and G. Klein, *The Soviet and East European Dictionary* (Oxford, 1984), 343.

YOUNG POLAND MOVEMENT (Ruch Młodej Polski [RMP]), clandestine anti-communist organization established in 1979 in Gdańsk* by a group of young people, which began its formation in 1969. Members of the group were active in the Movement for the Defense of Human and Civil Rights (ROPCiO)* and the Students' Solidarity Committee and cooperated with the Gdańsk Academic Priesthood (Duszpasterstwo Akademickie), the Workers' Defense Committee (KOR),* and the Confederation for an Independent Poland (KPN).* They published and distributed political leaflets and periodicals and developed propaganda and self-educational activities. On July 29, 1979, a communiqué was issued announcing the establishment of the RMP, and on August 18, 1979, its *Ideological Declaration* was accepted. It emphasized neo–National Democratic, Christian Democratic, anti-Soviet, and anti-communist ideas, declared that human rights and national sovereignty were the most important values of the movement, and announced that it would fight for national moral improvement, for free access to uncensored knowledge and information, and in defense of national culture and consciousness. The RMP, led by such activists as Jacek Bartyzel, Piotr Dyk, Grzegorz Grzelak, A. Hall,* Marek Jurek,* Arkadiusz Rybicki, Jan Samsonowicz, and Andrzej Słomiński, had no clearly established structure. After imposition of Martial Law,* some of its leaders were interned or hid underground and the group's activities were limited. When Martial Law was lifted, RMP members gathered around the underground publication *Polityka Polska* (''Polish Politics''). In September 1988 they returned to the RMP banner. The RMP was a good school for future leaders of the Christian-National Union (ZChN),* Liberal-Democratic Congress (KLD),* Democratic Right Forum (FPD), and other political organizations of the reborn democratic Poland. D. Cecuda, *Leksykon Opozycji Politycznej 1976–1989* (Warsaw, 1989), 96–98.

ZABŁOCKI, JANUSZ Z. (1926–), veteran of the Home Army (AK),* journalist and editor of several Catholic periodicals, such as *Więź* (''The Link'')* and *Ład* (''The Order''), member of the PAX Association* in 1950–55, and co-founder of the Clubs of Catholic Intelligentsia* in 1956. In 1965 he became a Sejm* deputy, from 1972 he served as vice-chairman and, from 1977, chairman of the *Znak** parliamentary group. In 1976 he founded, and in 1977–81 presided over, the Polish Club of Catholic Intelligentsia. During 1981–84 he chaired the Parliamentary Club of the Polish Catholic-Social Union (PZKS).* During his long political career he tried to find a compromise between socialism and his Catholic faith. *Who's Who in the Socialist Countries of Europe*, ed. by J. Stroynowski, vol. 3 (Munich, 1989), 1331; G. Polak, *Kto jest kim w Kościele katolickim* (Warsaw, 1996), 431.

ZAGAJEWSKI, ADAM (1945–), existential poet and writer describing Polish realities under communism. In the 1970s he was a key representative of the poetic group Nowa Fala (''New Wave''). From 1979 he has been a member of the Board of Directors of the Polish PEN Club. Harassed by censors,* he left Poland in 1982 and settled in Paris, where he co-edited the quarterly *Zeszyty Literackie* (''Literary Notebooks''). *Dictionary of Polish Literature*, ed. by E. J. Czerwinski (Westport, Conn., 1994), 451; J. Zieliński, *Leksykon polskiej literatury emigracyjnej* (Lublin, 1989), 140; P. Kuncewicz, *Agonia i nadzieja. Poezja polska od 1956* (Warsaw, 1993), 466.

ZAHORSKI, ANDRZEJ (1923–92), historian, professor at Warsaw University,* and expert on the late 18th century. *Who's Who in the Socialist Countries of Europe*, ed. by J. Stroynowski, vol. 3 (Munich, 1989), 1334.

ZAIKS, association of writers established in 1918 and affiliated with several international writers' organizations. Its goal was to represent Polish writers and to protect their rights. ZAIKS reached 3,400 members in 1965. *Nowa Encyklopedia Powszechna PWN*, vol. 6 (Warsaw, 1996), 62.

ZAKOPANE, major winter-sport and health resort in Poland, but also an important cultural center located in the Tatra Mountains, near the border with Slovakia. *The New Encyclopaedia Britannica*, vol. 12 (Chicago, 1990), 888.

ZALESKI, AUGUST (1883–1972), diplomat, Minister of Foreign Affairs during 1926–32 and 1939–41, and President*-in-Exile during 1947–72. Most Poles in exile did not recognize Zaleski as President. When he refused to step down in 1954 after his first term in office, the Council of Three* was established to lead Polish political institutions in exile. G. Lerski, *Historical Dictionary of Poland, 966–1945*, with special editing and emendations by P. Wróbel and R. J. Kozicki (Westport, Conn., 1996), 675; T. Radzik, *Z dziejów społeczności polskiej w Wielkiej Brytanii po drugiej wojnie światowej, 1945–1990* (Lublin, 1991); *Warszawa nad Tamizą*, ed. by A. Friszke (Warsaw, 1994); W. Hładkiewicz, *Przywódcy "Polskiego" Londynu, 1945–1972* (Zielona Góra, 1993), 5–9.

ZAMBROWSKI, ROMAN (1909–77), member of the State Council (Rada Państwa)* from February 1947 to May 1955 and an activist of the reformist "Puławska group" within the Polish United Workers' Party (PZPR).* A member of the Communist Party of Poland (KPP) from 1928, he spent World War II in the USSR and served as chief of the Political-Educational Department of the Polish Army* there. In 1944 he joined the Polish Workers' Party (PPR)* and soon became Secretary of its Central Committee* and a member of the Politburo,* where he was responsible for state administration. He occupied several important apparatus posts, such as Deputy Speaker of the Sejm* during 1947–52, Minister of State Control in 1955–56, and President of the Supreme Control Chamber (NIK).* During the March events of 1968,* he was removed from his position because of his Jewish heritage. T. Mołdawa, *Ludzie Władzy 1944–1991. Władze państwowe i polityczne Polski według stanu na dzień 28 II 1991* (Warsaw, 1991), 445; Z. Błażyński, *Mówi Józef Światło. Za kulisami bezpieki i partii* (London, 1985), 47–49; G. Sanford and A. Gozdecka-Sanford, *Historical Dictionary of Poland* (Metuchen, N.J., 1994), 227.

ZAMOYSKI, JAN T. (1912–   ), scion of the aristocratic Zamoyski family, veteran of Polish freedom fighting, member of the Senate* in 1991–93, founder and president of the reborn, but small, National Democratic Party (SND) from 1991. *Kto jest kim w polityce polskiej*, ed. by R. Ignasiak (Warsaw, 1993), 327.

ZANUSSI, KRZYSZTOF (1939–   ), film director who gained international renown with such films as *Structure of Crystal* and *Year of the Calm Sun*. *Who's Who in the Socialist Countries of Europe*, ed. by J. Stroynowski, vol. 3 (Munich, 1989), 1340.

ZAORSKI, JANUSZ (1947–), film director and producer, member of the Radio and TV* Council from 1988, and its chairman in 1991. *Kto jest kim w polityce polskiej*, ed. by R. Ignasiak (Warsaw, 1993), 328.

ZAPIS ("The Record"), underground literary quarterly published from 1977. *Zapis* published such important works as *Kompleks polski* ("The Polish Complex") and *Mała apokalipsa* ("The Little Apocalypse") by T. Konwicki,* and *Wielki strach* ("The Great Fear") by J. Stryjkowski.* *Dictionary of Polish Literature*, ed. by E. J. Czerwinski (Westport, Conn., 1994), 88; J. Karpiński, *Polska, Komunizm, Opozycja* (London, 1985), 315; D. Cecuda, *Leksykon opozycji politycznej 1976– 1989* (Warsaw, 1989), 202.

ZAREMBA, ZYGMUNT (1895–1967), theoretician of the Polish socialist movement and leader of the Polish Socialist Party (PPS).* He joined the PPS in 1912 and belonged among the most important party leaders of the interwar period. In 1939 he co-organized the defense of Warsaw* and built a clandestine organization of his Party in occupied Poland. Though a key leader of the Polish underground state, he was, by happenstance, not among the 16 Polish statesmen arrested by the NKVD in March 1945. He continued his activities in the underground, but threatened with arrest, he left Poland for France in 1946. There, he rebuilt the PPS in exile and was among its main leaders. *Słownik Historii Polski 1939–1948*, ed. by A. Chwalba and T. Gąsowski (Cracow, 1994), 239–243; A. Friszke, "Przedmowa" [Introduction] to Z. Zaremba, *Wojna i konspiracja* (Cracow, 1991), 11–31; A. K. Kunert, *Ilustrowany przewodnik po Polsce podziemnej, 1939–1945* (Warsaw, 1996), 606.

ZARĘBSKI, ANDRZEJ (1957–), Solidarity* activist, spokesperson of the government of J. K. Bielecki,* Sejm* deputy in 1991–93, and member of the Radio and TV* Council from 1993. *Kto jest kim w polityce polskiej*, ed. by R. Ignasiak (Warsaw, 1993), 328.

ZARZYCKI, JANUSZ (1914–), Polish Army* general and communist official. He joined the Polish Workers' Party (PPR)* in 1942 and belonged to the general staff of its People's Guard. Arrested by the Germans in 1943, he went through Auschwitz and Buchenwald. In 1945–48 he served as chief of the Main Political Board of the Polish People's Army, and in 1948–49, as chairman of the Union of Polish Youth (ZMP).* Sidetracked during 1949–56, he returned to power during the "Polish October" of 1956,* serving as Deputy Minister of Defense and chief of the Army Main Political Board in 1956–60. Mayor of Warsaw* (president of the capital's National Council) in 1956 and 1960–67, he was purged for his opposition to the March events of 1968.* R. F. Staar, *Poland, 1944–1962: The Sovietization of a Captive People* (New Orleans, 1962), 134–136; Z. Błażyński, *Mówi Józef Światło. Za kulisami bezpieki i partii* (London, 1985).

ZASP (Związek Artystów Scen Polskich [Union of Artists of the Polish Scenes]), artists' trade union* established in 1918. In 1950 it was dissolved and replaced by SPATiF (Stowarzyszenie Polskich Artystów Teatru i Filmu [Union of Polish Artists of Theater and Film]). In 1981 SPATiF returned to its old name, but the union was suspended and liquidated after imposition of Martial Law* in December 1981. It was rebuilt in 1983 and developed in 1989. *Nowa Encyklopedia Powszechna PWN*, vol. 6 (Warsaw, 1996), 1050.

ZAWADZKI, ALEKSANDER (1899–64), Silesian miner and President of the State Council (Rada Państwa)* from 1952 until his death. A member of the Communist Party of Poland (KPP) from 1923, he headed its super-clandestine Central Military Department. During World War II Zawadzki worked as a miner in the Soviet Kuznietsk Coal Basin. He joined the communist-controlled First Polish Army* in 1943 and was one of its top political commanders. Simultaneously, he belonged to the leaderships of the Union of Polish Patriots (ZPP) and the Bureau of Polish Communists in the Soviet Union.* In 1944 he joined the Polish Workers' Party (PPR),* its Central Committee,* and the Politburo.* After the 1948 "unification," he held these positions in the Polish United Workers' Party (PZPR).* He also served as governor (wojewoda) of Silesia in 1945–48, Deputy Premier in 1949 and 1950–52, and president of the Central Council of Trade Unions (CRZZ). T. Mołdawa, *Ludzie Władzy 1944–1991. Władze państwowe i polityczne Polski według stanu na dzień 28 II 1991* (Warsaw, 1991), 445; Z. Błażyński, *Mówi Józef Światło. Za kulisami bezpieki i partii* (London, 1985), 46–47.

ZAWIEYSKI, JERZY (1902–69), writer, publicist, liberal Catholic intellectual, member of the State Council (Rada Państwa)* from February 1957 to April 1968, and friend of Primate S. Wyszyński.* An actor by profession, he spent the years 1929–31 in France, where he was influenced by the "Personalism" of Emmanuel Mounier. In the 1930s Zawieyski organized amateur theaters, and during World War II he participated in the anti-German resistance. Later he contributed to the prestigious *Tygodnik Powszechny* ("The Universal Weekly"),* was active in the Clubs of Catholic Intelligentsia* after 1956, and in 1957 became a member of the Sejm* and the chairman of the Parliamentary Catholic Club Znak.* He died shortly after he was removed from the Sejm and the State Council for his criticism of the March events of 1968.* C. Miłosz, *The History of Polish Literature* (Berkeley, Calif., 1983), 508; *Dictionary of Polish Literature*, ed. by E. J. Czerwinski (Westport, Conn., 1994), 454–464; T. Mołdawa, *Ludzie Władzy 1944–1991. Władze państwowe i polityczne Polski według stanu na dzień 28 II 1991* (Warsaw, 1991), 446; A. Micewski, *Ludzie i opcje* (Warsaw, 1993), 93.

ZBoWiD (Union of Fighters for Freedom and Democracy), veterans' organization established in September 1949 with the fusion of 11 groups of veterans and former German political prisoners active in Poland from 1945. The organization was reshaped into the Union of Army Veterans of the Republic of Poland

and Former Political Prisoners (Związek Kombatantów RP i b. Więźniów Politycznych) in 1990. Membership in ZBoWiD was considered helpful in a professional career and was associated with privileges. Controlled by the Polish United Workers' Party (PZPR),* before 1956 ZBoWiD did not accept former members of the Home Army (AK)* and other military formations the Party considered anti-communist. The union, which reached 188,000 members in 1965 and 800,000 in 1986, helped to organize historical celebrations and build monuments. ZBoWiD was a tool in the political fighting between various Party factions. M. Moczar,* for example, based his political network and campaign in the 1960s on ZBoWiD. The union's Main Council was headed by J. Cyrankiewicz* in 1949–72, P. Jaroszewicz* in 1972–80, M. Moczar in 1980–83, and H. Jabłoński* in 1983–90. The Main Board of Directors was presided over by F. Jóźwiak* in 1949–56, J. Zarzycki* in 1956–64, M. Moczar in 1964–72, S. Wroński* in 1972–80, W. Sokorski* in 1980–83, and Józef Kamiński in 1983–90. T. Mołdawa, *Ludzie Władzy 1944–1991. Władze państwowe i polityczne Polski według stanu na dzień 28 II 1991* (Warsaw, 1991), 325; *Nowa Encyklopedia Powszechna PWN*, vol. 6 (Warsaw, 1996), 1050.

ZHP (Związek Harcerstwa Polskiego [Union of Polish Scouts]). See **Scouting.**

ZIEJA, JAN (1897–1991), Catholic priest, military chaplain in the Polish-Bolshevik war of 1919–20, veteran of the anti-German resistance during World War II, founding member of the Workers' Defense Committee (KOR),* and activist in the democratic opposition* in communist Poland. J. J. Lipski, *KOR: A History of the Workers' Defense Committee in Poland, 1976–81* (Berkeley, Calif., 1985); M. H. Bernhard, *The Origins of Democratization in Poland: Workers, Intellectuals, and Oppositional Politics, 1976–1980* (New York, 1993).

ZIELIŃSKI, TADEUSZ (1926–   ), Polish ombudsman in 1992–96. A candidate during the presidential elections of 1995,* he was supported by the Union of Labor (UP),* the Polish Socialist Party (PPS),* and the Party of Retirees, but he won only 3.5% of the vote. *Kto jest kim w polityce polskiej*, ed. by R. Ignasiak (Warsaw, 1993), 332.

ZIEMBIŃSKI, WOJCIECH (1925–   ), editor and artist, veteran of World War II, founding member of the Workers' Defense Committee (KOR),* activist in the Crooked Circle Club* and in the democratic opposition* in communist Poland. J. J. Lipski, *KOR: A History of the Workers' Defense Committee in Poland, 1976–81* (Berkeley, Calif., 1985); M. H. Bernhard, *The Origins of Democratization in Poland: Workers, Intellectuals, and Oppositional Politics, 1976–1980* (New York, 1993).

ZIĘTEK, JERZY (1901–85), official of Silesian local governments, member of the State Council (Rada Państwa)* during 1963–80, and its Deputy President in 1980–85. During 1919–21 he participated in the Silesian Uprisings; after 1922 he worked in autonomous Silesian self-government. During 1930–35 he represented the Non-Party Bloc of Cooperation with Government (BBWR) in the Sejm.* Ziętek spent World War II in the USSR, where he joined the communist-controlled Polish Army* in 1943. A member of the Polish Workers' Party (PPR)* from 1945 and of the Central Committee* of the Polish United Workers' Party (PZPR)* from 1964, he served as deputy governor (wicewojewoda) of Silesia during 1945–50 and its governor in 1973–75. In 1950–64, he was deputy president of the Katowice* Provincial Council, and he presided over this nominal self-government during 1964–73. Ziętek was considered by many to be the embodiment of a true Silesian political activist. T. Mołdawa, *Ludzie Władzy 1944–1991. Władze państwowe i polityczne Polski według stanu na dzień 28 II 1991* (Warsaw, 1991), 447.

ZIMAND, ROMAN (1926–92), literary historian, writer, and dissident.* Deported by the Soviets to Central Asia from his native Lvov, he returned to Poland in 1945 and joined the communist youth movement and the Polish Workers' Party (PPR).* A journalist in the "thaw"* weekly *Po Prostu* ("Plainly Speaking"),* he was deeply involved in the de-Stalinization process in Poland and, in 1957, was expelled from the Party. He became an activist in the Crooked Circle Club* and a faculty member at the Literary Research Institute (IBL) of the Polish Academy of Sciences (PAN).* Interned under Martial Law* and dismissed from work, he returned to IBL in 1985. *Who's Who in the Socialist Countries of Europe*, ed. by J. Stroynowski, vol. 3 (Munich, 1989), 1356.

ZIMIŃSKA-SYGIETYŃSKA, MIRA (1901–97), actress and educator. Singer in Warsaw's* literary cabarets before the war, she participated in the anti-German resistance and the 1944 Warsaw Uprising. In 1948, together with her husband, T. Sygietyński,* she created the famous state song and dance ensemble *Mazowsze* ("Mazovia") and then served as its director and artistic manager. *Who's Who in the Socialist Countries of Europe*, ed. by J. Stroynowski, vol. 3 (Munich, 1989), 1356.

ZIÓŁKOWSKA, WIESŁAWA J. (1950–   ), economist, vice-chairperson of the Union of Labor (UP)* and its Parliamentary Club since 1992, and Sejm* deputy since 1989. A member of the Polish United Workers' Party (PZPR)* during 1974–90, she was an organizer and leader of the Polish Social Union (PUS)* and the Greater Poland Social-Democratic Union (Wielkopolska Unia Socjaldemokratyczna) in 1990–92. *Sejm Rzeczpospolitej Polskiej. II Kadencja. Przewodnik* (Warsaw, 1994), 198.

ZIÓŁKOWSKI, JANUSZ A. (1924–   ), professor of sociology at Poznań* University and Secretary of State for International Affairs in the presidential chancellery of L. Wałęsa* from January 1991. A Solidarity* sympathizer and a member of the Civic Committee,* Ziółkowski participated in the Round Table Negotiations* in 1989. As Secretary of State he collaborated harmoniously with the Minister of Foreign Affairs, K. Skubiszewski,* and helped to create a new line of Polish foreign policy. G. Sanford and A. Gozdecka-Sanford, *Historical Dictionary of Poland* (Metuchen, N.J., 1994), 230; *Kto jest kim w polityce polskiej*, ed. by R. Ignasiak (Warsaw, 1993), 334.

ZLP. See **Union of Polish Writers.**

ZMP. See **Union of Polish Youth.**

ZMS. See **Union of Socialist Youth.**

ZMW. See **Union of Rural Youth.**

ZNAK ("The Sign"), Catholic monthly devoted to religious life, theology, philosophy, and history, published since 1946 in Cracow.* In 1950–52 it appeared irregularly, and in 1953 only one issue was published. Later *Znak* was suspended until 1957, when the Znak publishing house was established and began to publish books and the periodical *Znak.* The publishing house has been directed by J. Woźniakowski,* and the periodical had been edited, in succession, by Hanna Malewska, B. Cywiński,* and Stefan Wilkanowicz. J. Karpiński, *Polska, Komunizm, Opozycja* (London, 1985), 321.

ZNAK ("The Sign"), group of progressive Catholic writers and intellectuals gathered around *Tygodnik Powszechny* ("The Universal Weekly")* and the monthlies *Znak* ("The Sign")* and *Więź* ("The Link").* In 1957 the group received several seats in the Sejm* and established the *Znak* parliamentary caucus. It constituted the only opposition in the Sejm and included between three and five deputies (K. Łubieński,* S. Kisielewski,* S. Stomma,* T. Mazowiecki,* and J. Zawieyski*), although in 1957–61 it had eleven deputies. *Znak* openly criticized the government's policies during the March events of 1968.* Split by the Gierek* regime in 1976, the movement influenced many future Solidarity* leaders and opposed the activities of the PAX Association* and the Polish Christian Social Association,* which opposed the Roman Catholic Church* hierarchy. A. Bromke, "The 'Znak' Group in Poland," *Poland since 1956,* ed. by T. N. Cieplak (New York, 1972), 80–94; G. Sanford and A. Gozdecka-Sanford, *Historical Dictionary of Poland* (Metuchen, N.J., 1994), 230; J. Karpiński, *Polska, Komunizm, Opozycja* (London, 1985), 321.

ZNP. See **Union of Polish Teachers.**

ZOMO (Motorized Units of the People's Militia), special police units trained to fight riots and to disperse demonstrations, established in 1956. Developed in the 1980s, ZOMO was used often and became the infamous symbol of the Jaruzelski* regime. Jaruzelski himself received a nickname "ZOMOza," derived from the name of ZOMO and the Central American dictator Somosa. ZOMO was dissolved in September 1989. M. H. Bernhard, *The Origins of Democratization in Poland: Workers, Intellectuals, and Oppositional Politics, 1976–1980* (New York, 1993); *Nowa Encyklopedia Powszechna PWN*, vol. 6 (Warsaw, 1996), 1038; B. Juryś, *Byłem w ZOMO* (Warsaw, 1991).

"ZRYW" ("Spurt"), group within the Labor Party (SP)* organized by Z. Felczak and F. Widy-Wirski* and sponsored by the Polish communist authorities, which planned to use it to crush the SP. A. Micewski, *Ludzie i opcje* (Warsaw, 1993), 7.

ZSL. See **United Peasant Party.**

ZYCH, JÓZEF (1938–), lawyer, peasant politician, Deputy Speaker from 1991, and Speaker of the Sejm* from March 1995. In 1989 he was an organizer and leader of the Polish Peasant Party "Revival" (PSL "Odrodzenie"). In 1990 he joined the newly reunited Polish Peasant Party (PSL),* became deputy president of its Main Council (Rada Naczelna) and chairman of the PSL Sejm caucus. Considered a reasonable and moderate politician, he is a strong rival of W. Pawlak* in the PSL leadership. T. Mołdawa, *Ludzie Władzy 1944–1991. Władze państwowe i polityczne Polski według stanu na dzień 28 II 1991* (Warsaw, 1991), 448; *Kto jest kim w polityce polskiej*, ed. by R. Ignasiak (Warsaw, 1993), 336; G. Sanford and A. Gozdecka-Sanford, *Historical Dictionary of Poland* (Metuchen, N.J., 1994), 231.

Ż

ŻABIŃSKI, ANDRZEJ (1938–   ), Party official and leader of a hard-line faction in the Polish United Workers' Party (PZPR)* in the early 1980s. An activist of the communist youth movement, he served as chairman of the Socialist Youth Association (ZMS)* in 1967–71. During 1969–85 he was a Sejm* deputy, and in 1971 he became a member of the Party Central Committee.* In 1980 he joined the Politburo* and gained the powerful position of Party First Secretary in Katowice* Province. There, he animated intense anti-Solidarity* activities and tried to oppose what he thought to be the overly conciliatory policies of Gen. W. Jaruzelski,* who sidetracked Żabiński after imposition of Martial Law in Poland.* *Who's Who in the Socialist Countries of Europe*, ed. by J. Stroynowski, vol. 3 (Munich, 1989), 1331.

ŻANDAROWSKI, ZDZISŁAW (1929–   ), member of E. Gierek's* leadership group. A Party member from 1948, he joined its Central Committee* in 1968 and its Politburo* in February 1980. During 1954–56 he served as first secretary of the Warsaw University* Party organization, during 1960–69 as secretary of the Warsaw* City Party organization, during 1971–77 as chairman of the Party Organizational Committee, and from April to October 1980 as member of the State Council (Rada Państwa).* In 1980–81 he was removed from all positions, deprived of the People's Poland Builder order, and forced to retire from the Sejm.* *Who's Who in the Socialist Countries of Europe*, ed. by J. Stroynowski, vol. 3 (Munich, 1989), 1339; T. Mołdawa, *Ludzie Władzy 1944–1991. Władze państwowe i polityczne Polski według stanu na dzień 28 II 1991* (Warsaw, 1991), 448.

ŻENCZYKOWSKI, TADEUSZ (1907–97), youngest deputy of the Sejm* in 1938, veteran of the Polish resistance during World War II, political refugee in Western Europe from 1945, deputy director of the Polish Program of Radio Free Europe,* and prolific and outstanding historical writer who opposed communism but never used anti-communist demagogy. A. K. Kunert, *Ilustrowany przewodnik po Polsce podziemnej, 1939–1945* (Warsaw, 1996), 616; *Warszawa nad Tamizą. Z dziejów polskiej emigracji politycznej po drugiej wojnie światowej*, ed. by A. Friszke (Warsaw, 1994), 72, 100, 112, 143.

ŻOŁNIERZ WOLNOŚCI ("Soldier of Freedom"), newspaper published by the Defense Ministry as its semi-official organ. Originally, *Żołnierz Wolności* was published for the soldiers of the First Division of the communist Polish Army* in the USSR during 1943–45. Between 1945 and 1950 the all-Polish Army daily was called *Polska Zbrojna* ("Armed Poland")—a title taken from an interwar Polish Army newspaper. In 1950 the title was changed to *Żołnierz Wolności*. The newspaper, six pages long, appeared six times per week, selling about 100,000 copies, until the fall of communism in Poland. It presented a stiff communist line and played an important role in the propaganda and indoctrination campaign. Several times, in 1968 and 1980–81, its publications signaled the future plans of the communist authorities. J. Karpiński, *Polska, Komunizm, Opozycja* (London, 1985), 329.

ŻÓŁKIEWSKI, STEFAN (1911–91), sociologist, historian, literary critic, politician, and author of numerous works on culture, literature, and politics. A member of the Polish Workers' Party (PPR)* from 1942, he was active in the communist resistance, edited its underground periodicals, and was appointed a member of the National Home Council (KRN).* During 1945–48 he edited *Kuźnica* ("The Forge"), a communist cultural flag periodical. In 1948 he established and headed the Institute of Literary Research (IBL), and from 1949 he was a professor at Warsaw University.* He was expelled from the university in 1969 for his solidarity with students persecuted after the March events of 1968.* In 1948 and 1955–56 he chaired the Science and Culture Department of the Central Committee* of the Polish United Workers' Party (PZPR);* he also served as long-time member of the Sejm,* as Minister of Higher Education in 1956–59, as scientific secretary of the Polish Academy of Sciences (PAN),* and as editor of several periodicals. *Who's Who in the Socialist Countries of Europe*, ed. by J. Stroynowski, vol. 3 (Munich, 1989), 1361; M. Dąbrowska, *Dzienniki Powojenne 1945–1965*, vol. 1, ed. by T. Drewnowski (Warsaw, 1996), 177.

ŻUKROWSKI, WOJCIECH (1916–   ), writer. A veteran of the September Campaign of 1939 and the Home Army (AK),* he joined the Polish People's Army* in 1945; he served as war correspondent in North Vietnam from 1954 and diplomat to New Delhi from 1956. In 1972 he became a Sejm* deputy and was on the Sejm Commissions for Culture and Foreign Affairs. He also co-edited several journals and chaired the Society for Polish-Soviet Friendship. He supported Martial Law,* and in 1982 he joined the Patriotic Movement of National Revival (PRON).* *Who's Who in the Socialist Countries of Europe*, ed. by J. Stroynowski, vol. 3 (Munich, 1989), 1363.

ŻUŁAWSKI, JULISZ (1910–), poet, writer, and translator. He fought in the September Campaign of 1939 and spent World War II in a German POW camp for officers. After the war he joined the editorial staff of *Kuźnica* ("The Forge") and *Nowa Kultura* ("The New Culture"), important communist cultural periodicals. During 1978–83 he presided over the Polish PEN Club. *Who's Who in the Socialist Countries of Europe*, ed. by J. Stroynowski, vol. 3 (Munich, 1989), 1363; M. Dąbrowska, *Dzienniki Powojenne 1945–1965*, vol. 1, ed. by T. Drewnowski (Warsaw, 1996), 177.

ŻYCIE WARSZAWY ("Warsaw Life"), daily published in Warsaw* since 1944. It became very popular in the 1950s and had several local editions in Polish provincial capitals. The daily published essays on politics, economy, and culture as well as the news. *Nowa Encyklopedia Powszechna PWN*, vol. 6 (Warsaw, 1996), 1090.

ŻYGULSKI, KAZIMIERZ (1919–), government official and sociologist. A veteran of the Home Army (AK)* in the Lvov region, he was deported by the Soviets to Siberia and returned to Poland in 1956. He started a scientific career and served as deputy rector of the State Higher School of Theater and Film, Minister of Culture in 1982–86, and from 1983 Presidium member of the National Council of Culture (Narodowa Rada Kultury). *Who's Who in the Socialist Countries of Europe*, ed. by J. Stroynowski, vol. 3 (Munich, 1989), 1366; A. Kępiński and Z. Kilar, *Kto jest kim w Polsce inaczej* (Warsaw, 1985), 409–421.

ŻYMIERSKI-ROLA, MICHAŁ (1890–89), Marshal of the People's Poland. Born as Michał Łyżwiński, he graduated from the Jagiellonian University* in Cracow* in 1914 and then participated in the Polish struggle for independence, served with the Piłsudski Legions, fought in the 1919–20 Polish-Bolshevik War, and occupied several commanding positions in the Polish Army.* Charged with fraud in 1926, he was imprisoned until 1931. He left for France, but in 1938 Żymierski-Rola returned to Poland. During World War II he joined the Polish Workers' Party (PPR)* and its People's Guard. In 1944 he became a member of the Presidium of the National Home Council (KRN),* commander-in-chief of the Polish People's Army, and the head of the Defense Department of the Polish Committee of National Liberation (PKWN). Promoted to Marshal in 1945, he served as Minister of Defense in the Provisional Government of the Republic of Poland* and in the Provisional Government of National Unity (TRJN)* until 1949, when he became a member of the State Council (Rada Państwa).* Unjustly accused, he was imprisoned in 1952. Rehabilitated in 1956, he was nominated vice-president of the National Bank of Poland and president of the Commercial Bank. Although he retired in 1968, he was used by the Gierek* and Jaruzelski* regimes for symbolic and ceremonial purposes. *Who's*

Who in the Socialist Countries of Europe, ed. by J. Stroynowski, vol. 3 (Munich, 1989), 1366; G. Sanford and A. Gozdecka-Sanford, *Historical Dictionary of Poland* (Metuchen, N.J., 1994), 232; A. K. Kunert, *Ilustrowany przewodnik po Polsce podziemnej, 1939–1945* (Warsaw, 1996), 617.

1945

January 1 Polish Committee of National Liberation (PKWN), also known as the Lublin Committee, declares itself the Provisional Government* of Poland.

January 4 Despite British and U.S. protests, Stalin recognizes the Provisional Government.*

January 17 Red Army* takes Warsaw.*

January 19 Red Army* takes Cracow.* Gen. L. Okulicki* dissolves the Home Army (AK).*

January 27 Red Army* reaches Auschwitz and Katowice.*

February 4–11 Yalta Conference.*

March First issue of *Tygodnik Powszechny* ("The Universal Weekly")* appears in Cracow.*

March 27 Soviets arrest 16 leaders of the Polish underground state and deport them to Moscow for trial.

April 22 E. Osóbka-Morawski,* Premier* of the Provisional Government,* signs a 20-year treaty of friendship, mutual assistance, and postwar cooperation with the Soviet Union.

May 7 Germany surrenders to the Allies. The end of World War II in Europe.

June 18–21 Trial of 16 leaders of the Polish underground state in Moscow.

June 19 Polish troops seize Cieszyn.* Later, under Soviet pressure, Poland returns the region.

June 28 Provisional Government of National Unity (TRJN)* is created.

July 5 Britain and the United States officially recognize the Provisional Government of National Unity (TRJN)* and withdraw their support from the Polish Government-in-Exile.*

July 17–August 2 Potsdam Conference.*

August 2 Amnesty* for soldiers of the anti-communist underground.

August 6 Delegacy for Armed Forces* dissolved.

August 16 Treaty between Poland and the USSR fixes their new border at the Curzon Line. Poland officially loses 69,290 square miles in the east and gains 39,596 in the west.

September 2 Freedom and Independence (WiN)* organized by former members of the Home Army (AK).*

September Concordat with Vatican is broken by the Provisional Government of National Unity (TRJN).*

November 13 Ministry of ''Recovered Territories''* is formed.

November 16 Decree about ''crimes particularly dangerous in the time of State reconstruction'' is issued.

December 6–13 First Congress of the Polish Workers Party (PPR)* meets in Warsaw.*

1946

January 3 National Home Council (KRN)* passes the act on the nationalization* of industry.

February Volunteer Reserves of the Citizens' Militia (ORMO)* is organized.

February 5 Churchill's Fulton speech (''Iron Curtain'').

February 14 Polish and British representatives of the Allied Combined Repatriation Executive in Berlin agree on deportation of millions of Germans* from Poland to the West. First national postwar census takes place in Poland, which has 24 million inhabitants, including 2.3 million Germans.

June 30 Referendum* on the issues of the western border, reforms, and the Senate.*

July 4 Kielce pogrom.*

August 5 Soviets end occupation of the ''Recovered Territories''* and give control over them to the Polish administration.

September 26 Provisional Government of National Unity (TRJN)* deprives six Polish generals and 70 high-ranking officers of Polish citizenship on the grounds that they served in a ''foreign army''—the Polish Resettlement Corps.

1947

January 4–February 3 Trial of the leaders of the Freedom and Independence (WiN).* The sentences range from two years' imprisonment to capital punishment.

January 8 Premiere of the first Polish movie after the war.

January 19 First postwar parliamentary elections held.

February 4 B. Bierut* becomes President* of the Polish Republic.

February 8 New government is formed by Premier J. Cyrankiewicz.*

February 19 New Sejm* passes the Little Constitution.*

February 22 Amnesty* act passed in the Sejm.*

April Authorities start the "Battle of Trade."

April 4 Deputy Minister of Defense, Gen. K. Świerczewski,* killed by the Ukrainian Insurgent Army (UPA).*

April 28 Beginning of the Action Vistula.*

July *Kultura** is first published in Rome.

July 2 Three-Year Plan accepted.

July 9 Poland, pressured by the Soviet Union, rejects the Marshall Plan.

July 23 United States ends World War II aid to Poland.

September 14 Communist authorities of Poland denounce the 1925 Concordat with the Vatican.

September 22–27 Council of nine communist parties meets in Szklarska Poręba to form the Cominform.* Poland is a founding member.

October 21 S. Mikołajczyk* secretly leaves Poland.

1948

January–February Central Planning Office, influenced by economists from the Polish Socialist Party (PPS),* is attacked by the Polish Workers' Party (PPR).* C. Bobrowski,* the socialist head of the office, resigns in February.

January 26 USSR and Poland sign a five-year trade treaty.

February–May Warsaw Military Court tries members of the National Armed Forces (NSZ)* and the National Party (SN). The sentences include several death sentences.

March Premier J. Cyrankiewicz* goes to Moscow to meet with J. Stalin and to discuss unification of the workers' movement in Poland.

May 3 Communist authorities of Poland ban celebration of Constitution Day.

June 26 New five-year trade agreement between Poland and the USSR is signed to counterbalance the Marshall Plan.

July 6–7 Plenary meeting of the Central Committee* of the Polish Workers' Party (PPR)* condemns J. Tito and Yugoslavia.

July 22 Communist youth organizations unite to form the Union of Polish Youth* (ZMP).

August Catholic weekly, *Tygodnik Warszawski* ("The Warsaw Weekly"),* is shut down and its editorial board arrested.

August 25–28 Congress of "Intellectuals for Peace" in Wrocław.*

August 31–September 3 During a plenary meeting of the Central Committee* of the Polish Workers' Party (PPR),* W. Gomułka* is removed as General Secretary and is replaced by B. Bierut.* The Stalinist period* starts.

November 5–19 Warsaw military court tries six Socialist activists for belonging to the secret Socialist organization and attempting to overthrow the existing system by violence. The same court tries eight members of the Freedom and Independence (WiN)* organization from the Lublin* region and gives eight death sentences.

November 12   S. Wyszyński* becomes Primate* of Poland.

December 15–21   Unification Congress*; the Polish Socialist Party (PPS)* and the Polish Workers' Party (PPR)* form Polish United Workers' Party (PZPR)* as a result of a forced merger.

1949

January 11   Ministry of the "Recovered Territories"* is closed by the government.

January 20   W. Gomułka* resigns as Deputy Premier and is replaced by A. Zawadzki.*

January 25   Poland becomes a founding member of Comecon.*

February 10   Central Planning Office is dissolved and replaced by the Commission for Economic Planning.

March   Special Bureau—Tenth Department of Ministry of Public Security—in charge of acts of sabotage and espionage, is established.

July 1   Central Council of Trade Unions (CRZZ)* is created.

July 13   Pope excommunicates all members of communist parties who are Roman Catholics.

August 5   Authorities issue a new law that guarantees freedom of religion but foresee heavy penalties for people forcing religion on others or trying to use religion as a means of political pressure.

September 30   Poland, pressed by the USSR, revokes its 1946 treaty of friendship and mutual assistance with Yugoslavia.

October 28   Government of Poland expels the International Refugee Organization and the International Red Cross, claiming they are agents of the West.

November 6   K. Rokossowski* becomes Minister of National Defense and Marshal of Poland on the "request" of the Polish government.

November 11–13   Plenary meeting of the Central Committee* of the Polish United Workers' Party (PZPR)* elects K. Rokossowski* a member of the committee and removes W. Gomułka,* Z. Kliszko,* and M. Spychalski.*

November 27–29   Polish Peasant Party (PSL)* and so-called Lublin Peasant Party (SL) unite to form United Peasant Party (ZSL).*

1950

March   Poland withdraws from the International Monetary Fund and the International Bank of Reconstruction and Development because, according to the official governmental announcement, they had become "open instruments of American imperialism."

March 20   First National Exhibition of Visual Arts opens period of Socialist Realism* in Poland.

April   K. Pużak,* Secretary General of the Polish Socialist Party (PPS),* dies in Rawicz prison.

April 14   Agreement is signed between the government and the Episcopate* referring to, among other things, the teaching of religion in school, the activities of the Catholic University of Lublin (KUL),* and the Roman Catholic press.

June 1   Number of Polish provinces (województwo) is increased from 14 to 17 with the creation of three new administrative units in the western territories.

June 25   North Korean troops invade South Korea.

July 6   German Democratic Republic signs a border treaty with Poland in Zgorzelec. The treaty recognizes the Oder-Neisse Line* as a legitimate border between the two states.

July 9   Communist-controlled remnants of the Labor Party (SP)* are added to the Democratic Party (SD).*

July 21   Six-Year Plan (1950–55) is accepted by the Sejm.*

August 20   Poland withdraws from the World Health Organization.

October 28   Emergency session of the Sejm* devaluates the Polish currency, the złoty (3 new zł. to 100 old zł.).

October 29   Soviets tie Polish currency, the złoty, to the Soviet ruble, which reduces convertibility of the złoty into Western currencies.

December 3   Second postwar census is held; Poland is populated by 25 million inhabitants.

1951

February 15   Poland and the USSR exchange 185 square miles of Polish territory in Lublin* Province (parts of the Hrubieszów and Zamość districts) for a Soviet region of similar size in the Bieszczady Mountains—a signal that the Polish-Soviet border is movable.

March   Warsaw Regional Military Court tries a group of leaders of the Jehovah's Witness movement for "spying and hostile anti-Polish propaganda." The same court tries several activists of the Labor Party (SP).*

June 29–July 2   First Congress of Polish Science held in Warsaw* establishes the Polish Academy of Sciences (PAN).*

July–August   Supreme Military Court tries four generals: S. Tatar,* Franciszek Herman, J. Kirchmayer,* and Stefan Mossor. Sentences range from 10 years in prison to life imprisonment.

July 21   Monument to Feliks Dzierżyński is unveiled in Warsaw.*

July 31   W. Gomułka* is arrested.

August 2   W. Gomułka* is imprisoned for "nationalist deviation." He spends three years under house detention.

October 8   Warsaw Regional Military Court sentences five activists of the Polish Peasant Party (PSL)* as "spies and agents engaged in subversive activities, and close collaborators of Mikołajczyk."*

1952

January 5   Poland loses most-favored-nation trade status in the United States. The Americans raise tariffs and other duties on Polish goods imported into the United States.

March 1   Polish communist government formally protests against activities of the U.S. House of Representatives committee investigating the Katyń* case.

April 5   Agreement between the Polish and the Soviet governments is signed regarding the construction of the 30-storey Palace of Culture and Science in Warsaw.*

May   Governmental announcements that detergents, meat, fats, sugar, and sweets will be sold with coupons.

July 22   New Constitution, based on the 1936 Soviet Constitution, is accepted by the Sejm.*

October 26   Parliamentary elections.

November 20   First meeting of the new Sejm.*

November 30   Archbishop S. Wyszyński* is informed that he will be elevated to Cardinal in January 1953.

December 15   Opening of the large exhibition "Such Is America."

1953

January 1   Rationing system is abandoned, but the prices of several commodities are raised.

January 21   Four Roman Catholic priests and three laypersons are tried by the Cracow Regional Military Court for contacting Polish émigré institutions and a Western intelligence center. Three priests are sentenced to death.

February 9   Communist authorities pass a law giving them the exclusive right to make all appointments to religious offices.

March   *Tygodnik Powszechny* ("The Universal Weekly")* is suspended.

March 5   Stalin's death.

March 19   Following the Soviet example, the Polish communist government accepts the rule of collective leadership. B. Bierut* resigns as Premier* to be succeeded by J. Cyrankiewicz.* Bierut keeps the post of First Secretary of the Polish United Workers' Party (PZPR).*

August 24   Polish communist government follows the Soviet example and renounces German reparations to Poland.

September 22   Bishop of Kielce,* C. Kaczmarek, is sentenced to 12 years' imprisonment for heading an "anti-state and anti-people center."

September 25   Cardinal S. Wyszyński* is arrested.

December 5   Col. J. Światło,* vice-director of the Tenth Department in the Ministry of Public Security, asks for political asylum in West Berlin.

1954

March 10–17   Second Congress of the Polish United Workers' Party (PZPR).* One of its main topics: the very bad condition of agriculture* caused by collectivization.*

May   Premiere of the STS (Students' Satirical Theater).*

June 18   Poland resumes its cooperation with UNESCO, interrupted in 1949.

July 21   First furnace of Nowa Huta* is put into operation.

September 28   First press conference of Col. J. Światło* in Washington, D.C. Radio Free Europe* starts broadcasting Światło's texts.

November   Inauguration of "Bim-Bom,"* satiric student theater.

December 7   Ministry of Security is abolished and replaced by the Ministry of Interiors and the Committee of State Security.

December 13   W. Gomułka* is released from house arrest and admitted to the hospital of the Ministry of Public Security.

1955

January 21–24   Third plenary meeting of the Central Committee* of the Polish United Workers' Party (PZPR)* criticizes the activities of the political police.

May 14   Warsaw Treaty* is signed.

July 21   Palace of Culture and Science is handed over to the Polish government by the Soviets.

July 31–August 14   "Fifth World Festival of Young People and Students for Peace and Friendship" is held in Warsaw.*

August 19   Weekly *Nowa Kultura* ("The New Culture") publishes *A Poem for Adults* by A. Ważyk.*

September   *Po Prostu* ("Plainly Speaking")* becomes a vehicle of political "thaw."*

November 26   *Dziady* ("Forefathers' Eve"),* by Adam Mickiewicz, is staged for the first time after the war on the centenary of the poet's death.

1956

January 5   Crooked Circle Club (Klub Krzywego Koła)* has its first meeting.

February 14–25   Twentieth Congress of the Soviet Communist Party is held in Moscow.

March–April   *Po Prostu* ("Plainly Speaking")* and *Nowa Kultura* ("The New Culture") publish articles about injustices done to the soldiers of the Home Army (AK).*

March 12   B. Bierut,* First Secretary of the Polish United Workers' Party (PZPR),* dies in Moscow.

March 20   E. Ochab* is elected first secretary of the Polish United Workers' Party (PZPR).*

March 21   Party *aktiv* is familiarized with N. Khrushchev's Twentieth Congress "Secret Speech."

April 10   W. Gomułka* is officially rehabilitated.

April 23   Amnesty* is passed by the Sejm* (over 35,000 people released from prisons).

May 4   J. Berman,* second highest in the Polish communist hierarchy, resigns his posts.

May 29   W. Gomułka* writes to the Politburo* for permission to speak at the Central Committee* Plenum.

June 23–25 Workers of Poznań's* ZISPO machine-building plant choose and send their delegates to Warsaw* for discussions with government officials.

June 26 Minister of the Machine Industry promises to consider the demands of Poznań* workers.

June 27 Authorities in Poznań* renege on promises given to the workers earlier; strike in Poznań.

June 28 "Black Thursday" in Poznań.* Strikes spread in Poznań, followed by street demonstrations. The Polish Army* uses force against demonstrators, and bloody clashes result. Street fighting in Poznań.

June 29 Premier J. Cyrankiewicz* announces that the Poznań* uprising was prepared by "the imperialist centers" and "the reactionary underground."

June 30–July 6 Special Central Committee* Commission looks for the causes of the Poznań* uprising. Work stoppages occur in other cities in solidarity with Poznań.

July Government calls off its collectivization* policy.

July 10 USSR agrees to give Poland economic aid of 100 million rubles.

July 17 Attorney general states that 53 persons were killed during the Poznań* uprising.

July 18–28 Seventh Plenum of the Central Committee* acknowledges economic factors as the main reason for the Poznań* uprising. E. Gierek* is elected to Politburo.*

August 5 Polish United Workers' Party (PZPR)* restores the membership of W. Gomułka.* Some Politburo* members begin unofficial talks with him.

August 25–26 More than 1 million Poles participate in a pilgrimage to Jasna Góra monastery in Częstochowa* to celebrate the 300th anniversary of the defeat of the Swedes there and the recognition of the Virgin Mary as Queen of the Kingdom of Poland.

September Prosecution begins in Poznań* for participants in "Black Thursday."

September 18 USSR and Poland sign an agreement for large-scale Soviet aid to Poland.

October 8–10 Politburo* evaluates the situation in Poland as "critical." H. Minc* resigns.

October 15 W. Gomułka,* M. Spychalski,* Z. Kliszko,* and W. Loga-Sowiński* return to the Central Committee.*

October 18 Ambassador of the USSR to Poland, Ponomarenko, informs E. Ochab* that N. Khrushchev and a delegation of the Presidium of the Communist Party of the Soviet Union will arrive in Warsaw* the next day.

October 19 Red Army starts moving in the direction of Warsaw.* N. Khrushchev visits the Eighth Plenum of the Central Committee* of the Polish United Workers' Party (PZPR),* which begins that same day, and meets W. Gomułka.*

October 20 Soviet delegation leaves for Moscow.

October 21 W. Gomułka* is appointed First Secretary of the Polish United Workers' Party (PZPR).*

October 23 Hungarian uprising starts.

October 24 W. Gomułka* speaks at the rally of some 400,000 people on Parade Square in Warsaw.*

October 29 Cardinal S. Wyszyński,* released from internment, returns to Warsaw.*

November 1 Red Army* enters Hungary.

November 7–20 Session of the Sejm* approves changes in the composition of the government and the State Council (Rada Państwa).*

November 13 Marshal K. Rokossowski* is relieved of his posts as Vice-Premier and Minister of Defense and returns to Moscow with a group of Soviet officers.

November 14–18 W. Gomułka* travels to Moscow to sign the Five-Point Declaration, putting Soviet-Polish relations on a partnership footing.

November 15–18 Polish-Soviet talks in Moscow result in declarations forgiving the Polish debt, stipulating conditions for stationing Soviet forces in Poland, organizing repatriation* of Poles living in the USSR, and scheduling grain deliveries and loans for Poland.

November 18 Crowd in Bydgoszcz* attacks and destroys the radio station that jammed Western broadcasts.

November 19 Workers' Councils Act is passed by the Sejm.* The act admits workers to the administration of their enterprises.

November 21 Polish delegation in the United Nations abstains from the vote condemning Soviet intervention in Hungary.

December 10 In street riots in Szczecin,* demonstrators break into the Soviet consulate.

December 17 Poland and the USSR sign an agreement permitting the Red Army* to remain "temporarily" in Poland.

December 25 *Tygodnik Powszechny* ("The Universal Weekly")* is reinstated.

December 31 The number of the cooperative farms drops from over 10,000 in September to 1,534.

1957

January 2 Union of Socialist Youth (ZMS)* is formed.

January 20 Parliamentary elections are held.

January 22 Bohdan Piasecki, the son of the leader of the PAX Association,* B. Piasecki,* is kidnapped in Warsaw.* The body of the murdered boy is found in December 1958.

February 10–11 Union of Peasant Youth (ZMW)* is formed.

February 27 New government of J. Cyrankiewicz* is formed.

March 25 Repatriation* agreement is signed in Moscow by representatives of the Polish and Soviet governments.

May 15–18 Central Committee of the Polish United Workers' Party (PZPR)* holds J. Berman* and S. Radkiewicz* politically responsible for the activities of the Security Bureau (SB)* in 1945–56.

August 12–14   Strike of tram operators in Łódź.*

October 2   *Po Prostu* ("Plainly Speaking")* weekly is closed by the authorities. The decision is followed by several days of clashes between the police and students. At the United Nations, the Polish Foreign Minister, A. Rapacki,* reveals a plan to create a "nuclear free zone" out of the two Germanys, Czechoslovakia, and Poland.

November 11   Warsaw provincial court sentences R. Romkowski,* former Deputy Minister of Public Security, to 15 years' imprisonment; J. Różański,* former director of the Investigations Department in the Ministry of Public Security, to 14 years; and A. Fejgin,* former director of the Tenth Department in the Ministry of Public Security, to 12 years.

1958

February   First issue of the monthly *Więź* ("The Link")* is published.

May   M. Wańkowicz* returns to Poland.

July   Hanna Rewska is sentenced to three years' imprisonment for distributing copies of the Paris *Kultura* ("Culture").* She is released after an appeal.

October 28   New Pope, John XXIII, is elected.

1959

January–February   Fr. Marian Pirożyński, who "strove to engage in unauthorized publishing activity," is sentenced to two years' imprisonment.

March 10–19   Third Congress of the Polish United Workers' Party (PZPR)* is held. W. Gomułka* criticizes the Yugoslav communists, and E. Ochab* announces: "We communists are sure that cooperative farming is the future of Polish rural areas."

July 31   Government proclaims a "Meatless Mondays" campaign to deal with meat shortages.

August 2–5   U.S. Vice President Richard M. Nixon visits Poland and enjoys an enthusiastic welcome.

September   J. Chałasiński* is removed from his posts, including that of deputy secretary general of the Polish Academy of Sciences (PAN),* for his paper "Sociology and Social Mythology in Postwar Poland," presented during the Fourth World Sociological Congress in Milan and Stresa.

December 3–5   Meeting of the Union of Polish Writers (ZLP)* delegates is held. A. Słonimski* is replaced by J. Iwaszkiewicz* as president.

1960

April 17   Riots in Nowa Huta* in defense of the cross removed by the authorities from the future site of a church building.

July 16   Celebration of the 550th anniversary of the Grunwald victory over the Teutonic Knights. A. Ford's film *The Teutonic Knights* is shown in Olsztyn.

November 17   Poland regains most-favored-nation trade status in the United States.

December 6   National census is held in Poland, which now has 29.7 million citizens.

1961

April 15   Fourth postwar elections to the Sejm* are held.

July 14   Sejm* passes law according to which all citizens have to report their presence to local authorities when staying in a given place for more than three days.

July 15   New law on education withdraws religious instructions from schools and adds an eighth grade to the elementary school curriculum.

August 19   New regulation, issued by the Ministry of Education, stipulates that all centers of religious instruction should be registered and controlled by state authorities.

December 21   H. Holland* jumped, or was pushed, out of a window of his apartment during a search of it by police.

1962

February   Authorities close the Crooked Circle Club* in Warsaw.*

February 9   Anna Rudzińska, secretary of the Crooked Circle Club* and the Polish Sociological Society, is sentenced to one year's imprisonment for "preserving texts with improper content."

Spring   Club of Explorers of Contradictions (Klub Poszukiwaczy Sprzeczności) meets for the first time.

October   Authorities organize demonstrations to protest the U.S. blockade of Cuba.

December   First volume of *The Great Universal Encyclopedia* appears.

1963

March 7   Poland and West Germany sign a three-year commercial agreement.

April   Nurses go on strike in Warsaw.*

April 1   Prices of coal, electric power, gas, central heating, and water utilities are raised.

June   New weekly, *Kultura* ("Culture"),* replaces *Nowa Kultura* ("The New Culture")* and *Przegląd Kulturalny* ("The Cultural Review").

June 21   New Pope, Paul VI, is elected.

July 1   Last Stalinist, R. Zambrowski,* is removed from the Politburo* and the Central Committee.*

September 15   Prices of milk, alcohol, and matches are raised.

December 28   Northern section of the Friendship Pipeline is opened.

1964

March 14   Thirty-four intellectuals sign the "Letter of 34,"* protesting against cultural policies of the government. The authorities answer with reprisals against the signers.

July 20   Amnesty* is announced to mark the 20th anniversary of the People's Poland.

July 21   *Warsaw Nike*—a monument "To the Heroes of Warsaw, 1939–45"—is unveiled in Warsaw.* The inscription on its plaque, quoted above, and the form given to the monument were designed to avoid direct homage to the Warsaw Uprising.

August   A. Zawadzki* dies and is replaced as Chairman of the State Council (Rada Państwa)* by E. Ochab.*

September 26   Gen. M. Moczar* is elected president of the Union of Fighters for Freedom and Democracy (ZBoWiD).*

October 14   L. Brezhnev replaces N. Khrushchev as First Secretary of the Soviet Communist Party. Shortly after this change Brezhnev, A. Kosygin, and Y. Andropov met with W. Gomułka,* J. Cyrankiewicz,* and Z. Kliszko* "in the Białowieża Forest region."

November 9   Warsaw* provincial court sentences M. Wańkowicz* to three years' imprisonment for sending to his daughter abroad a text on the literary situation in Poland. Wańkowicz is arrested but never goes to prison.

November 14   Authorities temporarily arrest K. Modzelewski* and J. Kuroń* after police searched their houses and found a manuscript critical of the regime.

November 24   Polish United Workers' Party (PZPR)* expels K. Modzelewski* and J. Kuroń,* who write an open letter to the Party critical of its policies.

December 12   M. Moczar* is appointed Minister of the Interior.

1965

February 2   A manager of the Warsaw Meat Trading Enterprise is sentenced to death and later executed for the systematic, fraudulent seizure of public property. Four others accused are sentenced to life imprisonment.

March 19   J. Kuroń* and K. Modzelewski* are arrested in connection with their "Open Letter" to the Party.

April 8   Poland and the USSR renew, for the next 20 years, the 1945 treaty of friendship, cooperation, and mutual assistance.

May 30   Elections to the Sejm* and the People's Councils.

July 19   Sentencing in J. Kuroń* and K. Modzelewski* trial: three years in prison for Kuroń and three and one-half years for Modzelewski.

September 17   Jan Nepomucen Miller is sentenced to three years in prison for publishing several articles in an émigré periodical in London. These articles included "false information about the situation in Poland."

November   Letter of the Polish bishops to the bishops in Germany.*

December 10   *Życie Warszawy* ("Warsaw Life")* starts a propaganda campaign against Polish bishops.

1966

January 7   Authorities restrict Primate S. Wyszyński* from travel abroad.

January 13   Ceremonies opening the millennium of Polish Christianity start in Rome without S. Wyszyński.*

April 16–17   State-sponsored millennium celebrations* in Gniezno and Poznań.* W. Gomułka,* participating in the celebrations, criticizes the idea of Poland as a fortress of Christianity.

May–June   Church celebrations of the millennium take place in Częstochowa* and Warsaw* without the participation of Pope Paul VI, who does not receive government permission to enter Poland.

August   Cultural Revolution is proclaimed in China.

September   Copy of the picture of Our Lady of Częstochowa is intercepted by police on its way from Warsaw* to Katowice.* The authorities prohibited the circulation of the icon in the country.

October 21   During their celebration of the 10th anniversary of the "Polish October" of 1956* at the University of Warsaw,* members of the Socialist Youth Union (ZMS)* urge the release of J. Kuroń* and K. Modzelewski* from prison. Re-legation from the Polish United Workers' Party (PZPR)* and Warsaw University follows.

October 22   Polish United Workers' Party (PZPR)* expels L. Kołakowski* for his address at the October 21 demonstration.

December   Pope Paul VI tries to visit Poland again, but the government does not allow him to enter the country.

December 18   Minister of Education closes four theological seminaries.

1967

March–April   Poland renews its friendship treaties with Czechoslovakia, the German Democratic Republic, and Bulgaria.

March 22   A. Michnik's* student rights are suspended.

April 15   Gdańsk* Shipyard is renamed after Lenin.

May 3   J. Kuroń* leaves prison.

June 5   Outbreak of war between Egypt and Israel. Public opinion favors Israel and condemns the Soviet-supported Arab states.

June 6   Polish government condemns "the aggression of Israel," breaks diplomatic relations with it, and starts an "anti-Zionist" campaign.

June 19–24   Sixth Congress of Trade Unions is held. In his speech on Israeli history, W. Gomułka* compares the Israeli Army to the Nazi Wehrmacht and suggests that "Zionist circles of Polish Jews" should move to Israel.

July 2   K. Modzelewski* leaves prison.

September 6–12   Gen. Charles de Gaulle, accompanied by his wife and a large group of French officials, visits Poland and receives an enthusiastic welcome from the population, especially in Silesia, where he calls Zabrze "the most Polish of all Polish towns."

October 8–11   Premier Indira Gandhi of India visits Poland.

October 26   During a trial closed to the public, N. Karsov is sentenced to three years in prison for allegedly preparing to send abroad material deemed harmful to the regime.

November 24   Tenth Plenum of the Central Committee* is held in Warsaw* to discuss shortages in market supplies. The government announces a 16.7% average increase in meat and poultry prices.

November 25   Adam Mickiewicz's *Dziady* ("Forefathers' Eve")* is staged by K. Dejmek* at the National Theater in Warsaw.*

November 26   First Polish cars produced under the Italian "Fiat" license appear in Warsaw.*

December 19–21   Conference of Foreign Ministers of the Warsaw Treaty Organization* devoted to the Middle East crisis is held in Warsaw.*

December 29   Government stops all aid to Polish Jews* and to persons who helped the Jews during the war. This decision is rendered by the Joint Distribution Committee.

1968

January 3–5   A. Dubchek appointed First Secretary of the Czech Communist Party.

January 30   The play *Dziady* ("Forefathers' Eve"),* by the great Polish poet A. Mickiewicz, is closed down because of its anti-Russian tone. Students organize a protest at the statue of Mickiewicz; police arrest some protesters.

February   Students protest the ban of *Dziady*.*

March 2   Union of Polish Writers (ZLP)* condemns governmental policy toward the play *Dziady*.*

March 4   A. Michnik* and H. Szlajfer,* organizers of the protest of January 30, are ejected from the University of Warsaw.*

March 8   Student rallies and protests take place at the University of Warsaw.* "Worker-activists" and riot police enter the campus and beat and arrest the students.

March 9   Protest meeting is held in the main hall of Warsaw Polytechnical University.

March 11   Student movements and demonstrations spread to most academic institutions in Poland. The media start a propaganda campaign against "Zionists" and "Stalinists."

March 12–19   Rallies, demonstrations, strikes, and clashes with police occur at the universities in Cracow,* Łódź,* Toruń,* Poznań,* and Wrocław.*

March 19   W. Gomułka* announces that J. Szpotański* is sentenced to three years' imprisonment for writing a satirical poem.

March 25   Purges at the universities* start. Professors B. Baczko, L. Kołakowski,* Z. Bauman,* M. Hirszowicz, W. Brus,* and S. Morawski are fired from Warsaw University.*

March 29   Large numbers of students are ejected from the universities, with 1,616 from Warsaw University* alone. M. Moczar* and his Party faction intensify the "anti-Zionist" campaign. Thousands of Jews* and Poles of Jewish background emigrate.

April 9   E. Ochab* resigns from the State Council (Rada Państwa).* M. Spychalski* replaces him as Chairman.

April 11–18   Gen. W. Jaruzelski* becomes Minister of National Defense.

April 18   Warsaw Treaty Organization* starts military maneuvers in Czechoslovakia.

April 28   First student riots occur in Paris.

July 14–16   Communist leaders of Bulgaria, East Germany, Hungary, Poland, and the USSR meet in Warsaw* and send an ultimatum to the Czechoslovak Communist Party to stop reforms.

August 20–21   Warsaw Treaty Organization* starts military invasion in Czechoslovakia.

October 29   Polish troops leave Czechoslovakia.

November–December   Trials of the so-called commandos,* students of Warsaw University,* are held in Warsaw.*

November 11–16   Sixth Congress of the Polish United Workers' Party (PZPR).* L. Brezhnev participates in the congress and presents his "Brezhnev Doctrine." M. Moczar* is ousted from his position as Interior Minister.

1969

January 15   J. Kuroń* and K. Modzelewski* sentenced to three and one-half years in prison each.

February–April   More prison sentences meted out after March 1968 events*: A. Zambrowski, two years; I. Lasota,* I. Grudzińska, and T. Bogucka, one and one-half year.

February 10   A. Michnik,* B. Toruńczyk,* and H. Szlajfer* are sentenced to prison (three years and two years, respectively) for participating in March 1968 events.*

June 1   Elections to Sejm* and People's Councils.

August 22   During the burial of P. Jasienica,* J. Andrzejewski* publicly condemns the regime for its obscurantism.

1970

February   Negotiations in Warsaw* begin between Poland and West Germany to normalize mutual relations.

February 9   Trial of the Taternicy* starts.

May 11   Gen. W. Anders* dies in London.

August 12   USSR and West Germany sign a treaty on the renunciation of force. The treaty recognizes the Oder-Neisse Line* as Poland's western border.

December 7   Poland and West Germany sign an agreement normalizing their relations and also recognizing the Oder-Neisse Line* as Poland's western border.

December 8–12   Third postwar census is held: Poland has 32.6 million inhabitants.

December 12   Government increases prices of basic foodstuffs.

December 13   Strikes and demonstrations in Gdańsk,* Gdynia,* and Sopot.*

December 15   Headquarters of Citizen's Militia in Gdańsk* is attacked by demonstrators; building of the District Committee of the Polish United Workers' Party (PZPR)* is set on fire. Politburo* decides to use armed forces against the riots.

December 16   Gdańsk* Lenin Shipyard is surrounded by militia and army. Strikes and riots also continue in Elbląg,* Pruszcz Gdański, and Tczew.

December 17   Many Gdynia* Shipyard workers are killed on their way to work in the morning. Szczecin* Shipyard goes on strike, and its workers go to the streets. Altogether, 48 people are killed and 1,165 wounded in Gdańsk.*

December 18   W. Gomułka* suffers a stroke.

December 20   Plenary meeting of the Central Committee.* E. Gierek* replaces W. Gomułka* as First Secretary of the Polish United Workers' Party (PZPR).* Gierek rescinds the price increases. M. Spychalski* resigns as Chairman of the State Council

(Rada Państwa).* Gomułka, B. Jaszczuk,* Z. Kliszko,* M. Spychalski,* and R. Strze-lecki* are removed from the Politburo.*

December 23 P. Jaroszewicz* replaces J. Cyrankiewicz* as Premier.* The latter be-comes Chairman of the State Council (Rada Państwa).*

December 30 Minimum wage is raised.

1971

January 8 Vatican officially moves the dioceses of the "Recovered Territories"* from German ecclesiastical jurisdiction to Polish Roman Catholic Church* administration.

January 14 E. Gierek* announces that the Royal Castle in Warsaw,* destroyed during World War II, will be reconstructed.

January 22 Sit-down strike in Szczecin* Shipyard.

January 24–25 E. Gierek* meets with workers on strike in Szczecin* and Gdańsk.* He promises democracy and better living conditions ("Will you help?"—"We will help!").

February 6–7 Eighth plenary meeting of the Central Committee* discusses the De-cember events.* Z. Kliszko* and B. Jaszczuk* are removed and W. Gomułka* is sus-pended from the Central Committee* for their "serious errors."

February 11–15 Textile industry in Łódź* goes on strike.

February 15 Price hike is revoked; strike in Łódź* ends.

March 3 Meeting between Primate S. Wyszyński* and Premier P. Jaroszewicz*—the first meeting between a Primate and a Premier of Poland in 25 years.

March 9 Polish Press Agency informs that "Captain Czechowicz Has Carried out His Mission" as a Polish communist spy in Radio Free Europe* in Munich.

June 24 E. Gierek* changes the current Five-Year Plan (1971–75) to calm the popu-lation.

October Warsaw Provincial Court tries the leaders of the Ruch Movement.*

October 5 Jerzy Kowalczyk tries to blow up the lecture hall of the Teachers' Training College in Opole.*

December 6–11 Sixth Congress of the Polish United Workers' Party (PZPR)* is held, with L. Brezhnev, G. Husak, and E. Honecker present. J. Cyrankiewicz* and M. Moczar* are removed from the Politburo.* The slogan of the Congress is "May Poland grow in strength and may her people be more prosperous." The newly elected Central Commit-tee* does not include W. Gomułka.*

1972

January 1 Peasants relieved from mandatory deliveries.

March 28–29 H. Jabłoński* replaces J. Cyrankiewicz* as Chairman of the State Coun-cil (Rada Państwa).*

May 10 During a plenary meeting of the Central Committee,* E. Gierek* speaks about building a "second Poland."

May 17   West German Parliament ratifies the 1971 Polish-German treaty including the Oder-Neisse Line* as the western border of Poland.

May 31–June 1   President Richard Nixon visits Poland.

September 14   Poland and West Germany decide to establish diplomatic relations.

October 2–6   E. Gierek* visits France and is received with full state honors. France gives Poland credit of 1.5 billion francs.

October 20   M. Szczepański* is appointed chairman of Radio and TV* Committee.

November   Strikes in Gdańsk,* Łódź,* and Silesia.

1973

February 7   Decision is made to form the Federation of Socialist Polish Youth Unions. *Gleichschaltung* of the Polish youth movement starts.

March 26–27   Socialist Union of Polish Students (SZSP)* emerges.

Spring   First issue of *Aneks** quarterly is published.

October 6–24   Yom Kippur War between Israel and several Arab states. Shortages of gasoline in Poland and price increases for electricity and other forms of energy follow.

November 22   Administration reform: 49 small provinces (województwo) are created in place of 17.

December   Government permits 50,000 ethnic Germans* to leave Poland for West Germany.

1974

July   Celebrations of "The 30th anniversary of the People's Poland."

July 5   Official relations between the Polish People's Republic and the Vatican are revived.

July 18   Amnesty* act is issued to commemorate the 30th anniversary of Polish People's Republic.

July 19–22   L. Brezhnev visits Poland and receives the Grand Cross of the Virtuti Militari Order.

October 8–13   E. Gierek* visits the United States.

December 12   "Letter of 15" is signed on behalf of Poles living in the USSR.

1975

May 28   Administrative reform implemented. Following the French model and strengthening central government against regional self-government, the authorities replace 16 provinces (województwo) with 49 and liquidate counties (powiat).

August 1   Poland signs the Helsinki Accord, which recognizes the postwar boundaries as permanent and guarantees basic civil rights.

September   Several unexplained fires break out in Warsaw.* The arsonists are not found.

October 9   Representatives of the German and Polish governments sign an agreement in Warsaw,* according to which about 125,000 ethnic Germans* will leave Poland and, in return, Germany will pay Poland 1.3 billion German marks. In addition, Germany will grant Poland a long-term loan of 1 billion marks.

November 29   Modern Gdańsk* refinery begins operations.

December 5   "Letter of 59" intellectuals is signed, protesting against planned changes in the Polish Constitution. That same day the Central Railway Station in Warsaw* is opened.

December 8–12   Seventh Congress of the Polish United Workers' Party (PZPR).*

December 29   Parliamentary Committee to sketch a draft for constitutional amendments is created.

1976

January 9   Episcopate* sends a letter to the authorities protesting planned changes in the Polish Constitution.

January 31   Group of 101 intellectuals sign a letter to the Sejm's* constitutional committee protesting the planned changes of the Polish Constitution and the restriction of civil rights.

February 10   Sejm* votes for the constitutional amendments, which involve an alliance with the Soviet Union and the leading role of the Polish United Workers' Party (PZPR).*

March 21   Elections to the Sejm* and the People's Councils are held. 98.27% of eligible voters participate in the elections, and 99.43% of them, according to the electoral committee's communiqué, votes for the Front of National Unity* candidates.

May   Prof. E. Lipiński* writes an open letter to E. Gierek.*

May 3   Program of Polish Independence Agreement (PPN)* is announced.

June 24   Without preparing the public, Sejm* decrees food price increases up to 60%.

June 25   Strikes and clashes with police occur in Radom,* Ursus,* Płock, Łódź,* Starachowice, Grudziądz, and Nowy Targ. The authorities moderate the price increases.

July   "Letter of 13" against sentences in Ursus* and Radom* trials. "Letter of 14" sent to the Sejm,* with Open Letters of J. Andrzejewski* and J. Kuroń.*

July 2   E. Gierek* and P. Jaroszewicz* meet with Party activists in the sports arena in Katowice.*

July 17   First trial of Radom* strike participants takes place in Warsaw.*

August 13   Sugar rationing begins.

September 23   Workers' Defense Committee (KOR)* issues its first appeal.

1977

March 26   Movement for the Defense of Human and Civil Rights (ROPCiO)* is established.

May 7   S. Pyjas,* student and Workers' Defense Committee (KOR)* affiliate, is killed in Cracow.*

May 24–30 Hunger strike in St. Martin's Church in Warsaw* protests police persecutions in Poland.

July 19 Sejm* passes an act of amnesty.*

September NOWa,* an independent printing house, comes to life. The first issue of the underground biweekly *Robotnik* ("The Worker")* appears.

October Three new underground periodicals appear: *Głos* ("The Voice"),* *Spotkania* ("Encounters"), and *Puls* ("The Pulse").*

December 1 E. Gierek* visits Pope Paul VI in the Vatican to talk about a possible new concordat.

December 29–31 U.S. President Jimmy Carter visits Poland, praises Poland's respect for human rights and religious freedom, and surprises the Polish public.

1978

January 11 Association of Academic Courses (TKN)* starts its activities.

February 25 K. Świtoń* organizes Founders' Committee of Free Trade Unions (KZWZZ) in Silesia.

April 29 Committee of Free Trade Unions is organized on the Baltic Coast and in Ursus.*

June 24 First stage of the construction of the Katowice* Ironworks (Huta Katowice) is officially completed.

June 27 First Polish cosmonaut, M. Hermaszewski,* is sent into orbit on the *Soyuz 30* spaceship.

July Provisional Committee for the Self-Defense of Farmers is formed in the Lublin* region.

October 16 Cardinal K. Wojtyła is elected as Pope John Paul II.*

November 14 "Experience and the Future" (DiP)* conversatory is organized.

December Polish hard currency debt reaches $15 billion.

December 7 Fifth postwar census is conducted in Poland, which now has 35 million inhabitants.

December 16 L. Wałęsa* and other members of the Committee of Free Trade Unions hold a memorial service for victims of the December 1970 events.*

1979

February 15 Explosion caused by a gas leak in the *Rotunda*, one of the main Warsaw* offices of the General Savings Bank (PKO). Forty-nine people are killed.

April 17 Lenin monument in Nowa Huta* slightly damaged by a bomb explosion.

June 2–10 First Papal visit* to Poland.

October 1 Confederation for an Independent Poland (KPN)* is organized.

November 11 Independent rally takes place at the Tomb of the Unknown Soldier in Warsaw* to commemorate the anniversary of Polish independence in 1918. Organizers of the rally are later arrested and tried.

December 16 L. Wałęsa* and the Committee of Free Trade Unions hold a memorial service for victims of the December 1970 events* and demand that a monument be erected on the site of the 1970 massacre. Police break up the service and arrest participants.

1980

February 11–15 Eighth Congress of the Polish United Workers' Party (PZPR).* E. Babiuch* replaces P. Jaroszewicz* as Premier.* The latter is not elected to the Central Committee.*

March 23 Elections to the Sejm* and the People's Councils; according to the official communiqué, the candidates of the Front of National Unity* received 99.52% of all legal votes.

May 3 Police arrest several people participating in a public celebration of May 3, Constitution Day, in Warsaw.*

June 18 Explosion at the Lenin Shipyard in Gdańsk* kills 8 and injures 60. Workers express their concern about working and safety conditions.

July–August Wave of strikes goes through Poland, involving more than 300,000 workers. The strikers receive a pay increase of 10% to 15% within hours after the strike.

July 1 Food prices are unexpectedly raised; meat prices increase by almost 100%.

August 14 Strike in Gdańsk* Shipyard.

August 16 Inter-Factory Strike Committee (MKS)* is organized in Gdańsk* Shipyard with L. Wałęsa* as its chairman.

August 18 Inter-Factory Strike Committee (MKS)* formulates a list of 21 demands. Strike in Szczecin.*

August 22 Government Commission starts talks with the Inter-Factory Strike Committee (MKS)* in Gdańsk.* In Rome, Pope John Paul II* holds a special mass for the strikers.

August 24 Group of Experts, affiliated with the Inter-Factory Strike Committee (MKS)* in Gdańsk,* is established. E. Babiuch* is dismissed as Premier* and replaced by J. Pińkowski.* M. Jagielski* is appointed Deputy Premier to start negotiations with the strikers.

August 26 Primate S. Wyszyński* in his homily in Częstochowa* urges the strikes to stop.

August 29 Strikes occur in Silesia.

August 30 Plenum of the Central Committee* decides to sign the agreement with the workers. The agreement is signed in Szczecin.*

August 31 Gdańsk Agreement* is signed by L. Wałęsa* and M. Jagielski.*

September 1 Striking workers of Gdańsk* and Szczecin* return to work, but strikes continue in other regions of Poland until mid-September.

September 4 Agreement between the authorities and striking workers is signed in Jastrzębie-Zdrój.*

September 6 S. Kania* replaces E. Gierek* (now ill) as First Secretary.

September 10   Independent Student Association (NZS)* is organized.

September 17   Solidarity* is proclaimed.

September 21   Sunday Mass is broadcasted on the radio throughout Poland for the first time since the 1940s.

October 3   Solidarity* organizes a one-hour strike to force the authorities to put into effect the Gdańsk Agreement.*

October 9   C. Miłosz* receives the Nobel Prize in Literature.

October 24   Warsaw District Court registers statutes of Solidarity* with stipulations recognizing the leading role of the Party and limiting the right to strike. Solidarity calls a general strike for November 12. S. Kania* goes to Moscow.

November 10   Polish Supreme Court accepts Solidarity's* status without additional stipulation about the leading role of the Party and strike limits. The text of the Gdańsk Agreement* is added as an appendix to the statute. Solidarity withdraws threat of strike.

December 1–2   E. Gierek* is removed from the Central Committee* of the Polish United Workers' Party (PZPR).*

December 5   Central Council of Trade Unions (CRZZ)* ceases to exist. Members of the Warsaw Treaty Organization* meet in Moscow to discuss the situation in Poland.

December 9   Soviets initiate military maneuvers around Poland that build tension and provoke Western warnings about possible intervention in Poland.

December 12   Foreign ministers of NATO warn the USSR that an invasion of Poland would end the East-West détente.

December 16   Dedication of a memorial in Gdańsk* commemorating workers killed during the December 1970 events.*

1981

January 1   Authorities dissolve the government-controlled Central Council of Trade Unions (CRZZ).*

January 15   L. Wałęsa* meets Pope John Paul II* in Rome.

February 9   Gen. W. Jaruzelski* replaces J. Pińkowski* as Premier* and requests a 90-day period of peace.

February 19   Independent Student Union (NZS)* is registered.

March 8   Rally at Warsaw University* commemorates the March events of 1968.*

March 8–9   Independent Self-Governing Trade Union of Individual Farmers Solidarity (Rural Solidarity*) is established with J. Kułaj* as its chairman.

March 19   J. Rulewski* and a dozen of other Solidarity* leaders are beaten by police in Bydgoszcz.* Tension mounts.

March 19–26   Warsaw Treaty Organization* maneuvers in Poland and neighboring countries are extended in response to unrest in Poland.

March 20   Solidarity's* National Coordination Commission (KKP)* announces strike readiness.

March 22   Politburo* warns against anarchy threatening socialism in Poland.

March 24 National Coordination Commission (KKP)* announces general strike on March 31.

March 27 Four-hour national warning strike is held.

March 30 Talks between L. Wałęsa* and M. Rakowski.* Wałęsa, on television, calls off the general strike.

April 3 First issue of *Tygodnik Solidarność* ("The Solidarity Weekly").*

April 7 In his address to the Party Congress in Prague, Czechoslovak communist leader G. Husak states that the Warsaw Treaty Organization* will not tolerate the undermining of socialism in Poland.

April 15 "Horizontal structures" movement of the Party meet in Toruń.*

May 3 Large and numerous Constitution Day rallies.

May 12 Rural Solidarity* is registered by a Warsaw Court.

May 13 John Paul II* is seriously wounded by an assassin, which adds to tension in Poland.

May 28 Primate* S. Wyszyński* dies.

June 9 Eleventh Plenum of the Central Committee* of the Polish United Workers' Party (PZPR).*

June 28 Mass service and rally, attended by over 150,000 people, commemorates the 1956 Poznań* uprising.

July 7 Archbishop J. Glemp* becomes new Primate.*

July 14–20 Ninth Congress of the Polish United Workers' Party (PZPR).* About 80% of all delegates are new. A secret ballot with multiple candidates, used for the first time, results in a new Politburo,* with only four former members re-elected. S. Kania* is elected First Secretary by secret ballot.

August 5 General strike organized to protest food price hikes.

September 5–10 First part of National Congress of Solidarity* in Gdańsk.* Message is sent to the working people of the Soviet bloc. The Soviets respond with fleet maneuvers off Gdańsk.

September 26–October 7 Second part of Solidarity* congress. L. Wałęsa* re-elected chairman.

September 28 Workers' Defense Committee (KOR)* dissolves itself.

October Father J. Popiełuszko* of St. Stanislaus Kostka parish in Warsaw* begins to read a "Mass for Poland" every month.

October 4 New food price hikes announced by the authorities.

October 16–18 Gen. W. Jaruzelski* replaces S. Kania* as First Secretary of the Polish United Workers' Party (PZPR).*

October 23 Gen. W. Jaruzelski* sends army units into the countryside ostensibly to help in food procurement.

November 4 Talks between Gen. W. Jaruzelski,* Primate J. Glemp,* and L. Wałęsa* try to set up a Council for National Consensus. Solidarity* asks for an end to strikes for three months.

November 11   For the first time since 1938, Poland celebrates Independence Day.

November 20   Independent Students' Union (NZS)* announces a national student strike.

November 24   Sit-in strike in the Higher School of Fire Brigades Officers (WOSP). Soviet Marshal V. Kulikov, commander of the Warsaw Pact,* visits Warsaw* for consultations with Gen. W. Jaruzelski.*

December 2   Motorized Detachments of the Citizens' Militia (ZOMO)* takes the Higher School of Fire Brigades Officers (WOSP) by force.

December 8   Primate J. Glemp* appeals to Solidarity* and the government to negotiate.

December 11–12   Congress of Polish Culture in Warsaw.* Solidarity's National Commission meets in Gdańsk* and asks for a national referendum on a non-communist government in Poland.

December 12–13   State Council (Rada Państwa)* pronounces Martial Law.* Military Council for National Salvation (WRON)* is established. Mass arrest of workers and intellectuals starts.

December 13   Strikes and riots in many cities in response to Martial Law.*

December 14   Polish Army* surrounds the Gdańsk* Lenin Shipyard and cuts Western news cables—a news blackout.

December 15   Strikes suppressed in Manifest Lipcowy mine in Jastrzębie-Zdrój,* in Świdnik, in the Gdańsk* Lenin Shipyard, and in Warsaw* Steelworks (December 16). Nine miners die in Silesian mine "Wujek"* during clashes with Motorized Detachments of the Citizens' Militia (ZOMO).*

December 17   U.S. President R. Reagan blames the USSR for Martial Law* in Poland.

December 20   Polish ambassador to the United States defects in protest against Martial Law, followed by the ambassador to Japan four days later.

December 23   Strike crushed in Katowice* Steelworks. U.S. President R. Reagan announces sanctions against Poland.

December 28   Last sit-in strike ends in the Silesian mine "Piast."

December 29   United States imposes economic sanctions against the USSR for imposition of Martial Law* in Poland.

1982

January   Beginning of "the verification action" against journalists. Hundreds are fired.

January 9   Jaruzelski*-Glemp* talks. The Military Council for National Salvation (WRON)* creates Civic Committees of National Salvation (OKON).

January 11   Foreign ministers of NATO meet in Brussels, condemn the Soviet role in "the system of repression in Poland," and ask European countries to participate in economic sanctions against the USSR.

January 13   Solidarity's* All-Poland Committee of Resistance (OKO) is created by E. Szumiejko.

January 27   Large price increases are announced, effective February 1. Economic reform laws pass.

March 20   Polish People's Republic Association of Journalists replaces the old Association of Polish Journalists (SDP).*

April 22   Solidarity's* Provisional Coordinating Committee (TKK)* is established.

May 1   Clashes take place between police and anti-government demonstrators during the May Day celebrations.

May 3   Motorized Detachments of the Citizens' Militia (ZOMO)* attacks demonstrators in Warsaw,* Toruń,* Cracow,* Elbląg,* Gliwice, Szczecin,* Lublin,* and Gdańsk.*

June   K. Morawiecki* organizes Fighting Solidarity* in Wrocław.*

July   Solidarity's* Provisional Coordinating Committee (TKK)* creates Solidarity-Abroad Coordinating Bureau, with its seat in Brussels.

July 20   Patriotic Movement for National Revival (PRON)* comes into being.

July 21   On the eve of the communist holiday of July 22, Gen. W. Jaruzelski* announces the restoration of international telephone service and the release of many internees.

August 31   Protests mark the second anniversary of the Gdańsk Agreement.*

September 3   Interned members of the former Workers' Defense Committee (KOR),* J. Kuroń,* J. Lityński,* A. Michnik,* and H. Wujec,* are arrested.

October 8   Sejm* announces new trade union laws. Solidarity* and four other groups are de-legalized.

October 26   Sejm* passes several restrictive bills, including "social parasite" legislation and anti-alcohol laws.

November 13   L. Wałęsa* is released from internment.

November 14   L. Wałęsa* returns home in Gdańsk.*

December 18   Sejm* gives the government special powers for the period of suspended Martial Law.*

December 30   Martial Law* is officially suspended, although most of its measures have already been written into the penal law. Militarization of key industries continues.

1983

January 3   New regime-supported trade unions* begin to form to replace the dissolved Solidarity.*

May 7–9   First National Congress of the Patriotic Movement for National Salvation (PRON).*

May 12   Eighteen-year-old high school student G. Przemyk is stopped by police when he and his friends celebrate the completion of school exams; he is beaten to death.

May 28   Warsaw* Military District Court sentences Z. Najder,* the director of the Polish section of Radio Free Europe,* to death in absentia.

June 16–23   Pope John Paul II* visits Poland.

July 16   Front of National Unity* is dissolved and its role taken by the Patriotic Movement for National Salvation (PRON).*

July 22   Martial Law* officially ends and the Military Council of National Salvation (WRON)* is dissolved.

August 25   M. Rakowski* meets the employees of the Lenin Shipyard in the room where the Gdańsk Agreement* was signed in 1980. Rakowski is not well received.

August 29   Union of Polish Writers (ZLP)* is dissolved by the authorities because it had "become in practice an instrument of political anti-state opposition."

October 5   L. Wałęsa* is awarded the Nobel Peace Prize.

1984

January 13   M. Szczepański,* former chief of Polish Radio and TV,* is sentenced to eight years in prison.

February 7   P. Bartoszcze,* a leader of Rural Solidarity,* dies. The police autopsy points to murder.

June 8   B. Lis,* a member of Solidarity's Provisional National Committee, in hiding since December 13, 1981, is arrested.

June 17   Local government elections are boycotted by Solidarity.* Official turnout is 74.77%.

July 22   Sejm* passes a general amnesty* act "to mark the 40th anniversary of the Polish People's Republic."

October 19   J. Popiełuszko* is abducted, tortured, and killed by members of the secret police.

December 27   Trial of the murderers of F. J. Popiełuszko* begins in Toruń Provincial Court.

1985

January   Government announces new price increases. When Solidarity* threatens a strike, the increases are halted.

February 7   Killers of Fr. J. Popiełuszko* are sentenced to imprisonments from 14 to 25 years.

February 13   Police interrupt a meeting with L. Wałęsa* and arrest W. Frasyniuk,* B. Lis,* and A. Michnik.* They are later tried for "activity intended to cause unrest" and participation in the "activity of an illegal organization called the Provisional Coordinating Committee."

March 10   Konstantin Chernenko dies and is replaced by Mikhail Gorbachev.

April 1   Prices for electricity, gas, and coal are raised.

April 26   Poland and other members of the Warsaw Treaty Organization* renew their commitment to it for the next 20 years.

April 30   Authorities transfer Solidarity* property to the All-Poland Alliance of Trade Unions (OPZZ).*

May 1 and 3   Anti-regime demonstrations in several towns and cities.

July 1   Food prices are raised.

October   Solidarity* urges a boycott of general elections.

October 13   In elections to the Sejm,* voting turnout, according to official data, is 66%.

November 7   First meeting of the new Sejm.* Z. Messner* replaces W. Jaruzelski* as Premier.*

November 12   W. Jaruzelski* takes the position of Chairman of the State Council (Rada Państwa),* replacing H. Jabłoński.*

1986

January 11   B. Borusewicz,* a member of the Provisional Coordinating Committee of Solidarity,* is arrested in Gdańsk.*

April   Media report the Chernobyl accident several days after the disaster and after the radioactive cloud has passed over the country.

April 22   Warsaw Provincial Court sentences a group of leaders of the Confederation for an Independent Poland (KPN).* L. Moczulski* receives a prison term of four years.

May 31   Z. Bujak,* a member of the Provisional Coordinating Committee of Solidarity,* is arrested after almost five years of hiding in the underground.

June   Poland is formally admitted to the International Monetary Fund and the World Bank.

July 17   Third amnesty after imposition of Martial Law.*

September   Organizational committee of the Agricultural Foundation* is created.

September–October   Various structures of Solidarity* begin to function openly. No legal sanctions are applied.

September 11   General amnesty for most political prisoners.

November 19   Solidarity,* illegal in Poland, becomes a member of the International Confederation of Free Trade Unions and the World Confederation of Labor.

1987

January 12   Pope John Paul II* receives Gen. W. Jaruzelski* at the Vatican.

March   Authorities raise food prices by 10% and fuel prices by 40%.

May 1   Anti-government demonstrations and clashes with the police take place during the May 1 celebrations.

June 1   Orange Alternative* movement is established in Wrocław* on International Children's Day.

June 8–14   Pope John Paul II* visits Poland and meets with Gen. W. Jaruzelski* and L. Wałęsa.*

July   Mass graves are discovered near the village of Giby in the Suwałki region. The discovery is followed by the establishment of the Civic Committee for the Search for the Inhabitants of the Suwałki Region Who Disappeared in July 1945.

September 3   Cracow Industrial Society is registered.

September 4   Society for Economic Activity is established in Warsaw.*

September 26–29   U.S. Vice-President George Bush visits Poland.

October 12   The authorities announce a November referendum* on "Further Reformation of the State and the National Economy."

October 25   National Executive Committee of Solidarity* is organized.

November 15   Polish Socialist Party (PPS)* is reorganized in Warsaw.*

November 29   Referendum* on reforms fails as a result of a Solidarity-led boycott.

December   Polish debt to Western countries reaches $39.2 billion.

1988

January 1   Jamming of Radio Free Europe* is stopped.

January 30   Authorities announce new price hikes.

February   Sporadic strikes and demonstrations are provoked by the governmental austerity program.

April   Gas, electricity, and other heating costs rise by 100% and coal by 200%.

April–May   Strikes at Nowa Huta,* Stalowa Wola, and Gdańsk* to demand re-legislation of Solidarity.*

June   Only 55% of the people vote in the local elections, boycotted by Solidarity.*

June 17   New military oath is accepted. It includes a reference to "brotherhood at arms with allied armies" instead of the "brotherly alliance with the Soviet Army and other allied armies."

July 11   Mikhail Gorbachev visits Poland.

August   Strikes in Szczecin,* Lower and Upper Silesia, Gdańsk,* and Stalowa Wola for higher wages and restoration of Solidarity.*

August 23   L. Wałęsa* calls for negotiations with the government.

August 27–28   Eighth plenary meeting of the Central Committee* is held. Some of its members support an agreement with the opposition.

August 31   L. Wałęsa* meets Gen. C. Kiszczak,* S. Ciosek,* and Bishop J. Dąbrowski. Kiszczak proposes the Round Table Negotiations.* After the talks Wałęsa asks for the strikes to end.

September   L. Wałęsa* announces that he is ready to negotiate with the authorities.

September 16   Introductory meeting in Magdalenka of the representatives of Solidarity* and the government.

September 19   Z. Messner* resigns as Premier.*

September 27   M. Rakowski* becomes Premier.*

October   Round Table Negotiations* fail to be convened.

October 31   Government closes the Lenin Shipyard in Gdańsk.* Massive demonstrations follow.

November 4   British Prime Minister Margaret Thatcher meets L. Wałęsa* in Gdańsk.*

November 7   M. Rakowski* states that re-legalization of Solidarity* is out of the question.

November 30 TV debate between L. Wałęsa* and A. Miodowicz,* leader of government-sponsored trade unions. Wałęsa clearly wins the debate.

December 9–12 L. Wałęsa* visits France, invited by President François Mitterrand.

December 18 Group of intellectuals form the Citizens' Committee to assist L. Wałęsa.* H. Wujec* is elected secretary of the committee.

December 20–21 Tenth Plenary Session of the Central Committee* of the Polish United Workers' Party (PZPR)* changes the leadership of the Party. S. Ciosek* and L. Miller* become secretaries of the Central Committee.

1989

January 16–18 Central Committee* of the Polish United Workers' Party (PZPR)* agrees to discuss legalizing of Solidarity* and open Round Table Negotiations.*

January 27 Solidarity* and the Catholic Church* agree to start Round Table Negotiations.*

February 6–April 5 Round Table Negotiations.*

March 7 Polish government officially accuses the USSR of committing the 1940 Katyń* massacre.

April 5 Government and Solidarity* sign the Round Table Agreement.

April 7 Sejm* accepts some constitutional amendments, including creation of the Senate.*

April 13 State Council (Rada Państwa)* announces that parliamentary elections will take place on June 4.

April 17 Solidarity is registered as a legal union.

May 8 First issue of *Gazeta Wyborcza* ("The Electoral Gazette")* appears.

June 2 *Tygodnik Solidarność* ("The Solidarity Weekly")* appears for the first time since its liquidation during Martial Law.*

June 4 First round of the first postwar parliamentary elections* that are partially free. A spectacular victory for Solidarity.*

June 18 Second round of the parliamentary elections.

June 23 Citizens' Parliamentary Club* is formed.

July 3 *Gazeta Wyborcza* ("The Electoral Gazette")* publishes A. Michnik's* article "Your President, Our Premier."

July 4 New bicameral Parliament opens.

July 6 During a speech to the Council of Europe, M. Gorbachev promises not to interfere with reforms in Poland and Hungary,

July 9–11 U.S. President G. Bush visits Poland and meets L. Wałęsa.*

July 17 Poland re-establishes diplomatic relations with the Vatican.

July 19 Joint session of the Sejm* and the Senate* elects W. Jaruzelski* President* of Poland.

July 25 W. Jaruzelski* asks Solidarity* to join the governmental coalition. L. Wałęsa* refuses.

July 29   M. Rakowski* resigns as Premier* and replaces W. Jaruzelski* as First Secretary of the Polish United Workers' Party (PZPR).*

August 1   Government ends all price controls and rationing of food. Panic in the food markets.

August 2   President W. Jaruzelski* appoints C. Kiszczak* as Premier.*

August 19   C. Kiszczk* resigns as Premier* and President W. Jaruzelski* appoints T. Mazowiecki.*

August 24   T. Mazowiecki* forms the first non-communist government in over 40 years.

September 12   T. Mazowiecki's* government is sworn in.

September 19   Poland and the European Economic Community sign a trade agreement.

September 22   Independent Students' Association (NZS)* is registered.

September 29   ZOMO (Motorized Units of the People's Militia)* is dissolved.

November 8   PRON (Patriotic Movement of National Revival)* dissolves itself.

November 9–14   West German Chancellor Helmut Kohl visits Poland.

November 17   Monument of Feliks Dzierżyński is dismantled.

November 19   L. Wałęsa* visits the United States, addresses the Congress, and asks for more help for Poland.

December 4   During a meeting of the Warsaw Treaty Organization* in Moscow, the USSR, East Germany, Poland, Hungary, and Bulgaria condemn their 1968 invasion of Czechoslovakia.

December 8   Government of T. Mazowiecki* announces austere policies to end the economic crisis in Poland.

December 28–29   Sejm* and the Senate* approve the economic plan of the Mazowiecki* government, known later as the Balcerowicz* Plan, formally end the existence of the Polish People's Republic, return to the prewar flag, and rename the state the Republic of Poland.

1990

January 1   Beginning of economic reforms, known as "shock therapy." Prices increase sharply and złoty is devalued.

January 16–19   Strikes over the governmental economic policy in the Silesian coal mining region.

January 25–28   Polish United Workers' Party (PZPR)* dissolves itself during its final Eleventh Congress. On the next day, the Social Democracy of the Republic of Poland (SdRP)* is formed.

January 27   Lenin Shipyard* in Gdańsk* changes its name to Gdańsk Shipyard.

February 15   Premier T. Mazowiecki* and the leader of Solidarity,* L. Wałęsa,* meet to discuss growing opposition among workers to the negative consequences of economic and political reforms. The meeting marks the beginning of a split between the supporters of Mazowiecki and Wałęsa. Solidarity demands early free parliamentary and presidential elections, removal of the communists from governmental positions, and creation of new jobs for those people who became unemployed because of the economic restructuring.

February 16   Paris Club agrees to reschedule Polish debts.

March   Soviet authorities admit, for the first time, that it was the Stalin regime and the NKVD who were responsible for the 1940 Katyń* massacre.

March 7   K. Kozłowski* becomes the first civilian Deputy Minister of the Interior.

March 8   West German Parliament renounces all claims to Polish "Recovered Territories,"* the former German lands given to Poland after 1945.

April   L. Wałęsa* hints that he will run for President.*

April 3   B. Komorowski* and J. Onyszkiewicz* become the first civilian Deputy Ministers of Defense.

April 11   End of censorship* in Poland.

April 19–25   Second Congress of Solidarity* re-elects L. Wałęsa* as its leader. The rift between Wałęsa and T. Mazowiecki* becomes publicly apparent.

May 2   During his official visit to Poland, the West German President states that Poland's borders* are permanent.

May 10   Security Service (SB)* is dissolved.

May 14   Center Alliance (PC)* is established.

May 21–25   Railway workers strike in Silesia and Pomerania against governmental economic policy.

May 27   Local elections are held, Poland's first completely free, multiparty elections since before World War II.

June 21   Joint West and East German Parliaments pass a resolution confirming Poland's borders.

June 27   Organizational meeting of the Democratic Right Forum.

June 29–30   First convention of the Liberal-Democratic Congress (KLD).*

July 13   Sejm* approves the Law of Privatization of State Estates.

July 16   Citizens' Movement for Democratic Action (ROAD)* is established.

August 2   Minister of National Education, H. Samsonowicz,* issues a special instruction introducing religious education to schools.

September 5   Solidarity* withdraws its logo from the first page of *Gazeta Wyborcza* ("The Electoral Gazette").*

September 17   L. Wałęsa* officially announces his candidacy for President* of Poland.

November 5   T. Mazowiecki* officially announces his candidacy for President* of Poland.

November 14   Foreign ministers of Poland and a united Germany sign a treaty guaranteeing Poland's borders.*

November 20   Miners strike against governmental economic policy.

November 25   First ballot of the presidential elections. The division of the vote— 39.96% for L. Wałęsa,* 23.10% for S. Tymiński,* and 18.08% for T. Mazowiecki*— forces a runoff election between Wałęsa and Tymiński.

November 26   T. Mazowiecki* resigns as Premier.*

December 2–18   J. Olszewski* tries unsuccessfully to form a cabinet.

December 9   L. Wałęsa* wins the runoff election with 75% of the vote.

December 22   L. Wałęsa* takes the presidential oath.

December 29   President L. Wałęsa* nominates J. K. Bielecki* as Premier.*

1991

January 3   Citizens' Parliamentary Club (OKP)* splits in two.

January 12   Cabinet formed by J. K. Bielecki* is accepted by the Sejm.*

January 16   Forty political parties are registered in Poland.

February 15   President L. Wałęsa* meets Czechoslovak Premier V. Havel and Hungarian Premier J. Antall in Visegrad; formation of the Visegrad triangle.

February 23   M. Krzaklewski* is elected head of Solidarity* and succeeds L. Wałęsa.*

February 25   Foreign and Defense Ministers of the Warsaw Treaty Organization* countries sign an agreement to dissolve the pact.

March 13   Party X* is formed and registered.

March 15   Seventeen Western countries forgive $16.5 billion of Poland's $33 billion foreign debt.

March 19–26   President L. Wałęsa* visits the United States.

April 4   Red Army* begins its withdrawal from Poland.

April 12   Warsaw's* Stock Exchange* inaugurates its activities in the building of the former Central Committee* of the Polish United Workers' Party (PZPR).*

April 16   Company stocks are traded for the first time since 1939.

April 18   International Monetary Fund approves a $2.5 billion loan to Poland.

April 20   Z. Bujak* leaves the Citizens' Movement for Democratic Action (ROAD)* and establishes the Democratic-Social Movement (RDS).

May   Sporadic strikes in Lublin,* Lubin,* Warsaw,* Białystok,* and Starachowice.

May 20   Polish currency, the złoty, becomes convertible.

June 17   Premier J. K. Bielecki* and German Chancellor H. Kohl sign a treaty of friendship and mutual assistance between Poland and Germany in Bonn.

July 1   Warsaw Treaty Organization* is formally dissolved.

July 27   Poland joins Hexagonale.*

October 27   Parliamentary elections* take place, and 29 separate groups enter the Sejm* and the Senate.* As a consequence, the government of J. K. Bielecki* falls.

November 8–13   B. Geremek* tries unsuccessfully to form a government.

November 23   *Gazeta Wyborcza* ("The Electoral Gazette")* has a circulation of 870,000.

December 6   J. Olszewski* is appointed Premier.*

December 23   J. Olszewski* forms his cabinet.

1992

January 1 Government increases prices of electricity (20%), gas (70%), and hot water (100%).

January 9 Russia cuts in half gas deliveries to Poland.

January 12–13 Solidarity*-organized protests against price increases.

January 13 Declaration of Polish-Lithuanian friendship is signed in Vilna.

February 11 J. Onyszkiewicz* resigns as Deputy Minister of Defense.

February 14 L. Kaczyński* is elected President of the Supreme Control Chamber (NIK)* by the Sejm.*

March 5 H. Gronkiewicz-Waltz* is elected President of the National Polish Bank by the Sejm.*

April 6 Defense Minister J. Parys announces that a group of military commanders have prepared a military coup d'état. A conflict between J. Parys and President L. Wałęsa* begins.

April 23 Treaty of friendship between Poland and Belorussia is signed in Warsaw.*

May 6 Presidents of Poland, Hungary, and Czechoslovakia meet in Prague and express their desire to be linked to the West European security network.

May 18 Treaty of good neighborliness and cooperation is signed by Poland and Ukraine. Defense Minister J. Parys resigns.

May 22 L. Wałęsa* and Russian President B. Yeltsin sign a pact of cooperation between Poland and Russia.

May 26 L. Wałęsa* withdraws his support of the Olszewski* government.

May 28 Sejm* asks Interior Minister A. Macierewicz* to produce a list of state officials who cooperated with communist secret police during 1945–90.

June 4 Interior Minister A. Macierewicz* presents the Sejm* with a list of 64 parliamentary deputies and state officials who cooperated with communist secret police during 1945–90.

June 5 Olszewski* government is ousted by a no-confidence vote in the Sejm.*

June 5–July 10 W. Pawlak* tries, unsuccessfully, to form a government.

July 10 H. Suchocka* forms a new government.

August 19 Government accepts the Program of General Privatization (Program Powszechnej Prywatyzacji).

August–September Strikes in several large state factories.

September 1 Former communist Premier P. Jaroszewicz* and his wife are murdered in their home.

September 20 Coalition for the Republic (KdR)* established by J. Olszewski's* Movement for the Republic (RdR),* A. Macierewicz's* Polish Action (AP), and K. Morawicki's* Freedom Party (Partia Wolności, formerly Fighting Solidarity).*

October 4 Forum of Democratic Right, headed by A. Hall,* leaves the Democratic Union (UD).*

October 14   Russian President B. Yeltsin sends L. Wałęsa* photocopies of the March 5, 1940, document ordering the execution of over 20,000 Poles, partially in Katyń.*

October 28   Last Russian combat troops leave Poland.

November 24   Treaty signed between Poland and the International Monetary Fund for $700 million loan.

December 17   Thousands of coal miners strike, protesting low wages and plans to reorganize the mining industry.

1993

January 7   Sejm* passes a law strictly limiting abortion.*

February 15   L. Wałęsa* signs a strict anti-abortion law.

March 18   Sejm* rejects the governmental Program of General Privatization (Program Powszechnej Prywatyzacji).

April 30   Sejm* passes a privatization plan, later approved by the Senate* and signed into law by President L. Wałęsa.*

May 28   Government of H. Suchocka* falls. Sejm* accepts a new electoral law with a 5% threshold for parties and an 8% threshold for coalitions.

May 29   President L. Wałęsa* dissolves the Sejm.*

June 1   President L. Wałęsa* signs a new electoral law, accepted by the Sejm* on May 28.

June 22   European Community formally invites Poland, the Czech Republic, Slovakia, Bulgaria, Hungary, and Romania to apply for membership.

June 27   L. Wałęsa* disassociates himself from Solidarity* after it refuses to endorse his candidates in parliamentary elections scheduled for September.

July 5   Government establishes a value-added tax (VAT) of 22% on most goods and adds more excise taxes on gasoline, automobiles, alcohol, and tobacco.

August 16   Unemployment reaches 15.2% of the workforce (2.8 million people).

August 25   Russian President B. Yeltsin visits Warsaw,* signs a trade agreement and an accord to construct a natural gas pipeline with Poland, and lays a wreath at a memorial commemorating the 1940 Katyń* massacre.

September 18   Last Russian military units leave Poland.

September 19   Parliamentary elections; only four parties cross the 5% electoral threshold and enter Parliament. Spectacular victory of the Polish Peasant Party (PSL)* and the Democratic Left Alliance (SLD).*

October 14   First session of the newly elected Sejm.*

October 18   W. Pawlak* is nominated Premier* by President* L. Wałęsa.*

October 26   Government of W. Pawlak,* the first non-Solidarity cabinet after 1989, is sworn in and takes office.

December 8   Republican League is registered in Warsaw.*

December 29   W. Pawlak* explains, in his Sejm* speech, that his government will continue the economic policy of the previous government despite his election promises to end it.

1994

February 2 Poland joins the "partnership for peace" program launched by NATO in January.

February 4 Deputy Premier and Minister of Finance M. Borowski* of the Democratic Left Alliance (SLD)* resigns to protest the policies of Premier W. Pawlak,* of the Polish Peasant Party (PSL),* who made important decisions without consulting other ministers in the coalition government. A split in the SLD-PSL coalition appears.

March Interior Ministry investigation confirms "numerous irregularities" in the activities of the police in the Poznań* region.

March 10 London Club agrees on 42.5% reduction of Poland's $13,200 million debt to some 300 commercial banks.

March 14–15 W. Pawlak's* first visit to Moscow.

March 17 *Radio Maryja* of Father Rydzyk* receives an all-Polish concession.

April 8 Poland applies for membership in the European Union.*

April 16 President L. Wałęsa* threatens to dissolve the Sejm* and to call new parliamentary elections. The confrontation between Wałęsa and the ruling coalition dramatically intensifies.

April 23 Democratic Union (UD)* and the Liberal Democratic Congress (KLD)* agree to merge to form the Freedom Union (UW).* T. Mazowiecki* is elected its chair, and former KLD leader D. Tusk* its deputy chair.

April 26 President Algirdas Brazauskas of Lithuania and President* L. Wałęsa* of Poland sign a Treaty of Friendship and Cooperation in Vilna. The treaty was preceded by months of difficult negotiations in which Lithuania pressed for formal condemnation of Poland's 1920 annexation of Vilna.

May Solidarity-organized strikes in mining, heavy industry, and the media.

May 12 Right-wing "confederation," the Convenant for Poland (PdP), is established by five parties.

July 1 Sejm* votes to postpone ratification of a concordat with the Vatican until after the adoption of a new Constitution.

July 6–7 U.S. President B. Clinton visits Warsaw* and addresses the National Assembly.

September 2 Sejm* accepts L. Wałęsa's* veto of legislation liberalizing abortion.*

September 8 Last Russian soldiers leave Polish soil.

September 30 President L. Wałęsa* meets a group of Polish Army* generals during a dinner in the town of Drawsko. The generals express their no-confidence vote toward the Ministry of Defense and demand direct presidential supervision over the Army. Some in the Polish political establishment call the dinner in Drawsko an attempted coup d'état.

1995

January 1   Polish currency, the złoty, is redenominated. The new złoty is worth 10,000 old zloty; 1 U.S. dollar is worth 2.4 złoty.

January 13   A. Olechowski,* the Foreign Minister of Poland and an ally of L. Wałęsa,* resigns to protest the Pawlak* government's international policy.

January 30   Polish and Russian government representatives sign an agreement in Warsaw,* writing off mutual debts after Russia pays $US 25 million to Poland.

February 7   W. Pawlak* resigns as Premier* following President L. Wałęsa's* threat to dissolve Parliament. Wałęsa had persistently accused Pawlak's government of delaying economic reforms and of corruption.

February 16–17   Russian Premier Victor Chernomyrdin visits Poland to sign an agreement on the construction of the 650-kilometer Polish section of a gas pipeline from Siberia to Western Europe.

February 17   Acting Polish Minister of Defense J. Milewski* and U.S. Secretary of Defense William Perry sign a defense cooperation agreement in Washington, covering the sharing of military information and joint military maneuvers.

March 1   J. Oleksy,* a leader of the Democratic Left Alliance (SLD)* and the Polish Peasant Party (PSL)* coalition, replaces W. Pawlak* as Premier* of Poland.

April 1–2   Second Congress of the Freedom Union (UW)* elects L. Balcerowicz* as its new president, replacing T. Mazowiecki,* and J. Kuroń* as its candidate in the presidential elections of 1995.*

April 8   Liberal-Conservative Movement (RLK) is established in Warsaw.*

April 30   L. Wałęsa* announces that he will stand in presidential elections of 1995.*

September 6   Speaker of the Sejm* J. Zych* announces that presidential elections will be held on November 5, with a second round on November 19 if no candidate gains an absolute majority of votes.

November 5   First round of the presidential elections of 1995.*

November 19   A. Kwaśniewski* defeats L. Wałęsa* in the second round of the presidential elections of 1995.*

November 28   The Foreign, Interior, and Defense Ministers, W. Bartoszewski,* A. Milczanowski,* and Z. Okoński, respectively, resign after the victory of A. Kwaśniewski,* because their portfolios were appointed after consultation with former president L. Wałęsa.*

December 19   Outgoing Interior Minister A. Milczanowski* presents documents that, in his opinion, prove that since 1983 Premier* J. Oleksy* has collaborated with the Soviet, and later with the Russian, secret services.

December 23   A. Kwaśniewski* is sworn in as President* for a five-year term.

Sources: J. Karpiński, *Poland since 1944: A Portrait of Years* (Boulder, Colo., 1995); G. Prins, *Spring in Winter: The 1989 Revolutions* (Manchester, 1990); *Keesing's Record of World Events; Chronology of 20th-Century Eastern European History*, ed. by G. C. Ference (Detroit, 1994): P. Majer, *Polska i świat 1989–1992. Kalendarium przełomu*

(Warsaw, 1993); J. Kuroń and J. Żakowski, *PRL dla początkujących* (Wrocław, 1995); *Poland's Permanent Revolution: People vs. Elites, 1956 to the Present*, ed. by J. L. Curry and L. Fajfer (Washington, D.C., 1996); A. Andrusiewicz, *Polska 1991–1995. Kalendarz wydarzeń* (Rzeszów, 1997).

SELECTED BIBLIOGRAPHY

Andrews, Nicholas G. *Poland, 1980–81: Solidarity versus the Party*. Washington, D.C.: National Defense University Press, 1985.

Ascherson, Neal. *The Polish August: What Has Happened in Poland*. New York: Penguin Books, 1981.

Ash, Timothy Garton. *The Magic Lantern: The Revolution of '89 Witnessed in Warsaw, Budapest, Berlin, and Prague*. New York: Random House, 1990.

Ash, Timothy Garton. *The Polish Revolution: Solidarity, 1980–1982*. London: Granta Books, 1991.

Barnett, Clifford R. *Poland: Its people, Its society, Its culture*. New York: Grove Press, 1958.

Bernhard, Michael H. *The Origins of Democratization in Poland: Workers, Intellectuals, and Oppositional Politics, 1976–1980*. New York: Columbia University Press, 1993.

Bethell, Nicholas. *Gomułka: His Poland and His Communism*. Harmondsworth, Engl.: Penguin Books, 1972.

Bielasiak, Jacek, and Simon, Maurice. *Polish Politics: Edge of the Abyss*. New York: Praeger, 1984.

Blazynski, George. *Flashpoint Poland*. New York: Pergamon Press, 1979.

Blit, Lucjan. *The Eastern Pretender: Bolesław Piasecki, His Life and Times*. London: Hutchinson, 1969.

Bromke, Adam. *Poland: The Protracted Crisis*. Oakville, Ont.: Mosaic Press, 1983.

Bromke, Adam, and Strong, J. W., eds. *Gierek's Poland*. New York: Praeger, 1973.

Brumberg, Abraham. *Poland: Genesis of a Revolution*. New York: Vintage, 1983.

Brzezinski, Zbigniew. *The Soviet Bloc: Unity and Conflict*. Cambridge, Mass.: Harvard University Press, 1961.

Bugajski, Janusz. *Ethnic Politics in Eastern Europe: A Guide to Nationality Policies, Organizations, and Parties*. Armonk, N.Y.: M. E. Sharpe, 1994.

Chęciński, Michael. *Poland, Communism, Nationalism, Anti-Semitism*. New York: Karz-Cohl Publishing, 1982.

Cieplak, Tadeusz N., ed. *Poland since 1956*. New York: Twayne Publishers, 1972.

Clarke, Roger, ed. *Poland: The Economy in the 1980s.* Harlow: Longman, 1989.

Coutouvidis, John, and Reynolds, Jaime. *Poland, 1939–1947.* Leicester: Leicester University Press, 1986.

Curry, Jane Leftwich. *The Black Book of Polish Censorship.* New York: Vintage, 1984.

Curry, Jane Leftwich. *Poland's Journalists: Professionalism and Politics.* Cambridge: Cambridge University Press, 1990.

Curry, Jane Leftwich, and Fajfer, Luba. *Poland's Permanent Revolution: People vs. Elites, 1956 to the Present.* Washington, D.C.: University Publishing Associates, 1996.

Czerwinski, E. J., ed. *Dictionary of Polish Literature.* Westport, Conn.: Greenwood, 1994.

Davies, Norman. *God's Playground: A History of Poland*, vol. 2. New York: Columbia University Press, 1984.

Dziewanowski, M. K. *The Communist Party of Poland: An Outline of History.* Cambridge, Mass.: Harvard University Press, 1976.

Dziewanowski, M. K. *Poland in the Twentieth Century.* New York: Columbia University Press, 1977.

Embassy of the Republic of Poland to Canada. *Poland, 1996: The Economic Situation.* Ottawa, 1996.

Gerrits, Andre. *The Failure of Authoritarian Change: Reform, Opposition and Geopolitics in Poland in the 1980s.* Aldershot, Eng.: Dartmouth, 1990.

Graham, Judith. *Current Biography Yearbook, 1996.* New York: H. W. Wilson Company, 1996.

Groth, Alexander J. *People's Poland: Government and Politics.* San Francisco: Chandler, 1972.

Hahn, Werner G. *Democracy in a Communist Party: Poland's Experience since 1980.* New York: Columbia University Press, 1987.

Hann, C. M. *A Village without Solidarity.* New Haven, Conn.: Yale University Press, 1985.

Held, Joseph, ed. *The Columbia History of Eastern Europe in the Twentieth Century.* New York: Columbia University Press, 1992.

Horak, Stephan M. *Eastern European National Minorities, 1919–1980.* Littleton, Colo.: Libraries Unlimited, 1985.

Johnson, A. Ross; Dean, Robert W.; and Alexiev, Alexander. *East European Military Establishments: The Warsaw Pact Northern Tier.* New York: Crane Russak, 1982.

Kamiński, Bartłomiej. *The Collapse of State Socialism: The Case of Poland.* Princeton, N.J.: Princeton University Press, 1991.

Karpiński, Jakub. *Countdown: The Polish Upheavals of 1956, 1968, 1970, 1976, 1980.* New York: Karz-Cohl, 1982.

Karpiński, Jakub. *Poland since 1944: A Portrait of Years.* Boulder, Colo.: Westview Press, 1995.

Keesing's Record of World Events. Cambridge: Harlow, 1945–1996.

Kemp-Welch, A. *The Birth of Solidarity: The Gdańsk Negotiations, 1980.* London: Macmillan, 1983.

Kennedy, Michael. *Professionals, Power, and Solidarity in Poland: A Critical Sociology of Soviet-Type Society.* Cambridge: Cambridge University Press, 1990.

Kersten, Krystyna. *The Establishment of Communist Rule in Poland, 1943–1948.* Berkeley: University of California Press, 1991.

Kierzkowski, Henryk; Okolski, Marek; and Wellisz, Stanisław, eds. *Stabilization and Structural Adjustment in Poland*. London: Routledge, 1993.

Kolankiewicz, George, and Lewis, Paul. *Poland: Politics, Economics and Society*. London: Pinter Publishers, 1988.

Korbonski, Andrzej. *Politics of Socialist Agriculture in Poland, 1945–1960*. New York: Columbia University Press, 1965.

Kuroń, Jacek, and Modzelewski, Karol. *Revolutionary Marxist Students in Poland Speak Out*. New York: Merit Publishers, 1968.

Laba, Roman. *The Roots of Solidarity*. Princeton, N.J.: Princeton University Press, 1991.

Landau, Zbigniew, and Tomaszewski, Jerzy. *The Polish Economy in the Twentieth Century*. London: Croom Helm, 1985.

Lane, Arthur Bliss. *I Saw Poland Betrayed: An American Ambassador Reports to the American People*. Indianapolis: Bobbs Merrill, 1948.

Lepak, Keith J. *Prelude to Solidarity: Poland and the Politics of the Gierek Regime*. New York: Columbia University Press, 1988.

Lerski, George J. *Historical Dictionary of Poland, 966–1945*, with special editing and emendations by Piotr Wróbel and Richard J. Kozicki. Westport, Conn.: Greenwood Press, 1996.

Leslie, R. F., ed. *The History of Poland since 1863*. Cambridge: Cambridge University Press, 1980.

Lewis, Flora. *The Polish Volcano: A Case of Hope*. London: Sacker and Warburg, 1959.

Lewis, Paul. *Political Authority and Party Secretaries in Poland, 1975–86*. Cambridge: Cambridge University Press, 1989.

Lipski, Jan Jozef. *KOR: A History of the Workers' Defense Committee in Poland, 1976–81*. Berkeley: University of California Press, 1985.

Łopiński, Maciej; Moskit, Marcin; and Wilk, Mariusz. *Konspira: Solidarity Underground*. Berkeley: University of California Press, 1990.

Malcher, George C. *Poland's Politicized Army*. New York: Praeger, 1984.

Mason, David S. *Public Opinion and Political Change in Poland, 1980–1982*. Cambridge: Cambridge University Press, 1985.

Micewski, Andrzej. *Cardinal Wyszyński: A Biography*. San Diego: Harcourt, Brace, Jovanovich, 1984.

Michnik, Adam. *Letters from Prison and Other Essays*. Berkeley: University of California Press, 1985.

Michta, Andrew A. *Red Eagle: The Army in Polish Politics, 1944–1988*. Stanford, Calif.: Hoover Institution Press, 1990.

Mikołajczyk, Stanisław. *The Rape of Poland: The Pattern of Soviet Aggression*. New York: Whittlesey House, 1948.

Miłosz, Czesław. *The Captive Mind*. New York: Knopf, 1953.

Miłosz, Czesław. *The History of Polish Literature*. Berkeley: University of California Press, 1983.

Misztal, Bronisław. *Poland after Solidarity: Social Movement versus the State*. New Brunswick, N.J.: Transaction Books, 1985.

Morrison, James F. *The Polish People's Republic*. Baltimore: Johns Hopkins University Press, 1968.

Myant, Martin. *Poland: A Crisis for Socialism*. London: Lawrence and Wishart, 1982.

Narkiewicz, Olga. *The Green Flag: Polish Populist Politics, 1867–1970*. London: Croom Helm, 1976.

New Catholic Encyclopedia. New York, 1967.

Ost, David. *Solidarity and the Politics of Anti-Politics: Opposition and Reform in Poland since 1968*. Philadelphia: Temple University Press, 1990.

Piekalkiewicz, Jaroslaw. *Comunist Local Government: A Study of Poland*. Columbus: Ohio University Press, 1975.

Ploss, Sidney I. *Moscow and the Polish Crisis*. Boulder, Colo.: Westview Press, 1986.

Podgórecki, Adam. *Polish Society*. Westport, Conn.: Praeger, 1994.

Poland: Country Profile. London: Economist Intelligence Unit.

Polonsky, Antony, and Drukier, Boleslaw. *The Beginnings of Communism in Poland*. London: Routledge, 1980.

Raina, Peter. *Political Opposition in Poland, 1954–1977*. London: Poets and Painters Press, 1978.

Raina, Peter. *Independent Social Movements in Poland*. London: London School of Economics, 1981.

Roos, Hans. *A History of Modern Poland*. New York: Alfred A. Knopf, 1966.

Sanford, George. *Polish Communism in Crisis*. New York: St. Martin's Press, 1983.

Sanford, George. *Military Rule in Poland: The Rebuilding of Communist Power, 1981–83*. London: Croom Helm, 1986.

Sanford, George, ed. *The Solidarity Congress, 1981: The Great Debate*. London: Macmillan, 1990.

Sanford, George, and Gozdecka-Sanford, Adriana. *Historical Dictionary of Poland*. Metuchen, N.J.: Scarecrow Press, 1994.

Schaufele, William E. *Polish Paradox: Communism and National Renewal*. New York: Foreign Policy Association, 1981.

Schöpflin, George. *The Soviet Union and Eastern Europe*. New York: Muller, Blond, and White, 1986.

Simon, Maurice D., and Kanet, Roger E., eds. *Background to Crisis: Policy and Politics in Gierek's Poland*. Boulder, Colo.: Westview Press, 1981.

Staar, Richard F. *Poland, 1944–1962: The Sovietization of a Captive People*. New Orleans: Louisiana State University Press, 1962.

Staniszkis, Jadwiga. *Poland's Self-Limiting Revolution*. Princeton, N.J.: University of Princeton Press, 1984.

Starski, Stanisław. *Class Struggle in Classless Poland*. Boston: South End Press, 1982.

Stehle, Hansjakob. *The Independent Satellite: Society and Politics in Poland since 1945*. London: Pall Mall, 1965.

Strzelecki, Jan. *Solidarity: Poland, 1980–81*. Cambridge: Cambridge University Press, 1983.

Stypułkowski, Zbigniew. *Invitation to Moscow*. London: Thames and Hudson, 1951.

Syrop, Konrad. *Spring in October: The Polish Revolution of 1956*. Westport, Conn.: Greenwood Press, 1976.

Szajkowski, Bogdan. *Next to God . . . Poland: Politics and Religion in Contemporary Poland*. London: Frances Pinter, 1983.

Szajkowski, Bogdan, ed. *Political Parties of Eastern Europe, Russia, and the Successor States*. London: Longman, 1994.

Szczepański, Jan. *Polish Society*. New York: Random House, 1970.

Szulc, Tad. *Pope John Paul II*. New York: Simon and Schuster, 1995.

Taras, Raymond. *Ideology in a Socialist State: Poland, 1956–83*. Boulder, Colo.: Westview Press, 1986.

Taras, Raymond. *Poland: Socialist State, Rebellious Nation*. Boulder, Colo.: Westview Press, 1986.

Taras, Raymond. *Consolidating Democracy in Poland*. Boulder, Colo.: Westview Press, 1995.

Taras, Raymond C., ed. *Handbook of Political Science Research on the USSR and Eastern Europe*. Westport, Conn.: Greenwood Press, 1992.

Tischner, Józef. *The Spirit of Solidarity*. San Francisco: Harper and Row, 1984.

Torańska, Teresa. *"Them": Stalin's Polish Puppets*. New York: Harper and Row, 1987.

Touraine, Alain. *Solidarity: Poland, 1980–81*. Cambridge: Cambridge University Press, 1983.

Tworzecki, Hubert. *Parties and Politics in Post-1989 Poland*. Boulder, Colo.: Westview Press, 1996.

Wandycz, Piotr. *The Price of Freedom*. London: Routledge, 1992.

Weschler, Lawrence. *The Passion of Poland: From Solidarity through the State of War*. New York: Pantheon Books, 1984.

Weydenthal, Jan de. *The Communists of Poland: An Historical Outline*. Stanford, Calif.: Hoover Institution Press, 1986.

Weydenthal, Jan de; Porter, Bruce; and Devlin, Kevin. *The Polish Drama: 1980–1982*. Lexington, Mass.: Lexington Books, 1983.

Woodal, Jean, ed. *Policy and Politics in Contemporary Poland*. London: Frances Pinter, 1982.

Zdaniewicz, W. *The Catholic Church in Poland, 1945–1978*. Poznan, Poland: Pallottinum, 1979.

Zieliński, Janusz G. *Economic Reforms in Polish Industry*. London: Oxford University Press, 1973.

Zurawski, Joseph W. *Poland: The Captive Satellite. A Study in National Psychology*. Detroit: Endurance Press, 1962.

INDEX

Bold font indicates that a given person or phenomenon has an entry in this dictionary. Bold font numbers show where this entry is located. Some persons and phenomena appear in the chronology section of this dictionary which is indicated in the index

About the Author

PIOTR WRÓBEL is Associate Professor of History and a holder of the Konstanty Reynert Chair of Polish Studies at the University of Toronto. He is the author of seven books and numerous articles on Polish history, and he worked extensively on G. J. Lerski's *Historical Dictionary of Poland, 966–1945* (Greenwood, 1996) after Lerski passed away.

ISBN 0-313-29772-X

EAN

90000>

9 780313 297724

HARDCOVER BAR CODE